Unless Recalled Earlier

DATE DUE

DEMCO, INC. 38-2931

studies in jazz

Institute of Jazz Studies
Rutgers—The State University of New Jersey
General Editors: Dan Morgenstern and Edward Berger

1. BENNY CARTER: A Life in American Music, *by Morroe Berger, Edward Berger, and James Patrick, 2 vols., 1982*
2. ART TATUM: A Guide to His Recorded Music, *by Arnold Laubich and Ray Spencer, 1982*
3. ERROLL GARNER: The Most Happy Piano, *by James M. Doran, 1995*
4. JAMES P. JOHNSON: A Case of Mistaken Identity, *by Scott E. Brown;* Discography 1917–1950, *by Robert Hilbert, 1986*
5. PEE WEE ERWIN: This Horn for Hire, *as told to Warren W. Vaché, Sr., 1987*
6. BENNY GOODMAN: Listen to His Legacy, *by D. Russell Connor, 1988*
7. ELLINGTONIA: The Recorded Music of Duke Ellington and His Sidemen, *by W. E. Timner, 1988; 4th ed., 1996*
8. THE GLENN MILLER ARMY AIR FORCE BAND: Sustineo Alas / I Sustain the Wings, *by Edward F. Polic;* Foreword *by George T. Simon, 1989*
9. SWING LEGACY, *by Chip Deffaa, 1989*
10. REMINISCING IN TEMPO: The Life and Times of a Jazz Hustler, *by Teddy Reig, with Edward Berger, 1990*
11. IN THE MAINSTREAM: 18 Portraits in Jazz, *by Chip Deffaa, 1992*
12. BUDDY DeFRANCO: A Biographical Portrait and Discography, *by John Kuehn and Arne Astrup, 1993*
13. PEE WEE SPEAKS: A Discography of Pee Wee Russell, *by Robert Hilbert, with David Niven, 1992*
14. SYLVESTER AHOLA: The Gloucester Gabriel, *by Dick Hill, 1993*
15. THE POLICE CARD DISCORD, *by Maxwell T. Cohen, 1993*
16. TRADITIONALISTS AND REVIVALISTS IN JAZZ, *by Chip Deffaa, 1993*
17. BASSICALLY SPEAKING: An Oral History of George Duvivier, *by Edward Berger;* Musical Analysis *by David Chevan, 1993*
18. TRAM: The Frank Trumbauer Story, *by Philip R. Evans and Larry F. Kiner, with William Trumbauer, 1994*
19. TOMMY DORSEY: On the Side, *by Robert L. Stockdale, 1995*
20. JOHN COLTRANE: A Discography and Musical Biography, *by Yasuhiro Fujioka, with Lewis Porter and Yoh-ichi Hamada, 1995*
21. RED HEAD: A Chronological Survey of "Red" Nichols and His Five Pennies, *by Stephen M. Stroff, 1996*
22. THE RED NICHOLS STORY: After Intermission 1942–1965, *by Philip R. Evans, Stanley Hester, Stephen Hester, and Linda Evans, 1997*
23. BENNY GOODMAN: Wrappin' It Up, *by D. Russell Connor, 1996*
24. CHARLIE PARKER AND THEMATIC IMPROVISATION, *by Henry Martin, 1996*
25. BACK BEATS AND RIM SHOTS: The Johnny Blowers Story, *by Warren W. Vaché, Sr., 1997*
26. DUKE ELLINGTON: A Listener's Guide, *by Eddie Lambert, 1998*
27. SERGE CHALOFF: A Musical Biography and Discography, *by Vladimir Simosko, 1998*
28. HOT JAZZ: From Harlem to Storyville, *by David Griffiths, 1998*
29. ARTIE SHAW: A Musical Biography and Discography, *by Vladimir Simosko, 2000*
30. JIMMY DORSEY: A Study in Contrasts, *by Robert L. Stockdale, 1998*
31. STRIDE!: Fats, Jimmy, Lion, Lamb and All the Other Ticklers, *by John L. Fell and Terkild Vinding, 1999*
32. GIANT STRIDES: The Legacy of Dick Wellstood, *by Edward N. Meyer, 1999*
33. JAZ2Z GENTRY: Aristocrats of the Music World, *by Warren W. Vaché Sr., 1999*
34. THE UNSUNG SONGWRITERS: America's Masters of Melody, *by Warren W. Vaché Sr., 2000*
35. THE MUSICAL WORLD OF J. J. JOHNSON, *by Joshua Berrett and Louis G. Bourgois, III, 1999*
36. THE LADIES WHO SING WITH THE BAND, *by Betty Bennett Lowe, 2000*
37. AN UNSUNG CAT: THE LIFE AND MUSIC OF WARNE MARSH, *by Safford Chamberlain, 2000*

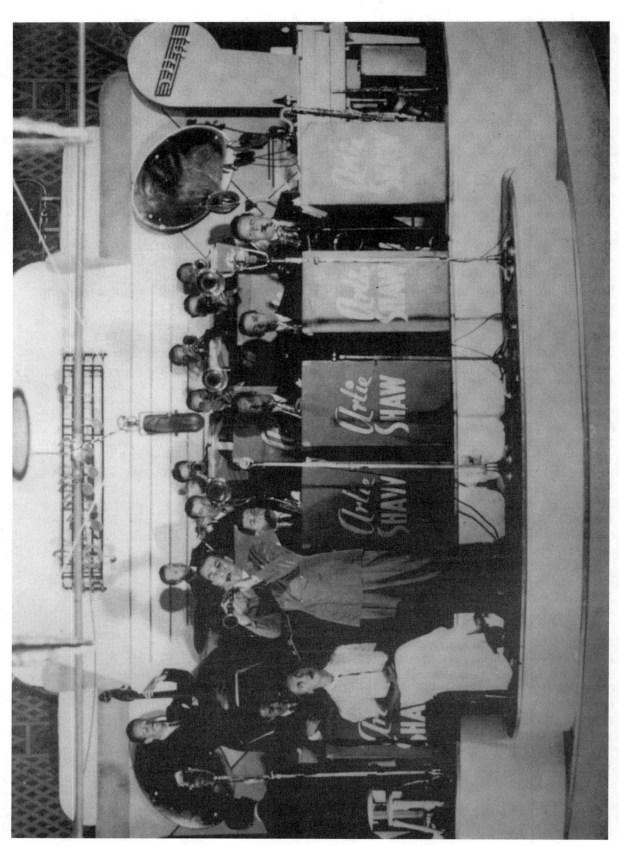

Frontispiece: The "Begin the Beguine" Band, summer 1938. Back row: Sid Weiss (b); Cliff Leeman (d); Johnny Best, Claude Bowen, Chuck Peterson (tp). 2nd row: Harry Rodgers, George Arus, Russell Brown (tb). 3rd row: Les Burns (p, with back turned); Al Avola (g); Tony Pastor (ts); Les Robinson (as); Ronnie Perry (ts); Hank Freeman (as); note Freeman's baritone sax in front of him, and his bass clarinet and B-flat clarinet to the right of his stand. Front: Patty Morgan (v); Shaw.

Artie Shaw

*A Musical Biography and
Discography*

Vladimir Simosko

Studies in Jazz Series, No. 29

**The Scarecrow Press, Inc.
Lanham, Maryland, and London
and
Institute of Jazz Studies
Rutgers—The State University of New Jersey
2000**

SCARECROW PRESS, INC.

Published in the United States of America
by Scarecrow Press, Inc.
4720 Boston Way, Lanham, Maryland 20706
http://www.scarecrowpress.com

4 Pleydell Gardens, Folkestone
Kent CT20 2DN, England

Copyright © 2000 by Vladimir Simosko

British Library Cataloguing in Publication Information Available

Library of Congress Cataloging-in-Publication Data

Simosko, Vladimir.
    Artie Shaw : a musical biography and discography / Vladimir
Simosko.
        p.   cm. — (Studies in jazz series ; no. 29)
    Includes bibliographical references and index.
    ISBN 0-8108-3397-2 (cloth : alk. paper)
    1. Shaw, Artie, 1910–   . 2. Jazz musicians—United States
Biography. 3. Shaw, Artie, 1910–   Discography. I. Title.
II. Series: Studies in jazz ; no. 20.
    ML419.S52S56   2000
    788.6'2165'092—dc21
    [B]   99-24345
                                                   CIP

♾ ™ The paper used in this publication meets the minimum
requirements of American National Standard for Information
Sciences—Permanence of Paper for Printed Library Materials,
ANSI/NISO Z39.48–1992. Manufactured in the United States of
America.

Contents

Foreword by Artie Shaw   *vii*
Editor's Foreword by Dan Morgenstern   *viii*
Preface   *ix*

  1:   Artie Shaw in Context: A Historical Perspective   1
  2:   New York to New York: 1910–1930   17
  3:   Sideman; New York: 1930–1936   25
  4:   String Swing: 1936–1937   43
  5:   Art Shaw and His New Music: 1937–1938   51
  6:   "Begin the Beguine" to the Palomar: 1938–1939   63
  7:   Hollywood to Hollywood: 1939–1940   73
  8:   Hollywood to New York: 1940–1941   85
  9:   Artie Shaw and His Orchestra: 1941–1942   93
10:   The Rangers; Navy Band 501: 1942–1944   99
11:   Artie Shaw and His Orchestra: 1944–1945   105
12:   Artie Shaw on Musicraft: 1946   111
13:   Artie Shaw "Longhair": 1949   115
14:   Artie Shaw and His Orchestra: 1949–1950   119
15:   Artie Shaw on Decca: 1950–1953   123
16:   Artie Shaw and His Gramercy 5: 1953–1954   131
17:   Spain to Los Angeles: 1950s–1990s   139

Introduction to the Discographies   143
Artie Shaw Sideman Discography: 1928–1936   147
Alphabetical List of Tune Titles with Artie Shaw as Sideman: 1928–1936   165
Artie Shaw Discography: 1936–1954   171
Appendix 1: Alphabetical List of Tune Titles with Composer Credits and
    Recording Dates   211
Appendix 2: Discographical Addenda and Ephemera   229
Appendix 3: Artie Shaw as Composer/Arranger   231
Appendix 4: Artie Shaw and Vocalists   237
Appendix 5: Annotated Selective Bibliography   245

References   *249*
Name Directory   *251*
Name Index   *271*
About the Author   *281*

Foreword

The first time I saw Vladimir Simosko's name was when someone sent me an article he had written about my Gramercy 5. That title, by the way, was simply the prefix of one of the numbers in the 1940 New York telephone directory, as were several others I used for various small groups formed from the big band I led that year—the Chelsea 3, the Regent 4, the Vanderbilt 6, the Trafalgar 7, and of course the eponymous (as in John O'Hara's novel) Butterfield 8.

Back to Mr. Simosko . . . since then he and I have had many telephone conversations, and we also spent several days together when he came down here a few years ago to discuss one of his early drafts of this book. Most of the published material I've read about myself is riddled with error and discrepancy and at times sheer foolishness, and I was impressed by Vladimir's genuine concern for accuracy and awareness of musical values.

I find it difficult to be objective about a book dealing with me and my work. However, I can state that this one is definitely an "authorized version." Many of my personal recollections and observations are here, and, viewed purely as a small fragment of history, the text contains a great deal of information I had completely forgotten.

Mr. Simosko obviously has done a lot of hard work compiling all this data, and I must admit I'm pleased that much of the music holds up quite well after all these years. But I can't help thinking of the story about a schoolboy who, when asked to hand in a report on a book about penguins, wrote: "This book tells me more about penguins than I care to know."

Oh well. Anyway, here's Vladimir's big fat book about me and my many bands and my rather sporadic recording career. I hope you'll find it interesting, illuminating, and perhaps even useful, as a carefully researched reference source. I know I will.

ARTIE SHAW
Newbury Park, California
25 August 1994

Editor's Foreword

Artie Shaw put away his clarinet, from which he had coaxed such unique sounds, in the summer of 1954, but his music still commands attention, and so does the man. Nearing 90, Shaw remains as fiercely independent of mind and mercurial of temperament as ever, and he is still actively involved in the creative process as he completes his literary magnum opus, a trilogy that will be part autobiography, part novel.

Meanwhile, before the reader is the definitive survey of Shaw's musical career and recorded legacy. A labor of love by Vladimir Simosko, who discovered Shaw when he was a teenager studying the clarinet, this book is the result of decades of dedicated research. It was worth the time and care.

Prior attempts to deal with this material have been either incomplete or inaccurate, and Shaw's work as a sideman has never before been dealt with in depth. For the first time, we have a clear picture of what Shaw played and recorded (including solos, thankfully) before becoming a bandleader. That alone is a major contribution to the history of jazz and popular music, but there is much more. Shaw's fertile years at the helm of big bands and small groups, even his classical activities, are documented in unprecedented detail. Among other things, this brings into proper focus his important but often overlooked work as arranger.

It is ironic that Shaw's enormous popularity as an icon of swing served to obscure his stature as a creative jazz musician, but in recent years that key aspect of his contribution has begun to get proper critical attention. Simosko's book, which bears the not readily imprimatur of its subject, enhances our understanding and appreciation of a musical legacy that will remain a source of joy and inspiration to lovers of jazz, and of the clarinet.

Dan Morgenstern
Series Editor

Preface

Research for this work began in 1957, when, as a fourteen-year-old clarinet student, I first REALLY HEARD an Artie Shaw record. My teacher, Frank Stark, a band director and jazz player around Pittsburgh in those years, had encouraged me to improvise to learn my way around the instrument, and to listen closely to all clarinetists to develop an idea of how the instrument should sound. I was already familiar with my father's collection of Swing Era 78-rpm records, many by Benny Goodman or featuring various other clarinetists. I'd also had my own copy of Artie Shaw's *The Pied Piper of Hamelin* album of records for children, many years earlier. Nevertheless, the focused listening inspired by Frank Stark's advice to look for conceptual models caused me to hear music in a new way, and soon afterward, when I heard Shaw doing "Frenesi" on the radio, the impact of his sound, control, and phrasing on the instrument was overwhelming.

From that point, I simply habitually acquired almost everything I encountered concerning Shaw's music, including records, articles, photos, and mentions in books of all sorts. My motive was to answer the questions I'd had since first hearing Shaw play. What was the story behind that breathtakingly flexible, conceptually strong, yet delicately subtle clarinet playing? What were the stories behind each of those distinctive bands he led? What kind of leader was he? How much music was there? How was the unity within and among the performances achieved? (The point was seldom made that Shaw had arranged the bulk of his output himself, and composed a healthy percentage of the best of his bands' repertoire).

Of course, Shaw's autobiographical *The Trouble with Cinderella* immediately provided the definitive insights into Shaw's character and development. The career that had produced the music was also fascinating, representing the acting out of a specific artist-versus-society confrontation, but a detailed account was not available. It quickly became obvious that a clear, chronological account of Artie Shaw's musical career and recorded output, which I had been trying to assimilate piecemeal, didn't exist in any one source. Accordingly, this book represents the one source I had been looking for since 1957.

I must stress that there was no intention of providing a detailed account of Artie Shaw's personal life or his career apart from his music. As Shaw approved of this approach, it seems justified. Even so, not every story I heard concerning Shaw has been included—only those with adequate verification and not refuted by Shaw himself. Only when specifically referring to his music or musical career, and seeming of importance, have any spurious stories been refuted in the text.

The major resource center for information was the Institute of Jazz Studies at Rutgers University. In 1968, I became part-time curator when the collection was acquired, and began setting it up in the Dana Library in Newark, New Jersey. My work there, and the contacts available, enabled me to acquire the bulk of the source material for this work over the next few years. I perused all the music periodicals for the relevant years out of general interest, continuing my habit of photocopying or making notes on information concerning Shaw. Several key publications, such as *Billboard* among others, had to be researched in other libraries, such as Lincoln Center and Princeton University. In 1973, I was able to meet Artie Shaw in person, thank him for his music, and discuss this project on the telephone with him a few times.

The first result of these efforts was my paper, "Artie Shaw and His Gramercy Fives" in the *Journal of Jazz Studies*, vol. 1, no. 1 (Fall 1973), pp. 34–56. By then, I also had been in touch with important Shaw collectors and researchers (as acknowledged in that paper), and with the major record companies for which Shaw had recorded. A proposal for a biodiscography on Shaw, prepared in collaboration with fellow collector/researcher John Harding, was sent to prospective publishers in 1975, but for various reasons that project was abandoned soon afterward.

By 1988, when Martin Williams encouraged me to submit my efforts on Shaw to him at the Smithsonian Institution Press, which had published my earlier book (on Eric Dolphy, written in collaboration with Barry Tepperman), the number of "new" Shaw recordings and the amount of available information on Shaw in my files had grown considerably. Accordingly, I prepared an entirely new draft, and recontacted Shaw.

Fortunately, Shaw was willing to spend time discussing this project on the telephone over the next few years. His secretary at that time, Midge Hayes, also went over the draft I had sent him. In 1991, I was able to meet with Shaw at his home near Los Angeles and go over the draft with him thoroughly. He made many suggestions, corrected much misinformation from published sources, and told many new stories clarifying various details or phases in his career.

While on study leave from my full-time job as Head of the Music Library at the University of Manitoba, I revisited the Institute of Jazz Studies at Rutgers University to make another pass through available research material. The cooperation of the staff there was invaluable.

The number of other individuals who contributed significantly over the years toward the information contained in this work is very large, beginning with Frank Ellisher telling me the story of his helping out the band while they were at the Willows in Pittsburgh in 1937. My uncles, John Zawaski and Andrew Z. Williams, provided the photos they took of the 1939 band at the Stanley Theatre in Pittsburgh. Fred Turco, of Oak Lawn Books in Providence, Rhode Island, also was a major source of recordings and books. In essence, Mr. Ellisher and my uncles began my collecting habit, and I could not have continued it without Mr. Turco after I moved to Canada in 1974. Successively, my parents and wives assisted with my collecting and recurring involvement with this project over the years, not in the least by their patience. Special thanks also are due to Martin Milgrim for assistance in finding certain rare recordings; Hugh Larimer for access to his collection of jazz books and magazines; Bob Strassmyer, the authority on Cleveland dance bands, for information on Shaw's Cleveland phase; C. P. Gerald Parker, for his inexhaustible sources of contacts among collectors; Bozy White, the Bunny Berigan researcher and collector; and Martin F. Bryan of Vintage Recording Co. in St. Johnsbury, Vermont, for various rare early "sideman" items. Recontacting John Harding, after many years, I was provided with significant assistance in cross-checking various data and exchanging photos and dubs of rare recordings. Finally, Rochelle Kantorowich provided invaluable volunteer proofreading assistance.

In this study, I followed the form used in my earlier book on Eric Dolphy. An introductory chapter summarizes the musician's career in the contexts of jazz history and social setting. The rest of the work provides a more detailed account of the career and known recordings, with contemporary review and interview quotes providing atmosphere and direct insights. The discography lists all known recordings and preferred issues of them, and is separate from the text to facilitate easy reference. Appendices and indexes supply additional details on topics that did not seem to warrant such thorough attention within the rest of the text.

Adapting this form to Artie Shaw's musical life, it seemed logical to break down the account into chapters detailing each phase of his career, and the discography to reflect the known surviving recordings of these successive phases. (However, the idea of listing all known releases of all performances recorded has been dismissed, as this would clutter the discography with much virtually useless information, often impossible to verify.)

Shaw was immersed in the music business as a performer for thirty years, from the summer of 1924, when he began to study saxophone, until the summer of 1954, when he ceased performing. It is this period of activity that is the focus of this work. The exact mid-point of this career was the year 1939, and Artie Shaw was the most popular musician in the music business at that time. Swing, a particular form of big band jazz, had been *the* popular music of that era for about three and a half years as 1939 began. Following Shaw's abdication from his position as the most popular musical figure of the day toward the end of that year, popular tastes began leaning toward bands with a distinctly more commercial, entertainment-oriented style, and jazz was never again so closely intertwined with popular tastes.

In examining Shaw's career and musical orientation, hopefully it becomes apparent that a pinnacle of good taste was achieved in musical popular culture that year. Moreover, not only was the reigning pop star also a major jazz artist—that, after all, had been the case since Benny Goodman inaugurated the Swing Era and became King of Swing in 1935—but Shaw also was almost entirely responsible for the character and arrangements of the music made under his own name, a rare situation in the music business among pop stars. This alone would have earned him a place of significance and prominence in any era. The combination of these factors surely represents an unusual situation in history. Consequently, the chapters on the development and success of the band Shaw was leading during that period are the longest, as are those sections of the discography (since more has been preserved and made available from that period of his career).

Throughout, I have tried to present a balanced account appropriate to what Shaw's musical legacy represents. Accordingly, earlier chapters leading up to his enormous success sketch out the phases of his development as a musician and his attitudes toward what he was doing, highlighting significant events in this development. Later chapters reflect the essential features of his subsequent work and career as a musician, again with aspects of his personal life only sketched in as background data when relevant. It should be obvious in context why, for example, his two prewar string orchestras are discussed in separate chapters and why the division is where it is, while the discography lists all his 1940–1942 string ensembles in one section; or why appendices seemed appropriate for the discussions of his work with singers while a leader, and of his role as composer/arranger in his bands. The indexes, of course, are to provide ready reference to tunes he recorded as a sideman (with dates and the bands he recorded them with), as a leader (with composer credits and dates of recording), and on the relevance (in context) of individuals mentioned in the text or discography.

A complete bibliography of all references I've encountered while preparing this work would be enormous, and would contain mostly repetitive and often misinformed clichés. Most references used are fully cited in context: this not only makes it easier for the reader or researcher to see what was said where; it also provides insight, in context, into the attention Shaw received in the media as his career ebbed and flowed over time. Any extensively used or quoted sources are also listed or described in the bibliography.

Transcriptions of solos and arrangements have been ignored. The music was meant to be heard, not studied in written form, which in any case could not provide any insight into the feel of the interpretations. Anyone who cannot hear the subtlety and depth of Shaw's playing, and of his arranging as performed by the working bands he led, would not be helped by such a map. Those who can hear these qualities would not need one.

Inevitably, errors will be found. Typos and inadvertent mistakes crop up with every proofing, causing awe that they had survived so many earlier proofings. Inevitably, more data will surface as well, and I hope many more "unknown" recordings. I will be looking forward to such information.

I also would like to thank Professor Paul Hammer and Dr. Bernie Rose, both of the University of Manitoba School of Music, for reading the draft and making suggestions, and Jeff Solylo and Chris Rutkowski for assisting with the computer.

Vladimir Simosko
Winnipeg, June 1999

Chapter 1

Artie Shaw in Context:
A Historical Perspective

Artie Shaw and his music cannot be understood or appreciated on any but the most superficial levels without an understanding of the medium within which he worked and the "stage setting" against which the drama took place.

On the surface, Artie Shaw is world famous as a clarinet-playing bandleader popular during the Swing Era, just prior to World War II. A slightly closer look reveals the glamour image, which included eight wives, among them the famous movie actresses Lana Turner, Ava Gardner, Doris Dowling, and Evelyn Keyes, as well as best-selling novelist Kathleen Winsor. Various Hollywood adventures and his dashing abandonment of his musical career on several occasions also contributed to Shaw's public image as an iconoclastic, unpredictable celebrity. Decades later, watchers of late-night television may have become aware of Shaw as an articulate guest on many talk shows. In the early 1980s, filmmaker Brigitte Berman did a two-hour Academy Award–winning documentary for the National Film Board of Canada titled *Artie Shaw: Time Is All You've Got*. For those who saw it, this film would have generated a deeper appreciation of the complex nature of Artie Shaw and his career, and the greater depths lurking there. Documentation of other aspects of the Artie Shaw phenomenon includes his autobiographical *The Trouble with Cinderella*, first published in 1952, and two collections of short fiction published under his own name.

Even jazz buffs and record collectors tend to perceive Shaw primarily as one of the great figures of the Swing Era and perhaps acknowledge his supreme virtuosity as a clarinetist, without recognizing his deeper role and influence. Sadly, some of the superficial coffee-table jazz books emerging in the 1980s and 1990s have even naively attempted to dismiss Artie Shaw as merely a "multitalented dilettante" whose place in jazz history was as Benny Goodman's competition for the title of "King of Swing" following Shaw's 1938 super-hit recording of "Begin the Beguine." Such misinformed dismissals are, of course, easily refuted by a closer examination of Shaw's career and legacy. It quickly becomes obvious that Shaw was in fact a master jazz artist of unusual depth and sensitivity, who clearly outclassed his peers and contemporaries on several levels of activity.

Even Shaw seems to have had a restricted appreciation of his own significance. In his autobiography he wrote:

> Primarily, I have always tried to play music that would satisfy me, within the limitations of the fields I've worked in. . . . Given the imperative necessity to please enough people to continue making enough money to be able to pay good enough musicians to play the kind of music I felt more or less satisfying. . . .
>
> But judging from any strictly creative viewpoint, I have never actually been a musician at all. In my opinion, no public performer in any mass medium can ever be creative in any real sense. At best, a performer can only RE-create, interpret, modify, seek—and sometimes find—new values in the creative work he is interpreting, performing, re-creating; but the fact of the creating itself, the making of something where nothing existed before, this is the domain of the composer, and the composer only—when it comes to making music. In the same sense as it is the playwright who makes the theatre, the writer the book business. ([1], pp. 385–86)

Well, this perspective can be argued both ways. In one sense, only God is creative. Even the composer, playwright, novelist, and so forth, are merely interpreting their impressions and feelings, re-creating life situations and, in a sense, being performers as well. From the other side of this view, even the slavishly imitative performer is "making something where nothing existed before." Every performance is different and new. Also, Shaw composed pieces for his bands, and developed a style of improvising on the clarinet that evolved over the years but remained distinctive.

"Improvisation" has been defined as "spontaneous composition," and in an art form where originality is highly valued, Shaw earned the highest respect. While it could be argued that these achievements are variations on the idiom within his medium, it also could be argued that, in the process, Shaw defined a distinctive career. By the choices, decisions, and development as a musician he made along the way, he created Artie Shaw, the icon. The career itself makes a statement where nothing existed before, and also left a body of work that defines the music of Artie Shaw.

Shaw himself refers to "the Artie Shaw business" as something separate from the human being inhabiting what became a public image. Shaw deals with his own perceptions and insights lucidly in his autobiography, revealing himself to be an intellectually oriented and acutely conscious individual who found himself in the sometimes awkward position of simultaneously pursuing a wide-ranging self-education while making a living being Artie Shaw the celebrity.

However, it is the body of work defining the music of Artie Shaw, and the career producing the music, in the process making its own statement, that are the focus of interest here. For this reason, the "Ex–Artie Shaw" of later years and any more intimate gossip-oriented examination of his personal life would be of little relevance to any attempt to develop a clearer perception of this career and music, and what it represents. On the other hand, any account of his career and music would be meaningless outside the context of its medium and the larger social backdrop.

This larger social backdrop was North America, primarily from the 1920s through the early 1950s. The medium was the music business, but despite Shaw's overwhelming popularity during his peak years, his music should be understood in the context of jazz history rather than as pop music of its day. Shaw certainly has earned his place in the history of popular culture, but his career and music can be more fully appreciated as a chapter in the history of jazz as an evolving art form.

Social histories and jazz histories abound, but certain points should be kept in mind for fuller understanding. Jazz history itself cannot be understood divorced from the history of the times. A detailed account of the history of the second quarter of the twentieth century (plus a few years on either side) is beyond the scope of this work, even from a jazz viewpoint. Nevertheless, some grasp of the mood of the times is necessary, as is a brief survey of the broad contours that heavily influenced the details.

Both jazz and the twentieth century had their immediate genesis during the latter half of the nineteenth century. The Industrial Revolution and assorted new inventions provided the technological and sociological background for various developments that did not radically change life on a mass scale until World War I and its aftermath. In the same period, jazz began to develop out of the folk roots of the African American experience blended with European harmonic sophistication, and before the end of World War I the first jazz records were becoming a popular rage. Thus it was not until the early 1920s that familiar features of the twentieth century were becoming the norm in North America.

Jazz is in a rare position among art forms. It offers documented evidence of its history and development almost from its inception. Because recordings had become practical enough to offer a widespread repertoire to a mass audience by the beginning of the century, many examples of pre-jazz "roots" in music were preserved even before some of the earliest jazz groups were recorded. Photography and cinema also were developing roughly contemporaneously with sound recording technology, providing an immediate visual documentation of the era and glimpses of early bands and personalities as well.

The first commercially successful record players began reaching a curious public in the late 1880s with Berliner's machines. By the turn of the century, various types and manufacturers of equipment were available. The Columbia and Victor companies were among the leaders in the field, and Enrico Caruso's operatic arias were million-sellers in the opening years of the twentieth century. Ragtime was *the* popular music of the era, but as the piano didn't record well at that time, records of ragtime piano playing were rare at first. Before technology had improved enough to permit adequate records to be made, ragtime piano performances were recorded on piano rolls. Early ragtime records featured banjos, xylophone ensembles, and even saxophones. (Saxophones were a relatively recent addition to the musical instrument family, having been invented by Adolph Sax around 1840.) "Coon Songs" and other manifestations of minstrel show entertainment also were popular, and represented another dimension of pre-jazz roots. Vaudeville musicians making records included the ragtime saxophone ensemble The Six Brown Brothers and the virtuoso saxophonist Rudy Wiedoeft.

A legend persists about the New Orleans cornet player Buddy Bolden. He is often credited with leading the first authentic jazz band, before 1900 (despite equally convincing documentation that the first "Dixieland" band was led by the white drummer Jack Laine in New Orleans even earlier). Bolden apparently had made a cylinder recording prior to his running amok during a New Orleans parade and being incarcerated in a mental institution in 1907. Obviously, the insight into early jazz that this recording could provide, should it ever surface, assuming it still exists, would be invaluable. Unfortunately, no trace of it has ever been found. (In one of those ironies of history, Artie Shaw's earliest recordings in 1928, featuring his arrangements and alto saxophone solos, have something of the same intriguing aura: they were never issued, although test pressings are known to have been made and circulated. Of course, these would be primarily of interest to Shaw specialists and students of the Swing Era, and have not achieved the widespread legendary status of the Bolden cylinder, with its potential insights into this earliest acknowledged jazz stylist.)

Another early figure important to jazz history is James Reese Europe. Europe led a large black ensemble in the pre–World War I years. They often accompanied the dance team of Vernon and Irene Castle, who provided a ballroom dance show similar to the virtuoso showmanship later provided by Fred Astaire and Ginger Rogers. During the war, Europe led a military concert band that entertained the troops in France and England. His recordings generally are cited as among the documentation of pre-jazz roots. Europe was credited with great potential, but he was stabbed to death during an argument with his drummer in 1919.

Most sources on jazz history note that Freddie Keppard, the Creole New Orleans cornet giant, was offered the opportunity to record with his jazz band in 1916. He refused, preferring not to offer documentation that would allow others to "steal his stuff." Thus, the next band to be offered the opportunity, the Original Dixieland Jazz Band (ODJB), a white group also from New Orleans, became the first group to record authentic jazz, in 1917.

The ODJB's first record, "Livery Stable Blues"/"Dixie Jass Band One-Step" recorded for Victor, was a million-seller. Ironically, the group had actually had a prior record date for Columbia, but the record was not released at once, and credit for the earliest available jazz record subsequently went to Victor. Comparison of the ODJB's records with other records up to that time reveals that jazz was indeed a distinctive new approach, although the ragtime roots were clearly evident. The fact that they were a white group notwithstanding, blues inflections also were evident from their first recordings. Unorthodox use of their instruments was a feature as well, although the barnyard animal effects on "Livery Stable Blues" is more in the spirit of novelty entertainment than avant-garde experimentation.

The ODJB was a sensation at Reisenweber's at Columbus Circle in New York. They appeared in a Chaplin short and toured England in 1919. Suddenly jazz had displaced ragtime as the latest popular music fad. Imitations began to appear, and established performers such as The Six Brown Brothers, Rudy Wiedoeft, and James Reese Europe can be heard on records incorporating elements of the ODJB's approach. Other early jazz bands to record included Jimmy Durante's and Wilbur Sweatman's. Sweatman, a clarinetist who often led a circus band and closed his vaudeville acts by playing three clarinets at once, is also remembered for having Duke Ellington as his pianist for a while. He recorded under the name "Wilbur Sweatman's Jazz Band" as early as 1918. His performances indicated close ties to the ragtime roots and some flamboyant clarinet playing.

James Reese Europe's last records in May 1919 clearly show the influence of the ODJB when compared with their records and his own earlier records. Rudy Wiedoeft went on

to be a major influence on most early jazz sax players because of his prodigious technique. He made several records in that era that were million-sellers, but he never developed into a jazz performer.

The New Orleans ensemble style was thus first revealed on the ODJB's records, and despite inspiring imitations, for a time they were the style's only widely known authentic example. This style featured a front line of cornet or trumpet playing melodic lead; trombone providing a lower counter-melody pattern with slurs and fills; and clarinet providing decorative arpeggios. They would improvise variations on the melody being performed, adhering to their roles and the harmonic structure of the piece. The ODJB's rhythm section consisted of just piano and drums at first. The piano provided harmonic and rhythmic support, and the drummer would supply a distinctive, propulsive rhythmic foundation. Other instruments associated with rhythm section roles included the banjo or guitar and the string bass or tuba (the players frequently "doubled"), augmenting both rhythmic and harmonic support. Generally everybody played all the time, with rhythmic accents in their phrasing often interlocking kaleidoscopically in the same manner as the roles of various drummers in African percussion ensembles. This similarity is easily identified by careful listening to and comparison of African drum ensembles with authentic New Orleans jazz.

The European contribution of course was the melodic and harmonic character of the pieces performed. The simultaneous improvisations generally would be confined to the prominent intervals in the chord structure, with passing tones and vocalization techniques occurring ad lib. Although other instruments would take the lead occasionally, to give the trumpet or cornet player a bit of a rest, solos were virtually unknown. "Breaks"—brief unaccompanied solo flurries by one or another instrument—often were features of performances, but these characteristics were the only "solo" passages. Thus, the improvisations even in the most freewheeling climaxes were more the variations-on-the-melody approach rather than creative new melodic ideas superimposed on the structure.

The "feel" of the music was lighter and more buoyant than its most obvious parent style, ragtime. It is easy to imagine, when ragtime was the most popular music of the day, what would happen as the musicians loosened up as the night progressed. The bands would play at parties, picnics, and taverns, with the atmosphere growing more lively and the urge to "jazz it up" given rein as the inebriants flowed and the behavior grew uninhibited.

Besides ragtime, the repertoire of the entertaining bands or pianists would include minstrel and vaudeville tunes, and folk songs from the various ethnic communities of the clientele. They would also play scaled-down versions of the repertoires of the community concert bands, which would perform in the kiosks of the parks of nearly every town on Sundays and holidays. It should be remembered that improvisation was common even in the European classical tradition prior to the twentieth century, so at that time, spontaneous variations would not have been as wild an idea as might be later supposed.

Thus, rudimentary jazz was developing spontaneously anywhere musicians could let it out. Naturally it would evolve more readily in the less-inhibited environments where the liveliness of the occasion would stimulate more flamboyant improvisations. New Orleans, with its famous Storyville red-light district and potpourri of diverse ethnic inhabitants, was a logical spawning ground for such developments. With the New Orleans ensemble approach evolving into a tradition representing the most sophisticated manifestation of this tendency, and with the first group to record and become famous playing jazz hailing from New Orleans, the city's reputation was secure. By 1920, jazz had definitely arrived.

As the 1920s began, the United States was emerging from World War I with a new identity as a major world power. Euphoria was in the air. Peace and prosperity were coupled with the new lifestyle made possible by the new technological innovations. Automobiles and airplanes, radios and record players, movies and telephones, all on a scale previously unimaginable, were reshaping values and behavior. Fashions and decor were changing also. Everything was fresh and new, at least for the young and healthy not lost in rural backwaters. Between the new media and the war's influence, the entire population was inexorably affected.

The "Roaring '20s" also were referred to as the "Jazz Age," with the cliché images of gangsters and flappers, classic cars and Prohibition, and the hot jazz band in the cellar speakeasy.

In retrospect, it seems odd that record companies were slow to pick up on the market for jazz recordings. The "race records" market did not get under way until 1920, with the popularity of Mamie Smith's earliest blues disc. Record companies then began to develop their lists of such material. In the early 1920s, small independent record companies began to record jazz regularly. One of these was Gennett Records, with a studio in Richmond, Indiana, known as the first recording studio in the Midwest. Gennett developed a remarkable catalog of classic jazz recordings in the early 1920s. Its artists included the New Orleans Rhythm Kings, a white group largely from New Orleans then performing at the Friar's Inn in Chicago, who began recording for Gennett in 1922.

In California, Kid Ory's Sunshine Orchestra, consisting of black New Orleans musicians, also was recording in 1922. They recorded for the Sunshine label, a black-owned company with limited distribution, in typical New Orleans ensemble style. In 1923, Gennett recorded another black New Orleans group, King Oliver's Creole Jazz Band, that featured the young Louis Armstrong and the Dodds brothers, the pioneer drummer Warren "Baby" Dodds and the outstanding clarinetist Johnny Dodds.

In 1924, Gennett recorded the Wolverines, featuring Bix Beiderbecke, the young white cornet player with a unique and distinctive style. By this time soloists were performing well-developed creative improvisations on records regularly, but this development had not been recorded prior to 1922. On one of the records that the New Orleans Rhythm Kings made for Gennett, "Tiger Rag," the brilliant clarinetist Leon Roppolo performed a long virtuoso clarinet solo that clearly was beyond the concept of thematic variation. Roppolo improvised an original new melodic idea on the structure of the tune, a musical statement independent of the original composition except for the harmonic foundation.

The idea of such solos caught on quickly. King Oliver featured himself and his young protégé Armstrong both on unison cornet breaks and for solo features in an aggressive, powerhouse style. He also featured clarinetist Johnny Dodds for some rough-hewn, expressive clarinet spots. With the Wolverines the next year, Beiderbecke demonstrated a dialectical antithesis to their solo approach by recording lyrical, melodically flowing solos with a clear, longing tone. By 1924 and 1925, Muggsy Spanier was recording with his Bucktown Five and Stomp Six groups featuring his own Armstrong-inspired trumpet and clarinetist Volly DeFaut in substantial solos. By that time Armstrong had left Oliver to work in New York with Fletcher Henderson, inspiring all musicians who heard him with his powerful approach and original ideas.

Fletcher Henderson had begun as house pianist for the Black Swan record company, the first black record label, which formed in 1921 as a subsidiary of Pace Phonograph Corporation. In providing backgrounds for various blues and popular singers, Henderson used emerging local jazzmen and ultimately formed the first jazz big band. They landed a long run at the popular New York City nightclub, the Club Alabam, on West 44th Street. The band included Coleman Hawkins, appropriately called the "Father of the Tenor Saxophone" as he was the first man to develop a distinctive solo style on the instrument. Hawkins thus became the first role model for budding saxophonists in jazz, but even he showed a dynamic expansion of conception following Armstrong's tenure with Henderson.

Thus, by the mid-1920s, jazz had developed considerably as an art form. The collectively improvised ragtime-with-blues approach of the New Orleans pioneers and Harlem Stride pianists had evolved into a style featuring virtuoso soloists, and the first jazz big bands had begun to appear.

Even popular dance orchestras were exhibiting the influence of jazz. Paul Whiteman had established some of the groundwork for the blending of jazz and classical influences with his combination of symphonic textures, "hot" jazz soloists, and occasional sophisticated arrangements. His premiering of George Gershwin's "Rhapsody in Blue," with Gershwin on piano, represented a landmark in this genre, although the jazz content was minimal. Whiteman's first recording of the piece, in 1924 with the composer again at the piano, occupied a 12-inch 78-rpm record. This performance was far jazzier in interpretation than the usually heard orchestral version. Whiteman's later use of jazzmen such as Bix Beiderbecke, Frank Trumbauer, the Dorsey brothers, and Jack Teagarden, to name a few, and of arrangers with jazz orientation such as Bill Challis, was an indication of his leanings. Whiteman even was called the "King of Jazz" and was widely considered to have made jazz "respectable" by these practices. He had one of the most popular dance orchestras in the country, and with his first record, "Japanese Sandman"/"Whispering" in 1920, he joined the ranks of million-sellers. Whiteman's long career extended into the television era. His contribution to jazz was slight beyond providing work for his jazz soloists and influencing most dance orchestras and public tastes toward jazz.

Another popular and influential group was the California Ramblers. This was a recording group consisting of studio musicians in New York who began turning out jazz-oriented dance music during the early 1920s. Its personnel included Red Nichols, Tommy and Jimmy Dorsey, Adrian and Art Rollini, and other significant early jazz performers. However, Chicago was considered the center of jazz activity, because of its wide-open nightlife, the gallery of major jazz stars working there, and of course the documentation of these figures by Gennett Records. With the early recordings by Louis Armstrong, Earl Hines, and the group of white musicians known as the Chicagoans, the sounds of the era achieved fuller definition. This was enhanced by the replacement of acoustical recordings with the improved fidelity made possible by electrical recording technology, beginning in 1925.

Artie Shaw began taking his first steps into the music business during 1924–25. Then in his mid-teens, he was self-taught, and learned by the usual method of studying the masters. Although jazz had been documented on record only since 1917, young musicians already had a substantial body of material for study. The youngsters later to gain fame as the Chicagoans were learning jazz the same way at the same time.

The practice of studying the recordings of the masters for guidance and inspiration has remained the usual way for aspiring jazz performers to begin. After a young musician identifies role models and develops a conception of how to sound, playing jazz with others refines skills and the ability to improvise interactively. The budding musician's own personality then has the opportunity to emerge. Although some performers remain slavish imitators of the masters

throughout their careers, the ideal in jazz circles always has been to establish a personal style. Ideally, the musician also continues to grow as an artist, evolving with changing conditions and personal maturity. However, this is rare. Even many of the most creative innovators have exhibited the tendency to crystallize their styles and continue without significant changes in their approach, after a certain point.

Shaw made it a point to work with musicians from whom he could learn. First in his hometown of New Haven, Connecticut, and in the latter 1920s in Cleveland, he worked hard to develop his skills as a multi-instrumentalist, and also learned to arrange music for the dance orchestras with which he worked. He has affirmed that his earliest musical idols and stylistic role models were Bix Beiderbecke and Frank Trumbauer (2). As individual stylists they were unique, with more advanced harmonic conceptions than was the norm in that era and a lyrical, melodic approach. Their music on their many records together from the latter 1920s was highly distinctive, and had a great impact on Shaw.

> They were the greatest influence on my style. Later came Louis [Armstrong]. I went to Chicago to see him many times. I wasn't thinking in terms of the clarinet then, but Jimmy Noone made the greatest impression as far as clarinet players go. (2)

The clarinet had been one of the primary instruments in jazz from the beginning. Larry Shields, with the ODJB, was the first clarinetist to gain prominence as a major influence through recordings. He had a clear-toned, flowing style, smooth and florid. These traits were identified with the Creole school of New Orleans clarinetists. They also were evident in Leon Roppolo's work with the New Orleans Rhythm Kings (NORK), and were derived from the French classical approach to the instrument. This style was personified by the Tio family of clarinetists and teachers in New Orleans, and by the legendary Alphonse Picou. However, these men were not noted for their improvisational prowess, and it remained for their pupils to add creative virtuosity to this foundation. Sidney Bechet, Albert Nicholas, Barney Bigard, and Omer Simeon were among the early jazz soloists whose styles were shaped by studying with the Tios. Bechet developed an extremely personal style that featured a wide, rapid vibrato, but he later became more identified with the soprano saxophone. Both Bechet and Nicholas became expatriates to Europe after some impressive early recordings. These included Bechet featured with Clarence Williams in 1923 and Nicholas with the Jazz Wizards in 1925. In the latter 1920s, Bigard achieved considerable prominence with Duke Ellington, and Simeon had recorded with Jelly Roll Morton and others.

Jimmy Noone also was from New Orleans and a pupil of the Tios. His influence on other clarinetists spread from his work in Chicago with major bands and on an impressive series of recordings beginning in 1923. Noone's virtuosity and musical imagination had a great impact on all who heard him. Apparently, he was the primary influence for young clarinetists in the 1920s. Even Jimmy Dorsey in New York exhibited Noone's influence, and the Chicagoans, including Frank Teschemacher, would go to see him play and sit in. Despite his prowess and prominence, Noone continued to study, even taking lessons from famed classical clarinet teacher Franz Schoepp, who also counted among his pupils such future clarinet stars as Buster Bailey and Benny Goodman.

Johnny Dodds also had studied with Lorenzo Tio Jr., although Dodds exhibited the rougher, more vocalized style of clarinet playing that served as an antithesis or alternative style for the instrument. Many of the younger stylists showed blends of elements from both the smooth and rough-hewn approaches, a successful synthesis that afforded a wider range of expressiveness.

Benny Goodman, only a year older than Shaw, grew up in Chicago. He was immersing himself in the nightlife at an early age, and recorded his earliest clarinet solos with Ben Pollack's jazz-flavored dance band in 1926. Meanwhile, in New York, Jimmy Dorsey had begun recording with the California Ramblers in 1924, being featured in solos on both alto sax and clarinet. Dorsey's technical proficiency and articulate, imaginative solos made him one of the great figures of the era and a major influence on other musicians.

Also in New York in this period, Duke Ellington was emerging as one of the most creative composer-arrangers in the history of the art form. Ellington brought a new sophistication to arranging concepts by employing unusual voicings in blending instruments in his band, and by writing to feature the unique musical personalities of his soloists. Like Fletcher Henderson, Ellington was fortunate in obtaining an extended engagement in a major New York night spot which included regular broadcasts. This provided exposure, security, and the opportunity to try out ideas with some of the best musicians available working in the band. At the same time, the Harlem Renaissance generated an upsurge of black pride and a curiosity among white audiences, who found black entertainment an exotic and stimulating diversion.

Against the backdrop of the excitement of the Roaring '20s, parallel improvements in cinema and radio entertainment contributed to the stimulation pervading the culture, and provided increasing work for musicians. Performing in the orchestra pit in theaters for silent films and stage shows, and at dances and in nightclubs, kept most musicians busy. Only the best could aspire to studio work in the radio stations, the most elite, prestigious positions.

Record sales also were reaching all-time, unheard-of peaks in the late 1920s, with over 100,000,000 units consistently being sold annually. Of course, only a fraction of these were jazz or jazz-oriented music. As with radio, however, the work was essentially anonymous. Only the big stars or bandleaders were named. Often pseudonyms were used. As in every era, there were celebrities with larger-than-life status, "stars," but these were usually movie and radio personalities or Broadway and vaudeville "names." Rudy Vallee emerged as a major popular singer in this period, but only occasionally were individual virtuoso musicians so acclaimed, such as was Rudy Wiedoeft.

With the stock market crash at the end of October 1929, the era ended. The 1930s began with the population preoccupied with basic survival and a search for some escape from the well-named Great Depression. The early 1930s witnessed a slump in the recording industry along with everything else. By 1932, record sales had dropped to a tiny fraction of previous totals, with sales figures quoted as low as 6,000,000 for the year. Obviously a significant source of income for musicians had evaporated. With the advent of "talkies" (as films with sound were called) another formerly reliable source of work had vanished, as musicians no longer were required to provide accompaniment to the movies in theatres across the continent. Prohibition ended in 1933, putting speakeasys out of business, although many converted to legitimate nightclubs. Many superb musicians were unable to work and considered themselves fortunate to get other jobs, outside music. Yet, radio was on the upswing, as the dominant entertainment medium of the era. More than ever, the best position for a musician was with a radio station, and obviously only the very best could hope for such a prestigious situation.

It is therefore a clear testimony to Artie Shaw's ability and professionalism that he was hired to play lead alto sax on the radio in Fred Rich's house band with the Columbia Broadcasting System (CBS) in New York, in 1931. Shaw had finished up the 1920s as musical director, arranger, and lead alto saxophonist for Austin Wylie, who had the top band in Cleveland at the time. He then spent much of 1930 working in Irving Aaronson's Commanders, one of the most famous dance bands in the nation, in Hollywood and on a cross-country tour, before becoming stranded in New York. He subsequently spent six months jamming with the best musicians in Harlem, where he played regularly with Willie "The Lion" Smith and became good friends with such emerging major jazz figures as Chick Webb and Billie Holiday, while waiting for his Musicians' Union card. Then, in the front ranks of the best white musicians in New York (black musicians were segregated from such employment opportunities at the time), he sat out the worst years of the Depression as a staff musician at CBS or, later, as a freelance musician in the studios.

Jazz was continuing to evolve despite the limited opportunities for the musicians to work or record in the early 1930s. Logical stylistic possibilities and extensions would occur naturally to the more creative musicians at any time. Style also is affected by changes in atmosphere and social conditions. The eminent folklorist Alan Lomax explored the relationship between style and culture in his monumental study, *Folk Song Style and Culture* (Washington, D.C.: American Association for the Advancement of Science, 1968). Lomax showed that nuances of style in the arts are a reflection of values and life-style in the culture. Consequently, the evolution of style in jazz also is a reflection of the musicians responding to their environment. Life-style and attitudes in the early 1930s were so different from what they had been in the 1920s that changes in artistic expression were inevitable. It is interesting that the hypervitality of the jazz of the 1920s subtly evolved into a smoother, lighter approach. This feeling eventually dominated most popular music of the 1930s and became known as "swing."

The concept of swing was not new. In fact, Baby Dodds, one of the great jazz drummers of all time and the most important jazz drummer of the New Orleans tradition, who started performing before 1910, stated in *The Baby Dodds Story As Told To Larry Gara* (rev. ed.; Baton Rouge: Louisiana State University Press, 1992):

> When I first started playing in New Orleans. . . . Those days they didn't call it jazz, but they called it swing. (p.12)

Many song titles incorporated the word, the most famous and definitive being Duke Ellington's "It Don't Mean a Thing If It Ain't Got That Swing." This song title summarized the prevailing attitude toward the propulsive, levitating feel characteristic of jazz from its inception. As a stylistic label, however, it applied to the overall feel of the music during the Swing Era, also identified as the Big Band Era in jazz history because of the simultaneous popularity of big bands playing this style.

The precise nature of this stylistic evolvement in jazz is easy to hear if one listens to a wide cross section of prominent jazz musicians' work chronologically through the time period in question. The rise of virtuoso soloists during the 1920s to a dominant role in the music was an affirmation of the euphoria and individuality that marked the era. Stylists were encouraged to develop their individuality (within limits), so that a wide variety of approaches were explored very quickly. The "language" of the music developed its own "vocabulary," and its most eloquent spokesmen and innovators had a dominant effect on the styles of younger musicians, who utilized them as role models while blending influences from many sources in finding their own personal expression. As noted, this often involved a synthesis of apparently opposite orientations toward the music. For example, combining the aggressive, flamboyant "hot" style with the smooth, flowing melodic approach that emerged in the same period provided the essential characteristic of the swing style. The lighter feel to the rhythm and the more sophisticated harmonic textures that characterized the style of the Swing Era were logical developments in response to the greater expressive freedom the soloists were putting forth. These elements also can be perceived as a direct response to the mood of the early Depression years, incorporating a certain introspective attitude with a less aggressive flamboyance, while retaining a badly needed sense of euphoric freedom as an antidote to the economic situation.

In the big band field, this development can best be illustrated by comparing the direct, call-and-response-between-sections approach of Fletcher Henderson with the moody, harmonically sophisticated tone colors of Duke Ellington, as the two premier big band leaders of the 1920s evolved. Listening to other jazz-oriented big bands performing in the early 1930s, including certain jazz dates led by Red Nichols, Glen Gray's Casa Loma Orchestra, Benny Carter (one of the great creative arrangers of the era as well as an influential instrumentalist), and of course Henderson and Ellington especially, proves the swing style was being played by big bands years before the style became the dominant popular music in North America.

Precise technical descriptions of what was happening musically in such transitions are meaningless. The music itself developed intuitively, by ear, with theoretical discussions following later by those concerned with such matters. Those who understand the music (or "musical language") can hear these developments clearly, and would not need a map. Those who do not understand the music would be baffled by such an analysis. In any case, precise notation cannot capture the *feel* of the music, which is its most essential ingredient. Such an exercise would therefore be futile, except for those attempting to write arrangements based on these styles. Even then, more would be gained by studying the published versions of complete arrangements from that era, or even more important, the original recordings. No two bands would play the same arrangement the same way, and even the same band on the same day generally evidences differences in interpretation when alternate takes are compared. In any case, the interpretative feel of the music, intuitive in that era, would have to be learned by imitating records. The culture no longer exists. The style is natural only to survivors of that era, although imitations persist. Naturally, only the original contemporary recordings document the style adequately.

Fortunately, recordings exist in abundance. Films and photographs also serve to document the era, although Hollywood's treatment of jazz always has been to trivialize it. Appearances by the big bands in movies were more often embarrassing than representative, and often performances were marred by irrelevant dialogue. The best visual documentations of the big bands were the film shorts. A band was then featured for a number or several numbers, usually without interference or distractions. Sound recordings exist in three basic categories: commercial studio records; radio broadcast air checks of live appearances; and radio transcription recordings. Transcription recordings were marathon recording sessions providing radio stations with studio-quality material for broadcasting, as commercial studio records were for home use only and not licensed for broadcast. Hundreds of recordings by each of the most popular bands of the Swing Era survived, and go in and out of print regularly.

Artie Shaw naturally was part of the scene during the transition from the 1920s styles to the swing of the 1930s. Working in the radio studios as one of the top saxophonist/clarinetists in New York, he was called for countless radio shows, transcription dates, and commercial recording sessions during his period as a sideman. However, the commercial nature of most of the music he was involved in playing was incompatible with his intellectual development, the program of self-education he had been pursuing, and his aesthetic tastes. Although he derived fulfillment and musical pleasure from playing jazz, this generally occurred in informal jam session settings, or while sitting in with bands in Harlem. Despite the security of his situation, Shaw became disillusioned with the music he was forced to play to make a living and walked out on his musical career at the height of the Depression, in 1933, to live on a ramshackle farm and write a novel. Eventually, however, he found he had to return to music to earn a living and finance his further education.

The Swing Era officially started in 1935, when Benny Goodman took his radio show dance band on the road performing the Fletcher Henderson arrangements he had been playing on the air. Audiences who had heard the broadcasts gave him an overwhelming reception, and the big band swing fad became recognized as a commercial, moneymaking business.

Radio and records had continued to be the favorite forms of entertainment in the homes of those who could not afford a nightlife. But the Depression was easing, and the public increasingly was finding the means to go out to movies and dances. The theaters offered the latest Hollywood escapism and remnants of vaudeville, and ballrooms offered bands performing popular songs and the latest from Tin Pan Alley for dancers. The new swing style was embraced wholeheartedly by a public conditioned by jazz-flavored popular music. The mood of the population coincided with the euphoric freedom inherent in the music, and swing helped lift the morale of the entire continent out of the Depression despite the war clouds looming over Europe and the Far East. The popular big bands became the centerpieces for theater shows, where the public could see them along with the latest escapist film and some leftover vaudeville. Dancing to the big bands in the big ballrooms became a favorite pastime.

Record sales once again escalated, to previously unimaginable figures. Creative jazz soloists were elevated to the status of pop stars and became cult figures. Benny Goodman was "King of Swing."

Artie Shaw got into the band business almost by accident. As a free-lancing studio musician of proven ability, he was offered a spot in the world's first swing concert, in 1936. He decided to blend his interest in classical music with his jazz ability and featured himself in a unique chamber-jazz context amidst the usual big bands and combos performing typical swing. He was a sensation and was immediately offered contracts and the opportunity to record. Although his ambition still was to save up enough to retire and go off to a farm to write, as he'd done in 1933, the prospect of making the money playing his own music was irresistible.

Shaw assembled a group that was an extension of his experimental chamber-jazz ensemble. They made some records and performed in a few ballrooms and theaters, but the public was responding to the big bands. Shaw's group, performing his unique arrangements, was too subtle. Although an artistic success, as far as the public and the businessmen in music were concerned, the band was a flop.

Miffed, Shaw decided to give the public what it obviously wanted, a conventional big band, which he referred to as "the loudest goddamn band in the world." Obsessed now with success (he spelled it "$ucce$$" in his autobiography), he gruelingly drove himself to shape the band into the kind of unit and sound he wanted. Still using many original compositions and his own arrangements, he added a repertoire of the most attractive popular songs by the highest quality popular composers of the day. Nevertheless, he uncompromisingly defied the rigid racial barriers of the era by hiring black singer Billie Holiday. Shaw wanted success, but on his own terms.

When Shaw's record of "Begin the Beguine" became one of the most popular and biggest–selling records in popular music history, he suddenly found himself a superstar. Temperamentally unsuited to handling the maelstrom of attention and flood of trivia with which he was deluged when he opened at the Hotel Lincoln in New York City for the fall and winter of 1938–39, he felt that everything had suddenly become a madhouse. Yet, on January 16, 1939, he was part of a delegation of entertainers, along with singer Gertrude Niesen, actor John Garfield, and actress Frances Farmer, to discuss the political situation with President Franklin D. Roosevelt. In the midst of his first flush of success, Shaw felt concern about the coming war.

It is worth noting that the Swing Era also affected Europe. American jazzmen visiting England and the Continent had been sensations since as early as 1919, and European musicians were catching on to the style, notably the superb Belgian Gypsy guitarist Django Reinhardt, as documented on recordings with the Quintet of the Hot Club of France. European recordings by American jazzmen, some of whom had been residents of Europe for years, also were widely available before the war. The Nazi regime naturally banned swing as a product of the black and Jewish "races" and therefore as "decadent" and unsuitable because of its corrupting influence on Germanic youth. In fact, the real threat in the music was its euphoric freedom and individuality, obviously in direct contrast to Nazi discipline and uniformity. The film *Swing Kids* clearly and evocatively depicts one aspect of this phenomenon as it was experienced in Nazi Germany in 1939. One of the great ironies of the era was that Hitler's cultural police did not feel it necessary to ban Artie Shaw's records at first, as they somehow thought he was the son of George Bernard Shaw (perhaps because of Artie Shaw's widely known literary interests) and, thus, Shaw could be neither black nor Jewish and therefore okay.

In the spring, Shaw, a celebrity publicized as the most popular musician in the country, collapsed on stage from a rare blood disorder. Following his near-death experience, he again considered quitting the music business, but was talked into continuing with his band. Nevertheless, the pressures of the business side of his career, and the frantic behavior of fans, finally led to his highly publicized walkout six months later.

Still at the height of his fame when he returned after a few months' rest, Shaw reentered the music business, again on his own terms. This time he featured a large orchestra with a string section, enabling him to experiment with a wider palette of tonal colors. He refused to play anything but extended hotel and ballroom engagements on the West Coast, and he recorded several more hit records with his own arrangements, often using Latin rhythms, and with a small combo. Nevertheless, after about a year he retired again to rest and study.

It was in this interlude, to the best of Shaw's memory, that he made one of his rare overt "political" gestures within the music business. Always impatient with the business practices of the booking agents, the strain of touring schedules imposed by the agencies, and the competitive practices imposed on the music business by interagency rivalries motivated by monetary concerns, Shaw tried to organize the top band leaders into withdrawing from their agencies and forming a cooperative booking agency.

During the late 1930s and up to World War II, some deplorable practices were common in the way bookers and other agencies dealt with their clients. As documented in contemporary music magazines, musicians were intentionally subjected to grueling tours and long jumps between one-night stands, to undermine morale and eliminate potential rivals even within the same agency, with tradeoffs between agencies as part of business deals stimulating such practices as well. Uncooperative musicians whose ideas conflicted with the agencies' policies also were subjected to

this treatment as a disciplinary measure, with the threat of not getting work at all offered as the alternative. While not all agencies were so unscrupulous, and even the best-intentioned booker might have to schedule bands on such long jumps and grueling tours just to keep them in action, there is no doubt that many musicians and bands gave up or were eliminated through accidents on the road caused by intentionally exhausting scheduling that could have been avoided through cooperation and intelligent planning among the various agencies that made up the business.

Shaw felt that he had been subjected to such practices prior to his sudden popularity, and wanted to eliminate the problem for everyone by having the top bands control their own bookings. Instead of competing, they would exchange locations cooperatively, dividing the territory and sharing the exposure. With plenty of work available for all bands at the height of the Swing Era, other bandleaders could join and perform at other spots, filling in and being groomed for the top positions.

Even Glenn Miller (who had taken top position in the popularity polls after Shaw's walkout and subsequent self-imposed withdrawal from touring in favor of remaining at one location for most of the life of his 1940–41 orchestra) was in favor of the idea, as was Tommy Dorsey, another very popular bandleader with an acute business sense. However, to Shaw's chagrin, Benny Goodman refused to join the venture. Without Goodman's cooperation, the idea was doomed before it could be tried.

It is not clear why Goodman refused to consider the venture. Perhaps the alleged rivalry between the two clarinetists that was stirred by the musical press influenced Goodman's opinions. Apparently, Goodman took the idea of there being a rivalry far more seriously than Shaw, who always maintained it was nonsense. Shaw noted,

> There never was any contest. Even back in the days when we played together in the studios. I always played lead. No contest. (2)

In any event, Shaw's status as a controversial and iconoclastic figure within the music business would have been ensured even without such an overt political move. A less popular figure probably would have found himself unable to work at all after taking on the agencies at such a level. The history of jazz contains many stories of outstanding musicians whose careers were obliterated because of their being "controversial" in their critique of dubious business ethics. (The impressively interesting tenor saxophonist Lucky Thompson a generation later comes to mind.) Shaw's efforts to perform such a maneuver to outflank the established powers in the business, following his outspokenness on so many earlier occasions, provides great insight into why he often was referred to in disparaging or sneering ways in the musical press. Even Gunther Schuller, who certainly should know better, made some astonishing comments about Shaw's personality and motives in his controversial book *The Swing Era* (New York: Oxford University Press, 1989, pp. 692–714), thereby carrying on the tradition of character assassination and inaccurate criticism of Shaw's music a full 50 years after Shaw's initial critiques of the music business.

It must be stressed, therefore, that at this point in Shaw's career, the bulk of the music he had performed under his own name had been arranged or coarranged by Shaw himself. As noted, he had been a skilled arranger since his Cleveland days, and he continued sketching out or providing models for *everything* his bands played and providing final adjustments to the material his arrangers scored, even in his later orchestras. Goodman, of course, had relied on Fletcher Henderson, Edgar Samson, and others. Glenn Miller, who also was a skilled arranger, nevertheless hired Jerry Gray as his arranger, at Shaw's suggestion. This was after Gray had been with Shaw for about four years as Shaw's main orchestrator, in a musical relationship Shaw once described as similar to that of Billy Strayhorn with Duke Ellington (2). Shaw did use the work of other arrangers in later bands, but few bandleaders were as responsible for the total effect of the music under their names as Shaw, and few produced a body of work in such consistently good taste, particularly in his prewar bands. In addition, Shaw was his own chief virtuoso soloist, continuing to provide breathtaking solos, awesomely intricate or exquisitely lovely, as the arrangement required. Still only thirty years old at this point, he already had recorded eight records that quickly became million-sellers.

When he again reentered the music business with a new band in the late summer of 1941, it was an extension of his prior experimental big band with a string section. This time, Shaw hired top arrangers instead of doing all the arranging himself. Of course, the band also played his old arrangements and he composed and arranged new material for it himself, but for the first time as a leader he was featuring others' material. By this time, after Shaw's earlier hit records with a string section, many other successful bandleaders also were adding string sections.

There was nothing new in dance orchestras having string sections, but jazz-oriented swing bands had not previously included strings. Shaw's own arrangements with his earlier bands, and the arrangements by others that he was using in his new orchestra, were incorporating jazz and classical elements in their more advanced writing that anticipated the so-called Third Stream movement of the coming decades. In *Artie Shaw: Time Is All You've Got*, Shaw stated that if the war had not disrupted everything, he might have continued with this orchestra for quite a while.

When the United States entered the war, Shaw enlisted in the Navy as an ordinary seaman. However, he was soon promoted and put in charge of a band, without his requesting the change. Characteristically, Shaw went right to the top. He visited James Forrestal, then U.S. Secretary of the Navy, to request a reassignment to form a quality band that would tour battle areas to help boost the morale of the troops, where they most needed it. Forrestal agreed. The band toured the South Pacific battle zones, saw action, and nearly broke down from fatigue and illness. Shaw emerged so depressed by his view of the war, and life in general, that he was hospitalized and received a medical discharge. He then underwent psychoanalysis with May Romm in Los Angeles for one and a half years, and with Abram Kardiner in New York for two and a half years.

World War II was an all-out effort on the part of the United States to save the world for democracy as far as the population was concerned. Emerging victorious with the atomic bomb and various postwar technological developments enhancing life-styles, the country went into a postwar reevaluation phase. The GIs settled down with their brides, and the Baby Boom was well under way. A mellow life in suburbia became the American ideal.

During the war, popular musical tastes shifted to appreciation of sentimental singers, for obvious psychological reasons. Also, the draft and rationing during the war had curtailed much of the big band scene and its audiences. Furthermore, the recording ban by the Musicians' Union during the war had prevented new records by instrumental musicians but allowed singers and vocal groups to record.

Meanwhile, jazzmen were responding to the hyperpace of the new era by expanding their expressive freedom with still more adventurous harmonic and rhythmic innovations. Thus, the style known as "bebop" developed among the avant-garde musicians of the day.

Essentially, the classic bebop style of the 1940s can be appreciated as a logical extension of the gradual stylistic changes that had been evolving throughout the history of the art form. The leading innovators and their immediate predecessors can be heard contributing to this development on contemporary recordings, although the recording ban prevented many of the more adventurous and short-lived bands from recording at all. As always, certain key innovators were catalysts for the development of the new style. Most of them spent their formative years working in the big bands during the prewar years.

The Swing Era was not entirely preoccupied with big band jazz. Popular groups included the "corny" and "sweet" bands as well as assorted smaller ensembles. Other styles of music also generated huge popular followings, including country music, polkas, blues, and boogie-woogie, which was a jazzy style of piano blues. Even the best of the big bands performed silly and insipid popular material along with big band jazz. Most big bands also featured small ensembles from within the band, allowing more freewheeling jazz performances.

Some of these small groups performed in the older Dixieland style, such as Tommy Dorsey's Clambake 7 or Bob Crosby's Bobcats. Others were offering significantly different material, including Benny Goodman's quartet, featuring Lionel Hampton's vibraphone; Chick Webb's Little Chicks, featuring Wayman Carver's flute; and Artie Shaw's Gramercy 5, featuring Johnny Guarnieri's harpsichord. It should be noted that Shaw is frequently mentioned in the literature on jazz as being harmonically advanced relative to his contemporaries and therefore more of an influence on the next generation of musicians. It is worth noting as well that his big bands were remarkably free of the silly novelty tunes and syrupy, insipid ballads relative to the repertoire of almost all other bands of the era.

Some of the most creative innovators emerged from the small groups and big bands of Count Basie, Duke Ellington, Benny Goodman, and the then-obscure Jay McShann. The Basie band featured startlingly modern tenor sax solos from Lester Young, and a new style of drumming from Jo Jones. Ellington's bassist, Jimmy Blanton, and Goodman's guitarist Charlie Christian innovated styles on their respective instruments that served as guidelines for the next generation, although sadly neither lived to participate. McShann's band launched Charlie Parker, prototypical bopper and one of the most influential musicians in jazz. It is interesting to note that Basie's and McShann's bands emerged from Kansas City, performing in a unique style that has been identified with that city, and that Charlie Christian came from Oklahoma.

The earliest manifestation of the Kansas City style was Bennie Moten's big band records of 1932. This band included Count Basie and several charter members of Basie's band a few years later. As another wide-open city in that era, Kansas City's nightlife afforded its musicians lots of opportunities to work and try out ideas.

When Lester Young first recorded in 1936 in a small group out of Basie's band, he seemed to burst on the scene with a totally individual style that was fully developed and mature. His style represented an antithesis to Coleman Hawkins's robust, swaggeringly powerful approach. Young acknowledged admiration for Frank Trumbauer, and was closer to the lyrical, melodically flowing music of the Beiderbecke-Trumbauer material than anything else in jazz. His sense of phrasing and harmonic ideas were extremely advanced, and Young is universally acknowledged as the model for the entire "cool" style of saxophone playing that emerged over a decade later. Interestingly, Shaw expressed the greatest admiration for Lester Young while discussing musicians of that era in personal communications. A good summary of Shaw's 1991 comments on Lester Young was communicated to Loren Schoenberg in a 1984 interview, which was quoted in his liner notes to the MusicMasters CD 65026 (originally titled *Artie Shaw '1949'* and reissued as *Last Recordings Vol.II: The Big Band*). Shaw stated:

> Hell, Lester Young had more of an effect on me than any clarinetist. Lester and I were friendly, and we would go out and jam together when he was with Count Basie. We also sat around in his hotel room in Harlem playing, just the two of us. . . . Bill (Basie) said something of interest to me: "When Lester plays, I kind of lose the band." You know, Lester played in another dimension than the band did . . . he would go off into another place. . . . Lester played MUSIC first, jazz second. When Lester would play something, and I would follow him, we were kind of meshing. It was a very interesting kind of juxtaposition of two quite different sensibilities doing almost identically the same thing. He knew I dug him, and I knew that he dug me. "Dig" is a good word there—not just understood, not just heard, but dug. Got underneath. . . . He played better clarinet than guys who played "better" clarinet than he did. The formulation of the idea in his head, musically, came out of his horn.

Basie's entire rhythm section also represented a stylistic breakthrough into the next wave of innovation. Basie's sparse, stimulating solos and subtle accompaniments to others' solos, Walter Page's walking bass, Jo Jones's light, infectiously swinging drumming, with only occasional accents from the bass drum and the timekeeping cymbals, and the overall rhythmic feel generated by the section working together with Freddie Green on rhythm guitar, provided the foundation for the new stylistic movement.

Charlie Christian, innovating a style of guitar playing derived from adapting a Lester Young–inspired solo style to the electric guitar, came to prominence with his features in Benny Goodman's sextet. Later, at jam sessions at Minton's Playhouse and Monroe's Uptown House, where the young avant-garde players were working out the new style in the early 1940s, Christian played with Charlie Parker, Dizzy Gillespie, Thelonious Monk, and drummer Kenny Clarke. After Jimmy Blanton died of tuberculosis, Oscar Pettiford emerged during the war years as the prototype for modern bassists. Monk was providing radical new approaches to the piano, and Parker and Gillespie defined the new style on alto sax and trumpet, respectively, becoming the greatest exponents of the bebop conception.

Parker and Gillespie worked in big bands led by Earl Hines and later Billy Eckstine during the war years. These were the most advanced big bands during that period while the "modern jazz" aesthetic was being developed. Recordings by bands led by Benny Carter, Stan Kenton, and later Georgie Auld and Boyd Raeburn demonstrated the development of arranging styles during the later war years and immediate postwar period. In the later 1940s, Gillespie's big band and Woody Herman's Second Herd were among the best performing in this style.

Despite the vitality of the new music, and the relevance of the style to postwar conditions, its sophistication was lost on the general public. Listening to the bebop combos and big bands, it is easy to sense the mood of the culture, which had just emerged from winning the most destructive war of all time and was getting used to having jet planes and atom bombs. But public tastes seemed to turn instead toward ever more insipid vocalists, and jazz was relegated to being an increasingly underground phenomenon. These were the final years in the waning popularity of big bands, and the hyperenergy of the new solo stylists was incomprehensible to most of the population.

Artie Shaw had not been in a position to participate in the development of this new style. Much of the time, of course, he was off the scene, serving in the Navy. Following his recovery period on the West Coast, he put together another superb big band, without strings, in 1944. Again, he used other arrangers, and he hired several forward-looking stylists as sidemen. However, with the decline of popularity of big bands generally, he found himself with an excellent but underappreciated unit. Accordingly, he broke up this fine band after about a year, and devoted much of 1946 to experimenting. Recording with a studio orchestra, he used his own arrangements and several vocalists, most often Mel Tormé, in trying to elevate the treatment of popular songs to an artistic level. An eclectic musician, he also recorded a set of children's records, *The Pied Piper of Hamelin*, for which he had written the script and composed and arranged the music in 1941. There were only a few instrumentals in this series of recordings, with relatively little jazz interest. Following these experiments, he again retired from the music business to devote himself to writing. For two years he did no public performing. He was not inactive musically, however, as he was undergoing a disciplined artistic metamorphosis into the classical idiom.

When Shaw reappeared in 1949 as a classical soloist, he was well received by most classical reviewers. Yet the jazz and popular music critics were hostile. They were looking for his old hits. Few seemed to appreciate his motivations in immersing himself in this idiom. He had been involved in classical music since the beginning of the 1930s, and his experiments with fusing jazz and classical elements into a coherent artistic expression had appeared off and on since his first appearance as a leader. Yet his contributions in this direction have never been fully acknowledged, and his 1949 experiments also remain undervalued. After several months and some superb recordings, wanting to earn money for a new farm, he again formed a quality big band.

Unfortunately, while Shaw was off the scene, another recording ban had assisted the final demise of the Big Band Era. Vocalists still were flourishing, and the public was growing more apathetic toward jazz as the prominence of the bebop style prevailed. Shaw's 1949 big band was one of his best, but by the beginning of 1950 he had disbanded because of public disinterest. Again, he cynically decided to give the public what it wanted, and he toured briefly with a nostalgia unit. He also made a series of recordings for Decca, again arranging popular songs for vocalists. These exhibited little jazz content aside from Shaw's masterful solos. He then dropped out of sight again, once more retiring to a farm to write. This time the result was his autobiography, published in 1952.

During the late 1940s and early 1950s, two movements in the jazz world were occurring simultaneously, while the big bands were disintegrating and the bebop movement was alienating the public. One movement was the "Dixieland Revival." The other was the development of so-called cool jazz.

The Dixieland Revival originated with the rediscovery of the New Orleans pioneers still active in the South. Increasing interest in jazz history had led to the first books on the subject emerging during the 1930s, and researchers were turning to the sources for information. Discovering that many of the pioneers still were able to play well, these researchers brought them out of retirement or obscurity. After the war, interest in the older styles began to grow. Many previously unrecorded pioneers were documented by Bill Russell's American Records label, including trumpeter Bunk Johnson, a contemporary of King Oliver and another mentor of Louis Armstrong. Along with Johnson, clarinetist George Lewis, the same age as Armstrong but unrecorded and obscure, was brought into prominence and became a central figure in the revival. It is worth noting that when Lewis was asked who his favorite clarinetist was, he said, "Artie Shaw" (Tom Bethell, *George Lewis: A Jazzman From New Orleans* [Los Angeles: University of California Press, 1977] p. 113).

Older figures were encouraged by lucrative offers to return to their original styles, including Louis Armstrong, who formed a Dixieland group that included clarinetist Barney Bigard, trombonist Jack Teagarden, and pianist Earl Hines. Sidney Bechet and Albert Nicholas were flourishing in Europe. Jimmy Dorsey formed his Dorseyland Jazz Band, a small group out of his dance band, playing some of the better Dixieland jazz in that period. Imitators began to gain great popularity, including the Dukes of Dixieland and groups led by Bob Scobey and Turk Murphy. Clarinetist Pete Fountain and trumpeter Al Hirt, both from New Orleans, recorded together, playing superb music in this era before going on to become commercial parodies of the style. Fountain was a musical clone of his mentor Irving Fazola, a star with Bob Crosby's big band and Bobcats. Fountain went on to star on Lawrence Welk's television show in the latter 1950s, where he performed excellent Dixieland jazz regularly in special features and became a pop star.

While the clarinet was regularly featured with the early stylists, it had fallen out of favor with the modernists. It allegedly was too difficult an instrument to adapt to the technical demands of the new style. However, several outstanding clarinetists made excellent records in the new style, especially Buddy DeFranco, who had emerged from Tommy Dorsey's band to work with Boyd Raeburn and, by the late 1940s, to win polls as top clarinetist. Clarinetist Tony Scott also played bebop early in the development of the style, recording with Dizzy Gillespie in 1945. Scott went on to experiment in the 1960s and later with cross-cultural blends, including recording an album with Japanese classical musicians performing on koto and shakuhachi in their traditional styles. John LaPorta, Bill Smith (later known as William O. Smith, the contemporary composer and avant-garde clarinetist), Sam Most, and Jimmy Giuffre also provided ample documentation of their work as outstanding clarinetists in the modern idiom in the early 1950s. Giuffre also was associated with the Third Stream movement and recorded many excellent albums in the cool style, remaining active in more avant-garde contexts as well.

The cool jazz movement also began in the late 1940s. It represented a restrained, cerebral approach to the innovations in harmony and rhythm of the bebop pioneers. The style can be perceived as a logical extension of the approach to jazz exhibited by Bix Beiderbecke and Frank Trumbauer in the 1920s. As noted, Lester Young was the stylistic role model for saxophonists in this trend. Miles Davis's famed "Birth of the Cool" nonet of 1948, which recorded a number of excellent examples in this genre in 1949–50, is usually cited as the trigger for this movement. This band contained sidemen who had worked with Claude Thornhill's unusual big band of the late 1940s: Thornhill was a skilled and imaginative arranger whose original ideas were executed by his arranging staff, including Gil Evans and Gerry Mulligan among others. Evans and Mulligan also arranged many of the Miles Davis nonet pieces. Blind pianist Lennie Tristano was another central figure pioneering this style. Lee Konitz, who had played alto sax with Tristano, Kenton, Thornhill's band, and Miles's unit, was the quintessential cool jazz alto player, although eclipsed by Paul Desmond's work with Dave Brubeck. Brubeck was perhaps the most successful popularizer of the style, which actually succeeded in attracting a bit of an audience, especially among beatniks and the college crowd. Gerry Mulligan also was very successful with this approach from the early 1950s onward.

For a while, jazz almost seemed to be recovering a popular following. The Dixieland Revival had generated a popular following in a nostalgia mood, and cool jazz was appealing to intellectually oriented modernists. At least the

cool jazz movement was an appropriate reflection of the style and mood of the era, when a relatively restrained and sedate approach to life seemed to prevail. Television had taken over as the primary medium for home entertainment, and the Baby Boomers were in school. Fans of the Swing Era and former GIs were facing approaching middle age in front of their television sets in suburbia as the relatively mellow Eisenhower years got under way. The Cold War was becoming a fact of life and a conservative and relaxed aura prevailed, despite the paranoia generated by Senator Joe McCarthy's House Un-American Activities Committee.

In the early 1950s, the "Red Scare," concern that subtle communist infiltration was undermining the American way of life, stimulated a gigantic congressional investigation led by McCarthy's committee, which intimidated everyone with witch-hunt tactics and pounced on the slightest clue and flimsiest evidence, destroying careers and blacklisting celebrities.

Artie Shaw was among those adversely affected by these developments, being called to testify before McCarthy's committee in 1953. Shaw confessed to being in favor of world peace. When asked why he attended a communist-sponsored World Peace Congress, he replied that if there had been a Republican one, he would have gone to that, too. This remark earned a round of applause from onlookers. Shaw was let off, but the next thing he knew, the Internal Revenue Service was after him for $82,000 in back taxes. He scrambled around trying to pay this off, but ultimately he was forced to sell his farm.

Despite these pressures, Shaw then surprised the jazz world by reemerging to appear with an updated Gramercy 5 combo, playing the then-current cool style, during the fall and winter of 1953–54. Performing this style of modern jazz was the obvious approach for Shaw, whose personal aesthetic roots were from the same sources. He always had been impatient with nostalgia, and his own music always had been post-Dixieland despite a handful of convincing performances in that style from his sideman recordings. Popular music still was dominated by silly or insipid vocal stylists. Rock and roll, still in its infancy, was just a white version of black rhythm-and-blues styles.

Consequently, Artie Shaw can be seen as totally contemporary and as a vivid reflection of the times once again in 1953–54, just as he was during the peak of his popularity at the height of the Swing Era. His playing was better than ever. He expressed interest in touring with his new Gramercy 5, along with a string quartet for performing classical repertoire as well, for the college audiences. Interestingly, this type of programming later became a feature of the so-called Third Stream recitals.

Although Shaw was unable to fulfill this plan at the time, a set of four LPs issued by the Book-of-the-Month Club in 1984 contained exactly this programming. The set was titled

Artie Shaw—A Legacy (BOMR 71-7715) and included many of these Gramercy 5 recordings along with Shaw performing classical repertoire with a string quartet (as well as some other items of great interest in the Shaw discography). This collection therefore represents the culmination of his mature artistry and reveals his musical intentions and interests at the time he left the music business entirely, at the age of forty-four.

The evolution of Artie Shaw as an artist, therefore, can be seen as a reflection of the times in which he was living, and of the evolution of jazz as an art form up to the time he left music. Stylistically, his music represented the range of jazz styles, from the New Orleans ensemble style on one rare item, through the cool jazz that was the epitome of modern jazz in the early 1950s. His recordings reveal him to be one of the most interesting soloists performing at each successive stage from the early 1930s until his retirement. Only the flamboyantly aggressive bebop style, which was avant-garde in the mid-1940s, was not represented. Throughout one important stage in the evolution of jazz, the period during which it was the most popular form of music in North America, Artie Shaw was performing some of the best music the era offered, and for a while was the most popular musician active. This is even more remarkable when it is recalled that he functioned as his own arranger and chief soloist, and was the composer of four of the eight tunes that he recorded that were million-sellers at the time. No other bandleader of the Swing Era could make such a claim. Few were virtuoso soloists. Very few did any arranging, let alone *all* their own arranging. Only a handful achieved Shaw's level of popularity (only one at a time could be No. 1) or had such a proportion of original tunes become million-selling records. Most important from an artistic viewpoint, very few continued to evolve as artists or remained so contemporary during their careers.

Beyond all that, there is another side to Shaw: the writer/ intellectual whose career was also an acting out of an existential statement. Throughout his active career, Shaw was constantly appalled by the commercial aspects of the music business, and consistently made comments in interviews and wrote articles about his views on the music scene. He made it clear that he felt stress from the conflict between the motives and goals of an artist on the one hand, and the pressures and demands of the music business and the materialistic society in which he functioned on the other. Shaw acted this out by consistently trying to escape from the music business, both prior to his rise to fame and later, when it meant walking out on a million-dollar business. Even his recorded legacy reflects aspects of this conflict of interest. As a sideman early in his career, he deplored the commercial music he was required to perform, although he loved the occasional opportunities to play some good jazz. As a leader, he would alternate long periods of relentlessly un-

compromising artistic integrity with brief phases of "giving the public what it wants" before walking out yet again. Careful listening to his overall legacy makes the approach/ avoidance conflict audible, although his own clarinet playing was always impeccable and inspiringly beautiful.

His life exhibited several contrasts of similar intensity. These help explain his character and lend insight to further appreciation of his music and career. One is the extreme contrast between the poverty and loneliness of his childhood in New York and New Haven and the wealth and frenzy of his later life as a pop star and Hollywood celebrity, hounded by newsmen, fans and hangers-on. Another is between this wildly public life as a popular bandleader and his perennial desire to retire to a reclusive life on a farm and write. Either extreme was in bizarre contrast to his war experiences in the South Pacific. Besides the stress of battle contrasted with performing, he was alternately met on this tour with either "Oh, it's Artie Shaw! What can we do for you?" or "Who do you think you are? This isn't Hollywood!" There also are the much-publicized marriages, which feature the contrast between what he apparently was looking for in a wife and the glamorous movie stars and celebrities he actually married after his rise to celebrity status. Nevertheless the major contrast professionally was between what Shaw wanted to do musically and what the public demanded of him. It was the conflict of interest between his goals as a developing artist and the pressures of the music business, which molded his career and demonstrated his integrity.

The portrait that ultimately emerges is of a frustrated, intellectually oriented artist devoted to his medium but desperately trying to escape the commercial pressures and to resist the trivialization of his art. Inadvertently becoming a celebrity and a controversial figure, he continued trying to create as he felt appropriate, but he alternated these efforts with occasional experiments along more popular lines, retiring each time he became consistently regarded as a celebrity instead of as an artist. Finally, he refused to continue the game.

It sounds like the plot of an existential novel on artistic alienation. With added elements such as "son of a poor Jewish tailor" and "marries a succession of glamorous movie stars," it seems too improbable to be believed. Nevertheless the resulting body of work, both literary and musical, is of surprisingly high quality. It is an artist's legacy, after all, on which he is ultimately evaluated.

It was as a clarinetist that Artie Shaw made his greatest impact. Although he started as a saxophonist and played lead alto sax and/or baritone sax in countless bands on record and radio shows, doubling as required on clarinet, bass clarinet and flute, he seldom recorded solos on anything but clarinet (although a few alto sax solos from his sideman days have surfaced). He began being featured regularly, on records and radio shows, from about mid-1931. By then there was plenty of tradition to draw from for comparison, but Shaw proved himself to be among the most interesting soloists of the era at the age of twenty-one. These earliest performances, with Fred Rich's Fred's Friendly Five on radio show transcriptions, among others, revealed Shaw to be aurally identifiable, if not as distinctively original as he would later become. His uncanny control of every nuance of his sound already was a feature of his work. Several of his performances on these broadcast transcriptions were within Dixieland-styled arrangements, and his clarinet was fluently exciting in that idiom. His jaunty, round-toned low-register improvisations from this period are also of particular interest. Although he performed many featured sub-tone chalumeau spots as a sideman, most were melodic statements without much decoration, and this style did not appear in his later work, as a leader.

Throughout the early and mid-1930s, Shaw made many records as a sideman and eventually as leader of his own bands. Consistently, his solos revealed stylistic evolution and a maturing conception, developing toward what it would become by the time he began recording for RCA's Bluebird label in the summer of 1938. By then, both his style on clarinet and his band's style were fully formed and well defined. Growing out of the full-toned, smoothly fluid approach of so many of the best clarinetists, Shaw's sound became even fuller and richer, exhibiting uncanny control of the extreme upper register. Every phrase and nuance seemed impeccably placed for maximum expressive effect. His solos had taken on the impact of the direct communication of a fully formed musical idea. Shaw was no longer just playing the clarinet. He was making music with a sound totally under control and breathtakingly flexible. His ideas had strength, imagination, and subtlety. He also seemed to have a cunningly sophisticated sense of the appropriate way to play whatever piece he was performing.

Shaw's improvising produced such intelligently conceived solos, with such interesting harmonic choices, that many listeners believed they had been composed beforehand. Of course, alternate takes and broadcasts of live performances of the same pieces proved he was improvising fresh ideas almost constantly. On rare occasions he would repeat himself, as on the two versions of "I Get a Kick Out of You" recorded for both Thesaurus and Decca with his 1949–50 band. Such instances seem appropriate, as if he were quoting himself or repeating an anecdote. Even with this absolute mastery, he continued developing as a clarinetist. His playing changed with his environment and the conditions affecting him. This is natural for all artists providing honest expression as opposed to mere craftsmanship.

It is fascinating to follow the transformations in Shaw's style as a clarinetist in chronological order from his earliest available extended solo features with Fred's Friendly Five onward throughout his career. Each stage offers a new dimension to his artistry and musical persona. Even within the context of his sideman work, an evolutionary trend is apparent between his earliest work and the solos after his return from the Bucks County farm. Careful listening reveals an evolution even between 1934 and 1936. Shaw's playing after he became a leader also changed from band to band. Particularly obvious are the differences in Shaw's playing with his 1937–38 band, as revealed on his records for Brunswick/Vocalion and the Thesaurus transcriptions, and with the 1938–39 band heard on his records for Bluebird and available air checks. His playing changed again within the contexts of his 1940–42 string orchestras. Also particularly obvious are the transformations in his playing after the war, with his 1944–45 band, and again following his immersion in the classical idiom when he returned to playing in 1949. He was again developing a new approach to the clarinet with his final group in 1953–54. He has often stated that the recordings with these last groups were the best playing he ever did.

Chapter 2

New York to New York: 1910–1930

Artie Shaw was born on the Lower East Side of New York City on May 23, 1910, the only child of Jewish immigrants from Eastern Europe. His mother, Sarah Strauss, from a village in Austria, met and married Harry Arshawsky, from Russia, in New York. There, they ran a small dressmaking business out of their basement apartment on Second Street. For a while their business flourished, and they moved it into a loft, where they employed a number of people and hit a peak of modest prosperity. For a time, Harry Arshawsky also had a photography studio on nearby Avenue C on the Lower East Side, "Arshawsky's," in an effort to escape from the dressmaking business.

Unfortunately, the photography studio venture was not a success, and eventually it had to be sold at a loss. During World War I, the dressmaking business also dwindled, and after filing for bankruptcy the family moved to New Haven, Connecticut, to try again.

Setting up home and business on York Street, the Arshawskys enrolled Arthur at the Dwight Street School, where he first encountered anti-Semitism. On the lower East Side of New York, there was nothing unusual about his name or about being Jewish. However, in WASP-ish New Haven, seven-year-old Arthur Arshawsky suddenly found himself inexplicably bullied, called names, and chased by stone-throwing classmates. The awe he felt as a city boy exploring a new suburban environment was met with mockery from his peers. By nature shy and introspective, Arthur reacted by withdrawing into reading. An uncle who was a housepainter brought him a "whole barrelful of books" found abandoned at one of his jobs. From this beginning, Arthur developed into a lifelong compulsive reader. A quick learner with nearly total recall, he was able to skip a grade at the Dwight Street School. This further estranged him from his classmates, as he was now smaller and younger than the rest.

At age eight, he had a classic near-death experience because of almost drowning. He related in a personal discussion,

I saw The Light, heard the music, everything. Then they started me up again. I always thought it was a hallucination. (2)

While these events were taking place, Arthur also was having his "first brush with The Muse" in the form of piano lessons. Bored and disgusted with the tedium of practicing through his Czerny method book every day, he argued constantly with his mother over the merits of the experience. He once earned a quarter for playing "Traumerei" for a friend of his mother. Far from inspiring him into the music business, however, the event merely prompted the observation that there must be an easier way to earn a quarter. Nevertheless, he went on to earn a local reputation as a wizard with the ukelele a few years later during a stint with the Boy Scouts.

Meanwhile, family fortunes had dwindled further. The Arshawskys moved to a less expensive apartment on Grand Avenue. There, Arthur began associating with some mischievous youths exhibiting tendencies toward a future of utter delinquency. However, his parents moved yet again, to a better neighborhood on Orange Street. There they remained, while Arthur finished grammar school and went on to attend New Haven High School, known as Hillhouse High by its students.

In *The Trouble with Cinderella*, Shaw provided a vivid and sympathetic portrait of himself at this stage:

I was 13 years old when, toward the end of my freshman year at Hillhouse, I discovered a new form of entertainment and amusement. At that age I had developed into a lonely, withdrawn, overly bashful kid, with few friends and a tendency to keep pretty much to myself. The original shyness engendered in me by some of my early Dwight Street School experiences had crystallized into a general introspective set. My life had fallen into a pattern which had very little to do with any of the normal social aspects of high school life. I went to school, meaning I put in the requisite amount of time involved in attending classes and so on—but I was actually no part of it. By that time my feeling of being an alien, an outsider, an outgroup member, had become so much a part of my whole attitude toward life that I was unable to integrate myself with any school activities outside of those I was forced to take part in. ([1], p. 52)

This "new form of entertainment" consisted of waiting at the side door of Poli's Palace Theatre on Church Street in New Haven, and slipping inside whenever anyone exited, before the door closed again. Poli's was a vaudeville theater, and Arthur was fascinated by the acts, which opened a fantasy world of glamour and excitement. He was particularly entranced by acts that included musicians on stage, although the regular theater pit band held no such fascination.

> I watched them with rapt and breathless interest, staring at them with wild surmise. The clincher came when, along toward the middle of the act, one of the musicians, all dressed up in a blue-and-white striped blazer, came down to the footlights, knelt down on one knee (looking sharp as a tack and rakish as all get-out to me as I sat entranced in my stolen seat), and played a tune named "Dreamy Melody" on a shiny gold saxophone. ([1], p. 55)

It has been reported that this inspirational vision was a young saxophonist named Ernie Warren, who made records with Paul Specht's orchestra and a small group out of Specht's outfit called The Georgians a few years later. In one of those intriguing coincidences life frequently offers, Shaw's first recordings after he settled in New York were made with Specht's orchestra in 1931. While this makes a good story, Shaw stated in private conversation that this was *not* Ernie Warren: "Ernie had left New Haven by then. I knew Ernie, it wasn't him. I don't know who it was" (2).

Arthur promptly began trying to convince his parents that he should take up the saxophone. Shaw noted that his mother was fairly easy to convince, once she understood what a saxophone was and that it had something to do with music, although she was more in favor of his returning to the abandoned piano. His father, however, was quite against the enterprise. Eventually a compromise was reached: Arthur could earn money for a saxophone by working that summer at Gorn's Delicatessen on Orange Street. Upon earning the required $40 he promptly quit, tore over to Wrozina's Music Shop on Centre Street, and acquired his first saxophone. According to Shaw, this was one of the happiest moments of his life. After a few days, however, he was back at Wrozina's trying to find out how to play it.

The head salesman at Wrozina's agreed to provide Arthur with five free lessons, and he was introduced to the mystique of reeds and embouchure, swabs and key oil. The instrument was a C-melody saxophone, roughly between the tenor and alto saxes in size and tone quality, although appearing similar to an undersized tenor. This type of saxophone was a popular instrument in its day. Because it was pitched in C, the melody could be played directly from sheet music, requiring no transposition. In later years it was considered obsolete. Frank Trumbauer was the most prominent jazz player to have recorded extensively on the instrument, and his tone is said to have inspired Lester Young, a proposition that seems less bizarre after listening to Trumbauer's recordings in the 1920s and early 1930s. The instrument can be heard in a very avant-garde setting on certain recordings by multireed player Kalaparusha Maurice McIntyre, but it no longer is widely used.

Shaw reported that he took only two of the promised five lessons, as his teacher, Henry Hill, was too insistent on practicing scales before trying more ambitious musical adventures. Accordingly, the neighborhood was exposed to the raucous sounds only a determined neophyte saxophonist experimenting with more energy than skill can produce. After a few months, he felt confident enough to enter an amateur-night contest at a local vaudeville theater. He played "what I fondly believed to be a version of a lively little classic entitled 'Charley My Boy' " ([1], p. 62) with the pianist in the pit band. To his astonishment, he won the $5 first prize, which raised his status with his family. Encouraged by this success, he acquired a copy of a popular record by then-reigning saxophone star Rudy Wiedoeft playing a typical virtuoso piece, "Saxophobia," and began a regimen of marathon practice sessions, learning from records by the master players.

Feeling the need to gain experience performing with other musicians, Arthur teamed up with Gene Beecher, a high school friend who played banjo. Together they played the vaudeville circuit on amateur nights, booked in as a sort of "professional amateur" act to beef up the quality of the evenings' entertainment. After a number of such appearances their amateur status grew suspect, and the boys went on to form a band with a few other aspiring young musicians. Shaw recalled his activities with his Peter Pan Novelty Orchestra, consisting of sax, violin, piano and drums, as six or seven months of innocent, simple pleasure and unadulterated fun. Another group reportedly consisted of Billy Berman, trumpet-playing older brother of trumpet star Sonny Berman; pianist Johnny Ferdinandus; drummer Ted Pearlman; plus Beecher and Arshawsky. This group, the Bellevue Ramblers, originally led by Bernie Disken, played at dances, after basketball games, and later at the Liberty Pier at Savin Rock. By then, Harry Arshawsky had left his family to seek his fortune in California, so money from these gigs was needed to supplement the family income.

When not playing, Arthur would hang around bandstands watching the local professionals at work. The top band in New Haven was Johnny Cavallaro's Orchestra, working at the Cinderella Ballroom, located at the corner of Orange and Court Streets. Among its personnel were future stars Tony Pestritto (later known as Tony Pastor) on tenor sax and trumpeter Charlie Spivak. One night while he was performing with his own band, Arthur spotted Cavallaro's drummer, Dave Yudkin, in the audience. Arthur was beginning to attract the notice of the local professionals as well.

Impressed by his prowess, Yudkin arranged an audition for Shaw with Cavallaro. Shaw described this audition in detail in *The Trouble with Cinderella* ([1], pp. 72–76), and the story has been told with slight variations elsewhere. Essentially, Cavallaro, although impressed by the newcomer's jazz ability, could not hire him because Shaw could not sight-read the band's arrangements. Shaw promised to remedy the situation and be back in a month. Cavallaro agreed. A month later, Shaw had learned to read music. He came back and passed the audition without difficulty. Cavallaro took him down to the Musicians' Union, then bought him a tuxedo. Arthur Arshawski had made the transition to professional musician.

He also was a fifteen-year-old high school student, however, and the hours he began keeping, working as a musician, left him little time for sleep before school. Feeling it absurd that a professional musician should spend his days as a high school student, Arthur eventually contrived to flunk himself out. Despite his mother's efforts and recriminations, he was then free to devote himself exclusively to music.

Aside from appearing at the Cinderella Ballroom, Cavallaro also was often booked for one-nighters elsewhere, such as fraternity parties at the nearby Wesleyan University. On Cavallaro's nights off, Arthur often would work with other bands, including Eddie Wittstein's Society Band and Les Laden's Yale Collegians. The latter organization was a college outfit that occasionally hired a professional musician to fill its ranks. Rudy Vallee also worked in this band at the time and described their working behind Rudolph Valentino's stage shows in Waterbury, Meriden, and New Haven in his autobiography, *My Time Is Your Time* (New York: I. Obolensky, 1962, p. 42). He recalled Arthur Arshawsky as

a young Jewish boy of rather sullen demeanor, who had little or nothing to say about himself or the study of the saxophone. . . . This close mouthed young man was obviously a very fine performer and a solid musician.

The need for him to double for clarinet passages in many of the arrangements these bands were performing led Shaw to acquire a straight B-flat soprano sax as a substitute for the clarinet, which he had not yet learned to play. Also during this period, he decided to change his name. He reduced Arthur Arshawsky, the English version of his Hebrew name (Abraham Isaac Arshawsky) given him by the rabbi on the traditional eighth day after birth, to just plain Art Shaw. Aside from its convenience as a stage name, this enabled him to avoid issues over his being Jewish.

In 1926, the Cavallaro band went to Bantam Lake Resort near Litchfield, Connecticut, for a summer commitment. While there, the older men in the band decided to teach young Art about the manly art of boozing. After a couple of boilermakers, Shaw passed out in the cabin, wearing only a red bathing suit. He awakened to discover that the band already was performing behind the silent films preceding the dance in the ballroom. Without remembering to change, he snuck into the theater and took his place. When the lights went up and he was spotted, Cavallaro chased him out into the lake, swinging a banjo at him and declaring him fired.

Several young musicians who had been appreciating the band then asked Shaw to join them for a promised job at the Joyland Casino in Kentucky. Accordingly, Shaw rattled off in an old jalopy with Ralph Platt and The Kentuckians to Lexington, only to have the job close unexpectedly within a week. Stranded, Shaw hocked his horns. He spent days reading Jack London in the public library and evenings seeking a gig. He slept in the park and washed dishes for meals. Finally he was hired by a band led by Blue Steele, and toured with them through Tennessee and Georgia until he was able to save enough money to get home.

Back in New Haven, Shaw was again hired by Cavallaro. This was for a job in Florida, and it was on the condition that Shaw learn to play the clarinet parts on clarinet. Shaw tried to learn en route, but he was barely competent on arrival. This incurred Cavallaro's wrath once again. However, Shaw survived the gig and by the time they returned to New Haven he was able to handle the parts.

By this time Shaw also was playing baritone sax, and he felt confident enough to audition for the lead alto sax chair with a band of New York musicians, led by Alex Hyde, who were to be performing at the Olympia Theatre in New Haven and needed to supplement their personnel with local talent. Shaw wrote in *The Trouble with Cinderella*:

The first thing I knew, I was up there making an audition; and the next thing I knew—and this damn near floored me altogether—I had been hired!

We had to play three or four stage shows daily, and between shows there were constant rehearsals for the following week's show. We reported for work at least a half hour before curtain time. . . .

The most important thing I learned from that whole job had less to do with the music itself than with the way a professional musician was supposed to behave. . . . In time I began to learn to conduct myself more in accordance with my status as a professional musician working with other professionals who took their means of livelihood fairly seriously. . . . In addition there was also a good bit of stuff I was managing to learn about music. . . .

I began to learn a new method of sight reading. The idea was to read three or four, or even more, bars ahead of where you were playing. I found out about new methods of tone production, and the various kinds of tones that could be used in different types of ensemble playing—dry tone, warm tone, the use of vibrato—wide and narrow—and when to avoid vibrato altogether. I was introduced to the whole matter of dynamics—which up until then had never even entered my mind. All I had ever known about dynamics was that a fellow either played loud or soft, depending on how many other musicians he had to be heard over—but now I learned that this is one of the most important things an orchestra player has to be aware of, and that he must modulate his own playing in accordance with it in almost every note he plays. In short, I had to learn so many technical and non-technical aspects of the seemingly simple procedure of blowing a horn in a dance band, that after a few weeks of it my head buzzed. I remember that I used to go home nights and have a terrible time getting to sleep at all. Round and round in my mind would go the "lessons" of each day.

But eventually the practical training began to show results; and I'll never forget the time when, after one of our shows during which I had played a short solo passage, the trombone player came over to me down in the dressing room and said, "That was damn good, Art. Sounded like a real pro."

I was so happy to hear that from him that I seriously think I wouldn't have taken a thousand dollars instead. Not that anyone would have made the offer—but still, I mean it.

And speaking of money, I was now making more than I had ever made before in my life, or, for that matter, even thought of making. The scale on that job—union scale, that is—was eighty-odd dollars a week. And on top of that, there was scarcely a week when I didn't work some dance job at least once or twice, generally on Saturday and Sunday nights, after the last show at the Olympia Theatre. ([1], pp. 104–107)

Shaw continued his account of his Olympia Theatre engagement:

[B]ecause of a new shift in policy on the part of the Publix Theatre Presentation people, the Olympia Theatre orchestra had to take on a new job. This was still back in the silent motion picture days; and it was decided that in addition to playing four stage shows a day the orchestra had to play in the pit during the movie. Although this was a new and valuable experience for me, with a type of music I had never played before, nevertheless it also made for a pretty tough job, with very long hours indeed. Not only did we continue with our four stage shows daily, and our constant rehearsing for next week's show, but now there was additional rehearsing for the movie score, plus the hour and a half or so we had to put in playing the score four or five times a day during each showing of the picture.

At first, the novelty of this new kind of music was intriguing enough so that I didn't particularly mind; but after a couple of months the grind began to wear me down. After all, I was still a kid, and although intensely devoted to learning the mysteries of my craft, I was young enough to feel a restless urge to get out of there once in a while. . . . After a couple of months of the new routine, I began to dread the idea of being cooped up in the theatre all day, from around ten in the morning to as late as eleven-thirty at night on Saturdays. ([1], pp. 109–10)

Despite this morale problem, Shaw was so successful in the Olympia orchestra that after the engagement Hyde wanted him to go to New York to join the California Ramblers. This was a popular recording unit in the 1920s that included such musicians as Red Nichols and the Dorsey brothers. Shaw, exhausted by the grueling schedule at the Olympia and feeling he needed more seasoning before taking on New York, was more intrigued by an offer from some musicians he had met in Florida: Chuck Cantor, whose brother Joe Cantor led a band at a Chinese restaurant in Cleveland, and Willis Kelly, lead trumpet player in Joe Cantor's Far East Orchestra. Shaw accepted their offer to play lead alto sax with Joe Cantor's band in Cleveland.

In 1927, Cleveland was experiencing a fad for Chinese dine-and-dance restaurants. The Far East Restaurant at 1614 Euclid Avenue offered a lunch show, largely attended by office girls who ate chow mein and danced with each other. The dinner show lasted two hours, and after an hour's break the band reassembled for dancing until 1 a.m. After settling into an apartment with his mother, Shaw pursued the endless rounds of this seven-day-a-week schedule, punctuated with after-hours jam sessions, for about a year.

While with Cantor, Shaw decided to try writing arrangements for the band. Knowing what he wanted to hear, but knowing nothing about the mechanics of writing out an arrangement, he attacked the challenge by laying all the parts on the floor and crawling from part to part writing in each instrument's contribution. The results were not very satisfactory. Shaw then developed his approach, scoring before writing out individual parts, until he was turning out good arrangements regularly. In discussing his work with Cantor, Shaw said:

My first records were with Joe Cantor, about 1927–28, for Gennett Records. They had this studio by the train tracks out there in Richmond, Indiana. We went in and did a session which was all my arrangements. I featured myself a lot on alto. Lots of notes everywhere; I was trying to put in too much at once. I remember we did a piece called "Frisco Squabble" and my first arrangement for the band, "Wabash Blues," and a couple of others. Willis Kelly was in that band, and a guy named Les Arquette, who played tenor sax and sang. He was the sex appeal for the girls. (2)

As noted in the discography, certain details concerning this session differ slightly from Shaw's memory of the event sixty-five years later. Sources indicate that the session was recorded on August 13, 1928, and "Wabash Blues" was not one of the titles cited. Although test pressings were distributed at the time, surviving copies could not be located for review.

After completing his year's contract with Cantor, Shaw worked for a while in a band led by drummer Merle Jacobs. In Cleveland's *The Plain Dealer* for Sunday, November 16, 1980, an article titled "Minstrel of big-band era in Cleveland keeps beat" profiled Merle Jacobs. Jacobs reminisced briefly about Shaw, stating, "When Shaw left me to go with (Austin) Wylie, he took half my band with him. I haven't forgiven him yet!" Shaw noted,

> Yeah, I remember working with Merle Jacobs. It was a small group. I took a cut in pay to work in that band because they were playing jazz, and you didn't get much chance to play jazz around there in those days. I ran into Merle not long ago. He's a promoter in Las Vegas and I saw him when I was up there lecturing at the University of Nevada. I may have taken half the band with me when I left, but what he didn't say was that I probably brought them along when I came. Johnnie "Scat" Davis was in that band, and [Clarence] Hutchinrider. We were glad to get a chance to play some jazz instead of the commercial dance music we were doing with Cantor or Wylie. (2)

At the time Shaw was hired by Austin Wylie, Wylie was leading the top band in Cleveland, at the Golden Pheasant Chinese Restaurant at 944 Prospect Avenue. Intriguingly, trombonist Jack Jenney (later active in the New York radio and recording studios, intermittently a bandleader, and a star sideman with Shaw's 1940–41 orchestra) was in Austin Wylie's band at that time, gaining his earliest professional experience. Wylie's band was prominent enough to be cited regularly in the musical press and also was broadcasting frequently.

Within a short time, Shaw was turning out arrangements regularly for Wylie as well as for the house band at WTAM radio. In *The Trouble with Cinderella*, Shaw's descriptions of his activities in this period indicate he had developed into a workaholic. Furthermore, exhaustion from his work schedule was compounded by bouts of insomnia. It also was clear that he was miserable from loneliness and sexual frustration.

Fortunately, Shaw found a close friend in Claude Thornhill, then playing piano with another band working in Cleveland. He got Thornhill hired into Wylie's band by writing several arrangements for two pianos. After some struggle Shaw managed to convince his mother that he needed to be independent of her attentiveness. Afterward, he and Thornhill shared an apartment. He also fell deeply in love with a girl named Betty. He described their close but platonic relationship rhapsodically in his autobiography. Nevertheless, his workaholic syndrome coupled with the grueling schedule and insomnia continued.

Early one morning, Shaw was hyper from lack of sleep and bored after finishing an arrangement. Idly leafing through the newspaper, he spotted an essay contest on how the upcoming National Air Races of 1929, which were to be held in Cleveland, would benefit the city. To pass the time before going to work for the lunch show, he worked on an entry. To his surprise, he won the prize—a trip to Hollywood.

While in Hollywood, Shaw had a brief, strained reunion with his father, and some awkward moments being photographed with a few celebrities. Staying at the Roosevelt Hotel, he went into the Blossom Room to watch stars such as Charlie Chaplin, Jean Harlow, and other famous personalities of the day dancing to one of the nationally famous dance bands of the era, Irving Aaronson's Commanders. Shaw was delighted to find that the band contained two of his friends from New Haven: Charlie Trotta, who had played trumpet in Hyde's band at the Olympia, and Tony Pestritto. Their reunion inspired them to recommend to Shaw that he join Aaronson's band when it was scheduled to be reorganized following their upcoming tour with the Cole Porter musical *Paris* starring Irene Bordoni.

Shaw returned to Cleveland indecisive. He had become virtually the musical director of Wylie's band, writing arrangements and playing lead alto sax. He felt that Wylie's band was of more musical interest than Aaronson's, which was far more entertainment oriented. Clearly, Austin Wylie had one of the more newsworthy bands of the day, if contemporary issues of *Billboard* were any indication. For example, the June 8, 1929, *Billboard* noted on page 26: "Austin Wylie Set For Summer" and went on to state that Wylie's band had recently concluded six months at the New Picadilly Restaurant. It was then to be at the Willow Gardens for the summer, with nightly radio broadcasts over WTAM. The same issue noted on page 53 that Irving Aaronson's Commanders, having just closed with Irene Bordoni's *Paris* musical, were at the Palace Theater in New York.

Mention of both groups occurred at intervals in *Billboard*, along with the other leading bands of the day. These included orchestras led by Paul Whiteman, Gus Arnheim, Guy Lombardo, Ted Weems, and Ben Bernie, along with less often mentioned orchestras such as Duke Ellington's, Cab Calloway's, and Glen Gray's Casa Loma Orchestra. Nevertheless, Wylie's band was regional; Aaronson's was national.

When the *Paris* show played Cleveland, Aaronson and his musicians went to hear Shaw's work with Wylie and were impressed. Their offer was repeated, but Shaw still was unable to decide. Among other considerations were his friends Claude Thornhill and, of course, Betty.

On the other hand, Shaw's insomnia had begun alternating with a deep, coma-like sleep from which it was difficult to arouse him. This often was causing him to be late for work. Wylie's having to come after him put Shaw in an awkward position with both Wylie and the other men in the band. Also, Thornhill and Betty were encouraging him to go with Aaronson, as it represented a real big-time break. Finally, Betty threatened to break off their relationship if Shaw didn't accept Aaronson's offer.

Consequently, at the end of his two-year contract with

Wylie, Shaw cabled his acceptance to Aaronson, climbed into his "shiny red Auburn roadster," and drove to Hollywood.

With Aaronson, Shaw felt a mixture of scorn and jealousy toward the entertainment aspects of the band's presentations. For instance, each member of the band had a unique specialty act. This would involve singing or clowning while accompanied by the band's pianist, Chummy MacGregor. Shaw tried joining the show by arranging a version of "Dinah" featuring himself as vocalist. It was not a success. Aaronson's evaluation of Shaw's stage presence was succinct: "The kid has the personality of a dead lox" ([1], p. 185). Shaw was thereafter spared the responsibility of functioning in this capacity, and remained on the bandstand during the acts.

The lack of musicality in Aaronson's band, combined with Shaw's involvement with a young starlet, resulted in his first attempt to get out of the music business. Reasoning that if the famous movie star Lou Ayres had been a banjo player, a saxophonist also could become a movie star, Shaw inquired about breaking into Hollywood, to no avail. He summarized the appeal of the environment beautifully in *The Trouble with Cinderella*:

> There was a feel, a smell, an atmosphere, a golden, glamorous haze, that suffused everything during those days. My girl put it all into words one night when we were taking a long drive out through the orange grove countryside south of Los Angeles. The air was heavy with the scent of orange blossoms, and in the distance there was the sighing of a summer wind and the boom of the Pacific surf. And I was just nineteen, and my girl was the most magically, breath-takingly beautiful girl in the whole wide world, and she loved me, and everything was magic and loveliness and everlastingly right with everything I knew or cared to know. And as we drove through the summer night, she leaned back against the leather seat—the top was down and the wind blew through her hair and the sky was crammed chockfull of blue-white diamonds, and as she looked up at the star-studded velvet darkness she sighed deeply and murmured, "This whole place is made for love." ([1], p. 193)

During their engagement at the Blossom Room of the Roosevelt Hotel on Hollywood Boulevard, Aaronson's band occasionally backed the young Bing Crosby, who often would stop by to ask to sit in for a few songs. Besides the advantages of being heard by the Hollywood stars and executives who frequented the place, Crosby also had a girlfriend staying there at the time whom he was eager to impress. He was in Hollywood with Paul Whiteman's orchestra, with whom he had come to some fame as part of Whiteman's vocal group, The Rhythm Boys, which also included Al Rinker and Harry Barris. They were appearing on the Old Gold radio show and making the movie *King of*

Jazz at that time, and Crosby was indulging in youthful excesses with alcohol despite Prohibition. An auto accident outside the Roosevelt one evening resulted in Crosby being jailed, although Whiteman was able to arrange for him to be let out to work on the movie. Impatient with their recurrent antics, Whiteman let The Rhythm Boys go shortly after their Hollywood commitments ended that spring.

Shaw's recollection of Crosby at that time was very positive:

> Even in those days, you knew there was something special about him. He was doing something that hadn't been heard before. It was his own. (2)

Following their extended engagement at the Blossom Room, Aaronson's band moved to the Granada Cafe at 68th and Cottage Grove in Chicago. The June 28, 1930, issue of *Billboard* noted on page 27 (datelined June 21, 1930) that "Irving Aaronson Is Set" to open at "Casa Granada on Cottage Grove beginning Monday," replacing Ted Weems, whose band had been at that location since September 1929. The July 23, 1930, *Variety* had an ad for the band on page 64, listing personnel and noting they were broadcasting nightly over CBS (WBBM Chicago). Aaronson's band remained at the Granada well into September 1930.

This was a particularly influential episode in Shaw's life. He took full advantage of his stay in Chicago. He had made pilgrimages to Chicago during his Cleveland years to catch the jazz masters at work. He recalled seeing Louis Armstrong's Hot Five live in their one public appearance, at a concert featuring OKeh recording artists (2). Nevertheless, staying for the entire summer, jamming with the best, was an experience Shaw referred to as the peak of his jazz education up to that time.

It was in this period that he decided to concentrate on the clarinet as his primary expressive voice. He reminisced in his autobiography about meeting the great trumpet player Muggsy Spanier when they were both sitting in with Earl Hines's band at the Grand Terrace Ballroom. He also wrote a lengthy account of one experience of sitting in with some of The Chicagoans at a marathon dance contest. After describing how various musicians drifted in and out of the session as the night wore on, including pianists Joe Sullivan and Jess Stacy, Shaw wrote in *The Trouble with Cinderella*,

> There was one trombone player, Floyd O'Brien, who had one of the most peculiar, lazy, deliberately mistaken-sounding styles I've ever heard. He would almost, but not quite, crack a note into little pieces, and each time you thought he was about to fall apart he'd recover and make something out of what started out to sound like a fluff—until after a while you began to get the idea that this guy not only wasn't making any mistakes at all, but had complete control over his horn. He would come so damn close to mistakes that you couldn't

see how he was going to get away with it; but he always recovered somehow—and this trick of almost, but never quite, making the mistake, and each time recovering so that the things he played went off in altogether unexpected and sometimes quite humorous directions, was what made his style so peculiar to start with—although it's impossible to give the flavor of it in language.

Also on this same session was the clarinet player I mentioned a moment ago—Frank Teschemacher. I sat next to him and watched him while he played. We were all slightly drunk on bad bootleg gin, but it didn't seem to affect his playing any. He too had this odd style of playing, but in an altogether different way from O'Brien's. Even while he'd be reaching out for something in his deliberately fumbling way, some phrase you couldn't quite see the beginning or end of (or, for that matter, the reason for in the first place), there was an assurance about everything he did that made you see that he himself knew where he was going all the time; and by the time he got there you began to see it yourself, for in its own grotesque way it made a kind of musical sense, but something extremely personal and intimate to himself, something so subtle that it could never possibly have had great communicative meaning to anyone but another musician and even then only to a jazz musician who happened to be pretty damn hep to what was going on.

The bizarre thing about that particular session was that while all this subtle and intricate musical stuff was going on, while we were all playing and passing bottles of gin around from one to another, out there on the dance floor were all those pooped out, broken down Marathon Dance contestants; and no matter what we played, no matter whether the tempo was draggy or bright, there they shuffled like the walking dead, hanging grimly, wearily, on to each other, leaning together like tired trees in a hurricane, clutching one another for dear life, like punch-drunk fighters in a nerveless clinch at the end of the last long round of a tough fight, and that was what it was like all the time we were there, right up until we finally quit around seven a.m. and packed our horns and left the joint with those living corpses still clinging desperately to each other, shuffling wearily two by two around the dance floor in the damnedest caricature of dancing I have ever seen in a lifetime of watching plenty of caricatures of that particular form of activity. ([1], pp. 198–99)

This also was the period during which Shaw discovered classical music. Like most jazzmen, Shaw had, up to that time, dismissed the "longhairs" as dull. One day, visiting a record store just off The Loop, he was startled to hear something uniquely captivating floating out of a listening booth. The clerk gave him copies of the material in question, and Shaw settled down to study "The Firebird Suite" by Stravinsky.

Within a few minutes I was trying to recover from the greatest musical shock of my life. When I finished, I carefully replaced the records in their jackets, and, clutching the album

tightly to make sure no one tried to get it away from me, went back to the clerk.

"Got anything else like this?"

"Do you mean something by the same composer?"

"Yeah—and any other guy who writes stuff like this."

. . . I went home lugging all those records, the 4 albums and the one single record. All Stravinsky—including "The Fire Bird Suite" which was what I'd heard in the booth, and "Le Sacre du Printemps." The single record was Debussy's "L'Apres-midi d'un Faune" [*sic*].

That was my introduction to a whole new musical world. ([1], p. 202)

As a result of these new interests, Shaw's relations with the other men in Aaronson's band were strained further. They found his new musical tastes to be incomprehensible.

Meanwhile, in an attempt to enhance the musicality of Aaronson's band, Shaw, Pestritto, Trotta and MacGregor campaigned enthusiastically for bringing in Toots Mondello to join the saxophone section. Mondello, however, was used to playing lead alto, and resented playing second to Shaw. Shaw obligingly switched to tenor sax, which he particularly enjoyed because this new role involved more jazz solo opportunities.

Aaronson's only known record date while Shaw was with the band occurred in Chicago, on August 22, 1930, although Shaw has stated that he has no recollection of ever recording with Aaronson (2). The two titles recorded that day were apparently dance tunes with vocals (see discography for details). Discographers also often have attributed Shaw with being among the personnel of several Irving Aaronson record dates held during 1928, but obviously that would have been far too early for Shaw to have been with Aaronson.

The September 13, 1930, *Billboard* noted on page 2, "Whiteman for Granada Cafe," due to open in October. The same page also noted, "Ben Bernie for Chicago," to be appearing at the Granada. However, Aaronson's departure date was not mentioned.

Following their stay at the Granada, Aaronson's band moved on to New York, where they opened at the Beacon Theater at 74th and Broadway on October 10, 1930. *The New York Times* Entertainment Section for that date billed the Beacon show as including "Aaronson's Commanders IN PERSON—America's Most Famous Band" along with the movie *Moby Dick* starring John Barrymore. Within a week of their opening, Shaw had the auto accident related in his autobiography which resulted in his being stranded in New York.

The New York Times for October 16, 1930, noted on page 7: "Car Kills Man, Pair Held." It went on to state, "Arthur Shaw, 20, of 2842 Grand Concourse, and Betty Goldstein, 19, of Hotel Marseilles," in a car with Ohio license plates, struck and killed a man named George Woods, age 60, a chef on a yacht, on Broadway at 91st Street. The car drove on, but witnesses took the license number, and the police found the couple in the car on Columbus Avenue shortly afterward. It was reported that Shaw had stated that he thought he had hit a traffic stanchion.

The circumstances of the accident, which had occurred in the early morning hours of Wednesday, October 15th, resulted in a lawsuit, which caused Shaw to have to remain in New York when Aaronson's band moved on from the Beacon Theater. *The New York Times* gave their closing date as November 26, 1930, with Will Osborne and his orchestra opening there on November 28th. The December 6, 1930, issue of *Billboard* stated on page 22 that Irving Aaronson's

Commanders were performing next at The Regent, in Paterson, New Jersey.

Legal fees for the drawn-out proceedings of the lawsuit concerning the accident quickly exhausted Shaw's savings. He found himself broke and stranded, unable to work because of Musicians' Union regulations requiring a six-month waiting period in residence before new arrivals could be granted a Local 802 card. Shaw had to move back in with his mother, who had returned to New York and resumed her dressmaking business when Shaw left Cleveland for Hollywood the year before.

In despair, Shaw restlessly walked the streets, or rode the subway trains back and forth for hours. He had reached one of the extreme low points of his life.

Chapter 3

Sideman; New York: 1930–1936

It was 1930, and the effects of what was to be known as the Great Depression were just beginning to settle in across the nation. Artie Shaw, at 20, already had reached a level of poverty, loneliness, and despair in keeping with the norm of that era. Shortly before coming to New York, while still in Chicago, he had learned of his father's death ([1], pp. 205–14). Shortly after arriving, he had accidentally killed a man, and he was facing a manslaughter charge and possible imprisonment. Unable to work as a musician because of the Local 802 Musicians' Union rules, he was again dependent on his mother's talents as a seamstress and was in debt because of legal fees. His writings on this period in his autobiography are moving statements on the human condition, in keeping with the existentialist literature on despair. Wandering about New York City, he eventually discovered Greenwich Village and spent much time walking around gazing at the windows, fantasizing a better life. In *The Trouble with Cinderella*, he wrote:

> I don't think I can ever really forget that phase of my life. For, aside from anything else that may have happened inside me as a result of it, and aside from anything else I learned from what I had to go through during this period—there was one thing it taught me, something quite valuable for a man to learn. Despite Donne's statement that no man is an island unto himself, I know that there are certain respects in which each man is an island, and that the possibility of bridging the terrible void that exists between these islands that we are and live on and within, is far slimmer than most human beings are ever given the time or opportunity to realize.
>
> As to whether it is better or worse for a man to learn this particular lesson—that I can't say. I only know that to me, at the age of nineteen [*sic*], it was a bitter lesson; and that ever since that time, ever since I first really learned it, I have never, or rarely, been able to escape the realization of it, not even at the peak of my career as a bandleader when, night after night, I stood up in front of my band surrounded by thousands of eager-eyed kids listening and watching and devouring with their eyes and ears this publicity-created symbol I represented and in a sense had become, and through which I acted as a kind of focal point for the daydreams and fantasies of thousands of other seventeen, eighteen, and nineteen-year-old kids not too unlike what I myself might have been like at their age, no matter how dissimilar our background and lives might appear on the surface.
>
> And because I had learned this lesson, because I had become aware of the vast void between the islands of ourselves, I have never since been able to entirely dispel that original loneliness and lose myself in the crowds for whom I performed. If anything, the larger the crowds and the warmer the waves of admiration and love that I have felt pouring up from them, the more intense the loneliness and sense of isolation I have felt standing up there between the two separate worlds of my band on the one hand, and the audience on the other; with myself drifting, apart, between these two worlds, like a separate island, or some sort of lost planet, alone in dark, cold, outer space, wandering, like Shelley's moon, "companionless among the stars that have a different birth."

Those few months I've been writing about were so filled with inner turbulence that it is hard for me now to disentangle fantasy from reality. There were all sorts of pointless little adventures I got myself into; furtive excursions into the twilight world of New York's dim, dark recesses, where I mixed with the debris of a vast city and brushed up against other night-wanderers like myself, castoffs from life, rejects, marred and imperfect products of the civilization factory—with some of whom I made brief and abortive contact before drifting on.

At length, through some accident I can't remember, I found my way to Harlem; and there I found temporary haven, a place to light for awhile. Also, I found a friend.

This was a Negro piano player named Willie Smith, who was known all over Harlem as "The Lion." He worked every night from around midnight to six, seven, even eight in the morning in a little cellar joint called the Catagonia Club—or, as it was more familiarly known to its patrons, Pod's and Jerry's.

After my first visit there, I felt that this tiny little joint, with its dim lighting, its small bar over at one end of the room, its sprinkling of red-and-white checkered tables, was what I had been looking for. It reminded me of the South Side Chicago hangouts I used to frequent. The clientele was more or less the same, but more important than the clientele was the whole atmosphere of the place. I felt at home here, for the first time since I had arrived in New York.

Mainly, it was the music that attracted me. And that was Willie Smith's department—for it was he, The Lion, who dominated this little joint with his piano playing. ([1], pp. 221–24)

Shaw later wrote a short story "fictionalizing" his meeting with The Lion. This was published as "Snow/White In Harlem, 1930" in his collection of short stories, *The Best of Intentions* (Santa Barbara, Calif.: John Daniel and Company, 1989). This story also was chapter 10 of his work in progress, the long novel *The Education of Albie Snow*. He discussed his relationship with The Lion extensively in *The Trouble with Cinderella*, where he noted,

The Lion was, as I now know, one of the very few "originals" I have ever encountered in jazz music. From a purely harmonic standpoint, he was far ahead of most of his contemporaries. ([1], p. 27)

Willie "The Lion" Smith was one of the key musicians in the Harlem Stride school of piano playing. The style originated at Harlem rent parties and was first prominently displayed by James P. Johnson on recordings made as early as 1921. Stride was characterized by loping bass lines from the left hand, incorporating unusually large intervals. The most prominent pianist performing in this style was Thomas "Fats" Waller.

The Lion also wrote about Shaw's visits to Pod's and Jerry's in his autobiography, *Music on My Mind* (New York: Doubleday, 1964, pp. 168–169), describing the scene from his perspective:

There were times when we had sitting-in, but the Lion discouraged it at first so the place wouldn't turn into another Rhythm Club. To sit-in with me they had to be able to run chords or, in other words, play in all the keys. I wanted men who could transpose, memorize, and improvise. A good minister or lecturer doesn't have to use The Book—a good one can make it up as he goes along. If you want to hear improvising, get to a Baptist minister, a priest, or a rabbi.

When Sidney Bechet came back from Europe he used to come down and join in on soprano sax. At the time I had Arthur (Traps) McIntyre working with me on drums. And for several months a handsome young man named Shaw would bring his clarinet in every night and play along. He had just arrived in New York and was having a dickens of a time getting organized in music. Shaw was waiting out his New York union (802) membership card—a man who wants in can't take a steady job until he's been in town for six months—and so he came in to play with the Lion every night for free.

My boy Artie was a good student and the Lion was proud of him when we went out to jam after finishing our nightly stint at P.'s & J.'s. He wrote about our association in his autobiography: "Playing with the Lion was a brand-new kind of musical experience . . . and I would do my best to get with it, until after a while I began to get the drift, to latch on to

what he was doing to the point where I could have some general predictability of where we would end up."

We would visit Basement Brownie's or Goldgraben's blind pig. Sometimes we both played in these places until both of us felt as though we couldn't stay awake another minute. One morning at Goldgraben's, a place where they had a tile floor and booths along the side, Pops Bechet, who was particular about clarinet players, came up to ask about Shaw.

"Lion, who is the musicianer?"

"Artie Shaw," I said.

"He is a good blues man."

I said he was.

Artie used to encourage me to get my tunes written down and published.

Benny Carter has spoken of his association with The Lion during his own formative years. The demands were formidable. Tunes were played at breakneck speed with key changes every chorus if The Lion was in that sort of mood. A horn player would require a fluent and prodigious technique. Carter called his experiences working with The Lion a major factor in the development of his style (Benny Carter, personal communication with author, 1973).

Through his association with The Lion, Shaw met and jammed with other musicians around Harlem. It was in this period that he became good friends with the great drummer and bandleader Chick Webb and with singer Billie Holiday. Gradually, he also got to meet the prominent white "Downtown" musicians, who also would come to Harlem to sit in.

After finally getting his union card, Shaw began getting work. He moved in with bassist Artie Bernstein, living in the Roxwell Apartments at 50th Street and Seventh Avenue. Violinist Harry Bluestone also lived there, and Bix Beiderbecke, Eddie Condon, and trombonist Will Bradley were frequent associates in jamming at the apartment or wandering off to sit in at a club. With the others, Shaw began hanging out at Plunkett's, a speakeasy at 205½ West 53rd Street in the shadow of the "El." Plunkett's was a clearinghouse and meeting place for the Downtown musicians. Having integrated himself among the most prominent musicians in New York by proving himself at countless jam sessions and sitting in at clubs, Shaw was recommended by Tommy Dorsey to Fred Rich, director of the house band at CBS, for filling a saxophone opening. Shaw played his audition without a hitch. Unexpectedly, however, the job went instead to a friend of one of the studio contractors.

That spring, Shaw played jobs with bands led by Joe Moss, Leo Reisman, and the Dorsey brothers. In May 1931 there were two appearances at college parties with the Dorseys while Bix Beiderbecke, with whom Shaw had roomed briefly during this period, was also in the band. According to Richard M. Sudhalter in *Bix: Man and Legend* (New Rochelle, N.Y.: Arlington House, 1974, p. 398), the first of these gigs was at Princeton University on Friday, May 8,

1931. The band also included trumpeter Bunny Berigan and saxophonist Eddie Miller in addition to Beiderbecke, Shaw and the Dorseys. Sudhalter noted, "Bix experiences circulation trouble during the ride home, must be helped to his room." Sudhalter reported that a week later, the same horn men, with some changes in the rhythm section, did another college date, this time at Yale; on this occasion the pianist was Lennie Hayton. Shaw wrote fictional descriptions of these encounters and gigs in his novel, *The Education of Albie Snow*, as well.

In a 1951 interview/article by Leonard Feather (" 'Happy at Last!' Says Shaw," in *Down Beat*, June 29, 1951, pp. 1–3, 9), it was stated that:

> He made his first records with Roger Wolfe Kahn and with Specht, playing alto on the latter's "Dancing in the Dark" and "You Forgot Your Gloves." (3)

Shaw noted, however, that he worked with Kahn only in the latter half of 1932. He confirmed that his first record session in New York, soon after getting his New York City Musicians' Union card, was with Paul Specht and his orchestra on Specht's May 28, 1931, record date (2). Specht had been leading a prominent theater and ballroom orchestra since the early 1920s. At the time Shaw joined, other members included trumpeter Charlie Spivak and trombonist Russ Morgan. As noted, Shaw already had recorded several unissued sides with Joe Cantor for Gennett in 1928, and two titles with Irving Aaronson in Chicago the preceding summer, but as far as he could recall, not at all between those sessions (2).

On Paul Specht's "You Forgot Your Gloves" and "Million Dollar Baby," which were recorded on that session, Shaw can be heard providing strong lead alto sax work with the section, and clarinet obbligatos behind the vocalist. The performances were exuberantly peppy and well within the style of the day. Concerning these earliest of his New York sideman recordings, Shaw stated,

> The music was awful. Also, I didn't know how to play for the recording studio. Once I got into CBS, I learned how to get the sound that would record well. My sound had been big, but hadn't had the edge that picked up through the mike with the proper bite. (2)

Although they recorded another tune that day, it was not "Dancing in the Dark." However, three days later Ben Selvin recorded this tune on a matrix number only two titles beyond those for the Specht session. In his excellent study of Benny Goodman's career, *B.G.—On the Record* (New Rochelle, N. Y.: Arlington House, 1969), D. Russell Connor listed this session as with mostly unknown personnel. Despite the presence of a sub-tone clarinet solo, Connor noted Goodman's participation as "a possibility only" ([4], p. 81).

As Shaw was not yet with CBS, however, his presence in a Selvin-led unit that early would seem unlikely.

During that June, Red Nichols began rehearsing a band for a July 8, 1931, opening on the roof terrace of the Park Central Hotel at 56th Street and Seventh Avenue. Shaw, Will Bradley, Artie Bernstein, and Harry Bluestone all were in the band, as well as guitarist/singer Tony Sacco. Shaw was by then rooming with Sacco at the Plymouth Hotel on 49th Street. Sacco remembered Shaw as a "bookworm," although there were occasional nights of "booze, broads and weed" (letter from John Harding quoting Sacco, 1976). These diversions have been perennial extracurricular activities for many musicians. Shaw recalled this type of recreation as a feature of his Chicago days as well, but stressed that for him, music always came first. Sacco also noted that Shaw inevitably went off after the Park Central closed to sit in at after-hours sessions, seldom bothering to take his own instruments. He was relying on borrowed horns. Perhaps some of this behavior was a reaction to Bix Beiderbecke's death in early August.

Sacco also recollected Shaw being on the recording date by the Park Central Orchestra on August 24, 1931. However, it has been reported that Shaw did not have any solos on the resulting records, which were dance tunes in the hotel ballroom style of the day (letter from John Harding summarizing comments from Tony Sacco, 1976).

While with Nichols that summer, Shaw was again approached by Fred Rich to audition for the lead alto sax chair at CBS, replacing Lyle Bowen with the house band. One story described pianist Sammy Prager as Shaw's sole accompanist in an empty studio for this audition, witnessed from the recording booth by the appropriate "top brass" of CBS. Another version had Shaw performing the audition unaccompanied on that occasion, which would have been just a formality at that point anyway. Of course, Shaw passed easily and this time was offered the position. Still smarting from the rejection that spring, Shaw accepted but on the condition that his salary would be 25 percent higher than that offered. To Shaw's surprise, Rich agreed, and Shaw left Nichols for CBS in late August.

Fred Rich, who had been musical director at CBS studios since 1928, opened a new radio show, *Friendly Five Footnotes*, for the Jarman Shoe Company in September 1931. Shaw recalled this show as his "first gig for CBS" (2). The band was billed as Fred's Friendly Five although it featured several sizes of ensembles. At one point in one of the show transcriptions, announcer David Ross mentioned that "Friendly Fred and his twenty-piece orchestra" were ready to go. ("Friendly Fred" was given credit both for "his own original tap dance" and for being the vocalist, in David Ross's program announcements.) Nevertheless, it is apparent that many of the jazzier numbers employed a smaller ensemble. Their theme song for opening and closing these broadcasts was "I've Got Five Dollars" (the price of a pair of Jarman's "Friendly Five" shoes at that time) and featured the sounds of a tap dancer, an obvious trademark for a shoe company. Shaw stated that he remembered that "they had a guy tap dancing on a board" for making those performances, but could not recall who it was (2). Shaw reminisced fondly about this gig in one of our discussions:

> I remember Joe Venuti sitting right in front of me. Tommy Dorsey was right behind me. Bunny Berigan was in that band . . . Manny Klein . . . top musicians in New York at the time, but the music was execrable.
>
> We did them as transcriptions. It took a few sessions. We just went in and played into the mike. What happened after that I don't know. (2)

In making transcriptions, the studio's house orchestra would record tune after tune in long, marathon recording sessions, and these recordings would be used later interspersed with dialogue and advertisements for broadcasts as needed as the season progressed. Thus, all the music for the *Friendly Five Footnotes* programs actually had been recorded around the end of August, before the show went on the air in mid-September, rather than being performed on the air as the broadcasts occurred.

It should be mentioned that Bunny Berigan researcher Bozy White, who spoke with many surviving members of the CBS house band from this era during the 1950s and later, stated in private discussions that although Berigan was with the Fred Rich CBS band in this era, he was not heard soloing with Fred's Friendly Five on these programs and may not have participated. Sammy Prager, one of the pianists with the band at that time, had told him that Berigan and Lyle Bowen went into the pit band of a Broadway musical that season, explaining both their absences from the CBS house band in that period. This musical was Sammy Fain's *Everybody's Welcome* and the pit band was the Dorsey Brothers' Orchestra. In *Tommy Dorsey: On the Side* by Robert L. Stockdale (Metuchen, N.J.: Scarecrow Press, 1995), it was stated that Fred Rich was angry with Tommy Dorsey for luring Berigan away from CBS for the show (p. 248), which did not open until October 13, 1931, at the Schubert Theater. Stockdale also maintains Dorsey's absence from the Fred's Friendly Five transcriptions on the same grounds, erroneously stating that these sessions occurred in September and October 1931, but the transcriptions obviously were recorded earlier than he had noted, and Dorsey and Berigan would not yet have had to leave CBS for participation in the musical.

In 1975, Aircheck Records issued two LPs of material from these shows. These included some of the announcements by David Ross and some of the period "aviation news bulletins" by Casey Jones, introduced on some shows as "the famed speed-demon air pilot and vice president of Curtis-Wright Corporation" (Casey Jones is, in fact, pictured and identified as such in many aviation history books). The advertisements and aviation announcements included on the LPs simulated the actual shows, adding evocations of the era. On most titles, Shaw's lead alto sax work is prominent. Paul Small was named as the vocalist in the liner notes to the Aircheck label releases; however, radio listings for these broadcasts in *The New York Times* named "Larry Murphy, tenor, with Rich's orchestra" from the middle of September 1931 into April 1932, when another program began appearing in their 9:45 p.m. Friday time slot on WABC. Nevertheless, a different singer in the later transcriptions was definitely identified by Martin F. Bryan as Elmer Feldkamp.

The liner notes to the Aircheck releases stated that there had been twenty-six programs of four tunes each, believed to have been recorded in two sessions in the fall of 1931 (although they obviously were recorded earlier). The writer, Martin L. Kite, suggests that the clarinet solos were by either Tony Parenti or Jimmy Dorsey; however, Shaw has confirmed that these were all his work (2). Martin F. Bryan of Vintage Recording Co. also has affirmed that programs exist that are numbered up to twenty-eight (see discography). This may imply that enough shows were prepared for three seasons, as radio shows were prepared in groups of thirteen per season. Thus, there would be twenty-six for two seasons, thirty-nine for three seasons, etc. Since these shows were on the air for only six months, twenty-six shows seems more likely, with the show labeled "#28" possibly having a typo.

These transcriptions include the earliest performances featuring Artie Shaw soloing extensively that have become available. Only nine of the twenty-seven issued performances had clarinet solos. "One Man Band" also offered some short clarinet breaks and ensemble passages with Shaw soaring excitingly. Another issued tune, "Alabamy Bound," had one of Shaw's rare alto sax solos.

On the nine issued titles with good solo exposure for Shaw's clarinet, he revealed a looser, more uninhibited approach to his attack, phrasing, and tone than his later work displayed. However, nuances of expression and development of ideas were easily recognizable as Shaw, and the insight provided into his early work, both as a soloist and for his sax section lead alto, was invaluable. These rare albums contained only about 25 percent of the material known to have been recorded for this series (see discography).

Some of the performances, especially by the smaller ensemble, contained some excellent jazz. Shaw noted that the principal soloists were Manny Klein on trumpet, Tommy Dorsey on trombone, Joe Venuti on violin, and Shaw. There were also a few restrained but interesting bass clarinet solos, "probably by Rudy Adler, who used to play all the woodwinds for situations like that in the studios in those days" (2). It should be noted that reedman Jack Towne reportedly has claimed that he was the bass clarinetist on these items, but Shaw did not recall Towne in this context at all, and reaffirmed Adler as the most likely candidate. Also, although Tommy Dorsey routinely occupied the first chair trombone spot with the CBS house band in this era, Lloyd Turner allegedly was cited as the jazz trombone soloist on these shows by some of the surviving band members; when this was mentioned to Shaw, he merely stated, "No, that's Tommy. Turner may have been there, but that's Tommy soloing" (2).

"Copenhagen" was performed Dixieland style, uptempo, and included some exciting moments from Shaw's clarinet. A smaller ensemble also did "Some of These Days" and "Somebody Stole My Gal" in similar arrangements, with excellent Shaw solos following the period vocals. "Nobody's Sweetheart" and "San" seemed to be by the same group, with different variations in solo order. "San" had two clarinet solos, the first a sub-tone low-register improvisation. "Bugle Call Rag" was given a laid-back dance band treatment, with a good Shaw feature. A noticeably larger ensemble was used for the remaining three issued titles that featured Shaw's clarinet solos. "Roll On Mississippi," "Goin' to Town," and "Dixie Jamboree" seemed unwieldy and cluttered compared to the smaller groups, but Shaw was well featured. This included another *chalumeau* solo on "Goin' to Town."

Shaw was given solo space on only a few of the unissued pieces known from these sessions, as listed in the discography. These include a short, peppy clarinet solo on the first version of "Sugar" and some nice chalumeau spots on "Sweet Jenny Lee" and, more briefly, on "Was It Wrong?" (where Shaw traded four-bar phrases with the bass clarinetist). There also was another fine alto sax solo on "Linda." "Tiger Rag" was another potent Dixieland number after the fashion of "One Man Band" or "Copenhagen" as discussed above, with some particularly hot clarinet passages. Again, many of the unissued numbers expose Shaw's lead alto sax section work clearly and interestingly.

Altogether, Shaw was well exposed soloing on clarinet (or, twice, on alto sax) on sixteen of the pieces known to survive from these transcriptions. On their best performances, the ensemble supplied some of the more exciting and inspiring jazz of the era. In discussing these programs, however, Shaw stated, "I hated the artificial peppiness. Most of that reminds me of why I quit to go live on the farm as soon as I could" (2).

Nevertheless, these and other transcriptions, and the commercial records Fred Rich's groups made in this period, offer additional documentation of Shaw's early work, with, possibly, occasional moments of jazz interest.

Not long after this beginning at CBS, Shaw found himself performing on his Hollywood friend Bing Crosby's radio shows. Crosby had gone on from being fired by Paul Whiteman following his Hollywood adventures to being featured on his own radio show, *Presenting Bing Crosby*, on CBS six evenings per week beginning on September 2, 1931. Crosby recalled this major break with enthusiasm in his autobiography, *Call Me Lucky* (New York: Simon & Schuster, 1953, p. 80):

> When I finally did appear, I was a new voice with a different style, and I stirred up interest. . . . I did my first commercial for Cremo Cigars. For a while I was on a CBS sustaining program, but sustaining or singing for Cremo, no one ever had a hotter orchestra accompanying him than I had: Freddie Rich was the conductor, and he was backed by such musicians as Joe Venuti, Artie Shaw, Eddie Lang, and Manny Klein, to name a few.

Unfortunately, surviving transcripts of most of these radio shows could not be located for review. Nevertheless, given Crosby's stature and popularity, it is likely that many, if not all, such transcriptions have survived and may surface eventually. It is rumored that Larry Kiner, the "personalities" collector who has issued many rare items on his various collectors' label recordings, has a large number of these Crosby programs. However, there were no distinctive Shaw passages on the issued titles from the first of the Crosby CBS shows (see discography).

By November 1931, Crosby had acquired Cremo Cigars as a sponsor. *The Cremo Singer* radio show also was on the air featuring Bing Crosby six evenings per week in the same time slot as Crosby's earlier show: 7:00–7:15 p.m. with a repeat for the West Coast 10:00–10:15 p.m. Two broadcast excerpts from this series were issued on John Newton's "Personalities On Parade" series in the late 1980s. These were from November 7th and 9th. The November 9, 1931, show was issued almost intact. No features for Shaw were on this material either. These shows were preserved on rather worn aluminum discs and consequently are only available in very low fidelity. The orchestra was identified by the announcer as Carl Fenton's, who took over conducting the Cremo shows during late 1931 and early 1932 with essentially the same personnel. It is of interest to observe that Crosby sang with less than perfect intonation on these pieces, and that his performances were punctuated by some relatively uninhibited scat singing, whistling, humming, and occasionally the solemn recitation of the lyrics instead of singing them over the orchestral backdrop. Although Carl Fenton and his orchestra were given the opportunity for an instrumental on the broadcast dated the 9th, no soloists from the orchestra were featured, either on this instrumental or on any of the available performances featuring Crosby.

Fred Rich and his orchestra also made several Hit-of-the-Week records in the late summer and fall of 1931, but exact dating of these sessions has not been possible. Aside from some lead alto sax passages characteristically similar to Shaw's work in that period, and a sub-tone melody passage on one title that is aurally identical to Shaw's work on similar passages, there is nothing of interest to Shaw scholars on those performances. The records from Fred Rich's one documented Columbia Records date under his own name while Shaw was in the band, on September 10, 1931, could not be located for review, although D. Russell Connor, in his *B.G.—On the Record*, has attributed the clarinet to Jimmy Dorsey, implying that enough can be heard to form an opinion. Intriguingly, Stockdale, again in his *Tommy Dorsey: On the Side*, indicated that Tony Parenti played clarinet and alto sax and that Jimmy Dorsey's presence was only a possibility. (As noted, on the Aircheck Records releases of the Fred's Friendly Five material, the clarinet and alto sax work was attributed to either Dorsey or Parenti, as well.) In any case, this music was all in the commercial dance idiom.

Shortly after starting to work at the CBS Studios, Shaw noticed a tall, gaunt, scholarly looking clarinetist named Guy D'Isere who played with the CBS Symphony. He always carried his clarinet in a big briefcase bulging with books and sheaves of papers. Shaw was impressed, but embarrassed himself by revealing his literary naivete despite his voracious reading habits. In spite of this awkward start to their relationship, D'Isere eventually became Shaw's mentor. D'Isere provided guidance and stability as Shaw groped for knowledge and insight in pursuing his self-education and intellectual development. Shaw would assist D'Isere with his hobby, which was publishing his own translations of classical Greek plays on his home press. Shaw wrote with gratitude and respect of their relationship in *The Trouble with Cinderella* ([1], pp. 40–44).

Musically, Shaw was finding life at CBS less rewarding. The commercial nature of the music and business orientation of the productions left no room for musical values. Because the sponsor was paying for music, not pauses, there were no pauses, not even when a Grand Pause was scored into a composition by classical composer Richard Wagner.

At one rehearsal, Shaw had just begun a restrained, "radio-ized" solo when the producer interrupted the music with,

> "How many men are playing in that spot?"
> "Just solo clarinet and rhythm section—5 men altogether. Just for that 16-bar spot," said the conductor.
> Silence. Conference in the control room. Then—"No good," the loudspeaker rasped. "The sponsor's paying for 35 men, and 35 men are what he wants to hear."
> "But you can't play ensemble all the time," said the bewildered conductor.
> "The sponsor doesn't care about that—he's paying for a full orchestra and he doesn't want to hear 5 men. Fill it in."
> "But—" and the conductor subsided.

> By the time we went on the air that night, it had been "filled in" and this time the whole orchestra was playing ensemble throughout. I assume the sponsor was happy. ([1], p. 258)

Shaw reported widespread cynicism among the studio musicians as they endured similar absurdities day after day. In his manuscript for his novel, *The Education of Albie Snow*, Shaw has included fictionalized versions of some of these events and the musicians' reactions. Projected as a trilogy, the first volume, some 1,900 pages in manuscript draft, had the working title *Sideman*. Shaw also described the overall situation at CBS in private discussions:

> There was a relatively small group of us who were playing in the studios at that time. Only a few of us were jazz players; there were lots of straight readers in the sections also. It was usually the same bunch, no matter who was conducting.
> Bunny Berigan and Manny Klein did most of the jazz trumpet work. Tommy Dorsey was there, of course, and sometimes Miff Mole, featured on trombone. I was hired to play lead alto, but would almost always solo on clarinet, whenever there were any solo opportunities. Usually there wasn't. Jimmy Dorsey was often on 2nd alto. Benny Goodman was sometimes there, too. I think we may have done a show series together under Ben Selvin at that time. It's not unlikely we may even have had solos on the same show on different numbers, with some of those bands.
> I remember one show where we were rehearsing a number, and Benny thought there was something interesting in the lead alto part. He leaned over and said, "Hey Pops, can I try that?" I didn't care; I said "Sure!" Then we ran through it again. The conductor stopped us and said, "Who's playing that lead alto?" Benny waved, and the conductor said, "Give it to Shaw!"
> There were different conductors for different shows, and there would usually be some singer, or a vocal group. But the musicians were pretty regular. It was just a job. We'd just show up and play. We were all pretty cynical about the quality of the music. Lots of it sounded the same. It was the early 1930s equivalent of muzak. (2)

Shaw worked as a staff musician for CBS in this situation until late spring or early summer 1932. Additional radio shows under Fred Rich and others, on which Shaw performed, undoubtedly survive on transcriptions. One such show was the *Blue Coal Minstrels* program. Imitating a minstrel show format complete with comic dialogue between "Bones" and "Mr. Interlocutor" and advertising "cleaner-burning Blue Coal" for furnaces, each reviewed show had an instrumental by "Larry Briers and his Orchestra," which all featured brief but very Shaw-like solo work, on either clarinet or alto sax (see discography). Each show also featured vocals by an unidentified quartet, operatic-styled tenor Fred Vettel, and (on reviewed shows) two otherwise unidentified female singers referred to as "Blue Coal Mammy" by the announcer. One of these female singers sounded suspiciously like early Kate Smith, although there is some controversy concerning this tentative identification. Shaw was uncertain about the singers, stating,

> Not much there to be completely certain. That's probably me [on clarinet and alto sax solos] but I don't recall that show. It's hard to remember *everything* from that far back, you know!
>
> I don't know who those singers are. I never paid much attention to who was singing or conducting. The shows were so silly it was hard to stand it. We'd go in and record, and what they did with the stuff after that I don't know. It was just a job I couldn't wait to get away from. (2)

There also were a number of commercial record dates with pseudonymous bands led by Fred Rich, Ben Selvin and others occurring in this period that may have featured Shaw (it has not been possible to review all of them). It is therefore interesting to speculate whether many of the other sessions from this period listed in D. Russell Connor's *B.G.—On the Record* as being "possible" or "non-B.G. recordings" or in Stockdale's *Tommy Dorsey: On the Side* might have included Shaw instead of some of their attributions or among those unidentified.

Ben Selvin was the recording contractor for Columbia since the early 1920s. During his long career, which evolved into his later position among the company's top executives, he reportedly recorded over 9,000 titles under various pseudonyms and was bandleader on numerous radio shows ([10], p. 500). Selvin recalled,

> Artie Shaw did a few sessions with some of my bands—but I have no information as to titles of tunes or dates. It must be remembered that we recorded thousands of titles under 9 different names: The Cavaliers, The Newport Society Orchestra, The Bar Harbor Society Orchestra, The Knickerbockers, The Harmonians, The Kentucky Serenaders, etc., etc. (letter from Ben Selvin to John Harding, 1961)

Concerning Selvin's recordings and radio shows in this period, Connor noted,

> Gene Krupa did not participate in many BG–Selvin sessions, contrary to the assumption of other discographers. As Gene remembers it, he worked for Selvin at a later time than Benny, and more often with another clarinetist of some repute: Artie Shaw. ([4], pp. 41–42)

While Benny Goodman was widely known to have recorded extensively for Selvin up to late 1931, after that point Goodman was less regularly featured. He was listed for only one Selvin date in that period, in June 1932. As noted in *B.G.—On The Record*,

Benny readily admits he was "difficult" in those days. He was cocksure of his ability, and no one was going to tell him how to play the clarinet. Occasionally, some conductor tried . . . and that was the final bar in that working arrangement. ([4], p. 100)

Thus, the various radio shows such as the Devoe Painters program under Ben Selvin, for example, would be other places to look for Shaw features on surviving radio show transcriptions from early 1932. On *Devoe Painters Show #3* (see discography), Shaw had a stunning clarinet solo on "Happy Feet" and was also featured briefly on "Cheerful Little Earful." Oddly, *Devoe Painters Show #1* sounds like a different band, and did not feature Shaw.

Shaw noted in discussing his work at CBS that he often played in Ben Selvin's band on radio shows, and also on records released under a wide variety of pseudonyms, during this period (2).

> We did countless sessions of that typical material, and it makes me uncomfortable to listen to it now. Those clarinet solos on the *Devoe Painters Show* were unquestionably me, but it was rare to get any chances for even that much. They used the best musicians in New York for some of the worst music.
>
> The jazz players like Bix and Jack Teagarden were really unsuited to that sort of thing. They played from the head and from the heart, not from paper. They weren't trained for that. They really suffered sitting in Paul Whiteman's Orchestra all night just for a chance to play 8 bars or 16 bars every once in a while.
>
> It was having to play sessions of that sort day after day which made me determined to get out of the business and off to that farm. (2)

Thus, inevitably, most of the Selvin material reviewed had no clarinet or alto sax features. It was rare even to hear any clarinet sub-toned melody passages on the bulk of the available material. Shaw's strong lead alto sax section work often was the only clue that he might have been on the date.

One Ben Selvin record session that has been confirmed as featuring Shaw was recorded on May 12, 1932. There were occasional jazzy solos, but the music was in the style of the dance music of the day. A vocal group was featured on all four titles. Shaw had short solos on clarinet on all four titles also, and on "Whistle and Blow Your Blues Away" played an alto sax solo as well. This was one of the few alto sax solos confirmed by Shaw as his work (2). Shaw's clarinet solos in this period seem more restrained than his playing with Fred's Friendly Five the preceding summer. Intriguingly, on "Crazy People" he trades four-bar phrases with what sounds like the same bass clarinetist heard doing the same thing with Shaw on the Fred's Friendly Five numbers.

Meanwhile, Shaw was following D'Isere's advice in his literary pursuits and taking extension courses at Columbia University in his spare time. It was during this period that Shaw became friends with Max Kaminsky, one of the better trumpet soloists in that era. In his autobiography, *My Life in Jazz* (New York: Harper & Row, 1963), Kaminsky recalled,

[W]hen Artie was working in the CBS house band and playing some club dates on the side, we were both hired by Leo Reisman to play a coming out party at the Biltmore. Leo carried on in his special eccentric way all evening, lying down on the bandstand and swinging up his legs and hollering "Yeah!" when things got rolling. This was the closest we ever got to swinging in society bands. During an intermission Artie and I talked about how dreary and banal this kind of music was. Artie had a strong desire to play jazz and of course there was hardly any place to play it then. At the end of the evening we went over to Artie's apartment on 57th Street for more talk. Artie was always interested in learning and improving himself—I believe at the time he was taking courses at Columbia University in journalism or writing— and his apartment was loaded with records and books. When I spotted a whole collection of Louis's early recordings in his huge library of symphonic music and jazz records, I was done for, and we sat around till morning playing the records and talking. ([5], p. 94)

Shaw's disillusionment with the music business was growing critical, and he was becoming inspired by the idea of writing. He had heard about a group of intellectuals who were buying up farms in Bucks County, Pennsylvania, not far from New Hope. This area became renowned as an artists' colony. Shaw set himself the goal of saving up enough money to purchase such a farm in Bucks County himself, and then retiring from the music business to live there and write a novel about his late friend Bix Beiderbecke. Beiderbecke already was becoming a legendary martyr figure, having drunk himself into such a state of debilitation that he had died of pneumonia the preceding summer, at the age of twenty-eight. Frustration and depression over the commercial nature of the music business were widely known to be the reasons behind his—and many other musicians of the era—turning to drinking as an escape.

An interesting item of news may contribute a clue as to why Shaw decided when he did to go on the road, rather than remain with CBS, given his personal motivations at the time. The May 14, 1932, *Billboard* noted on page 16 that CBS, like everywhere else adversely affected by the Depression, was laying off over one hundred staff members. All the remaining staff were taking a 15 percent pay cut. Shaw knew he could make more on the road anyway, and apparently an offer from Vincent Lopez did the trick. Lopez had a very successful dance orchestra, and spent long periods at the prestigious St. Regis Hotel on Fifth Avenue at 55th.

Billboard announced on page 27 of its July 16, 1932, issue that Vincent Lopez and his orchestra would be leaving the St. Regis Hotel on July 18th for a tour of the Midwest.

It also was around this time that Shaw eloped with Jane Carns, the daughter of a doctor in Ashtabula, Ohio. They had met several summers earlier, apparently while the Joe Cantor band was playing at a summer resort on Bantam Lake. The bride was not yet at the age of consent, however, and her father had the marriage annulled. Shaw spoke of his pain and confusion during this process in the documentary film *Artie Shaw: Time Is All You've Got*. While continuing on the road, he did not hear from Jane or her family for months. Shaw wrote with poignancy and humor in a fictionalized account of such a situation in his novel manuscript *The Education of Albie Snow*. He described his characters' initial meeting at a summer resort gig, their reunion after several years, and their prompt elopement while Albie was taking a vacation from the radio and recording studios. Shaw's fictionalized account of the family pressures on the couple and their subsequent estrangement was particularly vivid and moving.

In Leonard Feather's long interview/article on Shaw in *Down Beat* (3), there was a story about how Shaw got into Vincent Lopez's band, and details concerning Shaw's allegedly having had little or no respect for Lopez. However, Shaw emphatically refuted this point concerning his opinion of Lopez (2). In his autobiography, *Lopez Speaks* (New York: Citadel Press, 1960, p. 268), Lopez recalled Shaw's brief tour with his band that summer:

Just before we left for our date at the Schroeder Hotel in Milwaukee that preceded our engagement at Chicago's Urban Room, I met another performer headed for fame. On Joe Ribaud's recommendation (he was my contractor) I hired (Artie Shaw) to play first saxophone and clarinet. He was a brilliant musician, but the talent that bordered on genius had a temperament to match.

Lopez went on to relate that he had been rehearsing the band extra hours at the Schroeder in preparation for their important Chicago opening, which was set for October 1st. One day after a rehearsal, Shaw gave notice on the ground that Lopez was a "slave driver." Lopez's drummer, Johnny Morris, clarified this by stating, "After we got as far as Milwaukee, (Shaw) got an offer from Roger Wolfe Kahn, and gave Lopez his notice" (3). Lopez continued his tour without Shaw.

Roger Wolfe Kahn was the son of multimillionaire Otto Kahn, had a reputation as a daredevil pilot (he was pursued by the "air police" for some unauthorized low-level flying in June 1932, according to *The New York Times*), and loved music. From the early 1920s he led a sometimes heavily jazz-flavored band that occasionally made records with prominent jazzmen. During the World War II years, he worked as a test pilot.

Rumors and discographical citations of earlier records by Roger Wolfe Kahn featuring Shaw evidently were in error, as Shaw noted in conversation that he only worked with Kahn "during the 1932–33 tour" (2). Although he often has been cited in the personnel on Kahn's May 4, 1932, record date, Shaw stated,

> I had nothing to do with that. I was still at CBS and too busy for other things. When I joined Kahn, I stayed right through into the Gershwin show. There was no association before or after. (2)

Shaw confirmed that he worked initially with Kahn at the Palace Theater, and later at the Hotel Pennsylvania, with Gertrude Niesen singing with the band (2). *The New York Times* for Friday, July 22, 1932, contained an ad in its entertainment section concerning the Kahn band opening "Tomorrow" (Saturday, July 23, 1932) at the Palace, and the band was listed for that location until being replaced by Kate Smith the following week.

On August 5, 1932, Shaw did record with Roger Wolfe Kahn's orchestra. He recalled playing the baritone sax feature for Kahn's record of "Just Another Night Alone." This was a sixteen-bar, slightly decorated melody statement, the only clear exposure of Shaw's baritone sax work to have surfaced.

> I just did that because I was told to; it's what was required at that point. I never enjoyed soloing on the bigger horns; you don't have the control of the air you have on smaller instruments like the clarinet. (2)

Roger D. Kinkle also cited Shaw having a clarinet feature on "Sheltered By the Stars" from the same session in his *The Complete Encyclopedia of Popular Music and Jazz 1900–1950* (New Rochelle, N.Y.: Arlington House, 1974, p. 1737). Although Shaw did play excitingly during the final chorus, his improvisation was largely drowned out by the closing ensemble, as if he had been placed too far off-mike. In the introduction to that piece, however, Shaw had a two-bar flute break shortly after the opening ensemble, his only clear exposure on the instrument. He also could be clearly heard providing his usual strong lead alto work in the sax section. He did not solo in the other titles recorded that day, although the reed section had well-exposed flute ensemble passages during "You've Got Me in the Palm of Your Hand" and Shaw of course played the lead. During "I Can't Believe It's True" there are some short breaks leading into ensemble passages where he is very briefly heard on clarinet and later alto sax.

During that summer or fall, the Roger Wolfe Kahn Orchestra made a Vitaphone film short called *The Yacht Party*.

The twenty-two-year-old Shaw was well featured, standing up and soloing on clarinet on "Way Down Yonder in New Orleans" and clearly visible playing alto sax in the sax section, surrounded by his baritone sax, clarinet, and flute. He also had clarinet solos on "Crazy People" and "Dinah" during the course of the film. This music short also featured singer Gertrude Niesen singing with Kahn's band on one number. (The January 28, 1933, *Billboard* mentioned on page 15 that Niesen, "still in her teens," was a rising star, "having been heard with Roger Wolfe Kahn's Orchestra on stage and hotel engagements" that season.) The acrobatic, double-jointed dancer Melissa Mason was featured on screen during "Dinah," and The Kahn-a-Sirs, a male vocal quartet, also was featured twice (see discography for details). The final number, "Lullaby of the Leaves," was partially drowned out by the sound of an airplane motor. The visuals show Kahn in helmet and goggles waving out of the open cockpit of a biplane. The band was filmed craning their necks upward, with these scenes alternating with the little biplane flying off into the clouds wagging its wings, as if Kahn were conducting with the plane. The effect of the entire film was nevertheless not as absurd as the usual rock videos of more recent vintage, which are logically its aesthetic descendants. Shaw stated in conversation that he recalled making this film only "vaguely" (2).

Shaw also recalled the famed Chicago pianist Joe Sullivan being with the band during their New Orleans tour (2). The Kahn band played an extended engagement at the Roosevelt Hotel in that city. Obviously, this tour, and *The Yacht Party* film, would have to have been made between their Palace Theater and Hotel Pennsylvania engagements. However, in his article on Joe Sullivan's career, "Notes for a Bio-Discography on Joe Sullivan (Part II)" in *Annual Review of Jazz Studies 1* (New Brunswick, N.J.: Transaction Books, 1982, p. 136), writer Norman Gentieu dated Kahn's New Orleans tour as taking place in the spring of 1933. As the timing of Shaw's career demonstrates, Gentieu's dating was undoubtedly too late.

In an interview quoted in Gentieu's article, Sullivan recalled how Shaw kept up his self-education while on the road:

> Artie Shaw, by the way was with that band. Oh, that was wonderful. We used to look over there. He was the highest paid musician in the band, and Charlie Teagarden and I, we were almost like little old sidemen . . . so here would be Artie Shaw—the music stand is here and he's having all these books, you know, which were too deep for me even to understand. And someone would have to punch him. We had all those big arrangements that cost Roger Wolfe Kahn thousands of dollars and Artie'd pick up the clarinet, he'd go through the things and put it down and start reading again.

In *The Trouble With Cinderella*, Shaw recalled their stay in New Orleans as lasting "six weeks or so."

But although you got to play some decent jazz with an outfit like that (which was at least stimulating from a musical standpoint), it was plain to see you weren't getting anywhere. Travelling around that way, from one place to another, never staying in any one place for any length of time . . . I was still trying to find time for reading and learning to write—and this business of living out of a suitcase was hardly conducive to that. ([1], p. 280)

A photo of Kahn's band on the stand was published in Brian Rust's *The Dance Bands* (New Rochelle, N.Y.: Arlington House, 1972, p. 68), showing Shaw sitting in the band, surrounded by his alto and baritone saxophones and flute, playing clarinet. Flute ensemble passages also can be heard on Kahn's record of Duke Ellington's "It Don't Mean a Thing If It Ain't Got That Swing" (Columbia 2722), made at their recording session in November 1932, during their stay at the Pennsylvania. This arrangement included a superb long clarinet solo by Shaw, and part of this performance was used in the sound track of *Artie Shaw: Time Is All You've Got.* The other side of that original 78-rpm disc, "A Shine on Your Shoes," had no feature for Shaw. Kinkle noted that Shaw was featured on another tune from this session, "Fit as a Fiddle," but this disc could not be located for review. Kahn's records with this band have been very rare because of the limited number of pressings being made during that especially low period of the Great Depression. Unfortunately, LP or CD reissues have not surfaced at this writing. Despite the period vocals in their movie and on the 78-rpm discs it was possible to review, the band sounded very good for the time, and the unusual exposure for Shaw's sideman capabilities on flute and baritone sax was unique.

According to *The New Yorker*'s "Goings On About Town" columns over the relevant period, the Kahn band played the Pennsylvania Grill on Seventh Avenue and 33rd Street from October 14 through November 17, 1932. During that period, anticipating the breakup of his orchestra because of lack of work, Kahn arranged for the band members to work in George Gershwin's new Broadway musical *Pardon My English*, which opened at the Majestic Theatre in New York on January 20, 1933.

Pardon My English evidently began rehearsals in late November 1932, and played tryouts in Philadelphia on December 2nd, Brooklyn on the 26th, and then in Boston, before beginning its run at the Majestic. This was not one of Gershwin's more successful efforts. The show lasted only forty-six performances, closing on February 27, 1933. Shaw stated,

That was really Kahn's band working in that show. Kahn worked it out with Gershwin for him to use us. Gershwin would come and sit in with us occasionally. He was trying to get something going, but the show didn't take off.

There wasn't much to the show musically. I had memo-

rized the book in no time, but the conductor got upset when I showed up without the music. "Put it up there anyway," he said. So I spread it on the stand upside down and turned the pages backwards.

I was interested in writing and painting in that period. The music we had to play was so incredibly bad I couldn't wait to get out of the music business. Shortly after that show closed I was able to get away to the farm. (2)

In early 1933, Shaw also was again actively freelancing in the New York radio studios as well as playing in the Gershwin show. Rumors of Shaw's presence on Bing Crosby's Columbia record date of January 26, 1933, persist, but the exposure for the clarinetist is minimal, and in reviewing those performances, Shaw stated, "Could have been anybody!" (2) Joey Nash recalled Shaw in Adrian Rollini's band on the session featuring Nash's vocals recorded in February 1933. D. Russell Connor placed Benny Goodman and Shaw together in Al Goodman's orchestra on the Will Rogers show that season ([4], p. 111). One show, consistently mentioned by Shaw as a low point in aesthetic mindlessness, was called *Manhattan Melody-go-round*, which had gone on the air in late 1932. Being again confronted by such musical drudgery further increased his desire and determination to leave music and go off to a farm to write.

Following the closing of the Gershwin show, Shaw was able to initiate his first retirement from the music business. Finally, he had saved the money needed to buy that farm in Bucks County. Together with Marge Allen, a nurse, Shaw purchased the farm of poet Isadore Schneider for $3,000, putting it in both their names. Marge Allen later became Shaw's first wife (discounting the annullment of the year before). Shaw abandoned the security of his musical career to live there and to write that novel about Bix Beiderbecke. "I was 23 at the time. What I was looking for was a period of uninterrupted and unharassed time" ([1], p. xii).

The depiction of the little farm in *Artie Shaw: Time Is All You've Got* evoked the beauty of the rural atmosphere and the back-to-nature solitude Shaw was seeking. In *The Trouble with Cinderella* he referred to it as "25 weedy acres with a dilapidated old house on it" near Erwinna, Pennsylvania ([1], p. 262). In his new introduction to the DaCapo edition, he added that it had a ramshackle barn, a wood stove and a fireplace for cooking and heat, kerosene lamps for light, an outdoor well with a kitchen pump for water, and an outhouse in the back ([1], p. xii). He and Marge Allen lived frugally, and Shaw cut firewood for extra money. He teamed up with a partner, a local resident named John Coffee, to truck the wood to Greenwich Village to sell. "He had the truck," Shaw explained (2). Shaw has mentioned that this work did not particularly suit him. "Once I almost severed my thumb," he recalled in one discussion (2).

Writer John Wexley, who lived there, and Shaw's old

friends Claude and Polly Thornhill were some of the few visitors to the farm that year. Both Wexley and Thornhill's widow, Polly Haynes, recalled the situation vividly in the Berman film; she especially noted the intensity of Shaw's personality. In personal discussions, Shaw related that Thornhill had tried to get him to return to music in that period.

> One time Claude and Polly Thornhill came down and Claude tried to interest me in joining Ray Noble's band. I just said "No!" It had taken me everything I could do to get out of that scene. Listen to what the music business offered in those days. There just weren't any good bands playing at that time. It was the equivalent of elevator music, shopping mall music. I didn't want to go back to that. (2)

Primarily, of course, Shaw spent that year working on his manuscript. His frustration mounted as he gradually realized that he did not feel he knew enough about what he wanted to say. Finally one day his frustration became critical. In *The Trouble with Cinderella* he wrote:

> All I knew was that I didn't know anything. I was obsessed with a sense of my own total, abysmal ignorance. . . . A week or so later I moved back to New York City and started figuring out ways and means of going about the business of filling in the large gaps in my small store of formal education. . . . On the other hand, since I hadn't touched a saxophone or clarinet during the entire year, I now had quite a time getting back to being able to produce musical sounds on either of them again. . . . These were the only tools by which I could expect to support myself while I embarked on the next lap of my quest for knowledge. ([1], pp. 265–68)

Although in *Artie Shaw: Time Is All You've Got* it is stated that Shaw returned to New York in the fall of 1934, Shaw actually had returned to active playing by February 1934: a blurb in *Melody Maker* dated February 10, 1934, noted that Shaw, Berigan, and tenor saxophonist Babe Russin were again with the CBS house band. Nevertheless, Shaw stressed that he was actively freelancing in all the studios, rather than being locked into any set format, and that immediately after his return from the farm he began playing baritone sax for Richard Himber. Vocalist Joey Nash, who was featured with Himber during 1933–35, also remembered Shaw in Richard Himber's orchestra on all their Studebaker radio shows and Victor record dates from early 1934 on, including their first Bluebird record session on March 19, 1934. Nash also sang on all titles from Adrian Rollini's record date of March 24, 1934; Shaw confirmed his solos on all takes from that session.

Shaw affirmed working with Himber regularly from the time he returned to music from his farm until beginning to tour with his own band in late 1936. He performed the sub-

toned low-register clarinet passages heard on many Himber records from these sessions. When asked about his activities with Himber in this period, Shaw stated unequivocally, "Himber never did anything without me" (2). This included many radio broadcasts and transcriptions for Studebaker, Pure Oil, and other sponsors, and at least the three cited World Transcription sessions, in addition to the Victor records, as listed in the discography. While musicians often called in a substitute when ill or on other engagements, Shaw noted that he seldom did this, as he regarded commitments seriously, and therefore he was certain that he was in the sax section on all Richard Himber sessions during 1934–36. Unfortunately, aside from the low-register subtone melody passages, Shaw was not often featured as a soloist with Himber, and neither dubs nor reissues of any of their airchecks or broadcast transcriptions have surfaced at this writing.

The version of "Put On Your Old Gray Bonnet" featuring a good Shaw solo that is heard on the sound track of *Artie Shaw: Time Is All You've Got* was taken from a performance by Ben Selvin's orchestra for *The Taystee Breadwinners* radio show of March 27, 1934, according to Robert L. Stockdale's *Tommy Dorsey: On the Side* (Metuchen, N.J.: Scarecrow Press, 1995). This show, sponsored by Taystee Bread, went on the air over radio station WOR in November 1933, with personnel varying slightly from week to week. Other programs in this series do not feature Shaw, according to collector John Harding, although it is likely that Shaw participated in other shows in this series around this time on which he is evidently not aurally identifiable. Several of the earlier shows reportedly featured Benny Goodman.

Shaw was also on Ed Wynn's *Texaco Fire Chief Hour* radio show with Don Voorhees and his orchestra, on the air that season. Nothing could be located concerning transcriptions from this show while Shaw was with that band, although a photo of the band on stage has survived that shows Shaw among the reedmen. This photo was shown in *Artie Shaw: Time Is All You've Got*. Voorhees' orchestra performed for Wynn's program for two years, beginning in the fall of 1932 (at which time Shaw was with Kahn). For the 1934–35 seasons, Voorhees was replaced by Eddie Duchin and his orchestra for that show.

Shaw also vividly recalled working alongside Benny Goodman in Johnny Green's orchestra on singer Ruth Etting's radio show, although he thought that this might have occurred in early 1933 (2). However, research indicates that Johnny Green had played for the Ruth Etting show during 1934. In an interview on page 14 of the May 31, 1952, *Melody Maker*, the composer/bandleader Johnny Green identified Shaw as the clarinetist for a sixteen-bar solo on one of the pieces recorded at Green's August 1, 1934, record date, "A New Moon Over My Shoulder." If so, Shaw played virtually unadorned melody on this piece in an uncharacteristically stiff and thin-toned manner, and was not featured otherwise on the records made at that session. Shaw again stated, "That could have been anybody!" (2) Intriguingly, on another tune from that session, the vocalist was Peg La Centra, a teenaged singer already making a name for herself. In fact, the August 18, 1934 *Billboard* had an article on page 9 headlined "Peg La Centra Own Show" [*sic*], noting that she had evolved from being an announcer and radio actress in Boston to singing on her own show on NBC.

Two weeks later, Shaw was present for a vital, straightforward jazz date under trumpeter Wingy Manone's leadership. There was no doubt of Shaw's identity, since Manone named a few members of his group in his opening patter on both takes of "Never Had No Lovin' " and referred to "Artie Shaw" both times. This Manone date included an all-star roster of personnel. Pianists Teddy Wilson and New Orleans pioneer Jelly Roll Morton shared the session for two tunes apiece. The quality of the personnel and performances made this a classic session. Shaw was in good form as well as in good company. Oddly, these superb performances were not released at the time. A collectors' label, Special Editions, issued two titles on 78-rpm records several years later, but the other tunes and comparably fine alternate takes only surfaced in the 1970s on the equally rare Rarities collectors' label.

The two sessions with Red Norvo's Swing Septet in September and October 1934 were also straightforward jazz sessions of high quality. Allegedly, these were the first records on which the style of the music was referred to as "swing" on the record label. Previously, the word had been part of tune titles or an adjective to describe the feel of the music, rather than the name of a style. Shaw had substantial solos on three of the titles recorded at these sessions. No clarinet can be heard on "The Night Is Blue," and Shaw was absent from an additional take of "Old Fashioned Love." Norvo's xylophone and the absence of the usual trumpet gave these performances a distinctive character. "Tomboy" was taken fast. Both takes were excellent, hard-swinging jazz. "I Surrender Dear" was performed as a romantic ballad, with Shaw's clarinet sensitively lyrical on both takes. "Old Fashioned Love" was taken medium-fast. Shaw's solo on the alternate take was superior to that on the originally issued version.

Shaw also had a nice eight-bar solo on the Alice Faye recording of "My Future Star." Brian Rust cited it in his *Jazz Records A–Z, 1932 to 1942* (Hatch End, England: The Author, 1965) as recorded on the same date as the earlier Norvo session, despite the gap in record matrix numbers. This session was more of a popular vocal feature in nature, rather than strictly jazz. However, Miss Faye sounded very good. Her style did not lend itself to sounding stilted and dated, as so many singers of that era did. Shaw did not have a solo on "Yes to You" from the same session. Two Chick

Bullock records listed by Rust as being made on the same day with adjacent matrix numbers may have included the same band, but copies of the recordings could not be located to check for Shaw features.

Shaw confirmed participating on two record dates with the popular singer/trumpeter Johnnie "Scat" Davis in October 1934 (2). While Shaw had the clarinet obbligato passages behind the leader's vocals on all reviewed titles, he was only featured for brief solos on two of them (see discography). Interestingly, Rust had again attributed the clarinet work to Jimmy Dorsey.

On November 20, 1934, Shaw participated in another jazz-oriented record date. This time the leader was Shaw's old idol, Frank Trumbauer, and Shaw was again well featured. Although "Blue Moon" had the character of a typical period dance piece, complete with dated vocal, and "Down t' Uncle Bill's" included some novelty vocal entertainment, there was some good solo space for Shaw on all four titles. "Troubled" and "Plantation Moods" were instrumentals offering more substantial solo work within good arrangements. Shaw's two solos on the latter were brief but effective. "Troubled" was the most interesting number of the session from a jazz perspective, with particularly good solos from Shaw on both alto sax and clarinet, working up to a climactic ending with Shaw's clarinet soaring over the ensemble. The drummer, usually listed as "Jack Williams" in discographies, was actually John Williams, father of the well-known film and television composer/arranger of the same name who was born in 1932.

The recordings Shaw made with Norvo and Trumbauer enhanced his reputation in the jazz world of that period. Along with the Manone session, these performances provided the most interesting settings yet to have surfaced for Shaw's sideman work during that era. There also were many more recordings with Richard Himber's orchestra throughout that season featuring vocalist Joey Nash, with occasional sub-toned melody passages from Shaw's clarinet.

Meanwhile, Shaw had resumed his studies at Columbia University. His wife Marge was also taking courses in psychology there at the time, in connection with her work as a nurse. Unfortunately, Shaw quickly learned that he would be required to earn his high school equivalency if he wished to enroll in a degree program, despite his already having taken numerous extension courses. Grimly facing the frustration of attending these relatively trivial classes given by cynical or indifferent instructors, Shaw plunged into his studies with his usual frightening intensity and determination. He wrote enthusiastically of his studies in mathematics and logic. However, personality conflicts with rigidly unimaginative instructors and a more intimate glimpse of what academia was really like quickly demolished his new plan to work toward an instructorship somewhere himself, eventually.

And all at once I found myself right back where I had started when I had come back to New York City from Bucks County. My whole world had suddenly collapsed. All my aspirations had exploded in my face. I couldn't figure out where I was or what to do. The only thing that seemed to make any sense at all was to go on back to music again, try to save up some more money, and see what might turn up. . . . A few months later, I was once more working my head off in the radio and recording studios, making several hundred dollars a week playing on soap and cereal programs. Now and then there would be a recording session, where there was a chance to play something a little less sickening than the music required by the advertisers and sponsors for whom I did most of my work, but even that was not enough.

Now I had no goal at all; and I had to try to accustom myself to working in a vacuum. There seemed to be no road ahead from where I stood. As far as I could see, looking into whatever future lay ahead of me, I would have to go on playing an infinite succession of radio programs in which the dull mediocrity of the music was enough to kill anyone's taste for music of any kind whatsoever. ([1], p. 279)

Shaw spent 1934–36 playing in radio orchestras led by conductors such as Howard Barlow, Peter van Steeden, Sigmund Romberg, Andre Kostelanetz, Jack Shilkret, Nat Shilkret, Victor Young, and of course Richard Himber. When asked about working with figures such as Young and Romberg, Shaw said,

Yeah, I worked with Young occasionally, but most of that material was awful—1930s muzak, with only the occasional necessarily restrained 8-bar solo, not enough to relieve the tedium. Sigmund Romberg was the only one of those pop-composer/conductors whose music did much for me. At least it was more interesting material. (2)

As a freelance musician with a substantial reputation, he also was often called to participate in record dates. Countless singers and bandleaders could have included him on any of hundreds of records made in that period. He mentioned working occasionally with the ARC house band organized by Russ Morgan, who took over that responsibility for the company in August 1934, for record sessions in this period. However, he noted this material was "usually pretty corny," with only the same sort of rare, restrained solo opportunities described earlier. The same problems concerning identification of sidemen on records also applied to this period. There is no doubt that careful listening to records and broadcasts made in New York City during 1935 would turn up an occasional Shaw solo. It is likely more would have been attributed to Shaw by collectors and discographers if it had not been erroneously reported in several sources that Shaw had retired to his farm in Bucks County in 1935, instead of 1933.

An example of the difficulty in tracing Shaw's sideman

sessions was provided at the January 15, 1935, recording session that produced "You Fit Into the Picture." This Chick Bullock record featured a clarinet solo obviously by Shaw, but it was the only record Bullock made that day. The previous record matrix numbers, also recorded that day, featured singer Connie Boswell (of The Boswell Sisters). These were slow, sentimental ballads with a string section and only ensemble backings (no solos), and it did not sound like the same band. Only those three titles were recorded at ARC on that date. As it was rare that a band would assemble in a studio and only make one side, it would seem probable that Shaw was involved on all three titles. Chick Bullock also made many other records with indefinite personnel in 1934–35, but there was no evidence of Shaw's presence on the records that could be reviewed, except for those cited in the discography.

The December 22, 1934, *Billboard* noted in its "Air Briefs" column by Jerry Frankel on page 10, "Studebaker is spotting electrical transcriptions in all corners of the world, bringing the Himber Orchestra with Joey Nash to the various countries." Nash also noted that the Studebaker show was almost unique in being on both NBC and CBS by the same sponsor. Unfortunately Nash also was the name of a rival car manufacturer, and the March 23, 1935, *Billboard* announced on page 11 in Frankel's column that Nash was off the show because of his name.

Joey Nash sang on most Richard Himber records made that first year Shaw was with the band. He wrote the liner notes to the two-LP set *Richard Himber and His Ritz-Carlton Hotel Orchestra Featuring Joey Nash 1934–1935* (AXM2-5520). Included was the following story:

The Studebaker Champions Hour rehearsals were chaotic clambakes. Himber was constantly uttering pejorative remarks about the band's playing. Musicians screamed insults at Dick. Acid comments and taunts were volleyed back and forth 'till 30 seconds before going on the air. . . . Dick's threats to have the entire orchestra expelled from the musicians' union were greeted with jeers. When he gave the band, en masse, their notice, they were always back for the next show. . . . On one program, unknown to Dick, the CBS studio clock was put ahead 3 minutes and when his baton gave the down beat for the program's opening, announcer David Ross stuttered and stumbled over his introductory words; discords, eerie trills, caterwaul glissandos, pure cacaphony poured from the band. The baton fell to the ground and so did Dick, horror stricken.

The band's sight–reading ability was super-extraordinary. There never was a need to go over a song again and again. Once through from introduction to coda and there'd be cries of "next number."

Shaw recalled "the time we almost gave Himber a heart attack" with the above-mentioned time-change trick (2).

This was in response to Himber's verbal abuse, which was particularly resented as Himber was notorious for underpaying his men. Apparently, he often added musicians for broadcasts at less than scale. Finally the March 16, 1935, *Billboard* reported on page 7, "Himber AFM Hearing." Himber was being cross-examined by the American Federation of Musicians over his paying under scale. The April 6, 1935, issue noted on page 7, "$1000 AFM Fine for Dick Himber" for this practice, going back to 1933 at the Essex House and continuing with his Ritz-Carlton Hotel band and NBC broadcasts.

Through it all, Shaw kept doing his job and continued pursuing his self-education. He stated,

> You have to realize we were just doing our job. It's what we did for a living. We didn't think in terms of history or attach any more significance to these records and broadcasts than a ditch-digger would to a ditch or an accountant to a bill. Most of the music was appalling anyway. The occasional jazz date was a rarity. I was interested in books, art, writing. I loved music, but what we did in the studios was just a job. (2)

Of course, Shaw continued attending jam sessions after hours. In Arnold Shaw's *52nd St.—The Street of Jazz* (New York: Da Capo Press, 1977), Manny Klein was quoted concerning one memorable night when Shaw jammed with Jimmy Dorsey in an alto sax duel at the Famous Door:

> [Artie Shaw] was one of the great clarinet players, but his original instrument was the alto. And he was a fantastic lead alto. . . . On this particular night, it was Jimmy Dorsey's playing that annoyed Artie . . . he kept shaking his head. Finally, he got up and said, "Are you coming?" I stared at him: "Where are we going?" He motioned with his hand: "To get my horn." So I drove him up to his apartment, somewhere on Central Park West in the 90s. When we returned to the [Famous] Door, he got on the stand—and he played! You never heard such sax playing in your life. He was a demon! But that was Artie Shaw, a meshuggener [crazy man] if there ever was one. (pp. 116–17)

During the winter of 1935–36, Bill Challis led a radio orchestra as a vehicle for his arranging, which included Shaw playing lead alto and taking occasional clarinet solos. Challis had a substantial reputation as one of Paul Whiteman's arrangers and for his work with Jean Goldkette's bands, which had featured Bix Beiderbecke and Frank Trumbauer. In addition to broadcasting regularly, Challis recorded at least two sets of material for World Transcriptions.

In 1983, Circle Records, a collectors' label based in Atlanta, Georgia, issued a two-LP collection of the World Transcriptions material. According to the liner notes, sixteen titles were recorded at the World Studio at 711 Fifth Avenue on Monday, February 24, 1936, between 4 and 11 p.m. The additional issued titles were cited as being recorded at a previous session, although the World numbers were higher (see discography). In discussing the Challis transcriptions, Shaw referred to them as some of the better documentation of his sideman work during this period (2). Shaw actually was featured on fewer than half the numbers released. On some pieces he was only featured for straight melody or sub-toned passages, as with Himber.

On the eight titles on which he can be heard improvising, "Rockin' Chair" offered the least exposure, with only a four-bar break. Fortunately he was given more space on the remaining numbers that featured him. On "Great Day" he had a chorus except for the bridge. On "New Orleans" he was given a full chorus and the bridge again later. "Clarinet Marmalade" offered two sixteen-bar excursions plus a four-bar break. The exciting "Let Yourself Go" had a sixteen-bar clarinet solo. "Riverboat Shuffle" offered a two-bar break as well as a sixteen-bar solo. At the second session, Shaw had his best feature on "Diga Diga Doo," which included two-bar and four-bar breaks early in the arrangement, a sixteen-bar solo, two later eight-bar spots, and fills during the last chorus. "Mimi" also featured a full chorus of improvisation from Shaw.

As usual with transcription service material, these performances were issued under a pseudonym: "Bob Conley and his Orchestra." Vocals were cited as by "Betty and the Troubadors," but were actually by Bea Wain and The Bachelors. The band broadcast for thirteen weeks during the winter of 1935–36, in addition to making these transcriptions. However, air checks by the band have not surfaced.

Shaw also was on the air in Lennie Hayton's orchestra for Ed Wynn's radio show, sponsored by Plymouth over WABC/CBS at 9:30 p.m. on Thursdays that season. In *Metronome* (March 1936, p. 34) a "Radio Reviews" write-up of Wynn's show noted that the lineup of Hayton's band was almost the same as the one he used on the *Your Hit Parade* show (which Hayton had debuted in April 1935). The review then listed trumpeter Charlie Margulis, trombonists Jack Jenney and Jack Lacey, Art Shaw, pianist Frank Signorelli, and bassist Artie Bernstein, among others, with vocals by the King's Men and the Rhythm Girls. Again air checks have not surfaced and apparently Lennie Hayton's band never made transcriptions for any company in that era.

Commercial record dates known to have included Shaw became more common beginning in January 1936. However, the results still were uneven. Quality ranged from dismal commercial tedium (with only brief solos offering a spark of interest to jazz listeners or Shaw scholars) to brilliant jazz sessions with all-star personnel in good form.

From January, four commercial record dates known to have included Shaw have surfaced to date. The records made with The Boswell Sisters on January 6th had them in good form, but Shaw was given solo space only on "The Music

Goes Round and Round." The Himber session on January 13 featured Shaw only for a sub-tone clarinet melody statement. Manny Klein's record date on January 20 did not feature any Shaw solos. On the Bob Howard session of January 28, otherwise good performances by a small band including Bunny Berigan and Babe Russin as the other horns, were marred by the period vocals of the leader, but Shaw was given generous solo space. On "Whose Big Baby Are You?" he was featured for eight bars. "Much Too Much" was an unusually structured AABA-form piece with the "A" sections twelve bars long. Shaw decorated the melody with low-register passages during the "A" sections of the first chorus, with Frank Signorelli's piano featured on the bridge. On the other two performances, Shaw had good sixteen-bar solos.

April 1936 was a vintage month, although it started off slowly with a typical commercial dance music date for Jack Shilkret on the 2nd; Shaw was only featured for a couple of four-bar breaks on "A Little Robin Told Me So."

On April 6th, Shaw was shown off to great advantage with Richard Himber. Shaw recalled this record date as the best of all his sessions with Himber; he soloed on all titles except "Would You." On "Tormented" Shaw performed his solo in a rhapsodically lyrical approach that anticipated the effect achieved with his own bands later.

On April 13th, Bunny Berigan made one of his classic record sessions as a leader. Shaw was featured for some outstanding obbligato passages behind Berigan's vocal on the excellent original version of "I Can't Get Started." Chick Bullock sang on the remaining titles the group recorded, but his vocals usually were edited out of LP and CD reissues of this session. Shaw was featured for a good solo on "Melody from the Sky," and the band recorded two other titles that day: "A Little Bit Later On," with a fine Shaw clarinet solo, and the wonderfully titled "Rhythm Saved the World," with no clarinet solo, although Shaw can be heard clearly, if slightly off-mike, during the Dixieland-style ensemble passages. However, company files, the same ones that cited Eddie Condon as present on guitar (although Condon stated in his autobiography that he was in the hospital that day), noted that Shaw had been replaced by Paul Ricci for those performances. Discographers and record album jackets have perpetuated this error, despite Shaw's well-exposed solo work. Bozy White, the Berigan authority, interviewed Forrest Crawford (the tenor saxophonist on the date) concerning this session, and related in personal discussions that "it was Shaw on all titles. Crawford didn't have his union card yet and could only perform if he was called as a substitute. So, Paul Ricci was contracted and Crawford went as his substitute. Ricci wasn't even there, and Shaw was the only clarinetist."

On the 21st, Himber made another World Transcriptions session which included Shaw features on some titles, but this set could not be reviewed. However, some of the tunes Shaw soloed on at their Victor record date earlier in the month were among those recorded.

On April 24, Shaw and Claude Thornhill went into the studios to cut a test pressing of a Thornhill original. Shaw stated that Thornhill "just wanted to try something, so we went into a studio and did it. It was sort of similar to something Willie The Lion would have done" (2). Shaw has a copy of this recording in his personal collection.

The records made with Frank Trumbauer's group on April 27th also were excellent jazz-oriented performances. Even the vocals were outstanding, as the vocalist was Jack Teagarden. He also was so well featured on trombone that the date seems more a Teagarden session than a Trumbauer session. Shaw was well featured on all four titles, playing at the consistently high level he displayed on earlier recordings when he had the opportunity to do more than a few obbligatos, fills, or short breaks. On page 25 of the June 1936 issue of *Metronome*, there was a review of "'S Wonderful"/"The Mayor of Alabam'" from this session, which began, "The Trumbauer sides show off some mighty good clarinet work by the not-often-enough-heard Artie Shaw."

During May 1936 Shaw participated in the world's first swing concert, as leader of his own group. This event was organized by Joe Helbock, proprietor of the Onyx Club. The Onyx Club, located on West 57th Street, was an important jazz club and musicians' hangout in that era. Joe Helbock was intensely interested in jazz. The preceding summer, Benny Goodman had catapulted Swing into the public consciousness, and Helbock felt that the time was right to promote the new style. Shaw was among those invited to appear. He was asked to fill a three-to-five-minute interval with a small group performance while the stage setup was being changed.

Shaw decided to offer "something just a tiny bit different" amidst the succession of big bands and jazz combos making up the rest of the program. He composed a piece for string quartet, clarinet, and pianoless rhythm section. Since it was in the key of B-flat and was meant to fill an interlude, he called it "Interlude in B-flat."

The concert took place at the Imperial Theatre on West 45th Street on May 24, 1936, one day after Shaw's twenty-sixth birthday. The audience, made up primarily of musicians, people in the music business, and jazz fans, was overwhelmed by "Interlude in B-flat." Jazz critic Leonard Feather later wrote, "Artie's one number, 'Interlude in B-flat,' broke up the show" ([1], p. 297).

In explaining his concept in composing "Interlude in B-flat," Shaw wrote in his autobiography,

> From time to time during that period, I used to get together with a few fellows who had a string quartet, and spend an evening playing some of the clarinet and string quartet literature—the Mozart quintet, the Brahms ditto, stuff like that.

. . . I happen to like the sound of clarinet and strings, and used to enjoy these little sessions enormously. In fact, it had at times occurred to me to try writing something in the jazz idiom for this combination. Now it suddenly occurred to me that this might be a good idea for this swing concert of Helbock's. ([1], pp. 293–94)

Shaw also stated in private conversation that he had been sketching out arrangements of this nature as early as the period on his Bucks County farm (2).

On the strength of his Imperial Theatre appearance, Shaw was offered the opportunity to form his own band, make some records, and perform in some of the night spots with this new idea. He protested that he just wanted to get away to write, but the idea of financing this ambition by performing his own music, instead of the usual commercial drudgery, appealed to him.

Shaw continued freelancing in the studios while he worked on building a library, establishing personnel, and eventually rehearsing the band before taking it before the public. He continued performing on many radio shows in this period, including with guitarist Dick McDonough's band on WEAF for Borden's Ice Cream. On June 4th and 23rd, McDonough's band, which also included Bunny Berigan, recorded eight titles, which featured good Shaw solos on "Way Down Yonder in New Orleans" and an intriguing arrangement of "Dear Old Southland" (tango passages and quotes from "St. Louis Blues" were written into it). On other titles, Shaw was featured only in playing obbligatos behind vocals, except for a short break on "The Scene Changes." Unfortunately, although Peg La Centra was the singer on these Borden's Mel-O-Roll shows, she did not appear on any of McDonough's record dates.

Shaw also was cited in the personnel for Carl Hoff's band for the *Your Hit Parade* radio show that summer. The Carl Hoff orchestra was profiled on page 22 of the August 1936 issue of *Metronome*, lending insight into the situations Shaw was facing in the studios:

Carl Hoff, the young Californian, swings the stick for the Wednesday evening edition of *Your Hit Parade* programs, heard over both NBC networks (10 p.m. E.D.S.T.). As a batoneer, Hoff is comparatively a newcomer to the airwaves, having served as an arranger for such units as Ted Weems, Vincent Lopez, Paul Ash, and others. He is known particularly in the profession for his musical scores for motion pictures.

Among his favorite jobs were the Walt Disney cartoons of Mickey Mouse and also *Merry Melodies*. In a more serious strain, he has worked on a number of feature films which include *Trader Horn*, *The Kid from Spain*, and *Hallelujah, I'm a Bum*.

He prefers dance music for light work, but for more concentrated endeavor prefers concert arrangements of popular compositions. Since forming his own orchestra, he has worked across the country—Los Angeles, Chicago, and New York—and had one of the first orchestras to broadcast from the west coast.

When an orchestra leader accepts a contract for the Hit Parade, he also accepts a formula from the sponsor and producer which calls for rhythm and unadulterated melody. It is understood that tone colors are to be added. No melodic distortions or tricky passages are permitted, and always, the vocal accompaniments must not detract from the song as it was written. That in itself is difficult to conform to because an arranger may fall into a natural climactic development which may alter a note or two of the original melody. Of course it will be ruled out, so, constructions of these orchestrations for the Hit Parade must be planned according to a "made to order" formula and Carl Hoff is capable of executing orders because of his varied experience.

The bulk of arranging for the current broadcast is handled by himself but on a program of such magnitude, it is physically impossible for one person, so to assist he employs Dewey Bergman for the sweet tunes and Danny Gool for the swing arrangements. Danny and Dewey score the overflow which Carl cannot handle himself.

There are thirty men in the Hit Parade orchestra, leaving room for plenty of color. As vocalists in this unit, Bob Simmons is tenor soloist and Glen Cross, baritone. Ruth Dick lends the feminine touch, and for group singing we find the Leader's Trio (an Ed Smalle unit). Gordon Cross, Eddie Ellington and Glen Cross comprise the trio.

Full personnel for the large Carl Hoff orchestra also was provided, and Shaw is listed as playing lead alto, flute, and clarinet (see discography). Shaw stated,

Oh, yes, Carl Hoff. I remember that! Hoff didn't know what to do with us. I mean, he had all those superb musicians and such trivial arrangements. We were so bored with that trite material we'd get pretty rowdy at those sessions. I recall a water pistol fight with the brass section, with the water pistols filled with cheap dime store perfume. That left the studio smelling pretty strong. There was so little to the music, we had to do something to break the monotony. (2)

Nevertheless, the performances by Carl Hoff's orchestra recorded for World Transcriptions at about this time do not sound quite that completely vacuous. Among other points of interest, they occasionally featured some intriguing lead alto sax passages and some short alto sax solo opportunities, and none of the titles listed in the discography featured vocals. Shaw felt there was not enough exposure for the alto sax to be sure, but he thought it might be him (2).

When Ray Sinatra took over the *Your Hit Parade* show for additional Wednesday night broadcasts later that summer, Shaw remained with the orchestra, even though he already was appearing at the Silver Grill with his own band (according to John Harding). When asked about working with Ray Sinatra, Shaw stated, "Oh yes, Ray Sinatra! He was always doing a lot with vocal groups" (2).

Performances identified as being transcriptions by this orchestra at about this time included a few nice but restrained Shaw clarinet solos and some vocals by Joey Nash. Shaw had associated Nash only with the earlier Richard Himber period; nevertheless, Joey Nash sang on other transcriptions, allegedly also from this period, identified as by Emile Coleman and his orchestra. Although this band sounded superficially similar to Ray Sinatra's, or for that matter Richard Himber's, there were no features by which Shaw could have been identified as being present on those items.

Shaw also worked in Frank Cornwall's band on the Squibb Dentifrice radio programs. Their shows were broadcast on Monday, Wednesday and Friday mornings over WOR during July and August 1936, beginning July 3rd. Violinist Cornwall's group grew out of his trio, which also included accordionist Phil Papile and bassist Marcus Messing. For the broadcasts, he added reedmen Shaw and Eddie Light, Dick McDonough on guitar, Lem Leach on vibraphone, and Caspar Reardon on harp. Transcriptions of shows featuring this unusual instrumentation were rumored to have been preserved, but this could not be confirmed. In any case, Sid Stoneburn reportedly replaced Shaw not long after the show opened.

Shaw, Berigan and an excellent rhythm section that included McDonough, pianist Joe Bushkin and drummer Cozy Cole backed Billie Holiday on July 10th for her first record date under her own name. All four titles were superb, with Shaw well featured. These records also were among the very best featuring Shaw as a sideman. All concerned performed memorably. Bozy White has related that Billie Holiday told him on two separate occasions that she was very pleased with those records and thought Berigan and Shaw had been terrific.

Another record date on July 20th under vocalist Chick Bullock's name regressed back to period vocals and relatively routine dance arrangements typical of the era. Shaw had some solo space on "Take My Heart" and several short hot breaks on "You Dropped Me Like a Red Hot Penny," but a low-register clarinet spot on "You're Not the Kind" was less evidently Shaw, and there was no feature on "These Foolish Things."

Also on July 20th was Bunny Berigan's first Thesaurus Transcriptions recording session. Shaw also had been listed in the personnel for this set, but he has denied being the clarinetist heard briefly performing obbligatos behind the vocalist on two numbers, or taking a short solo on "Sing Sing Sing" (2). The obbligatos sounded quite similar to Shaw's work in such cases, so it is therefore understandable that his presence was inferred, since there were not any good clarinet features by which to have made a judgment. Bozy White's research on Berigan could not determine who the lead alto and clarinet soloist was. Even members of the band

with whom White had discussed this session could not recall, which makes it even more unlikely that it was Shaw. Shaw stated,

> Bunny and I made a lot of sessions together, and I was on some under his name, but I was never in his big band. Those Rhythm Makers things were just ways for us to make some money to keep our bands going, so we'd go in with our bands and do the sessions. I'm not sure who he had with him then. Maybe it was Joe Dixon. (2)

Shaw made several more record dates as a sideman before opening with his own band at the Hotel Lexington. He was featured briefly with Richard Himber on July 27th, with Jack Shilkret and his orchestra on the 31st, and with Dick McDonough's band again on August 5th. *Metronome* stated on page 41 of its September 1936 issue, "Fine Artie Shaw clarinet work on Richard Himber's 'Me and the Moon' " (from the July 27th session).

Even after Shaw's band opened at the Hotel Lexington, he continued to make occasional record dates as a sideman, recording with Jack Shilkret, Chick Bullock, Dick McDonough, Richard Himber, and Mildred Bailey. He has stated that he needed the money to finance his band, and wasn't busy during the day, so this activity continued until he left New York to begin to tour with his own bands (2). Most of this material was commercial, slightly jazzy dance music. Shaw has confirmed his own work, where possible, on any items listed in the discography.

The recordings with Mildred Bailey were a considerable improvement over the usual commercial sessions. They featured arrangements by Eddie Sauter and included such sidemen as Ben Webster and Johnny Hodges in good form, not to mention Mildred Bailey's excellent singing. However, Shaw was featured only for a brief introduction to "For Sentimental Reasons" and was absent from a fourth title recorded at the same session.

Shaw also may have performed on a later sideman session or two. As noted, he was certain he ceased such activity once he began touring with his own bands, but he was not certain whether this would have been after the tour of colleges in November 1936 (which was followed by the busy Paramount Theatre engagement and subsequent trip to Dallas, as described in chapter 4), or if he continued accepting sideman dates after returning from Dallas until he left New York again to tour with his next group in the spring of 1937. When questioned, Shaw stated that it was possible he may have performed on records as a sideman as late as early spring 1937, to help finance his new band. He could not recall any sessions specifically from that period, and was quite confident there would have been nothing more of that sort of activity afterward, once he'd left on the road with his "New Music" band (2).

Chapter 4

String Swing: 1936–1937

The Imperial Theatre concert was significant in other ways besides providing Artie Shaw with his big break. As noted, it was the first official swing concert in New York and one of the first jazz concerts of its type (a succession of noted groups appearing briefly, one after another, before a concert audience). The aforementioned OKeh Records concerts in Chicago, which featured their performers in a similar format, predated the Imperial Theatre concert by a decade, but were not jazz-only concerts. Furthermore, it was the Imperial Theatre event that inspired John Hammond's "Spirituals to Swing" concerts a couple of years later, and all later jazz concerts and festivals, including Norman Granz's "Jazz at the Philharmonic" series. Yet it seldom gets the attention it deserves in jazz literature. For example, the *New Grove Dictionary of Jazz* (ed. Barry Kernfield [London: Macmillan, 1988]) failed to mention it in expected contexts. "Imperial Theatre" did not even appear in its index. The best discussion aside from the original *Down Beat* review (June 1936, pp. 1, 8, 9) was in Arnold Shaw's *52nd Street: The Street of Jazz* (New York: Da Capo Press, 1977, pp. 85–87ff.). Curiously, details differ from the *Down Beat* review.

Occasionally when it has been mentioned, the date of the concert has been given incorrectly. This included the Aircheck collectors' label release of "Interlude in B-flat," which unaccountably misdated the performance as April 8, 1936. In view of this concert's importance to jazz history, as well as to Artie Shaw's career, it is appropriate to examine the event in greater detail.

The Imperial Theatre was in the heart of Broadway's theater district, on West 45th Street, a few blocks south of organizer Joe Helbock's Onyx Club. The Onyx Club had been a musicians' hangout since its nights as a speakeasy during Prohibition. Shaw recounted in his autobiography that when it became necessary after Prohibition for Helbock to acquire a liquor license for the club, he took up a collection among frequenters of the place. Contributors became "charter members" of the Onyx Club. Among these individuals were Tommy Dorsey, Manny Klein, Bunny Berigan, and Artie Shaw. The musicians would jam regularly on the premises. As 52nd Street evolved as the place to hear the best jazz,

the Onyx Club became one of the "in" places to go. Helbock became something of a jazz authority by osmosis. In the liner notes to *Artie Shaw—A Legacy*, Shaw summarized the genesis of this important event by simply stating, "It suddenly seemed to Joe (Helbock) like a good idea to rent a legitimate Broadway musical theatre and put on what he called a swing concert."

Marshall Stearns's original copy of the program is in the Institute of Jazz Studies Archives at Rutgers University, with annotations and corrections. Shaw also has a copy. It is large, glossy, and full of advertising. Advertising income for the program was quoted at $1,000 by *Down Beat*. Details on attendance and income also were cited: the concert was sold out at $2.75 per seat, for a total seat sales figure of $2,300. There were seventeen bands participating in the concert, which was a benefit for the Musicians' Union.

The concert began at 9:00 P.M. on Sunday, May 24, 1936, when announcer Paul Douglas of NBC introduced the Glen Gray Casa Loma Orchestra. They were followed by an eight-piece harmonica band, which the *Down Beat* reviewer called "just about acceptable from a novelty standpoint." They, in turn, were followed by Wingy Manone's group and Stuff Smith's band. Then, quoting in full:

Next came Artie Shaw and his string swing ensemble which stole the show for novelty. . . . He has what is probably the only new creation in modern music within the past five years. . . . A combination consisting of a legit string quartet plus a rhythm section and Shaw featured on clarinet. . . . Arrangements were by Shaw, I believe, and were distinctly outstanding. . . . Intro on first selection, which was probably original, had four bar string (no rhythm) playing sustained harmonics à la Debussy and Ravel ("La Valse" not "Bolero") then with a fanfare of rhythm, Shaw came in for some dynamic clarinet work that will probably keep Goodman awake for several nights to come . . . absolutely masterful on technique and tone. . . . Rates with Goodman any day . . . after each chorus strings would pick up modulations in subdued style and then rhythm would whip back into high style swingin' with Shaw playing variations on the theme. . . . Second selection was "Japanese Sandman" and proved that idea could be adapted to popular selection with plenty guts. . . . Applause tore down house and necessitated many a bow. . . . Four Star stuff. (p. 8)

Shaw also described this performance in detail and with great humor in his autobiography ([1], pp. 294–98). Seldom noted was Artie Shaw's return to the stage later in the program with Bunny Berigan's group, which also included Joe Bushkin on piano and Eddie Condon on guitar, among others, although photos of this group on stage at the concert have been published in several sources.

Also in the show were Red Norvo's Swingtette, with and without Norvo's wife, singer Mildred Bailey; Bob Crosby's orchestra; Tommy Dorsey's Clambake 7; a small group out of Paul Whiteman's orchestra, introduced by Whiteman, which featured Frank Trumbauer and Jack and Charlie Teagarden; Adrian Rollini's group; Frank Chase's Saxophone Sextet; solo appearances by pianists Willie "The Lion" Smith and Meade Lux Lewis, and by harpist Caspar Reardon; the Carl Kress–Dick McDonough guitar duo; and Louis Armstrong, who concluded the program with his band.

The recording of "Interlude in B-flat" from this concert is the earliest item under Shaw's leadership in the discography. It was notable for Shaw's blending of jazz and classical elements ("shades of Ravel," Shaw said of one part of his arrangement) and for the absence of a piano, which opened up the harmonic texture of the piece and enabled the string quartet to be heard clearly.

As noted, as a result of this performance Shaw was promptly invited to contract for recordings and appearances with his own group. He signed with the Rockwell-O'Keefe Agency, and less than three weeks after the concert, had a studio group recording for Brunswick Records. He had enlarged his ensemble by adding trumpet, trombone, tenor sax, and piano. Shaw said this was "in order to give the band more flexibility and a greater range of tone color." Shaw did all the arrangements himself. Interestingly, their first recording was an expanded arrangement of "Japanese Sandman," the tune that also had been reviewed at the Imperial Theatre along with "Interlude in B-flat." This song had been a major hit for Paul Whiteman, and had been recorded at his first record date in 1920. Along with another instrumental, "A Pretty Girl Is Like a Melody," Shaw's band also recorded two vocals that featured guitarist Wes Vaughan. He sang so stridently on "No Regrets" that his singing was edited out of later LP issues. Almost all discographers have listed a remake of that title a week later, as well.

Shaw's arrangements exhibited subtlety, sophistication, and imagination. There were good solos by his old friend from Joe Cantor's band, Willis Kelly, on trumpet, and by Tony Zimmer on tenor sax. Shaw, naturally, was the princi-

pal soloist, exhibiting the fluency and intricacy of phrasing that characterized the best of his sideman work.

As noted, over the eight weeks leading up to his band's next record session for Brunswick, Shaw continued to work in radio orchestras and make records and transcriptions as a sideman to finance his new band. Nevertheless, he also was working hard to build his band's library for their opening at the Hotel Lexington at 44th Street and Lexington Avenue. To assist with writing out the orchestrations of the arrangements he was sketching in preparing a book for his distinctive ensemble, Shaw hired violinist Jerry Gray (who also would lead the string section) and pianist Joe Lippman into the band. He also added another trumpet to the brass section, and hired Peg La Centra as the band's vocalist. Originally from Boston and still in her teens, Peg La Centra already was a veteran of many years in commercial radio, and as noted, Shaw had recorded with her in Johnny Green's band in 1934, and was working with her on Dick McDonough's radio show for Borden's Ice Cream that spring. He also brought in Tony Pastor, formerly known as Tony Pestritto, his old friend since New Haven, for the tenor sax chair and vocals. The rest of the personnel Shaw would use at the band's debut at the Lexington was almost established.

For their second record date, the band again recorded two instrumentals and two vocals, both by Peg La Centra. Her vocals on "South Sea Island Magic" and "It Ain't Right" revealed her singing to be far superior to most vocalists of the day. She had an appealing, rich voice with a throaty vibrato and a slight Boston accent that added up to a distinctive style. Although thoroughly evocative of the era, her work retained interest more than that of many other singers of the day. She seemed to blend appropriately with the refined textures of Shaw's arrangements, and sounded convincing on virtually all of her performances throughout her tenure with Shaw's bands. Her excellent intonation also was a major asset. On the Dixieland-flavored "It Ain't Right" she also proved she could swing effectively.

The two instrumentals recorded at that session, "Sugar Foot Stomp" and "Thou Swell," revealed the jazz capabilities of the band. The creative use of the string quartet made these among the more interesting records of the era, and again Shaw's clarinet work was outstanding.

By the time of this second date, the results of Shaw's first recording session were getting good reviews in magazines such as *Billboard* and *Metronome*, appearing in the former's "Best Records" column and all four sides getting positive attention on page 16 of the August 1936 issue, listed under "Art Shaw." The records were issued with "Art Shaw and his Orchestra" on the labels. Glen Gray, writing an article on swing music and stylistic trends for *Billboard*, suggested, "Maybe Artie Shaw's swinging strings will hit the bull's eye."

The band opened at the Hotel Lexington on August 21st

as scheduled. In *The New York Times* under "Hotels and Restaurants" for that date the Lexington ran an advertisement that read:

TONIGHT! For the first time in New York:
ART SHAW and his Orchestra bring "SWEET SWING" to
the Silver Grill featuring Peg La Centra

At last something entirely new in dance music! A dance orchestra combining, at the same time, a complete swing band with a dreamy string ensemble. Come for dinner or supper dancing in the gay Silver Grill and thrill to the newest musical sensation, "Sweet-Swing."

The October 1936 *Down Beat* reported on page 3 that their music was well received, and listed the personnel for the band. By then Ben Plotkin had replaced Sam Rosenblum on second violin, and Shaw's old friend from the Cavallaro band, Dave Hudkins, was on drums. The article stated,

Artie's new type of instrumental swinging has been marvellously received by New Yorkers and may point to a new development of hot music. They are broadcasting over CBS and Mutual networks, and have recorded for Brunswick.

They also ran a photo of Peg La Centra captioned "Sings With Artie's String Swing" in a later issue.

George T. Simon gave the band a very good review in the October 1936 *Metronome* on page 22, which was reprinted in his book *Simon Says* (New York: Galahad Books, 1971). He said,

The Silver Grill, an oval shaped room with tables on tiers, was one of the greatest rooms in which to hear a band. It was intimate and had fine acoustics.

After praising the band's musical versatility and singling out individual band members one by one for praise, he wrote:

The band satisfies, too, from a showmanship angle. Shaw, a cleancut looking chap, presents a pleasing, reserved front. Quite obviously he knows what the dancers want for not only does he contrast his tempos nicely, but he also sets tempos that are thoroughly danceable. Showmanship credit too to Peg La Centra who sings for the crowd, rather than at it, and who does it well. And don't overlook the aforementioned Tony Pastor, whose kidding around and screwy faces help bring the mob up to the bandstand. ([6], pp. 68–70)

Pastor's singing, gravelly and hip, proved to be a regular attraction with Shaw's bands for the rest of the 1930s, along with his restrained tenor sax solos. As a singer, Pastor also managed to provide vocals that have not dated as badly as those of most of his contemporaries.

On the band's next record date, September 17th, Pastor sang on one tune, and Peg La Centra on the other three pieces recorded that day. These records were more audience oriented, with the La Centra vocals in the slower, mellower style of dance music. Pastor's "novelty" vocal was the only up-tempo number of the session.

After a couple of weeks at the Lexington, Shaw's agent, Tommy Rockwell, told him the band was getting complaints from the management. Thinking the concerns were musical, Shaw confronted the manager, Charlie Rochester, about whether the band was shaping up adequately. However, Rochester's complaint concerned the band's drawing power, not its music. Shaw quoted Rochester's indignant response to Shaw's defense of his band, in *The Trouble with Cinderella*:

You're talking about music. I don't give a good goddamn about music. I don't know a goddamn thing about music. I'm paying you to play so we can get some goddamn customers in the joint and make some dough. What the hell do you think I'm running here—a goddamn concert hall or something? If you want to take your pants down on that goddamn bandstand every night and take a crap up there, and if people'll pay to come in here and see you do it—I'll pay you to take a crap up there every night. That's how much I give a good goddamn about what kind of music you're playing. ([1], pp. 305–6)

Shaw said this speech came as a shattering disillusionment, as he finally realized he wasn't in the music business; he was in the entertainment business. Despite the encouragement and attention of the music world, he was not generating a popular following.

One night a young girl marched up to Shaw backstage after a show and said, "I'm Judy Garland. I'm a singer with Metro; I just had to tell you how great your music is" (Gerold Frank, *Judy* [New York: Harper & Row, 1975], p. 92). Of course Shaw was impressed. Frank went on to describe Shaw's reaction:

"How old are you?" he demanded, and when she told him fourteen, he hugged her in delight. "My God, sweetie, you're really something! Do you realize that nobody but musicians like what we're doing? The public hasn't the foggiest idea."

He marvelled that a girl so young should have the ear and the perception to appreciate such music. ([7], pp. 92–93)

The band was broadcasting thirty-minute spots every Saturday and Sunday night throughout their stay at the Lexington. The first week there was an extra broadcast on Wednesday as well, and Shaw and at least part of the band were featured on the CBS *Saturday Night Swing Club* show on September 12th. However, none of these shows have become available.

Charlie Barnet told a story on himself in his autobiography, *Those Swinging Years* (Baton Rouge: Louisiana State University Press, 1984, pp. 75–76), which involved Shaw and Claude Thornhill as accessories. One night around this time, Barnet was drinking at the Onyx Club and managed to convince Shirley Lloyd, vocalist with Ozzie Nelson's band at the time, to elope with him. They took along Shaw and Thornhill, who happened to be there, and a jug. By the time they found a justice of the peace they were in Armonk, New York, and it was 4 a.m. The justice of the peace detected their condition and refused to cooperate until Shaw managed to talk him into it. According to Barnet, by the time they got back to New York City, the idea didn't seem so inspired, and the marriage was promptly annulled without consummation.

After six weeks at the Lexington, the band was booked into the French Casino, a theater-restaurant located at Seventh Avenue and 50th Street. Contemporary advertising in *The New York Times* announced:

SHOW—Clifford C. Fischer's Sensational
* FOLIES d'AMOUR *
On the Cocktail Lounge An Intimate Revue.
DINING—Unexcelled Cuisine,
Table d'Hote Dinner 6:30 to 10 P.M. Supper 10 P.M. to closing.
DANCING to 3 Orchestras: Vincent Travers, Art Shaw, Eddie South

The band opened on October 10th, booked for a six-week engagement. They continued broadcasting on CBS. Shaw was having the air shots transcribed so that the band could hear itself. In "Zeke Zarchy" by R. Gulliver (*Jazz Journal*, December 1983, pp. 14–15), Zarchy remembered the floor show as "lots of naked girls and things like that. It was great fun . . . in order to get to our bandstand we had to go through the girls' dressing room. We loved that part of it."

On October 30, the band recorded again for Brunswick. There were two vocals by Peg La Centra, one by Pastor, and an instrumental. La Centra's vocals were smooth and sophisticated, although "There's Frost on the Moon" was as bouncy and jazzy as the features Pastor usually got. Indeed, his feature, "Take Another Guess," was ebullient with good humor. The instrumental, "Skeleton in the Closet," featured some more interesting scoring, including an eight-bar quote from Shaw's theme, "Nightmare," as a musical pun.

On their broadcast two days following this record date, the same four tunes were performed "live," and an air check circulates among collectors. It is not known whether this air check was preserved through a copy made by the station or whether it was one of the recordings Shaw had made himself in order to discuss the fine points of their performances with the band (a practice he was known to use at this time). The

broadcast versions of these pieces were as similar as alternate takes to those commercially recorded, although the slight extra "edge" usually present in live performances was evident, giving the band slightly more sparkle.

During their stay at the French Casino, Mike Michaels was dismissed from the trombone chair, being replaced temporarily by Sonny Lee, then Jerry Colonna before Moe Zudekoff (later known as Buddy Morrow) joined for the rest of the band's existence.

The band closed at the French Casino on November 20th, and embarked on a tour of colleges. There was another Brunswick Records session ten days later which featured Peg La Centra on three titles. The fourth piece was another fine instrumental, "The Same Old Line." Although two of the vocals were up-tempo, more in the manner of "There's Frost on the Moon," none of the performances were quite at the level of inspiration of the band's earlier sessions.

Some of the tunes recorded by the band were pop pieces that were being recorded by many performers at that time. It was the practice of the recording industry to make "covers" of likely songs, in hopes of getting a hit record. Cover performances of songs from popular movies also were frequently recorded. For example, with this band Shaw recorded three pieces from the 1936 Bing Crosby movie, *Pennies from Heaven*. These titles were "Skeleton in the Closet" (which was performed in the movie by Louis Armstrong), "Let's Call a Heart a Heart," and "One Two Button Your Shoe." Coincidentally, all three of these records had been released, and "Skeleton in the Closet" was doing well on *Billboard*'s charts, when the band went into the Paramount Theatre on Times Square to open along with the movie *Pennies from Heaven* on December 9, 1936.

The stage at the Paramount was on an elevator, so that the entire band could be lowered out of sight when it was time for the movie, and raised again for their shows. Along with *Pennies from Heaven* and a Betty Boop cartoon, audiences would see:

In Person: ART SHAW and his Band,
Al Bernie, Peg La Centra, 4 Modernaires,
Extra Added Attraction Jane Cooper

"Plus Dan Baker at the organ," according to *The New York Times* advertisements at the time. The ads featured a dominant picture of Crosby. It was clear that the movie was the main attraction.

Personnel changes had brought drummer George Wettling into the band some months earlier, but adding another member of The Chicagoans to his rhythm section temporarily for the Paramount engagement caused Shaw some interesting situations. Eddie Condon recalled his brief tenure with Shaw's band in his autobiography, *We Called It Music* (New York: Holt, Rinehart & Winston, 1947, p. 247):

Just before the opening his guitar player went to a hospital with appendicitis and I replaced him. The band wore uniforms and ugly brown suede shoes. At one point in the performance I had to stand up, put my right foot on a chair, and play a sixteen-bar solo. Otherwise both my feet were hidden by a music stand. Wettling's right foot was hidden by his bass drum: his left was visible to the audience. We wore the same size shoe, and since each musician had to buy his own uniform and accessories, we shared a pair of the brown suede atrocities. George wore the left one, I wore the right one. The band sat in the pit, which was elevated for the stage show. The movie was *Pennies from Heaven* with Bing Crosby and Louis Armstrong. I stayed in the pit and watched it again and again. During one performance I had Colin Campbell, a friend, with me. When it was time for the stage show Colin said, "I'd better get out of here or I'll be lifted up with the rest of you."

"Sit by the organ," I said. "It doesn't go up."

But it did. I turned around just in time to see Colin frantically scrambling off as the spotlight picked us up.

Bassist Ben Ginsberg recalled Condon's antics while at the Paramount (personal communication via John Harding, 1976). They were next to each other on a high tier with a sheer drop behind them. When the spotlight was focused on Ginsberg for his bass solo on "Streamline," Condon would clown under his breath in an effort to get Ginsberg to laugh. He would also sway the tier slightly, which would be enough to create insecurity in a bass player standing near the edge attempting to perform a solo.

As if Condon's sense of humor wasn't enough, he also was notoriously incapable of reading music. According to some reports he would sometimes reach the end of the pieces sixteen bars ahead of anyone else. Finally, Shaw's regular guitarist Tony Gottuso recovered from his appendicitis operation and returned to the band before the engagement ended. Consequently, he was able to play on the band's next record date, the day after their closing at the Paramount. Gottuso remained with the band into the new year, but was replaced in Dallas by Mike Bryan.

At their December 23rd Brunswick Records session, the band recorded six titles. These were all instrumentals, and of consistently high quality. There were four titles by the full group, including three jazz standards and Shaw's original composition "Cream Puff." The horns and piano were omitted for the remaining two titles, returning to the instrumentation featured on "Interlude in B-flat." These included another Shaw original, the very fast "Streamline," and a beautiful rendition of "Sweet Lorraine" taken at a moderate tempo. Shaw commented on being pleased with his arrangement of "Sweet Lorraine" in private discussions (2). This pared-down ensemble also appeared in public, being announced as the "Streamliners," as noted in reviews of the Dallas engagement later that winter.

Over the Christmas holidays, the band had a break before traveling to their next engagement at the Adolphus Hotel in Dallas, Texas. A blurb in *Billboard* had reported that "Art Shaw's Swinging Strings" would be at the Penn Theatre in Philadelphia for a "battle of the bands" opposite Clyde McCoy over the holidays; however, this engagement was canceled.

The Adolphus Hotel was one of the hotels in the Hitz chain. The band had been booked by Rockwell-O'Keefe for a tour of several locations owned by Ralph Hitz in various cities, with the Dallas booking as the first. The band arrived in Dallas shortly after the new year began.

The January 3, 1937, *Dallas Morning News* Entertainment Section had an ad for the Adolphus which announced:

Starting at Dinner—January 6th—Art Shaw and his Orchestra, Featuring Peg La Centra. Dallas! Here's that man Shaw bringing you something entirely new in dance music . . . a dance orchestra combining a swing band and a dreamy string ensemble. Be a member of the welcoming committee when he opens in the gay Century Room Wednesday.

After their opening, the band was scheduled to perform three shows daily at the hotel: luncheon music, and dinner and supper dancing. They also did radio broadcasts over WRR in Dallas five separate times in the interval from the 3rd through the 6th alone, publicizing their opening. They also continued to broadcast daily throughout their stay at the Adolphus. (Researcher John Harding calculated that a total of sixty broadcasts would have occurred for the band during the engagement.) The *Dallas Morning News* reviewed the band's opening the next day, in an article titled "Shaw Presents Novelties at Century Room":

More novelties than one would have thought possible appeared on the floor show presented by Art Shaw and his band at the opening of the orchestra Wednesday night in the Century Room. The show opened with a special swing arrangement of the old jazz favorite "Ding Dong Daddy From Dumas" with Tony Pastor, orchestra vocalist, singing incidentally, and then Towne and Knott, dance team, came out to perform their numbers. Peg La Centra, the individualistic featured singer with the orchestra, sang next a selection from George Gershwin's *Porgy and Bess*. The Shaw orchestra is one of the few popular orchestras able to play the music of the folk opera but it includes enough variety in its instrumentation to achieve the necessary effects.

Highlight of the show was the rendition of "Streamline," an original composition of Art Shaw himself. This was played by the "Streamliners," comprising the string section of the band and Shaw's clarinet. A torrid rendition of "King of Jazz" by the whole group brought the programme to a finale.

Despite the favorable press attention and exposure, the band failed to go over in a big way. After a week, the dance team changed to John and Edna Torrence. Just two weeks later, it was announced that Shaw's engagement was to be cut short, and Al Bernie, a mimic popular since the vaudeville circuits, would be added to the bill during the last week. Bernie, of course, had also appeared on the same bill with the band at the Paramount.

Zarchy also was quoted (in a 1976 letter from John Harding) describing conditions at the Century Room as

almost sheer hell. The room was panelled in its entirety in glass and mirrors, and even the supporting pillars were panelled in glass. With only 3 brass and 1 sax we were too loud for the room, and there was a constant battle between the management and Artie. We were forced to play in whispers most of the time, but the band itself was a joy to play in—all fine musicians and of course Artie himself—he was a giant. Despite the all glass room, there was something to look forward to in just going to work.

Nevertheless, Zarchy quit at the end of the Dallas booking. *Metronome* noted on page 39 of its February 1937 issue: "Curtis Hurd, fine trumpet man, has joined forces with Artie Shaw's band at the Adolphus Hotel in Dallas!"

The band ended its engagement February 2nd. Their next booking, a hotel also in the Hitz chain in New Orleans, was canceled. Shaw and the band were stranded in mid-tour. By the time they got back to New York, Shaw was broke and thoroughly discouraged, with only a Brunswick recording date in mid-February to look forward to.

All four titles from this last Brunswick session by the band were very good performances. The band was playing at the top of its form, and the arrangements and solos again offered the sophisticated musical twists and surprises that made their recordings so enjoyable. The instrumental, "Love Is Good for Anything That Ails You," was among the best of the band's many fine instrumentals, which is saying a lot. Peg La Centra's three vocals were among her best work with the band as well.

Frank Dailey, a former band leader and manager of the Meadowbrook Ballroom in Cedar Grove, New Jersey, was a great admirer of the band and booked them into the Meadowbrook for four weeks beginning February 17th. The band broadcast on WABC beginning Friday, February 19th, on Tuesdays and Fridays. Nevertheless, as Shaw noted, "The public made its indifference only too plain. So I saw, read, and accepted the handwriting on the wall—and at the end of that job broke up the band. . . ." ([1], p. 311)

In the liner notes to *The Complete Tommy Dorsey Vol. V: 1937* (AXM2-5573), Lee Castle related how Tommy Dorsey recruited him out of Shaw's band at this point:

Tommy came and sat in with us at the Meadowbrook. He sat next to me in the band. After we played a bit, he whispered, out of the side of his mouth, "Why don't you join my band?

I think you'd be real happy with me." I looked at him like he was nuts. But when word got out that Artie didn't know what he wanted to do and might break up his outfit, I got a call from Tommy. I opened with him at the Pennsylvania Roof. . . . Tommy didn't even audition me, just hired me from the time we played together that one night.

While still at the Meadowbrook, however, Shaw took the band into New York for a recording date for the Thesaurus Transcription Service as one of the Rhythm Makers. The National Broadcasting Company began recording sixteen-inch transcription disks that were pressed in plastic and played at 33 1/3 rpm in 1935. These were leased to radio stations for broadcast. The recordings were made in marathon sessions at RCA studios in New York, with twenty or more titles recorded at each session, only one take per title. Many bands participated in this series, all anonymously billed as the "Rhythm Makers' Dance Orchestra," with even the vocalists given pseudonyms.

On this Thesaurus session the String Swing band recorded twenty titles. Nine of them were previously recorded for Brunswick, including three of Peg La Centra's best vocal features ("No More Tears," "Was It Rain?" and "Moon Face") and six of the best instrumental band features, including all four recorded by the full band at the classic December 23, 1936, session. These performances exceeded the high standard set by the band's Brunswick records of the same pieces. Among the eleven new titles, there were five Peg La Centra features. "All Dressed Up and No Place to Go" and "When Your Lover Has Gone" were outstanding, both because of the intriguing arrangements and because the band was fully warmed up. The six new instrumentals included a longer than usual performance of "The Mood That I'm In" and an interesting arrangement of "Swing High, Swing Low." The untitled blues and the remaining items were of similar high quality and further documented the band's book.

Collectors had to wait until 1985 for this Thesaurus session to become widely available in chronological order on the Swingdom collectors' label LPs. However, only some of the Brunswicks had been reissued since their original 78-rpm issues, scattered on various Epic LPs that have been long-out-of-print collectors' items. Eventually, they appeared complete and in order on the Ajaz label, another fairly obscure bootleg collectors' edition series. Finally, in the 1990s, CBS issued them complete and in chronological order on two CDs. At long last this band could be heard in its total output, generally (but not in every case) in the fidelity available from current technology for reissues. Only then did the full effect of the band's legacy become apparent, as the subtleties and contrasts in the voicings were lost when reproduced from the original well-used 78s. Additional CD reissues also have since also appeared on other collectors' labels.

The band's music can be heard to be a rather unique offering. Glenn Miller recorded three titles with similar instrumentation in April 1935, but never followed up, and Shaw's approach was distinctive (see appendix 3). The band evoked its era, but there were touches that sounded very advanced. It is apparent that Shaw knew exactly what he wanted and got it—jazz-oriented dance music with new tone colors in superior taste. He did this without compromise to his musical integrity by arranging popular material to the level of art while supplying genuinely exciting jazz.

However, the band was disbanded as a result of public apathy. Their last broadcast from the Meadowbrook was on March 9th. There were thirty titles recorded for Brunswick, twenty for Thesaurus, plus the few air checks, to document this musical approach.

During early March 1937, while the Shaw band was at the Meadowbrook, swing history was being made at the Paramount Theatre by Benny Goodman. He was playing to capacity crowds and causing riots among the jitterbugs with his best band at its peak. At that point Shaw decided to go along with the trend and form a swing big band with conventional instrumentation, and went right to work assembling personnel and arrangements for the new band with his usual intensity.

Shaw has stated that he may have made some sideman dates in this interval to help finance the new band, but he could not recall anything specific. One Dick McDonough session offered one short, suspiciously Shaw-like alto solo, but there was too little exposure, and no significant clarinet work on the session, to be certain of a positive identification. Shaw was sent dubs of these performances but could only say, "I don't remember this, but after all this time, you can't remember *everything*! Maybe—who could tell?" (2)

On Sunday afternoon, March 14, 1937, however, Shaw took time out to appear with his clarinet along with Duke Ellington on piano and Chick Webb on drums in a trio context. This unique event was part of an all-star swing jam-session concert organized by Irving Mills and held at his Master Studios in New York by the United Hot Clubs of America. Reportedly over 400 fans attended, and several photos from this event, taken by photographer Charlie Peterson, have been published (one of which appeared in the 1992 edition of *The Trouble with Cinderella*), but no recording is known to have been made. Shaw was sure none had been made. "It was part of a series of little jam sessions. I think we played the blues, and maybe something else, two or three numbers maybe. That's all there was to it" (2).

The review of this event in *Tempo* (April 1937) cited this set as the program's highlight, and Phil Cohen, producer of the CBS *Saturday Night Swing Club* show, was reportedly so impressed by the overwhelming response that he booked this trio for his show for later in April, according to Jim Prohaska's article "Irving Mills—Record Producer: The Master and Variety Labels" (*IAJRC Journal* 30, no. 2, Spring 1997). However, Shaw has stated that he did not believe this trio had appeared elsewhere or ever recorded or broadcast. Shaw was reportedly a guest on the *Saturday Night Swing Club* show on March 20th, but the exact context is not known.

Chapter 5

Art Shaw and His New Music: 1937–1938

Less than a month separated the last broadcast with the string band on March 9, 1937, and the opening of Shaw's conventional big band at the Raymor Ballroom in Boston, Massachusetts, on April 2, 1937. After breaking up the string group, Shaw immediately began collecting a library for the new band and was auditioning sidemen "by the hundreds," according to reports, at Nola Studios at 111 West 57th Street.

Shaw retained Jerry Gray and Joe Lippman, to assist him with orchestrations for the new arrangements he was preparing for the new band. In addition, Ben Ginsberg stayed on as bassist and copyist, and George Wettling and Tony Pastor also remained from the former band. *Metronome* announced, "Artie Shaw Drops Strings," in its April 1937 issue and listed the personnel on page 14:

Malcolm Crain, Tom DiCarlo, Tweet Peterson (trumpets), Charlie Castaldo, George Arus (trombones), Les Robinson, Warren Kirk, Tony Pastor, Fred Petry (saxes), Jack O'Brien (piano), Al Avola (guitar), Ben Ginsberg (bass), George Wettling (drums)

However, Harry Rodgers recalled joining Shaw as trombonist and orchestrator, on March 22, 1937. Rodgers remembered the day clearly, as he had just completed his first record date playing in Glenn Miller's band, and bumped into Shaw and Ronnie Lanthier as he left the studio. Lanthier had been Tommy Dorsey's road manager. Shaw had just hired Lanthier and bought Tommy Dorsey's band bus at the same time. Lanthier knew Rodgers from several occasions when Rodgers had done arranging and copyist work for Dorsey, and introduced him to Shaw. Shaw hired Rodgers on the spot.

At about this time Wettling decided to go with Bunny Berigan's band. Soon after he influenced Bunny to swap pianists with Shaw. Wettling and Lippman were on Berigan's April 1st record date, and Shaw had Les Burness for his pianist. Meanwhile, Shaw needed a drummer, and he went to the Roseland Ballroom to hire Cliff Leeman away from the Hank Biagini orchestra. While there, he was impressed by Biagini's lead alto saxophonist, and proceeded to hire Les Robinson as well.

Initially, the band's book contained whatever arrangements Shaw could gather. He wrote in *The Trouble with Cinderella*,

Some of them I got on credit. Some had been pirated from the libraries of various bands around the country and peddled to me by a guy who used to hang around bands and make himself a buck that way. ([1], p. 311)

Money was short. Shaw described the economics of the situation in his autobiography. He could not even afford to paint over the sign on the bus he had bought from Dorsey. They were stopped three times under suspicion of having stolen it. On one occasion, in Boston, Lanthier was even arrested and the bus impounded because the police had just heard Tommy Dorsey broadcasting from New York. Shaw had to temporarily abandon the bus and driver and rush to their next engagement by public transportation. Following this, the band scraped together the money to repaint the vehicle.

They played the Raymor two nights a week, and traveled around to colleges and the chain of New England ballrooms on nights away from the Raymor, playing one-nighters. On April 9th, the two bands booked into the Roseland State Ballroom in Boston were Shaw's and Berigan's. Their appearance together was billed as "A Sensational Battle of Swing Music, featuring the stars of the CBS Saturday Night Jam Sessions, Art Shaw and his Orchestra vs. Bunny Berigan" (*Boston Post*, April 9, 1937, p. 27). They "battled" again at Reed's Casino, Asbury Park, New Jersey, on Sunday, April 14, 1937 (*Metronome*, May 1937, p. 41).

By the end of the month, Shaw had taken his new band into the Thesaurus Transcription Service studios and recorded twenty-six items. In addition to the usual twenty titles, they produced a transcription disc with an announcer simulating a location broadcast, including opening and closing themes and announcements. This special transcription featured different performances of three of the titles also on the regular transcriptions recorded that day, plus "Night and Day." For this occasion, a different theme song was used, another Shaw original, "The Bus Blues." As Shaw explained in the Berman film, his theme song had been "Nightmare" since his first broadcast from the Lexington in 1936. However, since the Rhythm Makers Orchestra was otherwise anonymous, Shaw could not use as distinctive a theme as "Nightmare" on this occasion.

The first disc held four excellent jazz pieces. "Milenburg Joys" was a jazz classic from the 1920s and the other three were originals by Shaw, including a full version of "The Bus Blues" and the other versions of "Born to Swing" and "Ubangi" (later retitled "The Chant"). The band sounded crisp and swung nicely. Arrangements and solos were excellent, and all four performances were exciting.

In contrast, the next three discs resembled commercial dance items of the day, and the band sounded relatively stiff and uninspired. This included the five titles featuring vocalist Dorothy Howe. Although remembered by band members as "a gorgeous chick," she sang stiffly and with uncertain intonation on all her numbers here, only loosening up a bit on "I've Got Beginners Luck." "Twilight in Turkey" was an unusual arrangement, and "Night over Shanghai" and "Study in Brown" reflected the band's jazz potential. However, only with the fifth disc did they regain the quality exhibited at the beginning. This disc included two more Shaw originals and two jazz standards.

On May 6th, en route from Boston to Washington, D.C., for an opening at the Capitol Theatre, as the band bus passed through New York the musicians were able to observe the German dirigible Hindenberg floating majestically over the city, complete with Nazi swastikas painted on its fins, on its way to Lakehurst, New Jersey, after its Atlantic crossing. It made a strong impression on the band members, greatly reinforced when news of its blowing up while attempting to dock later that day reached them.

The band made its debut at the Capitol Theatre without its music. The bus had been delayed again, and they performed their "Nightmare" theme from memory and then ad-libbed a long blues number with many choruses of solo features. At last the music arrived, and as the parts were passed across the stand the audience realized what had been going on and burst into energetic applause.

Finishing their week at the Capitol, the band returned to New York for its first Brunswick record date on May 13th. Buddy Saffer, who had been playing second alto sax and was remembered only as "a tall skinny guy who wore glasses" by Les Robinson, who sat next to him, left the band upon their return from their engagement at the Capitol Theatre. He was replaced briefly by Art Masters.

They recorded four titles at the May 13th session, including two good instrumentals and two titles featuring Tony Pastor's singing. All four titles were up-tempo, rousing performances, with Pastor sounding more relaxed and his usual high-spirited self, in contrast to the stiff performances on most of his spots from the earlier Rhythm Makers session.

On May 18th they recorded again for Brunswick. This time they did four instrumentals, and all were good evidence of the band's quality and jazz orientation. Hank Freeman had replaced Art Masters in the interval. Freeman had been with Berigan and was impressed by Shaw and the band at their joint appearances. In the second alto sax chair, Freeman doubled on bass clarinet or baritone sax as arrangements required.

Intriguingly, saxophonists Freeman, Les Robinson, and Tony Pastor were with the band for the rest of its existence, except for a brief period when Robinson was out sick. The fourth saxophone chair, however, continued to change periodically over the next year and a half.

Beginning May 21, the band began a lengthy run at the Willows, a ballroom in Oakmont, a suburb of Pittsburgh, Pennsylvania. The facility had an NBC hookup coast to coast, giving the band its first radio exposure over KDKA every Saturday. However, another setback threatened the band at this point, and nearly caused it to fold. The incident became a favorite story of Frank Ellisher, who for many years ran a musical instrument repair shop and dealership in the Werner Building in Pittsburgh. He related in private conversation:

> Artie Shaw was playing at the Willows in Oakmont. One day, I got a call from a music company in New York asking me to confiscate some instruments from the band. It seems that a few of the musicians had received their horns on a free trial and skipped town without paying for them. But I felt sorry for the band. They told me that if I took their instruments, they would have to call it quits.

Ellisher loaned the band his own horns so they could continue their Willows engagement. "Some of them bought the instruments, and the others returned theirs. I didn't lose a penny on the deal," he would say with pleasure. Shaw's comment on hearing this story was, "I didn't know anything about that!" (2)

The band was held over at the Willows until June 24th. The band's appearance at the Willows was briefly reviewed by Sid Dickles in the July 1937 *Metronome* on page 35, under "Pittsburgh":

> The Willows up at Oakmont, Pa., for many years the leading nitery of these parts excepting the past two or three years while the spot was under the mismangement of many would-be promoters, is once again back in the city's limelight as a "go place." As a lead-off choice, Artie Shaw with his new swingapators, made the lid-lifter bring back memories of the good old hay-days of The Willows when the name bands would literally make the walls bulge. Artie came through and

indeed wlth flying colors! As for our conception of the band, it is not strictly of Brother Goodman's element, having many reversions to the style of Tommy Dorsey.

Unquestionably, Shaw's clarinet work is the inspired interest of the unit. Les Burness does himself well at the piano; Tony Pastor's tenoring is near-sensational; Georgie Arus handles the sliphorn with the greatest of ease; and Tom De-Carlo's [*sic*] torrid corneting is worthy of mention.

However, with it all, the band is plenty rough in spots but this will all be corrected in due time, as the new Artie Shaw band is just what the word implies. Dorothy Howe is Shaw's canary, with Tony Pastor also on the lyrics. Woody Herman moved into the Willows on June 25th.

Immediately after this engagement, Peg La Centra returned to work with Shaw, replacing Dorothy Howe.

On June 26th, Shaw opened at The Plaza at Hunt's Inn in Wildwood, New Jersey, for another month's engagement. The Plaza was near Ocean Pier, and the band spent much leisure time at the beach. The August 1937 issue of *Metronome* noted on page 43:

> Artie Shaw was at Hunt's Plaza, Wildwood, for the first two weeks of July. This is Shaw's new outfit and has only been together three months. Outfit is extremely powerhouse and until the brass stop over-blowing it will not be a top band. However, the swell arrangements by Artie and several of the men were well received and did much to overcome the otherwise adverse brass.
>
> — S. Hillerson

On July 12th they went back to New York for their second Thesaurus Transcriptions marathon recording session. These recordings showed the band sounding more polished but still an embryonic version of what it would become the following year. While the weaker performances from the April session were clearly outclassed, the band seldom achieved its former peak levels. Most titles seemed intended as dance numbers. Although Shaw played beautifully throughout, many of the pieces simply were not distinctive. Even Peg La Centra sounded a bit awkward on a few of her nine vocal features. Pastor did not sing on this session. Nevertheless, there were several outstanding performances. "The Loveliness of You" and "If I Had You" exhibited Shaw's clarinet particularly well. The versions of "All Alone" and "Because I Love You" were superior to the performances of these pieces at their initial Brunswick date in May.

The band returned to New York twice more that month, for a *Saturday Night Swing Club* broadcast on July 17th, and for another Brunswick Records date on the 22nd. Peg La Centra sang two of her best features from the Thesaurus session for Brunswick. The two other tunes were the first under Shaw's leadership to have become available in alternate takes. Both "Sweet Adeline" and "How Dry I Am"

were good performances. A different master was used for their initial issues on Brunswick from those released later on Vocalion. This happened several times among Shaw's later records for the company. Intriguingly, in most cases the more imaginative version seemed to have been saved for the Vocalion release.

After closing at The Plaza the band embarked on a series of one-night stands, with only occasional longer stays in one spot. *Metronome* reported that a one-nighter at Roton Point Park in late July had a poor turnout. On August 4th the band again recorded for Brunswick, featuring Peg La Centra on her last two performances with Shaw, and the first Artie Shaw originals by this band to be commercially issued. "The Chant" of course was recorded earlier for Thesaurus, titled "Ubangi." "Fee Fi Fo Fum" was an intriguing composition with witty twists and allusions as the arrangement unfolded. This composition also has been attributed to Al Avola in some sources. Shaw's arrangement of "The Blues" (later retitled "The Blues March" on LP issues) occupied both sides of a ten-inch 78-rpm disc. An alternate take also appeared on Vocalion, but oddly only the "A" side of the two-part record.

The band was mentioned in the musical press as having performed a fifteen-minute blues number on the air that summer. *Billboard* consistently praised each new record by the band as it was released, referring to them as underrated and undeservedly obscure. During September 1937, the band returned to The Plaza at Wildwood for another week, but otherwise they only played occasional one-nighters. Trumpeter Johnny Best left the band and the music business for a time, apparently having tired of all the scuffling.

For the band's next Brunswick Records session on September 17th, Shaw brought in his old friend Charlie Spivak to fill Best's chair. Bea Wain (as Beatrice Wayne) replaced Peg La Centra as female singer, and Shaw added scat singer Leo Watson for three tunes. This six-title record date included three Shaw compositions, one of them the first full recording of Shaw's theme, "Nightmare." This also has appeared in an alternate take, which had a deeper and more involved solo from Shaw than the commonly reissued take. Shaw was in excellent form on all titles, and "It's a Long Way to Tipperary" was one of the band's best records. *Metronome* reviewed this session in its November 1937 issue (p. 25):

> ARTIE SHAW: "It's a Long Way to Tipperary"/"Nightmare." "Shoot the Likker to Me John Boy"/"Free Wheeling." "If It's the Last Thing I Do"/"I've a Strange New Rhythm." (B.7975, 7976, unknown).—There's a great improvement in this Shaw band; much cleaner attack than it's ever possessed, smarter arrangements, better intonation—all aided greatly by fine recording balance and the fact that Charlie Spivak played first trumpet on the date. "Tipperary"

features fine biting brass, plus good Shawisms. Artie's "cry-in-the-jungle" clarinet features the reverse, one of these weird, monotonous, three-note progressions. "Shoot" is good, too, with emphasis on the much-used, accented fourth-beat stuff. "Wheeling" has some sending passages by brass and unison saxes, with Artie and drummer Cliff Leeman getting off on a swell duo coda. Spivak's lead and Beatrice Wayne's fine vocal feature "Thing," while various and sundry good points are incorporated in "Strange." All in all this batch is a highly pleasant surprise. (Note: What's Shaw doing now, though?).

Billboard continued praising Shaw's records. The following reviews were typical in style and content:

2 October 1937: More delightful swing gutterals are forthcoming from Art Shaw with "Fee Fi Fo Fum" and "Chant" (Br 7952). Latter side is a cannibalistic venture with the chordage of "I'll Be Glad When You're Dead You Rascal You" with plenty pagan pipings by Shaw to a tom tom accomp. Musical mate is scored grooving for a four note lick.

30 October 1937: Art Shaw continues to cut a deep groove for himself among the solid senders with a sock "It's a Long Way to Tipperary," his clary predominating the sock arrangements. Plattermate shows the Ellington influence for his own conception of a "Nightmare" (Br 7965) Shaw leaning his gobblestick the Barney Bigard way.

Ace Hudkins (formerly drummer Dave Hudkins, earlier known as Dave Yudkin, the New Haven drummer who brought Shaw to Cavallaro's attention) was Shaw's road manager at this time. One day that season, he was given the responsibility of taking Shaw's clarinet back to the Plymouth Hotel, where the band was living at the time. On the way, Hudkins stopped at a barbershop. He failed to notice that he had left without the clarinet until he had arrived back at the hotel. He ran back to the barbershop, but the clarinet was gone. Shaw's reaction was reported to have been fantastic. He was particularly upset over losing his mouthpiece. Apparently it was some time before he was again satisfied with his instrument.

Around this time, Max Kaminsky joined the band as lead trumpet man, replacing the recently departed Johnny Best. As described earlier, Shaw and Kaminsky had been friends since 1931. By fall 1937 their friendship was well established, so that Shaw did not hesitate to send his road manager over to Kaminsky's apartment to wake him up and badger him into coming along for a one-nighter in Bridgeport, Connecticut. In his autobiography, Kaminsky described his starting with the band:

When Artie's manager talked me into getting on that bus to Bridgeport, the band had been getting very little work and Shaw was in a great deal of financial trouble. . . . Artie was looking for someone to give him the one big idea, the big

break. I had a fair name then, and I had ideas and was experienced, while most of his men were beginners. It was a very immature band at the start and had no definite style. . . . I played two or three nights with Shaw and was still struggling with the book and trying to get the band to play on pitch, since it's up to the lead trumpet to carry the band and give it a tone and set the time. Then, on the fourth day, when we played at the Connecticut State Teachers College, things began to happen. ([5], pp. 95–96)

Unfortunately, following this vivid insight, Kaminsky's recollections exceeded credibility on several points. He tried to take credit for virtually everything that transpired for Shaw and the band. This included giving Shaw the idea of using a string quartet with the earlier band, suggesting Shaw hire a black singer and introducing him to Billie Holiday (not knowing or forgetting about Shaw's long friendship with Billie and their earlier records together under her name), and suggesting the arrangement of "Begin the Beguine" that became Shaw's first big hit record. Nevertheless, Kaminsky's musicianship and long experience were indisputable assets to the band. At the October 1937 recording sessions for Brunswick and Thesaurus, the brass sections sounded brighter and more together, and there were more frequent and hotter jazz trumpet solos on these recordings.

The October Rhythm Makers session included more jazz arrangements than the earlier Thesaurus recording dates. This time there were only six vocals, five by Tony Pastor, and "A Strange Loneliness" by twenty-year-old Dolores O'Neill, the band's new female vocalist. When she recorded the same number at the Brunswick Records date later that week, the arrangement was taken a little faster because of the three-minute time limit on 78-rpm records, resulting in the arrangement sounding less effective. Members of the band remembered her as "a pretty girl with a sound all her own, a soulful quality." Unfortunately, she was only with the band over a six-week period during which no further opportunities to record occurred.

In *Metronome* (November 1937, p. 52), Joseph F. Sroka reviewed musical activities in his area under "Scranton" and noted: "Art Shaw's initial appearance at the Casino under the Buddy Club auspices drew fairly well with Scranton's own Dolores O'Neill handling the vocals."

She also was still with the band at the "Geo. F." Pavilion in Johnson City, New York, on Friday, November 12th for a one-nighter at which they were intriguingly, prematurely and prophetically billed as:

The New King of Swing
A R T S H A W
and his Orchestra
Featuring
DOLORES O'NEILL

The admission charge has been lowered for this one engagement only, so that every swing fan may hear this band that has sky rocketed to the top and promises to be the sensation of the year.

Admission 50 cents.

O'Neill went on to some prominence with Bob Chester's orchestra, and continued working during the 1940s. She also returned to sing with Shaw's 1950 band. However, by the December 1937 recording sessions, Shaw's female singer was Nita Bradley, who then was married to Cliff Leeman, Shaw's drummer. Nita Bradley sang five of the twenty titles at the December Thesaurus session. Tony Pastor sang six more titles, for a total of eleven vocal numbers that date, more than any other Thesaurus set. The remaining numbers were jazz oriented and included several originals and jazz standards. Of particular interest were another full version of "Nightmare," the first recording of Shaw's "Non-Stop Flight," and a version of "I'll Be With You in Apple Blossom Time" with a Tony Pastor vocal.

At the band's Brunswick Records date at the end of the month, they did several of the same numbers, including three of Nita Bradley's features, "Non-Stop Flight," and "I'll Be With You in Apple Blossom Time" without Pastor's vocal and with a shuffle-rhythm added, another of the band's outstanding records. Alternate takes appeared of Pastor's and one of Nita Bradley's vocals from this session.

That fall and winter of 1937–38 was a rough period for Shaw and the band. Work was sporadic and scattered all over the northeast quadrant of the country. Personnel changes were frequent: the entire trumpet section changed over a period of a few months, and that winter Ben Ginsberg tired of the scuffle and took his bass over to Eddie Duchin's band, to be replaced by Sid Weiss. Shaw described the overall situation in an article he wrote titled "Music Is a Business," published in *The Saturday Evening Post* of December 2, 1939 (pp. 14, 15, 66ff):

We'd finish at Scranton, Pennsylvania, at two in the morning, grab a bite to eat, crowd into the truck and two used cars we had picked up, and make Youngstown, Ohio, three hundred and fifty miles away, by noon the next day. We had devised a system for getting the equivalent of two nights' sleep for a one-night hotel fee. When we hit a town in the morning we'd register and turn in immediately, sleeping until it was time to show up for the engagement. Finished playing, we'd return to the hotel and sleep the night through, driving to our next date the following day. That happened every other day and saved us plenty of much-needed money.

Time and again I was on the verge of throwing it all up. Everything seemed to happen to make things tough. We had what we considered a choice engagement to play a Cornell college prom at Ithaca. The two cars went on ahead, with the truck following. The truck landed at Utica, ninety miles away. We played for the prom with four men, the drummer beating it out on a large dishpan!

Gas for the cars was always a problem. They were old and they drank it fast. Once we had to resort to using a police teletype system to send an urgent message to New York for gas money. Two things kept me from quitting: The knowledge that if I did I was through for good, and because I could see the band shaping up. (8)

In *The Trouble with Cinderella*, Shaw described having to give the men only half their week's salary because the band wasn't getting work. The men accepted the situation, as they felt they were all in it together. Later, on the bus to the next job, a crap game got under way. Shaw had a winning streak and cleaned out the whole band. Then, he just gave them their money back again, as the other half of that week's salary. There were no complaints. Another story involved their bus coming upon a rickety bridge during a snowstorm late one night. The driver was concerned that the bus exceeded the load limit posted for the bridge. The men had to decide whether to get out and carry their stuff over, letting the lightened bus follow; give up and go back; or stay aboard and take a chance. They decided to risk it, and there was a moment of tense silence as the bus crept across. Upon reaching the other side, there was a relieved burst of chatter and they continued on their way ([1], pp. 336–39).

Kaminsky related some stories about the morale of the band as well, in his autobiography:

One afternoon when he had the band booked for a dance in Philadelphia, instead of telling us we had to make it, even though he knew we were exhausted, he made a little speech about how far it was and how he felt it was too hard for us, too much to ask of us. Of course we insisted on doing it. Another time, after we had travelled 600 miles from Boston to Pittsburgh in a snowstorm, only about 6 people showed up for the dance. Since this was before we had been on the air, we weren't known yet and nobody bothered to come out on a stormy night to hear us, but Artie made a big point of thanking these people and saying how happy he was that at least somebody showed up, inspiring us at the same time, too, by making us feel we were all in this great crusade together. ([5], p. 103)

Shaw wrote in *The Trouble with Cinderella*,

My whole life at that point was concentrated on this one job. To keep a group of musicians together, to replace those who couldn't take the life we had to lead in order to stay together, who drifted off one at a time either to go home and give up or to take jobs with other bands where they could make some money—to keep going long enough to build this band of mine to stand out from other bands in such a way as to demand attention from the public—to do all this in spite of the handicaps, financial or otherwise, under which I had to compete with other, more successful, already-famous organizations—this was the one thing into which I focussed my entire energy, and all the drives that had been building up inside me since I had started in as a musician back there in New Haven.

I used to lie awake night after night figuring out ways and means of going on with this thing I had started, this band that had become an obsession with me. I worried and schemed, planned and connived. I fought with agents, quit agencies, signed up with others and fought with those agents. I argued with musicians, dance-hall managers, dance promoters— even dancers. When people came up to me during work and said something I didn't like, I told them to go to hell. ([1], p. 332)

Among other problems, Shaw's relationship with Marge wasn't surviving the strain, and before the end of 1937 their marriage was over. In his autobiography, he wrote:

I was a wild man, a crazy man . . . all I knew was that I had started something and I wasn't going to quit it until I'd either licked it or it had licked me . . . it was one big long battle, one big long rat-race—with me as the head rat. And talk about tension—! At about that time I began to develop a little thing called migraine. But even that didn't matter too much. I learned to depend on aspirin—and later, when that got too weak to do the job, I began to keep large bottles of Empirin compound with codeine in my clarinet case, right where I could get at it real handy. ([1], p. 333)

He switched agents, leaving Rockwell's General Amusement Corporation (GAC) to sign with the Music Corporation of America (MCA) in the fall, but recognizing that his lack of bookings was related to MCA's conservative musical orientation, he switched back to GAC by February 1938.

He also was dissatisfied with his recordings, despite the favorable commentary in the musical press, and with his library of arrangements as well:

I spent a good bit of time listening to what other bands were doing on records. This was during a time when I had made up my mind to sacrifice the small amount of revenue I could get by making records myself. I hadn't liked the records I had made thus far: and since I couldn't quite figure out what kind of records I did want to make I decided to quit recording entirely until I had made up my mind.

At this same time I also decided to scrap another whole library of arrangements. . . . I made up my mind to replace this library, one arrangement at a time, until I had built up a new one. But this time I had some idea as to the kind of new one I wanted . . . I wasn't aiming at any so-called style. I wasn't interested in that. It seemed to me that the best "style" a band could have would come out of playing the best music it could. Each tune would more or less dictate the style of its own arrangement—and after that it was up to me and the men in my band to make each arrangement sound as good as we possibly could. ([1], pp. 329–30)

Except for the last recording session for Thesaurus in February 1938, no performances by the band in its transition period have surfaced. It was still the same band, not yet showing the transformation Shaw was working toward. A few performances still were relatively bland dance arrangements of limited jazz interest, despite good solos by Shaw, Kaminsky, Arus, Petry, and Pastor. Nita Bradley was featured on all four vocal titles recorded at that session. Of particular interest was the first recording of Shaw's ballad "Any Old Time." One extraordinary instrumental was Raymond Scott's "Powerhouse," sounding quite modern in context, and rather more sophisticated than would be expected after his "Toy Trumpet" or the bizarreness of his "Twilight in Turkey" from the April 1937 session. Shaw's own "Meade Lux Special" was big band boogie woogie style, common in that era but not among Shaw's material. The instrumental rendition of "Indian Love Call" provided an interesting comparison with the more famous version featuring Pastor's vocal from the band's first RCA record date the following July. Most intriguing was a New Orleans styled octet version of "Sweet and Low" with Burness on celeste, displaying Shaw as a great New Orleans style ensemble clarinetist. With Kaminsky oriented in that direction as well, the performance was a unique item in Shaw's recorded legacy. Although brief, it was of very high quality.

On February 19th the band again was reported featured on the CBS *Saturday Night Swing Club* show. Unfortunately no air checks or transcriptions have surfaced from the five-month interval following the Thesaurus session and prior to the July 1938 RCA date. Shaw, of course, was busily developing his new book and his concept of how he wanted his records to sound, which evolved after studying the hits of the day. He wrote in *The Trouble with Cinderella*,

The thing that each of these hit records had, it seemed to me, was a crystal-clear transparency. Not only in the recording, but in the arranging as well. You could hear every single last instrument on the record. The arrangement itself was simple, essentially; as a result even a lay listener could (so to speak) see all the way through the surface of the music right down to the bottom, as when you look into a clear pool of water and see the sand at the very bottom of the pool.

That was the image that occurred to me. And from there on in, that was what I tried to get every arrangement to sound like, whether I made it myself or not. And if anyone brought in an arrangement which fell short of this criterion I had established for myself—that arrangement was out.

All this took a long time. Not only the arranging, but the development of a blend between the various sections of the band as well as the blend in the sections themselves—but by the time the whole thing was finished, the musical job was done. It was as simple as that.

That is, if anybody thinks it's simple.

It's actually about the toughest thing you can do. Anybody

can work up a set of tricks. The toughest thing is always the least tricky, the least gimmicky, the least fancy, and don't ever let anybody kid you about that. And that goes for anything—not only music. ([1], pp. 331–32)

Shaw often had expressed dissatisfaction with the recordings he made that first year with the band. When some of the Brunswicks emerged after many years of being nearly forgotten collectors' items, he complained in a *Down Beat* interview with John McDonough titled "Non-Stop Flight from 1938" (January 22, 1970, pp. 12, 13, 38):

I'm sorry to say I have no control over that. . . . If I did, I would say no. Here they are taking masters that were made long before I felt that I was ready to do anything that would come back and haunt me later. Generally, when you have no control over something, it doesn't represent you. I wasn't settled when I made those things. (9)

When Artie Shaw took his band into the Roseland State Ballroom in Boston on March 22, 1938, the band was almost exactly a year old. Their recorded legacy included three dozen titles for Brunswick Records and over one hundred titles for Thesaurus, certain pieces for both. Despite Shaw's reservations, the Brunswicks generally were well received by reviewers, and some of them sold relatively well at the time. Original compositions by Shaw were represented by eight of the Brunswicks and double that number of Thesaurus titles. Many of the arrangements were held over and appeared again, either on broadcasts later, or re-recorded for RCA.

Listening to their entire output in chronological order would show the development of the band over the year. Even the weakest and dullest items revealed the band's early struggles and repertoire, and as noted, superb performances appeared as early as the Shaw originals at their first Thesaurus session. Of course, it is evident that many of the recordings did not represent the band at its best, even in that period. In fact, some of the early recordings were relatively uninteresting as jazz, despite good solos by Shaw, George Arus on trombone, tenor saxophonists Fred Petry and Tony Pastor, Johnny Best, Tom Di Carlo, or Max Kaminsky on trumpets, and Les Burness on piano.

Nevertheless, it also is undeniable that a healthy percentage of their performances and arrangements were superb examples of big band swing of the day. There were, of course, the many Shaw originals, and some of his arrangements of standards even survived to be recorded later on broadcasts and even for Bluebird. There also was material by Benny Carter ("Take My Word" and "Symphony in Riffs"), Larry Clinton ("Study in Brown" and "Let 'er Go"), Duke Ellington ("Azure"), Fletcher Henderson ("Stealin' Apples"), Luis Russell ("Call of the Freaks"), Fats Waller ("Honeysuckle Rose"), plus the aforementioned Raymond Scott

items, and many other excellent arrangements of good material. Even some of the vocal and novelty items came across well, although Shaw consistently emphasized, "I used vocalists only because it was commercially necessary, and whenever possible, it was a put-on, like Tony Pastor doing 'Indian Love Call' or 'Rosalie.' " (9)

The March 1938 issue of *Metronome* offered an intriguing insight into the timetable of the band's evolution on page 24:

ARTIE SHAW'S SWING BAND—A swell example of good swing, and one which most of the nation seldom does hear, has been turned in recently by Artie Shaw's band over some NBC remotes. Here's a bunch that really settles into some swell rhythmic grooves, which are obviously inspired by what it's playing, and possesses the knack of propelling that bit of inspiration to its listeners. The arrangements, the intonation, and the ensemble work are vast improvements over any similar work the band has ever shown before. Shaw's colossal clarinet is an accepted factor, while Maxie Kaminsky's trumpet, Tony Pastor's tenor, Sid Weiss' bass, and Cliff Leeman's drums all add plenty of individual highlights to the entire performance. Shaw's band has always shown signs of reaching brilliant heights. Unless its recent performances are just flashes in the pan, the crew has definitely arrived. (Editor's Note: Recent fan mail, especially from New England readers, shows tremendous excitement and appreciation for the work of Shaw's band.)

It is likely that some of the broadcasts for NBC referred to, and broadcasts later from the Roseland for CBS, have been preserved on air checks and would provide documentation of the metamorphosis of the band in this period. Unfortunately, to date none have surfaced.

The April 1938 *Down Beat* gave another glimpse of the Shaw band in action that spring, in an article on page 9 by Bob Doucette titled "Studes Cry 'More' As Dean Tries To Shush":

Artie Shaw is back in Boston for an undetermined length of time and I hope that it's for many weeks. Artie is making the Roseland State Ballroom his headquarters and working club dates from there, on the off-nights. Billy Holliday [*sic*], *the beautiful sepia thrush, took over the Shaw vocals, March 14. What a combination the Shaw and Holliday one is. Something to make the "cats" lick their chops about. Shaw is set for two CBS shots a week, starting March 22nd. According to events that happened the past week, the Shaw band is really giving out. Too much so, according to the dean and president of the Pine Manor Girls Jr. College ultra smart girls' school in Wellesley. First the dean and then the president pleaded, even demanded, that Artie "stop playing that kind of music." However, the "studes" were really in jazz heaven and let the boys in the band know it by their enthusiasm. So Artie stuck to his guns and insisted upon playing the brand of music that the "studes" contracted for and expected to get. Even though he knew and was in fact told, that he'd never play at the same school again unless he resorted to smaltz [sic]. More power to Shaw!*

"I'll tell you what was happening," Shaw said in personal conversation.

> The band couldn't get work until we hooked up with Si Shribman. It turns out I was making Benny Goodman nervous. He told his agent he'd quit if I wasn't stopped. Willard Alexander told me this years later. Benny could be very nasty. Anyway, we were hardly working. Those Thesaurus dates were to get some money to pay the band. My lawyer (Andrew Weinberger) connected me with Si. We were to broadcast from the Roseland two nights a week and the rest of the time Si booked us around New England. He gave us $1000.00 a week and was supposed to make up any shortfalls if expenses went over, in exchange for 10% of the gross. That was our contract. The radio time was most important. Radio could make a band in those days. (2)

The Shribman brothers operated a ballroom chain of twenty dance spots around the New England area and surrounding territory. Charlie Shribman had been booking bands into these locations since the mid-1920s. His older brother Si joined him in the business in the early 1930s. Some of their premises included Nuttings-on-the-Charles in Waltham, Massachusetts; the Bal-a-Lair in Shrewsbury, Massachusetts; Kimball's Starlight Ballroom in Lynnfield, Massachusetts; Canodie Park Ballroom in Salem, New Hampshire; the Danceland in New London, Connecticut; and other locations as far afield as Reade's Casino in Asbury Park, New Jersey and another spot in Old Orchard Beach, Maine. According to George T. Simon in his book *The Big Bands*:

> The most effective personal manager I ever knew was a large, quiet, stolid Bostonian named Si Shribman, who, along with his brother Charlie, owned and/or operated a string of New England ballrooms. Si evidenced a great love of bands in general and a great faith in a few new leaders in particular— young unknowns like Artie Shaw, Glenn Miller, Tommy Dorsey, Woody Herman, Claude Thornhill, and Tony Pastor. To them, Si gave more than mere advice. He lent them money to get started, then kept them working in his ballrooms and on college dates, which he booked, until they'd had a chance to develop musically and to establish themselves financially. Leaders loved Si Shribman, not only for what he did for them but also because of the quiet, gentlemanly way in which he treated them. He was both a rare manager and a rare man. ([10], p. 47)

At the time, apparently, "owning a piece of the band" was a new twist for Shribman, and so was installing a radio wire. NBC reportedly was not interested in a Boston remote, but CBS agreed and plugged it into their coast-to-coast na-

tional hookup. The band moved to the Boston area for some one-nighters while waiting for their opening at the Roseland State.

The story of Billie Holiday coming with the band has been given in several versions. Shaw stressed that very little that appears in Billie's autobiography, *Lady Sings the Blues*, is accurate, at least in connection with her working with him.

> She'd been on drugs a lot by the time she was working on that book with Bill Dufty. That does things to people's memories.
>
> She was very scared being in that band. Billie and then Helen Forrest were the only singers I could relate to musically—we had 14 singers in and out of that band, I don't even remember most of them. But you had to have a female singer if you wanted to work. Some of those tunes were so silly, but you had to do them so you could get work and be able to play what you wanted to play. I would've wanted Billie for my band back in our Harlem days if I'd had a band then. So when she left Basie and I heard she was out of work, I went looking for her.
>
> I got in the car one night after work, I think it was one in the morning. Maxie Kaminsky was with me, he was a trumpet player in the band. Maxie knew Billie too, and we both got in the car, drove down to New York, down to Harlem, asked around, found out where Billie was living with her mother in some little flat, and went up and got her. And that was it. She went up to Boston and she joined the band. No contracts, no nothing. She trusted me, I trusted her. (2)

It was not a completely unique situation, as black singer June Richmond was working with Jimmy Dorsey's band— they even made some records that month. However, Shaw insisted that Billie sit on the bandstand with the band, instead of just coming out for her scheduled numbers, and he featured her heavily.

Unfortunately, Shaw almost immediately began to run into difficulties over Billie's presence in the band. In the May 1938 *Down Beat* George Frazier wrote an article titled "Should Shaw Tell Pluggers To Go To Hell?" which appeared on page 4:

> When Billie Holiday left Count Basie in what is now a cause celebre, she was immediately hired by Artie Shaw. As a musician of unimpeachable taste, Shaw appreciates her artistry. To him as to so many of us—she is the finest songstress in the business today. Not one of those specious performers who catch on like a forest fire, she is, instead, a profound artist whose talents are too subtle for immediate consumption by the mob. . . . When Shaw hired her I knew, for one thing, that he would give her every opportunity in his rapidly improving band and that, for another, his two network broadcasts a week would do wonders toward popularising her. . . . At her own sort of thing, tunes like "Trav'lin," "I Must Have That Man," etc.—Billie is quite unbeatable; and as far as I'm

concerned (and Shaw too) that is enough. But not so with the professional representatives. With Artie a valuable plug right now, they are anxious to sell him their wares and they insist that a tune needs a vocal if it is to click completely. Well, I suppose that there is truth in that. But it so happens that Holiday simply doesn't give a damn for the run-of-the-mill Tin Pan Alley output. She is at her best when she's singing a song that she feels deeply and not when she is mouthing inane words in a gracious attempt to please some plugger. The sad result of all this has been a despicable whispering campaign to induce Artie to fire Billie and to replace her with a girl less talented and not so demanding.

Artie is deeply shocked at what has been going on. He is completely satisfied with Billie's work, knows that her vocal-isin' is a magnificent stimulus to guys like Maxie, Tony Pastor, Les Burness, Sid Weiss and himself, and feels that no band—gray or colored—can boast so fine a girl singer. If he had the complete say, I am sure that he would tell the pluggers to go to hell. But there is another factor that plays an important part. At the moment, he is working out of Boston under the aegis of Si Shribman, whose office holds a virtual monopoly on the band business in New England. . . . My current gripe stems from his attempt to run Artie's band. He turned down the sane suggestion that Shaw take on a male singer who would supplement Billie by doing pops and decreed that the band hire an extra girl. That, if it happens (auditions are being held at this writing), will be rather pathetic. It will be a rank injustice to Billie and simply too bad for any girl naive enough to try to sing from the same platform. . . . I grant that certain icky souls haven't found Holiday to their taste, but I feel reasonably certain that she appeals to the people who count. The kid's up against something pretty tough right now, though. And don't let anyone tell you that racial prejudice doesn't enter into the question. There are some bad people in Boston, chum.

Shaw naturally fought to retain Billie Holiday, for musical reasons:

The combination was kind of electrical. Something happened, some kind of chemistry happened up on that stand. Sometimes we'd go on the air and we'd do a half-hour of the blues. This was in an orientation where you were supposed to do eight popular songs or the song publishers would come up with razors and kill you, and we did a half-hour of the blues. . . . Maybe a third of it would be Billie extemporizing, making up her own blues lyrics. And we would start slow, build it up, change tempos, do all kinds of things. (2)

The band broadcast from the Roseland State twice a week, at 6:30 p.m. every Tuesday and Saturday of their three-month engagement, playing the other Shribman ballrooms and college dances on other nights. *The New York Times* also was noting in their radio programming listings that the Shaw Orchestra was featured on WABC at 12 midnight on Tuesdays, beginning March 22nd. In a *Jazz Journal*

interview with Shaw, the issuing of broadcasts and air checks was brought up. Shaw stated:

We broadcast from Boston . . . when Billie Holiday was singing with the band. None of that has ever surfaced. I know the stuff exists somewhere, but I've never been able to find it. I've been told that there's a whole bunch of stuff like that lying around, and that somebody is just sitting on it. That may well be true, so one of these days somebody might hear it. Billie sang superbly with that band. It was the first year she joined the band, the first time a black singer had ever worked steadily with a white band. Anyway, I don't know where these recordings are, but one of these days I'm sure they'll surface.

Shaw was invited to guest on Paul Whiteman's Chesterfield radio show at CBS, broadcast over WABC from 8:30–9:00 p.m. on April 15th. Shaw drove down to New York with just his rhythm section men, Burness, Weiss, and Leeman. They did quartet versions of two Shaw compositions, "Meade Lux Special" and "Streamline," for the broadcast. Again, air checks of this material have not surfaced to date. This was the first of several references to Shaw performing with small groups out of his band that season, on the air and in public.

On Easter Sunday, April 17, the Shaw band had a one-nighter at Reade's Casino in Asbury Park, New Jersey. *Variety* (May 18, 1938) noted that "Reade's booking weekends as they did last year," with Shaw opening the season. It also was noted that the establishment had a Mutual radio wire.

At the Hotel Somerset in Boston, on April 20th, Johnny Best returned to the trumpet section, replacing Tweet Peterson. Best took over the lead work, although Kaminsky was still with the band. By Kaminsky's own account, he was becoming unreliable, even missing sets occasionally, because of personal problems. A few other personnel changes occurred that spring: tenor saxophonist Fred Petry was replaced briefly by Cliff Strickland, who a few years later was leading an Artie Shaw-styled band as a clarinet player. Strickland was replaced after a short time by Ronnie Perry. Tex Mulcahy was added to the trombone section, giving the band a six-man brass section. Mulcahy shortly was replaced by Ted Vesely. Vocalist Nita Bradley returned to do the pop songs, leaving Billie to concentrate on her specialties.

Despite Kaminsky's problems, he was enthusiastic when both the Shaw band and his old boss Tommy Dorsey were booked for the Dartmouth prom for a "battle of the bands" event. "We actually blew Tommy off the stand," Kaminsky wrote ([5], pp. 98–99). Kaminsky also wrote of Shaw's old Harlem friend Chick Webb sitting in with the band in that period:

Chick Webb's band, with Ella Fitzgerald singing in it, was working right around the corner from Roseland State Ballroom then, at Lavargi's [*sic*], and Chick used to drop around occasionally to sit in with us—and what a spark he'd give us. . . . A jazz musician never feels so happy playing as when he's playing with a great drummer. That's about the greatest feeling you can get.

It was this kind of feeling, the feeling of wanting to play, that gave the Artie Shaw band its great punch. ([5], pp. 101–2)

Metronome (May 1938, p. 45) noted the proximity of the Shaw and Webb bands under "Boston News":

The Back Bay section of the Hub City has been rockin' solid for the past few weeks to the rhythm of Chick Webb and Art Shaw. Chick and his great swingstress Ella Fitzgerald are still packing them in at Levaggi's [*sic*] while right next door at the State, the new Shaw–Holiday combo is drawing record gates. The addition of Billie Holiday to Shaw's band has put this outfit in top brackets. Band is plenty solid with leader Shaw stealing the show with his clarinet work. "Wee Maxie" Kaminsky, Tony Pastor and Les Burness are the most consistent performers in the band. Drummer Cliff Leeman, the nucleus of a very solid rhythm section is getting plenty of attention from the fans with his wild man act. Most interested of all seems to be Nita Bradley, who drops over from her Hi-Hat spot at every chance. Some of Webb's band sneak in more than often to catch Shaw's music. Webb has been NBC'd twice weekly and Shaw is filling CBS ether.

The Shaw band also outplayed the Red Norvo band that spring, as was documented by J. F. Considine from Boston in a review that appeared on page 27 of the June 1938 *Metronome* titled "Swing Shakes Bay State." This write-up profiled several big band appearances for May, including a Benny Goodman concert at Boston's Symphony Hall. Concerning the Shaw band, Considine noted:

The greatest attraction of the month was the battle staged at Nutting's on May 16, between Art Shaw and Red Norvo. Shaw, who had previously nicked T. Dorsey at Dartmouth, also edged Norvo who was making his initial N. E. stand. Billie Holliday [*sic*] and Mildred Bailey waged a war within a war with Nita Bradley, re-engaged by Shaw, doing her bit between rounds.

On Sunday, May 29, Shaw and his band flew down to New York to play the Martin Block "Carnival of Swing" concert at Randall's Island. The band clearly was attracting more attention.

The June 1938 *Down Beat* had a long feature article on the band on page 6 titled "Cripes! Shaw Doesn't Sound Like Goodman!" subtitled, "Poor Publicity Has Hurt Artie, But He Leads Way Back to Solid Jazz." This article was written by John Munro. His highly interesting write-up began,

This is to acquaint the brethren with the biggest hunk of jazz dynamite now languishing in the shade of the old one-night stand.

After rejecting the prevalent idea that Shaw's band was in any way a copy of Goodman's, Munro went on to a very intelligent observation on why its records did not do the band justice:

This kind of music takes plenty of warm-up and sweat before it comes out nice and easy. On the dance stand the boys will play "Moten Swing" for 15 minutes or more at a stretch, and the music is truly unbelievable. But when you try to compress such stuff into a 3-minute disc or the requirements of the networks, the band just tightens up and produces a caricature of its best music.

There isn't a single drip of sentimentality in the Shaw music. His originals are either hard-boiled little rhythm pieces, or magnificent mood pictures like "Nightmare" or "Monsoon" or "Streamline." He is a brilliant and fluent composer, and at least half the band's active book is stuff he has written and arranged himself. For the rest he plays mostly the good old jazz classics, and a few of the newer pieces that have merit. Above all else he hates icky pop tunes, and when he has to include them to appease the jingoes, he wraps them up in bitter jazz phrasing that would split your sides for its broad sarcasm.

Another feature of this band, shared by very few, and certainly not the Goodman boys, is its thorough relaxation. In the Shaw music there is plenty of room for those easy going, rollicking instrumental rides that stretch out for chorus after chorus. For example, there is a nameless little number the band does, which now takes about 30 minutes without interruption, and gets longer every time they play it—a perfect sample of collective improvisation by inspired jazz artists. Les Burness starts it out soft and easy on his boogie woogie piano, and after a turn or two, the rest of the rhythm section chimes in.

Artie's notes are pure. The music tumbles easily out of his clarinet—the notes always pure and justly shaded and the rhythmic pattern eternally fresh. There is never any hint of straining, or scratchiness, or banality in this flow of jazz. When he has wound up his ideas, the whole band pitches in for a crescendo that rises steadily over several choruses. The persistent rhythm and piling noise catches the band in a sort of hypnosis, where they give and give until you think for sure something will have to pop. Suddenly it cuts off sharp, and in handsome relief there is George Arus blowing a swell one out of his trombone. Maxie and the boys up back play around with a new staccato background for this; and up front Artie gives the saxes their individual notes for a new end chorus he has just thought up. And so it goes, on and on. . . .

The gradual painstaking assembly of this great band will some day be one of the real yarns of the music business . . . the band has had plenty of tough breaks, rotten schedules, layoffs, pay cuts, and the rest of the one night misery. But despite a constant pressure of outside offers the boys have hung together. They like Artie and they like his music. This kind of spirit can't help showing up.

The Shaw crew has been tremendously lifted in the past few months by the presence of Maxie Kaminsky and Billie Holiday. One of the great little guys of jazz, Maxie really fits now for the first time in his troubled career. He has become the spark plug of the Shaw brass section, and his hard bitten solo playing hops up the whole band. Billie, a long shot by Shaw, is paying off a hundred to one. Her lilting vocals jibe beautifully in the Shaw style and her stuff is going big with the customers. Most of all the personality and musicianship of this real jazz gal have won and unified the whole band, and these days more than one solo is being played straight at Billie.

Munro went on to profile each member of the band and to provide a capsule summary of Shaw's career to date.

During June 1938 the band continued at the Roseland State Ballroom in Boston, broadcasting at midnight Tuesdays and 6:30 p.m. Saturdays, according to *Down Beat*. They also played three weekends at the Hampton Beach Casino in New Hampshire, starting June 4th. There, they had a CBS hookup for their first radio broadcasts away from the Roseland. Capacity crowds were reportedly in attendance all three weekends, with 1,650 reported in attendance on the 4th.

In the July 1938 *Down Beat* Bob Doucette wrote,

Artie Shaw has been the only band to draw consistently in these parts and the reason is due in great part to the swell air shows that Artie has been putting out. (p. 31)

The band placed high in the *Metronome* polls that spring and was reported to have broken attendance records "all across Shribman's chain," as well as being held over at the Roseland. Shaw's Brunswick records were doing very well in the jukeboxes and it was widely reported that he had signed with RCA and would record in July. The July *Down Beat* contained an article by John Hammond titled "Hammond Throws Hat in Air for Shaw & Discovers More Blues Pianists" (pp. 4, 26), which stated:

I would like to throw my hat high up in the air for Artie Shaw's band up in Boston. He hasn't the greatest soloists in the world, but the band plays as if it loved music, and there is no higher praise than that. Aside from Artie's brilliant playing there is Billie Holiday's singing, and don't let anybody tell you that Billie isn't still the greatest of all the girl singers with bands.

Intriguingly, the same issue featured an article titled "Columbia Swing Club Celebrates Second Anniversary" on page 1, with its *Saturday Night Swing Club* broadcast of June 25th featuring "the Artie Shaw Trio, from Philadelphia" among an all-star list of performers. The "Philadelphia" connection was due to the Shaw band playing a one-nighter at the Philmont Country Club in Philadelphia on that date as well. Also in June, Ben Cole signed on as Shaw's road manager, as the band continued playing one-nighters on nights off from the Roseland and began touring away from Boston. During this period Max Kaminsky's personal problems continued to escalate. Shaw stated in personal conversation,

I'd have to go over to his apartment and he'd be in bed with his girl, and I'd have to drag him out and yell, "If you don't come play I'll break your neck." (2)

In his autobiography, Kaminsky mentioned girl troubles as one of the reasons he left the band when they left the Boston area to tour. He was replaced by Claude Bowen. The personnel who would record "Begin the Beguine" were then in place.

A series of one-nighters outside Boston, beginning the last week of June with the aforementioned Philadelphia appearance, included:

June 25:	Philmont Country Club, Philadelphia
June 26:	Roton Point, South Norwalk, Connecticut
June 28:	Johnson City, Pennsylvania
June 29:	Parkersberg, West Virginia
June 30:	Charlestown, West Virginia
July 1:	Gwynn Oak Park, Baltimore, Maryland

The band's appearance in Baltimore, Maryland, on July 1st drew 1,500 fans, and reportedly impressed the audience with "10-min. Jam Sessions Held By Shaw At Dance," according to a write-up with that headline by Henry Kramer Jr. in the August *Down Beat* on page 26:

Baltimore's swing-gates have had an elegant time these past few weeks at the new Gwynn Oak Park ballroom. Art Shaw and ork were right in the groove when they jived out plenty of swing. The crowd nearly went wild when Billie Holliday [*sic*], the ork's colored canary, sang "You Go to My Head." Both she and Art were swarmed with alligator autographers at the intermission. Art and his licorice stick with several other members of the ork held about seven or eight ten-minute jam sessions.

The crowd went so haywire that Gwynn Oak's managers brought Jimmy Dorsey to the ballroom for another swing session.

Intriguingly, the Shaw band was also featured for a fifteen-minute broadcast from this location over station WFBR that night.

Their road tour continued with an appearance at the Sunnybrook Ballroom in Pottstown, Pennsylvania, on July 2nd. They also were reported appearing at the nearby Hershey

Park Ballroom in Hershey, Pennsylvania, at around that time.

The band, which by this time had vocalist Patty Morgan replacing Nita Bradley as the "white girl singer" contrasting with Billie, played the Palais Royale in Toronto on July 6th. On July 9th they played at the Million Dollar Pier in Atlantic City, New Jersey, where the often-published photo of Shaw and Billie Holiday performing together was taken.

A July 9, 1938, *Billboard* ad noted Paul Whiteman's Chesterfield show was switching to Wednesday evenings beginning on the 13th, and indicated that this show would feature a guest appearance by the "Art Shaw quartette."

The band played a longer stay at the Lakeside Casino in Hartford, Connecticut, in mid-July, closing the day before their first RCA recording session, which was held in RCA's "Studio 2" on East 24th Street in New York City on July 24, 1938. (This was the studio in which *all* of Artie Shaw's New York records for RCA eventually were made.) The first tune recorded that day was the version of "Begin the Beguine" that became Shaw's biggest hit and one of the best-selling records ever made.

Clearly, the band's reputation and the audiences' responses were increasing steadily at this point. At the Lakeside Casino, a poll among audiences indicated that Shaw's ranked with Goodman's, Dorsey's and Sammy Kaye's as one of the most popular bands. In an article in *Metronome*

Shaw allegedly was quoted as stating he'd be "King of Swing" within the year, a statement he later refuted in a letter to the editor published in the August 1938 issue on page 1. In the original article, "Boston Debates Artie Shaw's Swing" by J. F. Considine (*Metronome*, July 1938, p. 30), the opinion was expressed that

> The Shaw band will have to go commercial if Artie expects to reach the heights to which he aspires. The band has been sensational here as far as the cats are concerned but the dancing element complained that steps to the Shaw rhythms are complicated. It is generally felt that more pop tunes will have to replace some of Shaw's long-winded originals. "The Blues," in particular, a 35-minute number, ranks among the hepsters but is an ordeal to dancers. Whether or not the band's popularity will rise without some modification in policy is dubious.

A photo of the band taken that summer clearly showing the personnel of the band at that point was published on the cover of the September 1938 issue of *Metronome*. The photo had an unidentified white singer on the bandstand, not Billie Holiday as one might have hoped: it is Patty Morgan, who was mentioned in the September 1938 *Down Beat* as singing with the band, as well as Billie Holiday, at Shaw's engagements at the Palais Royale in Toronto for both the early July and early August appearances.

Chapter 6

"Begin the Beguine" to the Palomar: 1938–1939

"Begin the Beguine" had not been in the band's book long. As noted, Max Kaminsky tried to take credit for the conception of the piece in his autobiography, stating, "One day at a rehearsal, when I started to noodle around with the song, Artie told his arranger to copy it that way" ([5], p. 101). In the liner notes to RCA AXM2-5517, Bert Korall quoted several band members on the subject of this piece. Hank Freeman reminisced about a discussion with Shaw, Jerry Gray, and Chuck Peterson on how to arrange "that Cole Porter number that never made it," and Peterson suggested the rhythmic approach. The story continued that Shaw and Gray then worked up the introduction. Al Avola recalled Jerry Gray bringing the arrangement to an afternoon rehearsal. Shaw stopped the band after a few bars, not liking the "beguine" rhythm. "Artie wouldn't stand for that," Avola stated. "So he said, 'Let's do it in 4/4 time,' so we changed the time but kept Jerry Gray's chords." According to Avola, they tried it that night at the Roseland, and the crowd liked it. In conversation, Shaw shrugged these stories off with, "Everyone wants to get in on the act."

Shaw had to convince RCA to record it. The era when the producer of a record session became artistic director as well had not yet begun, but the trend was there. "Begin the Beguine" was issued on the "B" side of "Indian Love Call," which had Tony Pastor singing and the band responding with vocal asides like a Greek chorus. The piece was a take-off on Tommy Dorsey's big hit "Marie," which had similar vocal exchanges.

The rest of the six titles recorded that day included three excellent Shaw compositions: "Comin' On," "Back Bay Shuffle," and "Any Old Time." The latter was the ballad Nita Bradley sang for Thesaurus. It was sung this time by Billie Holiday. The session was completed by a superb arrangement of "I Can't Believe That You're in Love with Me." It was evident on all performances that the band had evolved significantly in style and execution since their last Thesaurus date. Hank Freeman was quoted in the liner notes to RCA AXM2-5556 saying that Shaw "was almost entirely responsible for the way we sounded. He taught us about phrasing. . . . Artie showed us how to do things, without being overbearing."

Bert Korall quoted Les Robinson in the liner notes to RCA AXM2-5556 as stating,

Artie had a lot to do with the teamwork that made us special. He was marvelous writing for the saxes. He sketched the choruses; someone else would voice them. But they all had the Shaw "feel." The section things were like solos, only arranged for saxophones.

Unfortunately, the quality of "Any Old Time" was the only commercially recorded evidence of the effect of Billie Holiday singing with the Shaw band. Because Billie was under contract to Brunswick Records at the time, RCA had to withdraw the record shortly after its release. Shaw explained, "She failed to mention that she was under contract to Brunswick and didn't have the right to record for anybody but Brunswick. She re-signed with Brunswick after promising she wouldn't." Corporate jealousies and business policies prevented this extraordinarily vital artistic combination from further documentation, leaving the frustrated artists helpless.

Following this important record date, the band continued on the road. On July 28th, they were at Summit Beach Park near Akron, Ohio, where despite a pouring rain the crowd gave the band a "terrific ovation." From the July 30th weekend through August 5th, the band was again at Wildwood, New Jersey, at the Ocean Pier. On the 6th, a Saturday night, at Gateway Casino in Somers' Point, New Jersey, the Shaw band drew the largest crowd for them that summer, numbering "several thousands" according to *Metronome* (September 1938, p. 28). On the 7th, a one-nighter at Olcutt Beach drew 1,500. They then went to Toronto for four nights at the Palais Royale, August 8–11, where Dick MacDougal reviewed them briefly for *Metronome* (September 1938, p. 27), calling them "a Godsend" and noting that the vocalists were Billie Holiday and Patty Morgan. The same issue carried a photo of a buxom, Swedish-looking young woman on page 2, captioned "Audree Warner joined Artie Shaw's band as featured ballad singer late in August."

The band spent August 12–18 at the Eastwood Gardens in Detroit, then went on a string of one-nighters:

19th: Sandy Beach Park, Russell's Point, Ohio
20th: Dunbar Caves, Clarkesville, Tennessee
21st: Coney Island, Cincinnati, Ohio
22nd: Joyland Park, Lexington, Kentucky
23rd: Stonebrook Park, Stoneboro, Pennsylvania
24th: Hecla Park, Bellefonte, Pennsylvania
25th: Summit Beach Park, Akron, Ohio
26th: Club Fordham Pavilion, Budd Lake, New Jersey
27th: Beach Point Casino, Mamaroneck, New Jersey
28th: Canadarago Park, Richfield Springs, New York
29th: Waldamere Park, Erie, Pennsylvania
30th: Maple View Ballroom, Washington, Massachusetts
31st: Madison Square Garden, New York City

The Madison Square Garden appearance was *The New York Daily News* Harvest Moon Dance. Two bands were engaged, the other being Nano Rodriquo's Latin band.

The Shaw band was appearing at the Westwood Symphony Gardens in Dearborn, Michigan, the Friday before Labor Day. In early September 1938, they were at Summit Beach Park again, and returned to the Eastwood Gardens in Detroit from September 8th through 11th. *Variety* commented on Shaw's return date there less than a month after their first engagement, and noted that this closed the summer season for the Eastwood Gardens.

The above list of one-nighters was the tour recalled somewhat distortedly in Billie Holiday's autobiography (with William Dufty), *Lady Sings the Blues* (New York: Doubleday, 1956, chapter 8), which included the famous incident when a Southerner yelled from the dance floor after one of Billie's numbers, "Have the nigger wench sing another." As Shaw related in *Artie Shaw: Time Is All You've Got*, Billie responded with an obscenity, potential grounds for a race riot. Shaw related that he had been prepared for such an incident and had several men ready to hustle Billie into the bus and drive away, while the band distracted the audience with a lively number.

Shaw remembered one night around this time as "the best jazz night of my life," in the article/interview by Robert Palmer in *The New Yorker* "Profile" titled "Middle-Aged Man without a Horn" (19 May 1962, pp. 47ff):

I remember a night someplace in Pennsylvania—everybody tired, hungry, beat after a long jump on the road—and suddenly it happened. It was the best jazz night of my life. Don't ask me how. Most nights, I halfway hoped for rain, so nobody'd turn up. That way we could play without interference—the crowd almost always got between me and the music. But on this night everything worked. It was a BIG crowd, too, as I remember. . . . The band just took over; suddenly it had a life of its own . . . nobody needed leading. Man we nearly tore the roof off that place. I could see people looking up out of the sea below, mouths wide open. (11)

Some writers have implied that Shaw and Billie were lovers in this period. Shaw emphatically refuted this in private discussions. "Aren't we interesting enough without that?" he asked incredulously. "We were very, very dear friends, that's all." He also refuted stories that Billie and drummer Zutty Singleton were in the band at the same time. "Zutty was along much, much earlier, in 1936, the string band, and only lasted a short time. It was great, but too soon to have a black drummer with a white band" (2).

Shaw emphasized their musical rapport as the basis for his friendship with Billie. "She could also be very, very funny, an aspect of her personality that was often overlooked" (2).

Shaw summarized his attitude at that point in a quote from Korall's liner notes to AXM2-5517:

Music was everything to me then. The audience was totally irrelevant. They were there because they had to pay the tab in order for me to pay the musicians, so we could continue to do what we were doing. I don't like to make invidious comparisons . . . but I have never read about anyone that the world calls an artist who hasn't had exactly that attitude—that you do what you do for the love of what you're doing. And if it works, fine. If you're lucky enough, sooner or later, mostly later, the audience will buy it. The miracle was that the audience bought it at all.

By September, life on the road began to take its toll. Les Robinson, who had developed a bad cold, was hospitalized for pneumonia when the band returned to New York, and George Koenig substituted on lead alto while Robinson was out sick. Trombonist Ted Vesely dropped out, and was replaced by Russell Brown. On September 16, 1938, Shaw himself collapsed on stage shortly after another "battle of the bands" in New York City, this time with Tommy Dorsey. George T. Simon wrote a review of this event in the *Metronome* issue for October 1938 on page 11, headlined "Artie Shaw Collapses in Swing Battle," subheaded "Contest at New York Benefit Reaches Sad Anti-Climax As Exhaustion Rather Than Dorsey Overcomes Clarinetist." The entire review was reprinted in his book, *Simon Says*. Simon said,

Prior to the unfortunate collapse, Shaw's Solid Senders had been outswinging Tommy's lads in no uncertain terms, though for all-around good dance music, the Dorseyers stood out among the 4 bands WNEW's Martin Block had assembled for the occasion (Claude Hopkins and Merle Pitt ended 3rd and 4th respectively). Holding back nothing, Artie and his men shelled out as few white bands have ever shelled before. Their rhythmic attack was devastating; their pace scorching; their effect upon the assembled jitterbugs downright murderous. It was an awful shame that the first to succumb to this band's terrific barrage was its leader. ([6], p. 394)

Shaw recovered in time to appear with the band for a broadcast on the *Magic Key of Radio* show on NBC from

2:00 to 3:00 p.m. on Sunday, September 18th. An air check survived from this show, featuring the band performing "Begin the Beguine" and "What Is This Thing Called Love?" with the latter performance offering some slight fluffs in Shaw's clarinet technique (one of the very few such examples in all his prodigious output), as if his recovery were not yet quite complete.

At about the same time, reviews of "Begin the Beguine" were beginning to appear, along with a few for Vocalion reissues of some of Shaw's Brunswick releases. The September 17th *Billboard* reviewed the latter's "Nightmare" without noting that it was an alternate take, but included the comment "Shaw is currently building his name and fame in the hinterlands." Instead of putting Shaw on the 75-cent Victor records along with such bands as Benny Goodman and Tommy Dorsey, RCA released Shaw's records on the budget 35-cent Bluebird label, at less than half the cost.

According to Shaw, officials at the company thought "Art Shaw" sounded too much like a sneeze and began labeling his records as by "Artie Shaw," but as noted he had been referred to as "Artie" all along in the press and by friends, as on Wingy Manone's 1934 record.

On September 27th, the band again recorded six titles for RCA. They remade two of the classic Shaw originals for Bluebird, "Nightmare" and "Non-Stop Flight" (earlier recorded for both Brunswick and Thesaurus); provided impressive renditions of two standards (the exquisite ballad "Yesterdays" and the up-tempo arrangement of "What Is This Thing Called Love?" heard on the *Magic Key of Radio* broadcast); and recorded the first two pop songs to be sung with the band by Helen Forrest, who had just joined Shaw that month.

In her autobiography, *I Had the Craziest Dream* (New York: Coward, McCann & Geoghehan, 1982), Helen Forrest related that Shaw had been impressed by her singing as early as 1937, and had approached her to join his band, but she hadn't felt ready. Also, she and the drummer of the band she was singing with at that time "sort of fell in love," and she hadn't wanted to leave him (12). However, by the end of the summer of 1938, she felt ready to take on the challenge offered by Shaw. After their September record date, she went with the band to the Chase Hotel in St. Louis, Missouri.

Down Beat (November 1938, p. 2) reported Shaw's band broke the house record for attendance there on opening night, September 30th, bringing in 1,091 dancers, and broke their own record the next night by drawing a crowd of 1,432.

The band was booked into the Chase Hotel for a three-week stay, with a radio wire with the Mutual network, but continued to do one-nighters on nights off. On October 17th, at the Savoy Ballroom in Chicago, the band attracted a crowd of nearly 5,000 people, and *Billboard* (October 29,

1938, p. 14) reviewed their appearance in typical period style:

ARTIE SHAW (Reviewed at Savoy Ballroom, Chicago)

Here's something to write home about if you are a swing fan and want to tip off the ol' folks to a band that will send 'em via the gutbucket route. Shaw and crew have been around now for two years, but his present style and personnel are the result of much refurbishing. Now, with six brass, four reed and four rhythm, this ork is groomed for solid, low-down syncopating and doesn't disappoint.

Shaw hits below the Mason-Dixon line on most of his arrangements, dispensing a brand of swing that is both hot and erratic but still confined enough to be called solid. The maestro himself holds up a good portion of the ork's showman-ship with his hot chorus rides on the clary against a hard, thumping background supplied by the rhythm section. His improvisations are not fancy but are plenty clear and true, and altho these solos cut off the rhythm strain for the dancers, it is worth while to halt the hoofing for an earful of Shaw. Rest of the boys bang away with lots of verve and the sum total adds up to a barrelfull of hot stuff, expertly handled, and which should more than please the present generation of swing-lovers.

The song department affords a wide assortment of contrasts. Tenor sax man Tony Pastor, ebony-colored Billie Holiday and newcomer Helen Forrest are cast for the vocalizing. Pastor works out on the more novel numbers and gives a good account of himself on this score, due to an enthusiastic delivery. Miss Holiday, late of the Count Basie Ork, is of that phenomenal species of singer who has no true singing voice yet can sell a song with a lot of passion and restrained emoting. In her field she is probably tops. Miss Forrest, recent addition, has plenty of rough edges needing smoothing, but gal is conscientious about her work and has a good chance to win out.

—Humphrey

The records from Shaw's first Bluebird session were discussed in the October *Down Beat* (p. 21) with the Shaw originals, "Comin' On" / "Back Bay Shuffle," meriting a positive review. The remaining titles were merely listed, although "Begin the Beguine" was just beginning to have an impact. In *Artie Shaw: Time Is All You've Got*, Shaw told of playing a dance in Indiana during this period just after the records had been released. When they played "Begin the Beguine," there was such wild cheering that Shaw thought some of the dancers had been doing something spectacular, but the band couldn't see anything. Later the number was requested again, and was followed by more wild cheering. Shaw turned to the band in surprise and said, "Looks like we've got a hit!"

On October 28, 1938, Artie Shaw and his orchestra opened at the Blue Room of the Hotel Lincoln, which spanned the block between 44th and 45th Streets along Eighth Avenue in mid-town Manhattan.

In *The Saturday Evening Post* article, Shaw stated, "The Lincoln had not been a good spot for bands, but that didn't bother us. We knew we had it this time." Not only had the feedback on the road caused them to realize that they had a hit, giving them the confidence to accept a long engagement in New York, but the Lincoln had an NBC radio hookup and the band would be broadcasting nightly, coast to coast. He continued:

Our opening night there was a madhouse. From then on I couldn't think straight. My life wasn't my own. Photographers from *Life* magazine, autograph hunters, everything all at once, plus all kinds of disagreeable pressures being put upon me. (8)

One of the disagreeable pressures related to Billie Holiday, but Shaw noted that the usual stories are garbled. Helen Forrest, in her autobiography, wrote:

When I joined the band, Billie Holiday was still with it. . . . She treated me well. The band's vocal arrangements were written for her, so I sat around. She'd say to Artie, "Why don't you let this child sing?" He'd say, "She hasn't got any arrangements yet." And she'd say, "Well, let her use mine. But don't let her sit there doing nothing all night." The Diana Ross movie about Billie, *Lady Sings the Blues*, shows a musician in her white band turning her on to drugs, but I never saw a sign of anything harder than marijuana while I was with Artie's band and Billie looked clean to me. The funny thing is everyone says she finally gave up when the band got to New York for its big opening at the Lincoln Hotel and she wasn't allowed to sit on the stand, but the fact is there wasn't any room for any singers on the bandstand and we both waited at a table up front for our turn. Maybe the fuss was because we sat together. The fact is Billie had told us she was leaving long before. Artie knew it when he hired me, which was one reason he hired me. We weren't together with the band for more than a month or two. ([12], pp. 57–59)

Helen Forrest also vividly described the role of the singer in the swing bands of the day, and her reaction to Shaw's band:

It was an outstanding band and I learned a great deal just listening to it. I had to listen to it a lot because like the other singers of the band days I sat on the bandstand and smiled a lot and kept time to the music and had to look like I was listening. I really was. Many singers with lesser bands were not. I sang maybe a couple of songs a set, which lasted about an hour. I never sang an entire song. The band would start and finish and I'd sing a chorus in between. That was the custom in those days. The band was the thing and the arrangements were written for the band, not the singer, not even on the vocal numbers. ([12], p. 57)

Within a couple of weeks of their opening at the Lincoln, the Shaw band had been signed to do the Old Gold *Melody and Madness* show with Robert Benchley, and scheduled to make their first film short for Vitaphone, titled simply *Artie Shaw and His Orchestra* and including a version of "Begin the Beguine." From November 17, 1938, the documentation of the band's music has become awesome as collectors' labels have continued to issue air checks from the Blue Room and transcriptions from the Old Gold shows. The band's live recordings had that extra edge and excitement that performing before an audience tends to bring out in performers. The Bluebird records had the sense of controlled polish and often deeper feeling that focusing on perfection enabled Shaw to bring out in the band. Outstanding performances both from record dates and from the various broadcasts were common, and left little doubt concerning the metamorphosis Shaw had effected in his band over the intervening year.

Shaw also made a few more personnel changes. Around the time Billie left near the end of November, Bernie Privin joined the trumpet section replacing Claude Bowen, and Les Jenkins replaced Russell Brown on trombone. George Wettling began substituting for the ailing Cliff Leeman around the beginning of December, until Buddy Rich joined at Christmas. Pianist Bob Kitsis and Shaw's future tenor sax star Georgie Auld allegedly joined the same day, December 16th.

The band was broadcasting five nights per week. On page 15 of the December 1938 *Down Beat* their broadcast schedule was listed as follows:

ARTIE SHAW—CBS—Sunday, 10 p.m. (Old Golds)
NBC red—Tuesday and Wed., 12 midnite,
NBC blue—Thursday, 11 p.m., Friday, 7 p.m.
(Hotel Lincoln, NYC)

The band or Shaw alone also made guest appearances for other venues. On page 16 of the December *Metronome*, an article headlined "New York Jam Spread Thick" discussed radio station WNEW's planned jam sessions for November. These sessions were held on Wednesday evenings at 6 p.m. for Martin Block's *Make Believe Ballroom* show, which ordinarily had played phonograph records. For the second show in the new series, evidently on November 9, 1938, the lineup was listed as:

Yank Lauson [*sic*], trumpet; Tommy Dorsey, trombone; Artie Shaw, clarinet; Chu Berry, tenor sax; Jess Stacy, piano; Alan Reuss, guitar; John Kirby, bass; O'Neil Spencer, drums.

However, there was no indication of what was performed. Nevertheless, one title was "Limehouse Blues" and it has been issued on a Chu Berry LP on the Merritt collectors' label, although the performance was incomplete. Shaw and

Lawson soloed before Berry, who was followed by Stacy. The LP version faded shortly after Stacy's piano solo, as Tommy Dorsey's trombone solo began. Fidelity was accurately described as "dim" in Eddie Lambert's review of this record in *Jazz Journal International* (June 1985, pp. 25–26). Furthermore, there were some skips, evidently in the master, during Shaw's spirited solo. The LP also unaccountably dated this performance as November 11, 1938, which would have been a Friday.

The same article noted that the BBC (British Broadcasting Corporation) had held a "mammoth band carnival" at Manhattan Center in New York on November 15th as a benefit for needy Local 802 musicians. The biggest attractions included Shaw's band, as well as Jimmy Lunceford's and "Jitterbug Betty Hutton of the (Vincent) Lopez outfit." The November 29, 1938, *Billboard* noted that Benny Goodman, Tommy Dorsey, Paul Whiteman, and the other bands involved were "following each other in 15-minute segments" from 9:00 p.m. through to 6:00 a.m. the next morning.

Shaw's guest appearance with Paul Whiteman's orchestra at Carnegie Hall on December 25th was also a major event. Other guests included Louis Armstrong, among others, and part of the program was broadcast. Shaw was featured on an original composition based on the blues, for which he dictated a score to one of Whiteman's arrangers, Irving Szathmary, who did the orchestration. In the liner notes to *Artie Shaw—A Legacy*, Shaw said he did not have time to rehearse the piece. He simply showed up and played it with the orchestra. Reviews were enthusiastic. Immediately after the performance, moderator Deems Taylor blurted, "You just can't DO that on a B-flat clarinet," no doubt due to Shaw's amazing facility in the upper register. One reviewer evidently picked up on that comment and erroneously surmised that Shaw had been using an E-flat clarinet on this occasion. It is also interesting to note that Paul Whiteman's drummer was George Wettling, who had been substituting in Shaw's band for the ailing Cliff Leeman since the beginning of December and had just been replaced by Buddy Rich. Fortunately, Shaw's blues performance was among the broadcast items. The recording appeared on a collector's label LP in the 1970s and eventually in the Book-of-the-Month boxed set, *Artie Shaw—A Legacy*, as noted in the discography.

Shaw made some interesting comments concerning the changes in personnel he made in the band late in 1938, in the liner notes to RCA AXM2-5517:

At one point, I guess it was late 1938 . . . I decided to hire the kind of men who played differently than I would have them play. I desired more than a mirror image of myself. Georgie Auld gave me what I was after. Bernie Privin added a different sound. And when Buddy (Rich) joined, more changes took place, all for the better. With people like this in the organization, it took on a more bubbling and vivid quality

and gave me reason to feel quite encouraged about the band's future possibilities.

His comments on the subject were continued in the liner notes to RCA AXM2-5556:

I remember having to let one of the men go when we really began to make it. "I was good enough to go this far," he said. And I answered, "Up to now, the audience would forgive errors. But now that we're up there, the people expect more. They come to hear us anticipating something quite special. And we have to be equipped to give it to them. When you're on the rise, the audience sits there receptively and is grateful for anything that's surprisingly good. But when you're top dog, the people challenge you each time around. The collective attitude is: 'Show me!' "

I asked a lot of my musicians . . . they had to deliver, I would tolerate no less. I didn't care how they occupied themselves off the stand. But what came out of those horns was crucial to me. . . . I was looking for individualists, who would add character to the organization. Georgie was one of the people who had the qualities I was seeking. He brought a new sound and a wealth of jazz feeling to the band. . . . And Buddy provided a spark we never had before.

By the end of the year, the band's personnel had stabilized with the lineup it would have for most of the rest of the band's existence. Shaw, feeling the need for a rest, flew to Cuba right after New Year's Day 1939 for a holiday. He was having trouble adapting to the fact of becoming a celebrity. The well-known story about Shaw looking at the lighted windows of the New York City skyline and telling his girl, "Behind every one of those lighted windows is a person, and someday every one of them is going to know my name," became a fulfilled prophecy. He wrote in *The Trouble with Cinderella*,

Overnight I found I had "arrived"—which in show business means a complete metamorphosis. I am not overstating at all when I say this occurs suddenly. One moment you're barely making ends meet—barely managing to meet your expenses, such as the payroll for your men, agency and management fees, publicity expenses, and so forth. The next moment you find yourself making thousands of dollars a week even after paying all these expenses. . . . All at once you're a new kind of creature, a totally different type of being from what you were a week ago. For some reason people begin to stare at you and treat you differently. For a while this can be terribly confusing. ([1], p. 336)

To Shaw's dismay, not only did he no longer have any peace, but even his friends began regarding him differently. In *The Saturday Evening Post* article he wrote:

The bigger our success, the more dissatisfaction there seemed to be in the band. Billie Holiday, who had gotten along fine with Helen Forrest, began to resent her. Georgie Auld came in for $125 while the rest of the band, getting scale, objected. Buddy Rich joined us and the older guys didn't like it when he got so much applause. Instead of a bunch of guys that were happy to be struggling toward a common objective, we became a bunch of cliques, and I became gradually estranged from my men. (8)

Shaw elaborated on this in *The Trouble with Cinderella*:

At first it was fairly subtle. The men began to treat me more as an employer than as a friend of theirs.

I soon noticed that they were beginning to behave strangely toward me . . . so I learned to keep to myself and thus avoid embarrassment all the way around.

From then on I used to eat with the band manager, or by myself, up in my hotel room, whenever that was possible. But there was another reason why eating alone began to become an obsession. I tried going into restaurants . . . I'd sit there trying to mind my business, but unable to ignore the stares of people who had recognised me and were busily pointing me out and whispering about me to others. ([1], pp. 339–40)

Artie Shaw and his orchestra won the *Down Beat* popularity poll as the leading swing band for 1938–39. The magazine devoted extensive coverage to the contest in its issues for December 1938 and January 1939. On the Old Gold show of January 22, 1939, Shaw was given a congratulatory trophy by Robert Benchley. The January 23, 1939, issue of *Life* ran a three-page "Life Goes to a Party" feature on Shaw, which included a beautiful photo of the band at work in the Blue Room, a shot of Shaw and Benchley clowning, and photos of jitterbugs dancing on the tables (pp. 60–63). The Shaw-Goodman "rivalry" was stressed in *Down Beat*. This media-conjured "controversy" had been annoying Shaw since the previous summer, when *Metronome* published the article erroneously stating that Shaw had said he would be "King of Swing" within the year. As noted, Shaw had promptly refuted that article in a letter to the editor. Of course, comments and comparisons had occurred even earlier. In a sense, this was inescapable. After all, both men were sons of poor Russian-Jewish immigrants, had been top studio men in New York, played clarinet, and were leading exciting swing bands of conventional instrumentation. It might be an interesting sociological study to contemplate the phenomenon of the two top-drawing popular musicians during the latter half of the 1930s answering this particular description. Nevertheless, they had very different approaches within the context of big band swing. John Munro had discussed this in his June 1938 *Down Beat* article titled "Cripes! Shaw Doesn't Sound Like Goodman!" already described. Despite the differences in their approaches and the effects of their music, the media and

much of the public persisted in playing the "Who's best?" game. Of course, the criteria were economic rather than aesthetic. The recorded legacies confirm their differences and their respective greatness.

Over 140 performances have been issued of the Shaw band from its period at the Lincoln, during which time the final shifts in personnel occurred. A few of their broadcasts were issued intact, including their opening and closing theme statements and announcements. The Old Gold shows were edited for existing issues, usually leaving only performances featuring Shaw and his band with their regular singers. Dick Todd, a baritone pop singer from Canada, was added to the band for these shows, but only a few of his performances have been issued at this writing. Shaw noted that he did not always play on Todd's romantic ballad features, and occasionally would just let the band back him (2).

There were five record dates for RCA's Bluebird label, producing twenty-eight titles. The ten tunes recorded on January 17th and 23rd appeared in a Bluebird album released in February 1939. The fact that these ten tunes were issued in an album was an indication of the status the band's work had achieved. This album represented the band's repertoire well, except for the absence of original Shaw compositions.

Shaw also made his second movie short, for Paramount, in early January 1939, according to *Billboard*. Titled *Class in Swing*, this film included an announcer "explaining" what the band was doing by talking over the performances. Although annoyingly intrusive, this did serve an educational function for exceedingly musically naive viewers.

On January 30, 1939, the band played a dance at Syracuse University, announced as their first engagement away from the Lincoln. The March 1939 issue of *Down Beat* announced on page 7, "In Syracuse, Artie Shaw thrilled 600 couples at the Syracuse U. senior ball."

The band was booked into the Strand Theatre in New York City for February 3, 1939, the day following the Hotel Lincoln closing. The Strand Theatre, at Broadway and 47th Street, offered another stage show and film package. The film was *Wings of the Navy* and the blurb on the Strand's advertisements asked, "Can America defend herself in the air?" Then, in larger format: "In Person: 1939's Newest Swing sensation! ARTIE SHAW." The February 4th *Billboard* music section listed several Shaw records as hits. RCA's ad for Victor and Bluebird records showed Shaw's face over the words "Bluebird Artist Artie Shaw Shovels in the Shekels for Coin Machine Operators." The jukebox trade was regarding Shaw as a "Nickel-Nabbing Magnet," according to a later ad. Shaw wrote in his article for *The Saturday Evening Post*:

When we went into the Strand Theatre it was even worse. People jumping up on the stage, cops, riots—things that were almost impossible to live through. (8)

When Shaw opened at the Paramount in Newark on February 17th after two weeks at the Strand, Goodman was opening at the Schubert a few blocks away, and the media made much of the event. *Time* magazine headlined "Jitterbugs in Jersey" on page 39:

Last week Newark, N.J. was the field of the jitterbug's equivalent to ordeal by battle. Benny Goodman, who for four years has reigned in adolescent hearts as the King of Swing, was playing on the stage at the Schubert Theatre. Within shagging distance, at the neighboring Paramount, was Artie Shaw, young pretender to the throne, and his band, which in six months has zoomed to fame on the strength of a few rousing records. A clear-cut battle for supremacy was forecast: the theatres are of approximately equal size; each was showing a grade B film; and the acts accompanying the bands were similar. Both leaders are ace clarinetists.

The expected jitterbug riots occurred on the opening day. Shaw's vocalist had to burrow to his microphone through the ecstatic exhibitionists swarming the stage. At the Paramount, a boy hurt himself jumping from a box. At the Schubert, a girl swooned clean away.

At week's end Benny Goodman could claim technical victory. Box-office receipts were approximately equal ($24,000), but the Paramount, where Artie Shaw was playing, had a 99-cent top to the Schubert's 75 cents. Addicts of Shaw's exciting recordings of "Begin the Beguine" and "Back Bay Shuffle" were disappointed by their idol's cold stage personality. Goodman's matchless trio and quartet and the smooth rendition of old favorites like "One O'Clock Jump" and "Don't Be That Way" won back wavering allegiance.

Elsewhere, however, headlines proclaimed "Art Shaw Noses Out Goodman Ork in Newark Battle." A *Metronome* editorial deplored the idea of the rivalry.

The band moved to the Earle Theatre in Philadelphia for the week of February 24th. The theater was so mobbed with kids, the school board lodged a formal complaint because of all the absenteeism, and traffic was snarled in the streets. Shaw recalled the situation in Philadelphia in *The Trouble with Cinderella*:

After the first show, when I tried to leave my dressing room to go out for a breath of air, I started towards the stage door but was told by the doorman that I'd better not try going out in the street. I asked him why not, and for an answer he opened the stage door just a tiny crack.

The whole street was jam-packed with kids! Traffic was completely halted and there were half a dozen mounted policemen trying to disperse this rioting mob of youngsters, with no apparent success whatsoever. ([1], pp. 341–42)

Helen Forrest noted in her autobiography:

We were stars. I don't know if I deserved to be one yet, but I was. Anyone in a popular band was a star of sorts. The top performers were stars. The singers, who were more easily identified than the musicians, were stars. And the bandleaders were the biggest stars of all. Many of our fans were respectful, but others went into a frenzy over us. ([12], p. 68)

When the band began to travel in March, Dick Todd ceased appearing on the Old Gold show. He had several hit records for Bluebird at the time, and was working in other contexts around New York as well. According to Sheldon O'Connell in his *Dick Todd: King of the Jukebox* (Providence, R.I.: OLB Jazz, 1987, p. 27), a contract dispute arose with the show's sponsors. Todd wanted to remain in New York to continue his other activities and demanded conditions to continue with the show which the sponsors would not meet. Interestingly, aside from Todd's participation on the Old Gold show with Shaw, he reportedly composed lyrics for Shaw's composition "Pastel Blue" and later recorded it with a new title, "Why Begin Again?"

Following their week in Philadelphia, the band moved on to Pittsburgh for a March 3rd opening at the Stanley Theatre. *Down Beat* reported in its April 1939 issue, "Pittsburgh Goes For BG; Shaw Reported Snooty" in an article by Milton Karle appearing on page 31:

Shaw gave local newspapermen the rottenest treatment any bandleader ever gave them. General opinion around town was that Shaw's crew had a case of superiority complex and was working under a noticeable strain.

Nevertheless when they closed on March 11th, they were reported having brought in $22,000 that week.

The band returned to New York for another Bluebird record date on March 12th, producing six more sides. Shaw's "Pastel Blue" was recorded as an instrumental, and Helen Forrest sang "Any Old Time" as one of her three vocal features that day. Later that day, they did another Old Gold show, which provided three excellent instrumentals.

A tour of colleges followed, including a dance at Temple University in Philadelphia on the 13th, and Princeton University's junior prom on the 17th (*Down Beat*, March 1939, p. 28). Also on the 17th, they had another recording date, producing three vocals by Helen Forrest, one vocal by Pastor, and two instrumentals, the same balance as the previous two recording sessions. However, this time the instrumentals were the Shaw originals "One Night Stand" and "One Foot in the Groove."

More one-nighters followed. The Shaw band played the Palais Royale in Toronto again on March 20th. This was followed by a night in Buffalo, New York, at the Broadway Auditorium on the 21st, where they packed the place despite a bad snowstorm. In the liner notes to AXM2-5533, Buddy Rich recalled stuffing the windows of the band bus with newspapers and clothes to keep warm during a snowstorm. He continued:

> I must admit, though, the large, appreciative audiences made you forget a lot of the inconveniences. I remember many a night getting off the band bus, after coming God knows how far, in unbelievable weather. And there it was. Another ball-room, club or auditorium. But the people who patiently waited for us, got the juices going in me. Because they were so devoted, so enthusiastic, you wanted to be great for them.

Helen Forrest also enjoyed the crowd:

> When we were in a theatre or at a ballroom we were really within reach and we loved it, we loved the adulation, all of us except Artie. Artie hated this sort of hysteria. He did not want to be touched, reached for, screamed at. He wanted to perform his music in the purest possible way and be appreciated for it in the purest possible way. He thought too many of the people were crazy and he used to say, "I don't know what the hell gets into them." The only way he used his popularity was with the ladies, but even then he didn't go for the ones that pushed to the front of the bandstand or waited at the stage door. . . . The boys in the band . . . weren't as selective. The girls were there and the guys took them. The girls crowded around the bandstand with their shining faces looking up in awe at the musicians . . . and the guys went off into the night with them. Most of the girls were young . . . but they loved the music and so they loved the musicians who made the music and they were soft touches for the guys. . . .
>
> On the other hand, the boys in the band protected me as if I were a kid. I wasn't, but I was a little like one, new to the business and all, and really inexperienced. Guys would come around the bandstand trying to make time with me, and Georgie or Tony or someone would come over and tell them to beat it, to let the lady alone. Some of the men who came around were good-looking and I didn't always want to be left alone, but the fellows in the band were like big brothers to me and they were determined to protect me even when I didn't want to be protected. It was nice, but it was annoying at times, too. ([12], pp. 68–70)

Of course, the band was drawing well. At the Ritz, in Bridgeport, Connecticut, the band drew 3200 on a Tuesday. At the Willard in Washington, D.C., a crowd of 2,000 showed up, and the band was reported to have brought in $3,500 that night (*Metronome*, May 1939, pp. 10, 42). The band was constantly in the news. The March issue of *Swing* wrote up the band's making of their second Vitaphone movie short in Brooklyn, complete with stills and candid photos. Band members recalled this film, *Symphony of Swing*, as having been made during their stay at the Strand in early February 1939. The March 1939 issue of *Upbeat* contained an article by Shaw titled "I'm Not A Monster" in which he defended himself for having intellectual interests (pp. 7, 27). Artie Shaw fan clubs banded together into the International Association of Artie Shaw Clubs, located at 247 Park Avenue in New York City (*Metronome*, May 1939, p. 25). There was even a Society for the Prevention of Artie Shaw, apparently a sort of tongue-in-cheek anti-fan club, oddly originating in Cleveland and occasionally issuing bulletins with all the flair of the Flat Earth Society. *Metronome* also mentioned that Oglethorpe University had buried a time capsule called the "Crypt of Civilization" containing, among other things, records purported to document three categories of music of the era: classical, sweet, and swing. These included unnamed items by Toscanini, Richard Himber, and Artie Shaw. Curiously, while *Metronome* reported the date the capsule was to be opened as "8113 A.D.," *Down Beat* announced the date of opening as "7937 A.D." A time capsule containing a copy of "Begin the Beguine" also was reportedly buried at the site of the World's Fair.

The March 1939 *Metronome* noted on page 56, "Shaw Series Just Published," concerning the publishing by Harms, Inc., of six of Shaw's hits "arranged in the modern manner by Artie Shaw." An advertisement for this series also appeared on page 6 of the same issue. The ad read:

> Now Ready—
> THE MODERN ARRANGEMENTS YOU'VE BEEN WAITING FOR!
> THE NEW ARTIE SHAW DANCE SERIES
> Every orchestra will want these new
> Artie Shaw Arrangements in its books!

Titles were listed as:

> "Begin the Beguine"
> "What Is This Thing Called Love?"
> "Softly as in a Morning Sunrise"
> "I Cover the Waterfront"
> "Indian Love Call"
> "Night and Day"

All indicated "Scored by Jerry Gray," and they were each priced at 75 cents. That month, *Down Beat* had a similar advertisement for these same orchestrations and also published a transcribed notation for Shaw's clarinet solo on "Copenhagen." The preceding month, both *Down Beat* and *Metronome* had extensive write-ups on the band. *Metronome* offered a review of the band on page 12. This was reprinted intact in *Simon Says* ([6], pp. 122–26). *Down Beat* had an article by R. Whitney Becker titled, "Sure, Artie's Band Is Great, But Give His Men Their Share of Credit." He went on to profile each member of the band in true fan magazine style on page 4:

Chuck Peterson—plays trumpet, French horn and trombone. Single, born at Herne, Texas 1915. Studied journalism and was once a reporter for the *Detroit Times*. Is a crack swimmer and likes to entertain friends. Once played under John Philip Sousa in Detroit; later worked with Henry Biagini. Easy to get along with.

Bernie Privin—also a trumpeter. Single, born in Brooklyn 1919. Doubles on mellophone. Has been a Union man less than a year, but already has played with Tommy Dorsey, Bunny Berigan and Shaw. Likes motorboating and is a cousin of David Sarnoff, President of RCA.

John (Colonel) Best—trumpet. Single, born in Shelby, N.C. in 1913 and has played with Biagini, Joe Haymes and Charlie Barnet. Originally studied for a commercial career and once wrote a tune called "South Washington Street Blues." He's related to Nathaniel Greene and Nathaniel Macon of Revolutionary War fame.

George Arus—trombone. Friends call him the "Swami of Swing." Single, born in Union City, N.J. in 1911. Also plays fiddle. Played with JXYZ Radio Station Ork in Detroit before joining Shaw. Favourite interests are wine, women and more women. Does a fine job of cutting the boys' hair when they haven't time to visit a professional barber.

Les Jenkins—trombone. Became nationally renowned for his fine work with Tommy Dorsey. A friendly, half-serious guy who asks no favours. One of the newest additions to Shaw's band and certainly one of the most popular.

Harry Rodgers—trombone. Boys call him "Muscles." Born in 1914 in Brockton, Mass. Arranges the pop tunes for Artie. Is an alumnus of Al Kavelin, Frank Dailey and Glenn Miller bands and his favourite hobby is arranging and listening to bands. Has played with Favien Sevitsky and other longhairs.

Georgie Auld—tenor sax. Joined Artie Christmas after making a name for himself and his horn with Bunny Berigan. Born in 1919 in Toronto and is still single. Likes to take his girl around, listen to good bands, sleep and mess around on alto sax. Is an expert horseman and motorcar driver. Currently his jittery, gutty tenor style is the most imitated in the nation.

Hank Freeman—alto and baritone sax. Single, born in New Haven, Conn. in 1918. An alumnus of Berigan, Barnet, Joe Haymes and Leon Navarro. One ambition is to find a good reed. Likes fishing and once caught a large bass with his teeth, therefore gaining much publicity. Real name is Henry, but don't call him that!

Les Robinson—alto sax. Leads the smooth Shaw reed section. Another former Biagini man and likes to go to shows and talk on the telephone. Home is in South Bend, Ind.

Tony Pastor—tenor sax. Plays first tenor, with Auld on second. Married and most fond of spaghetti, sometimes inviting the boys to his house for huge samples of the dish. He's a Hartford product, likes to rollerskate and is the only original member of Shaw's first band. Handles all the male vocals, sings huskily, in coloured style. Noted especially for his killing vocal on Artie's Bluebird record of "Indian Love Call" with the boys shouting "cheep cheeps" in the background.

Sid Weiss—bass. Born in 1914 in Schenectady, N.Y. Married and played with Wingy Manone and Barnett. Is a nut on

the movie photography subject. Wife was president of the Washington Hot Club when he married her and she also is hep and a good critic. Played symphony stuff under Harold Bauer at one time.

Al Avola—guitar. Single, born in 1915 in Boston. Studied commercial art and law and is a member of the Massachusetts bar. Still dabbles in art occasionally. Played in Boston Junior symphony, also handles a violin, and was acclaimed a child prodigy when he was 6 years old. A great admirer of Segovia, he is now experimenting with a new method of playing the Spanish guitar. Real name is Alexander Albert Avola. Writes tunes occasionally, his "Fee Fi Fo Fum" stacking up as one of Artie's best platters.

Bob Kitsis—piano. A graduate of Harvard, class of '38, where he studied medicine and music. Single, born in 1917 in Boston. It was only recently he auditioned for Artie and landed the job, although he had never played in a band before! Interests also include concert music, good literature, Harvard–Yale games and Hedy LaMarr.

Buddy Rich—Drums. A real youngster, born in 1918. Has worked with Joe Marsala and Bunny Berigan, among others. Musicians claim him to be the fastest drummer among the whites. Fine showman. Has been playing the skins since he was 3 years old when he was a standard vaude drum act.

Helen Forrest, by her own account, was born in Atlantic City, New Jersey, in 1918 (not Washington, D.C., in 1916, as Becker had it). She was singing with her brother's dance band in Washington, D.C., when Ziggy Elman, the trumpet star with Benny Goodman, talked Shaw into going to see her.

Despite having sung on various radio shows under several pseudonyms, she regarded going with the Shaw band as her first major experience. In the liner notes to RCA AXM2-5533, Helen Forrest was quoted as saying,

I must say I was frightened. But Artie was just fantastic—so helpful and gentle and considerate. Artie treated me like a queen. That was unheard of, in those years. When a girl started with a band, she was nothing. If Artie and the guys hadn't been so nice, I might have been turned off and not continued in the profession. As it was, Artie was very supportive and all the musicians were my buddies and protectors. . . . Artie played a beautiful, romantic type clarinet and inspired me to sing. His approach to material formed the basis of what would be my style.

In her autobiography, she described her relationship with Shaw as a person:

He never came after me and it never occurred to me to go after him. He liked me and I liked him. We were friends, as much as a bandleader and a band singer can be. We were together a lot and we talked a lot. I learned a lot about music and about life from him. His interests went beyond music into every aspect of life. As I have said, he was the most intelligent man I ever met and you had only to listen to him to learn from him. I took my troubles to him and we talked them over and he helped me with a lot of good advice. I wish I could have helped him with his love life. Ha! ([12], p. 69)

She wrote frankly of the sexual politics of the vocalists in the bands:

There always was a lot of talk about the girl singers in the all-boy bands. A lot of it was true, too. There were singers who took on all the guys in their band at one time or another. They were all together in this thing and the girls didn't want to play favorites. Tonight, the brass section. Tomorrow night, the reeds. You know. And of course there were the girl singers who just got involved with one guy and really had a hot romance with him and maybe wound up marrying him. And the girl singers who put out for the leader. A lot of them had hot romances with their leaders and quite a few wound up marrying them. But there also were the girls who stayed straight. I was one of those . . . and it seems to me that if you set your standards high and stuck to them the guys would accept it. Oh, they were always fooling around. Georgie Auld, for one. He'd make a pass, half-kidding, ready to make more of it if I'd let him, I'm sure, and I'd say, "Hey, Georgie, I don't want it, I'm not looking for it, and I don't need it, so please lay off," and he'd laugh and that would be the end of it.

Once in a while on overnight trips we'd take trains. On one trip, we had a sleeping car with those enclosed bunks. I had gotten into my bunk and was almost asleep when I felt someone in the bunk with me, feeling me. I let out a screech and leaped out of the bunk. The lights came on and all the guys were leaning out of their bunks laughing. Georgie leaned out of mine. He'd gone in as a gag and all the guys were waiting to see how far he got. I laughed too. It was funny. It was all in fun. I just wanted to keep it that way. ([12], p. 71)

She went on to describe Georgie Auld coaxing her into drinking with him one night so that he could make a pass at her. She got sick and retreated to her room, locking the door. Members of the band called to her through the door, trying to make sure she was all right.

I think they were scared because they knew Georgie had tried to get me drunk so he could make a pass at me. They were just trying to help. . . . The next morning I felt awful. I don't think I talked to Georgie for two weeks.

Later, when she decided to marry the boyfriend she had been so reluctant to leave, Shaw's reaction was warm and caring.

When I told Artie . . . he said, "I know your family must be worried about your travelling with a bunch of men and I know you must feel trapped at times among so many men, but you also must know we respect you and love you and would never take advantage of you, so you don't have to get married to feel safe with us. You are becoming a big star . . . you've seen enough by now to know it's not good to be married in this business, it just doesn't work out too well. Do yourself a favor, give yourself some more time." ([12], p. 73)

The band was scheduled to work its way across the country to open on April 19th at the Palomar Ballroom in Los Angeles, replacing the George Olsen orchestra at that location. They were booked for the Palace in Cleveland for the 14th, and the next two nights at the Aragon Ballroom in Chicago. However, Shaw was ill with strep throat and the effects of a new drug, sulfanilamide, and these bookings, among others unspecified, had to be canceled (*Metronome*, May 1939, p. 47; also *Down Beat*, May 1939, p. 3). Consequently, when the bookings were dropped, George Arus flew to Pittsburgh to see a dancer he'd met there.

Shaw was still sick on his opening night in California, and collapsed on stage.

In all, I was some 6 weeks in recovering after passing out cold right in the middle of an opening night before a record crowd at the Palomar Ballroom. ([1], pp. 349–50)

The Palomar reported the crowd at 8,785 that night. Shaw then had his second vivid "near death" experience, paralleling the vision he had experienced at age eight, when he'd nearly drowned. "Again, The Light, music, the whole thing. Again, I thought of it as a hallucination" (2).

When he regained consciousness and opened his eyes, he found himself looking right into the face of Judy Garland. They had remained close friends since the night she had gone backstage at the Lexington to compliment his music. Shaw often said she was "like a little sister" to him.

Shaw had been unconscious for five days, and had almost died from a usually fatal blood disease called agranulocytosis. Meanwhile the band continued with its appearance at the Palomar, with Pastor leading. Air checks of broadcasts from the Palomar and transcriptions from their Old Gold shows of the Artie Shaw band without Shaw have surfaced to document their work during the interval Shaw was out sick. The band sounded good. They swung hard, and hearing the familiar Shaw pieces without clarinet solos by the leader made an eerie contrast. Tony Pastor or Georgie Auld filled in the solo opportunities on tenor sax. Bernie Privin and Johnny Best also took some of Shaw's solo spots on trumpet.

Chapter 7

Hollywood to Hollywood: 1939–1940

When Shaw had recovered enough to leave the hospital, he began taking walks and long drives with Judy Garland, just talking as he recuperated. However, Judy had developed a major crush on him. She was making the movie *The Wizard of Oz* at that time, and was even getting criticism for taking so much time away from the studios to be with Shaw. In the biography *Judy*, by Gerold Frank, their relationship was beautifully described:

One of Shaw's first memories when he finally came to was of Judy's face hovering over him: "That absolutely marvelous little face, with freckles, the brown eyes, the reddish hair, looking at me with consummate tenderness"—mythlike, dreamlike, not real. He could hear her whispering, "You're going to be all right, Artie. . . . Don't worry. You'll be all right." She had come there many times, the nurses told him. Whenever he awoke, it seemed she was there, leaning over him, the Constant Nymph, encouraging him, comforting him, willing him to get well.

When he grew strong enough to leave the hospital for a little while each day, Judy appropriated him as her private outpatient, taking him on long drives. She gave him her warmth, her enthusiasm, her delight in him, and he was overwhelmed by tenderness for her. He had never had a sister, and she was close to what he would have wanted if he had had one. He never thought of her as someone to be made love to, the idea had simply not occurred to him. When he wanted that, there were others to whom he turned; with Judy it was pure delight in her as an adorable companion, a joy in being with someone he loved in a very idealistic way.

He could hardly contain himself in teaching her, in conveying to her his own excitement about himself, themselves, the world. He knew he was on the top. He was young, he was handsome, he had money, and in this city in which they found themselves, this dreamland. . . . He would joke with her as they drove, saying, "You're little Frances Gumm from Grand Rapids, and I'm little Arthur Arshawsky from the Lower East Side of New York, and look where we are!" He would have her stop the car, and breathe deeply. "Smell the wind, Judy, when it's right, like now, it's all orange blossoms, you can smell the fragrance of the whole San Bernardino Valley." And the people here, gifted, talented, each beautiful in his own way, gathered here, in this one incredible town, from all over the world. . . . "We're the chosen few, Judy, we're the chosen people! We've got no place to go but up, and it's never going to end!" Judy would laugh, and cling to him, and he would hug her, and try to convey to her what an absolutely marvelous creature she was, eager, lovely, outgoing, thirsty for knowledge, just beginning to feel the wonder of being young and alive.

He was amazed, as he had been in New York, that she should have understood the music he and his band played at the Hotel Lexington three years before. And her sense of humor! That laugh of hers, that belly laugh that caught everyone and rendered them helpless, it just burst out of her. She would roll on the floor, clutching her stomach, howling with glee. He could make her laugh, and, laughing together, they were two golden people in a golden world. ([7], pp. 123–24)

Shaw related a grimmer side to his psychological orientation at that point, however. In *The Trouble with Cinderella* he wrote:

During that 6 weeks of convalescence I had a lot of time. And I did a lot of thinking. And out of all this thinking I arrived at my decision that enough was enough. As soon as I could finish up certain contractual obligations, I was going to get out of the whole thing. . . . What was the sense in remaining a sideshow freak, gaped at and stared at and pawed at by thousands of "fans" wherever I went? . . . what about all that other stuff I had been trying to do when I was going to school and trying to figure out a few things about myself and the world I lived in? ([1], p. 350)

In *The Saturday Evening Post* article he wrote,

I was plenty frightened when they stretched me out on an operating table and began pumping other people's blood into my veins. A number of magazine and radio station polls had elected me King of Swing, but the bugs inside me had no respect for royalty. I overheard a nurse whisper something about one chance in a hundred, and that capped the climax.

They wouldn't let me talk or move a muscle, but they couldn't stop me from thinking—even with a temperature of 106. I looked back into the months that had been a buildup for this let down. The one-night stands, the long brutal jumps from town to town in rainstorms and blizzards, the bottles of aspirin I had consumed to keep me going and blowing. What for? To die at 28? (8)

Shaw rejoined his band at the Palomar on his twenty-ninth birthday, May 23rd. His Old Gold show broadcast that day was reviewed in the June 3rd *Billboard* on page 20:

Artie Shaw returned to the Robert Benchley program coincident with that show's shift from a Sunday CBS spot to NBC Tuesday. . . . Just to give convincing proof that he has fully recovered from the illness which kept him off the show some time, Shaw gave several corking clarinet performances, the three numbers the band played being jumperoos. In "Shoot the Likker . . ." (announced as "Shoot the Rhythm") Shaw played notes that just can't be believed. The band plays with a terrific zing, a zing few bands possess today. The last number, however, was a bum selection, a blare tune rather than a swinger.

On May 29, the National Swing Club held a concert at the Hippodrome in New York that featured many of the leading figures in music. A trophy for Band of the Year was presented to Shaw in absentia by Paul Whiteman. Although it had been anticipated that Shaw's mother would be on hand to accept the trophy, *Metronome* reported in its July issue's review of the event that the award was accepted for Shaw by bandleader Jan Savitt, who stated that he was proud to do so as Shaw had been so helpful to him in his own career.

The band was held over at the Palomar until late June. *Down Beat* announced its broadcasting schedule in its June 1939 issue on page 17:

NBC Blue: Tuesday 9 pm, Thursday 12:30 am.
NBC Red: Saturday 12:30 am; local stations
KNX and KEHE: heavy nightly schedule.

Several broadcasts from their stay at the Palomar have surfaced, along with three record dates to document them at that stage of their career. Over half of the records featured Helen Forrest. These included another fine original ballad by Shaw, "Moonray." Tony Pastor sang on three other titles. There were another four instrumentals as well, including Shaw's original composition "Traffic Jam." These were again among the band's best work.

A review of the entire show at the Palomar appeared in *Billboard* (June 10, 1939, p. 22), offering an enlightening glimpse of the era's entertainment context. After a description of the "mammoth nitery" in primarily economic terms, the review continued:

Shaw's band, while not a hot combination in the strict sense of the word, nevertheless hands out a good solid brand of commercial swing that makes those terp-minded patrons who

shell out for ducats satisfied. Shaw packs a couple of warblers that do a good job. Helen Forrest scored with "Sly Old Gentleman." Male half of the lyric spielers is Tony Pastor, who does okeh on some oldies. His best was "Them There Eyes."

Only one show and it hits the floor at 11:30. Strict ballroom stunt is supervised by Whitney Roberts, who stages a pillow contest. Divan cushions are thrown out on the floor. Couples dance until the music stops. Idea is to land on a cushion with your partner. Proceedings got plenty of laughs, winning couple getting bottle of champagne or two deluxe dinners. Stuff was rather drawn out and too dull to be entertaining.

Oivero Trio, two femmes and a male, did some perch work. Balancing the end of the pole on his forehead, male managed to keep everything upright while his two partners did various tricks high up. Good stuff that got plenty of gasps. This is an act that deserves the best.

Dub Taylor did a comic turn that was good for laughs. Fresh from the flicker *You Can't Take It With You*, Taylor employs several "bashful boy tricks" such as nose wiping, etc. His xylophone work was okeh and provided a good contrast to his gags. Also did "When Day Is Done" on the harmonica. He could do with some new material, but the crowd didn't seem to mind.

Searles and Lene presented a dance act that rounded out the bill very nicely. Starting out with a rhumba fox trot, they wind up with a terp routine to "Jungle Drums." Their appearance is okeh and steps are tops. They're in their 5th week. Windup found them pulling several planted jitterbug teams out of the crowd for some extra fancy limb tossing.

Whitney Roberts did a couple of dances . . . that went over all right.

New p.a. for Artie Shaw while he is on the coast is B. McDevitt.

June 10, 1939, was Judy Garland's seventeenth birthday. Shaw and Phil Silvers attended a party at her home. Their gift to her was a specially made home recording, an Artie Shaw–Phil Silvers comedy record they had prepared for her. The content of the record was not described except by the adjective "hilarious." Her biographer related,

Judy found Phil the funniest of men, and the three, Artie, Judy, and Phil, went everywhere together . . . music and books brought Judy and Artie together as much as anything else. ([7], p. 126)

Shaw would often bring her books to read "that he thought were beautiful and from which she would benefit." He also was constantly surprised by her low self-esteem. ([7], p. 127)

The extraordinary thing was that Shaw had no idea that Judy was in love with him physically, emotionally, intellectually. Sometimes when he took her home, and now and then when he hugged her, or was about to kiss her on the cheek, he found her lips on his, and she was kissing him, not as a sister but as a woman. It would surprise him. He would hold her by her shoulders and say, What are you doing? What are you up to, you idiot? And she would say, Nothing, nothing, and laugh. He thought she was having fun with him, playing sex games as young girls do. ([7], p. 128).

According to the July 1939 *Metronome* (p. 7), Shaw had a recurrence of his throat problems and had to be rehospitalized for tonsillitis. The article noted that the band would be beginning work on the M-G-M film *Dancing Co-ed* shortly. On the Old Gold show from June 27th, Shaw croakily accepted an award from *Radio Guide* for "best swing band of the year" but was excused from performing due to his tonsillectomy (see discography).

The band had been held over at the Palomar until the end of June, then went into the Golden Gate Theatre in San Francisco, opening July 4th. In *Billboard* it was reported that the band had brought in $22,000 for the week ending July 14th.

Down Beat reported that Shaw had been signed for two full-length films: *Broadway Melody* with Fred Astaire, and *Dancing Co-ed*. There were several references to his working on two films that summer, although it turned out to be only *Dancing Co-ed* starring Lana Turner. The band's work in the film was reported to be taking three weeks beginning July 12th, but they were on the road again by the beginning of August. The experience of making *Dancing Co-ed* provided still more stress for Shaw. First, he found himself expected to utter banal lines about "hep cats and alligators" in the film. In *Artie Shaw: Time Is All You've Got*, he described himself patiently trying to explain to the director of *Dancing Co-ed* that, in the film, he is supposed to be himself, Artie Shaw, and that Artie Shaw did not talk that way. The director's response was to cut Shaw's part to a minimum. Shaw then tried to buy his band out of the picture, but the contract was held, and they had to finish it. Shaw and Lana Turner, then eighteen years old and just beginning her rise to prominence, didn't get along. She would ignore Shaw and would sit at the other end of the set. In the biography *Lana: The Public and Private Lives of Miss Turner* by Joe Morella and Edward Z. Epstein (New York: Dell, 1971), the following dialogue was quoted:

"Say," Shaw kidded Lana, "If you don't talk to me I won't play your music right."

Lana took the remark completely seriously. "You wouldn't dare," she shot back.

Shaw, surprised, explained that he was only kidding and was trying to break the ice between them.

"You might have said something nicer," she said, not at all placated. ([13], p. 38)

Even the camera crew felt hostile toward Shaw after his rebellion. It was reported that the lighting crews "spent time planning how to 'accidently' drop a sun-arc lamp on the musician's head" ([13], p. 38).

The film was a mindless bit of fluff, with a silly plot concerning planting a showgirl (Lana) on a college campus and staging a dance contest with her as the secretly prepicked winner, to gain publicity. Shaw's contribution involved playing for the dancers, but dialogue marred the performances, which were just bits and pieces anyway. A promotional release contained a fiery version of "Traffic Jam" without interruptions or dialogue, however, and what footage of the band in action that emerged was excellent. Additional performances not used in the film emerged in 1997 on a Rhino CD (see discography).

Helen Forrest, missing the dating a bit, wrote of all this activity in her autobiography:

We went to Hollywood to make some shorts and then a feature. Musical shorts were popular in those days. Along with cartoons and newsreels, they played with the double features that movie houses ran if they didn't have big band stage shows. We made one short in the summer of 1938 and two in the summer of 1939. In the first, I sang, "Let's Stop the Clock." In the second, *Class in Swing*, I sang, "I Have Eyes." In the third, *Symphony in Swing*, I sang "Deep Purple." While we were making the first one, Artie met and had an affair with, ironically as it turned out, Betty Grable, who was making a movie called *Campus Confessions*. When we made the feature film *Dancing Co-Ed* in 1939, Artie met Lana Turner and started a romance which led to marriage. Artie always liked those campus co-eds. I did not sing a song in the movie. We filmed during the day and played the Palomar Ballroom at night while working the Old Gold *Melody and Madness* radio show in between. We supplied the melody, along with an added singer, Dick Todd, to do the boy ballads. Robert Benchley provided the madness. A writer who made movie shorts and feature films, he was a very funny fellow with a sly sense of humor. But I seldom saw him. He did his stint separately. The show was on once a week for almost a year from November 1938 through August 1939 and when we weren't in Hollywood we always had to get back there to do the show. ([12], pp. 74–75)

Metronome reported in its "Memphis" column on page 32 of its July 1939 issue that the Shaw band would perform four nights in late July at the Claridge. It also was reported that a vocal group called The Four Clubmen under the direction of Lyn Murray would be featured on the Robert Benchley–Artie Shaw Old Gold program, but none of their performances have surfaced at this writing.

The band began another series of dates in August:

2nd: Salt Lake City, Utah
4th: Municipal Auditorium, Kansas City

5th: Municipal Auditorium, St. Louis, Missouri
6th: Aragon Ballroom, Chicago, Illinois
7th: Ramona Gardens, Grand Rapids, Michigan
8th: Modernistic Ballroom, Milwaukee, Wisconsin

For six nights, August 11–16, the band played at the East-wood Park in Detroit, where 18,000 people were in attendance over the week. *Billboard* had a review in its September 9, 1939, issue, on page 13:

Smooth style of the Shaw band is responsible for a noticeably different reaction from the gapers in front of the stand when Artie and his men hold forth. Instead of indulging in rhythmic gyrations commonly called jitterbugging, Shaw's fans stand still and watch fascinated. The band's style is rather far on the sweet side of swing, but Shaw has numbers for adherents of both kinds of music and alternates them successfully.

Line-up is four sax, three trombones, three trumpets and four rhythm, Shaw leading with his clarinet but minus any flashy conducting tricks. He bows out of the spotlight often to give solos to Georgie Auld, sax; George Arus and Les Jenkins, trombones; and John Best, Bernie Privin and Chuck Peterson, trumpets. On numbers like "The Chant," almost a Shaw theme song, and blues items Artie's clarinet work is outstanding. Drummer Buddy Rich shines particularly in the long solo jungle-rhythm passage introducing "The Chant."

Helen Forrest and Tony Pastor, sax, attend to the vocals. Girl has a strong, clear voice but could stand a bit more personality. Pastor takes the comedy wordage and goes over well.

On August 17th the band played another one-nighter, at the G. E. Pavilion in Johnson City, New York, on their way east for an August 18th opening at the Ritz-Carlton Hotel in Boston for a two-week stay. There, Johnny Best left the band and Shaw flew trumpeter Harry Geller out from Los Angeles to replace him. This was the first personnel change since 1938.

Shortly after the Ritz-Carlton opening, Shaw's manager booked him into an appearance playing a concert on Boston Commons. *The New Yorker* "Profile" reported:

Shaw arose, threw aside his dressing gown, and outlined his plans for retiring on the spot. The manager at length soothed him and talked him around. At the appointed hour, 10,000 shoving, jostling fans showed up on the Common, and their humor was prankish. With great difficulty, Shaw played the concert; then he climbed into a limousine with the Mayor. But the crowd, despite 40 policemen in attendance, declined to open a way. Chanting, it took to rocking the car, which finally turned turtle, with a crash of glass. When Shaw had regained a measure of composure and mobility, he fought a retreating action on foot, fending off grasping hands all the way back to the Ritz. His lapels were ripped off, his jacket was split down the middle, his face was badly scratched, his hair was askew, his tie had been squeezed to a string, and his

trousers were limp bags. It required three hours of steady persuasion by the manager to coax him down to the ballroom that night. (11)

An almost-complete broadcast air check, an Old Gold show, and a Bluebird record date have become available to document the band during its stay at the Ritz-Carlton. Band members recalled that Shaw flew the band back and forth between Boston and New York to make the record date without interrupting their schedule at the Ritz-Carlton. Following their closing, the band went on the road again. They performed at Hershey Park, Pennsylvania, on September 1st; at the Million Dollar Pier in Atlantic City for two nights, September 2nd and 3rd; and moved into Canada for a one-nighter in Crystal Beach, Ontario, on the 4th.

The band was then booked for three days at the Canadian National Exposition (CNE), from September 5 to 7, 1939, following Benny Goodman and preceding Tommy Dorsey. A large ad in the Toronto *Globe and Mail* on Tuesday, September 5, 1939, included a photo of Shaw and a blurb that read:

ARTIE SHAW
He's here for three days of glorious swing!

Go often—crowd around the bandstand and see this famous band in action! Dance to music such as you've never heard before. The dance floor is the largest in Canada. There are seats for those who just wish to watch. Prices are reasonable. Artie Shaw will play afternoons and evenings today, Wednesday and Thursday. Reserve tickets for the Old Gold Broadcast at 9 p.m. tonight may be obtained from any CNE Ticket office. Reserved seats for broadcast $1.00. Includes dancing. Afternoons 50¢. Evenings $1.00.

The band's visit was mentioned briefly but vividly by El-wood Glover in his introduction to the book *The Bands Canadians Danced To* by Helen McNamara and Jack Lomas (Toronto: Griffin House, 1973):

The memorable CNE Tent where the big names would play and where I used to emcee the American network shows of Tommy Dorsey and Artie Shaw (the Old Gold Summer Show in the Fall of '39 with Artie Shaw's band, the four King Sisters and Warren Hull . . . wow!) (p. vii)

The Canadian National Exhibition publicity was over-shadowed by dark headlines concerning Hitler's invasion of Poland and the torpedoing of the *Athenia*, a passenger ship that had a number of Torontonians aboard, by a German submarine. Nevertheless, attendance and the enthusiasm of crowds at the CNE over the holiday were noted by the *Globe and Mail*. There was even a gossip blurb in the entertainment section to the effect that Betty Grable had taken a part in a New York play to be near Artie Shaw when he would be playing in New York later that season.

Helen Forrest told a particularly revealing story about this tour into Canada in her autobiography:

> We were always on the move and we never really knew where we were. We were always exhausted and punch-drunk, but we just went on and on. Every time we were on the bandstand we got fresh life and made beautiful music. The people loved us for it. We got a lift from the fans and inspiration from their cheers.
>
> The boys used to bring bottles in brown bags aboard the bus and drink the stuff straight, passing it around, especially on cold winter trips. Life on the bus and on the road was so difficult I can understand why so many used hard drugs to get by, but I never got into that and I never saw any of it in my day. Liquor and marijuana were what I saw. Marijuana was bad business in those days. As I understand it, the stuff was so straight and so strong it was practically a hard drug. And so many of the guys were turned on to it that the bus used to fill up with that sickening, sweet-smelling smoke so you could hardly breathe. They used to keep the front window seat for me and even on the coldest days I'd have my window wide open so I could breathe. The smoke would get in my hair and I'd stick my head out of the window to try to get the smell out. My gown would hang in the back of the bus and by the time we finished a trip it would smell like a "joint." I'd grab it when we got in and try to air it out, but I went up on the bandstand smelling like a joint many a night, and I didn't even smoke.
>
> One time we were getting on a bus on our way to Toronto when one of them asked me to hold a brown bag for him. It was tied up with a thick rubber band. Georgie had his hands full with his instrument case and I had one of those huge handbags. Without thinking, I said okay and stuffed it into my bag. We got to the Canadian border at Toronto and immigration authorities pulled out the luggage and went through it and boarded the bus and searched through it and even body-searched Georgie Auld, who was a Canadian from Toronto. They couldn't find anything, but they held us up for a long time until some of the boys suggested I make a fuss. I did. I said, "Guys, we have to get going. We've got a date to play in Toronto. We're running late. You haven't found anything. There's nothing to find. C'mon, give us a break." They finally did and let us pass on through. They never did search me. I don't know why it didn't dawn on me earlier, but I never thought about it from the moment I stuffed that bag into my purse until the moment I started to hand it back. ([12], pp. 81–82)

Helen reported she was furious with the musician who had turned her into an unknowing marijuana smuggler. "That was the one time I couldn't laugh off something as a bad gag," she wrote ([12] p. 82).

Artie hated it when the guys came to play drunk or stoned. He wouldn't stand for it. He got the reputation of being a tough boss because of that, but he didn't dissipate and he believed the guys that did couldn't play the music the way they should. That was one of the things that bothered him about the business. But the guys usually cooled it before a performance. Even though they really believed they played better when they were high on "hash." ([12], pp. 83–84)

Shaw's use of alcohol and marijuana on occasion already has been noted, but while he may have continued to use both when relaxing, his avoidance of it on the stand is well documented. In *The New Yorker* "Profile," he related:

> I once had a first trumpet, wonderful jazz man—well, his name was Charlie, that's enough—and he was giving me some trouble. I took him aside and said, "Charlie, you're throwing us out with this marijuana you're smoking. You're not blowing good at all." He said, "Look here, Artie, I blow better being a little on pot. It comes out cleaner." "Allright," I said, "we'll make a deal. Give me the sticks you'd use tonight, and I'll smoke 'em. Then you be the judge." Well, I smoked one, and, do you know, I began to rock; I'd never felt better about how I was playing." (11)

In discussing this incident, Shaw amended *The New Yorker*'s version of the conclusion of this story slightly, noting, "Later I told him, 'You're right, Chuck, let's both turn on every night,' but he just said, 'Uh-uh.' That was that" (2).

The delay at Canadian customs described by Helen Forrest had other consequences. The October 1, 1939, *Down Beat* had an article on page 1 by Walter McCarty headlined, "Promoter Sues Artie Shaw." The subtitle stated, "He Walks Off Stand; 2,500 Dancers Riot." On the same page, Shaw's manager, Ben Cole, wrote a further explanation of the situation. Cole's account set the stage:

> The train carrying Artie Shaw's musicians arrived 45 minutes late in Buffalo. We had 40 pieces of baggage to move. . . . By the time we arrived at the Peace Bridge, in a pouring rain, it was 8:20 p.m.
>
> Then we had to go through U.S. customs, Canadian customs and Canadian immigration. Then we had an 18-mile drive to Crystal Beach. We arrived there about 9:15 and it took 15 or 20 minutes to set up on the stand. Another band was playing and we had to wait for them to get off. However we were ready at 10 sharp and we started immediately.
>
> The promoter, one Tick Smith, was reported complaining that the band had arrived more than an hour late.
>
> Shaw himself was on time, but took a nap waiting for his boys to arrive at the Crystal Beach ballroom. . . . Smith, meanwhile, had to refund $200 to dancers who grew tired of waiting. Because of the late start, at intermission, the promoter told Shaw and Cole he was withholding $400 of the $2,000 promised the band for its night's work.

Controversy over what happened next was apparent from the following accounts. Cole related:

Words led to an ultimatum, Shaw and his boys did just what any other band would have done—they left the stand when it became apparent that the promoter would not pay according to the contract.

The crowd favored Artie all the way. They shouted and stomped, but they were faithful to Artie when they learned that the band wasn't being paid. . . . Artie spoke to the crowd. They didn't boo him—those were cheers. His talk quieted the mob and we left.

In the promoter's version of the story, "hundreds of dancers . . . booed Shaw and the band. . . . The crowd got so wild that Shaw, in leaving, asked that they quiet down. . . . Police were called and the riot was quelled."

Next day Shaw and band went to Toronto. A few days later, when he was driving across the Peace Bridge, a man stuck his face in Shaw's car and shoved him a sheet of paper. Artie, it was said, thought it was an autograph request and grabbed it. The paper, however, was a summons charging Shaw with breach of contract and slander to the tune of $10,000.

Following this trip and its unpleasant conclusion, the band moved on to the Palace Theatre in Cleveland, Ohio. They were booked for the week of September 8–14, 1939. On page 3 of their October 1, 1939, issue, *Down Beat* published an account of their Cleveland reporter, Eunice Kay, being brushed off by Shaw. The article, titled "Maybe He Will Look Before Shaw Ducks The Next Reporter," was accompanied by a photo of Miss Kay, an obviously very attractive young woman. However, *Metronome* was able to get an interview, briefly summarized in the account on page 50 of their November 1939 issue headlined: "Shaw Big in Cleveland But Band Disappoints—Still Yens For Strings And 30 or 40 Men."

After an unusually quiet summer, marked by complete absence of big names, Artie Shaw opened the Palace Theatre's fall season.

Opening day record was shattered and Shaw went on to complete one of the finest weeks the Palace has had.

Shaw, however, was disappointing with a complete lack of stage personality. Musically there were many things lacking in the band.

Shaw disclosed that he still intends to include strings in his band. He would like to have a complete string section, including violins, cello, and bass, with an enlarged band of 30 or 40 musicians.

Following the Palace closing on September 14th, the band had also been booked for a few one-nighters, according to *Billboard* (September 2, 1939, p. 13):

15th: Trianon Ballroom, Toledo, Ohio
16th: Castle Parma, Cincinnati, Ohio

17th: Idora Park, Youngstown, Ohio
20th: Hecla Park, Bellefonte, Pennsylvania

They then opened at the Strand Theatre in New York City on the 22nd for two weeks. Their opening night at the Strand was reviewed for *Billboard* (September 30, 1939, p. 21):

Nobody has to be told by now that Artie Shaw and his band are terrific. Playing here in conjunction with *Espionage Agent*, a choice Warner stinkeroo, they're about anything anybody could possibly ask. They're so good that they even make you forget the picture.

At the start, they rise out of the ork pit, with shadows thrown against the traveller, and go immediately into their foot-tickling, irresistible blasting hot tootling. Fourteen boys (divided into 4 sax, 6 brass, and 4 rhythm) plus Shaw and his clarinet, they're the whole show, despite the fact that there are a couple of other excellent acts on the bill. Even their background show accompaniment is more listenable than the prize packages of most outfits. The crew is billed as the band of the year, but in sober truth they rate with the great pop aggregations of all time.

After a brief hello from Shaw, who acts as a straight-forward and personable emcee throughout, the boys go into "Traffic Jam" and "Donkey Serenade," and have the customers (including this one) eating out of their hands. The Four Reilleys, 3 lads and a girl with a cute and effective series of tap routines, click handily at this point—incidentally, it's hard to see how any act could fail to be lifted by the band—and then Helen Forrest, band songstress, comes on for a couple of numbers. She seemed to this reporter an extraordinarily dull vocalist, but the crowd liked her, and Shaw finally had to beg off for her on the score of laryngitis. Maybe that was what was wrong.

Then the boys go into their signature, "Begin the Beguine," their rendition of which is just a shade less famous than Beethoven's "5th Symphony," and Tony Pastor, a good sax man, makes the mistake of singing 2 novelties.

The band "parade" is interrupted again for the knockout acro and comedy act of Dick, Don and Dinah, a standout trio who end with 3-high acrobatics that are amazing—so amazing that they drew a show-stop lasting well into Shaw's next number. And that's something. The band plays a couple more tunes, including "St. Louis Blues," before the picture, like taxes, inevitably rolls around again.

There are too many outstanding soloists in the Shaw aggregation to pick out any for special mention, except the drummer lad, who's one of the most engaging and terrific hidebeaters extant, and of course the maestro and his clarinet. One nice thing is almost all the lads are given ample opportunity to show their solo stuff.

Evans and Mayer, billed in the ads, failed to show.

House was packed the evening show opening day, despite the start of the Jewish holidays.

As Shaw related in *Artie Shaw: Time Is All You've Got*, dancers swarming the stage at the Strand nearly knocked his teeth out one night when one of them swung his girl in the air and her heels hit his clarinet. With intriguing timing, right after that show, a reporter, Mike Mok of *The New York Post*, asked him what he thought of jitterbugs. Shaw called them "a bunch of morons," as part of an overall critique of the music business in general. Dave Dexter reported on the incident in an article titled "Artie Shaw Fed Up With Music Racket," which appeared on page 1 of the October 15, 1939, *Down Beat*. Dexter quoted extensively from the Mok interview. Interestingly, both Dexter and an editorial in the November 15th issue defended both Shaw's position and his integrity.

The November *Metronome* contained another interview with Shaw, in which he stated Mok had exaggerated some of his statements. Nevertheless, basically he reaffirmed the essence of his comments. This was not surprising, as he had been expressing similar sentiments all along. He had even written out his views on the music business for an article in Tommy Dorsey's own music publication, called *The Bandstand*, as early as the previous winter. However, there was a general outcry from the offended public. Shaw's appearances on the Old Gold show were canceled and many thought this was a response to his comments. Shaw stated in *Metronome* (November 1939, p. 10):

The show gradually turned into a comedy which didn't do the band any good. Besides . . . the new schedule called for a West Coast show at 11 o'clock Saturday nights and I couldn't leave the Penn for that. And so when I asked for a one-week vacation because I was so tired, and they wouldn't give it to me unless I quit the show entirely, I quit the show entirely.

On the same page, *Metronome* reported that Lennen and Mitchell, the advertising agency for Old Gold cigarettes, refused to comment on whether the Mok interview had anything to do with it. Referring to the time remaining in Shaw's contract for the program, they explained Shaw's departure from the show by stating, "He asked us for a week's rest, so we gave him seven." However, Shaw stated in private discussions that the real reason behind the split was that he adamantly refused to read a cigarette commercial that they demanded he do (2).

This was probably the vacation Shaw took to go fishing in Canada, catching one fish, according to the stories. When asked if he really went into the woods with his clarinet for at least an hour a day on such excursions, he expanded on the story, relating that the location was along the Tabasintac River in New Brunswick, Canada, and was one of his favorite spots. He would practice a routine of exercises for clarinet called "Vade Mecum" (Go with Me), which was in the key of F-sharp, daily. "After going through that," he said, "you've done everything possible on a clarinet" (2).

He has stated, "The clarinet practically became an appendage of my body. We were playing all the time. . . . It got to the point where I could do anything I wanted on the instrument" (2).

However, his dissatisfaction had nearly reached the crisis point. He stated in the liner notes to AXM2-5533:

The 1939 ensemble was the best ever. I paid a fantastic amount of attention to the details of each chair, each section and how they blended. I gave as much as I could, considering that I was being pulled and torn by a lot of extraneous facts that come with success. I never put that much time into a band again. Unfortunately, I must admit we had begun to cater somewhat to public taste. The commercial aspects had not yet gotten in the way of the music. But the band was slicker. I don't think it was as artistic in the sense of taking chances, of doing things unpredictably.

Though my band was not designed to perform pop tunes, we got very deeply into them in 1939. We were playing what you call dance music and a lot of people requested these songs. And because we were number one, pressure was exerted on me and a lot of items found their way into our repertoire that I wouldn't ordinarily have looked at. When I hear the names of some of the tunes I say, "Oh, God, why?" Then I remember, being on a pinnacle, making enormous amounts of money, being scared to death. Before breaking through, I could say, "We don't play that. . . ."

It seems the higher you climb, the further you can fall . . . when you're big, big, BIG! and getting large advances from the record company, top money wherever you appear, and acclaim everywhere, you feel a great sense of tension. I guess it's fear of failure.

He continued in the liner notes to AXM2-5556:

By mid-1939, the pressures were enormous and had been building for some time. I had boxed myself into a situation with agents and lawyers and song pluggers and PR men and contracts and money. . . . But money had no meaning to me during those hectic months in 1939. My entire professional life had gotten out of hand. I remember thinking frequently of a 4-line poem . . . "He struck three chords / For beauty's sake / And one / To pay the rent." While there was enough for beauty's sake and the music remained primary, I could subsist emotionally. When it got to be four for the rent, I could no longer take it. There was nothing left for me . . . music, my reason for being in the band business, had taken a back seat. Success had distorted things and taken me away from my original goals . . . the band got into formulas. . . . Of course we did make good music, overall. But . . . a band capable of remarkable performances and taking major strides was caught in a trap created by success.

Besides the internal pressures of artistic conflict, there was the external action. In *The Trouble with Cinderella*, Shaw wrote:

If it isn't a theatre appearance you're getting ready for, it's a radio show. If it's not radio, it's records you've got to make. If it isn't any of these, it's a tour of one-night stands you're about to start on. And all through everything there seem to be hundreds and thousands of crazy people pushing and shoving and crowding and milling around in mobs, shrieking for your autograph, or your picture, or something, or just plain shrieking for no reason on earth you can figure out. Your whole life has become a kind of wild nightmare. ([1], p. 344)

The behavior of fans, in particular, was an irritation. In his biography of Buddy Rich, *Traps the Drum Wonder: The Life of Buddy Rich* (New York: Oxford University Press, 1991), Mel Tormé quoted Georgie Auld on one incident:

One show we did, as the pit was going down, this little broad jumped on top of the pit, grabbed hold of Artie, and started to dryhump him! He's holding his clarinet above his head; he don't want to break his reed. ([15], p. 44)

In the *Metronome* interview on page 10 of the November 1939 issue, titled "I Still Don't Like Jitterbugs" (reprinted in *Simon Says*), Shaw stated:

I want everybody to know that all I'm interested in is making good music. If they like it, they can have it! If they don't they can keep away from it. But let 'em concentrate on my music and not on me. ([6], pp.18–19)

In the liner notes to RCA AXM2-5556, Shaw offered a concise summary of his emotional state:

Progressively, I moved away from my musicians. I couldn't seem to communicate with anyone. I found it impossible to articulate the problems at the time. I can't tell you how lonely I was. But I was determined to get out, to relieve the tension.

This was the period when Shaw and Betty Grable were romantically involved. They had met in Hollywood earlier that year, and Betty Grable had come to New York to star in the Broadway musical *Du Barry Was A Lady* that fall. Songwriter Sammy Cahn, who was an acquaintance of Shaw's in that period, described the situation in his autobiography, *I Should Care* (New York: Arbor House, 1974, p. 248):

He and Betty . . . were much like people out of a Gene Kelly movie, dancing down the streets of Fifth Avenue at night after her show, shouting and laughing. And these two people were so much in love.

Yet, Shaw wrote in *The Trouble with Cinderella*:

It was one of the loneliest times in my life. I had a few friends, people who were not in the music business, and with

them I was able to be myself and still not be regarded as completely off my rocker. . . . I couldn't get anyone connected with me to agree, of course. Everyone told me I was crazy . . . even to think of any such thing as quitting. ([1], p. 350)

Sammy Cahn related that Shaw would occasionally avoid appearances, pleading illness, and Cahn would pose as his doctor and make an announcement. While there were stories to this effect in the media, naming Shaw's physician as "Dr. Dudley Bumpus," Shaw denied avoiding appearances (2). Cahn also reported witnessing some of Shaw's wristwatch-buying expeditions, which Shaw referred to in the Berman film as a way to prove to himself that he was making money, a tangible symbol. The watch collection allegedly grew quite large. Given Shaw's concern with time, the watches also represented a philosophic symbol.

The possibility of Shaw quitting was referred to several times in the various music magazines that fall. In addition, there were several items concerning Shaw that anyone with any sensitivity would find discouraging or at least in poor taste. *Down Beat* printed a photo showing Shaw and Betty Grable in a coy pose, smiling at each other. The photo was captioned, "Who Said This Wasn't The Real Thing?" The caption went on to speculate on the potential of their marrying, as Betty Grable had just divorced Jackie Coogan. However, the picture was a composite made by superimposing Shaw's face on another photo that apparently had shown Grable and Jack Benny together in a publicity pose. Around the same time, an interview with Billie Holiday by Dave Dexter in *Down Beat* quoted her as making some bitterly uncomplimentary remarks about Shaw and her stay with the band ("I'll Never Sing With a Dance Band Again—Holiday," in the November 1, 1939, issue, pp. 4, 20). Shaw even promptly contributed a rebuttal to *Down Beat* concerning this unfortunate diatribe. He also was reported being sued again, this time for having knocked over a drunken pedestrian in Boston a year or two earlier, after lengthy litigation in the interim. The lawsuit in Buffalo concerning the Crystal Palace incident was also still pending, and the music magazines were keeping track of the proceedings.

On October 19th, 1939, Artie Shaw and his orchestra opened at the Cafe Rouge of the Hotel Pennsylvania at 33rd Street and Seventh Avenue in New York City. Again *Billboard* provided a review (November 4, 1939, p. 12):

In the midst of all the fuss and fury surrounding Shaw's pungently expressed opinions of his constituents, his clarinet and his band continue as two of the better products of the Swing Age. If the gapers do inconsiderately gape they must at least be given credit for discrimination in their gaping.

Backed by the lift and drive of his 6 brass, 4 reed and 4 rhythm, Shaw's work is as brilliant and electrifying as always. Jazz has produced many fine things but few with the elemental appeal and the highly technical proficiency of a Shaw blues passage against the tom-tom rhythm of which he is so fond. This is virtuosity (in its own particular field) at the peak of its development.

The band never lets the music down. The anticipated beats, the bent notes, the precision supply the rhythmic lift that has always been one of the outfit's foremost attributes. But it's all too academically perfect, the performance cries out for a lightness of touch, a sense of bounce and a showmanship that Tony Pastor's comic vocals alone can't give it. Pastor is good, but not good enough to take away from that dead-pan facade which is the only blight on an otherwise nearly perfect job.

Helen Forrest's warbling has always left this listener cold. But the Shaw clarinet covers up a lot of sins. Open mouths are definitely not out of order when he puts the instrument up to his.

The contemporary reviews did not exaggerate the band's quality. Most of the complete broadcasts for the band's first three nights at the Cafe Rouge have been issued. About fifty performances have become available from the period the band was at that location. Their broadcast schedule was inadequately listed in the November 1, 1939 issue of *Down Beat* as:

NBC Blue: Thursday & Saturday 12 midnite. Other spots.

The Bluebird records emphasized the pop material Shaw was complaining about having to perform. Yet, although the relative shortage of instrumentals was disappointing, there was no loss of quality in their performances.

In early November, Al Avola had to leave due to illness and was replaced by Dave Barbour. Rumors that Tony Pastor would be leaving to form his own group were circulating. The November 1939 *Metronome* announced on page 9, "Rich Leaves Shaw," noting that the flamboyant drummer would be moving into Tommy Dorsey's band. According to discussions with Shaw, Rich was replaced by Ralph Hawkins three days prior to Shaw's famous walkout (2).

In *The Trouble with Cinderella*, Shaw wrote:

At the stage I was in then, any little thing would have been sufficient; and so, because of a slight unpleasantness with some idiot on the floor in front of the band, who was evidently trying to impress his partner by using me as a focal point for his witticisims, I suddenly decided I'd had it. Instead of kicking him in the teeth, I walked off the bandstand, went up to my room, and called my lawyer. When I got him on the phone, I told him I was leaving. ([1], p. 351)

According to contemporary reports, this occurred at about 11 p.m. on Tuesday, November 14, 1939. In *The Trouble with Cinderella*, Shaw went on to describe his confrontations with his lawyer, agents, band, and others concerned.

At one point, he described their bringing in a medium to try to convince him to reconsider quitting. Shaw was unyielding. Finally, following a last meeting with his band, he left New York on Saturday, November 18th.

I got in my car and started driving. It was snowing hard the day I left New York. I remember coming out of the Jersey end of the Holland Tunnel and suddenly realizing I was out from under all the misery and idiocy I'd been buried in for so long. The flood of relief that rolled over me made up for all the turmoil and trouble and talk-talk-talk it had taken to get out.

I was driving a big, heavy car, the heater was working, the snow was falling heavily outside, but it was warm inside the car—and that night I knew I wouldn't have to show up on a bandstand before a crowd of ogling strangers. That night I could check in at some hotel or tourist camp and be just plain Art Shaw again—Art Shaw, private citizen. I felt fine. ([1], p. 353)

By his own account, Shaw was at first undecided on where to go. He was reported to have called his mother from Tennessee on the 23rd. He related having called several friends on the West Coast, where he still had a house he had bought while based in Hollywood. However it had been rented to actress Flora Robson, who still had some time on her lease. Besides, friends were advising him to stay away from Hollywood if he really wanted peace and quiet. One of the close friends he had called was Judy Garland. She was quoted in *Judy* as stating:

My God, what did you do, walking out like that? You just don't know what's going on here. Where is Artie Shaw? That's all people talk about. You're the mystery man. You fell off the earth. ([7], p. 140)

He recalled hearing good things about Mexico, which had been in the music news that year fairly prominently, and decided it was "as good a place as any" and stopped in Acapulco, then just a small fishing village, not yet the resort it would become. He wrote of living quietly and keeping to himself:

During the day I swam, fished, took the sun and read. In the evening I sat on my terrace overlooking the town square, or went to the local bistro, or to listen to local musicians playing on the wharf. I did absolutely nothing I didn't feel like doing. I thought about music but didn't play. ([1], pp. 355–56)

The January 1940 *Metronome* headlined "Artie Shaw Wants a Mexican Band" on page 11. The article noted that Shaw was commuting to Mexico City from Acapulco and engaging with local musicians in jam sessions, although not playing in public. An accompanying photo showed him smiling out of the middle of a tux-clad Mexican band.

Meanwhile, the January 15, 1940, *Down Beat* had a blurb on page 21 concerning a *Down Beat* reporter running into Shaw in Mexico City. It related that Shaw had threatened to smash the reporter's camera if he tried to photograph him.

On January 12th Shaw broke his kneecap and tore several ligaments in his leg while rescuing Ann Chapman, an American heiress and student at the Geneva College for Women, from the surf at Acapulco where she had been knocked senseless by a breaker and was being dragged out by the undertow.

> I was the only one on the beach at the time who realized what had happened, and I was the nearest person to her anyway. So I tore out to where she lay drifting, and started to pull her in towards the beach. At that moment an enormous wall of water rose up, broke over both of us, picked us up like a pair of tiny chips, and flung us down every-which-way. ([1], p. 356)

Down Beat headlined "Artie Shaw Saves Girl From Death" and noted that a few days after being flown to Mexico City to have his leg set, he flew back to Los Angeles with his leg in a cast. His house on Summit Ridge Drive was again available. He then began working on some motion picture ideas with Borros Morros, the producer, concerning a film about the tribulations of a bandleader.

As for the band, after Shaw's exit Georgie Auld was elected leader. The men were understandably in shock. In the liner notes to RCA AXM2-5556, trumpeter Bernie Privin was quoted as saying,

> Prior to Artie's sudden escape to warmer climes, we had no inkling that a move was imminent. Before that memorable evening at New York's Hotel Pennsylvania, everything seemed essentially normal to the men in the band. We were doing beautifully. Evidence of strain on Artie? Yes. . . . After Georgie took the reins, Tony Pastor left to form his own band. Buddy Rich became a featured player with Tommy Dorsey. And the rest of the men, with a couple of replacements, tried to honor as many of Shaw's commitments as possible. We worked the Roseland . . . for a couple of weeks, then did some college dates. The money wasn't too great. We all took rather heavy salary cuts. I went from $125 to $50 per week. It all came to an end in Jacksonville, Florida.

Les Robinson, who had played lead alto with the band since its formation in 1937, stated:

> Artie's quitting was a terrible shock. . . . We had no idea, really, what was going on in Artie's mind. He didn't like signing autographs, or having the crowds get too close. Artie was always a private type of cat. But you had to respect him. Musically, he knew exactly what it was all about and he communicated what he wanted very well. There was never any doubt in the band about direction. It just didn't work without

Artie. The magic was gone. We didn't have our key soloist and that all-important source of discipline and professionalism that made the band great. Artie had a lot to do with the teamwork that made us special. Well, we made a few records for the Varsity label, played out the string. It didn't take too long to realize we couldn't make it on our own.

Georgie Auld was quoted as saying,

> There we were. Artie got into his red Packard and drove off. . . . I was deeply sorry to see it end. Artie and I had good rapport from the first night I was with the band. We never had one run-in through our entire association.
>
> And suddenly I was a band leader. It was a disaster. When it was over, we were all deeply depressed. After all, the band had been number one and we had a great sense of pride. I didn't look back. I joined Benny Goodman and tried to put my life back together.

Harry Geller, the trumpet man who had replaced Johnny Best in August 1939, also contributed his recollection of the aftermath of Shaw's walkout:

> Ben Cole, the band's manager, said Artie wanted to see me. I had not been with the band long and had come from Los Angeles with my wife to join him. I went to his room. There were several people in his suite. I could feel the tension. He told me, "I'm going to give you two first-class airplane tickets back home to the Coast, and a bonus for your trouble." I was enormously pleased and surprised. I must really say that as far as money and consideration are concerned, Shaw was really great.

Intriguingly, Buddy Rich's recollection was that he had been on the stand playing drums at the Cafe Rouge the night Shaw walked off:

> [Shaw] left during the first set. He didn't show up on the bandstand. "Where's Artie?" The room was packed. I sat down behind the drums, and I waited. We all started looking around at each other. Everybody in the brass section looking at me. I'm looking at them. Finally after about . . . 5 minutes of waiting, Tony Pastor got up in front of the band and called a set. Artie never came back. ([15], p. 51)

In the liner notes to RCA AXM2-5530, Rich was quoted on his feelings:

> The band was a hell of an experience. I think Artie was a very dedicated guy. He taught me a lot about music, behavior on the stand, things in general. I liked what we did—the good tunes, the show music, even the pop tunes. The band always sounded good. Even the ballads had a pulse.
>
> Artie had the whole field covered. He kept the band happy by giving us good music to play. He held onto the dancers because the beat was there. And he didn't lose the listeners because the musical content was more than acceptable.

Certainly, there is ample documentation that the men in the 1938–39 band appreciated Shaw's leadership and the experience of being with the band. In the liner notes to RCA AXM2-5517, Privin recalled,

> The pressures of success got to Artie. But he never was unreasonable as a leader. Rehearsals were handled with a firm, knowing hand. Generally we knew what was expected of us. There was a little distance between Shaw and the guys. But we knew he cared. For example, whenever we travelled it was first-class. He made sure we played good music, and that we were comfortable.
>
> For all the travelling and constant activity, there were few squabbles in the band. It may be hard to believe, considering all that was happening, but everyone got along pretty well. Tony Pastor . . . was a sweetheart. He kind of took care of the younger guys.

Robinson noted,

> The 1939 Shaw band had something that never again will be duplicated. It was a "team" band, everyone contributed. The blend of the sections and its overall sound didn't just happen. Shaw knew what he wanted and got it.

Nevertheless, the enormous success of Shaw's distinctive approach spawned imitators. As noted, several Artie Shaw–style bands emerged even as Shaw was quitting. Clarinetist Tommy Reynolds formed a blatantly Shaw-styled band in Boston, as noted in *Metronome*'s December 1939 issue. An article on page 10, titled "Tommy Reynolds Build-Up Like Artie Shaw's," noted that Reynolds was even working through the Shribman's chain of ballrooms in New England, as Shaw had, in getting started.

Also, during this period a lovely young woman named Ann DuPont emerged as leader of a male dance band. She was billed as "Queen of the Clarinet" and as a "female Artie Shaw" in *Down Beat*. An article on page 2 of the June 1939 *Down Beat* praised her playing as "a wild, uninhibited style" and "plays clarinet like Shaw." Although she flourished for a few years, she does not even appear in most reference books on jazz or in discographies, despite occasional similar praises and acclamations appearing in the music press well into the 1940s.

Chapter 8

Hollywood to New York: 1940–1941

Shaw had returned to Hollywood with the tentative project of scoring a film version of Gershwin's *Porgy and Bess*, but the deal fizzled out. He then found himself wondering what to do next. The February 1940 *Metronome* headlined on page 7: "Shaw To Lead Symphony!" Among other unfulfilled rumors was that a movie of Shaw's career was planned; the article also stated: "Shaw is also supervising the score and will act in the picture, which is strictly about the music industry, and which will be supervised for RKO by Borros Morros." The tentative title was *Second Chorus*, but that seems to be all that remained of this description of the film when it was made the following summer.

Shaw's social life with friends in Hollywood resumed, including his close platonic friendship with Judy Garland. Judy still was overwhelmingly infatuated with Shaw, despite his relationship with Betty Grable, who was still in New York. Gerold Frank gave an account in *Judy* of her getting Jackie Cooper to drive her to Shaw's house on a regular basis ([7], p. 142). Shaw, of course, still would have been convalescing with his broken knee.

One day Phil Silvers, who had become friends with Shaw in New York, took him to the MGM Studios to watch a scene being made for the movie *Two Girls on Broadway*. There, Shaw reencountered Lana Turner. Shaw admittedly was impressed with what he saw, but Silvers related in his autobiography, *This Laugh Is on Me* (Englewood Cliffs, N. J.: Prentice-Hall, 1973):

> Artie's disdain was monumental, but they made a date for that night. He insisted I come along, "because she might bring me down."
>
> As soon as we got into his car I knew he needed help. Lana wanted to visit a place called Victor Hugo's, which featured Guy Lombardo.
>
> Artie Shaw grooving on Guy Lombardo?
>
> He did it for her. Lombardo's musicians were in awe of Artie, tootled as if their fingers were stuck on flypaper. On the way home, Artie ran through the routine I'd heard so often: "I want a girl that will be satisfied with me alone on a desert island. . . ." The girl would agree, "Yes, just two people who need each other." And then they would roll into

bed for a pleasant jam session. Next day, all the philosophic rationalization would be forgotten. Artie was always brutally honest: He really did mean what he said. Every time.

> Lana crossed him up. "That's exactly what I want. A man who has the brains to be satisfied with me only."
>
> He was vehement. "Look, I'm sick of all this Hollywood crap. I want to break out."
>
> "Me too. Anywhere you say."
>
> Artie couldn't back out. He turned around, drove out to Paul Mantz's plane rental service, and chartered a plane to Las Vegas. To get married. I felt this was reaching too far for a joke, but Artie was flying against the petty restraints of slave society. Superman. He gave me the keys to drive his car home. (pp. 104–5)

In Lana Turner's autobiography, *Lana: The Lady, The Legend, The Truth* (New York: Dutton, 1982), she stated that their elopement took place on February 12, 1940. She wrote:

> We drove toward the ocean along Sunset Boulevard, and Artie did most of the talking—about how tired he was of the big-band business, about the concert orchestra he was planning that would make people take jazz music seriously, about how he wanted to write music and someday write books. He talked about Nietzsche and Schopenhauer (I'd never heard of them, and when I tried to read them later, I didn't get far). He said he was sick of jitterbugs and autograph hounds. What he wanted now were the basic things—a good, solid marriage, a home, and children. . . .
>
> Artie built me a romantic dream, with a white picket fence around it. His eloquence stirred me, and the evening took on a glow as we parked in a spot overlooking the ocean. We forgot about eating. We didn't kiss, but as we talked we held hands. Artie was right. I'd had my taste of fame and prosperity. Now it was time for more serious things. I told Artie that I didn't care if I never made another picture. And at the moment I meant it, or thought I did.
>
> It wasn't that I fell in love with Artie that night. I wasn't even physically attracted. But here was a wonderfully intelligent man, far more talented and famous . . . who took me seriously. ([14], p. 42)

Accounts differ as to details, but the various versions of their elopement amount to the same thing. Shaw's rage at hounding newspapermen besieging their house, Judy Garland and Betty Grable reacting with shock, Artie and Lana being front page news, and their realizing within three days that they had made a mistake, are universal elements in the tale. Lana was quoted as saying,

My elopement with Artie Shaw was typical of Hollywood at that time. The sudden marriage, the chase by reporters, the whim, the dashing action, that was the style in 1940, so I lived up to it. ([13], p. 43)

Shaw was quoted as saying,

The whole business had an unreal feeling about it. Even Lana, lying there next to me, seemed unreal. It had all happened so fast. ([13], p. 43)

When Betty Grable was asked if she was brokenhearted, she replied, "No, I wouldn't say that exactly," and went on to say, "It must have come on him very suddenly." Judy Garland's mother reportedly phoned Shaw to shout something about his breaking Judy's heart, which supposedly took him by surprise. He frostily informed her that there had been nothing romantic with Judy ([13], p. 44).

Judy and Lana also had been friends, but after the marriage Judy ceased visiting. When Shaw asked her why, Judy was quoted as replying, "Artie, she's a nice girl, but it's like sitting in a room with a beautiful vase" ([13], p. 48).

Artie Shaw's celebrity image was in high profile once again. For the fourth time in six months he was making headlines. First he had insulted his audiences. Then he had walked out on his musical career and disappeared. Then he broke his knee rescuing Ann Chapman from the Acapulco surf. Then came his surprise elopement with Lana. The musical world also was focused on Shaw's activities, anticipating the results of his plans to record with a large orchestra.

Shaw's interest in using strings was well known. Comments on using a string section had appeared in Shaw interviews several times. The December 15, 1939, *Down Beat* had two articles on Shaw on page 1. One was another detail in Shaw's perennial conflict with the music business. The headline "Shaw Pays Off Eli Oberstein; Suit Dropped" referred to one situation in the aftermath of his walkout. Oberstein, a top executive with RCA, was suing Shaw for lost commissions. Shaw charged Oberstein with coercion and threats. Shaw settled out of court by paying several thousand dollars. Clearly, his still owing RCA six sides was not a matter to be taken lightly. The other article on that page asked, " 'Mystery Man' Shaw To Use Hot Strings?"

The April 1st issue of *Down Beat* included, on page 19, an explanation from Shaw on why he was using a string section, titled "Here's Why Artie Is Using Strings":

"The general idea," he says, "is not to get away from swing music but to present dance music with more color than is possible with the usual brass and saxophone setup that has perhaps, due to constant usage, become monotonous. I will attempt to have a swing band playing as such, augmented by legitimate instruments playing legitimately."

"If possible," Shaw declares, "I should like to work this idea into a much needed laboratory for the creation and development of musical effects and innovations necessary to the growth of swing which I contend is a greatly misunderstood idiom."

In the liner notes to RCA AXM2-5556, Shaw was quoted as stating:

I was not deeply motivated in a musical way at this time. . . . I wanted to make nice records, do a professional job integrating the strings. . . .

I had come back to Hollywood with an idea. Instead of going on the road with a band and making umpteen thousand dollars a week, I would settle for much, much less and do some scoring work for pictures and recordings. One thing I didn't want to do was to get on that travelling treadmill again, but my agents kept at me. On the road I was a big asset to them. . . .

Finally for several reasons—I needed the money, I owed RCA six sides, I was restless and needed the stimulation of activity—I put together a 31-piece orchestra. And on March 3, 1940, we cut six sides, including "Frenesi."

An article on page 1 of the March 15, 1940, *Down Beat* by David Hyltone headlined "Shaw Using 31 Pieces!" and went on to say,

Artie Shaw's new band, which recorded for Victor-Bluebird last week, is terrific. Band includes 8 violins, 3 violas, 2 cellos, oboe, flute, bass clarinet, French horn, 4 saxes, 6 brass and 4 rhythm.

Listeners agreed it was a beautiful and melodic sounding group, with special arrangements by Artie and William Grant Still, the noted Negro composer and arranger. Most of the men were from movie studios . . . Dave Klein contracted the men.

Artie is set on staying in Southern California. He has his home out here now; it was recently purchased. He has just deposited his transfer card with Local 47 and told officials he planned to take a couple of weeks off for a trip east with his bride, as soon as he could make arrangements to leave the studio where he is working on a movie. Meanwhile his sponsors are trying to sell Artie for a radio commercial. . . .

The tonal colors available with the above instrumentation were well utilized in the attractive arrangements. "Adios

Marquita Linda" provided Shaw's best moments from the session with a generous clarinet solo.

Concerning the six pieces on this remarkable session, "Frenesi" and "Adios Marquita Linda" were songs Shaw had heard in Mexico that he liked. "Gloomy Sunday" achieved some fame as "the suicide song" and made the press that year for allegedly inspiring rejected lovers to end it all. "My Fantasy" borrowed its melodic line from Borodin's "Dance of the Polovetsian Maidens" and later, with new lyrics, became more famous as "Stranger in Paradise." "A Deserted Farm" is a composition by American composer Edward A. MacDowell, from his suite "Woodland Sketches." Shaw had been enjoying playing it on the piano in that period. He had William Grant Still orchestrate it in an entirely scored version, without improvised solos. The final number recorded at that record date was "Don't Fall Asleep," composed by Shaw with lyrics by his old friend Arthur Quenzer. Interestingly, passages in this arrangement echoed parts of Shaw's swinging 1939 composition "Man from Mars" (available only from air check versions). Even more from this composition can be heard surviving in Shaw's Gramercy 5 composition "Special Delivery Stomp" (recorded the following summer).

The three tunes sung by Pauline Byrne sounded good. Miss Byrne was the "Miss" in the vocal septet "Six Hits and a Miss" that was performing on Bob Hope's radio show in that era. However, the two Latin-flavored numbers, "Frenesi" and "Adios Marquita Linda," had a more distinctly original feel. While "A Deserted Farm" was not released for decades, "Frenesi" quickly became one of Shaw's biggest hit records. Shaw has said that he was not particularly happy with any of these records, as he had not been feeling much musical commitment that spring. He has said, "I never liked my record of 'Frenesi.' I don't think it was a good performance. We did it better later" (2).

Perhaps he was distracted by Lana. They visited New York in April, allegedly to tour the Lower East Side, erroneously described in contemporary gossip columns as "the ghetto in which he had grown up." Such distortions lend credence to the opinion that many of the allegations concerning Shaw in stories of their breakup were publicity-inspired concoctions from Lana's studio. Their greatly publicized trip coincided with the opening of Lana's latest movie, *Two Girls on Broadway*, at the Capitol Theater in New York. Lana also told of a poignant meeting with Shaw's mother while on that trip, in her autobiography.

Back in Hollywood, Lana's mother was irritating Shaw by always showing up unexpectedly. Shaw was able to stop that by watching for her one day and answering the door naked, saying, "Oh, I thought it was somebody else!" ([13], p. 46). Lana wrote in her autobiography that she was disgusted by Shaw's and Phil Silvers's getting high on marijuana and being silly. Many of the stories about their

domestic squabbles Shaw dismissed as nonsense, noting that they had servants and Lana was not expected to do domestic chores. Apparently tales of her having to wash his shirts in the bathroom sink and iron them and so forth were studio concoctions to create sympathy for Lana when the divorce publicity was lively. At one point, Lana supposedly was hospitalized for exhaustion, but actually the studio had set up an abortion behind Shaw's back. When he learned the truth, he was devastated. "That's what ended the marriage for me," he has said (2).

On May 13, 1940, Shaw returned to the Victor studios to record another five titles. This time he employed only twenty-three studio musicians, not counting the singers. He reduced the string section to ten men and eliminated trombones, oboe and flute. The two pieces sung by former Benny Goodman vocalist Martha Tilton were not as interesting as the Pauline Byrne vocals from the March session. Jack Pearce, who whistled and sang with uncertain intonation on "Mr. Meadowlark," represented the low point of the session. The outstanding performance was the instrumental "King for a Day," which featured Shaw extensively and in good form. Otherwise, the products of this record date were relatively dull. Nevertheless, Shaw played beautifully throughout.

Shaw and Lana still were in the news. Publicity events such as attending the ground-breaking ceremonies for the new Palladium Ballroom were photographed for the newspapers and magazines. Shaw also was in the news for being thrown from a horse and reinjuring his leg. Hollywood gossip reporters were thriving on rumors of the couple's marital difficulties. When they separated, they had been together slightly over four months. Lana filed for divorce on July 3, 1940.

In the music world, Shaw was in the news because of his signing for the movie *Second Chorus* and for George Burns and Gracie Allen's popular weekly radio show. Shaw began recruiting for his new orchestra in June.

The media again tried to use the idea of a Shaw–Goodman rivalry feud. The August 1, 1940, *Down Beat* headlined on page 1, "Artie Shaw Grabs Goodman's Men." However, in the article by Dave Dexter that followed, Goodman said,

> Artie did me a favor. All my band was on notice. Artie needed good musicians. So he offered to take some of my boys for his own outfit now working in the picture *Second Chorus* and on the Burns & Allen NBC show.

Goodman had been suffering painfully from sciatica since the preceding January, and finally, on July 10, 1940, headed for the Mayo Clinic in Rochester, Minnesota, for an operation. According to *Down Beat*, Shaw stepped in and fronted the band, which then finished their week at the Catalina Island Casino under the direction of Ziggy Elman and Kay Kyser.

Johnny Guarnieri, who had been Goodman's pianist, already had joined Shaw's new band in June. Shaw was using saxophonists Les Robinson, Jerry Jerome, and Bus Bassey, trombonist Vernon Brown, and drummer Nick Fatool from Goodman's band. Along with bassist Jud DeNaut, who had been with Shaw on the studio recordings earlier that year, they formed the nucleus of the new band. Shaw also hired some key men such as trumpeter Billy Butterfield and trombonist Jack Jenney, and there also was a nine-piece string section. Shaw has stated that the basic personnel for the band was set by the time they began the *Burns and Allen Show*. Shaw experienced union problems for not using Los Angeles musicians in his orchestra in that era: Spike Wallace, of the Los Angeles Musicians' Union, was insisting that Shaw use only LA musicians, and even threatened to have Shaw yanked off the *Burns and Allen Show* if he failed to comply.

The *Burns and Allen Show* with Artie Shaw and his Orchestra went on the air on Monday, July 1, 1940, and was favorably reviewed in the July 13, 1940, issue of *Billboard*:

> Artie Shaw, making his initial appearance since his alleged retirement, returns with a new ork containing a large string section. The music, with Shaw's clarinet leads, is, as explained in a talkfest with announcer John Heistand, a swing and classic hybrid. The effect is singularly okeh. The arrangements are good and Shaw's licorice stick has lost none of its potency since his layoff. The Smoothies are also spotted on this shot, getting across some okeh vocalistics.

It is noteworthy that this first show featured Shaw's latest big hit, "Frenesi."

Shaw's performances from the *Burns and Allen Show* broadcasts were unavailable and undocumented as far as most collectors and the public were concerned until in 1997 Hep Records in Scotland issued two CDs representing the majority of material actually broadcast by the orchestra (see discography). Apparently Shaw was featured for only one number per show, aside from fills from the band and some comedy dialogue, but the performances are superb. Although Shaw's new orchestra had barely been formed, even the earliest items are excellent. Alto-saxophonist Les Robinson was quoted by Burt Korall in his liner notes to RCA AXM-5572 concerning this band:

> Almost from the beginning the band "clicked." There was an unusual sense of togetherness about our performances. Most people who heard us thought we'd been on the scene for some time. The band had a distinctive "singing" quality, almost like a pipe organ, particularly when Butterfield was playing lead trumpet. He "sang" all over the place. The dy-

namics of this ensemble were really outstanding and ever so natural as well. . . . It balanced itself.

Korall also quoted tenor saxophonist Jerry Jerome:

> At the beginning all we did, aside from rehearse, was play the Burns & Allen radio show each week and wait for work to begin on the picture *Second Chorus*. Early in August we started filming. It was great fun, although there wasn't much to the picture.

The movie *Second Chorus* starred Fred Astaire and Burgess Meredith as rival trumpet players vying for a chair in Artie Shaw's band and for the attention of the female lead, Paulette Goddard. Their trumpet parts were dubbed by Billy Butterfield ghosting for Astaire, and Bobby Hackett for Meredith. Shaw again played himself in a fictional situation, this time with more dignity and remaining in character.

The orchestra was shown to advantage in a drastically edited version of Shaw's "Concerto for Clarinet" (initially referred to as "Hot Concerto" in the media), which Shaw composed for the film and later recorded as a twelve-inch 78-rpm double-sided disc for Victor. It primarily was a 12-bar blues performance, with touches of classical flavor at certain points in Shaw's arrangement and use of the strings, opening and closing with some spectacular clarinet cadenzas and including some excellent solos. The on-screen performance of this intriguing number times three minutes and twenty-five seconds on issued video copies, and Shaw complained about it having been cut radically (2). Another version made for the movie was, oddly, originally issued by the Armed Forces Radio Service in their Basic Music Library series, along with other Shaw material from his Victor recordings; this version times at four minutes and forty seconds, and aside from obvious differences in the solos, there are additional Shaw cadenzas after Billy Butterfield's trumpet solo, before the free-form clarinet/drum duo segment begins. This longer version became widely available only when it was reissued in 1997 on CD (see discography).

Another new Shaw composition written for the film was "Love of My Life," sung to Miss Goddard by Astaire, with Shaw and the band without strings performing the number, shown dimly visible in an out-of-focus shot through a glass door. Unfortunately this performance was marred by dialogue. A short version of "Everything Is Jumpin' " (also omitting the string section) was Shaw's only other substantial playing opportunity in the film, and provided a good view of the band. A few bars over the opening and closing credits were the only other moments Shaw was heard playing in the movie.

As with most Fred Astaire movies, *Second Chorus* was embarrassingly silly but sometimes fun. Shaw's few scenes showed him looking and playing well, with confident assertiveness and strength. Paulette Goddard was reported to have been very favorably impressed by the "Hot Concerto" feature for Shaw and the band. Her dance segment with Astaire was "Dig It!" (composed by Hal Borne and performed by a studio orchestra). Astaire's closing dance feature involved his dancing while conducting an enlarged orchestra playing "Poor Mr. Chisolm" (composed by Bernie Hanighen); Shaw was not involved except for handing Astaire his baton prior to the number. Astaire had only one other dance number in the picture, also not involving Shaw. Shaw's orchestra was not used for all musical segments: other groups of musicians are shown on-screen during various sequences. Hollywood's Local 47 Musicians' Union files, researched by Luiz Carlos do Nascimento Silva in 1997, show the schedule for the musicians for the film and distinguish between recording sessions and "sideline" appearances, which were for filming, not sound-recording. Various shifts of personnel are evident in the files, including enlarging or eliminating the string section, adding a woodwind section (presumably for the sequence where Astaire dances before the giant orchestra in the finale), and adding Bobby Hackett for the recordings for the sequences showing Astaire and Meredith playing trumpet on-screen (see discography).

Second Chorus was generally regarded as a failure by all concerned. The copyright was even allowed to expire, putting the movie in the public domain. As a result, it has been widely available for purchase in VHS and Beta formats since the early 1980s, and subsequently has been shown on television fairly often. Occasionally the "Hot Concerto" segment was edited out completely on these issues and screenings. Nevertheless, the film was interesting for Shaw's few scenes of dialogue and his performances with his new band.

Also in this period, Shaw again experienced stress from the music business aspects of his career. He had booked himself through the William Morris Agency to do the *Burns and Allen Show*, and his old agency, GAC, protested. Shaw had to fly to Chicago to confer with Musicians' Union President James C. Petrillo to resolve the controversy. Eventually, an arrangement was worked out for the agencies to split commissions in such instances. The media then announced that GAC had booked Shaw for the Palace Hotel in San Francisco for a September 12th opening, but Shaw affirmed that it was Morris that had booked him there (2).

Prior to the band's opening at the Palace, RCA recorded Shaw twice. The first session featured the debut of the Gramercy 5, the small group out of the band. The Gramercy 5 was a sextet (Artie Shaw AND his Gramercy 5) and included Billy Butterfield on trumpet, Shaw, and the rhythm section. Shaw stated that he had felt more constrained improvisationally with the large orchestra, so he decided to use key soloists with the rhythm section for a change of pace into

some looser jazz. There were several small groups out of the orchestra featured at shows, but only the Gramercy 5 recorded. Shaw took the names for these groups from the New York City telephone exchanges: Chelsea 3, Regent 4, Gramercy 5, Vanderbilt 6, Trafalgar 7; he noted that therefore the number "5" (not the word) is the appropriate way to spell it. He explained not recording the other ensembles with, "I didn't think they were quite what I wanted" (2). In later years, groups billed as the Gramercy 5 varied from quintets to septets, but by then the name had drawing power because one of the records made at this first record date, "Summit Ridge Drive," had become a million-seller during the war.

Shaw rehearsed the Gramercy 5 at his home on Summit Ridge Drive in Beverly Hills. He had had a harpsichord built for himself, and one day they decided to try using it and liked the results. Shaw noted that all Gramercy 5 performances were "head arrangements," with Butterfield's muted trumpet voiced a minor third below Shaw's clarinet, and drummer Nick Fatool usually using brushes. Bassist Jud DeNaut was quoted in the liner notes to RCA AXM2-5556:

> The group was about as much fun as anything I can think of. We weren't too well acquainted with the sound of the harpsichord at the time, nor was anyone else. But Johnny Guarnieri was truly fantastic, in a jazz way, on that instrument.

The September 1, 1940, *Down Beat* had an article on page 12 by Charlie Emge titled, "Shaw On 'Ancient' Kick, to Use Harpsichord in Hotel." In addition to describing the harpsichord as "an ancient forerunner of the piano," Emge announced that the band's Palace Hotel opening was scheduled for the 12th and noted that the band would routinely fly back and forth between Los Angeles, for the *Burns and Allen Show*, and San Francisco, for their hotel appearances.

The first record date for the Gramercy 5, on September 3, 1940, provided two original Shaw compositions and two pop songs. The opening number, "Special Delivery Stomp," grew out of a Shaw original performed by the 1938–39 band, "Man from Mars." It was an up-tempo, drivingly swinging performance. "Summit Ridge Drive," named for Shaw's street address, was a medium-tempo twelve-bar blues number. Of the pop songs, "Keeping Myself for You" was given a smooth, balladlike treatment, while "Cross Your Heart" was performed with a jaunty swing including some boogie-woogie harpsichord.

This September 3, 1940, Gramercy 5 session offers highly satisfying results and the classic status of the Gramercy 5 recordings already was justified by the level of these performances. The distinctive sound of the group, the infectious feel of the ensemble, the high quality of the solos, and Shaw being in good form were factors in evidence on all four titles.

The orchestra's record debut occurred on September 7th. The first item recorded was another excellent Shaw original, "If It's You," a vocal ballad used in the Marx Brothers' movie *The Big Store*. Anita Boyer sings it well, but her other feature on this date was a banal pop song. There also were two fine instrumentals recorded that day, a Latin-tinged version of "Temptation," which became another big hit, and an attractive version of W. C. Handy's "Chantez Les Bas" orchestrated by William Grant Still. To a certain extent, the repertoire of the band was encapsulated in microcosm in this recording session: some ballads and originals, some banal pop tunes of relatively minor interest, some Latin-flavored arrangements, and some intriguingly atypical material by noted figures.

The bulk of the orchestrations for this orchestra were done by Lennie Hayton (including integrating the string section into Shaw's earlier arrangements of tunes that had been hits with his 1938–39 band), with some contributions by William Grant Still and Ray Conniff. Shaw explained his methods in the quotes appearing in the liner notes to RCA AXM2-5572:

> I gave clear-cut instructions. In other words, I want the brass to do this, the reeds to do that, the strings and rhythm to thus and so, the modulations and punctuations to be placed here and there. I would also indicate whether I desired open or closed voicings.

At their October 7, 1940, record date they recorded five titles. Again, there were two vocals by Anita Boyer, including Shaw's "Love of My Life" and a relatively good pop song, "A Handful of Stars." There were two Latin-influenced pieces, "Marinella" (a Shaw composition) and "Danza Lucumi." But the masterpiece of the session was "Star Dust," in a completely new arrangement from that used with the 1938–39 band, with breathtakingly superb solos from all concerned. "Star Dust" turned out to be another multimillion-selling record for Shaw, whose solo has attained classic status. It is therefore of special interest that Shaw performed it a week later on the *Burns and Allen Show* as well, with significantly different solo statements.

Although the orchestra was broadcasting regularly from both the Palace Hotel and on the *Burns and Allen Show*, few air checks had surfaced until the Hep CDs emerged. These performances reveal the band in excellent form and offer new versions of several hit tunes Shaw had recorded, including many from the 1938–39 book rearranged to include the string section; tunes he would record with this new orchestra later (including several future hits, sometimes recorded for Victor within the week of the broadcast and showing remarkable variations in solos, as with "Star Dust"); tunes he would record with his next band (the 1941–42 orchestra); and in a few cases tunes he never recorded commercially

and that are not available from other known broadcasts. Also, an air check from the Palace Hotel dated October 26, 1940, revealed the band in good form for two Anita Boyer vocals that were never commercially recorded, and a rousing version of "Everything Is Jumpin' " from the 1939 band's book, rearranged for the enlarged orchestra (see discography).

Presumably, other broadcasts may eventually surface and appear on collectors' label recordings as well. However, the October 1, 1940, *Down Beat* noted on page 5, "Artie Shaw Loses Frisco Air Time." The article stated that the orchestra had lost its radio wire from the Palace Hotel because Shaw was not using any BMI (Broadcast Music, Inc.) tunes on the air.

BMI was a royalty collection agency set up by the networks to combat requests for higher royalties from ASCAP (American Society of Composers, Authors and Publishers), with whom most performers and songwriters were affiliated. For a while in this period, BMI even tried to forbid improvisation on the air, to ensure no ASCAP tunes were quoted by improvising soloists.

Shaw faced another problem in connection with royalties. When his record of "Frenesi" began to take off as a major hit in this period, the composer, Alberto Dominguez, turned up. This was quite a surprise to Shaw, who had thought it was a Mexican folk tune when he had heard a mariachi band performing it there. In *The New Yorker* "Profile," Shaw was quoted as stating:

> That little error cost me approximately a half million dollars. Under the usual system, I could have made a deal with the composer for 50% of the take in return for recording the tune. As it was, he got the money. (11)

Evidently, despite the BMI confrontations, the band continued to broadcast. A review of the orchestra's November 15, 1940, broadcast from the Palace Hotel appeared in the December 1940 *Metronome* on page 10, and mentioned the band's repertoire as consisting of Shaw's "Prelude in C Major," Anita Boyer singing "A Million Dreams Ago," the Gramercy 5 doing "Dr. Livingstone, I Presume?" and versions of "Frenesi" and "Diga Diga Doo," the latter being referred to as the best all-around number. This issue also had Shaw and the orchestra on the cover, and featured pictures of the orchestra and Gramercy 5 inside as well.

Jerry Jerome had some interesting reminiscences quoted in the liner notes to RCA AXM2-5572:

> I have very distinct memories of the Palace Hotel and San Francisco. We played one of the big rooms for dancing at the hotel. It might have been the Rose Room. Every night we rehearsed after we finished working. And it was just incredible the number of rats that ran around in the canopy over the band. The place was infested with them; the whole town was.

One night, I went up to the dressing room to change a reed on my horn. I put one foot up on a chair to get the reed out of the mouthpiece. I felt something heavy on my stationary foot. It turned out a rat was in my pants cuff. . . . Rats aside, San Francisco was a great city for musicians. A lot of local players came to hear the band. I must say Artie and our guys drew well because the performances were often extraordinary.

Band members all seemed to speak highly of the musical quality of the Palace Hotel engagement, which lasted until the orchestra went into the Hollywood Palladium on December 12, 1940.

A little over a week before their Palladium opening, there was a series of recording sessions, which preserved some of their best material. On the 3rd, recording for Victor, they again included two vocals by Anita Boyer, one of them another Shaw original, "Whispers in the Night." The three instrumentals also recorded that day ("This Is Romance," "What Is There to Say?" and the Duke Ellington—Juan Tizol composition "Pyramid") were all of high quality; an equally good alternate take of "What Is There to Say?" eventually also appeared, in the Bluebird *The Complete Artie Shaw* series. On the 4th, they recorded the "Blues" number from William Grant Still's "Lenox Avenue Suite" in two parts, taking up both sides of the 78-rpm release, plus two superb new Shaw compositions, both of which have since appeared in alternate takes as well: "Who's Excited?" and "Prelude in C Major" (which was cocomposed with Ray Conniff). On the 5th, the Gramercy 5 recorded four more titles, again two originals (including "Dr. Livingstone, I Presume?") and two pop tunes. The other new Shaw composition was "When the Quail Come Back to San Quentin," which had an interesting and humorous theme, including abrupt transitions and punctuations. The pop tunes were a swinging "My Blue Heaven" and a sedate, romantic version of "Smoke Gets in Your Eyes." Oddly, the RCA log sheets show the entire December 3rd session being rerecorded on the 5th as well, but without mentioning personnel or studio time. It is probable this was not a remaking session, involving new versions, but rather a dubbing session, involving transferring the original recordings (see discography).

Some confusion exists over the source and date of a Gramercy 5 performance preserved from a broadcast, "No Name Blues" (with the same personnel). It has been variously dated as from a *Tommy Dorsey Show* broadcast on March 9, 1940, which is unlikely as the group would not have been formed yet; September 3, the same day as the Victor recording session; and September 9, which is somewhat more likely as the *Burns and Allen Show* was broadcasting on Monday nights. However, Shaw was with Burns and Allen until March 24, 1941, and the Gramercy 5 was in any case featured on many broadcasts from their Palace Hotel and Hollywood Palladium ballroom locations during

1940–41. A blurb in the media mentioned the group appearing on the *Burns and Allen Show* as if it was a unique event, early in 1941; but it is not certain that this performance was from one of the unissued *Burns and Allen Show* broadcasts. Whether broadcast around the time of the group's first session, between their first and second date, or later that winter, "No Name Blues" was the most spirited of the eleven known performances by that edition of the Gramercy 5. Another Shaw original, it followed much the same shape and development as "Special Delivery Stomp" and "Summit Ridge Drive" (which was, as noted, also a blues), and was midway between the two in tempo. Shaw's two solos are among his best work, and Guarnieri, DeNaut, Butterfield, and Hendrickson soloed in that order between his offerings. Unfortunately, circulating versions suffer from a clipped ending, and one might wish for a cleaner recording.

Down Beat reported on page 9 of its January 1, 1941, issue, "Shaw's Palladium Opening One of Poorest in History." Estimates of the size of the audience in the huge ballroom were as low as 1500, despite outdoor publicity and newspaper ads for the event. Speculations for explaining the poor turnout included that a huge Christmas party the night before had pulled the punch out of the Shaw opening, and that "Shaw's well known indifference to the press" had cost him publicity. The Hollywood Palladium's management reportedly were happy with the business that night, however.

The orchestra's only record date during their six weeks at the Palladium occurred on December 23rd, when they recorded two relatively uninteresting vocals by Anita Boyer and the extended version of "Concerto for Clarinet." This performance was Shaw's first twelve-inch 78-rpm record, and occupied both sides for a total playing time of nine minutes and eighteen seconds, triple the length of the average 78-rpm record. Although Shaw shrugs it off as "just something scribbled out to fill a spot in *Second Chorus*" (2), it holds together well as a virtuoso display piece. It was published with Shaw's solos transcribed, and performed in schools and by other bands from time to time. Some of the cadenza passages had appeared before, and would again, just as the Russian Jewish folk tune cadenza done "frahlich" style at the end of "Dr. Livingstone, I Presume?" had also been heard earlier, but their effectiveness cannot be denied. The pieces were compositions, after all, and not everything has to be spontaneous improvisation in a solo. Most improvising performers tend to work out effective passages to be used as needed or as the idea to do so occurs.

Band members recalled Lana being involved in their Christmas festivities. Shaw and Lana had remained friends, and he related in *Lana* that he returned to his house one night to find that Lana had decorated it with a tree and presents. She jumped out of hiding giggling "Merry Christmas" and stayed over. Shaw said, "I liked Lana. She wasn't a malicious person." But rumors of a reconciliation did not prove true ([13], pp. 49–50).

Shaw had been broadcasting from the Palladium on NBC. However, programming disagreements again developed, and *Down Beat* had an article on page 3 of its January 15, 1941, issue headlined "I'll Play What I Want or Nothing at all—Artie Shaw." The orchestra continued to broadcast over local station KFWB after NBC canceled. Air checks from the last two nights of the orchestra's engagement at the Palladium have surfaced, but only three titles from the January 21, 1941, broadcast have become available, two of them slightly flawed. "Do You Know Why?" had an attractive Anita Boyer vocal but a clipped ending in available dubs. The Gramercy 5 performance of "Cross Your Heart" began, on available dubs, at a point over halfway through the first chorus, but the rest of the performance was vital and exciting, with extra solo space relative to the version recorded for Victor. Only "Alice Blue Gown" was complete on available dubs, and is at least as good a version as the only other known Shaw performance of the tune, from a *Burns and Allen Show* of the preceding summer.

The orchestra's closing night broadcast from the Palladium, January 22, 1941, is of particular interest. It was a historic occasion: the *Burns and Allen Show* was being transferred to New York, so the Palladium closing marked the end of the orchestra's West Coast engagements. Virtually the complete broadcast was issued on a Hep LP in the 1970s (reissued on CD; see discography), including a Gramercy 5 item ("Dr. Livingstone, I Presume?") and announcements. This displays the band "live," with the usual extra edge of excitement that live performances characteristically generate, and its performances in context.

The next day, January 23, 1941, the orchestra recorded four lush, romantic popular standards as instrumentals. These were all successful performances and have remained identified with this band. One of them, "Dancing in the Dark," became another of Shaw's million-selling hits in that era.

Announcements in the trade press indicated that Shaw would then be taking the orchestra on a theater tour, and several bookings were announced. However, further announcements indicated that the tour was cancelled so that the band could remain with the *Burns and Allen Show* in New York. (Nevertheless, on their February 10, 1941, show, Gracie mentions being in Chicago the previous week.) Some of Shaw's musicians elected to remain on the West Coast, but several key men remained with the orchestra. One of the replacements was Lee Castle, who had played trumpet with Shaw's original 1936–37 "Swing String" band.

The orchestra had one more Victor record date, in New York City on March 20, 1941, again performing four instrumentals of popular standards with Shaw in wonderful form. Their final appearance on the *Burns and Allen Show* was on March 24, 1941, and the orchestra's final number was "To a Broadway Rose" (which Shaw would record for Victor with his next orchestra). Shaw then broke up this orchestra, but remained in New York City. He had become dissatisfied with the Hollywood life-style and often complained of the insincerity of people who acted like friends but were just out for whatever they could get from him.

The orchestra had existed about ten months, from first rehearsals to disbanding. They had recorded twenty-eight titles for RCA Victor, and the Gramercy 5 made eight more. This band's documentation also includes their brief but effective spots in the movie *Second Chorus*; the few location broadcasts that have surfaced, including a few numbers by the Gramercy 5; and the thirty-three performances from the *Burns and Allen Show* issued on the Hep CDs. This accounting clearly illustrates the value of the surfacing of these *Burns and Allen Show* performances toward defining the legacy of this orchestra, which had several multimillion-selling hit records: many of their records are among Shaw's best known work, such as "Star Dust" and "Dancing in the Dark," among others.

The impact of Shaw's using the large string section also was considerable. It was not long before many of the big name popular swing bands included similar string sections, as a result of Shaw's popular success with this instrumentation, and a decade later, when Charlie Parker fulfilled his ambition to record with strings, the results seemed an updated version of what Shaw had begun with his various string groups, of which this orchestra made the greatest impression.

Chapter 9

Artie Shaw and His Orchestra: 1941–1942

Following his disbanding of his 1940–41 orchestra, Shaw again became the subject of speculation. The April 1, 1941, *Down Beat* headlined on page 2, "Shaw 'Retires,' Will Hunt 'Native' Music," and stated:

> Artie's plans are indefinite. He wants to remain in New York for a few weeks at least, browsing around and taking it easy, and then he hopes to return either to Mexico . . . or possibly Louisiana, where he feels he can unearth native American and Latin music. . . .
>
> Shaw says he is through with one-nighters, theaters, hotel and nitery location jobs, and any other work which cramps his independence. Radio and recording remain his chief interests, for through these mediums he can reach larger audiences and at the same time, not have to "punch a time clock" every night.

Shaw was quoted in the July 1941 issue of *Music & Rhythm* as stating,

> I'm happy, I think, for the first time in my life. I'm doing what I want to do exactly the way I want to do it. (pp. 6–7)

This article went on to state:

> Artie now spends most all his time at his bachelor apartment on New York's Central Park West reading current literature, playing symphonic and Ellington records, and most of all, arranging original music for performance on record dates.
>
> Shaw is one of the most maligned musicians who has ever played a one-nighter. His intelligence is a handicap in a business which has no respect for brains. Equipped with mental facilities which few of his colleagues can match, Artie was slapped in the face a little over a year ago with the most vicious "press" any dance band leader has ever gotten. . . .
>
> Many a novelist spends time in Shaw's apartment discussing current affairs, music, or philosophy. Artie does most of his work in the daytime, reserving his dinner hour for friends. After dinner he often stays home, entertaining.
>
> . . . One of his biggest ambitions is to see the music business cleaned up—more music, better music, more talented musicians, and less stress on money gains. Artie himself is

less concerned with accumulating a fortune than he is in arranging a two-bar voicing for four fiddles. He's making enough money, chiefly from records, to live nicely and have the things he wants. . . .

> "What is Shaw going to do?" That's the question everyone seems to be asking. The answer is this:
>
> "He's doing it, and has been for several months."
>
> Living his own life, playing the music he likes arranged as he likes it, with the musicians he admires most—that's Artie's answer.

As noted, this also was the period Shaw tried to organize the top bandleaders of the day to form a cooperative booking agency, as referred to obliquely in the above article's reference to cleaning up the music business. The article closed with a summary of Shaw's musical goals:

> Time will tell if Shaw, with his idealistic outlook, makes his mark in American music. American music—native music—is all he is interested in. His recent record of William Grant Still's "The Blues" typifies what he considers to be the real American music—a music which will live. Artie Shaw wants to popularize that music. He wants Negro composers and musicians to realize something for their efforts. Artie Shaw is an unusual personality with unusual ideas.

Some of the arrangements Shaw was working on included experimental scores for settings of children's folktales, including "The Pied Piper of Hamelin" and "The Emperor and the Nightingale." The former eventually was recorded for Musicraft in 1946, following a successful radio broadcast of an edited version of the original score, but Shaw never performed "The Emperor and the Nightingale." Shaw stated in private discussions,

> I was studying composition and arranging with Hans Byrns and David Diamond in that period, around the spring of 1941, and just did these settings as an exercise. I've never even heard "The Emperor and the Nightingale" but I'm considering having both pieces recorded in the near future for a CD release. It'd be interesting to hear the full versions. (2)

Some of the other arrangements Shaw was working on were recorded in June 1941. The June 1, 1941, *Down Beat* had an article on page 1 titled "Shaw Using Mixed Band On Records." The band was mixed in two senses. The rhythm section and the other horn men aside from Shaw were among the top black musicians in New York at the time. Aside from the racial mix, Shaw was again mixing the small jazz band sounds with the textures of a string section. He was quoted in the liner notes to RCA AXM2-5576 on his conceptions for this session:

I'd been doing a lot of studying with a guy by the name of Hans Byrns, who had been with the Berlin Opera (Orchestra). I was interested in a certain set of notions, having to do with composition, that he had developed. And I wanted to see how they would work out.

The charts were very carefully done. Perhaps I was too careful. What resulted represents something I was trying to hear. I wanted to ascertain what the contrast would be between essentially improvised sounds made by the jazzmen, reflecting blackness and primitivism of a sort, and the characteristically European strings.

The little venture was a success, up to a certain point. Not all the performances were top-level. The first take of "Beyond the Blue Horizon" was rejected back then . . . I wasn't crazy about every one of the tunes. "Love Me a Little Little" still sounds silly to me. But we were under great pressure to record pop things.

Shaw's sidemen included Henry "Red" Allen on trumpet and trombonist J. C. Higginbotham. These acclaimed masters had been appearing together on 52nd Street for some time in that period. Benny Carter was brought in on alto sax. Carter had been leading another in his excellent series of big bands that spring. Pianist Sonny White and drummer Beresford "Shep" Shepherd had been working with Carter that season. Guitarist Jimmy Shirley had been appearing on 52nd Street regularly with the Clarence Prophet Trio. Lena Horne, who had sung with Charlie Barnet's band, was the vocalist. She was very young at the time and sounded a little stiff, but nevertheless only her vocals from this record date were released on 78-rpm records. The large string section on this date also seemed unyieldingly stiff and kept the session earthbound despite the obviously high potential of the horns and rhythm section. Undoubtedly this was due to their being a studio-assembled group as opposed to a working unit having long experience with the conception and material. "Beyond the Blue Horizon" was remade later that summer with Shaw's then-working group with better results.

Less than two months later Shaw was rehearsing another large orchestra with strings, and preparing to go on the road. He had resisted pressure from his agents and even temporarily "retired" again for rest and study, but much of his earn-

ings had gone for taxes. In *The Trouble with Cinderella*, Shaw wrote of this venture,

By the time several more months had passed, I saw I was going to have to get hold of some money somewhere. In the end, despite my determination never to go out on tour with a band again, I had to do just that. ([1], p. 358)

Newsweek wrote up the new endeavor in its September 8, 1941, issue on page 74, headlined "Shaw's Swing Symphony":

Beneath the strains of wailing rhythm surging from a window at the corner of Broadway and 51st Street in New York City during the last fortnight, the voice of a young man, standing before a 31-man band, could be heard muttering "Smack it!" The young man was Artie Shaw; the orchestra, the new outfit he was readying for his first barnstorming tour of the country in two years. . . .

Now, at 31, Shaw has reorganized and expanded his band to include 15 strings, 7 trombones and trumpets, 5 saxophones and 4 rhythm instruments. It boasts 5 ex–band leaders, including Hot Lips Page, a featured trumpeter and the only dusky member of the outfit, and Jack Jenney, a trombonist, whose wife, Bonnie Lake, is the band's vocalist.

Dave Dexter wrote an extensive preview of the band for *Down Beat* as well. The September 1, 1941, issue headlined on page 1, " '$1,000,000 Talent' in Shaw Band." Noting that rehearsals had begun on August 15th, Dexter went on to describe the enthusiasm with which Shaw's sidemen responded to his offers. Many had left other bands to join his, and two men, Oran "Hot Lips" Page and Ray Conniff, had been leading their own bands and had abandoned them to join Shaw. Dexter wrote,

When Artie asks for something, he gets it. The guys who blow the horns like his way of doing things, his musicianship, and his ideas. Watching him rehearse is a revelation. Shaw gets discipline without ever asking for it; without flashing a "deathray" at his sidemen.

Artie will put much "new American music" in his books, including jazz arrangements of the blues and compositions by known and unknown American songwriters . . . music by Ellington, Handy, William Grant Still and other colored composers as well as the better music from the pens of Kern, Gershwin, Vernon Duke, Rodgers and Hart, De Rose and other top-notch writers will be emphasized.

Shaw was also quoted in the article, stating:

We hope it will be the finest outfit yet. The job ahead of us is tough and is going to take a hell of a lot of work on the part of every man, but I think we'll have something a little out of the ordinary to offer. The band is shaping up wonderfully so far.

Down Beat also published an article by George Frazier discussing and reviewing the new orchestra. Astonishingly, Frazier noted that he found it easy to compare the new band with Paul Whiteman's symphonic jazz of the 1920s, except that Shaw had updated things and had "assembled some of the most glowing talents in the profession and molded them into something, if not unique, at least immensely satisfying." Frazier also noted that Dave Tough's drumming had "enormous competence, impeccable taste, and one of the most miraculous beats in jazz," crediting Tough with providing the one major difference between Shaw and Paul Whiteman! He also found that the strings "blend well with the rest of the band and occasionally achieve something approaching loveliness."

The band was reported opening in Boston, but it also was reported to be beginning its tour with a one-nighter at Hampton Beach Casino in New Hampshire on August 29th. They also played Kimball's Starlight Ballroom in Lynnfield, Massachusetts, before returning to New York to make some records on September 2nd and 3rd, 1941.

On September 2nd, the full orchestra recorded six titles. One of these, "This Time the Dream's on Me," featured a vocal by Bonnie Lake, who unfortunately sounds a bit uncertain. The superb "Blues in the Night" was a feature for Hot Lips Page's dynamic singing and trumpet. Both of these titles were recorded in two takes, and the unissued takes circulate among collectors, the earliest instances of unissued takes from Shaw's Victor record sessions having become available. The four instrumentals also recorded that day are all superb: Thomas Griselle's "Nocturne," with its somberly lovely textures; Hoagy Carmichael's "Rockin' Chair"; a mesmerizing version of Vincent Youmans's "Through the Years"; and a fine, swinging version of the pop tune "If I Love Again."

Several other examples of unissued material by this band are in circulation, as noted in the discography. Generally, the unissued alternates are as substantial as the originally issued masters, with obvious variations in solo passages. This was especially apparent in Shaw's solo work, to the extent of providing more than obvious proof that Shaw created fresh solos almost constantly. However, on both "This Time the Dream's on Me" and "Blues in the Night" the unissued alternates reveal the overall performance sounding a bit less concentratedly inspired than the issued versions, as if they were warm-up takes. Four of the band's most substantial instrumental pieces completed the date, all apparently recorded in one take each, according to information from the RCA recording session log sheets. The somberly lovely "Nocturne" stood out as particularly distinctive.

The next day's recording session was with the small group and strings. For this date Shaw added Georgie Auld's tenor sax to the instrumentation used the preceding June, to provide richer sonorities. They recorded the remake of "Beyond the Blue Horizon" and two new Shaw arrangements, "Is It Taboo?" (in two takes, with the unissued alternate again in circulation) and the Shaw original, "I Ask the Stars." In the liner notes to AXM2-5576, Shaw referred to this session as producing

the best of the small-band-with-strings records. . . . All the charts are mine. The standout was our treatment of the pop tune of the day, "Is It Taboo?" It came closest to fulfilling my intentions, to achieving the level of excellence we constantly seek in our performances. The musicians on the date were from my 32-piece band, formed in August. Lee Castle, Ray Conniff, Les Robinson, Georgie Auld and I, in various combinations, formed the front line.

Shaw has also spoken with pride of his introduction to "Is It Taboo?" Although some reviewers had written disparagingly of Georgie Auld's work during this period, he performed in his best rhapsodic style and sounded fully involved and wholly appropriate, although his solos on the alternate takes show fewer imaginative variations than Shaw's.

On September 5th they played the Empire Ballroom in Allentown, Pennsylvania, and on the 6th the Steel Pier at Atlantic City, New Jersey, where a broadcast originated that has surfaced to supply the first evidence of the band's "live" flavor. It is fascinating to hear "Nightmare" with strings, recalling that Shaw originally had done it for his first string group, and to hear this orchestra do hits associated with the previous year's material ("Frenesi" and "Dancing in the Dark"), balancing the material the earlier band had done for the *Burns and Allen Show*, which usually is associated with this orchestra. But the outstanding revelation was the long swinging version of "There'll Be Some Changes Made," displaying the orchestra and soloists in excellent form.

Down Beat published "Artie Shaw's Itinerary for Next 2 Weeks" (September 15, 1941, p. 15):

The young man with a stick who once told off America's jitterbugs is now watching them pay cash money to see and hear his new band. Maybe no other leader could have gotten away with it, but Artie Shaw appears to be stronger at the box-office now than at any other time in his stormy career.

The SRO sign has been hung up on almost every date Shaw and his men have played since he started out 2 weeks ago in Boston.

The itinerary for Shaw's appearances following the Steel Pier was then listed as follows:

September 8th: Reading Fair, Reading, Pennsylvania
10th: Sunset Ballroom, Carroltown, Pennsylvania
11th: Brookline Country Club, Brookline, Pennsylvania

12th: Sports Arena, Rochester, New York
13th: Hershey Park, Hershey, Pennsylvania
14th: Ritz Ballroom, Bridgeport, Connecticut
17th: Foreman Field, Norfolk, Virginia
18th: Riverside Stadium, Washington, D.C.
19th: Auditorium, Roanoke, Virginia
20th: Auditorium, Charleston, West Virginia
21st: Yankee Lake, Brookfield, Ohio
22nd: London Arena, London, Ontario
23rd: Mutual Arena, Toronto, Ontario
24th: Auditorium, Ottawa, Ontario
25th: Forum, Montreal, Quebec
26th: (open)
27th: Waldemeer Park, Erie, Pennsylvania

The September 22, 1941, *Time* noted on page 32, "Artie Shaw on Tour," with a picture of Shaw and Page captioned "The boss is colorblind." This was a reference to Shaw having canceled a tour of the South and Southwest rather than put up with Southern hospitality:

In Eastern cities and towns last week, jitterbugs by the thousand laid their dollars on the line to hear a new dance band. The band belonged to dark, dapper, moody Clarinetist Artie Shaw, who 2 years ago pronounced his jitterbug followers morons, declared that the music business stinks, and, consigning the whole shebang to hell, left his band, got out of his contracts, went off to Mexico.

In the past year and a half, Clarinetist Shaw has gone through his 3rd marriage and divorce (to & from Cinemactress Lana Turner) and returned to music. Impatient, inquisitive, he brooded over the idea of a big band with which he could play concert jazz. . . .

Sadder but sweeter, Artie Shaw last week soft-talked the jitterbugs, dispensed autographs like grace notes. . . . Nevertheless Leader Shaw last week cancelled 32 such golden dates in the South and Southwest, where he has never played. Reason: he was asked to shelve Negro Paige [*sic*] during that part of his tour. The South can take all-Negro bands . . . against a Negro in a large white band it tends to draw the color line. But Artie Shaw, like most musicians, is colorblind.

The band quickly achieved another full schedule of bookings for October. They began the month with a week at the Palace Theatre in Cleveland, Ohio. After this, their published itinerary was:

October 10th: Trianon Ballroom, Toledo, Ohio
          11th: Castle Farm, Cincinnati, Ohio
          12th: Rink, Waukegan, Illinois
          15th: Park Ballroom, Collinsville, Illinois
          16th: Auditorium, Joplin, Missouri
          17th: Coliseum, Tulsa, Oklahoma
          18th: Auditorium, Oklahoma City
          21st: Auditorium, Topeka, Kansas
          22nd: Shrine Mosque, Springfield, Missouri

23rd: Playmor, Kansas City
24th: Turnpike Casino, Lincoln, Nebraska
25th: Party, Omaha, Nebraska
26th: Tromar Ballroom, Des Moines, Iowa
29th: Surf, Clear Lake, Iowa
30th: Victor session, Chicago
31st: Chicago Theatre, Chicago

Shaw had begun his tour with Dave Hudkins again functioning as his road manager. However, Hudkins was replaced by Mike Ventrano, who was also shortly replaced by Shaw's old boss, Austin Wylie. In this interval, Bonnie Lake was replaced by vocalist Paula Kelly. The Cerney Twins were accompanying the band on its theater tour as one of the acts.

On October 18th, in Oklahoma City, Shaw unveiled a small group out of the band. According to *Billboard*, the group was announced as the "Swing 8" and consisted of Shaw, Page, Jenney, and Auld plus the rhythm section. They were reported to have performed a twenty-minute piece that had the crowd on its feet. Max Kaminsky recalled touring with the band in his autobiography:

Artie was bigger than ever. People followed his bus and swarmed in to collect autographs whenever it stopped. . . . We were all paid wonderful salaries for those days, in fact, my kingly $175 a week was the most money I had ever made up to then. ([5], p. 125)

Billboard provided an illuminating review (despite the limitations of the reviewer in appreciating Shaw's string section) of the orchestra from its opening at the Chicago Theatre on October 31, 1941:

Chicago Theatre, Chicago (reviewed Friday Afternoon, October 31).
The unpredictable Artie Shaw made his local debut with a 32-piece band, including a 15-piece string section that does little to justify its presence. Shaw can more than get by with 16 men (seven brass, five sax and four rhythm) who can compete with the better swing outfits and probably come out on top. The "Symphonic Swing" section is dead timber here and only a financial burden to the theatre. As far as the box office is concerned, Shaw is still the draw, and the strings are of little added value. Nor does the section fit into the proceedings.

The band's standard instrumentation carries the load, opening with "Temptation" (introducing the leader's hot clarinet), and following with "Stardust" [*sic*] in which Oran (Hot Lips) Page rides off a torrid chorus on his highly trained trumpet. A spiritual, "Nobody Knows the Trouble I've Seen" further emphasizes the versatility of the band. Paula Kelly, cute songstress, was not too strong vocally at the opening show with "I Don't Want to Set the World on Fire" and "Time Was."
In "Begin the Beguine" Shaw makes further progress on

his clarinet climaxing his talents on that instrument. In the finale he scores with his "Hot Concerto." Preceding the wind-up is the engaging work of "Hot Lips" Page, who sings and plays the horn with equal gusto. Rolled off such Harlemites as "Saint James Inferno" [*sic*], "Happy Feet" and "Blues in the Night," and the mob wanted more.

While his boys looked too crowded on the bandstand and their suits could certainly stand a good pressing, Shaw made a neat appearance and his introductions were polite and brief.

Two outside acts strengthen the bill—Bobby Lane and Edna Ward, and Billy Rayes.

Lane and Ward are a refreshing acro pair, presenting a couple of novel routines that feature Bobby in some fine tricks. Their work is fast, clean, and different.

Billy Rayes is a good comedy juggler, depending on the delivery of his patter (which in itself is pretty good) and his juggling impressions of noted movie players for laughs. His dramatic Charles Boyer is not as important to the act as it used to be when few impersonators did Boyer. He should give it less of a play. His dancing and juggling exit still nets a couple of bows and an extra bit.

On screen, Warner's *Navy Blues*, pic is not as good as it should be. Business was big at the end of the first show.

The day before, at their first record date since beginning to tour, the band had recorded two pleasant vocals (Hot Lips Page's rendition of "Take Your Shoes Off Baby" and Paula Kelly singing "Make Love to Me") and two outstanding jazz instrumentals (Fred Norman's "Solid Sam" and Ray Conniff's "Just Kiddin' Around") featuring strong solos and interesting, sophisticated arrangements. On their next record date two weeks later, the focus was on swinging jazzy numbers, with the only vocal being Page's superb work on side "A" of the double-sided "St. James Infirmary." Ray Conniff's "To a Broadway Rose" and Marjorie Gibson's "Deuces Wild" also were excellent, and along with the orchestra's earlier sessions offered ample documented evidence that the Chicago Theatre reviewer's evaluation of the string section's effectiveness was a clear case of missing the point. The circulating unissued alternates from these sessions again offer clear evidence that the band's work was consistently at a high level, and of the usual particularly varied soloing from Shaw.

The band continued with its theater engagements. They were at the Earle Theatre in Philadelphia the week of November 14th, at the State in Hartford, Connecticut, the following week, and at the Metropolitan in Providence, Rhode Island, the week after that. Their last night at the Metropolitan was December 7, 1941. The management interrupted the show to have Shaw make the announcement that all service personnel should report to their bases immediately. The Japanese had just bombed Pearl Harbor.

Shaw has stated that he felt foolish leading a band and playing the same music once the country was in the war. He immediately put the band on notice and fulfilled a few more weeks of bookings before disbanding after their final Victor session. This took about six weeks. Their next engagement was the Loew's State Theatre in New York. Their opening was broadcast on the *Coca-Cola Show*, and the part of the broadcast air check that circulates among collectors indicated the band was in fine form. A *Billboard* review from the engagement is revealing:

Artie Shaw menage moved in here this week with Bob Du-Pont and the Colstons, two acts that have been making Shaw's theatre dates with him. Ork naturally takes up major portion of the full hour show, but the acts proved to have the most lift for this audience at show caught.

Band suffered from lack of real showmanship, part of which could be blamed on the theatre management itself. Piano and music stands were all draped with heavy, brass-colored material which had no eye appeal whatsoever. And Shaw is no sparkling personality on the stage. Despite these handicaps, however, band is crammed with top musicianship and this includes Shaw, too, who has that clarinet under perfect control.

Shaw's big crew is set up with 15 strings, seven brass, five reed and four rhythm. Library played included Shaw faves such as "Temptation," "Star Dust," "Begin the Beguine," and his original "Concerto for Clarinet." Arrangements and ork's execution were commercial and good. To highlight the string section, Shaw played another original tagged "Suite No. 8," a blending of concert style with syncopating swing from the brass and reeds.

Besides Shaw's own clary soloing, sliphorn artist Jack Jenney, Georgie Auld's tenor sax, and Hot Lips Page's trumpet are all heard as specialties. Ork's vocalist Paula Kelly warbles "Time Was," "I Said No," and "I Don't Want to Set the World on Fire." Gal's appearance and salesmanship make up for her lack of voice. The instrumental solo work by the Jenney–Auld–Page combo was all to the good, and went over here. Shaw's name and the preponderance of 32 men on stage seemed to hold the audience in awe. They heard good music.

Bob DuPont did his standard top job of manipulating the balls, Indian clubs and tambourines. Closed with his apple-eating routine while juggling a plate and napkin, and had the audience pleading for more.

The Colstons stopped things cold with their satirical dances. Polished off three numbers a la ballroom, tango, and hot style. Then had to come back for a speech and some more foolery. A top act for any spot.

Crowd was thin at late afternoon show first day. Pic was second Broadway run of MGM's *Shadow of the Thin Man*.

The orchestra's next recording session on December 23rd produced two pop-tune features for vocalist Paula Kelly and two outstanding extended instrumentals, both in the later-so-called Third Stream direction Shaw had been pioneering. These latter recordings were "Suite #8" and "Evensong," both composed and arranged by Paul Jordan, and were issued together, occupying one side each of a twelve-inch 78-rpm disc. "Evensong" returns to the moody depths evidenced in the earlier "Nocturne," while "Suite #8" uniquely begins with just the strings, in a classical approach, and then builds to a sudden transition into hot, jazzy big-band swing with exciting solos. These performances stand among this band's, and Shaw's, best work. As mood pieces or tone poems, as well as distinctive foreshadowings of the Third Stream approach, they are among the most evocative and interesting records of the era. It is therefore particularly welcome that an unissued take of "Evensong" (originally listed on the RCA log sheets as being titled "Dusk") circulates to reveal an equally intense and gorgeous rendition, the relatively minor differences providing an intriguing if subtle contrast to the issued performance.

At the orchestra's final pair of record sessions in January 1942, they recorded three relatively routine vocals by Fredda Gibson (later known as Georgia Gibbs), another feature number for Hot Lips Page's singing and trumpet ("Sometimes I Feel Like a Motherless Child"), and four dynamic, jazzy instrumentals that again exhibited that side of the band's work spectacularly well: a Paul Jordan arrangement of the popular "Hindustan," plus two titles he composed and arranged for the band ("Carnival" and "Two in One Blues"), and another excellent Ray Conniff composition, "Needlenose."

Immediately following these record dates, Shaw disbanded. The orchestra had lasted just over six months but probably would have continued indefinitely if the war had not come along, as Shaw mentioned in *Artie Shaw: Time Is All You've Got*. Their legacy consisted of twenty-eight titles recorded for Victor, several excellent unissued alternate takes in circulation among collectors, and the few air checks that have surfaced (see discography). Unfortunately, the Swing 8 was not featured on any of the air checks located so far. The string section lived on, hired intact by Tommy Dorsey.

The opening months of 1942 were uncertain and confusing for everyone. The war effort was suddenly all-consuming. Shortly after Shaw broke up his orchestra, *Down Beat* announced on page 1 of the February 1, 1942, issue, "Shaw in Hospital; May Be Drafted When He Leaves." He was reported entering Roosevelt Hospital in New York City for "an operation." The February 15, 1942, issue of *Down Beat* reported on page 1 that his contract had been purchased from GAC by the William Morris Agency, and that he would be forming a new band in March.

The March 1, 1942, *Down Beat* asked on page 1, "Shaw Set To Resume This Week?" The article noted that he had been resting in Hollywood for the past month on doctors' orders, and stated,

> That Artie can return, reorganize and start out again without springing something entirely new—either in personnel or orchestration—is considered impossible.

However, on March 3, 1942, Shaw married Elizabeth Kern, daughter of composer Jerome Kern, in Yuma, Arizona, and afterward brought her back to New York City to "a palatial apartment he maintained on Central Park South" (11). He then took out a conventional big band (without strings) organized for him by Lee Castle for a few weeks, "to raise money for the bride" (11).

This band, which featured vocalist Terry Leonard, opened its tour at the Capitol Theatre in Washington, D.C. Exact personnel was not published, and although this band reportedly did broadcast, no air checks are known, and they never recorded. They finished their tour in Detroit, where Shaw "made one of the few sentimental speeches of his life. From the stage, he said goodbye to the band and to the audience, and spoke feelingly about the war" (11).

Shaw's draft status also was a subject of speculation, and *Down Beat* reported that he would be training bands for the USO (April 15, 1942, p. 1). However, a few days after closing his theater tour, "the new Mrs. Shaw drove her husband to 90 Church Street in a Lincoln convertible" (11), and at 10 a.m. on April 28, 1942, he enlisted in the U.S. Navy.

> Shaw's first duty ship was a ferry, which took him to a minesweeper docked at Staten Island. When the minesweeper put to sea, Shaw, safely removed from land-based snarls (and from the sound of music), felt a blessed sense of peace. The galley was good, the men were congenial, and he liked the work. Unqualifiedly happy for perhaps the first time in his life, he returned to shore, only to learn that he had been made a chief petty officer and was being sent to Newport to form a band. Taking his bride along to his new station and establishing her in a cottage that rented for more than twice the amount of his Navy pay, he proceeded to look over his musical personnel. (11)

There, Shaw found that the quality of the musicianship in the Navy band he was expected to train was giving him severe migraines. With his characteristic directness, he discarded his uniform, put on his civvies, and went AWOL to visit James Forrestal, who was then the undersecretary of the Navy, to complain. He stated, "I want to get into the war, and if I have to run a band, I want it to be good!" (11). Forrestal sent him back with permission to recruit a band of top musicians for a special tour of the Pacific Theater.

Chapter 10

The Rangers; Navy Band 501: 1942–1944

In *The New Yorker* "Profile," Shaw's recruitment technique was described as:

> "They'll get you in this war anyhow," he would say, "and they'll put you to doing something else. When it's over, you won't be able to play. Your lip will be gone." And he would look hard at his victim. (11)

Actually, Shaw reported in private discussion that he had had no problem getting the men he wanted: they were eager to participate, and Claude Thornhill practically begged to be part of it (2).

Max Kaminsky wrote a long chapter in his autobiography on Shaw's Navy band, nicknamed The Rangers. Extensive accounts of the band's experiences were published by *Down Beat* and *Metronome* upon its return. The latter named Shaw "Musician of the Year" for 1943, for his contribution to the war effort. When regarded in historical context, the "Amazing Saga of Shaw Band" (as *Down Beat* headlined its account) still seems remarkable. It probably was the most important tour Shaw or any of his bands ever did, considering the work they were doing.

Kaminsky's accounts of his and Dave Tough's inductions were hilarious. Neither of them being acceptable physical specimens, the Navy doctors tried to send them home at their physicals. To get these holdovers from his 1941–42 orchestra into the Navy, Shaw had to provide Kaminsky with a letter for the Navy doctors. Tough was tougher to get through; Shaw had to go along to personally request a waiver. Kaminsky's account of reporting for duty at Pier 92 on West 52nd Street was another hilarious account of the jazz musician facing the military. Finally, he found the rest of the band there. Eventually, under Shaw's direction, they would march up and down the pier learning Navy band repertoire for state occasions until the recruitment was completed ([5], pp. 131–35).

The band was being organized during October and November of 1942. Shaw was able to recruit many former sidemen from his own and other major swing bands. Once the lineup was complete, they were herded onto a truck and driven to Penn Station, where they boarded a train for San Francisco. Kaminsky recalled their departure from New York:

> "Take a good long look," Dave said softly as the driver turned down Broadway. Even in the wartime dimout the Great White Way looked great to us. "I still feel I've been shanghaied," I said. ([5], p. 136)

In San Francisco the band was stationed at the Navy barracks on Treasure Island. Betty and Jerome Kern came to San Francisco and stayed at a hotel while the band was awaiting shipment.

Finally, the band sailed for Hawaii on the *Lurline*, a former cruise ship with an interesting history, converted into a troop transport for the war effort. They landed at Pearl Harbor on Christmas Day, 1942.

While at Pearl Harbor the band played concerts and dances for the servicemen at The Breakers, located on Waikiki Beach. On January 30, 1943, the only recording of The Rangers known to collectors was taken from a radio broadcast, when the band played "Begin the Beguine" as part of a birthday salute to President Roosevelt. Fidelity was very poor on circulating tapes. However, the band sounded in good form for their "Nightmare" theme statement and "Begin the Beguine," which featured Sam Donahue for the usual tenor sax solo.

The Rangers played at The Breakers for servicemen on Monday, Wednesday and Friday afternoons until April 1943. In the evenings, they would play at the Pearl Harbor Officers' Club. Otherwise, they toured around the Hawaiian Islands giving concerts at all the service camps.

The men lived in regular Navy barracks. Shaw, as a chief petty officer, was quartered in the Halekulani Hotel. Claude Thornhill stayed at a friend's apartment in Honolulu, according to Kaminsky ([5], p. 137). Kaminsky also described Admiral Chester Nimitz being taken with Claude Thornhill's piano playing ([5], p. 139). Ultimately, when The Rangers left Hawaii, Thornhill remained behind. Shaw noted that Thornhill had been along to perform between the band's sets, and that the regular band pianist throughout was former Charlie Barnet pianist Rocky Coluccio.

The band left Hawaii on the new battleship *North Carolina* destined for Noumea, the capital city of the island of New Caledonia and a principal naval base. Their second night there, The Rangers played on the aircraft carrier *Saratoga*. They were set up on the flight deck on one of the elevators while the troops were assembled below. The band was lowered into the aircraft hangar while playing their theme, and the response of the men below as the band was coming down was so enthusiastically powerful that Kaminsky and Shaw both described the event glowingly. This was the experience Shaw discussed as being so moving in the Berman film. Kaminsky reported the event with similar feeling in his autobiography ([5], pp. 143–44).

The band lived in barracks on the outskirts of Noumea in a makeshift wire-enclosed encampment that also served as a naval motor pool. Kaminsky wrote:

> Along with short water rations we were given lectures by Artie about being on guard against food poisoning and dysentery, since the refrigeration facilities were so poor that the Navy couldn't guarantee that the chow it fed its men wasn't tainted. After a couple of meals of bad meat, we decided that it wasn't worth the gamble, since it all tasted so terrible anyway, and we took matters into our own hands. As musicians with long experience of being on the road, most of us were used to foraging for ourselves. One of the men wangled several cases of tuna fish from some undisclosed source, and each day one of us would get a pass to go into town to buy a half-dozen loaves of fresh-baked French bread, and between candy bars and the food we were served when we played at officers' parties, we made out all right. . . .
>
> Every morning we would pile our instruments into one truck and climb into another truck to be driven down to the pier. Motor launches were waiting there to take us out to the destroyers and battleships anchored in the harbor, where we'd give concerts for the men. We also played at all the different camps around the island for the Marines and Seabees and Army troops. . . . the men in the South Pacific theatre were so starved for bands from home that they went wild at the mere sight of us. ([5], pp. 141–43)

From Noumea, the band also was flown out to other nearby camps and bases, and to hospitals to play for the wounded and sick. A small group from the band went into wards where the full band could not be accommodated. Where there was no piano, Harold Wax took along his accordion. In some of the wards the musicians were so moved by the condition of the soldiers that they could hardly play.

Original plans had called for a two-month schedule of tours from New Caledonia to surrounding bases. However, The Rangers completed their schedule after about a month of intensive effort, so that they could move on to entertain troops closer to the battle zone. They were moved north to Espiritu Santo, the northernmost island in the New Hebrides. From there they continued their routine of traveling to surrounding islands and bases. *The New Yorker* reported:

> [Shaw] had orders to play music for Navy morale, but nowhere had quarters been arranged for him and his men.
>
> "I was the lowest of the low," he says. "The brass considered our mission silly, and I heard a lot of 'You're not in Hollywood now.' " He became a champion scrounger, finding bunks, bedclothing and food for his men, and doggedly playing concerts whether anybody asked for them or not. . . .
>
> "We'd set up shop in some eerie tropical setting—palm trees all around, board benches, Navy boys sitting on them or on the ground—and when we'd swing into our old favorites, really socking it, you could see tears come to their eyes." (11)

The troops were overwhelmingly appreciative, showering the band with gifts. Shaw noted in *Artie Shaw: Time Is All You've Got* that in some places the officers also were glad to see them, offering to help, while on the next island he might even be refused a jeep to scout around looking for the best place to set up to entertain the troops and would receive the "Who-do-you-think-you-are" treatment. In *Metronome*'s article, "Musician of the Year" by Mike Daniels (January 1944, pp. 18–20), he was quoted as stating: "We hitch-hiked everywhere, sometimes on a large ship, then a smaller one, and sometimes by airplane. We travelled any way we could."

He also related in conversation:

> There was one son-of-a-bitch out there who almost got us all killed. We were all set to hitch a ride on a transport plane when this officious bastard ran out and ordered us off, saying we had to travel like other Naval personnel, and made us take a ship. It not only threw us off schedule, it was particularly dangerous just then. Everyone knew a Japanese sub was waiting out there. Sure enough the next ship in our little convoy got torpedoed and sank right there. (2)

Shaw, naturally, was not particularly concerned about officious naval regulations, and treated his men as he did in other bands he had led. This naturally included his perennial rule of "no drinking on the bandstand." On one occasion, he verbally disciplined Conrad Gozzo and Dave Tough for passing a beer between them during a set. This discussion was witnessed by a serviceman who had known Gozzo from back home. He later spoke of the incident as though Shaw was an unspeakable tyrant and reported being embarrassed for the men for having to tolerate such petty discipline. Such an interpretation lends insight into many of the anti-Shaw stories that have circulated. While the serviceman may not have known of Shaw's long-standing rule, Tough certainly did, having been with the 1941–42 orchestra. Furthermore, Shaw had known Dave Tough since the mid-1930s and was well aware that Tough was an alcoholic. Whitney Balliett, in a "Profile" on Dave Tough in *The New Yorker* (November 18, 1985, pp. 160–62ff.) quoted Shaw concerning Tough:

> I first knew Davy in the '30s when he was with Tommy Dorsey, and we'd go up to Harlem to listen to music. He was a sweet man, a gentle man, and not easy to get to. He was shy and reclusive. He had great respect for the English language. He read a lot and I read a lot, so we had that in common. During the 2nd World War, he was in my Navy band, and we'd get together once in a while and talk. He was an alcoholic, and, like all alcoholics, he always found things to drink. I'd assign a man to him if we had an important concert coming up—say, for the crew of an aircraft carrier—and that man would keep an eye on him all day. This was so he wouldn't get drunk and fall off the bandstand, which he had done a couple of times.

Shaw, of course, wanted Tough in his bands because of his musicianship:

> I think he was the most underrated big-band drummer in jazz, and he got a beautiful sound out of his instrument. He tuned his drums, he tried to achieve on them what he heard in his head, as we all do, and I think he came as close as you can get. He refused to take solos. Whenever I pointed to him for 12 or 8 or 4 bars, he'd smile and shake his head and go on playing rhythm drums.

The men were constantly running into individuals they had known back home. In his autobiography, Kaminsky told of being in the hospital briefly with dengue fever, a form of malaria, when Eddie Condon's brother Pat came to see him. Kaminsky thought he was hallucinating at first, but was so stimulated by the reunion that he got up from his sickbed and played the camp concert that night.

The Rangers went on to move through the Solomon Islands chain, moving closer to the battle zone. In July, they landed at Henderson Field on Guadalcanal, where fighting was still taking place. There were bombing attacks on the base every night. According to *Metronome*, the band experienced a total of seventeen bombing attacks. The tents where The Rangers were quartered "were so riddled by bullets they looked like mosquito netting," Kaminsky recalled.

> We always seemed to be in foxholes. They set up tents for us, but when that alarm went off—zoom! We were back in those foxholes so fast we moved like one man. ([5], pp. 144–45)

While on Guadalcanal The Rangers could listen to Radio Tokyo broadcasting American jazz. *Metronome* quoted in its January 1944 article,

"You even hear Artie Shaw records on Radio Tokyo," said Shaw. "One night we heard Jap propaganda announcers playing Shaw records and announcing in good English, that Shaw and his band were playing at the St. Francis Hotel in San Francisco. The idea was to make American boys homesick. Out there on a tiny island, thousands of miles from the mainland, the boys and I got quite a kick from that spiel."

Down Beat noted in its "Amazing Saga Of Shaw Band" article (December 15, 1943, p. 1):

> The Rangers were never more amazed than when they first heard Artie's "Begin the Beguine" piped from Tokyo between snatches of propaganda. It was while they were on Guadalcanal, too, that word came through from the States that bandleader Shaw's wife had given birth to a baby boy. There was a celebration that night, despite the fact that it took place amid the whine and roar of Jap bombs.

Kaminsky wrote:

> Needless to say, all our concerts were given in the daytime, and we competed with the chattering of monkeys, the screeching of parrots, and the whistles of the bright colored little parakeets, which were as common as our sparrows. But when the sirens blew to alert us for Condition Red—the warning that enemy planes were approaching—the jungle would become suddenly still, and not even a leaf seemed to stir in the hushed silence until you began to hear the hum of the planes and the scream of bombs and then the nightmare began again. ([5], p. 145)

The New Yorker "Profile" added:

> What with the makeshift quarters, the inadequate food, and the constant shifting around, the band grew tired and, on Guadalcanal, even sick. The island was being bombed every night, and nobody got much sleep. Dave Tough, already in precarious health, contracted dengue fever . . . and others began to break down. One night, Shaw was taking a walk along a jungle road when he suddenly went blank. An officer came along in a jeep and said, "Where you bound, Chief?"
>
> "I don't know," said Shaw.
>
> "Get in," said the officer quietly, recognizing the symptoms. Shaw burst into tears, but climbed into the jeep and allowed himself to be driven to the hospital.
>
> "I'd probably have been all right if the fellow hadn't been so damned kind," he says. (11)

Down Beat went on about the condition of the band:

> On Guadalcanal and some of the other battle zone islands, the heat would often reach 110 degrees. All of the men always carried a towel to wipe away sweat, and the extreme heat often caused the instruments to break down, cracking the metal parts of the horns and making the pads on saxes and clarinets fall off.

Shaw stated in the *Metronome* interview:

I found it not unusual to be playing a solo and have a pad drop right out of my clarinet. Salt water is murder on instruments. . . . Reeds are impossible to get out there. The guitar and bass men (Al Horesh and Barney Spieler) never could keep enough strings.

Kaminsky wrote,

By now my trumpet had acquired a greenish tinge, which I couldn't rub off, and our sheet music was so mildewed, fly-specked and dog-eared that it was as limp as pulp. ([5], p. 144)

Shaw related a particularly significant story in personal discussion:

On Guadalcanal, we'd get bombed or strafed every so often. Sometimes we'd be set up to play and have to run for the foxholes. One night bombs landed close by the foxhole I was in, one on each side, bracketing it. We were deafened, and my hearing never came back in my left ear. It had been in bad shape since an ear infection 10 years earlier, but after that, nothing. (2)

Finally, after several weeks on Guadalcanal, the band was flown out one night between air raids. Kaminsky related a vivid story of Dave Tough scrambling to transport his drums and finding an abandoned wheelbarrow in the jungle at the crucial moment ([5], p. 147). The Rangers then worked their way back through the same islands in reverse, to Noumea again.

Later in August The Rangers were shipped to New Zealand for a tour of hospitals and bases there. They also played concerts and dances for servicemen in Wellington and Auckland. After about a month in New Zealand, they were sent to Australia. William H. Miller wrote of the band's Australian tour in an article titled "Navy Band 501 Creates Furore In South Pacific" in the December 1, 1943, *Down Beat*. Miller's write-up included a "Profiling the Players" feature with capsule biographical profiles of each member of The Rangers. Concerning the band's tour, Miller wrote on page 1:

South Pacific—The advent in Australia of a real, snap-up, first-class American swing band is not merely a sensation—it is a milestone. Never before has one of the outstanding large outfits of the States visited our country. . . . It was fitting that the first group to venture such an expedition should be under the leadership of Art Shaw, for Shaw is justly well-known to thousands of Australians per medium of his recordings and radio broadcasts.

The band itself is a really fine organization. Shaw is not faced with one of the greatest difficulties that beset the civil-

ian maestro—a constantly changing personnel. The boys are in it now for the duration, whether they like it or not. In consequence, during the year of the group's existence they have come to know each other's outlooks and each other's playing, eventually merging into a compact whole whose unanimity and precision are delightful to hear.

Mostly they play pieces for which Shaw is famous, such as "Begin the Beguine," "Star Dust," "Frenesi," and "Softly as in a Morning Sunrise," with an admixture of stomp numbers, these also put over in the inimitable Shaw fashion.

Goodlooking and good humored . . . Art has a personality which puts his band across with the minimum of ballyhoo. . . . He rightly takes his wartime role very seriously, and will play only for servicemen, although he goodnaturedly arranges for the entree of local members of the musicians' union if possible. It is believed that he will not broadcast here because of this attitude.

. . . their reward reaches them nightly in the appreciation that shines in the eyes of the American servicemen who cluster round the stand, eager not to miss a note of music the like of which they thought they had left behind them long ago with all the rest of the familiar farrago of the good old days at home. And to such Australians as are lucky enough to hear it, the Shaw band is an unforgettable experience and lesson. . . . Its effect on the morale of troops wherever it goes is of inestimable military value.

However, the band's grueling experiences were taking their toll. Shaw wrote:

At that point, the whole outfit was beginning to show signs of wear and tear. We stayed on in Australia, however, and travelled up and down that whole continent for some months more before the whole band, including myself, began to come apart at the seams. By then our instruments were being held together by rubber bands and sheer will, having survived any number of air raids and damp spells in fox-holes; and the men themselves were for the most part in similarly varying states of dilapidation. ([1], p. 373)

In late October 1943, naval medics in Brisbane, Australia, declared The Rangers victims of combat fatigue and ordered them shipped home to San Francisco. The musicians had had to man battle stations while on shipboard all along, but this had been in the damage control area. Despite torpedo attacks and bombings, they had been relatively uninvolved. On their way home, however, they found that they were expected to stand watches on the guns. Kaminsky recalled,

Homeward bound on board a Liberty Merchant ship, which sailed alone to San Francisco in the Jap-infested waters without escort, Dave and I were assigned to watches on the twenty-millimeter gun turrets. It took the combined strength of both of us to lift the bombs and to cock the huge guns. They're lucky we didn't blow up the ship just trying to load the guns. To keep our spirits up, I used to bring my trumpet out on the long night watches and after opening the intercom system to the other turrets, I'd put in a mute and play for all the guys, very softly, all during the watch. ([5], p. 152)

The Rangers disembarked in San Francisco on November 11, 1943, in time for the men to get leave to visit their families for Thanksgiving. Several members of the band were sick enough to require hospitalization, including Shaw. He was placed in the U.S. Naval Hospital at Oak Knoll, California, just outside Oakland. Although the official diagnosis was "combat fatigue,"

the malaise that had stricken him on Guadalcanal was by no means cured. His migraine headaches recurred, he felt deeply depressed, and he drifted into a near-psychotic stupor. (11)

In December 1943, Shaw was let out of the hospital briefly to visit his family in Beverly Hills. There, he was interviewed for the *Metronome* feature where he was named "Musician of the Year" and photographed with his wife and infant son. The magazine described him as thinner, ill at ease, and nervous and fidgety. Shaw remained in the hospital "in a state of dysfunction" for a few months until he received a medical discharge in March 1944.

After his discharge from the hospital and the service, Shaw went into intensive psychoanalysis for his depression and immobility. Ultimately, at the rate of an hour a day, five days a week, Shaw stayed in analysis for a year and a half, but within a few months he was able to start functioning again and began to make plans for another band.

In Barry Ulanov's "Shaw in '44" interview (*Metronome*, September 1944, p. 18), they had a fascinating discussion on art and culture. Shaw stated, "There's no way to go but ahead," and Ulanov noted,

He made it clear that he was still going to experiment, that he was interested in the work of the young arrangers and composers who were welding the materials of so-called classical music and those of jazz into a richer, fuller, stronger, more broadly articulate art.

Artie studied composition some years ago with David Diamond, the young American composer, and has formulated a kind of musical credo emphasizing wider scoring, "rather than writing so close you lose everything." (16)

Shaw also expressed interest in pursuing the direction of his last band before the war, using strings and large-scale compositions. He was hoping to confine his activity to radio, pictures, and record dates, with a theater tour no more than once a year.

Unfortunately, Shaw's relationship with Betty was also strained. In July they separated, and Shaw was facing another divorce. He described it as "a pretty bitter business. My son Steve was involved."

In *The Trouble with Cinderella*, Shaw wrote:

I had to suspend further self-research for a time in order to get back down to earth and hustle up a few bucks again. My mother still had to be supported. I had recently been divorced and had to get out and earn some alimony money. There were a number of other expenses to meet and there was only one way I could dig myself out of the financial hole I had buried myself in.

I went out on tour once more. ([1], p. 375)

Shaw hired Benny Goodman's brother, Freddie Goodman, as his road manager and began recruiting men on the West Coast for his new band in the late summer of 1944.

Chapter 11

Artie Shaw and His Orchestra: 1944–1945

An Armed Forces Radio Service (AFRS) *Command Performance* broadcast dated June 10, 1944, was Shaw's first known recorded performance after leaving the Navy. It was a short version of "Long Ago and Far Away" featuring Shaw with a band including a string section. Shaw did not recall the circumstances of this broadcast, on which he and actress Bette Davis also read a short dedication of the performance to several named servicemen. Shaw had not had a working band with strings since early 1942, and suggested that this performance probably was with a studio group assembled for the occasion (2).

The September 1944 *Metronome*, which contained the "Shaw in '44" interview, also announced "Shaw Band Stringless" on page 9. The write-up consisted mainly of speculations on future sidemen, all of them incorrect. Only the fact that Shaw was recruiting for a new "stringless" big band was accurate.

Later in September, Shaw appeared on two Armed Forces Radio Service programs. The first, on September 25, was *Jubilee* broadcast #198, featuring the Count Basie band with Buddy Rich on drums and Shaw as guest soloist. According to Chris Sheridan in *Count Basie: A Bio-discography* (Westport, Conn.: Greenwood Press, 1986, pp. 216–18), when Lester Young and Jo Jones were drafted, Shaw and Rich replaced them temporarily, with Shaw performing Lester Young's parts on clarinet. This story also is related by Buddy Tate on page 124 of Stanley Dance's *The World of Count Basie* (New York: Scribner's, 1980). Shaw could not confirm this, noting that his life at that point was "a mess" and particularly chaotic (2). His separation and imminent divorce from Betty also was in the news, and he was in the midst of his psychoanalysis, trying to recover from his Navy experiences. In any case, his appearance on this show revealed him playing well, if sounding unusually hyper. He played "Oh Lady Be Good" with the full band and an original blues piece with just the rhythm section. Clarinet solos on other titles on this broadcast were attributed to Rudy Rutherford. Intriguingly, alternate takes of both titles featuring Shaw were issued on a Count Basie CD. The absence of audience noise indicates that these performances probably

were from the afternoon rehearsals mentioned in the broadcast. The "original blues" with the quintet was even better on the rehearsal recording than on the broadcast version. No two issues of this piece seem to use the same title for it, and the riff-like melody has not appeared elsewhere.

On September 30, 1944, Shaw, Basie and Rich were joined by an all-star group for an AFRS *Command Performance* broadcast of "Honeysuckle Rose." This was also a rather hyper performance which Shaw considers "raucous" (2). Photos from this session were widely published and erroneously cited as Shaw's first public appearance since leaving the Navy.

The media gave various dates for the beginning of rehearsals for Shaw's new band, even as early as August 1944, indicating great interest in its formation. Apparently they began rehearsing about late October or the beginning of November 1944. Shaw then took the band out for two weeks of one-nighters on the West Coast before beginning a theater tour on December 1st. They took time out from their string of one-nighters to make their first Victor recordings on November 23, 1944. This was Shaw's first studio recording session since January 1942.

For its initial recording session, the band performed two pop tunes with vocals by Imogene Lynn ("Ac-Cent-Tchu-Ate the Positive" and "Let's Take the Long Way Home") and two excellent jazz-oriented instrumentals, Jimmy Mundy's "Lady Day" and Ray Conniff's "Jumpin' on the Merry-Go-Round." With this band, as with his 1941–42 orchestra, Shaw was using other arrangers whose work interested him. The above instrumentals were arranged by their composers.

Their theater tour began with a week each at the Orpheum Theatre in Minneapolis followed by the Chicago Theatre in Chicago. They then split a week at the respective Palace Theatres in Akron and in Columbus, Ohio, before doing a week at the Palace Theatre in Cleveland. On December 29, 1944, they went into the Downtown in Detroit for a week. On January 9, 1945, they again recorded for Victor, this time in New York City.

Six titles were recorded at this session. The full band performed two popular standards arranged by Ray Conniff ("I'll Never Be the Same" and "'S Wonderful") and Buster Harding's excellent "Bedford Drive," as well as Imogene Lynn's best vocal feature to date, "Can't Help Lovin' That Man" (arranged by Bobby Sherwood). Again, the effect of the full band was powerful and crisply modern. The remaining two titles were by the new edition of the Gramercy 5: this 1945 unit had the brilliance of Roy Eldridge, a powerful soloist whose extremely individual ideas were an engrossing contrast with Shaw's; eighteen-year-old Dodo Marmarosa on piano; and twenty-year-old Barney Kessel on guitar. The 1945 Gramercy 5 thus provided a formidable array of solo talent with a decidedly hip orientation. Marmarosa and Kessel, of course, soon made names for themselves in the new music. Shaw was definitely highly inspired in this context, in great form and revealing his own stylistic evolution. The results were impressive small-group jazz. Both "The Sad Sack" (a medium-tempo minor blues) and the swinging "The Grabtown Grapple" were new Shaw compositions illustrating the updated musical conception of this group. Coupled with the spectacular soloists and the dynamic punch and infectious swing of their performances, the classic status of these Shaw originals was guaranteed.

During January 1945, the band played theater engagements at the RKO in Boston and at the Earle in Philadelphia, closing there on the 25th. The next day they opened at the Strand Theatre in New York City for five weeks. On opening night, Friday, January 26th, Paul Socon reviewed the band for *Billboard* (February 10, 1945, p. 27):

> New show brings back Artie Shaw and his ork to Broadway for the first time in couple of years. To prove that the guy is still plenty b.-o. by virtue of having plenty of good discs around while he was in the service for over a year, place was mobbed all day. And the 45-minute show Shaw dishes up won't disappoint his fans a bit. For, wisely enough, Shaw has selected tunes that feature himself thruout, and when backed by a band that's hitting plenty solid considering how new it is—some 4 months—stage stint comes off for the most part.
>
> Outside of his music, Shaw does little to help the goings on, sticking mainly to playing the clarinet and closely watching the solos taken by each man. Latter point is especially disconcerting on stage, for it seems as if Shaw is listening and judging at the same time, rather than getting behind his sidemen and helping sell his instrumentalists to payees. He exhibits little enthusiasm, which is bad. Musically, outfit walks off with honors. Wisely enough, Shaw has included plenty of old-timers made by disks in his tune line-up.
>
> There's "Star Dust" and "Begin the Beguine," latter especially a fave. And to link all the tunes together, Shaw is in there all the time, throwing in licks behind instrumentalists, his singer, Imogene Lynn, and altogether giving payees their money's worth. And, it's assumed that most of the standees paid to get in to see Shaw and his new band.
>
> Outside of Roy Eldridge, Negro trumpeter, Shaw is by far the most outstanding man in the band. When he's on his instrument, band has a beat, and altho there's still a stiffness about the outfit, there's little doubt that Shaw will again wind up with one of the big outfits around today. His tone and style are unmistakable, and his arrangements in keeping with the style that made a name for him prior to the time when he broke up his band.
>
> Then again, he's a very appreciative guy on stage, and while not exhibiting much enthusiasm for what's going on, he's obviously a more subdued guy than he once was. And he still plays plenty of music on his stick, enough to satisfy any of his fans who plank down their dough.
>
> Miss Lynn opens with "Ac-Cent, etc." not a good choice for the gal, but closer, "Must Have That Man," is a winner. "Ac-Cent" is for a novelty singer, who can frolic around on stage and sell lyrics and general feeling of the song. Miss Lynn, gal with a nice voice and keen on the eyes, warbles a good ballad but doesn't hit it off on the rhythm stuff. Shaw's Gramercy Five, combo of piano, drums, guitar, trumpet, bass and himself, do a quickie that sells. Finale is strictly an instrumental that sells sidemen in the band, but it's not a rousing walker-offer.
>
> Two acts with him are standard; Sunny Rice, enthusiastic fem tapster, and comedy team, Ross Wyse Jr. and June Mann. Latter pair have been seen here on many occasions but they get plenty of laughs and walk off to big hand. Little guy is showy dancer and smartly hides it behind laugh routines with gal. However, he lets it out at the end and they come back to plenty of claps. Miss Rice is a cute and saucy tapster and sells smartly.
>
> Pic is WB's *Objective Burma.*

Metronome also provided a review of the band at the Strand, by Leonard Feather, in its March 1945 issue (p. 24):

> The band plays nothing sensational, but there's a refreshing lack of bad taste and bombast. All the numbers, in this theatre at least, were helped by well-arranged lighting effects and good amplification.
>
> The show opened with a Buster Harding original, "Bedford Drive," a pot-boiler, but with excellent spots by Artie and his great guitar man, Barney Kessel, plus nice reed section work. "Stardust" [*sic*] had Ray Conniff playing a la Jack Jenney, more fine stuff by the leader, and a rhythm section producing sounds that are seldom so effectively blended on, or transmitted from, a theatre stage.
>
> Artie handsomely gave credit in his announcement to arranger Ray Conniff when the highly original orchestration of "'S Wonderful" came up. Blonde Imogene Lynn followed, Accentuating the Positive and doing a fair job on "It Had To Be You." There is no male singer, thank God.
>
> The Gramercy Five [*sic*], with the brilliant Dodo at the piano and a mutedly effective Roy Eldridge, cantered through a blues and an original; then Roy was joined by the full band for a superb job on "Body and Soul." Then came "Begin the Routine" or whatever they call it. . . . The show

closed with a fast instrumental blues in which several soloists shone very brightly.

The articulate Artie announced the show smoothly, though perhaps with not quite enough conviction. To sum up: Artie, Roy, Barney and Dodo are worth your money any time. The band isn't great yet, but it's on the right track; and that, in these days of symphonic swing and assorted swooners, is something for which we should be thankful.

After closing at the Strand on March 1, 1945, Shaw took the band on a cross-country tour ending back in Hollywood. On March 15th, Shaw and the rhythm section appeared on Bing Crosby's *Kraft Music Hall* radio show. Shaw explained that the band got a vacation upon arriving on the Coast, so he just brought back the rhythm section for this appearance (2). The group did two popular songs, "I Was Doing All Right" and "You Took Advantage of Me." Intriguingly, two performances of each piece have appeared on the Artie Shaw Club collectors' label LP titled *The Artie Shaw Gramercy 5* (ASG5). One version of each was from the broadcast air check, and the others were from a special pressing 78-rpm record, Music Hall 119. The double performances of each piece are as similar to each other as alternate takes. All four performances were superb. "I Was Doing All Right" was performed as a ballad, while the other tune was a swinging up-tempo rendition.

The April 1, 1945, *Down Beat* reported on page 7, "Shaw Signs For Dorsey Dancery," and noted:

Shaw had seven new men in his band when he arrived here from his cross-country tour. He said he'd lost some to draft calls and had had to make some changes for certain musical results.

The effect of a turnover of more than one-third of the band's personnel was not as noticeable as, for example, the effect of changing five key men in the 1938 band while they were at the Lincoln. Despite the large number of substitutions, Shaw retained his rhythm section and key soloists in this new lineup.

On April 5, 1945, the band recorded two excellent instrumentals for Victor, a beautiful version of "September Song" and another Buster Harding original, "Little Jazz." The latter title was a tour de force feature for Roy Eldridge; Shaw did not solo. On April 8th, the full band's earliest radio broadcast that has surfaced occurred. On this *Fitch Bandwagon Show*, they played Shaw's familiar arrangements of "Begin the Beguine" and "My Heart Stood Still," Roy Eldridge's feature "Little Jazz," and a long, hard-swinging version of "Limehouse Blues" that featured some particularly potent Shaw.

On April 17th, the band had another Victor record date. Shaw again featured the work of his new arrangers. "Summertime" was arranged by Eddie Sauter in a long version

for a twelve-inch 78-rpm issue. The other titles were not released at that time, and only became widely available in the LP era.

The band played a week at the Golden Gate in San Francisco, from April 25th through May 1st, then crossed the bay to play at the Orpheum in Oakland from May 3rd through May 9th. Beginning May 11, 1945, the band appeared at the Dorsey Brothers' Casino Gardens Ballroom on the Santa Monica Pier every weekend for six weeks. It was reported that the band was only playing weekends during this period, and that they had again lost their radio wire for not clearing their tunes with the networks in advance.

Shaw was again restricting his activities to rehearsing and recording while performing from one location. Aside from his Friday/Saturday/Sunday appearances at the Casino Gardens, he began recording regularly for Victor starting in early June. Over a ten-day period they went into the RCA studios seven times, with thirteen performances eventually released. Many were not issued at the time, however.

In late June the band returned to the San Francisco area. After performing at the Pacific Square June 29th through July 1st, they returned to Los Angeles and began playing weekends at the Rendezvous Ballroom, beginning July 4th. The day before, they had the first of a series of thirteen recording sessions for the month of July. This resulted in another twenty-one recordings eventually released featuring the band, and the beginning of the final Victor recordings Shaw made, by the Gramercy 5. These were completed by August 2nd. The band was reported stymied by transportation problems and only doing recordings following their Rendezvous appearances.

The recordings the band made during those two months from early June through early August 1945 are among the best in the Shaw discography. Along with the earlier recordings by this 1944–45 band, the best pieces and jazz originals were among the very finest material by big bands of the day. There were only a few pop tunes or vocal features that were of limited jazz interest to distract from the many exciting arrangements and solos, when examining the band's total output. In the liner notes to RCA AXM2-5579, Shaw stated:

I didn't feel terribly dedicated during this period of my life, because I was so busy putting myself back together [after the war]. But my playing was changing in a major way. It's hard for me to talk about it objectively. Yet it's clear I was moving from one thing to another, making changes, looking for better ways, as I was in life.

This would be reflected in his playing as a matter of course, since all artists reflect their inner state in their work. Although he was not composing or arranging as prolifically as he had in his earlier bands, his playing sounded like he was having fun and was happy with the music he was making.

However, things were not so happy at RCA. Eli Oberstein, a top RCA executive, apparently was trying to take control over what Shaw was doing in the studios. Shaw naturally insisted on retaining control himself. Some of the remakes of pieces being recorded and rerecorded that season were due to the studio technicians trying to insist that Shaw speed up the arrangements to keep performance time shorter for the ten-inch 78-rpm records (2). Only one extended performance was made, the Eddie Sauter composition "The Maid with the Flaccid Air," which approached the aura of some of Shaw's prewar, pre–Third Stream experiments. This performance was issued along with "Summertime" on a twelve-inch 78-rpm disc.

The recordings for RCA ended after the early August Gramercy 5 session. The 1945 Gramercy 5 records were among the best of Shaw's career, and all five performances from these last sessions were also original compositions by Shaw. "Scuttlebutt" (recorded July 31st) may be the best of the 1945 Gramercy 5 pieces in terms of its composition and impact. The remainder were recorded on August 1, 1945. The moody medium blues "Mysterioso" also featured excellent solo work and effective ensemble passages that are almost Ellingtonian, and the contrast between the two versions issued offers a graphic illustration of how different in effect two takes of the same composition on the same day can be. Shaw's rephrasing of the melodic statement radically altered the mood and impact of the piece, but it would be difficult to choose a preference, as both approaches to the theme worked effectively. "Hop Skip and Jump" had an almost surreal element in its thematic transitions and abrupt stops, a refinement of the type of humorous compositional statement evident in "When the Quail Come Back to San Quentin" from 1940. Finally, the smooth "Gentle Grifter" absolutely sparkled.

During September and October 1945, the band was featured on a series of Armed Forces Radio Service *Spotlite Bands* shows. They also were playing at the Casa Mañana in Los Angeles for four weekends, beginning September 15th.

The band's work on the *Spotlite Bands* broadcasts revealed it to be in excellent form, with the extra edge of excitement characteristic of live performances. There also were two features for the Gramercy 5 including Eldridge. One of these was a version of "Summit Ridge Drive," which had become a big hit for Shaw. The other was a performance of "Scuttlebutt" even more potent than their classic record made a few weeks earlier. In addition, there were two more Gramercy 5 performances from these broadcasts following Eldridge's departure from the band, played by just Shaw and the rhythm section, as on the Crosby show the preceding March. Several numbers not otherwise recorded by the full band were preserved, including an exciting version of "On the Sunny Side of the Street" with Shaw obviously having a good time.

The full band also performed two modern pieces on these broadcasts that were included on their last studio recording date, recorded at Shaw's expense and eventually issued on Musicraft. These were Buster Harding's "The Glider" and the Shaw original, "Let's Walk," which along with superb performances of "The Hornet" (also by Buster Harding), Shaw's "Love of My Life," and two pop tunes with vocals by Hal Stevens, were recorded in the studio in excellent fidelity. Hal Stevens had also recorded two dismal vocals with the band the preceding July. " 'Dismal' is right!" Shaw stated. "We were under tremendous pressure to record commercial tunes" (2). Fortunately, these later vocals were considerably more interesting, with Shaw playing a magnificent opening solo on "How Deep Is the Ocean."

Shaw has spoken highly of Roy Eldridge's solo features on five of the six performances recorded at this session, and of his muted section lead on "The Glider" and "Let's Walk." Nevertheless, discographies have consistently omitted Eldridge from the personnel of this session and dated it as occurring in mid-November 1945, after Eldridge had left the band. Eldridge also has consistently been left out of the personnel listings in the liner notes to issues of this material (which also sometimes err in citing a string section present), and the trumpet solos have been credited to Ray Linn. In fact, although the musical ideas do strongly evoke Eldridge, the solos were a bit more restrained and the tone a bit thinner than Eldridge's usual sound, leading to opinions that Ray Linn was "doing a Roy" in Eldridge's place after Eldridge had left the band. Concerning this discrepancy over Eldridge's participation, Shaw stated,

> I don't see how anyone could miss Roy. It's definitely him on there; it wasn't Ray Linn. Also there must be something wrong with that dating, as the session definitely occurred before Roy left the band; after the Victors, and before Roy left. (2)

In discussing the circumstances of Roy Eldridge leaving the band, Shaw explained:

> I'll tell you why I had to fire him. The racial pressures were getting to him. Once in San Francisco he wasn't allowed in the theatre where we were playing, even though his name was on the marquee, because he was black.
>
> I did what I could but there were lots of ugly incidents, and one day when he was mad about everything he pulled a knife on me. I said, "Roy, if I'm your enemy, who's your friend?" He started to cry and I took the knife away from him. Then I sat him down and told him, "Look at yourself, it's tearing you up. Go to Europe for a while." So I had to let him go. Later he did go to Europe and when I ran into him after he came back, he said, "Yeah, you were right, but

I had to come back anyway." There were no racial problems in Europe, but he missed the scene over here. (2)

Eldridge appreciated being with the band musically, despite the problems. In the liner notes to RCA AXM2-5579, Eldridge was quoted as stating:

Artie was a great director. . . . As soon as I began coming to rehearsals, I knew Shaw was okay. The band improved rapidly because he knew what to change and what to leave alone. And, fortunately, he had some good cats in the sections.

The charts were great—some experimental things, some straight-ahead items. We played essentially for dancing. But there were good jazz things in the book, like Buster Harding's "Big City Shout" and "Bedford Drive."

I stayed on the band for about 9 months. But there were more than a few racial problems. . . . It was great on the stand. But when I came off, I couldn't get anything to eat. . . . I don't like talking about things like that. I'd rather concentrate on the music and the musicians. Both were great in the Shaw band; a lot was going on.

Following Eldridge's departure, Ray Linn returned to the trumpet section. The band lasted less than another two months. After completing the *Spotlite Bands* series and Casa Mañana engagement, the band went into the Meadowbrook in Culver City, California. Another broadcast has surfaced from this period, a *Fitch Bandwagon Show* that featured the band on four pieces. (There also was an item by Betty Hutton on the broadcast, but it sounded like a different group and Shaw was not heard.) Shaw did not feature the Gramercy 5 on his last two available broadcasts. A few days after the band closed at the Meadowbrook, Shaw disbanded, on November 18, 1945. The band had lasted just over a year.

The band's final studio record date, as noted, was not for Victor. The disagreement between Shaw and Oberstein was making the musical press that season. *Down Beat* reported "Shaw–Victor Split Confirmed" in its December 1, 1945, issue on page 16. The article reported that Oberstein was complaining over Shaw's wanting to retain "the whole say" where his recordings were concerned and "demanded the right to record only his own choice of material. Oberstein thinks the choice of material should lie with the recording company."

The December 15, 1945, *Down Beat* noted on page 6, "Shaw Will Sign With New Firm." Shaw was quoted as stating:

Musicians who want to do things of lasting value simply don't belong in companies that are run by men like Oberstein. And a lot of them are finding it out—this isn't just my fight by any means. Oberstein told me what I should record, and how, despite that my contract clearly stated I was to have

full authority. Why should I, or any bandleader who wants to do things that are worthy of respect from musicians and people who know good music, take orders from someone like Oberstein?

RCA's revenge for Shaw's leaving was to not release many of the sides made by this excellent band for over a year, and then in limited pressing quantities. Some titles were not issued until well into the LP era. In retrospect, Shaw's desire to take more time in the studios to get as close to what he wanted as possible seems amply justified when listening to the results. Clearly, the predominance of good jazz arrangements and relative scarcity of banal pop tunes indicated Shaw was compromising less, but the pressure to record commercial pop material was still too great.

Shaw had continued discussing music and the music business in print that year, and his comments were, as usual, insightful and consistent with his previous statements. In the July 1945 *Esquire*, Leonard Feather wrote up a substantial interview/article titled "Artie Shaw's Long View of Swing Music" on page 76. Feather wrote,

Because he happens to be the most articulate of all big-time bandleaders, I cornered Shaw during his last New York trip to question him about classics vs. swing, about popular music vs. real jazz, about money vs. art, and about the bearing of these three conflicts on his own musical policy. I came away with a good story, despite the delightful distraction of Ava Gardner, who was sitting next to Artie opposite me. . . .

The music industry grows, declared Artie, in an inverse ratio to its musical honesty. "The more I have to make money, the less I can rehearse, the less I can worry about improving the music. Lately I've been working to pay off a year's economic obligations, so we've been playing theatres. . . . If that were all I could ever do, I'd quit the business again. . . .

"As long as I stay in the music game, I want to show that jazz has as much validity as any art form; it's only some of the people in jazz who lack validity."

The March 1945 *Metronome* had an article titled "Shaw Speaks His Mind" on page 5. Shaw had again been criticizing the music business and had been misquoted in some of the tabloids. Apparently he had said that jazz was in poor shape as an art form because of "lack of integrity of men in the business, from top to bottom, from bandleader to booker to record executive." The article went on to note:

Artie spoke out against swooning and screaming, but he admitted to us that it can be legitimate when it is a reaction to music and not to pulchritude and stage presence, when the tears and the bravos are for the composition and the performance and not for the cut of the performer's chin and shin and hairline. . . . [jazz] does suffer, even as all the other arts, from the crude, rude, elephantine interference of its commercial overlords. If Artie's outburst serves to call attention to the poor effect, to the clumsy ministrations of these men, then it was well conceived and directed. Even if it doesn't do more than ruffle their composure, it has achieved something. For the elephant's hide is thick.

The above-mentioned "Shaw in '44" article by Barry Ulanov, besides stating many of Shaw's aesthetic perceptions and insights, concluded with an astute evaluation of Shaw and his impact by Ulanov:

> Artie Shaw's is a remarkably alert and provocative mind. He is a voracious reader, a stimulating thinker, a seeker after knowledge. When you combine these things with his very large talent as a musician, you have the size and shape of a very large creative force. The energies of such a creative force usually contain a seemingly destructive element. Loosed upon an unsuspecting, insensitive and thus unsympathetic world, these creative energies are falsely marked destructive at least as often as they are cited as an expression of value and beauty. Artie Shaw has been the victim of this sort of crude appraisal at least as often as he has been properly praised as a forceful, forward-looking creator. To me at least, the size of Artie's musical achievement, the sound of his ideas, and the shape of his plans for the future add up to something entirely constructive. Individuals who have grudges against Shaw, perhaps justified, perhaps not, should be listened to only as individuals. There may be questionable limitations and constrictions and aberrations in the personality of Artie Shaw. But as a musician and as a musical thinker he must be counted on the side of what we who look forward to great things still to come in jazz naively call Truth and Beauty. That is the way Artie Shaw's music has always impressed me. (16)

During this time period, Shaw also was in the news because of his relationship with Ava Gardner. They had met the year before, and had been living together for some time, to the delight of the Hollywood gossip columnists. Ava was already making a name for herself as a movie star, and had been briefly married to Mickey Rooney, although she was still only about twenty years old when she met Shaw.

In his biography of Ava Gardner, *Ava* (New York: Coward, McCann & Geoghegan, 1983), Roland Flamini gave the following account of their relationship's beginning:

> Before she loved Artie Shaw, Ava loved Artie Shaw's music. Growing up in North Carolina, she had been swept up in the swing craze . . . she had swayed to his music on his coast-to-

coast radio program and Artie Shaw records had kept her company when she was a lonely newcomer to L.A. ([17], p. 77)

After seeing Shaw play, "she was immediately smitten," the story continued. Meanwhile, Shaw had seen a photo of Ava and was impressed. A mutual friend then introduced them. Shaw took Ava to see Basie and introduced her backstage, which impressed her. They finished the evening dancing at the Mocambo.

Members of Shaw's 1944–45 band recalled Ava present for Thanksgiving dinner at Shaw's house on Bedford Drive in Beverly Hills in 1944. However, Shaw stated unequivocally that most of the stories written about his relationship with Ava were blatantly untrue. While Ava was never regarded as intellectually oriented and was intimidated by Shaw's reading habits and circle of intellectual friends, Shaw refuted the tales of her trying to catch up with courses at UCLA, and of his throwing a book she was reading across the room, calling it "trash." (The book allegedly was Kathleen Winsor's historical novel, *Forever Amber*). "Never happened," he grumbled in personal discussions on these and other similar stories (2). Certainly, many tales of their alleged difficulties had the flavor of studio concoctions. Some stories were merely garbled. For example, Shaw did negotiate an improved contract for Ava with her studio at one point, but the usual versions of the story were considerably distorted (2).

The Hollywood code of those days forbade widely publicized "live-in" relationships and the couple felt pressured into marrying. They wed on October 17, 1945, in Beverly Hills. Shaw's mother was in attendance and appeared in photos (occasionally erroneously identified as Ava's mother). Flamini wrote,

> Artie's friends included William Saroyan, Robert Benchley, S. J. Perelman, John O'Hara, Gene Fowler and Dorothy Parker. And at Shaw's house on Bedford Drive . . . the conversation more often centered around books and writers than on movie gossip. ([17], p. 78)

Shaw did help Ava select books to read. Before visiting his friend Sinclair Lewis in New York, Shaw gave Ava *Babbitt* to read, and helped her get through it. Concerning their final breakup, Shaw simply said, "I was en route to New York City and Ava didn't want to go" (2). They were reported to have separated in September 1946.

Chapter 12

Artie Shaw on Musicraft: 1946

During the winter of 1945–46, details of the negotiations between Shaw and Musicraft began to appear in the musical press. Once released from his Victor contract, Shaw was reported signing "an attractive deal" with Musicraft, but although it was described as "unusual," in that Shaw was to have complete freedom in the selection of recordings and how often and where they would be made, Shaw stated that this was, in fact, his usual arrangement (2).

In all, twenty-two titles plus a three-disc album of children's records (*The Pied Piper of Hamelin*), were recorded between April and November 1946. Only six titles were instrumentals. In view of Shaw's often-stated negative views on vocalists and pop tunes, and comparing these recordings to his output for Victor with his last working band, this would seem surprising. In discussing these sessions, Shaw said that he was again trying an experiment.

I was interested in recording some jazz-flavored pop music. That's all I wanted to do and I think it worked well. Using a vocal group as another section was a new idea; with four sections for texture and accompaniment—brass, reeds, strings and voices—there was a wider palette of tonal colors. I particularly liked "Guilty" as a treatment of a pop tune. I did the intro to "What Is This Thing Called Love?" myself— Sonny Burke orchestrated the rest of the arrangement—and I thought that was pretty effective. But it was a mixed bag. Some of those tunes were so vacuous. I'm thinking of reissuing some of the best of that material—I've got the rights to it now—and calling it *Mixed Bag*! (2)

Shaw did not have a regular working group at the time, and was using studio musicians. Shaw sketched all the arrangements, which were orchestrated primarily by Sonny Burke, who was also recording director, or by Dick Jones. He used different combinations of instrumentation for different effects on various pieces, depending on how he wanted each piece to sound. Most of the records were with a big band including a string section, as with his 1940–42 orchestras, although the effect was quite different. Others were with a forty-piece group consisting of large string and woodwind sections, plus a rhythm section. The studio orchestras were organized for Shaw by Dave Klein. The commercial nature and intent of these recordings has never been in doubt.

Unfortunately, the same cannot be said of the personnel and recording dates. Shaw's old friend Harry Bluestone was credited as concertmaster and solo violinist (on the introduction, composed by Shaw, to "My Heart Belongs to Daddy") in the original liner notes to the four-disc album of 78-rpm records titled *Artie Shaw Plays Cole Porter*, issued in the summer of 1946. A few key section men also were named, but full personnel had never been published until Luiz Carlos do Nascimento Silva discovered the data in the files of Musicians' Union Local 47 in Hollywood, in 1997, and published this information in the *IAJRC Journal* (Winter 1998, pp. 17–20).

The initial Musicraft session in this series was held on April 30, 1946, and produced two tunes: "I Got the Sun in the Morning" and "Along with Me." The former was an attractive arrangement featuring Mel Tormé and his vocal group, the Mel-Tones, and became a hit record in that era. Shaw's clarinet wove in and out of the performance. This was one of the best and most interesting of the Musicraft records made that year. "Along With Me" followed a simpler arranging pattern and set the form for most of the subsequent Musicraft vocals. Shaw played the melody with slight decorations in a gorgeous-toned, rhapsodic style. The textures behind Shaw's passages, and the melody between them, were played by either the lush strings or the full band. After the first half of the performance, Mel Tormé sang for the rest of the piece, with similar "fills" but no more heard from Shaw's clarinet.

Of the sixteen vocal titles eventually recorded for this series of Musicraft records, all followed the form of "Along with Me" except "My Heart Belongs to Daddy" (featuring Kitty Kallen singing and an interesting use of Shaw's theme, "Nightmare," interpolated as an introduction to the vocal) and "What Is This Thing Called Love?" (with Mel Tormé and the Mel-Tones). These followed the more intricate and interesting approach that was used on "I Got the Sun in the Morning," with Shaw's clarinet weaving in and out of the proceedings. Twelve of these sixteen vocal titles featured Mel Tormé, half of them with his vocal group, the Mel-Tones. The other four titles featured one tune each by Kitty Kallen, Teddy Walters, songwriter Ralph Blane on his own composition "Connecticut," and Lillian Lane on Shaw's composition "When You're Around."

The recording sessions held during June 1946 were devoted to turning out the aforementioned Cole Porter album. These included the four titles using the strings-and-woodwinds ensemble. When the Cole Porter album was announced in the July 1, 1946, issue of *Down Beat* on page 7, the headline read, "Shaw Delights Salesmen With Coming Album," and noted:

> Check-up on Artie Shaw's recent activities for Musicraft indicates the Bad Boy of the bandleaders has come to terms with the sales department. . . . Looks like Shaw is turning out a neat batch of musicianly, marketable platters, which, though they won't move collectors, will move rapidly over the sales counters.

However, the September 9, 1946, issue of *Down Beat* noted on page 3, "Old Victor Pact Stymies New Shaw Album":

> RCA-Victor threw a monkey wrench into the Musicraft waxworks when it uncovered an old Artie Shaw contract that forbids the ex-Victor star from cutting "Begin the Beguine" for any other firm. "Beguine" was one of the sides of Musicraft's long-anticipated Shaw album of Cole Porter tunes.
>
> Twenty thousand copies of the album had already been printed by the time Musicraft found it was no dice. . . . Since Shaw did not cut any extra tunes at the initial recording session, further album production will be delayed until Shaw can recut a new Porter composition. . . . There are several rubs to Shaw recording another Cole Porter number. First, he does not have a regular orchestra and will have to first reassemble and rehearse a new (and very elaborate) unit. Second, Shaw is currently having considerable trouble with his teeth and is not playing his instrument.

This arrangement of "Begin the Beguine," an instrumental, featured the big-band-with-strings ensemble. It was an interesting version, with Skeets Herfurt playing an alto sax solo resembling the Tony Pastor tenor sax solo in Shaw's more familiar arrangement. Eventually, a version of "Love for Sale," also an instrumental and featuring a nice tenor sax solo by Babe Russin, was substituted. All tunes in the album were featured in the movie *Night and Day*, a "Hollywood-ized" biographical musical on Cole Porter starring Cary Grant, which was also being released around this time.

The *Artie Shaw Plays Cole Porter* album was carefully and cleverly laid out. A pair of instrumentals with the strings-and-woodwinds ensemble ("I've Got You Under My

Skin" and "In the Still of the Night") each had one of the aforementioned "interestingly arranged" vocals on the reverse (Kitty Kallen singing "My Heart Belongs to Daddy" and Mel Torme and his Mel-Tones on "What Is This Thing Called Love?") that used the big-band-with-strings lineup. A pair of vocals with strings-and-woodwinds backing had Mel Torme (without the Mel-Tones) singing on "Guilty" and Teddy Walters singing on "You Do Something to Me." These arrangements were of the simpler form and were backed by the two instrumentals by the big-band-and-strings ensemble, "Night and Day" and "Begin the Beguine" (replaced by "Love for Sale"). With this layout, listeners could stack their records to play either all four vocals, which would all be quite different from one another; all four instrumentals, which would feature two different ensembles; all four of the strings-and-woodwinds performances, which would involve two different singers plus two instrumentals; and so forth, thereby providing many different programming possibilities for appreciating this material.

Alternate takes of "What Is This Thing Called Love?" and "Night and Day" appeared on the Lion LP *Artie Shaw Plays Cole Porter and Irving Berlin*. This LP also is interesting for having all eight titles from the Cole Porter set of 78s, plus the Irving Berlin songs "I Got the Sun in the Morning" and "There's No Business Like Show Business" filling it out. Ironically, Shaw wasn't involved in the latter title: it was from a Mel Tormé recording session for Musicraft in 1947, and bore matrix number 5803.

During July 1946, Shaw was involved in a unique project involving the musical setting for the fairy tale "The Pied Piper of Hamelin" that he had prepared in the spring of 1941, while studying orchestration with Hans Byrns. Shaw was credited with script, arrangements, conducting, and of course clarinet solos on the three-disc set of 78s issued in an album by Musicraft. A similar version was broadcast on the CBS *Columbia Workshop* show on July 21, 1946, and a low-fidelity dub of this broadcast has been circulating among collectors. The Musicraft records were made a week later. It was an amusing version of the story, narrated by Harry Von Zell, later well-known on television as straight man for George Burns and Gracie Allen on the *Burns and Allen Show*. A smooth, sly-sounding, "cool cat" interpretation of the Pied Piper was read by Ed Max. Arthur Q. Bryan, the voice of Elmer Fudd in the cartoons, read the part of the mayor of Hamelin in his characteristic Elmer Fudd voice. The result was a pleasant bit of fun conveying the transcendent overtones inherent in the fable and therefore of interest beyond its obvious intent as a set of childrens' records. It would seem to have natural potential for a cartoon video version using the Musicrafts as the soundtrack. (In 1998, Shaw produced a CD test pressing reissuing this set, plus his version of "The Emperor and the Nightingale" that he had composed and arranged at the same time as "The Pied

Piper of Hamelin" in 1941, but this has not been issued at this writing.)

The remaining Musicrafts were recorded during the late summer and fall of 1946. Shaw inadvertently contributed to pioneering the practice of making records with overdubbing, when the problems he was having with his teeth prevented him from playing on one of the scheduled recording sessions. The September 23, 1946, *Down Beat* announced on page 7, "Use Movie Trick To Save Session":

Hollywood—Recording technique common in motion picture work but never before used in commercial platter waxing was utilized by Musicraft on an Artie Shaw session here recently. With a recording date set up, Shaw found himself unable to play because of a dental operation. To escape loss of several thousands of dollars for musicians and studio costs the session was run without Shaw's solos. Later the clarinet parts were dubbed into the 2 sides previously cut, Shaw listening to playbacks through earphones.

Although, as noted, this was common practice in movie studios, and Sidney Bechet once recorded a one-man-band record overdubbing all instruments himself on a version of "The Sheik of Araby" in 1941, overdubbing was by no means the common practice it subsequently became in later decades. Shaw stated that the tunes were "Love for Sale" and "a couple of others" done at the same time, and that this event was strictly a matter of expediency (2).

Shaw was in the news regularly that season for a variety of reasons. The aforementioned dubbing innovations were one item. The Cole Porter album was a related newsworthy topic, and *Down Beat* noted on page 7 of its October 7, 1946, issue, "Shaw Subs New Tune In Porter Album," which was rereleased that fall. The November 18th issue reviewed a number of the Victors finally issued by that company, along with some of the new Musicrafts. During the same period, Shaw also made headlines for his divorce from Ava Gardner and subsequent marriage to novelist Kathleen Winsor on October 28, 1946. They were reported honeymooning in Mexico. Then, the January 1, 1947, *Down Beat* noted "Shaw Buys Estate" on page 7. The write-up revealed that Shaw and his new wife were setting up housekeeping in Norwalk, Connecticut. He had again retired from public performance and was devoting himself to writing: "books, not music," he stressed (2).

During the period since the war experiences that had left him so shaken, Shaw also had become curious about politics and world peace. *The New Yorker* "Profile" summarized this activity succinctly:

A by-product of his all-round misery and of his aversion to war was that he began to join any number of organisations, some of them beyond doubt Communist-inspired.

"I was in favor of a 'World Peace Congress,' " he says. "I put my name to any group identified with words I was interested in, like 'democracy' and 'peace,' but I never even got close to Communism. Out of curiosity, I attended a couple of Communist meetings under the name of Witherspoon, but I asked so many impertinent questions that they told me, 'Witherspoon, you aren't Communist material.' " (8)

Shaw and Kathleen Winsor were reported separating in May 1948. Their divorce became final in December of that year amidst much publicity. The August 14, 1948, issue of *Time* contained a summary of assorted allegations and counterallegations in its "People" column. Gossip magazines reported details gleefully.

Around that same time, a "Draft Artie Shaw Back To Music" campaign began in the musical press. The September 8, 1948, issue of *Down Beat* reported a "Draft Shaw Movement Rolling" on page 2. Published information then became garbled, with Shaw noting in discussing these write-ups, "It didn't happen that way" (2).

Apparently, Shaw's old friend Dave Hudkins had formed a band using Shaw's old arrangements, featuring clarinetist Bob Keene. Shaw allegedly was to take over upon returning to music. When this didn't materialize, Hudkins continued with Heinie Beau playing the clarinet parts, still using the "Artie Shaw Orchestra" tag. Despite the fuss made in the musical press, Shaw dismissed the whole incident. In fact, as he stated in *Artie Shaw: Time Is All You've Got,*

In 1947 or thereabouts I found myself becoming more interested in getting away from the pop music forms and getting off into classical music. I decided that I would give up playing any jazz, any improvised music, for one year, just to see what would happen to my playing, what would happen to the tone production. And the whole sound of my clarinet changed, my entire concept of what a clarinet could sound like changed.

Chapter 13

Artie Shaw "Longhair": 1949

The January 14, 1949, *Down Beat* announced on page 3: "Shaw Scheduled for Classical Concert." The article noted that he would be appearing with the Rochester Civic Orchestra under Guy Frasser Harrison on January 9, 1949, at the Eastman Theatre in Rochester, New York.

The emergence of Artie Shaw as a classical soloist in 1949 was the occasion for considerable attention in the musical press. The January 12, 1949, issue of *Variety* announced on page 1, "Artie Shaw's Gonna Let His Hair Grow." *Wood Magazine* headlined in its February 1949 issue on page 1: "Shaw To Play Serious Music: To Perform Mozart Concerto." The February 1949 issue of *Symphony* had an article on page 2 titled "Shaw To Concertize." The February 25, 1949, *Down Beat* headlined on page 1, "Shaw 'Through With Dance Bands', To Play Longhair." This article continued:

> Artie Shaw announced that he is definitely through with the dance band business and, henceforth, will concentrate on longhair concerts exclusively. In an interview in the *Democrat and Chronicle* following his appearance with the Rochester symphony, Shaw outlined his future plans as consisting of "doing what I am doing right now."
>
> Shaw, who has been studying longhair music on both clarinet and guitar in New York City for the last several months, feels good about deserting jazz.
>
> "There is nothing strange about my forsaking swing, jazz or what have you after so many years of playing it," said Artie. "There is more to music than 'Star Dust.' Any real musician, like any good painter or writer, can't be content to stand still and do the same thing over and over again."
>
> Shaw is doing occasional guest appearances with symphony orchestras, the local spot being his first.
>
> He is set for Kansas City, with Denver booked for March 1, and an appearance with the National Symphony at Carnegie Hall, New York City, April 18.

Curiously, the Denver Symphony files indicated that Shaw had appeared with them on July 26, 1947, and July 6, 1948, with no indication of what was going on. Shaw had no recollection of ever appearing with them except to per-

form the world premiere of Nicolai Berezowsky's "Concerto for Clarinet and Orchestra" at the March 1, 1949, recital. Shaw has affirmed that his guest appearance with the Rochester Civic Orchestra on January 9, 1949, as noted above, was his first in this idiom (2).

In February it also was announced that Shaw had signed with Columbia Records to record an album of classical material, and the article noted that he had been appearing as soloist on "several longhair radio shows" that season:

> He will make several appearances in March on a new series of Monday night musicales over WQXR and will guest on the DuMont TV *Window on the World* show on Thursday (24th).

Unfortunately, this February 24, 1949, DuMont *Window on the World* telecast has never surfaced in any form. It was one of several TV appearances Shaw made that season. The exact dates of the March radio broadcasts, and their repertoire, also could not be determined, although Shaw has so far released two performances of chamber pieces on which he performed that were preserved from radio broadcasts in that period.

The dating problems were exaggerated in the Book-of-the-Month Club four-LP boxed set titled *Artie Shaw—A Legacy* (BOMR 71-7715). Concerning when the classical pieces in that set were recorded, the Mozart Clarinet Quintet and Krein's "Hebrew Sketches" were erroneously dated as from 1947 in the liner notes. They were actually from the above-mentioned radio broadcasts in March 1949. On these pieces, Shaw's playing was warm and tonally gorgeous as always. His rendition of the familiar Mozart work, and the unusual Krein piece, were excellent documentations of his competence in this style. In the liner notes to the Book-of-the-Month set, Shaw referred in some detail to his Mozart Clarinet Quintet performance:

> Anyone listening to this will note that the clarinet is being played with vibrato. Which of course is NOT the conventional way to play this piece. Usually, in this sort of music, it

is not the conventional thing. I've had clarinet players ask me, 'Why DID you use vibrato?' And I reply, 'Why do the strings use vibrato? Why shouldn't the clarinet use vibrato? Why should it come out sounding like a miniature foghorn playing with the strings?' Vibrato is simply a way of embellishing tone. You can play the instrument dead or with some embellishment. Besides, as you can hear, the vibrato here is very slight, very controlled. It's not wide, not even a wave; it's just a ripple. . . .

I showed up at the WOR studios one Sunday and talked the piece over for a few minutes with the string players. They were the staff quartet at the station. They had been playing there for some time, and I appeared as guest soloist. We went on the air that Sunday morning and played the piece through without rehearsing note one.

Concerning the Krein piece, Shaw noted in the liner notes,

Alexander Krein was a Russian composer. He wrote the "Hebrew Sketches" near the beginning of the 20th Century. Again, this is with the WOR staff quartet. It may even have been done on the same Sunday as the Mozart quintet; I don't remember. I did several guest appearances there, including a Mozart trio.

Shaw has stated that he also has a copy of this version of the Mozart Clarinet Trio from one of these broadcasts, and that he has plans to issue it eventually on a CD featuring his classical work (2).

At his first record date since the Musicrafts in 1946, Shaw recorded eight short classical performances for Columbia on March 11, 1949. The large studio orchestra, for which Shaw engaged conductor Walter Hendl, provided a setting for the attractive arrangements Shaw had prepared. Orchestrations were by Hershey Kay and, on Ravel's "Habanera," Arthur Hoeree. Shaw was thoroughly convincing throughout. The mood and texture of the performances were appealing and the cumulative effect of hearing them one after another on the side of the LP titled *Modern Music for Clarinet* (Columbia ML4260) that juxtaposed them was that of hearing a nicely balanced suite. Unfortunately, the LP and even rarer 78-rpm issues of these performances have been almost impossible to find since shortly after they were originally issued in 1949–50 (except for an occasional highly priced copy on the collectors' market). Shaw stated in discussing these performances:

I may try to reissue that material someday, or at least part of it. I wasn't that happy with some of the material. A couple of the pieces were pretty insubstantial. On the other hand, a few of them stand up pretty well. (2)

It is of interest to note that, in 1993, a recording occasionally could be heard on classical radio programs featuring Branford Marsalis performing the Shaw/Hoeree arrangement of Ravel's "Habanera" on soprano sax (from *Romances for Saxophone* on CBS Masterworks MK 42122). Shaw was not aware of this use of his material, but shrugged that off. However, he was appalled by Marsalis's using a soprano sax on this piece.

That's terrible! That piece is far too delicate for such a coarse instrument. I've played soprano; the range is OK, but the tone quality doesn't suit Ravel's writing and tonal textures. Maybe flute or violin would work, but soprano sax is wrong.

Well, what can you expect. Taste and musical values don't enter into the marketplace at all any more, if they ever did. Just listen to what else that guy has done. (2)

On March 18, 1949, Shaw appeared on the CBS-TV *Adventures in Jazz* show with his regular rehearsal accompanist, Virginia Passecantandro, on piano. They performed Ravel's "Habanera" and Alan Shulman's "Rendezvous" on this program. Obviously, it would be a fascinating documentation if a video dub of this show has survived.

Unfortunately, the only video documentation of Shaw in his classical phase to have surfaced was some brief film footage in *Artie Shaw: Time Is All You've Got*. This was a clip of Shaw performing excerpts from the andante movement of Norman Dello Joio's "Concerto for Clarinet" with the composer on piano. Shaw explained,

Norman Dello Joio had that film made for a class he was teaching at Sarah Lawrence College. That was about all there was to the film, just parts of the Andante. We never recorded the whole thing. I don't know where she (Brigitte Berman) got ahold of that item! (2)

According to the media, Shaw was to have performed the Mozart Clarinet Concerto at the New York Academy of Music on April 4th, but this engagement was later reported canceled.

Meanwhile, arrangements were under way for Shaw to appear with a large orchestra for the opening of the new jazz club called Bop City, located at Broadway and 49th Street in New York. Ralph Watkins, the owner, had invited Shaw to perform for their opening night, on April 14th. Earl Wilson quoted Shaw describing the arrangements for this engagement in his syndicated news column "It Happened on Broadway":

"It's a switch," Artie said. "When they first asked me, I said, 'You know I'm through with dance music.'

"They said, 'The guy's kind of hot for you. He'd let you play what you wanted to.'

"So I said, 'Here's the deal. I got to play concert stuff. It'll cost dough.' They said OK. So I threw them one more curve. I said, 'No serving drinks while we're playing.' They said, 'That's rough, but OK.'

"It's a heck of a deal . . . I'll get men from the Toscanini orchestra—finest men in the country."

Unfortunately, Shaw was not provided with the most appropriate environment for this experiment. By all accounts it was a tightly packed, sweltering, noisy crowd that greeted Shaw and his forty to sixty symphony men (depending on the pieces being performed) on their opening night. Reportedly, over 3,000 people made it into the club that evening, and the line outside extended for two blocks. Shaw conducted material by Prokofiev, Debussy, Tansman, and Ravel, and performed the Berezowsky "Concerto," Finzi's "Bagatelles for Clarinet and String Orchestra" and another of the later-so-called Third Stream items he had been experimenting with for over a decade, a composition by Fred van Eps titled "Blues." He was facing failed air conditioning and sound systems, photographers pestering celebrities in the audience such as Kirk Douglas and Ava Gardner, members of the audience who responded with boredom, and even a few catcalls. Shaw was quoted in a *Time*'s review (April 25, 1949, p. 62) as stating, "I was standing up there with egg on my face and I couldn't hear a thing."

An exceptionally vitriolic anti-Shaw review of this opening night appeared on page 1 of the May 20, 1949, *Down Beat*: "This Is Arty? P'Shaw, Says Mix" (by M. Levin). Another similarly snide review, in an apparently right-wing tabloid called *Mirror*, went so far as to claim that the presence of Russian composers in Shaw's programming, coupled with his earlier interest in the World Peace Conference in Paris, was enough "evidence" to accuse Shaw of being a communist. In addition, the *Mirror* article referred to Shaw's musical offerings as "complete torture," and was duly quoted by Levin. The same issue of *Down Beat* also had an article on page 16 titled, "Much Confusion As Ella, Shaw Open Up Bop City," detailing the effects of the three groups sharing the stand: Shaw's orchestra, Ella Fitzgerald's combo, and the Kai Winding Sextet. Ella and her trio, consisting of Hank Jones on piano, Ray Brown, bass, and Charlie Smith, drums, reportedly held the attention of the audience. Trombonist Kai Winding's group, with Gerry Mulligan on baritone sax, Brew Moore on tenor sax, George Wallington on piano, Curley Russell on bass, and Kenny Clarke on drums, was described as pleasing the bop fans. *Billboard*'s review (April 23, 1949, p. 48) was less prejudiced and observed, "The plain fact was that Shaw's music was way over this mob's head." Shaw observed in personal discussions:

After the first night's flop, the orchestra jelled, and it became one of the most exciting events of my life. Conductors flew in from Europe—thousands came. Does that sound unsuccessful? (2)

Shaw also added that, on the numbers on which he was playing clarinet, Hershey Kay conducted the orchestra.

Following the week at Bop City, Shaw continued appearing as a guest classical soloist in various contexts throughout that spring. His April 18, 1949, Carnegie Hall appearance with the National Youth Symphony conducted by Leon Barzin was reviewed in *The New York Times* the following day, on page 29:

Artie Shaw . . . got a chance to play Nicolai Berezowsky's "Concerto for Clarinet and Orchestra" before a serious audience instead of before the noisy one that hardly listened when he played it last week at the opening of the night club Bop City.

The orchestral part is so slight that it hardly seems a concerto. In fact, the work sounded more like a series of four clarinet pieces, but Mr. Shaw played it delightfully. His performance had wit, authority, musicality, and, in the andante, poignant expressiveness.

This performance was broadcast over WNYC, and eventually was issued in the Book-of-the-Month Club boxed set, but was misdated in the liner notes as being recorded in 1948. Shaw has stated in that set's liner notes that he would have preferred a recording by the Denver Symphony, with which he had premiered the piece on March 1st. In private discussion, he stated,

The kids did a marvellous job, but the orchestra just didn't have the dynamic coherence that developed with the other orchestra, with whom I'd had a chance to really rehearse it thoroughly. (2)

Shaw had known Berezowsky since his CBS period, when Berezowsky played violin with the CBS Symphony Orchestra. In the Book-of-the-Month set liner notes Shaw was quoted as stating,

When I decided I was going to do a year of serious concert playing to see what effect it would have on my overall playing, Nicky came to me with this concerto. It may have been written first as a viola concerto and then adapted for me. . . .

The first movement baffled the audience totally. But by the second movement they apparently began to understand that there also was humor in the piece, and at the end of that movement they finally unbent enough to laugh. The last movement is one of the toughest things I have ever played on the clarinet. Incidentally, no one else has ever played it on clarinet, as far as I know. There's one segment of ten or eleven seconds that I spent almost three months practicing. But the third movement is the one I find a really beautiful thing.

Nicolai Berezowsky. He was very Russian, with a heavy accent. So is the piece, come to think of it. I liked Nicky very much. I hope he's still alive and I hope he hears this. It's a tough piece. As a violinist, Nicky tended to forget that a clarinet player has to breathe now and then.

On April 20th, Shaw was scheduled to appear with the Philadelphia Pops Orchestra, in Philadelphia. Negotiations also were under way for a tour of Europe, extending to Israel, during May and June. However, these plans were eventually dropped. Shaw remained in New York, where he rehearsed for his second recording date for Columbia, held on May 31, 1949.

This recording session produced one ten-inch and one twelve-inch 78-rpm disc. Again the results were included as one side of the Columbia LP, *Modern Music for Clarinet* (ML4260).

The longer performances were both Alan Shulman compositions. Shaw was backed by the New Music String Quartet, which premiered a number of albums of contemporary string quartet compositions in that era. "Mood in Question" added Janet Putram's harp to the ensemble. The "Rendezvous (for Clarinet and Strings)", featuring Shaw with the string quartet, has been widely recorded by other artists, but the version by Shaw evoked a distinctive mood in keeping with his other recordings from this period. In discussing these pieces, Shaw recalled the long rehearsals he scheduled to work out the phrasing he expected from the classical performers to get the "feel" he wanted (2).

The shorter performances from this record date featured two popular songs, Gershwin's "The Man I Love" and Cole Porter's "I Concentrate on You." These were arranged by Shaw, with orchestrations by Hershey Kay and Alan Shulman, respectively. They both featured Shaw backed by a large ensemble consisting of strings and woodwinds plus a rhythm section. They were far more successful than the pieces with similar instrumentation recorded for Musicraft in 1946, "due to taking time for careful rehearsing," Shaw

said (2). An alternate take of "The Man I Love" is still unissued, but dubs from a well-worn test pressing have been circulating among collectors. The LP and 78-rpm issues are the same performance. Variations between the two "takes" were slight but noticeable. The new approach to the clarinet Shaw had been speaking of was particularly evident on these pieces, as they included improvisation to some extent and a jazz dimension supplied by both the rhythm section and aspects of the arrangements. Again, the Third Stream nature of these performances was evident and highly successful.

Meanwhile, Shaw continued with his classical guest soloist appearances. His appearances that season with various symphony orchestras included:

> The Dayton Symphony, the Norfolk Symphony, the National Symphony in Washington, D.C.—we played the Mozart and Dello Joio concertos there. Also, with Tommy Sherman's "Little Orchestra" we did a package tour of Town Hall in New York, the Brooklyn Academy of Music, and Newark, playing the Mozart Clarinet Concerto the first half and the Dello Joio the second half. (2)

Concerning the Dello Joio concerto, which Shaw had commissioned, he said,

> I don't think anyone else ever did it. The manuscript is in the University of Arizona collection. I do have one recording of it with the Connecticut Symphony when we did it up in Westport or somewhere. But the sound's not good. It was done on acetates. (2)

Shaw continued performing classical repertoire as a guest soloist in various venues until well into 1950. Meanwhile, however, during June 1949, word began to spread in the music world that Shaw was planning to form another big band.

Chapter 14

Artie Shaw and His Orchestra: 1949–1950

Shaw's return to jazz was heralded with considerable advance notice. *Variety* headlined "18-Piece Jump Band, Jazz Unit For Shaw" on page 45 of its June 8, 1949, issue. *Billboard* announced "Artie Shaw Goes To GAC" on page 19 of its July 2, 1949, issue, noting that he was under contract to GAC and had commissioned Mary Lou Williams, Dave Matthews, and Ralph Burns to prepare conventional big band arrangements for him. He was quoted as stating that he wanted to buy a farm and needed money for a down payment, but that if he had to have a band at all, he wanted a first-rate one. The July 15, 1949, *Down Beat* headlined "Shaw Books Concert Trip" on page 1. Plans were under way for a twelve-week tour of theaters with a package including Sarah Vaughan, but this tour was canceled. Plans for the new, modern big band continued to materialize, however, and the August 12, 1949, *Down Beat* featured an article on page 6 titled "Shaw Sets New Crew." The write-up noted that rehearsals for the band were getting under way.

The big band Artie Shaw led in the latter half of 1949 performed a varied book of arrangements. Some were the modern charts he commissioned from several sources, including Johnny Mandel, Ange Callea, and Al Cohn, in addition to those cited above, plus a few by Tadd Dameron, Eddie Sauter, Gene Roland, and John LaPorta. Other arrangements were items from his old book, the usual hits he was expected to play every night. And every so often he would slip in something such as Ravel's "Habanera" rescored for the band. The September 23, 1949, *Down Beat* noted on page 3, "This Time Shaw Will Play As Dancers Ask, He Says," and published his tour itinerary:

September 14th:	Symphony Hall, Boston, Massachussets
15th:	Providence, Rhode Island
16–18th:	State Theatre, Hartford, Connecticut
21–24th:	(one-nighters in Canada)
October 1st:	Pla-Mor Ballroom, Kansas City, Missouri
4th:	Arkota Ballroom, Sioux Falls, South Dakota

5th:	Tomba Ballroom, Sioux City, Iowa
6th:	Armar Ballroom, Marion, Iowa
8th:	Frog Hop Ballroom, St. Joseph, Missouri
9th:	Tromar Ballroom, Des Moines, Iowa
12th:	Kato Ballroom, Mankato, Minnesota
15th:	State University, Iowa City
16th:	Sagle's Ballroom, Milwaukee, Wisconson
18th:	Nightingale Ballroom, Kaukauna, Wisconson
21–22nd:	Purdue University, Purdue [*sic*], Indiana
23rd:	Inglaterra Ballroom, Peoria, Illinois
29th:	University of Minnesota, Minneapolis
30th:	Electric Park, Waterloo, Iowa
November 5th:	I.M.A. Auditorium, Flint, Michigan
7–21st:	Blue Note Cafe, Chicago, Illinois

Time reviewed the opening night in Boston (September 26, 1949, pp. 47–48):

A record-breaking crowd, including a good many of the jammy jitterbug type which apparently hides under logs in the daytime, was lured into Boston's huge Symphony Ballroom. The Shaw faithful, plus a few horn-rimmed jazz intellectuals, clustered around the bandstand, stood through it all without moving much but their gum-chewing muscles. Right there, any resemblance to success stopped.

When Artie's boys began unravelling Ravel's "Piece en Forme de Habanera" the crowd around the bandstand applauded politely, but even the most ardent jitterers had to stop dancing. Cried one in petulant exasperation, "Artie, you stink."

Others attempted more precise analysis: "It's all right to play Ravel, but not with this band and not in a place where people want to dance. Artie is O.K. when he plays the Shaw stuff that everyone likes—like 'Stardust' [*sic*]."

Shaw was quoted as stating,

I'll play enough of what I have to play to keep the band together. If they want 'Begin the Beguine' I'll even play that. But I want to play something for kicks, too.

Shaw also wanted to continue with his guest appearances as a classical soloist, and appeared with orchestras in this capacity while also touring with his big band. An example was an evening at the Temple Shalom in Chicago. On November 9th, during his Blue Note Cafe booking with his big band, Shaw took time to appear there with an orchestra (billed simply as "Symphony Orchestra") conducted by Alfredo Antonini. Shaw performed the Mozart Clarinet Concerto plus an item that was again in the Third Stream approach, called "Fantasie on 3 American Songs." This turned out to be versions of "Frenesi"–"Star Dust"–"Begin the Beguine" interpolated in an arrangement by Richard Maltby. Shaw said, "That was a nice piece, sort of Kostelanetz-ish" (2). A private recording of this performance circulates among collectors, revealing Shaw to have been in very good form, soloing over the orchestral backing with his characteristic poise in a confident, jazzy approach to these familiar melodies. It is not known whether the Mozart piece was also preserved.

At the Blue Note Cafe in Chicago, Shaw was pleased to find that their audiences were "ecstatic."

> Without question that was one of the greatest engagements of my life. That was when that band really came into its own. Up until then, the band's reception in the midwest was dismal. I really liked that band. But except for Chicago, the public didn't respond. (2)

Following the Blue Note engagement, Shaw became ill with a gallbladder attack. He lost some time out of his tour, but after his recovery they played at The Click in Philadelphia from December 12th through 26th. A review appeared in the December 31, 1949, *Billboard* on page 21. The personnel of the band at that time was listed (see discography) and the Gramercy 5, with Shaw, trumpeter Don Fagerquist, and the rhythm section, was praised.

Following the engagement at The Click, Shaw embarked on a ten-day schedule of recording projects that provided the band's entire recorded legacy. These included a series of titles for Thesaurus Transcriptions.

Although pianist Dodo Marmarosa often has been cited on record jackets and in discographies as being among the personnel on the band's recordings for the Thesaurus Transcriptions, he had left the band by the time of the Blue Note engagement. Shaw related that he had been happy to have Marmarosa in his band again, but that repeated performances of "Frenesi" had been annoying the pianist.

> Dodo was a funny cat. One night he said to me, "If we have to play that again, I'm gone." Later that night we got a request for "Frenesi" again, and we played it. I looked over at the piano, and no Dodo. That was it! (2)

Gil Barrios was the pianist who replaced Marmarosa, and who performed on all recordings by that band. Rumors that the band had been recorded while at the Blue Note were untrue. Shaw observed, "I'm sorry it wasn't. I should have done it myself! But there were no recordings made then—no broadcasts or anything" (2).

The Thesaurus Transcriptions were recorded during the last few days of December 1949 and the first week of January 1950. During the same time period, Shaw also was scheduled to record with the band for Columbia, but disagreements arose in the recording studio. Shaw asked to be released from his contract and Columbia agreed. "Within 24 hours," according to the media, Shaw had signed with Decca and recorded two sides for them with his band.

For their first Decca record date, Shaw added Machito's Latin rhythm section on two John Bartee pieces, "Orinoco" and "Mucho de Nada." These were the most fully Latin of all Shaw's experiments with Latin elements among his recorded material. The era of using the Afro-Cuban influence prominently in jazz was well under way by late 1949, with Dizzy Gillespie's big band experiments being the most heralded examples. Machito also had been appearing with a big band performing in the same basic style that eventually became popularly known as "Salsa."

Both of these John Bartee titles also were recorded for Thesaurus, along with a third John Bartee piece, originally titled "Gue-le-le," also in a Latin style. However the lack of the authentic Latin rhythm section gave the Thesaurus performances a different effect. Curiously, the version of "Mucho de Nada" recorded for Thesaurus did not appear on the Thesaurus Transcriptions discs issued, or in any discographies. When *Artie Shaw '1949'* (MusicMasters CIJD60234, reissued as *Artie Shaw: The Last Recordings Vol. II: The Big Band* on MusicMasters CD 65026-2) was issued in 1990, "Mucho de Nada" was inexplicably retitled "Afro-Cubana," while "Gue-le-le" was mistitled "Mucho de Nada." According to transcription authority Ken Crawford, the Thesaurus version of "Mucho de Nada" must have been taken from an unissued test pressing. "Gue-le-le" also has been spelled "Bue-le-le" in some sources.

The total documentation of this band included fifty-six performances (counting the "Nightmare" theme statement). Six of these were recorded for both Decca and Thesaurus, leaving fifty unique titles. Seven performances were by the Gramercy 5, including two titles for Decca with vocals by Mary Ann McCall, fresh out of Woody Herman's Second Herd. There were also five vocals each from Pat Lockwood, who was the band's regular vocalist to the end of the year, and Decca artist Trudy Richards, who replaced her for the Thesaurus session after the New Year.

Of the remaining thirty-three titles, which were all instrumentals by the full band, more than half used the arrangements Shaw had recorded with earlier bands. These included re-orchestrations for conventional instrumentation of previous arrangements for the orchestras with string sections on pieces such as "Star Dust" and "Moonglow" (balancing the string orchestras' rearrangements of Shaw's earlier hits with his earlier big band). One title, "Love Walked In," used the same George Siravo arrangement that Shaw already had recorded for Victor in 1945, but the Victor issue had not yet been released at that time. At these 1949–50 sessions, Shaw recorded this same arrangement for both Thesaurus and Decca.

Thus, there were only fifteen titles recorded by this band that had not already been recorded by one or another of Shaw's earlier bands using essentially the same arrangements:

"Cool Daddy"
"Fred's Delight"
"Gue-le-le"
"I Concentrate On You"
"I Get a Kick Out of You"
"Innuendo"
"Krazy Kat"
"Love Is the Sweetest Thing"
"Minnesota"
"Mucho de Nada"
"Orinoco"
"Similau"
"Smooth and Easy"
"So Easy"
"The Very Thought of You"

The only new composition cited as by Shaw alone on this list was "Cool Daddy" (although he also has been given co-composer credit for "Orinoco"). Among the others there were three items by Johnny Mandel ("Innuendo," "Krazy Kat," and "Minnesota"); two by Tadd Dameron ("Fred's Delight" and "So Easy"); two by Eddie Sauter ("Similau" and "Smooth and Easy"); and the three Latin numbers by John Bartee. The remaining new titles consisted of four popular songs. Two of these Shaw had recorded earlier with different arrangements ("I Get a Kick Out of You" and "I Concentrate on You"). Curiously, both were Cole Porter compositions and both were earlier done with strings-and-woodwinds ensembles, the former in 1946 for Musicraft and the latter in 1949 for Columbia. The two new titles, "The Very Thought of You" (arranged by George Siravo) and "Love Is the Sweetest Thing" (arranged by Johnny Thompson), were both compositions by Ray Noble.

Thus, the 1949 big band's recordings resembled the 1945 big band's repertoire in mixing a book of new arrangements by modern writers with "updated" versions of Shaw's older arrangements. In addition, with both his 1945 and 1949 bands, Shaw was showing obvious developments new to his clarinet style. With the 1949 band, he played brilliantly in-

tricate solos out of his new conception following his classical metamorphosis. This resulted in fresh and, in the context of the older, familiar arrangements, often startling improvisations.

Some of the vocal arrangements also were new and distinctive. At least some of them reportedly were done by Gene Roland, later prominent arranging for Stan Kenton. However, Shaw was, as usual, dismissive of the vocal efforts. He referred to Pat Lockwood as "an ornament to decorate the band" and recalled Trudy Richards only vaguely, and more in connection with the 1952 record date for which Shaw wrote arrangements and conducted but did not play. In fact, he did not play for some of the Thesaurus vocals either. He was considerably more enthusiastic about Mary Ann McCall's work with him on the two Gramercy 5 titles.

The same general repertoire situation existed for the Gramercy 5 items. Most of the pieces they recorded were familiar. Four of the Thesaurus instrumentals were previously recorded by Gramercy 5 units, and even "The Pied Piper Theme" had been derived from Shaw's *The Pied Piper of Hamelin* album of children's records. This edition of the Gramercy 5 did not have quite the impact of the earlier groups, although like the big band it also bore obvious resemblance to its 1945 counterpart. This was due primarily to the lack of new material combined with the difference in personnel. Only the vocals with Mary Ann McCall were new to the Gramercy 5 discography. These were the first records of Gramercy 5 performances including a vocalist.

Shaw's soloists for the recordings issued on MusicMasters included Don Fagerquist for all trumpet solos except "Star Dust" (for which Don Palladino performed the opening originally done by Billy Butterfield); Al Cohn for all tenor sax solos except on "I Cover the Waterfront" (which was by Zoot Sims); and trombonists Sonny Russo (on "Innuendo") and Fred Zito (re-creating Jack Jenney's solo for "Star Dust"). Solos on piano and guitar, of course, were by Gil Barrios and Jimmy Raney, respectively. Concerning drummer Irv Kluger, whom Shaw would also use with his final groups in 1953–54, Shaw told Loren Schoenberg (who wrote the liner notes for MusicMasters CD 65026-2):

Irv was a very vital player. He was a spark plug with the small groups, too. Irv fit right in. He was a very supple drummer. He had a lot of spark as a human being. It's like the difference between Chick Webb and other drummers. Buddy Rich and Sid Catlett were exciting drummers; and Dave Tough, in his own way, even though he was quiet, had a great psychic energy to his playing. Irv fit right in with them.

Following the final January 6, 1950, Decca session, Shaw disbanded. The band had lasted only about five months. Shaw then entered Lenox Hill Hospital for a gallstone operation. As noted, he had lost time out of his tour because of a severe gallstone attack a month or so earlier. He was reported planning to take the rest of January off to recuperate.

On February 20, 1950, Shaw was sufficiently recovered to appear again as a classical soloist. He performed Dello Joio's clarinet concerto with the Little Orchestra Society at Town Hall in New York. Reviewers praised both Shaw's performance and the composition, which Shaw had commissioned.

During March, Shaw again appeared at Bop City with a conventional big band organized for him by Lee Castle. Shaw and the band again received a devastating review in *Down Beat* (by the same offensive reviewer who had been so vitriolic over Shaw's Bop City engagement the preceding year).

This was the band, with slight personnel variations, that recorded four instrumentals, all Shaw arrangements, for Decca on April 4, 1950. On LP reissues of these performances, the band did sound listless. However, the original 78-rpm issues played these recordings somewhat faster, and the same performances then sounded correspondingly brighter.

A few days later, a septet called the Gramercy 5 with personnel out of this big band recorded two Shaw originals for Decca. Both performances were first-rate, and Don Lanphere's tenor sax was an interesting addition to the ensemble and solos. Shaw played superbly on "The Shekomeko Shuffle" (named after his new farm) and "Crumbum" (a moody minor blues composition). Lee Castle, who had been with Shaw as early as his 1936 band, held his own in this relatively modern setting. As usual on Gramercy 5 performances, the trumpet was muted and the drummer used brushes throughout.

Although this big band continued to be Shaw's working unit that spring, and his contract with Decca promised twenty sides yearly for three years, all of Shaw's remaining recordings with that company were with studio groups and other Decca artists with whom the company teamed him up for making records. It is unfortunate that so little documentation of this working band and the enlarged Gramercy 5 exists. Shaw's regular vocalist that season, Dodie O'Neill, was not even represented. Meanwhile, studio groups, usually including large string sections, obviously not performing arrangements Shaw was using on the road, were recording regularly with specially contracted singers.

Chapter 15

Artie Shaw on Decca: 1950–1953

As well as Artie Shaw, Decca had several major jazz performers signed for recording contracts at the beginning of the 1950s. These included Louis Armstrong, Ella Fitzgerald, Coleman Hawkins, and Billie Holiday, among others. Instead of recording Shaw with artists such as these, Decca teamed him up with pop singers such as Dick Haymes and Don Cherry, with vocal groups including the Gordon Jenkins Choir, and even had him record Christmas carols. Although Shaw was performing regularly with his working groups during much of this time, after the early April 1950 documentation of his existing big band and Gramercy 5, he only recorded with studio orchestras for Decca, despite the potential for interesting performances with his subsequent working units. Even while on tour with his big band during the spring of 1950, he would fly back to New York to record with studio groups, usually backing vocalists. Shaw has confirmed that he did all the arrangements recorded under his name for Decca during those years.

The session with Dick Haymes on April 27, 1950, was among the more interesting, as a result of Shaw's using the strings-and-woodwinds ensemble as a setting for Haymes's vocals, an idea he had used for backing singers Mel Tormé and Teddy Walters on two of the 1946 Musicrafts; these are at least as good. Unfortunately (from the point of view of the jazz lover), almost all of the Decca records made that spring and summer by Shaw were of commercial popular music with vocalists and contained little or nothing to interest the jazz buff, aside from occasional brilliant clarinet solos from Shaw.

A month later, having become disillusioned with the receptions his bands had been receiving on the road over the preceding year, Shaw broke up the band Lee Castle had organized for him for the Bop City appearance, and with which he had been touring since then. Shaw then returned to New York for two more Decca record dates. On May 29, he recorded two titles with the Gordon Jenkins Choir and a big band with strings. He related that when the Decca officials asked him to make a record with Gordon Jenkins, his reaction was, "Why?" and that Jenkins had arranged the choral passages, while he arranged the music (2). The re-

sults ("I'm Forever Blowing Bubbles" and "You're Mine You") are among the most saccharine commercial items in Shaw's entire output. Nevertheless, Shaw's own playing on these titles was impeccably beautiful as always.

Two days later, on May 31, 1950, Shaw again entered the Decca studios to record another pair of titles with an entirely different studio band except for the two alto saxophonists. This time the overly cute-and-perky-voiced Gwen Davies and a vocal trio sang "I Love the Guy" in Broadway-show style, while the other side featured Don Cherry singing "Just Say I Love Her" (also in an overripe show-tune style) but with some outstanding Shaw obbligatos and fills. Both items were recent pop tunes. The men in the vocal trio would reappear later, with the Chelsea 3 and Chickering 4 vocal groups (see discography).

At the beginning of June, Shaw re-formed a road band with only tenor saxophonist Don Lanphere, pianist Gil Barrios, bassist Teddy Kotick, and vocalist Dodie O'Neill remaining from the preceding ensemble. He also changed road managers, replacing Lennie Lewis, who had been with him since the preceding fall, with Milt Gray. This was the band that Shaw often has referred to as his personal "private joke." In *The New Yorker* "Profile" he stated:

I had a band boy named Tommy Thompson, and I told him, "You're the arranger now. Get the latest copy of *Variety*, pick out the ten top tunes, and buy stock arrangements of them all. That'll be the nucleus of our library." Well, do you know, people liked that band. I did all the things I'd shied off from all my life. I laughed, I ogled, I wagged my head. (11)

The June 9, 1950, issue of *The Wind Sock* (published by the Marine Corps Air Station at Cherry Point, North Carolina) contained a lengthy review of Shaw's appearance there, written by Private First Class M. L. Jones. It related,

Well over 1,500 Artie Shaw fans packed the theatre Tuesday evening. They expected, and received, for the most part, a flawless performance—one that combined the artistry of hot jazz pieces with the smooth tempos of the famed masterpieces turned out by the clarinetist when he was at the peak of his career.

Nostalgia was the theme of the performance. This the audience wanted and got. They wanted to hear the Artie Shaw of old; the man who dictated the popular music tastes of audiences of a few years back.

But the mass in front of the stage didn't seem to think that they were getting the quality of music that is typical of Shaw's bands. They left the theatre with variations of one question on their lips: What has happened to the Artie Shaw who left nation-wide audiences stunned with admiration?

The answer is simple. Nothing has happened to the Artie Shaw of old! He, personally, still produces thrilling, flawless clarinet solos. His clarinet renditions of FRENESI and BEGIN THE BEGUINE are as incomparable today as they were ten years ago.

What the audience did not realize—and the reason for the apparent lack of Shaw perfection—was that the clarinet virtuoso was conducting an orchestra that was entirely new to him! Tuesday's performance was the third time that particular orchestra had played with Artie.

For technical reasons, he was forced to disband the orchestra that he started his tour of one-nighters with. Last Friday, a scant one week ago today, he assembled the band that played here. . . .

Vocals by singer Dodie O'Neill were handled with her typical ease and grace. It is these qualities, plus her thrilling voice, that has made her a popular figure with top orchestras for a number of years.

SUMMIT RIDGE DRIVE, another selection that was eagerly awaited but cooly recognized by the audience, was courageously attempted by Artie's new Gramercy 5. Actually seven musicians—Ted Kotick on the bass fiddle; Teddy Cohen on the vibraharp; Gil Barrios on the Steinway; Stan Feldman on drums; Don Lanphere on tenor sax; Dick Mills on trumpet; and Shaw on clarinet, composed the jazz "quintet."

High spot of the performance, judging from audience reaction, came when comedian Tommy Thompson poured forth his assortment of gags. . . .

Although mistakes were made and those who attended with high expectations were a bit disappointed, many of Artie's fans definitely found traces of his old artistry in Tuesday's performance.

On June 15th, near Huntington, West Virginia, Shaw had an auto accident that left him shaken, although he made the next night's gig in Cincinnati. However, when the band performed in Allentown, Pennsylvania, and the promoter came up to Shaw and said, "You're the greatest thing we've had since Blue Barron!" (a cliche-ridden and commercially oriented but popular dance band of the era), Shaw canceled the rest of his summer tour and broke up that band as well. He aloofly retired to his farm to immerse himself in writing, still emerging occasionally to make a few records for Decca. On July 19th, he recorded four sides, one of them again

featuring Don Cherry (for a similarly dramatic rendition of "Don't Worry 'Bout Me"). "Blue Again," featuring the lovely Jane Ford, has never been issued; the remaining titles featured the Chelsea 3 vocal group for "It's a Long Way To Tipperary" and "Show Me the Way to Go Home." The latter title was as close to a comedy record as Shaw ever made. Robert Lissauer, in his *Lissauer's Encyclopedia of Popular Music in America 1888 to the Present* (New York: Paragon House, 1991), accurately described the lyrics as having "a post-carousal connotation," and the trio sings with all the flair of an inebriated "barbershop" group. Following another outstanding clarinet solo, Shaw himself sang half of the last chorus, "just for fun" (2). His singing voice was mellow and pleasant, sleepily restrained (in keeping with the content of the lyrics) with some appealing melodic variations; and Shaw proved, if nothing else, that he also was a better *SINGER* than Benny Goodman! This record therefore manages to be surprising for three reasons: Shaw sang; it was a "comedy-novelty" item; and despite (or because of) the bizarre context, Shaw's clarinet solo sounded inspiring enough to seem miraculous.

During August, Shaw again switched agencies. Since his big band bookings had been so unsatisfactory, he left GAC and signed with the Willard Alexander Agency. It was announced that he would be appearing with a sextet that September.

In fact, Shaw opened with a sextet on September 15, 1950, at The Iceland, a Scandinavian restaurant on Broadway noted for its smorgasbord. The Iceland was described by Leonard Feather, in the November 18, 1950, *Melody Maker* on page 3, as "a well-decorated and spacious basement with a huge smorgasbord table in one corner." Shaw's band, billed as his Gramercy 5, consisted of Shaw, vocalist Terry Swope, and the Billy Taylor Quartet that had been Taylor's working group that season: pianist Taylor, guitarist John Collins, bassist Joe Benjamin, and drummer Charlie Smith.

Terry Swope, who also sang with Benny Goodman's band for a while the preceding year, had been working with a vocal group called Four Jacks and a Jill when Shaw hired her. The group's leader sued Shaw and Swope for $100,000, claiming Shaw had persuaded her to break her contract with the vocal group. "Shaw settled out of court just before the Iceland opening and Terry went in with the Shaw combo," according to the *Down Beat* article headlined "Shaw Debuts Gramercy 5" (October 20, 1950, p. 18). In Feather's *Melody Maker* article, titled " 'Strictly for the loot'—says Artie Shaw," as referred to above, Shaw again expressed cynicism with his audiences and the music business and stated:

I just came down here to pick up a few fast bucks. It's strictly for the loot. You can't make it with music any more—the band business as we know it is dead! People don't follow bands and know all the soloists the way they did. . . .

With me right now it's just a matter of how soon can I get back to my farm.

Nevertheless, he recalled the engagement at The Iceland favorably, noting, "That was a good group. I enjoyed that gig" (2). This edition of the Gramercy 5 performed only the booking at The Iceland, which lasted about four weeks. It was never recorded, although the rhythm section was used for two of the studio sessions Shaw did for Decca in September, just before opening at The Iceland, which otherwise used entirely different personnel. Unfortunately for the jazz lovers, these sessions featured large ensembles performing Christmas carols and standards, rather than the group and repertoire Shaw had been featuring that season at The Iceland. The first session on September 12th, featuring a strings-and-woodwinds setting, was never even issued. Two days later, Shaw recorded a version of "Jingle Bells" with the Chickering 4 vocal group and the arrangement using some of the motifs in his earlier arrangement of "Show Me the Way to Go Home" and somehow managing to sound satirical. Another attempt to record "Blue Again" remains unissued from this session. Nevertheless, the big band version of "Where or When," also recorded on September 14, 1950, was a fine performance worthy of the bands Shaw had led the previous year.

Two other fine instrumentals also were recorded for Decca that fall, "Serenade in Blue" and "Autumn Leaves" (on October 5, 1950). These standards were performed in lush strings-and-woodwinds settings more reminiscent of those done for Columbia in 1949 than those for Musicraft in 1946. They concluded the subgenre of eleven titles Shaw had recorded with this distinctive instrumentation, which included the four for Musicraft, two for Columbia, two with Dick Haymes the preceding spring, and the version of "White Christmas" also made at the October 5th session, again with vocalist Gwen Davies but without the vocal trio.

Following the engagement at The Iceland, Shaw returned to his farm to work on writing his autobiographical *The Trouble with Cinderella*, which was published in 1952. During this interval, he emerged only on rare occasions for Decca record dates. He stated,

During those years, I was dream-walking. My mind was on my farm and my writing. For those records, I'd sketch the arrangements on my farm, show up and play, then get back to the farm to write. (2)

The farm Shaw had bought in 1949 and was working to pay for was a 240-acre dairy farm called "Picardy Farm" near Shekomeko, New York. It was about three hours by train from Manhattan. Shaw has described it as the most

peaceful refuge of his life. It was beautifully depicted in *Artie Shaw: Time Is All You've Got* as "the place where I thought I'd reached the end of my personal rainbow," as Shaw put it. When Leonard Feather visited him there for the interview that resulted in the *Down Beat* interview/article " 'Happy At Last!' Says Shaw" (3), he wrote:

Artie lives alone now in a big, handsome house, with several household and farm employees living on his land. He is glad that dairy farming, unlike the music business, involves a commodity where you don't have to deal direct with the customers. The milk cans are picked up and taken away regularly, and he expects to make a nice modest profit this year.

Between this and his royalties he can live comfortably, and if he wants anything more, he can always use music to help his plans, as he did last fall when, to pay for the addition of a new wing on a barn, he worked a few weeks at Iceland.

His views on music have not changed basically. He says the American public is getting better music than it deserves, and points out that the best-selling record he has made so far under his Decca contract is a "real piece of crap" that sold 250,000 while the record that he considers his best musically on Decca sold exactly 415.

Artie's own summation of his present life is simple and succinct. "I'm doing Bucks County again," he says, "but this time on the right scale. A dairy farm in those days was out of my reach. Now I know what I want to write, and I have the conditions in which to write it. Bucks County was in 1933, and it'll be a couple of years before I've rounded out this writing job. It'll have taken me just 20 years to get back to where I wanted to go. I sure went a long way around."

During January 1951, Shaw returned to the Decca studios for a few more recordings backing vocalists. Of the six titles with singer Don Cherry, apparently also featuring a vocal group, Shaw said he could not recall playing clarinet at all. When told copies could not be located to check, he said, "Just as well" (2).

The two titles with June Hutton singing with Gramercy 5 backing, however, Shaw felt were more vital: "Junie was good; she could sing. I enjoyed those records. I thought Junie was marvelous" (2). These performances are of special interest since they echo the format used at The Iceland in featuring a female vocalist with a Gramercy 5 consisting of Shaw and only a rhythm section backing. June Hutton was the younger half-sister of bandleader Ina Ray Hutton, with whom she sang while a teenager. She sounds effective on both the lightly swinging "Dancing on the Ceiling" and the torch-styled "My Kind of Love," and Shaw's short solos and obbligatos are masterful and interesting.

Shaw spent most of the next fifteen months at his farm working on his book, except for a trip to England in the fall of 1951. He had lined up an orchestra there to record more of his arrangements for Decca to fulfill his contract.

Down Beat summarized the situation surrounding Shaw's

trip to England in its December 14, 1951, issue, headlining on page 1: "AFM Bars Shaw Wax Date in G. B.; No Reason Given." Shaw was described sailing from New York on August 30th on the liner *De Grassi*,

> owing Decca 18 sides, which he planned to cut in England using a big orchestra with strings and woodwinds. British sidemen scale being about one-third of the American fee, this would have represented a saving of thousands of dollars, even after deducting his round-trip fare.

Although the American Federation of Musicians did not cite its reasons for blocking Shaw's recording project for Decca, speculation in published discussions indicated the prevailing opinion was that the Musicians' Union wanted the fees paid to American musicians. "All I know is, I couldn't make the sessions," Shaw told interviewers. Decca was reported having no comment. Shaw's longtime lawyer, Andrew Weinberger, was reported negotiating with Decca to have Shaw's travel expenses reimbursed despite the project having fallen through. Weinberger's comment on the ban was, "It does seem a pity that this decision was made more or less retroactively in Artie's case." Apparently, other American bandleaders, such as Toots Camarata and David Rose, had done the same thing earlier without any repercussions. A Decca representative was quoted as stating,

> Vic Schoen did a date over there with the Andrews Sisters only a couple of months ago. Artie just happened to be the victim when they decided to clamp down.

While in England, Shaw was interviewed and photographed extensively. He was touring, attending performances by British musicians, and working on editing his manuscript of *The Trouble with Cinderella* while he was in England as well. In discussions of his recording project, tunes were named that Shaw eventually did record for Decca with a similar large orchestra. However, some Latin arrangements that were discussed never emerged, except for a lightly Latin-flavored version of "That Old Black Magic."

Actress Doris Dowling had joined Shaw in England, and the couple was interviewed by Marshall Pugh in the November 10, 1951, issue of the *Daily Mirror* concerning their engagement. Doris Dowling was described as "age 28, the sloe-eyed star of *Lost Weekend* and *Bitter Rice*." She and Shaw flew back to the states together on a Stratocruiser, arriving in New York on November 11th.

By the following April, *The Trouble with Cinderella* was being published by Farrar, Straus & Young, and Shaw was back in the Decca studios to record again. However, he did not play clarinet, as he had not been playing for over a year and said he did not feel it worthwhile to get his embouchure back in shape for just the one date. This April 23, 1952, session produced two vocals featuring Trudy Richards,

whose style had changed somewhat since the Thesaurus recordings over two years earlier. She was, in 1952, showing the influence of then-current pop star "sob-singer" Johnnie Ray. An instrumental also was recorded which was not released at the time, but of course had no clarinet solo either. "I just stood there and waved my hands a little bit," Shaw said (2).

On June 29, 1952, Shaw and Doris Dowling were married. Shaw was also in the news for reviews of *The Trouble with Cinderella*, which generally were very positive and enthusiastic.

In August 1952 he returned to the Decca recording studios yet again, this time with his clarinet, singer Connee Boswell, and a rhythm section. Like the session with June Hutton, this was a clarinet-with-rhythm-section Gramercy 5. Shaw had recorded with Connee Boswell in the 1930s under the Boswell Sisters' name, and he also was reunited for this session with Bob Kitsis on piano. Connee Boswell sang in a throaty, torch-singer style on this session. Unfortunately, Shaw's contributions were mostly fills and obbligatos, but his work was again masterful and interesting throughout. Along with the titles with June Hutton, these records evoke the format of the unrecorded Gramercy 5 of The Iceland in 1950, which had featured vocalist Terry Swope.

Shaw continued enjoying his farm. He referred to this period in *Artie Shaw: Time Is All You've Got* as one of the healthiest periods in his life. Sometimes he would help with the haying, or drive a tractor and help plow a field. However, in the spring of 1953, "for various complicated financial reasons having to do with the IRS and back taxes," he took out a band once again. This tour was for "about 30 one-nighters around Texas and Oklahoma in 5 weeks, in April and May 1953" (2).

The April 23, 1953, *Down Beat* headlined on page 1, "Artie Shaw To Go On Road With Band Soon." The article noted,

> Drummer Tony Papa is organizing a group of 16 men and a girl for the one-nighters, most of which will take place in Texas and possibly Oklahoma . . . set up by GAC, starting probably April 16 in Little Rock, Ark.

In discussing this band, Shaw related that he had wanted to take out a good band again, but his bookers told him to stay with his old hits if he wanted a successful tour. He said,

> Somebody had a band out in Indiana, and the agency set up the tour. I just went out to Elkhart with about 10 arrangements and we went down to Texas and Oklahoma and did the dates. That's all there was to it! (2)

Actually, a frustrating but in retrospect amusing incident occurred while Shaw was in Elkhart to meet his new band.

The Monday, April 20, 1953, issue of *The Fort Worth Press* headlined in its "Amusements" section:

Not at all like they said—
ARTIE "THE SNOB" FOOLS 'EM; HE'S REAL NICE GUY
by Jack Gordon

Following a description of Shaw's willingness to joke with autograph hunters and his telephoning "his sixth and current spouse, actress Doris Dowling, who is expecting a child in June," from his suite in the Western Hills Hotel, and an account of Shaw's surprising Joe Landwehr, who ran the Lake Worth Casino where Shaw was to play, by his affability and ability to discuss cattle (Shaw was breeding Holsteins on his farm), Gordon told this story about Shaw's visit to Elkhart:

> Driving up to the leading hotel there, where Shaw was to appear, the bandleader saw a big sign over the door: "Welcome Artie Shaw."
> The hotel staff smothered Shaw and his young manager Vic Jaimel with hospitality. The two were literally swept from their car.
> "Later," relates Jaimel, "Artie wanted his car. Nobody knew where it was. Turned out the police had towed it in. Artie had to pay a 'no parking' fine and towing charge before we could get to the car."

Intriguingly, collector/researcher John Harding has a photo of Shaw and his car outside the Elkhart hotel in question. Harding noted that the marquee had actually stated, "Welcome to Artie Shaw and his Orchestra."

Gordon concluded the write-up by noting,

> At the Casino, Shaw played all the great ones identified with him: "Begin the Beguine," "Dancing in the Dark," "Summit Ridge Drive." The younger set wasn't out in numbers attracted by (Ralph) Flannigan or (Stan) Kenton, but as Artie said, "I recorded 'Begin the Beguine' in 1938. That was a long time ago."

Little was published in the jazz magazines about this band or the tour. Fortunately, collector/researcher John Harding was able to copy the band's itinerary from Shaw's datebook, which resides in the Artie Shaw Archives at the University of Arizona. This document showed that the band opened its tour at the Lake Worth Casino in Fort Worth on Saturday, April 18th. Following two days off, they did five nights at the Club Seven Oaks in San Antonio, April 21–25, where Shaw did an inconsequential interview for the local newspaper with writer Ed Castillo. The tour then continued as follows:

April 26: Alton Queen, Palacios
April 27: Dessan Hall, Pflugerville
April 28: Palladium, Houston
April 29: Auditorium, Shreveport
April 30: Pine Bluff, Arkansas
May 1: Westwood Supper Club, Little Rock, Arkansas
May 2: Field house, University of Arkansas (Fayetteville)
May 3: (flight to New York from Little Rock to appear before the House Un-American Activities Committee on May 4th)

As noted, Shaw had to interrupt his tour to appear before the House Un-American Activities Committee in New York on May 4th. Senator Joe McCarthy had been intimidating members of the entertainment industry, among others, with his House Un-American Activities Committee, in the relentless and, in retrospect, irrationally paranoid search for Communist infiltration. Witnesses were interrogated in vast numbers in attempts to prove conspiracy through a guilt-by-association method. Shaw confessed to being terrified by the whole process in *Artie Shaw: Time Is All You've Got*, which included short clips of the filmed interrogation. He related that he had tried to walk a fine line between trying to be cooperative without incriminating anyone, and revealing his contempt for the whole business.

Shaw's testimony before the committee was transcribed and published in an ominous document titled *Hearings Before the Committee on Un-American Activities, House of Representatives, 83rd Congress, First Session* (Washington, D.C.: GPO), in the section headed "Testimony of Artie Shaw Accompanied By His Counsel, Andrew D. Weinberger." This section occupied pages 1150–94. Shaw admitted to being in favor of world peace and to trying to learn about Communism by attending meetings under the name of "Witherspoon," but reaffirmed his devotion to America. Photos were widely published showing him wiping his eyes in a gesture the press interpreted as "weeping" before the committee, but which Shaw maintained was due to the bright Kleig lights focused on him. His testimony earned him a handshake from Committee Chairman Harold Velde, snide write-ups in the tacky tabloids, which referred to him as a "Communist dupe," and the label of "controversial figure" politically. Following his testimony at the hearings, Shaw immediately flew back via Tulsa to continue his tour:

May 4: (evening): VCT Hall, Fort Smith
May 5: Fox Theatre, Hutchinson, Kansas
May 6: Tower Ballroom, Pittsburg, Kansas
May 7: Cimmaron Ballroom, Tulsa, Oklahoma
May 8: Country Club, Wichita Falls, Texas
May 9: Officer's Club, San Antonio, Texas
May 10: NCO Club, Randolph Air Force Base, San Antonio
May 11: Country Club, Corpus Christi

May 12:   VFW Hall, Alice
May 13:   Officer's Club, Air Force Base, Byron, Texas
May 14:   Longhorn Ranch, Dallas, Texas
May 15:   Student's Union, Texas Tech, Lubbock, Texas
May 16:   Oklahoma Memorial Union, Norman, Oklahoma
May 17:   Meadow Acres Ballroom, Topeka, Kansas
May 18:   Airlane Ballroom, Strand Hotel, Chillicothe, Missouri
May 19:   (open)
May 20:   McClure, Illinois
May 21:   Springfield, Illinois
May 22:   North Riverside, Chicago
May 23:   Beloit College Fieldhouse, Beloit, Wisconsin

Researcher John Harding reported that the few reviews of the band in local papers during this tour were brief and trivial. The review written by Fairfax Nisbet for his "At the Night Spots" column in the *Dallas Daily News* concerning the band's appearance on May 14th was the most substantial:

Nearly 1,000 persons turned out to hear Artie Shaw and his band at the Longhorn Ranch, Thursday evening. They found the maestro is still one of the greatest on clarinet though the band lacks the verve and drive of his old organisation.

Shaw, who has definitely individual ideas on music, frankly admits this band tour is commercial, also that he isn't trying to put forth his own ideas of music, but gives the customers what they want. And they wanted his old numbers, "Frenesi," "Begin the Beguine," "Star Dust," "Dancing in the Dark" and the like. And they got those, or anything else requested.

In an article in the September 1953 *Metronome* titled "The Same Music Isn't Always The Same" (pp. 20 +), Shaw was quoted explaining his approach to doing the same old things again and again:

"It takes a lot of discipline," he says, "self-discipline. A guy can go out of his head repeating the same phrases night after night. But if he can prove to himself that they're not the same, then he's really got a chance. . . .

"Each time you play it, it's another numbered version of that arrangement. Try to think of it each time as a new version, one you've never heard before, instead of the same arrangement that you've been playing night after night. Each time it's a new situation in itself. Try to convince yourself, even if you're only doing so during the playing of the particular piece, that 'this is the first time I'm playing this.' In other words, forget all the other times. Don't play from

habit. Read the notes and try to think that they are fresh and new. . . .

"I know that after having played "Begin the Beguine" I don't know how many thousands of times, I've long passed the stage where I can find something new to play . . . but I find that if I don't think of any of the other times that I've played it before, I get much more of a kick out of it. Each version is a new one to me. I may play it in Dallas in 1953, and that's the Dallas 1953 version. . . . Believe me, I'm having much more of a ball playing with my band, even though we repeat an awful lot of numbers, than I've had in years.

"I didn't expect to reincarnate the spirit and the playing of my original band. I know that you can't do that. The guys did what they had to do well enough. It was a job for them and that was that. . . . It's too bad, though, that they couldn't have had as good a time as I did."

Apparently May 23, 1953, Shaw's forty-third birthday, was the last gig of this tour. Enigmatically, Shaw's next datebook entry showed him at the Club 86 in Geneva from May 29 through June 6th; he also listed himself at The Colisee in Hull, Quebec, from June 10 to 20, and returning to New York on the 21st. These were probably vacation excursions with his pregnant wife, although Shaw could not recall specifically, stating, "Who can remember stuff like that?" (2).

Early in July 1953, Shaw was again in the Decca studios fulfilling contractual obligations to that company. At these sessions he recorded some of the arrangements he had prepared for the English dates that never materialized, with a big band including a large string section. Again, this was a studio orchestra, which could not be expected to perform with anything but highly polished studio perfection. Even Shaw did not sound inspired, playing at times as if he were supplying obbligatos. However, on "These Foolish Things" Shaw sounded more involved for his solo, and improvised a brilliant cadenza at the end of the piece. These orchestra sessions were recorded on July 2 and 6, 1953. Halfway between the two dates, which provided the backgrounds over which she would later dub recitations, Doris Dowling gave birth to Shaw's second son, Jonathan, on July 4, 1953.

Shaw was again trying an experiment with these performances, with the narration of the lyrics for these eight tunes being overdubbed later by actor Robert Pastrone and Shaw's wife Doris Dowling; apparently this was done on July 17, 1953. Having the lyrics read instead of sung, and the orchestra engineered softer for dynamic balance during the readings, resulted in an effect that seemed pretentious and affected. It should be noted, however, that this approach also resembled the jazz/poetry mixed-media performances which became the rage in beatnik circles in the mid-1950s and has continued ever since. The album, a 10-inch LP titled *Speak to Me of Love*, did not sell well, and the narration was omitted in later issues of these performances. As these were

Shaw's last recordings performing with an orchestra, it is unfortunate that the opportunity was not used for him to play extensively over the orchestra throughout.

During that year also, *Down Beat* was serializing *The Trouble with Cinderella* with an installment in every issue, beginning on page 3 of the December 31, 1952, issue and concluding in the July 29, 1953, issue. Occasional relevant photos accompanied the text, but unfortunately these were not used in the original publication of the book, and later editions with photos used other material.

It was in this period that Shaw participated in an interesting experiment for the Conn instrument company, which was developing a new model clarinet. His involvement in this project explained his appearing in Conn advertisements later in 1953, and resulted in a curious artifact in Shaw's living room.

The artifact resembles an abstract sculpture. It consists of short pencil-thin cylinders of brass set into a flat board. The cylinders are set in rows and are of varying height along each row. The result is that the tops of the cylinders define a topographical contour resembling gentle waves on water. It is labeled "The Artie Shaw Tone."

The Conn company wanted me to try a new clarinet they were working on. They put me in one of those acoustic research chambers with contoured walls, and placed microphones all over the place.

Then they had me play long tones up and down the chromatic scale and work out on the instrument. They had equipment graphing out the sound frequencies and overtones. In the chamber it sounded fantastic.

Somebody made this model of the resulting sound-map. Each row was a note on the scale, and the pegs in each row represent the frequencies of the overtones. The height of each peg represents the relative volume of each overtone. Some come out stronger, so the peg is longer.

Their measurements were to help them to determine the response of the clarinet in an effort to design it for proper overtone resonance throughout the scale. On this model, you can see the wave forms were symmetrical and even.

In the chamber, and registering on their equipment, it was impressive, but when I used it in front of an audience with a band it was disappointing. Of course, they ran the advertisement anyway! (2)

One of the Conn advertisements appeared on page 6 of the December 2, 1953, *Down Beat*. A photo of Shaw smiling over "The New Conn 20N Constellation" was accompanied by a quote:

"A distinctive achievement" says Artie Shaw. Artie Shaw, most eminent of modern clarinet artists, says—"The first American clarinet that I can heartily endorse. Its tone, intonation and response are wonderful."

"All true," said Shaw. "Unfortunately it just didn't work out on the job" (2). As noted earlier, Shaw had used Selmer clarinets previously. When he began performing in public again in the fall of 1953, he was using another French clarinet, a Buffet.

Chapter 16

Artie Shaw and His Gramercy 5: 1953–1954

That fall, after the sporadic and relatively mediocre recordings for Decca over the past few years, and indifferent public appearances since his 1949–50 band broke up, Shaw surprised the jazz world by returning to the bandstand with a new, vital, and stylistically modern Gramercy 5. He still was facing an IRS bill of $82,000 in back taxes, and had to turn to performing again to help pay it off. However, he had decided to avoid the obvious nostalgia-ridden big band approach, and instead perform music he wanted to play.

Shaw's datebook indicated the initial rehearsals for the new group occurred on September 10, 12, and 15th. The Gramercy 5 that Shaw formed in that late summer of 1953 was a fascinating departure from most of his earlier work. The lineup of the ensemble was distinctive in his recorded legacy: it featured Shaw in a sextet format including a vibraphone in place of the usual muted trumpet for his Gramercy 5 instrumentation. Stylistically, Shaw was exhibiting a new approach to the clarinet as well as a new approach with the whole group conception, in that they were performing within what can be most easily understood as the then-current "cool" style of modern jazz.

Leonard Feather documented the group's inception in an article on page 8 of the September 19, 1953, *Melody Maker* titled "Artie Shaw Leads Again: New Debut Opposite Sharon Trio." (The Sharon Trio referred to British pianist Ralph Sharon's group alternating sets with Shaw at the Embers):

> Ralph Watkins, owner of the Embers, started trying to talk Artie into going into the club with a small combo (the only size group this room can accommodate). Rather than throw something together and disband it immediately—as he did on a Texas trip a few months ago—Artie decided he might as well do the job wholeheartedly.
>
> The way things look now, there will be two or three ex-Shearing men in this new Gramercy 5: Joe Roland on vibes, Denzil Best on drums, and Tal Farlow or Chuck Wayne on guitar.
>
> The bass player will be Tommy Potter. A pianist has still to be selected, and he may be required to double on harpsi-

chord—as in the old Gramercy group. Hank Jones has been playing the rehearsals and will probably stay.

> With these men, Artie will not only play 8 weeks at the Embers, but will later go on a tour of the country's top jazz clubs. Artie hasn't allowed time to pass him by. His clarinet has taken on a new, modern flavor that fits elegantly with the men around him.

It also was announced that Shaw, still under contract with Decca, would be recording for that label with the group. While this never materialized, hints that the group would be recording apparently led discographers to cite the four titles released on the Bell label as being recorded as early as September 1953. The initial personnel for the group included drummer Denzil Best, until Irv Kluger replaced him at The Embers about October 17th (according to Shaw's datebook), and Kluger was the drummer on all known recordings by this edition of the Gramercy 5. Kluger, of course, had been Shaw's drummer with the superb 1949–50 big band.

Down Beat noted on page 1 of its October 7, 1953, issue, "Best, Farlow In New Shaw Unit," confirming personnel and plans:

> After a break-in week at the Hi-Hat in Boston, Shaw moved into the Embers Oct. 1 for 8 weeks, with a tour following. Record contract for the unit is not yet set, though several major companies are reported interested.

The Hi-Hat engagement actually closed October 4th; intriguingly, rumors circulate of a broadcast from the Hi-Hat, and possibly others from The Embers may exist. *Billboard* and *The New Yorker* (in its "Goings On about Town" column) and Shaw's datebook all cite their opening at The Embers on Monday, October 5th.

The Embers, at 161 East 54th Street in New York City, was described in *Billboard*'s review of the group's opening night as a "plush East Side bistro." This review, titled "Gramercy 5 Show Unveils Commercial, Cooler Combo," on page 20 of the October 17, 1953, issue, continued:

Artie Shaw's return to the music business with his new Gramercy 5 Monday [5], pulled one of the biggest crowds in the history of The Embers.... Not only was it an overflow crowd, but it consisted of music, radio and TV celebrities, as well as top brass from the agencies and diskeries. The size of the opening night crowd pointed up again the aura of excitement and glamour that still surrounds top ork leaders of the swinging 1930s. The room was really jumping.

The band also received excellent reviews in such magazines as *Variety* (October 14, 1953, p. 78), *The New Yorker* (October 17, 1953, p. 134), *Time* ("Native's Return," October 19, 1953, p. 88), and later in the engagement, in *Down Beat* ("Shaw's New Gramercy 5 'Not Just A Copy Of Old' " by Nat Hentoff, November 18, 1953, pp. 1, 16) and *Metronome* (December 1953, p. 19), along with the above *Billboard* write-up. No other Shaw working group had received so much attention at its inception since the 1944–45 band was getting under way.

The New Yorker 's review of opening night captured the atmosphere:

The room was jammed with habitual first-nighters, full of mothlike excitement, who kept up a flutter of conversation all the time the combination was on the stand. On the other hand, it was irrelevantly gratifying to see that Shaw appeared unruffled by the noisy audience, in contrast to his celebrated touchiness of past years. Playing absorbedly, bowing slightly to applause, or smiling to himself while one or another of the Gramercy Five was executing a solo, he seemed completely relaxed.

Shaw began things with one of his old hits, "Frenesi." The Five set up a Latin-American background, Shaw's clarinet entered with the melody, and everything was dandy for the first chorus. Then the Six noodled around somewhat aimlessly for a few choruses in straight jazz fashion, after which they rode the number out to its finish, in much the same way they had begun. So it went with most of the other pieces, among them "How High the Moon," "Summit Ridge Drive," and "The Pied Piper," the last an extension of a theme Shaw once used on a record for children. The men were playing what is known in the trade as "head" arrangements, in which the opening and closing sections are set and the rest is left to the ingenuity of the musicians. Such leeway can, of course, result in some magnificent work when good musicians have had time to feel out one another's style. Shaw played beautifully, and always with the composure of a true artist. One moderately paced number, a Shaw original called "Lyric," was new to me and among the most appealing of his offerings.

Interesting details and insights appeared in the other reviews as well. Taken together, the various write-ups provided a vivid impression of the setting and the effect of the group, including glimpses of its repertoire. The review in *Time* was particularly vivid:

Clarinetist Artie Shaw was back in the music business last week, at 43. He mounted the bandstand at Manhattan's jazz-bent Embers, looked unsmilingly over the jabbering crowd and spoke into the microphone: "Ladies and gentlemen, I'd like to remind you that it's almost axiomatic that music sounds better against silence. Not dead silence—just enough so that we can hear ourselves play."

The clatter continued, but Shaw turned to the group he calls the Gramercy Five (nostalgically named after his 1940 recording combo), stomped out a beat and began to play. For a while he sounded like a musical D. P., playing as if he could not decide between his old swing style and something considerably more jittery and "progressive." He mixed old Shaw favorites ("Begin the Beguine," "Frenesi") with such new Shaw originals as "Overdrive" and "Lugubrious."

As the early crowd gave way to the late one, the little band began to perk up. Vibraphonist Joe Roland bent over his instrument like a chef over a hot stove. Guitarist Tal Farlow, who had gazed vaguely into space as he played, began to take an interest in the way his fingers rambled up and down the fingerboard. Clarinetist Shaw began to interpolate light-hearted musical comments on his own flights—the raised eyebrow of a grace note, the shrugging arpeggio, the delayed take, the impudent echo. His glum face relaxed into smiles, and the crowd began to hear the new Artie Shaw.

Metronome's review began humorously but also showed appreciation:

A slogan-maker at the next table described the group as "George Shearing with a clarinet." A slightly looped young lady asked vibist Joe Roland if his name was Red Norvo. A tweedy gentleman told the world at large that guitarist Tal Farlow was a Rumanian gypsy with 2 fingers paralyzed on either his left or right hand, or, maybe, both hands. It was, in short, a hip crowd at the Embers this night.

But through it all, apparently undisturbed by such madly veering elements, shaven headed Artie Shaw stood, led, and played with impeccable courtesy and artistry as did the new Gramercy 5. . . . Artie is magnificently himself: rather immutable but hardly dated. He uses an inverted megaphone into which he occasionally blows to get an effect remarkably like a sub-tone clarinet. . . . Within a framework of cute, sometimes clever arrangements, the solos were of consistently high quality, making this one of the top musical groups in the country whose essence promises greater things with maturity.

Concerning the above comment about "George Shearing with a clarinet" Shaw noted in private discussion,

That's not bad. I liked what George was doing at that time and wanted to use some of it. He was doing some interesting things with sound textures. (2)

It remained for Nat Hentoff to provide the most astute analysis of the new Gramercy 5 and Shaw's efforts (including the explanation of the enigmatic description of Shaw's playing into an inverted megaphone, as cited in the above *Metronome* review), in his review for *Down Beat*:

[T]he group swings as few other current jazz groups do. Denzil Best's quietly authoritative pulse is perfect for this context, and Tommy Potter has never sounded better both as soloist and resonant rhythm support. . . . As for the ensemble, soundwise this is going to be an interesting evolution to hear. Conscious of the limitations of the instrumental setup per se, Shaw nonetheless is building a set of tonal balances that may surprise you both on records and in a quiet club—something the Embers recently has not resembled until after 2 a.m.

For one thing, set up in front of the clarinet is a standup megaphone. . . . This one has been cut off halfway through the handholes on each side. Its aim is to mask the sound of the clarinet in certain ensemble passages, because the clarinet overtones are sharper than those of the vibes, guitar and piano.

By playing his clarinet into the megaphone on specific passages, Shaw acts as a blending bridge between the dissimilar overtones of the other instruments. In the process a ring develops between vibes, clarinet, guitar and megaphone that produces a sound which is a synthesis of the instruments.

Hentoff went on to describe the role of the piano as liberated from the "either-or" approaches of contemporary groups (either eliminated, or used percussively to "feed" chords):

Under the Shaw setup, Hank Jones functions largely as soloist and as accompanist for Artie on the latter's choruses. As a result, the rhythm section sound is lighter—Potter and Best certainly provide all the rhythmic push needed. Joe Roland, because he can play 4-part chords, is the chief feeder for Tal Farlow and Farlow, in turn, backs Joe.

During choruses by Tal or Joe, Shaw will play a riff to Jones who'll answer back, and that serves as a base for Shaw's chorus when it comes up. All during the set, each man will contribute a set of figures behind a soloist when and if he feels it fits. So there is a degree of flexible movement not only in individual solos but in and through them from the rest of the band.

Shaw, with his shaved head giving him a look of intense asceticism, expressed his perspective on what he was doing in an article he wrote for *See* magazine titled "Dixie, Swing, Bop or What?" (not published until September 1954, pp. 34–36):

Unfortunately, many people do not have the musical background to comprehend the complex forms most of our better young musicians are now playing. . . .

I find, however, that audiences will listen to complex jazz if they are given a simple melodic framework upon which to base their understanding. We have been playing advanced jazz to appreciative listeners.

We do play old numbers like "Summit Ridge Drive" which my old Gramercy 5 recorded years ago. But, as your old records will show, any similarity between the way we used to play those old numbers and the way we play them now is purely melodic.

Most of the things we play today were written especially for us—mostly mood pieces like "Lyric," "Sunny Side Up" and "Stop and Go Mambo"—and they're as modern as we can make them.

In popular music, unhappily, the nation's musical conditioning for more than a decade has been dominated by honkers and wailing vocalists of both sexes. These probably will continue. Frankly, I doubt if I will live to see a mass preference for good instrumental jazz over gimmicked vocal arrangements.

Progress is slow—in music as in life. But progress is being made, and I for one do not despair. . . .

As one of the few musicians trying to make a musical bridge between the generations, I understand why audiences still cling emotionally to music of the big swing band. It flourished in the 1938–40 period, the peak of contact between musicians and listeners.

A few years later, however, the jazz musician, becoming more specialized, began to play things the average person could not understand. The bizarre end result was "bop."

Today, after considerable frustration, a number of young musicians like Chet Baker and Dave Brubeck and their groups are playing "progressive" jazz which audiences listen to without rebelling.

Jazz is not presented as it used to be, and that is a hopeful sign. The big dance bands, with crowds shuffling around the floor in front of them, are gone.

The future of jazz probably will be determined in the small jazz rooms in most of our principal cities, where people can sit over drinks and listen inexpensively to music they enjoy. Such people, I believe, will be numerous enough to keep the better musicians busy. In the process, we are sure to develop an exciting new form of American jazz, a group of musicians who play it well, and—eventually—audiences for whom it has real meaning.

The November 14, 1953, *Melody Maker* noted in an article titled " 'I Play the Way I Feel Now'—Shaw" that Norman Granz, organizer of the Jazz at the Philharmonic tours and owner of Verve/Clef Records, was actively pursuing Shaw for recordings with this group. The article also reported that Shaw was "laying plans for a college tour" with a double bill featuring the Gramercy 5 and a classical string quartet. Although this plan never materialized, Shaw's eventual release of some of this Gramercy 5 material on *Artie Shaw—A Legacy* (BOMR71-7715), much of it previously unissued, was accompanied in that set by some of the classical material from radio shows featuring Shaw with a string quartet, providing similar programming to what he had evidently intended at this point.

The December 2, 1953, *Down Beat* published Shaw's touring schedule on page 15, headlined "Busy Schedule For Shaw Gramercy 5," noting:

> After the combo closes at the Embers here Dec. 5, it has been set to appear at the Rendezvous in Philadelphia, Dec. 7–19, the Colonial in Toronto, Dec. 28–January 2, a one-nighter in Uniontown, Pa., and the Alpine Village in Cleveland, Jan. 11–17.

However, Shaw's datebook indicated that they were at the Rendezvous, at 915 Walnut Street in Philadelphia, until the 20th, and moved into the Colonial Inn in Toronto the next day, December 21st. While at the Colonial, Shaw had an interesting conversation with a newspaperman named Alex Barris, who was writing a column titled "The Record Album" for Toronto's *Globe & Mail* newspaper at the time. In Barris's column for Friday, January 1, 1954, which appeared on page 10, Barris wrote:

> Had a talk with Artie Shaw the other night and found he's been doing a lot of recording in New York in the last week or so. He said there's a danger of a record strike and he wanted to stock up.
>
> Distribution is still uncertain. What Shaw did was to record three-minute stuff for a label called Bell, which is partly owned by Pocket Books and will have a similar mass distribution setup. Longer versions of some of the numbers have been cut with an eye toward LP, possibly on Norman Granz's Clef label.

Shaw's datebook may not have been complete, as the next entry was for the Encore in Chicago from January 8 through 31, with no indication of the Colonial closing or the above-mentioned Uniontown gig (which may, of course, have been canceled). An appearance at the Carousel Club in Pittsburgh also has been reported without dates being given, which may have occurred in this interval. Following the Chicago engagement, they did a week at the Yankee Inn in Akron, Ohio, February 1 through 6, 1954.

In an article titled "Shaw Denies Missing Dates" on page 16 of the April 7, 1954, *Down Beat*, Shaw was mentioned as opening at Cleveland's Alpine Village on February 8, 1954. There he was billed as "Musician, Composer, Author, and Don Juan" in the publicity, and performed to capacity audiences. However, before long, he found himself hassled by the proprietor concerning alleged missed dates, which Shaw denied having been booked for in the first place.

In any case, they closed at the Alpine Village on the 14th, according to Shaw's datebook, which listed them next at The Embers again from February 27 through March 17. However, the group was widely reported to have returned to The Embers from February 22 to March 8, 1954. For example, the February 20, 1954, issue of *The New Yorker* stated on page 6 under "The Embers" in the "Mostly for Music" section of its "Goings On about Town" column:

> On Monday, Feb. 22, Artie Shaw and his unique Gramercy Five return to town. Beryl Booker's Trio will move in the same day. . . .

Later mentions in that column of their activity at The Embers named the group's personnel, praised their work, noted that they performed "every night but Sunday" from 9 p.m. through 3 a.m. and were replaced on Monday, March 8th, by Erroll Garner's Trio, all in *The New Yorker*'s typically concise style.

It was evidently during this period that most, if not all, the recorded performances by this group were made after hours at Shaw's expense. It has been eventually concluded, on the basis of Shaw's consistent statements that the group was recorded after hours when the band was working at The Embers, that the recordings were made either in early December 1953 (those originally issued on 78-rpm discs) or during the late February–early March 1954 appearances, with most of them made during the latter period.

Concerning the aforementioned Bell records, Shaw refused to discuss them in any context, stating only,

> That was scandalous, the most disgusting episode of my career. Those guys were swindlers. It was the only time I took anybody to the Union. It sickens me to think about it.

He could not confirm whether these were made at the same time as the other recordings by this group or separately, and also had no recollection of the Clef 78-rpm disc or its contents. All six of these titles were shortened (or, in the case of "Imagination," speeded-up) performances of pieces recorded in longer versions appearing on Clef releases. However, Shaw did recall being annoyed at having to make shortened versions of pieces they normally played far longer on, "for three records" especially for Bell. He associated this episode with the approach of the Christmas season, "while working at The Embers." Bell, of course, only released two records, but three records' worth of this abbreviated material were made. The implication was that all six of these pieces might have been made in December 1953.

Shaw was certain that everything else was recorded during their second stay at The Embers, despite the implication in Alex Barris's *Globe & Mail* article that the longer "takes" already had been made of those titles in December, and ultimately dismissed the puzzle by shrugging, "Your guess is as good as mine!" (2).

In the liner notes to the four-LP Book-of-the-Month Club

boxed set titled *Artie Shaw—A Legacy* (BOMR71-7715), Shaw noted that the recordings by this edition of the Gramercy 5 were all recorded at Fine Studios in the NBC building at 711 Fifth Avenue in New York. Shaw stated in this album's liner notes booklet,

> The group sounded so good to me that I thought they should be recorded. . . . I decided that this stuff was going to be lost forever if we didn't record it. So after we'd finish work at 4 A.M. I would take the group into Fine Sound where we recorded the whole book. We'd go into the studio around 5 A.M. and play till we were exhausted. Talk about playing relaxed. Some of these tracks were recorded at 10 or 11 in the morning.

Shaw often has stated that these were the best records he ever did. By the time of these recordings the group had been working together about six months, and the performances were very tight and polished. Shaw has said that he used a Buffet clarinet for these recordings, although his usual instrument for most of his career was a Selmer six-ring model with articulated G-sharp key. He chose the Buffet for the small group because "it had a more woody, intimate sound," and he played it very softly, almost sub-tone, only inches from the microphone.

All of the features mentioned in the reviews were in evidence on the recordings, although the group's entire repertoire has not yet been issued. At least two titles, which were mentioned in write-ups of the group, have not been released: "Overdrive" and "Krazy Kat" (the latter a Johnny Mandel composition recorded by the 1949 band for Thesaurus and not to be confused with the Frankie Trumbauer piece with the same title). Shaw leased the tapes to Norman Granz after much persuasion from Granz, and Granz eventually issued nineteen titles by this group, two of them in two versions ("Sunny Side Up" and "Imagination," in short versions for the aforementioned 78-rpm release, and in longer takes for LP issue). In 1984, *Artie Shaw—A Legacy* was issued, containing sixteen titles, seven of them previously issued on the long out-of-print Verve/Clef LPs.

In 1992, Shaw released a two-CD set on the MusicMasters label, *Artie Shaw: The Last Recordings* (MM65071-2), containing twenty performances, including thirteen by this group. These included six alternate takes of titles originally issued on Verve/Clef, and one previously unissued title. The latter was the moody minor blues, "Crumbum" (mistitled "Mysterioso," another moody minor blues but a very different composition). The others, of course, had been available previously on the rare Verve/Clef issues and on the bootleg Ajazz collectors' label reissues. In 1993, another two-CD set was issued by MusicMasters, *Artie Shaw: More Last Recordings* (MM65101-2). This set included most of the Book-of-the-Month Club album's Gramercy 5 perform-

ances, and also contained two versions of the exquisite "Autumn Leaves" in both the originally issued, rare 10-inch LP version as well as a previously unissued alternate take. This totals twenty-nine individual titles released, twelve of them in more than one performance. "Imagination" was issued in three different takes. One excellent title ("Sunny Side Up") originally issued on Verve/Clef was left out of these packages, but turned up on a later Artie Shaw MusicMasters CD titled *Mixed Bag* (MM65119-2). Altogether, forty-two performances have been issued by this edition of the Gramercy 5.

The two-CD set issued in 1992 (*Artie Shaw: The Last Recordings*) created a critical stir. Reviewers realized that the work of a master had surfaced, and the quality of the music was widely recognized and highly praised. However, only seven of the twenty titles were actually from Shaw's last recording sessions with his last Gramercy 5, which of course differed from the earlier group with Joe Roland's vibes by omitting the vibraphone and substituting Joe Puma on guitar for Tal Farlow; Roland and Farlow had left the group in March. Thus, the final Gramercy 5 was a quintet instead of the usual sextet.

The April 21, 1954, *Down Beat* noted on page 22, "Shaw Inks Puma, Heads Westward." The article included information on Shaw's continuing tour:

> Shaw opened at the Falcon Lounge in Detroit March 31 for 12 days. He goes into the Terrace Lounge in East St. Louis April 13 for a week.

Shaw's datebook indicated that they closed at the Terrace on April 18th, and went next into the Casbah Lounge in the Sahara Hotel in Las Vegas from April 21 through May 17th. They then went into the Downbeat Club in San Francisco, from May 19th through June 1st.

While performing at the Downbeat Club in San Francisco in May, the Gramercy 5 was reviewed for the *San Francisco Chronicle* by noted jazz critic Ralph J. Gleason, on page 22 of the May 25, 1954, issue. Gleason wrote:

> One of the most delightful musical surprises this year has been Artie Shaw and the Gramercy 5 currently at the Downbeat Club . . . Shaw stands out. The Gramercy 5 has organization and, within that organization, plenty of freedom for the individual musician to express himself fully. Yet, the organized framework, the tight, tricky and intriguing beginnings and endings of numbers, the intricate melodic and harmonic passages, give the entire product an atmosphere of class. . . .
>
> Although the Gramercy 5 does play many of the tunes Shaw has made famous—gleaned from the repertoire of his past small and big groups and including everything from "Frenesi" to "Summit Ridge Drive"—it also offers a considerable number of new, bright sounding originals. In all of

them, old and new, the overall sound of the group is delightful, modern and, when the occasion calls for it, exciting.

The group fitted itself so well to the acoustics of the Downbeat that it sounded on opening night as if it had been playing there for years. The light, tasteful drumming of Irv Kluger, the bass solos of Tommy Potter and the guitar solos of Joe Puma all came through in a pleasing musical perspective. Star of the group, aside, of course, from Shaw, who has again demonstrated that the younger musicians must improve upon him before they can claim to have advanced the jazz clarinet, is pianist Hank Jones.

The Gramercy 5 is not only one of the best small groups in jazz today but it is a living testimonial to the importance of organization in jazz. It sounds better when you know what you're doing and, believe me, Mr. Shaw and his associates most certainly know what they are doing.

June 1954 was the date Shaw indicated for the series of recording sessions, again held at his own expense, documenting this last edition of the Gramercy 5. These sessions were held in Hollywood, California, although apparently during much of June and early July the group was performing again at the Sahara Hotel in Las Vegas, Nevada. In the liner notes to *Artie Shaw: The Last Recordings* (MusicMasters MM65071-2), issued in 1992, Shaw stated:

Our last job was in Las Vegas. We played at the Sahara for a month—the first so-called major attraction to play behind the bar in the cocktail lounge. . . . Tommy and Jimmy Dorsey had a band at one of the other hotels and used to fall into the saloon after work. . . . But the dough was good.

The band also was reviewed for *Melody Maker* ("Jazz Among The One-Arm Bandits," July 3, 1954, p. 3). This article described the setting:

There, in the Sahara Hotel, behind the slot machines behind the gaming tables behind the lounge behind the bar behind a huge cash register—stood Artie Shaw and clarinet . . . surrounded by the craziest bunch of blonde chicks during every intermission.

Charlie Barnet also recalled performing in a hotel across the street from the Sahara during Shaw's engagement there, in his autobiography. Following this engagement the Gramercy 5 disbanded.

Shaw also leased the Hollywood recordings by this quintet to Granz, who issued one LP containing seven titles. The convoluted issuing history of the material originally issued by Granz is of interest in view of the importance of these recordings and their earlier rarity. Curiously, this album by the final quintet, titled *Artie Shaw and his Gramercy Five #3* (Clef MGC-630) listed the former Gramercy 5 sextet personnel, while one of their albums, which was titled *Artie Shaw and his Gramercy Five #4* (Clef MGC-645), named

the personnel of this last quintet. The albums titled *Artie Shaw and his Gramercy Five #1* (Clef MGC-159) and *Artie Shaw and his Gramercy Five #2* (Clef MGC-160) were 10-inch LPs also by the earlier group, and all four had interesting cover art by David Stone Martin. Later, most of the contents of the two 10-inch LPs (with the exception of the beautiful "Autumn Leaves") were reissued on a 12-inch LP titled *Sequence in Music* (Verve MGV-2014). Another 12-inch Verve LP, titled *I Can't Get Started* (Verve MGV-2015), contained five previously unissued titles, all by the sextet with Farlow and Roland. These LPs had romantic photos of sultry women in monochrome colors. To add to the confusion, a Japanese release of material by this group appeared in the 1970s with a facsimile of the cover of the *I Can't Get Started* album, but including additional tracks from the earlier releases as well as the original contents of that album.

Most of the Bell, Clef, and Verve material also appeared on the Ajazz bootleg collectors' label in the 1970s, in slightly reduced fidelity. A few pieces also appeared on other such records, including "The Pied Piper Theme" by the group with Farlow and Roland on a Sounds of Swing label pressing titled *Artie Shaw: the Jazz Years* (SoS125). Also, two titles by the quintet, "Rough Ridin' " and "Dancing on the Ceiling," appeared in a boxed set issued by Redwood Jazz (RWJ1001), which erroneously dated them as from 1945!

The seven titles by this quintet that appeared on the two-CD set *Artie Shaw: The Last Recordings* included alternate takes (instead of the original issues) of two titles issued on MGC-630 (interestingly, these were "Dancing on the Ceiling" and "Rough Ridin'," the latter in a more vital version on CD), and one previously unissued title, giving a total of ten performances available by this final group. The 1993 two-CD set *Artie Shaw: More Last Recordings* included only one title by the quintet, "September Song" (which had been previously available only on MGC-630). As with the earlier sextet, this final Gramercy 5 recorded primarily much longer performances than would have been possible in the pre-LP era.

Their work also was intricate, highly polished, and out of the cool style. Many of the head arrangements performed by both the sextet and quintet were extended performances that included plenty of solo space for each member of the group. These longer pieces also tended to feature various ensemble patterns interpolated into the performances, as well as exchanges of shorter improvisational phrases between members of the group, interspersed among their solos and ensemble passages. Along with the absence of the vibes, there was less of a tendency for witty ensemble quotes from other songs in the quintet's work. Furthermore, Shaw sounded more deeply involved in some of his solos than ever, as if his style was evolving toward yet another level of development. Only the absence of original Shaw compositions among this last Gramercy 5 output prevents this ensemble from representing the epitome of Shaw's recordings. In this setting consisting of clarinet and rhythm, Shaw's conception as an instrumentalist was fully exposed and undiluted. Fortunately Shaw has said that there was still considerable unissued material from both groups in his vault, both previously unissued titles and additional alternate takes. Shaw stated that he may still release them also, eventually.

Following the breakup of this last Gramercy 5, Shaw recorded nothing else as a performer. He only played one more brief tour, in Australia that summer, before ceasing to play clarinet entirely; he was certain no recordings had been made in Australia.

The September 22, 1954, *Down Beat* featured an article on page 1 that headlined: "Australia Opening Up for American Jazzmen," beneath a photo of Shaw playing clarinet, with Buddy Rich on drums, an unidentified bassist in the background, and Jerry Colonna looking on.

This article explained that two American promoters, Benn Reyes and Lee Gordon, the latter living in Australia, were "challenging the formidable taxation and transportation problems involved" in such a venture.

They decided to take a gamble that cost almost $100,000 and play a series of 7 dates in Sydney, Melbourne, and Brisbane, July 23–August 1 [1954].

They rounded up talent including Ella Fitzgerald, Buddy Rich, Artie Shaw, and Jerry Colonna. The musicians travelled separately. . . . The tour was a success, taking in

$110,000 for the 7 days. It was played mainly in boxing stadiums seating as many as 8000 persons.

The article indicated there were some problems. Ella did not arrive until several days later, resulting in ticket sales plummeting and necessitating extra free concerts for disappointed ticket holders once she had finally arrived. Airport crowds were reported mistakenly cheering Ella's maid as she got off the plane, and otherwise failing to recognize anyone but Colonna, who by this time had acquired a substantial reputation as a comedian.

In discussing this final tour, Shaw described it as "ridiculous, a shambles" (2). He related:

Lee Ross signed me for this tour of Australia with Ella, Buddy, and Jerry Colonna. We had equal billing, all "stars." Well, it got to Jerry and Buddy. They were totally impossible. Buddy was completely insufferable. They started ACTING like stars.

I'd stopped off in Honolulu to visit some friends en route, and when I got to Australia, I found the schedule hadn't left any time for rehearsals. The band was impossible. I was so upset I was ready to cancel the tour and leave for New York. The promoters came and pleaded with me. I'd been drinking bourbon to incapacitate myself so I wouldn't have to go on, because I never drank and played.

I had to go on anyway, and the band couldn't even play my theme or anything, didn't know what a downbeat was. It was hopeless.

The quartet stuff went a little better. We had a local piano player, a bass player, Buddy and me; not a Gramercy 5, just this quartet.

Nothing was recorded by these groups. Thank God!

That was the last gig I ever played in my life. True! (2)

Chapter 17

Spain to Los Angeles: 1950s–1990s

Following his final performing tour of Australia, Shaw returned to his farm. He had finally given up on being a performer in the music business, but other problems were disrupting the quiet life he had tried to set up for himself. He still was being labeled a "controversial figure" and IRS claims for back taxes ultimately forced him to sell his farm. His marriage with Doris Dowling also was not working out. The July 13, 1955, *Down Beat* noted on page 6, "Artie Shaw Sells Farm," and also revealed that he and Doris had separated. They were divorced in 1956.

Still owing Decca some records, Shaw again entered their recording studios to conduct a studio orchestra without playing. The four titles recorded in November 1955 were similar arrangements to those he had recorded for Decca in July 1953, except for the lack of his clarinet, and often have been reissued along with them (see "Discographical Addenda & Ephemera").

Shaw wrote movingly of the loss of his farm in the new introduction to the 1978 Da Capo Press edition of his autobiography. Following all this, he decided he had had enough of The American Way, and left for Europe. Ultimately he settled in Spain, in the little village of Bagur, halfway between Barcelona and the French border. He had a house built, which he had designed himself, on a mountain overlooking the Mediterranean. On a trip to Paris in 1956, he met actress Evelyn Keyes. They returned to Spain together and were married in 1957. Evelyn Keyes wrote extensively of their life together in Spain and later in Connecticut in her autobiography, *Scarlet O'Hara's Younger Sister* (Secaucus, N.J.: Lyle Stuart, 1977). She described his intense interest in fishing, complete with equipment, a library, and excursions to interesting sites. He became similarly involved with astronomy, complete with a telescope, library, and star charts. She also described his temperamental domestic habits vividly, and his eventual impatience with the different pace and style of life in Spain. Trips to London and New York preceded Shaw becoming restless and returning to the United States in 1960.

In Connecticut, they lived in a large house on Lake Wononskopomuc near Lakeville. Shaw developed a passion for riflery, became an excellent marksman and opened a gun shop in Clinton Corners, Connecticut. Eventually he got into the film distribution business and started Artixo Productions, named for the Catalonian pronunciation of his name as he heard it in Spain. Artixo Productions operated out of New York City, and Shaw worked out of his offices there until well into the 1970s, long after he and Evelyn Keyes had ceased living together.

During 1968, Shaw became involved in a project to re-record many of his 1938–39 hits for Capitol Records. Walt Levinsky performed the clarinet parts, and Shaw coached and conducted the band (see "Discographical Addenda & Ephemera").

Throughout, Shaw continued to work on writing fiction. He worked on short stories, a novel, and even a musical, and admits to publishing extensively under a pseudonym, which he preferred to keep secret, as his own "private joke" on the rest of the world. However, a second book was published under his own name in 1965 by Fleet Publishing Corporation in New York City, titled *I Love You, I Hate You, Drop Dead!* This was an excellent collection of three novellas exploring different aspects of marriage and friendship in various situations.

Relocating to the Los Angeles area in the mid-1970s, Shaw was again seen briefly on-screen as an actor in the 1978 television movie *Crash!* In this film he played one of the survivors of an airplane crash. He continued to be an occasional guest on television talk shows, a practice he had begun in the early 1950s. On these shows he often would comment on the Big Band Era as well as discussing his more current projects. He also would give lectures at UCLA and elsewhere on various topics, including "The Artist in a Materialistic Society," "Psychotherapy and the Creative Artist," "The Swingers of the Big Band Era," and "Consecutive Monogamy and Ideal Divorce."

In 1983, Canadian filmmaker Brigitte Berman began a two-year project to make a two-hour documentary on Shaw. She spent three days interviewing him before the cameras in his home in California, and traveled to the locations where he had found refuge to capture their atmosphere.

These locations included the Bucks County and Pine Plains farms, the house he had designed in Spain, and his former Lakeville, Connecticut, home. Home movie footage by bassist Sid Weiss and clips from Shaw's movies were used along with still photos, intercut with the interviews with Shaw and with others who had known him, including Evelyn Keyes. The documentary concluded with footage of Shaw conducting and appearing with his then-current project, an Artie Shaw band with Dick Johnson performing on clarinet. (The band was continuing to tour as the 1990s conclude, with Shaw occasionally accompanying it to introduce and conduct the music.) Shaw also performed on piano for the film, demonstrating his "Nightmare" theme briefly, and performing MacDowell's "A Deserted Farm" more extensively, behind footage of his New York dairy farm. "I was just showing her [Berman] something. I didn't know she was going to use it," he said of these spots (2).

There also were glimpses of Shaw's home, where he has been living since 1973, during the interview segments, including his study where he had been working on his monumental novel, *The Education of Albie Snow*. Projected as a trilogy, the first volume had the working title *Sideman*, and ran over 1,900 pages in manuscript at last count.

> It's about a young musician coming up in the 1930s, working in the studios and eventually forming his own band, but that's all really just his day job. He's really interested in books, art, ideas, and being a writer. It's fiction, but fiction is the only way you can tell the truth without getting sued. A lot of it's true, but in fictional form. (2)

The Berman film, *Artie Shaw: Time Is All You've Got*, was released in 1985 to critical acclaim and won an Academy Award. The Book-of-the-Month Club set featuring Shaw's 1953–54 Gramercy 5, some 1949 classical material preserved from broadcasts, and performances of "Interlude in B-flat" and the "Blues" from Paul Whiteman's 1938 Christmas concert in Carnegie Hall, also were issued then. Enthusiastic critical acclaim for this and other reissues of Shaw's recordings encouraged him to rerelease material from his superb 1949 band and other recordings by his last Gramercy 5 groups on the MusicMasters CD label. Other similar reissues, such as the 1949 classical and so-called Third Stream material, and the Musicraft recordings featuring Mel Torme (with whom Shaw maintained frequent contact over the years), also were under discussion. The Shaw band featuring Dick Johnson also has recorded a considerable quantity of material, but Shaw was not particularly happy with the results.

Shaw's third book issued under his name was *The Best of Intentions* (Santa Barbara, Cal.: John Daniel, 1989). This was a fascinating group of six short stories. One of them, "Snow/White in Harlem, 1930," also was Chapter 10 in Shaw's novel manuscript, and recounts fictionally Shaw's meeting with Willie "The Lion" Smith in Harlem in 1930. The title story was a complete rewrite of one of the novellas in Shaw's earlier collection of fiction, "Grounds for Divorce." The two versions of essentially the same story becoming available provided an interesting opportunity for comparison.

Visiting Shaw in 1991 at his home in California revealed him more energetic and enthusiastic at the age of eighty-one than most people half his age. His legendary ability to converse intelligently on a phenomenal range of topics, coupled with his prodigious memory, left the impression of encountering a kaleidoscopic dynamo of intellectual activity.

His house, medium-sized and unpretentious, had a small yard well screened by lush shrubbery, and was located in a reasonably average suburban neighborhood. Glimpses of its interior in *Artie Shaw: Time Is All You've Got* and other segments on television when he was interviewed there do not give an adequate impression of the quantity of books and art objects in every possible corner. A surprising quantity of the art, both paintings and sculpture, were by Shaw, and were of impressive quality. He explained that his interest in art led him to try doing some as well. Enough was visible to indicate that a small one-man show of vital impact could be assembled, and he indicated there was more in storage. The rest of his art and art objects included originals and prints by many prominent as well as obscure figures. In one corner a portrait bust of Shaw as a young man stood on a shelf irreverently wearing a battered fishing hat.

His books were everywhere, stacked on all available surfaces, including stacks on the floor next to almost every chair. There were even books standing on the sides of most steps on his staircase, leading to his study.

The upper floor of his house had a loftlike openness and contained most of his library, record collection, and work area. Small rooms to the side held filing cabinets full of his writings. The computer on which he was working on his novel was near a window with a spectacular view overlooking the neighborhood, with a mountain range in the distance. "It was this study and this view that sold me on this house," he said. "Those mountains have symbolic value as well as being beautiful. That's the last refuge of the California Condor, an endangered species" (2).

Just below his study windows was his back yard. Most of it was taken up by a small swimming pool, edged by a path that left a narrow but lovely garden to fill the space to the edge of his property. Shaw designed the garden himself, showing a slightly oriental influence. It contained, among other plants, a number of large, beautiful roses. Different sets of wind chimes, carefully selected for their tuning, hung along the patio roof. It was very pleasant to be on that patio, hearing the unusually interesting wind chimes gently tinkling, looking across that beautiful garden at the mountains lining the horizon.

A lot of people think I'm crazy to live like this when I could be making lots of money being a celebrity and living in a mansion. I never wanted that. This way I have time to work on my book. I have a few close friends and various projects under way, and spend most of my time reading and writing. Lots of people don't understand that, but that's how I want to spend my time. (2)

Introduction to the Discographies

Most of the available material Artie Shaw recorded in the studios for commercial release originally was issued on 10-inch 78-rpm records. They often were reissued in 78-rpm format and, repeatedly from the early 1950s into the late 1980s, on many LPs and 45-rpm discs. Most of these issues, long out of print, are available only through collectors, used record dealers, and places such as the Salvation Army. These obsolete formats have been replaced by compact discs, but not all of Shaw's records have become available on CDs, although more are appearing regularly, along with considerable material never before available, including recordings from radio broadcast air checks and transcriptions.

Most of Artie Shaw's records under his own name have been reissued on various LPs in chronological order, and these are the obvious choices for study, until they appear similarly on CD. Consequently, other rare issues were ignored in this listing, except for broadcasts, where all known issues were cited. For studio sessions, only the original 78-rpm issue and the most complete LP and/or CD issue were listed. Grab-bag CD or LP collections were not included.

This should not generally inconvenience those seeking to identify details concerning Shaw recordings on issues not listed. It should be apparent, for example, that if a studio recording was issued on an RCA label, the Bluebird or Victor recording of the piece is the one on that issue. Variations from this format are apparent, e.g., where the original issue was on LP.

For Shaw's appearances as a sideman, the situation is more difficult. For example, nothing more could be discovered about Shaw's initial recordings with Joe Cantor besides what was listed in the discography and mentioned in the text. Most of the "sideman records" cited have not been reissued after their initial 78-rpm release, and often have been listed in discographies with wrong personnel, if at all. The situation with radio shows on which Shaw performed as a sideman is even worse. Most have never been issued and dubs may not even have circulated among collectors, so that they often still exist only as original radio transcriptions or air checks, if at all. The fan of Shaw's sideman period should be encouraged to explore other recordings from this era, but it takes a lot of careful listening and comparison to be able to identify a musician aurally from only a few bars of exposure, which is usually the best of cases. Longer solos exhibiting more substantial musical statements were relatively very rare. Further discussion of problems tracing

Shaw's sideman performances is in the introduction and "*NOTE*" entries for that section.

The discography on Shaw as a leader is divided into eleven sections reflecting different phases of Shaw's musical career. Comments pertaining only to entire but specific sections of that section of the discography will preface those sections. This discography also was annotated with quick reference information ("*NOTES:*") relevant to the session just listed, or the band's activity at that time. Of course, more complete information on Shaw's or the band's activities can be found in the text. Occasionally, broadcasting information was included in these notes even though the material may not yet have become available and the exact contents of such broadcasts remain unknown.

Format of the discography follows the procedure of citing each session headed either by the group name in bold type, "same" (personnel data as the preceding session) or minor personnel changes from the preceding session, and the place and date. Full personnel is listed if it is the first session by a given ensemble or if it is radically different from the preceding session, with instrumentation (where known) given using the indicated abbreviations. This basic information is followed by the details of the results of the recording session, with the master number to the left and record numbers to the right of each tune title. Songs with vocals show "v" (for vocal) and the initials of the singer after the title in parenthesis, for example "(vHF)" = "vocal by Helen Forrest."

The problem of "take" numbers deserves some discussion. Consultation with various discographers on the subject and examination of assorted published data on the recordings revealed frequent discrepancies; therefore, "take" numbers have been noted only when it was necessary to distinguish known issues of alternate takes, unless decipherable recording session log sheets were available for examination. It should be noted at the outset that during the 78-rpm era, when taping technology had not yet emerged, records were made "direct to disc" (to use the current terminology). The masters were cut in the studio and plated for pressing the actual issued discs. These masters were fragile, so to ensure against flaws or damage, most companies almost always made two issuable takes of every number being recorded. This usually was accomplished by recording as many consecutive performances as necessary. However, some companies also solved the problem by running two cutting tables simultaneously. In that case, both "masters" were identical and differentiated by a suffix (e.g., "take 1" / "take 1A"). Of course, in some cases more takes were necessary to get two "perfect" versions, but generally only the best two takes would make it as far as going through the plating process. It should be kept in mind that the recording industry was a business, with the usual bureaucratic concerns about time and money. Consequently, unnecessary retakes or extra test pressings would be anomalies.

Obviously, when two performances were recorded, if both survived the plating process and test pressings could be generated that indicated both would be acceptable to use as the pressing master, a choice would have to be made on which one to issue. Many companies assigned the preferred, issued take the designation "take 1," so that the alternate was designated as "take 2" even though it may have been recorded first. Sometimes, the choice of which alternate would be issued was left to the leader. Other, rejected takes (if any) usually were destroyed. The preserved takes (the issued master and the alternate, whether an identical "take 1A" or a different "take 2") were retained for possible reissue pressings. Alternate takes occasionally also were issued, usually for one of three main reasons: the previously unissued take would be used for a subsidiary label or leased overseas; the originally issued master may have become lost, damaged, or degraded; or someone simply grabbed the wrong one for additional pressings or reissues.

Since the master number and take designation generally were scratched into the master near the label, whether or not the information appeared on the label itself, identifying that information generally is easy if one has access to the original 78-rpm disc. Unfortunately, in most cases the original 78s are very rare, so this usually has not been possible. Even the Institute of Jazz Studies archives, while I was working there, had only a small sample of the more obscure items. Thus, to review performances, I have largely had to rely on LP or CD reissues or "tape dubs for research purposes" obtained from collectors, especially for Shaw's sideman recordings, and such detailed information as take numbers often was not forthcoming from these or other published sources.

Most of the Brunswick/Vocalion 78-rpm records under Shaw's name also have not been available to be examined, so it was not always possible to check for such data on these items either, although most seen showed "take 1."

Unfortunately also, RCA was *NOT* one of the companies that etched matrix and take numbers onto the disc. Only the record issue number was etched into the disc instead. Therefore, information on take numbers concerning the bulk of Shaw's records as a leader (and for a large percentage of his earlier sideman records) would only be available from the RCA files. Fortunately, access to copies of the original recording session log sheets for Artie Shaw's records for RCA was provided by collector John Harding. However, this proved to provide more confusion and uncertainty, as often there was no clear indication of which take actually was used. However, the log sheets indicated that in most cases among Shaw's records, only one take of each performance was recorded, as a second turntable was being used, providing the "1" / "1A" designated masters. Published information, including such data in liner notes to RCA's LP and CD reissues, presumably from the RCA files, unfortunately has frequently been cited with errors when it has been possible to check the data. When asked about the seemingly anomalous published data concerning large numbers of takes having been made for particular tunes, Shaw noted that one take was indeed usually enough, especially with his Bluebird records and all the Victor Gramercy 5 items (2).

Therefore, as noted, I have reluctantly decided to omit take numbers except when necessary to distinguish alternates that have been issued, or (for Shaw's own records for RCA) when the available information was clear. Also, known rejected takes usually are not listed in this discography, in the interest of clarity, as they apparently do not exist. The "*NOTES*" for the record dates provide specific information and call attention to any problems left unresolved.

It would have been fulfilling to have straightened out the issue of take numbers once and for all concerning all of Artie Shaw's records, both as leader and as sideman. Discographically, one yearns for complete data on each recording session: what time did it start, and in what studio? Were there any rejected takes before a "perfect" master was recorded for issue? *WAS* that one the master then considered "take 1" (as with many companies), or was a later master issued instead and designated "take 1"? Do any other takes (if made) still exist? However, to accomplish this with any degree of accuracy and consistency, access to all the relevant companies' files would have been essential, plus access to the original masters to verify the files. In many cases the original masters no longer exist (during World War II, for example, much of this material was recycled for the war effort). In many cases the original company files also do not exist. While I was curator of the Institute of Jazz Studies at Rutgers during 1968–71, I attempted to gain access to all the relevant companies' files, but was consistently not given permission to do so. As noted, since LP and CD reissues of this material by those same companies, and other published discographic information (all with data allegedly from company files), are frequently contradictory concerning master number data, it did not seem wise to risk perpetuating erroneous data.

For convenience, tables of abbreviations of instruments and record labels follow immediately in this introduction.

Table of Instrument Abbreviations

acc	accordion
as	alto saxophone
b	bass
bari	baritone saxophone
bcl	bass clarinet
bs	bass saxophone
bsn	bassoon
C-mel	C-melody saxophone
cel	cello
cl	clarinet
d	drums
Eh	English horn
Fh	French horn
fl	flute
g	guitar
p	piano
perc	percussion
reeds	various woodwinds used
tb	trombone
tp	trumpet
ts	tenor saxophone
tu	tuba
v	vocal
vibes	vibraphone
vl	violin
vla	viola
xyl	xylophone

It is assumed that in most band situations in this era the saxophone section members all were involved in "doubling" on other instruments. Many arrangements called for clarinet section passages from the saxophonists. The baritone saxophonist would double on bass clarinet. When Shaw was a sideman, primarily playing lead alto sax and clarinet, he occasionally would be called on to double on flute, baritone sax, and bass clarinet as well. Discographies usually list saxophonists under their primary instrument, however, and that procedure has been followed here, except that, when unusual doubling was expected, all saxophonists have been listed as performing on "(reeds)" for that session. Shaw occasionally had four-man sax sections without a regular baritone saxophonist, such as in his 1937–39 band. In this case, Hank Freeman may have been doubling on alto sax, baritone sax, clarinet and bass clarinet during the course of an evening. Similarly, in Shaw's 1936–37 "String Swing" band, the pianist occasionally played a celeste for ensemble textures, but instrumentation has been listed as "(p)" for the sake of clarity, except when he was performing exclusively on celeste.

Table of Record Label Abbreviations

AFS	Affinity (compact disc)
AFRS	Armed Forces Radio Service
Aircheck	Aircheck Records (not to be confused with "air checks")
AJ	Archives of Jazz and Folk
Ajaz	Ajaz or Ajazz (exists under both names)
ARC	American Record Company
ASC	Artie Shaw Club (England)
ASG5	*The Artie Shaw Gramercy 5* (Artie Shaw Club issue)
AXM2-	RCA Victor's *The Complete . . .* series
BB	RCA Victor's Bluebird 78s
BBG	Big Band Gems
Bell	Bell Records
BOMR	Book-of-the-Month Records *Artie Shaw—A Legacy* album
Br	Brunswick 78s
CAL	RCA Victor's Camden LPs
Clef	Clef Records (Verve subsidiary)
CK	Columbia compact disc
CLP	Circle LP
Co.	Columbia 78s
De.	Decca
FF	Fanfare Records
FTR	First Time Records
GE	Golden Era Records
Har.	Harmony (Columbia subsidiary label)
HBCD	Hindsight CD
Hep	Hep Records
HoW	Hit of the Week
HS	Hollywood Soundstage
HSR	Hindsight Records
IAJRC	International Association of Jazz Record Collectors
J	Joyce
JG	Jazz Guild
JHCD	Jazz Hour Compact Disc
Kayde	Kaydee Records
LL	Laserlight CD
Lion	Lion (M-G-M subsidiary)
Mel.	Melotone 78s
MCA	Decca LPs
MGC	Clef LPs
MGV	Verve LPs
MM	MusicMasters
Mus.	Musicraft 78s
MVS	Musicraft LPs
NW	(p. 157)
RWJ	Redwood Jazz
SB	Sunbeam Records

SE	Special Edition 78s	TT	Thesaurus Transcription Service
SOL	Solid Sender Records	TOM	The Old Master Records
SoS	Sounds of Swing Records	Vic.	RCA Victor
SW	Swingdom Records	Vo.	Vocalion 78s

Artie Shaw Sideman Discography: 1928–1936

During most of this period Artie Shaw was one of a pool of New York's finest saxophone/clarinet virtuosos making frequent but usually commercially oriented records, transcriptions, and radio broadcasts. Shaw, Benny Goodman, Jimmy Dorsey, Tony Parenti, Arnold Brilhart, and their other less famous counterparts made countless sessions performing in very similar styles, often only playing in the section, with no opportunity to solo. Most of the music contained on such recordings is primarily of interest as period pieces, evidence of the tastes of the day. Occasional jazz numbers, or jazz solos within otherwise commercial dance performances, are of interest to jazz scholars documenting activities of the musicians in question, and occasionally their prowess and creativity. Any serious study of Artie Shaw as an instrumentalist, therefore, necessitates also examining not only his early sideman work as a clarinet soloist, but also his work as lead alto saxophonist, and even the occasional rare alto sax solo and intriguing glimpses of his roles on baritone sax and flute, as documented on such sessions.

It is frequently impossible to determine personnel performing on records or broadcasts from this era. Sidemen generally were unlisted on record labels, pseudonyms often were used for the bands, and company files have been lost or destroyed in many cases. Where such files exist, they often are wrong, giving information derived from the contracts rather than from session notes, by which time substitutions may have occurred, or even are incorrect simply because of human error. Occasionally, the testimony or diary of participants can provide better information. Often, documentation of a musician's presence is possible only by the trained ear recognizing his solo style, as one knows a friend's voice on the phone. Of course, aural evidence is the best guide, but aside from the occasional solo that exhibited the personal style of a participant, musicians were very nearly undistinguishable in playing their section parts. The musicians also were interchangeable among bands from session to session and even substituted for one another in the middle of a session if a participant had another commitment to fulfill. Although Shaw's lead alto sax section work, where clearly exposed, seems distinctive enough to tempt attribution of Shaw's presence to such passages where the personnel has been uncertain, this alone would not be a "safe" method to attribute him to the personnel.

Many discographers, however well intentioned, have published inaccurate data, compounding the problem. It is unlikely that full information can be recovered concerning most of this material. The pool of musicians in the studios who made countless record dates and broadcasts in this era therefore often cannot be sorted out beyond educated guesswork based on careful listening to their occasional solos. Unfortunately, it is also often fruitless to try to track down surviving copies of much of this material in order to check by listening. Most of this material has never been reissued since its original 78–rpm release or broadcast transcription, and reissues on collectors' label LPs, or even those by the major record companies, may often be as rare as the originals.

The following list represents what could be confirmed by ear or by Shaw, or was supported by convincing data after comparing the existing discographical data with Shaw's memory and known activity.

Joe Cantor and His Orchestra
Richmond, Indiana, 13 August 1928

Joe Cantor(vl), Izzy George, Willis Kelly(tp), Charlie Stenross(tb), Artie Shaw(as), Les Arquette(ts,v), Vic Buynak(ts), Walt Bergner(p), Chuck Shank(g), Julian Woodworth(b,tu,v), Chuck Cantor(d)

14137	Heartbroken and Lonely (vTrio)	Gennett unissued
14138	WaDaDa (v)	—
14139	Frisco Squabble	—
14141	The Girl Friend	—

NOTE: Initial information from Artie Shaw, who stated that this was his first recording session and that the band had recorded all Shaw arrangements with Shaw heavily featured on alto sax. Above probable personnel identified by Shaw and R. H. Strassmyer from a photo of Joe Cantor's band on the stand at the Far East Restaurant (c. 1927). A request for more information in Bob Hilbert's column "Discographical Forum" in *Joslin's Jazz Journal* generated a reply from Richard J. Johnson of Aylesbury, England, with the above specific date, master numbers and titles. Each title was recorded in four takes except 14141 (three takes). (Mx #14140 was a version of "I Can't Give You Anything But

Love" by Julian Woodworth accompanied by piano only, also rejected.) Test pressings were made, and were distributed "to the customer" (presumably Cantor) but surviving copies could not be located for review. The masters reportedly were destroyed on 4 January 1929.

Irving Aaronson's Commanders
Chicago, 22 August 1930

Charlie Trotta, Jimmy Taylor(tp,v), Red Stanley(tb,v), Artie Shaw, Art Quenzer, Phil Saxe, Tony Pastor(reeds), Sal Cibelli, Jack Armstrong(vl,v), Paul Mertz, Chalmers Mac-Gregor(p), Ralph Napoli(g,bjo,v), Max Walker(b), Stan Johnson(d,v)

| 6104 | Why Have You Forgotten Waikiki? (v) | Br4883 |
| 6105 | Moonlight on the Colorado (v) | — |

NOTE: Earlier sessions reported as including Shaw with Aaronson were spurious. This was the only record session by Aaronson known to have occurred while Shaw was in the band. Records could not be reviewed.

Paul Specht and His Orchestra
New York, 28 May 1931

Charlie Spivak(tp), Russ Morgan(tb), Artie Shaw(cl,as), Johnny Morris(v), others unknown

W151572	You Forgot Your Gloves (vJM)	Co.2472, Franklin Mint 8090
W151573	Falling in Love (vJM)	—
W151574	I Found a Million Dollar Baby (vJM)	Co.2482

NOTE: Shaw featured for clarinet obbligatos on 151572 and 151574; 151573 not available for review. Shaw affirmed this was his first record session after getting his New York union card. FM8090 cites Pete Pumiglio as clarinetist.

Red Nichols
New York, 24 August 1931

Red Nichols, Don Moore, Snub Pollard, Johnny "Scat" Davis(tp), Will Bradley(tb), Artie Shaw(as,cl), Russ Lyon(as,cl,v), Babe Russin(ts), Harry Bluestone(vl), Paul Mertz(p), Tony Sacco(g,v), Artie Bernstein(b), Victor Engle(d)

E37098	I'm With You (vTS)	Mel.12236
E37099	If I Didn't Have You (vTS)	Mel.12238
E37100	River Stay 'Way From My Door (vTS)	Mel.12235
E37101	I Idolize My Baby's Eyes (vTS)	—
E37102	I Don't Know Why (vRL)	Mel.12236
E37103	In a Dream (vTS)	Mel.12238

NOTE: Shaw reportedly not featured (information from Tony Sacco via John Harding). All titles were issued under various pseudonyms (see text). Around late August 1931, Shaw left Nichols to work in the CBS house band under Fred Rich, and recalled the following as his "first gig for CBS" (2).

Fred Rich Orchestra
New York, c. late August 1931

collective personnel: Manny Klein, Bob Effros, possibly Bunny Berigan, unk.(tp), Tommy Dorsey, Jerry Colonna, Lloyd Turner, Charles Butterfield(tb), Artie Shaw(cl,as), Elmer Feldkamp(reeds,v), probably Jimmy Dorsey, Jack Towne, Rudy Adler(reeds), Joe Venuti, Lew Conrad, unk. (strings), Irving Brodsky, Sam Prager, Walter Gross(p), Eddie Lang(g), Hank Sterns(b), George Green, unk.(perc,-xyl), Larry Murphy(v)

#1:	I've Got Five Dollars (Theme)	Aircheck-12
	Hosanna (vLM)	
	Guilty (vLM)	
	What Is It? (vLM)	Aircheck-13
	Song of the Flame (Theme)	

#2:	(Theme)	
	Jericho (vLM)	
	Just One More Chance (vLM)	Aircheck-13
	Bend Down Sister (vLM)	
	The Riff Song (Theme)	

NOTE: No features for Shaw on shows #1 & 2.

#3:	(Theme)	
	New Sun in the Sky (vLM)	
	I Love Louisa (vLM)	
	Sugar	
	High and Low (vLM)	
	(Theme)	

NOTE: Shaw featured on clarinet on "Sugar."

#4:	(Theme)	
	Do the New York (vLM)	
	Me (vLM)	
	Goin' to Town (vLM)	

This Is the Missus   Aircheck-13
(Theme)

#5:   (Theme)
It's the Girl (vLM)
Sweet and Lovely (vLM)   Aircheck-13
It's Great to Be in Love
   (vLM)
(Theme)(long version)

NOTE: This show offered only three numbers as shown, instead of the usual four tunes. No features for Shaw on shows #4 & 5.

#6:   (Theme)
I Idolize My Baby's
   Eyes (vLM)
Was It Wrong? (vLM)
I'm With You (vLM)
Roll On Mississippi   Aircheck-12
(Theme)(long version)

NOTE: Shaw featured on sub–tone melody clarinet for "Was It Wrong?" and a clarinet solo on "Roll On Mississippi."

#7:   (no details)

#8:   (Theme)
Oh That Kiss (vLM)
Goodnight Sweetheart
   (vLM)
I Wouldn't Change You
   for the World (vLM)   Aircheck-13
Alabamy Bound
(Theme)(long version)

NOTE: Shaw featured for an alto sax solo on "Alabamy Bound."

#9:   (no details)

#10:   (Theme)
I Know That You Know   Aircheck-13
   (vLM)
I'm Just a Dancing
   Sweetheart (vLM)
If I Had to Go On
   Without You (vLM)
Dixie Jamboree   Aircheck-12
(Theme)(long version)

NOTE: Shaw featured on clarinet on "Dixie Jamboree."

#11:   (Theme)
California Here I Come
   (vLM)
Linda (vLM)
You Didn't Know the
   Music (vLM)
Charlie Cadet March
(Theme)(long version)

NOTE: Shaw featured for an alto sax solo on "Linda."

#12:   (Theme)
So Are You (vLM)
You Call It Madness I
   Call It Love (vLM)
With Love in My Heart
   (vLM)
The Ranger's Song
   (March)
(Theme)(long version)

#13:   (Theme)
I'll Make a Happy
   Landing (vLM)   Aircheck-13
Hiding in the Shadows   —
   of the Moon (vLM)
You Try Somebody Else   —
   (vLM)
Fine and Dandy
(Theme)

#14:   (Theme)
Tell Tales (vLM)
By the Sycamore Tree
   (vLM)   Aircheck-12
Dinah (vLM)
Out of a Clear Blue Sky
   (vLM)
(Theme)(long version)

NOTE: Shaw not featured on shows #12, 13, & 14.

#15:   (Theme)
Ay-Ay-Ay
I'm Sorry Dear (vLM)
Nobody's Sweetheart   Aircheck-12
   (vLM)
Freddie the Freshman
   (vLM)
(Theme)(different)

NOTE: Shaw featured on clarinet on "Nobody's Sweetheart."

#16:   (Theme)
Follow the Swallow
   Home (vLM)
You Try Somebody Else
   (vLM)
Sunny Skies (vLM)
(Theme)(long version)

NOTE: Shaw not featured. "You Try Somebody Else" differs from Show #13 version.

#17:   (Theme)
99 out of 100 (vLM)
One More Kiss (vLM)
Japanese Sandman   Aircheck-12
   (vLM)

Sweet Jenny Lee (vLM)
(Theme)(long; different)

NOTE: Shaw featured for a low-register clarinet solo on "Sweet Jenny Lee."

#18:   (Theme)
            My Bluebird's Back
                Again (vLM)
            Honest Really Truly
                (vLM)   Aircheck-12
            San
            Southbound (vLM)
            (Theme)(long version)

NOTE: Shaw featured for two clarinet solos (one low-register) on "San."

#19:   (Theme)
            Who's Your Little
                Whoosits? (vLM)
            There's a Blue Note in
                My Love Song (vLM)
            Some of These Days   Aircheck-12
                (vLM)
            Save the Last Dance for
                Me (Waltz) (vLM)
            (Theme)(long version)

NOTE: Shaw featured on clarinet on "Some of These Days."

#20:   (Theme)
            Sugar (vLM)   Aircheck-13
            Too Late (vLM)   —
            Somebody Stole My Gal   Aircheck-12
                (vLM)
            Now's the Time to Fall
                in Love (vLM)
            (Theme)(long version)

NOTE: Shaw featured on clarinet on "Somebody Stole My Gal"; "Sugar" was a different arrangement from the version on Show #3 and also featured a vocal instead of Shaw's clarinet solo.

#21:   (Theme)
            The Sun's in My Heart
                (vEF)
            Was That the Human
                Thing to Do? (vEF)
            Just Friends (vEF)   Aircheck-12
            Goin' to Town
            (Theme)(different)

NOTE: Shaw featured for a low-register clarinet solo on "Goin' to Town" (which also differed from the version on Show #4 in not having a vocal).

#22:   (Theme)
            Tell Tales (vEF)
            Snuggled on Your
                Shoulder (vEF)

Goodnight Moon (vEF)
One Man Band   Aircheck-13
(Theme)(fadeout)

NOTE: Shaw well exposed on clarinet on "One Man Band." "Tell Tales" was a different performance from that on Show #14.

#23:   (Theme)
            Mary I'm in Love With
                You (vEF)
            Evening in Caroline
                (vEF)
            Auf Wiedersehen My
                Dear (vEF)   Aircheck-12
            Copenhagen
            (Theme)

NOTE: Shaw featured on clarinet on "Copenhagen."

#24:   (Theme)
            Dancing on the Ceiling
                (vEF)
            Somebody Loves You
                (vEF)
            I Want to Count Sheep
                'Til the Cows Come   Aircheck-12
                Home (vEF)
            Bugle Call Rag
            (Theme)(long; different)

NOTE: Shaw featured on clarinet on "Bugle Call Rag."

#25:   (Theme)
            Rain on the Roof
            Two Loves (vEF)
            Loveable (vEF)
            Tiger Rag
            (Theme)(fades)

NOTE: Shaw featured on clarinet on "Tiger Rag."

#26–27:   (no details)

#28:   (Theme)
            Lo and Behold (vEF)
            How Long Will It Last?
                (vEF)
            What Makes You So
                Adorable? (vEF)
            Zonky   Aircheck-12
            (Theme)(long version)

NOTE: Shaw not featured.

From above undocumented shows (no feature on the issued title):

            Waiting for the Robert E.   Aircheck-13
                Lee (vLM)
            (other unknown titles)

NOTE: These "Fred's Friendly Five" transcriptions for the Jarman Shoe Company were recorded at several sessions starting around late August 1931. Different ensembles were used for different pieces (eliminating the string section on some numbers, etc.). Shaw recalls the soloists as Manny Klein on trumpet, Tommy Dorsey on trombone, Artie Shaw on clarinet and alto sax, Joe Venuti on violin, probably Rudy Adler on bass clarinet, and one or more of the pianists. Each show featured an "Aviation News Bulletin" by Casey Jones (announced as "the speed demon air pilot and vice president of Curtis Wright Corporation" on some shows), which always preceded the last tune. The liner notes to the Aircheck LPs noted there were twenty-six fifteen-minute programs of four tunes each. However, program transcriptions numbering up to #28 have been verified by Martin F. Bryan of Vintage Recording Co. These programs were scheduled from September 1931 through April 1932. *The New York Times* radio listings indicate that the shows, featuring "Larry Murphy, tenor," were aired over WABC on Fridays at 9:45 p.m.

Shaw also was in Fred Rich's orchestra regularly on Bing Crosby's CBS sustaining broadcasts (Crosby's first CBS radio broadcast was on 2 September 1931) and Crosby's Cremo Cigars shows during 1931–32. Carl Fenton replaced Rich as conductor on the Cremo Cigars shows during late 1931 and early 1932. To date, any transcriptions of this material featuring Shaw have not surfaced.

Bing Crosby Show
New York, 2 September 1931

similar personnel; Bing Crosby(v)

Just One More Chance (vBC)	Vic.LPV584, LSA309	
I'm Through With Love (vBC)	—	

NOTE: Shaw not featured. The announcer notes Crosby will broadcast "nightly except Sundays."

Fred Rich and His Orchestra
New York, 10 September 1931

similar personnel; unk.(v) for Crosby

151777	If I Didn't Have You (v)	Co.2536
151778	As Time Goes By (v)	—
151779	I'm Just a Dancing Sweetheart (v)	Co.2534
151780	Kiss Me Goodnight (v)	—

NOTE: Records could not be reviewed. In *BG—On the Record*, D. Russell Connor indicated the clarinetist was Jimmy Dorsey; this implies clarinet solo work can be heard. For obvious reasons, it is probable that this soloist was Artie Shaw.

add Cornell Smelser(acc), Trio(v)
New York, c. late September 1931

Little Girl (vEF&T)	HoW J4	
It's the Girl (vEF&T)	HoW K1	

NOTE: Sub-tone melody clarinet on "Little Girl"

add Ben Alley(v)
New York, c. late October 1931

I'm Just a Dancing Sweetheart (vBA&T)	HoW L1	
As the Backs Go Tearing By	—	

NOTE: Shaw not featured; however his characteristic lead alto sax work is clear.

Bing Crosby Cremo Cigars Show
New York, 7 November 1931

Bing Crosby(v) for Alley; Carl Fenton(cond) for Rich

I Cried for You (vBC)

same
New York, 9 November 1931

Where the Blue of the
    Night(Theme) (vBC)
Now That You're Gone
    (vBC)
This Is the Missus (vBC)
Hiding in the Shadows
    of the Moon
Goodnight Sweetheart
    (vBC)

NOTE: No features for Shaw on these Cremo Cigars show performances. These pieces were taken from well-worn aluminum acetates and consequently are in very low fidelity. Nevertheless, "Hiding in the Shadows of the Moon" was an instrumental by "Carl Fenton and his Orchestra" on which Shaw's clarinet lead is audible in some section passages. The other titles featured Crosby virtually throughout, singing, scatting, humming, and whistling, with no solo opportunities for any of the instrumentalists in the band.

Fred Rich Orchestra
New York, c. early December 1931

Helen Rowland, Paul Small(v) for Alley

You Call It Madness I Call It Love (vHR)	HoW M2	

Auld Lang Syne   —
Call Me Darling (vPS)   HoW M3
Comin' Through the Rye   —

NOTE: Clarinet has short arranged passages on the last title.

Blue Coal Minstrels
New York, c. late 1931–early 1932

similar personnel with Artie Shaw(as,cl), Joe Venuti(vl), Cornell Smelser(acc), Larry Briers(p,cond), Fred Vettel, Kate Smith, unk. female, unk. quartet(v)

#1:   Just Hear That Slide
            Trombone (vQ)
         Moan You Moaners
            (vUF)
         If You Can't Sing,
            Whistle
         Marching Home to You
            (vFV)
         Just Because She Made
            Those Googly Eyes
            (vQ)
         Blue Coal Theme (vQ)

NOTE: Shaw featured on alto sax on "If You Can't Sing, Whistle."

#2:   A Good Man Is Hard to
            Find (vUF)
         Roll On Mississippi
         Hiking Down the
            Highway (vFV)
         Ida (vQ)

NOTE: Shaw featured on alto sax on "Roll On Mississippi."

#3–14:   (no details)

#15:   Blues in My Heart (vKS)
         Bend Down Sister
         Sweetheart I'm On My
            Way (vFV)
         Annabelle Lee (vQ)

NOTE: Shaw featured on clarinet on "Bend Down Sister."

#16:   Guilty (vKS)
         Little Mary Brown
         You Were My Salvation
            (vFV)
         Oh Susanna (vQ)

NOTE: Shaw featured on clarinet on "Little Mary Brown."

#17–19:   (no details)

#20:   Way Down Yonder in the
            Cornfield (vQ)

Nobody's Sweetheart
If I Were King (vFV)
The Alpine Milkman
         (vQ)

NOTE: Shaw featured on alto sax on "Nobody's Sweetheart."

#21–26:   (no details)

NOTE: Other shows in this CBS radio series (there presumably were twenty-six) could not be located. The band was announced as "Larry Briers and his Orchestra" and Shaw confirmed his solos on all the instrumentals.

Ben Selvin and His Orchestra
New York, 4 February 1932

similar personnel; Paul Small(v)

152104	Rain on the Roof (vPS)	Co.2614
152105	Auf Wiedersehen My Dear (vPS)	—
351155	Carolina's Calling Me (vPS)	Har.1411
236106	Delishious / Delishious (vPS)	Har.6505

NOTE: Sub-tone clarinet melody on 351155; no features on the others. The Columbia 236000 series matrix numbers were for fine-groove "5-minute" recordings on budget labels, with both instrumental and vocal versions of the same piece on the same side; the 351000 series also was for their budget labels, e.g., Harmony (as above). Selvin made many recordings and broadcasts in this period with his regular band, which included members of the CBS House Band when Shaw was playing lead alto sax and clarinet. Shaw noted they were "always" in the studios making records or broadcast transcriptions in those days; unfortunately, not as many radio shows from this era are available for review as one would like. Many that have surfaced contain excellent performances scattered among the banal commercial tunes and announcements. Some occasionally featured Shaw, like the following:

Ben Selvin Devoe Painters Orchestra
New York, c. spring 1932

probably similar personnel; Male Quartet(v)

#3:   Cheerful Little Earful
            (vMQ)
         Can This Be Love?
         (unknown waltz)
         Happy Feet (vMQ)

NOTE: Shaw confirmed his clarinet solos on both vocal titles. Each show also featured announcements by Ben Selvin and a performance by the Male Quartet with only piano accompaniment. Band for show #1 sounded different and included an accordion, with no features for Shaw to confirm. Other shows have not been located. As most radio shows offered thirteen programs per season, presumably there was more from this series featuring Shaw.

Ben Selvin and His Orchestra
New York, 12 May 1932

Manny Klein, unk.(tp), Tommy Dorsey(tb), Artie Shaw(cl,as), Herman Wolfson(ts), probably Rudy Adler(reeds), Joe Venuti(vl), Carl Kress(g), unk.(p), unk.(b), possibly Gene Krupa(d), Male Quartet(v)

W152193	Crazy People (vMQ)	Co.2661, TOM-16
W152194	Is I in Love? I Is (vMQ)	—
W152195	Lullaby of the Leaves (vMQ)	Co.2654
W152196	Whistle and Blow Your Blues Away (vMQ)	—

NOTE: Shaw confirmed his clarinet solos on 152193 & 152194, sub-tone melody clarinet on 152195, and both the alto sax and clarinet solos on 152196 (2).

In the spring of 1932, Shaw left CBS to go on the road. He has stated that during the period he was with Roger Wolfe Kahn's orchestra, he did no other gigs.

Roger Wolfe Kahn and His Orchestra
New York, 5 August 1932

Charlie Teagarden, Ruby Weinstein, Frank Zullo(tp), Leo Arnaud, Andy Russo(tb), Artie Shaw, Larry Binyon, Del Porter(reeds), Harry Urbant, Julie Held(vl), Joe Ross(vla), Russ Carlson(p), Perry Botkin(g), Ward Ley(b), Chauncey Morehouse(d), The Kahn-a-Sirs, Del Porter(v)

W152249	You've Got Me in the Palm of Your Hand (vK)	Co.2695
W152250	Just Another Night Alone (vDP)	Co.2697
W152251	Sheltered By the Stars (vK)	—
W152252	I Can't Believe It's True (vK)	Co.2695

NOTE: Shaw featured on baritone sax melody passages on 152250; short flute break and clarinet spots on 152251; brief breaks on clarinet and alto sax on 152252, and can be heard in flute ensemble passages in 152249. Personnel from Rust.

similar; add Gertrude Niesen(v)
Vitaphone Movie Short *The Yacht Party*, c. fall 1932

Way Down Yonder in New Orleans	MGM (laserdisc), ML 103 928
Gosh Darn (vK)	—, —
Sweet and Hot (vGN)	—, —
Medley: Crazy Rhythm/ You're Driving Me Crazy/	—, —
Crazy People (vK)	—, —
Dinah	—, —
Lullaby of the Leaves	—, —

NOTE: Shaw filmed soloing on clarinet on the first title, and playing lead alto saxophone or clarinet; Shaw clarinet solos also heard on "Crazy People" and "Dinah."

Roger Wolfe Kahn and His Orchestra
New York, 9 November 1932

Charlie Teagarden, Ruby Weinstein, Angie Rattiner(tp), Andy Russo, Phil Giardina(tb), Artie Shaw, Max Farley, Larry Binyon(reeds), Harry Urbant, Julie Held(vl), Joe Ross(vla), Marlin Skyles(p), Perry Botkin(g), Ward Ley(b), Chauncey Morehouse(d), The Kahn-a-Sirs, Del Porter(v)

W152318	Fit as a Fiddle (vK)	Co.2726
W152319	A Shine on Your Shoes (vK)	Co.2722
W152320	It Don't Mean a Thing (vK)	—
W152321	Just a Little Home for the Old Folks (vDP)	Co.2726

NOTE: No feature on 152319 (The Kahn-a-Sirs sing "Louisiana Hayride"); clarinet solo on 152320 used in *Artie Shaw: Time Is All You've Got*; others not reviewed.

Adrian Rollini and His Orchestra
New York, 14 February 1933

Manny Klein(tp), Tommy Dorsey(tb), Artie Shaw(cl,as), Art Rollini(ts), Adrian Rollini(vbs,xyl,bs,goofus), Joe Venuti(vl), Charles Magnante(acc), Fulton McGrath(p), Eddie Lang(g), Art Miller(b), Joey Nash(v)

13049	Have You Ever Been Lonely? (vJN)	Mel.12629
13050	You've Got Me Cryin' Again (vJN)	Mel.12630
13051	Hustlin' & Bustlin' for Baby (vJN)	—
13052	You Must Believe Me (vJN)	Mel.12629

NOTE: Joey Nash confirmed Shaw was on this session, but in *Tommy Dorsey: On the Side* (Scarecrow Press, 1995), Robert L. Stockdale listed the vocalist as Dick Robertson (p. 313). Records could not be reviewed.

In early 1933, Shaw played for George Gershwin's Broadway musical *Pardon My English* and on Will Rogers's radio show in Al Goodman's orchestra, among other venues. Shaw probably also played on other, unidentified record dates in this period. One controversial session is Bing Crosby's Columbia record date of 26 January 1933, but while Shaw said he might have made some commercial records with Crosby as well as their many radio broadcasts, exposure for clarinet on that record date is inconclusive. Shaw spent the year from March 1933 to early 1934 on his Bucks County farm and confirmed that he did not play at all in that interval. He stated that immediately after returning to the New York City studios from his farm, he began playing baritone sax for Richard Himber with Arnold Brilhart on lead alto, and resumed freelancing (2).

Richard Himber and His Ritz-Carlton Hotel Orchestra
New York, 19 March 1934

Charlie Margulis, Bunny Berigan(tp), Tommy Dorsey(tb), Arnold Brilhart, Benny Goodman, Henry Wade, Artie Shaw(reeds), Lou Raderman, Murray Kellner, Jack Zayde(vl), Adrian Rollini(vibes), Ed Steinberg(p), Ernie Capozie(g), Jack Kimmel(b), Nat Levine(d), Joey Nash(v)

81957	When a Woman Loves a Man (vJN)	BB5418, AXM2-5520
81958	Love Thy Neighbor (vJN)	BB5419, —
81959	May I? (vJN)	—, —
81960	A Thousand Goodnights (vJN)	BB5418, —
81961	Ending With a Kiss (vJN)	BB5421, —
91962	It's Psychological (vJN)	—, —

NOTE: Data from Joey Nash in liner notes to AXM2-5520 (a two-LP album titled *Richard Himber and His Ritz-Carlton Hotel Orchestra Featuring Joey Nash 1934–1935*). No feature for clarinet on any of the above titles.

Adrian Rollini and His Orchestra
New York, 24 March 1934

Bunny Berigan(tp), Al Philburn(tb), Artie Shaw, Benny Goodman(as,cl), Art Rollini(ts), Adrian Rollini(bs,vbs), Fulton McGrath(p), Dick McDonough(g), Artie Miller(b), Herb Weil(d), Joey Nash(v)

14995-1	A Thousand Goodnights (vJN)	Vo.2672, SoS122
14996-1	Butterfingers (vJN)	—, —
14997-1	Waitin' at the Gate for Katy (vJN)	Vo.2673, SB134
14997-2	Waitin' at the Gate for Katy (vJN)	—, —
14998-1	Little Did I Dream (vJN)	—, SoS122
14999-1	How Can It Be a Beautiful Day (vJN)	Vo.2675, —
14999-2	How Can It Be a Beautiful Day (vJN)	—, —

NOTE: Artie Shaw has confirmed that he was the clarinet soloist on all takes. SoS122 is the Sounds of Swing collectors' label LP titled *Artie Shaw: The Sideman Years*. SB134 is a Benny Goodman album on the Sunbeam label, which erroneously identifies the clarinetist as Goodman.

Ben Selvin and His Orchestra
The Taystee Breadwinners, New York, 27 March 1934

collective personnel: Manny Klein, Ruby Weinstein, Sterling Bose(tp), Tommy Dorsey, Miff Mole, Charles Butterfield(tb), Artie Shaw, Benny Goodman, Jimmy Dorsey(cl,as), Art Karle, Art Rollini, Hank Ross(ts), Ben Selvin(vl,cond), Harry DaCosta(p), Perry Botkin, Carl Kress, George Van Eps(g), unk.(b,d), Bill Jones, Ernie Hare, Gypsy Nina, Harry DaCosta(v)

#21:	Theme (vBJ,EH)	(unissued)
	Love Thy Neighbor (vBJ,EH)	—
	Nothing Ever Happens to Me (vEH)	—
	Two Loves (vGN,HDC)	—
	Put On Your Old Gray Bonnet (vBJ,EH)	IAJRC 14

NOTE: Shaw solos on clarinet on last title, part of which is used in the soundtrack of *Artie Shaw: Time Is All You've Got*. Other shows in this series did not seem to feature Shaw (information from John Harding). Personnel from Stockdale's *Tommy Dorsey: On the Side*, which indicates *The Taystee Breadwinners* programs began broadcasting weekly over WOR in November 1933, with slightly varying personnel from week to week. As Shaw is documented as having returned to freelancing by February 1934 (see text), it is likely he participated in other programs in this series as well, even if reportedly not aurally identifiable.

Richard Himber and His Orchestra
World Transcriptions, New York, 7 June 1934

Charlie Margulis, Bunny Berigan(tp), Tommy Dorsey(tb), Artie Shaw, Henry Wade, Herman Wolfson(reeds), Lou

Raderman, Murray Kellner, Jack Zayde, Fred Fradkin(vl), Verlie Mills(harp), Adrian Rollini(vibes), Ed Steinberg(p), Ernie Capozie(g), Jack Kimmel(b), Nat Levine(d), "Stevens Male Trio," "Bill Jones"(Joey Nash?), "Alice Goodwin"(v)

673	Wild Rose / Sally
674	You Oughta Be in Pictures (v"SMT")
675	With My Eyes Wide Open I'm Dreaming
676	Cocktails for Two (v"BJ")
677	True (v"AG")
678	May I? (v"BJ")
679	Sleepy Head (v"AG")
680	Baby Take a Bow
681	Little Dutch Mill (v"SMT")
682	Waitin' at the Gate for Katy (v"SMT")
683	Thank You for a Lovely Evening (v"AG")
684	All I Do Is Dream of You
685	If I Love Again (v"AG")
686	Why Do I Dream Those Dreams
687	Good News
688	Carioca
689	Jangle Fever
690	Love Me (v"AG")
691	Once in a Lifetime
692	Goodnight Lovely Little Lady
693	So Help Me (v"AG")
694	If I Do It Again

NOTE: Himber's band, which reportedly consisted of only fourteen musicians for the above session, recorded these twenty-two titles for World Transcriptions (mx.#673-694) under the pseudonym "Larry Bradford and his Orchestra" with pseudonymous vocalists as indicated. It is possible but not certain that "Bill Jones" was Joey Nash (session could not be reviewed). Instrumental personnel of the Himber orchestra listed above was from Joey Nash in the liner notes to AXM2-5520 (referring to the 12 June 1934 session below). Nash stated that this personnel remained consistent for all remaining Victor sessions on which he participated, and also on their weekly *Studebaker Champions Hour* radio show broadcasts on both CBS and NBC. (Nevertheless, most leaders used occasional substitutions and even pickup groups on occasion, so dependable consistency of personnel is not likely.) Shaw noted that Arnold Brilhart always played lead alto, but that "shortly" after Shaw joined Himber, Brilhart left the band and Shaw played lead alto and all sub-tone clarinet passages on all following sessions with Himber until late 1936 (2). Thus, Shaw probably had

already switched from baritone sax to taking over lead alto from Brilhart by the above session.

Guy Russell(v) for pseudonymous vocalists
New York, 12 June 1934

82595	Night on the Desert (vJN)	Vic.24662, AXM2-5520
82596	Straight from the Shoulder (vJN)	Vic.24672, —
82597	Rollin' Home (vGR)	Vic.24662
82598	The Marines' Hymn (vGR)	Vic.24672

NOTE: Shaw performed the sub-tone melody clarinet passages on the first two titles above; no feature for clarinet on 82598; 82597 not reviewed.

same
New York, 13 July 1934

83378	Fun to Be Fooled (vJN)	Vic.24680, AXM2-5520
83379	Let's Take a Walk Around the Block (vJN)	—, —
83380	What Can You Say in a Love Song? (vJN)	Vic.24670, —
83381	You're a Builder Upper (vJN)	—, —

NOTE: Shaw not featured.

Johnny Green and His Orchestra
New York, 1 August 1934

Pee Wee Erwin, Henry Levine(tp), Phil Giardina(tb), Artie Shaw(cl,as), Jimmy Lytell(ts), Johnny Green(p), Perry Botkin(g), Peg La Centra, Bernice Parks, George Beuler(v), others uncertain

W15618	Two Cigarettes in the Dark (vGB)	Co.2943
W15619	The Fortune Teller (vPL)	—
W15620	A New Moon over My Shoulder (vBP)	Co.2940
W15621	By the Taj Mahal (vGB)	—

NOTE: Shaw apparently featured on clarinet on 15620 (information from Johnny Green interview; see text). No features on the others.

Wingy Manone and His Orchestra
New York, 15 August 1934

Wingy Manone(tp,recit), Dicky Wells(tb), Artie Shaw(cl), Bud Freeman(ts), Teddy Wilson(p), Frank Victor(g), John Kirby(b), Sonny Greer(d)

15629-A	Easy Like	Rarities LP66, Collector's Classics COCD-4
15629-B	Easy Like	Rarities LP67, —
15630-A	In the Slot	Rarities LP66, —
15630-B	In the Slot	Rarities LP67, —

Jelly Roll Morton(p) replaces Wilson; same session

15631-A	Never Had No Lovin'	Rarities LP66, Collector's Classics COCD-4
15631-B	Never Had No Lovin'	SE-5011-S, SoS122, Rarities LP67, —
15632-A	I'm Alone Without You	—, —, —, —

NOTE: All takes originally rejected; 78-rpm Special Edition SE-5011-S issued in the 1940s (reissued on SoS122 LP *Artie Shaw: The Sideman Years*). Entire session issued on Wingy Manone Rarities LPs in the 1970s and on Collector's Classics COCD-4 in the 1990s. Shaw well featured on clarinet on all performances.

**Red Norvo and His Swing Septet
New York, 26 September 1934**

Jack Jenney(tb), Artie Shaw(cl), Charlie Barnet(ts), Red Norvo(xyl), Teddy Wilson(p), Bobby Johnson(g), Hank Wayland(b), Bill Gussak(d)

16021-A	Old Fashioned Love	Co.3059, SoS122
16021-B	Old Fashioned Love	Merritt LP-3
16022-A	I Surrender Dear	Co.2977, SoS122
16022-B	I Surrender Dear	Merritt LP-3

NOTE: Shaw well featured on all takes. A "take C" of 16021 (without Shaw) was also issued on Merritt LP-3.

**Alice Faye / Chick Bullock
New York, 26 September 1934**

Artie Shaw(cl,as), Alice Faye, Chick Bullock(v), others uncertain

16065	My Future Star (vAF)	Mel.13220
16066	Yes to You (vAF)	—
16067	Lost in a Fog (vCB)	Mel.13185
16068	Just Once Too Often (vCB)	—

NOTE: Shaw featured on clarinet for a solo on 16065 & for obbligatos and short breaks on 16068; no feature on 16066 or 16067. This was probably an ARC House Band date under Russ Morgan, ARC recording supervisor at the time. As with many ARC dates, records were issued under a variety of 78-rpm labels, including Banner, Conqueror, Melotone, Oriole, Perfect, and Rex. Shaw stated he participated

in some ARC House Band dates as a freelance sideman in this period (see text).

**Red Norvo and His Swing Septet
New York, 4 October 1934**

Jack Jenney(tb), Artie Shaw(cl), Charlie Barnet(ts), Red Norvo(xyl), Teddy Wilson(p), Bobby Johnson(g), Hank Wayland(b), Bill Gussak(d)

W16033-A	Tomboy	Co.2977, SoS122
W16033-B	Tomboy	Merritt LP-3
W16034-A	The Night Is Blue	Co.3026, SoS122

NOTE: Shaw well featured on both takes of 16033, but cannot be heard on 16034 and may not have been present.

**Richard Himber and His Orchestra
New York, 5 October 1934**

same or similar to 7 June 1934 (see "NOTE" for that session)

84436	June in January (vJN)	Vic.24811, AXM2-5520
84438	With Every Breath I Take (vJN)	—, —
84439	Stars Fell on Alabama (vJN)	Vic.24745, —
84440	Tea for Two (vJN)	Vic.24750, —
84441	Avalon (vJN)	—, —
84442	If I Had a Million Dollars (vJN)	Vic.24745, —

NOTE: Sub-tone melody clarinet passages on 84436, 84439, 84440, & 84441; no features on 84438 & 84442. Rust noted Matrix #84437 was not used.

**Johnnie "Scat" Davis and His Orchestra
New York, 15 October 1934**

Johnnie "Scat" Davis(tp,v), Artie Shaw(as,cl), others uncertain

38844	You Gotta Give Credit to Love (vJD)	De.271
38845	College Rhythm (vJD)	De.272
38846	Take a Number from 1 to 10 (vJD)	—
38847	Between Showers (vJD)	De.271

NOTE: Shaw featured on clarinet on 38845 & 38846; others not reviewed.

**same
New York, 22 October 1934**

| 38866 | Don't Stop Me If You've Heard It (vJD) | De.256 |

38867	Were You Foolin' (vJD)	—
38868	A Hundred to One It's You (vJD)	De.257
38869	Congratulate Me (vJD)	—

NOTE: Shaw had clarinet obbligatos on 38866 & 38867; others not reviewed.

Richard Himber and His Orchestra
New York, 23 October 1934

same or similar to 7 June 1934 (see "NOTE" for that session)

84744	What a Diff'rence a Day Made (vJN)	Vic.24756, AXM2-5520
84745	When Love Comes Swinging Along (vJN)	Vic.24764, —
84746	Say When (vJN)	—, —
84747	Must We Say Goodnight (So Soon?) (vJN)	Vic.24756, —
84748	Were You Foolin'? (vJN)	Vic.24757, —
84749	Winter Wonderland (vJN)	—, —

NOTE: Sub-tone melody clarinet on 84744, 84745, 84747, & 84749; no features on 84746 & 84748.

Frankie Trumbauer and His Orchestra
New York, 20 November 1934

Bunny Berigan, Nat Natoli(tp), Glenn Miller(tb), Artie Shaw(cl,as), Jack Shore(as), Frankie Trumbauer(C-mel), Larry Binyon(ts), Roy Bargy(p), Lionel Hall(g), Artie Bernstein(b), Johnny Williams(d), Dick Robertson(v)

86219	Blue Moon (vDR)	Vic.24812, SoS122, RCA RR88
86220	Plantation Moods	Vic.24834, —
86221	Down t' Uncle Bill's (vDR)	Vic.24812, —
86222	Troubled	Vic.24834, —

NOTE: Shaw featured on clarinet on all titles and also alto sax on 86222.

Richard Himber and His Orchestra
New York, 5 December 1934

same or similar to 7 June 1934 (see "NOTE" for that session)

| 86087 | In a Blue and Pensive Mood (vJN) | Vic.24824, AXM2-5520 |
| 86088 | Autumn in New York (vJN) | Vic.24823, — |

86089	I Woke Up Too Soon (vJN)	Vic.24824, —
86090	Dancing with My Shadow (vJN)	Vic.24829, —
86091	Dawn (vJN)	—
86092	Flamenco (vJN)	Vic.24823

NOTE: Sub-tone melody clarinet on all four titles on AXM2-5520; others not reviewed.

Connee Boswell / Chick Bullock
New York, 15 January 1935

Artie Shaw(cl,as), Connee Boswell, Chick Bullock(v), others uncertain

16642	Blue Moon (vCBo)	Br7363, NW248
16643	Clouds (vCBo)	—
16644	You Fit into the Picture (vCB)	Mel.13298

NOTE: Shaw featured on clarinet on 16644; no feature on others.

Richard Himber and His Orchestra
New York, 11 February 1935

same or similar to 7 June 1934 (see "NOTE" for that session)

88611	Lullaby of Broadway (vJN)	Vic.24868, AXM2-5520
88612	Everything's Been Done Before (vJN)	Vic.24886, —
88613	Why Have a Falling Out? (vJN)	Vic.24869, —
88614	Things Might Have Been So Different (vJN)	—, —
88615	Zing! Went the Strings of My Heart (vJN)	Vic.24868, —
88616	I'm Going Down to Dance at Clancey's (vJN)	—, —

NOTE: Sub-tone melody clarinet on 88612 & 88614; two four-bar breaks on 88616; no features on 88611, 88613, & 88615.

The above was the last Himber session with Joey Nash as vocalist. By the next session, personnel cited by Nash may have changed. Rust listed Himber's personnel as shown for the next session, except with Arnold Brilhart instead of Shaw.

Richard Himber and His Orchestra
New York, 4 May 1935

Ruby Weinstein, Jimmy Roselli(tp), Jerry Colonna(tb), Artie Shaw, Pete Pumiglio, Jess Corneol(reeds), Sam Persoff, Lou Raderman, Jack Zayde, Irving Zir(vl), Adrian Rollini(vibes), Sam Amoroso(harp), Dave Levy(p), Ernie Capozzi(g), Jack Kimmel(b), Nat Levine(d), Stuart Allen(v)

89739	Footloose and Fancy Free (vSA)	Vic.25037
89740	Time Will Tell (vSA)	Vic.25042
89741	In the Twinkling of an Eye (vSA)	Vic.25036
89742	Give a Broken Heart a Break (vSA)	Vic.25037
89743	Reckless (vSA)	Vic.25036
89744	Love Me Forever (vSA)	Vic.25049
89745	I Wished on the Moon (vSA)	(rejected)

NOTE: Short alto sax breaks on 89740; sub-tone melody clarinet on 89742 & 89744; no features on 89739, 89741, & 89743; 89745 not reviewed.

same
New York, 19 June 1935

92289	Broadway Rhythm (vSA)	Vic.25124
92290	I Never Saw a Better Night (vSA)	Vic.25077
92291	Monday in Manhattan (vSA)	Vic.25074
92292	Thrilled (vSA)	—
92293	Kiss Me Goodnight (vSA)	Vic.25073
92294	On a Sunday Afternoon (vSA)	Vic.25124
92295	When You Are in My Arms (vSA)	Vic.25077
92296	Gringola (vSA)	Vic.25073

NOTE: Sub-tone melody clarinet on 92291; no feature on the others.

same
New York, 19 August 1935

92984	Something to Remember (vSA)	Vic.25128
92985	From the Top of Your Head (vSA)	Vic.25119
92986	My Foolish Heart (vSA)	Vic.25128
92987	What a Wonderful World (vSA)	Vic.25122
92988	Without a Word of Warning (vSA)	Vic.25119
92989	Farewell My Lovely (vSA)	Vic.25122

| 92990 | Love Makes the World Go Round (vSA) | Vic.25132 |
| 92991 | Take This Ring (vSA) | — |

NOTE: No features on 92985 & 92987; sub-tone melody clarinet on 92988 & 92989; others not reviewed.

The Boswell Sisters
New York, 8 October 1935

Russ Case, Ed Wade(tp), Will Bradley(tb), Artie Shaw (cl,as), Martha Boswell(p), Carl Kress(g), Dick Cherwin(b), Stan King(d), The Boswell Sisters: Connee, Martha, Helvetia(v)

| 60029 | Top Hat White Tie and Tails (vBS) | De.574 |
| 60030 | Cheek to Cheek (vBS) | — |

NOTE: Shaw not featured.

Richard Himber and His Orchestra
New York, 21 October 1935

same or similar to 4 May 1935 session (see NOTE for that session)

95536	Just One of Those Things (vSA)	Vic.25161
95537	Smooth (vSA)	(rejected)
95538	You Hit the Spot (vSA)	Vic.25189
95539	Thunder over Paradise (vSA)	Vic.25179
95540	If I Should Lose You (vSA)	—
95541	I Feel Like a Feather in the Breeze (vSA)	Vic.25189
95542	I'm Painting the Town Red (vSA)	Vic.25161
95549	Twilight Waltz (vSA)	(special pressing)

NOTE: Shaw not featured on reviewed titles; 95537 & 95549 not reviewed.

same
World Transcriptions, New York, 25 November 1935

1149	Where Am I? (vSA)
1150	Violets
1151	Red Sails in the Sunset
1152	Tesaro Mio
1153	I'd Love to Take Orders from You (vSA)
1154	Take Me Back to My Boots and Saddle (vSA)

1155	I Found a Dream
1156	Hunkadola
1157	Will Love Find a Way (vSA)
1158	Love Is Sweeping the Country
1159	What a Wonderful World
1160	I'd Rather Listen to Your Eyes (vSA)
1161	No Other One (vSA)
1162	Why Was I Born / Here Am I
1163	A Little Bit Independent
1164	Body and Soul

NOTE: World Transcriptions mx.#1149 through mx.#1164 recorded on this date by Himber's orchestra issued pseudonymously as by "Larry Bradford and his Orchestra" with vocals by "Stan Abbott" (Stewart Allen). Session could not be reviewed.

The Boswell Sisters
New York, 6 January 1936

Russ Case(tp), Russ Genner(tb), Artie Shaw(cl), Martha Boswell(p,v), Dick McDonough(g), Artie Bernstein(b), Stan King(d), The Boswell Sisters(v)

| 60302 | I'm Gonna Sit Right Down and Write Myself a Letter (vBS) | De.671 |
| 60303 | The Music Goes Round and Round (vBS) | — |

NOTE: Shaw featured on clarinet on 60303; no feature on 60302.

Richard Himber and His Orchestra
New York, 13 January 1936

Bunny Berigan, Ruby Weinstein(tp), Jack Lacey and/or Lloyd Turner(tb), Artie Shaw, Lyall Bowen, Paul Ricci, Jess Corneol(reeds), Lou Raderman, Jack Zayde, Irving Zir(vl), Abe Borodkin(cello), Adrian Rollini(vibes), Ed Steinberg(p), Ernie Capozzi(g), Harry Patent(b), Nat Levine(d), Stuart Allen(v)

98831	Cling to Me (vSA)	Vic.25235
98832	I'd Rather Lead a Band (vSA)	Vic.25243
98833	Get Thee Behind Me Satan (vSA)	—
98834	So This Is Heaven (vSA)	Vic.25235

| 98835 | Life Begins When You're In Love (vSA) | Vic.25239 |
| 98836 | Suzannah (vSA) | — |

NOTE: Personnel from Rust (who listed Brilhart instead of Shaw). Sub-tone melody clarinet on 98833; 98836 not reviewed; no features on the others.

Manny Klein and His Orchestra
New York, 20 January 1936

Manny Klein, Charlie Margulis, Ruby Weinstein(tp), Jack Lacey, Jack Jenney(tb), Artie Shaw, Toots Mondello, Paul Ricci, Jess Corneol(reeds), Sam Shapiro(vl), Frank Signorelli(p), Tony Colucci(g), Artie Bernstein(b), Chauncey Morehouse(d), Bea Wain and the Bachelors(v)

18531	Hot Spell (vBW&B)	Br7606
18532	Ringside Table for Two (vBW&B)	Br7605
18533	I'm in Love (vBW)	—
18534	Juba	Br7606

NOTE: Shaw not featured.

Bob Howard and His Orchestra
New York, 28 January 1936

Bunny Berigan(tp), Artie Shaw(cl), Babe Russin(ts), Frank Signorelli(p), Dave Barbour(g), Pete Peterson(b), Stan King(d), Bob Howard(v)

60404	Who's Big Baby Are You? (vBH)	De.689, Rarities LP9
60405	Much Too Much (vBH)	De.722, —
60406	Garbo Green (vBH)	—, —
60407	You Hit the Spot (vBH)	De.689, —

NOTE: Shaw featured on clarinet on all titles, also issued on Shoestring LP106.

The Boswell Sisters
New York, 12 February 1936

Russ Case(tp), Will Bradley(tb), Artie Shaw(cl,as), Martha Boswell(p,v), Dick McDonough(g), Dick Cherwin(b), Stan King(d), The Boswell Sisters(v)

| 60463 | Let Yourself Go (vBS) | De.709 |
| 60464 | I'm Putting All My Eggs in One Basket (vBS) | — |

NOTE: Shaw not featured.

Bill Challis and His Orchestra
New York, 24 February 1936

collective personnel: Charlie Margulis, Manny Klein, Angie Rattiner, Sammy Spear, Ruby Weinstein(tp), Jack Jenney,

Jack Lacey, Will Bradley, Chuck Campbell(tb), Artie Shaw, Alfie Evans, Ben Kanter, Larry Binyon, Frank Chase, Rudy Adler(reeds), Harry Bluestone, Kurt Dieterle, Jack Gosslein, Frank Siegfield, Lou Raderman, Max Pilzer, Vladimir Selinsky, Harry Urbant, Sol Deutsch(violins), Harry Waller, Ike Sear, Hank Stern(violas), Abe Borodkin(cello), Laura Newell(harp), Frank Signorelli(p), Dick McDonough(g), Artie Bernstein(b), Chauncey Morehouse(d), Bea Wain and the Bachelors: Bea Wain, Al Rinker, Kenny Lane, Johnny Smedburg(v)

1285	Life Is a Song	CLP-71
1286	Let's Face the Music & Dance	CLP-72
1287	Dardanella	—
1288	Rockin' Chair	CLP-71
1289	Great Day (vBW&B)	CLP-72
1290	Get Thee Behind Me Satan (vBW&B)	—
1291	Paris in the Spring (vBW&B)	CLP-71
1292	Clarinet Marmalade	—
1293	Dear Old Southland	CLP-72
1294	Paradise	—
1295	In the Still of the Night	—
1296	New Orleans	CLP-71
1297	On Treasure Island (vBW&B)	—
1298	Let Yourself Go (vBW&B)	—
1299	Riverboat Shuffle	CLP-72
1300	The Moon Was Yellow	CLP-71

NOTE: Arrangements by Bill Challis. Shaw solos on 1288, 1289, 1292, 1296, 1298, 1299; clarinet melody passages on 1287; short alto sax and sub-tone clarinet melody passages on 1294; sub-tone melody clarinet on 1300; no features on the rest.

same
New York, early March 1936

1325	Broadway Rhythm	CLP-71
1326	Sidewalks of Cuba	—
1327	Medley: It Happened in Monterey /	—
	In a Little Spanish Town /	—
	Ramona	—
1328	Diga Diga Doo	CLP-72
1329	More Than You Know	—
1330	Mimi (vBW&B)	—
1331	Temptation	CLP-71
1332	Rhythm in My Nursery Rhymes (vBW&B)	CLP-72

NOTE: Arrangements by Bill Challis. Shaw on alto sax and sub-tone clarinet melody passages on 1327; improvised clarinet solos on 1328 & 1330; alto sax melody passages on 1331; no features on the others. Date was given as "previous" to the 24 February session, but the World Transcription Service mx#s were higher, indicating a later recording date. The reed section played flutes in places. Challis stated in the liner notes that the jazz trumpet spots were played by Manny Klein while Charlie Margulis played lead. Shaw played lead alto and clarinet solos. Jack Jenney played the jazz trombone solos. Challis also noted Shaw may have been in and out of the "first session" but the features were confirmed by Shaw. The vocal team "Bea Wain and the Bachelors" was credited to Al Rinker's leadership. Personnel is "collective" as Challis remarked in the liner notes concerning musicians "coming and going during the session" due to other timetable commitments. The World Transcriptions were issued under pseudonyms as by "Bob Conley and his Orchestra" with vocals by "Betty and the Troubadors."

Jack Shilkret and his Orchestra
New York, 2 April 1936

Artie Shaw(cl,as), Chick Bullock(v), others uncertain

18914	A Little Robin Told Me So (vCB)	ARC60602
18915	There's Always a Happy Ending (vCB)	—
18916	Robins and Roses (vCB)	ARC60603
18917	One Hamburger for Madame (vCB)	—

NOTE: Clarinet featured only for two four-bar breaks on first title.

Richard Himber and His Orchestra
New York, 6 April 1936

same or similar to 13 January 1936

101061	I've Got a Heavy Date (vSA)	Vic.25298
101062	Would You (vSA)	—
101063	Every Once in a While (vSA)	Vic.25293
101064	When You Love (vSA)	Vic.25299
101065	Tormented (vSA)	Vic.25293
101066	Celebratin' (vSA)	Vic.25299

NOTE: Shaw featured for clarinet solos on all titles except 101062. This was the only Himber session featuring Shaw improvising extensively.

Bunny Berigan and His Boys
New York, 13 April 1936

Bunny Berigan(tp,v), Artie Shaw(cl), Forrest Crawford(ts), Joe Bushkin(p), Tommy Finelli(g), Mort Stuhlmaker(b), Cozy Cole(d), Chick Bullock(v)

19012	A Melody from the Sky (vCB)	Vo.3224, Epic LG3109, Classics CD734
19013	I Can't Get Started (vBB)	Vo.3225, —, —
19014	A Little Bit Later On (vCB)	Vo.3224, Epic(E)33SX1506, —
19015	Rhythm Saved the World (vCB)	Vo.3225, Epic LG3109,

NOTE: Shaw solos on clarinet on 19012 and 19014; obbligatos on 19013; ensemble improvisation on 19015. Despite previously published data, Artie Shaw was the only clarinetist on this session. Classics CD 734 reissued all four titles but edited Bullock's vocals out of 19012 and 19015, as did Epic LG3109.

Richard Himber and His Orchestra
World Transcriptions, 21 April 1936

same or similar to 13 January 1936

1345	Tormented (vSA)
1346	Just One More Chance
1347	Lost (vSA)
1348	How Deep Is the Ocean
1349	Would You (vSA)
1350	Touch of Your Lips (vSA)
1351	When You Love (vSA)
1352	Forever and Ever
1353	There's a Small Hotel (vSA)
1354	Summertime (vSA)
1355	A Melody from the Sky
1356	You
1357	No Greater Love
1358	Will I Ever Know (vSA)
1359	I Don't Want to Make History
1360	You Started Me Dreaming

NOTE: World Transcriptions mx.#1345 through mx.#1360 recorded on this date by Himber's orchestra issued pseudonymously as by "Larry Bradford and his Orchestra" with vocals by "Stan Abbott" (Stewart Allen). Session could not be reviewed.

Claude Thornhill–Artie Shaw
Universal Recording Co., New York, 24 April 1936

Artie Shaw(cl), Claude Thornhill(p)

	(untitled Thornhill original)	test pressing

NOTE: This private recording survives in Artie Shaw's collection. Shaw stated, "Claude just wanted to try something so we went into a studio and did it. It was sort of similar to something Willie 'The Lion' would have done" (2).

Frankie Trumbauer and His Orchestra
New York, 27 April 1936

Charlie Teagarden, Ed Wade(tp), Jack Teagarden(tb,v), Artie Shaw(cl), John Cordaro(cl,as), Frankie Trumbauer(C-mel), Mutt Hayes(ts), Roy Bargy(p), Carl Kress(g), Artie Miller(b), Stan King(d)

19113	Somebody Loves Me (vJT)	Br7665, Epic SN6044
19114	The Mayor of Alabam' (vJT)	Br7663, —
19115	Ain't Misbehavin' (vJT)	Br7665, —
19116	'S Wonderful	Br7663, —

NOTE: Shaw featured on clarinet on all four titles. Epic SN6044 is a boxed set of recordings featuring Jack Teagarden and issued under his name.

Dick McDonough and His Orchestra
New York, 4 June 1936

Bunny Berigan(tp), Artie Shaw(cl,as), Dick McDonough(g), Dorothy Dreslin, Chick Bullock(v), others uncertain

19373	Take My Heart (vCB)	ARC60807
19374	Stars in My Eyes (vDD)	—
19375	The Scene Changes (vCB)	ARC60808
19376	On the Beach at Bali-Bali (vCB)	—, Jerry Disc EVA1700-2

NOTE: Shaw featured on clarinet only for a two-bar break on 19375 and obbligatos on 19376. This may have been the band McDonough was then leading on the radio which also included Shaw and Berigan.

Buddy Clark(v) for Dreslin & Bullock
New York, 23 June 1936

19466	Summer Holiday (vBC)	ARC60907, Jerry Disc EVA1700-2

19467	I'm Grateful to You (vBC)	—, —
19468	Dear Old Southland (vBC)	ARC60908, —
19469	Way Down Yonder in New Orleans (vBC)	—, —

NOTE: Shaw had clarinet obbligatos on 19466 & 19467, and solos on 19468 & 19469.

Billie Holiday and Her Orchestra
New York, 10 July 1936

Bunny Berigan(tp), Artie Shaw(cl), Joe Bushkin(p), Dick McDonough(g), Pete Peterson(b), Cozy Cole(d), Billie Holiday(v)

19535-1	Did I Remember? (vBH)	Vo.3276, CK40790
19536-1	No Regrets (vBH)	—, —
19536-2	No Regrets (vBH)	Merritt 504
19537-1	Summertime (vBH)	Vo.3288, SoS122, —
19538-1	Billie's Blues (vBH)	—, —, —

NOTE: Shaw featured on clarinet on all four titles. Columbia CK40790 is a Billie Holiday CD. These titles, usually only two at a time (in their original pairings), also have appeared on several other Billie Holiday LP & CD issues.

Carl Hoff Orchestra
World Transcriptions, New York, c. mid-July 1936

Ruby Weinstein, Manny Weinstock, Don Bryan(tp), Felix Giardina, Floyd Turner, Sam Lewis(tb), Art Shaw(as,fl,cl), Larry Abbott(as,cl), Art Horn(ts,cl,bcl), Jess Corneol(ts,-fl,cl), Irving Cramer(bar,cl), Irving Prager, Jack Zayde, Pete Eisenberg, Murray Kellner, Julius Schector, Max Pilzer, Syban Shulman, Frank Pinaro(vl), Sol Deutch, Joe Rosenblatt(vla), Frank Prager(cel), Verlie Mills(harp), Sam Prager, Dewey Bergman(p), Aaron Levine(g), Gerald Prager(b), Mel Raub(tu), Al Lapin, Dave Grupp(d), Leader's Trio (Eddie Ellington, Glenn Cross, Gordon Cross), Bob Simmons, Glenn Cross, Ruth Dick(v)

1797	Oh Say Can You Swing?
1798	Now the Show Is On
1799	The Night Is Young
1800	Twinkle Twinkle Little Star
1801	With Plenty of Money and You
1802	Goodnight My Love
1803	You're Laughing at Me
1804	Who's Afraid of Love?
1805	This Year's Kisses
1806	Slummin' on Park Avenue

1807	When My Dreamboat Comes Home
1808	May I Have the Next Romance with You?

NOTE: Personnel from *Metronome* of Carl Hoff's *Your Hit Parade* radio show band at this time. Carl Hoff's World Transcriptions were issued under the pseudonym "Chet Harper and his Orchestra." There were no clarinet solos; but there were short alto sax breaks in several arrangements and short improvised alto sax solos on 1801 & 1805. Shaw stated that this "may" have been him (2). No vocals on above titles.

Chick Bullock and His Orchestra
New York, 20 July 1936

Russ Case(tp), Will Bradley(tb), Artie Shaw, Sid Stoneburn(cl,as), Fulton McGrath(p), Chick Bullock(v), others uncertain

19574	You Dropped Me Like a Red Hot Penny (vCB)	ARC61002
19575	These Foolish Things (vCB)	ARC61001
19576	Take My Heart (vCB)	—
19577	You're Not the Kind (vCB)	ARC61002

NOTE: Personnel as listed in Tom Lord's *The Jazz Discography Vol. 3* (Redwood, N.Y.: Cadence Jazz Books, 1992), except Lord did not cite Shaw, who was featured on clarinet on 19574 & 19576; sub-tone melody clarinet on 19577; no feature on 19575.

Also on 20 July 1936, Bunny Berigan led a big band through twenty titles for Rhythm Makers Transcriptions which briefly featured some Shaw-like clarinet and alto sax passages. While these passages frequently have been attributed to Shaw, he has firmly denied participation (2). Berigan authority Bozy White interviewed surviving band members, but none could identify or recall who it was that played lead alto and the clarinet solos and obbligatos in question (see text).

Richard Himber and His Orchestra
New York, 27 July 1936

same or similar to 13 January 1936

102975	Midnight Blue (vSA)	Vic.25365
102976	The World Is Mine (vSA)	Vic.25392
102977	Me and the Moon (vSA)	Vic.25365

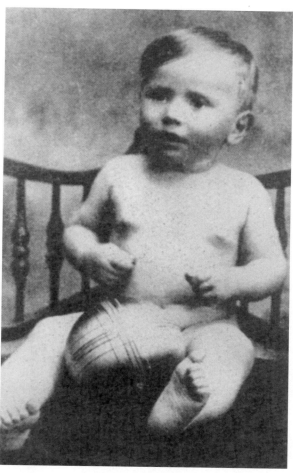

Artie Shaw as an infant, c. 1911. (Photos courtesy of John Harding, except where otherwise noted.)

Artie Shaw at age 4, c. 1914.

Shaw was a compulsive reader from childhood; the title of the book In Dubious Battle *by John Steinbeck seems appropriately symbolic of his career pattern.*

Joe Cantor's Far East Orchestra, c. 1927–28 (l to r): Artie Shaw, Charles Stenross, Walt Easton, Chuck Shank, Charlie Cantor, Willis Kelly, Les Arquette, Joe Cantor. (Photo courtesy Bob Strassmyer from Willis Kelly.)

Roger Wolfe Kahn and His Orchestra at the Hotel Pennsylvania, November 1932. This is the band that recorded for Columbia on November 9, 1932 (see discography). Back row (l to r): Larry Binyon (ts); Marlin Sykes (p, v); Ward Ley (b); Max Farley, Artie Shaw (reeds); Perry Botkin (g); Ruby Weinstein or Angie Rattiner, Charlie Teagarden (tp). Middle row (l to r): Joe Ross (vl); Roger Wolfe Kahn (with baton); Chauncey Morehouse (d). Front row (l to r): unknown (v); Julie Held (vl); 2 unknowns (v); Harry Urbant (vl); Andy Russo, Phil Giardina (tb); unknown.

Don Voorhees Orchestra on Texaco's Ed Wynn radio show; c. early 1934. Wynn is at the microphone with M.C. Graham McNamee; Voorhees is standing directly behind McNamee. Back row (l to r): Jack Pierce (tu); Joe Tarto (b); Fred Pfaff (tu); Sammy Lewis, Charles Butterfield Sr., Miff Mole, Charles Butterfield Jr., (tb). Standing at right: Dave Grupp, Harry Edison (perc.). 2nd Row: Henry Wade (behind Voorhees), Tony Parenti, Alfie Evans, Artie Shaw (directly in front of Miff Mole), Frank Chase (reeds). (Seated at right): "Pop" Evans, Joe Lindworm, Lloyd Williams, Fuzzy Farrar, Leo McConville, Benny Baker (tp). 3rd row: Lyle Bowen, unknown (hiding another unknown), Voorhees, Eddie Standard, Arnold Brilhart (directly in front of Shaw), Jimmy Crosen, Gil Koerner; unknown (reeds). In front of trumpets: Bill Trone (melophone); 2 unknowns (just behind the unidentified NBC announcer). Front row, between Wynn's back and the NBC announcer: Marty Quinto, 2 unknowns (g). On stage floor: Cities Service Quartet (v); McNamee, Wynn, NBC announcer.

Marge Allen, Shaw's first wife (discounting the elopement/annulment of summer 1932) with whom he shared the 1933–34 year on the Bucks County farm. They were divorced in 1937.

Artie Shaw in his "sideman days."

Imperial Theatre, May 24, 1936. Pictured (l to r): drummer Art Stern (hidden by his equipment); violinist Harry Bluestone; Shaw.

The New York Times *ad for the Silver Grill opening, August 21, 1936.*

Peg La Centra and Artie Shaw in the Century Room, Dallas, c. January 1937. Also visible at right is violinist/arranger Jerry Gray, with Tony Pastor just behind his head.

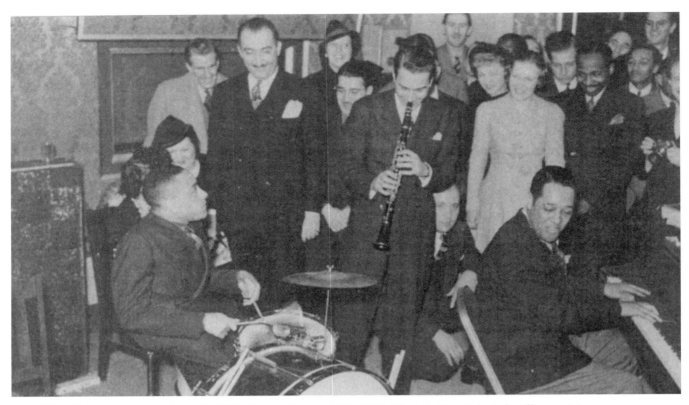

United Hot Clubs jam session, March 17, 1937. Pictured (l to r): Chick Webb (d), Artie Shaw (cl), Duke Ellington (p).

Shaw and Billie Holiday in Atlantic City, July 9, 1938.

Cover of Metronome *(September 1938).*

"Art Shaw" in a Selmer ad in the September 1938 Metronome.

Filming their first Vitaphone movie short, November 28, 1938. Pictured (l to r): Les Robinson (as), Tony Pastor (v, holding mike), Shaw, camera, and crew.

Shaw smiling in front of his band in a production still from the November 28–29, 1938, Vitaphone movie short. Front row (l to r): Al Avola (g); Ronnie Perry (ts); Hank Freeman, Les Robinson (as); Tony Pastor (ts). 2nd row: Chuck Peterson, Bernie Privin, Johnny Best (tp); Harry Rogers, George Arus, Russell Brown (tb). Rear: Sid Weiss (b); Cliff Leeman (d); Les Burness (p). Note Hank Freeman's baritone sax on the stand and the clarinets for doubling in the reed section.

Helen Forrest and Shaw in front of the band in their February 1939 Vitaphone movie short. Back row (l to r): Sid Weiss (b); Chuck Peterson, Bernie Privin, Johnny Best (tp); Buddy Rich (d); George Arus, Les Jenkins, Harry Rodgers (tb); Bob Kitsis (p). Front row: Al Avola (g); Georgie Auld (ts); Hank Freeman (hidden behind Shaw); Les Robinson (as); Tony Pastor (ts). Note Les Jenkins wearing a toupee for this film.

At the Stanley Theatre, Pittsburgh, March 1939.
Note the distinctive music stands, with nicknames:
Georgie Auld is "Killer," Hank Freeman is
"Spanky," and Les Robinson is "Dapper Dan."
(Photo courtesy of John Zawaski and Andrew Z.
Williams.)

Helen Forrest, who recorded more vocals with Shaw than any
other singer and went on to sing with Benny Goodman and
Harry James before becoming a major star as a single, in a
publicity photo, c. 1938–39.

Ad for Shaw's return to the bandstand at the Palomar.

Ad for Eastwood Gardens engagement.

Ad for Conrad reeds.

Lana Turner and Artie Shaw in a publicity shot for Dancing Co-ed *(July 1939). They eloped in February 1940 and separated the following summer.*

The King Sisters, who appeared with Shaw on the Old Gold Show, summer 1939. Seated (l to r): Yvonne, Donna. Standing: Louise, Alyce. In 1941 they were on the cover of the November 1st Down Beat.

Benny Goodman and Artie Shaw, 1939. Photo was taken when Shaw visited Goodman at Goodman's opening at the Waldorf that fall.

A classic photo of the 1939 band in action. Note the distinctive music stands with nicknames and caricatures. Back row (l to r): "Chuck" Peterson, Bernie "Crazyman" Privin, Johnny "Colonel" Best (tp); Buddy Rich (d). 2nd row: Harry "Muscles" Rodgers (ts), Les "Tex" Jenkins, George "Swami" Arus (tb); Al "Mouthpiece" Avola (g); Bob Kitsis (p). Front: Artie Shaw (cl); Georgie "Killer" Auld (ts; nickname on Auld's stand hidden by Shaw); Hank "Dapper Dan" Freeman, Les "Spanky" Robinson (as); Tony "Emcee" Pastor (ts); Helen Forrest (v). Freeman and Robinson have switched nicknames on this date; other photos of the band showing nicknames on the stands consistently have Freeman as "Spanky" and Robinson as "Dapper Dan."

Performing the "Concerto" sequence in Second Chorus *c. August 1940. Trumpets: Jack Cathcart, George Wendt (hidden by Shaw), Billy Butterfield. Trombones: Bruce Squires, Vernon Brown. Saxes: Jerry Jerome, Neely Plumb, Les Robinson.*

Fred Astaire, Paulette Goddard, and Artie Shaw in a publicity photo for Second Chorus *(August 1940).*

*The 1940–41 Gramercy 5 at a Victor recording session: (l to r) Johnny Guarnieri (harpsichord); Jud DeNaut (b); Billy Butterfield (tp); Nick Fatool (d); Artie Shaw (cl);
Al Hendrickson (g).*

The 1940–41 orchestra at the Hollywood Palladium. Back row (l to r): Jack Cathcart, George Wendt, Billy Butterfield (tp); Nick Fatool (d); Jud DeNaut (b); Fred Goerner (cello). 2nd row: Vernon Brown, Ray Conniff, Jack Jenney (tb); Alex Beller, Eugene Lamas (vl); Al Harshman, Keith Collins (vla). 3rd row: Bus Bassey, Neely Plumb, Les Robinson, Jerry Jerome (reeds); Johnny Guarnieri (p); Al Hendrickson (g); Ted Klages, Truman Boardman, Bob Morrow, Bob Bower (vl). Front: Artie Shaw and Anita Boyer. Note harpsichord and extra drum set for small-group performances, now naming only the Gramercy 5.

Shaw with his June 26, 1941, rhythm section. Pictured (l to r): Beresford "Shep" Shepherd, Billy Taylor, Sonny White, Shaw, Jimmy Shirley.

Artie Shaw, Henry "Red" Allen, J. C. Higginbotham, and Benny Carter at the Victor recording session, June 26, 1941.

Only Artie Shaw Could Have
Written This Clarinet Method!

AN INSTANT BEST SELLER!

ARTIE SHAW
CLARINET METHOD
Written in collaboration with Arnold Brilhart*

The praise and endorsements given this book by teachers,
professional stars and students has made it today's most
valuable addition to modern studies. Here is your greatest
guide to an up-to-date clarinet style offering the most
expert studies and exercises in technique development,
tonguing, scales, chords, improvisations and other ad-
vancements found only in this book.

Also contains Artie Shaw's own clarinet solos of Back Bay
Shuffle, Rose Room, I'm Coming Virginia, My Blue Heaven,
etc. Order your copy Today!   Price $2.00

*Designer of Enduro Reeds and Brilhart Mouthpieces

Ask your dealer to show you other Robbins Modern Methods
or write direct for free descriptive booklet.

*Four top bandleaders of
1941 meet with Maria
Kramer, owner of the Hotel
Lincoln (l to r): Artie Shaw,
Harry James, Maria Kramer,
Benny Goodman, and Blue
Barron. At that time, the
Harry James band with a
string section was perform-
ing at the hotel.*

*Ad for the "Artie
Shaw Clarinet
Method," c.
1941.*

The 1941–42 orchestra on stage.

*Oran "Hot Lips" Page,
Shaw, Max Kaminsky, and
Ray Conniff, c. 1941.*

Oran "Hot Lips" Page and Artie Shaw, c. late summer 1941.

Navy Band 501: The Rangers on stage. Sam Donahue is in the front row next to Shaw.

Shaw, still in uniform and just back from the Pacific, with wife Elizabeth (Kern) and son Steve, late 1943.

At the AFRS Command Performance session, September 30, 1944. Top row (l to r): Illinois Jacquet (ts); Tommy Dorsey (tb); Ziggy Elman (tp); Buddy Rich (d, hiding bassist Ed McKinney). Front row: Count Basie (p, posed here on vibes); Lionel Hampton (vibes); Artie Shaw (cl); Les Paul (g).

The 1945 band on stage at the Strand Theatre, New York, c. January 1945. Ray Conniff is the standing trombonist; Roy Eldridge is visible between baritone saxophonist Chuck Gentry and Conniff.

The 1945 Gramercy 5 (l to r): Dodo Marmarosa (p); Roy Eldridge (tp); Artie Shaw (cl); Barney Kessel (g); Morris Rayman (b); off-camera: Lou Fromm (d).

Mel Tormé and the Mel-Tones. Back row (l to r): Les Baxter, Mel Tormé, Bernie Parks. Front: Betty Beveridge, Ginny O'Connor.

Ava Gardner, Artie Shaw's mother, and Shaw at Ava and Artie's wedding.

Kathleen Winsor and Artie Shaw, c. 1947.

Pat Lockwood, Dodo Marmarosa, and Artie Shaw, c. fall 1949.

Trudy Richards, who recorded with Shaw in January 1950 and April 1952.

The 1949–50 band at the Blue Note, Chicago. Pictured (l to r): Gil Barrios (p); Pat Lockwood (v); Dick Niveson (b); Jimmy Raney (g); Shaw (hiding drummer Irv Kluger); Don Fagerquist, Don Paladino, Dale Pierce, Vic Ford (tp); Freddie Zito, Porky Cohen, Angie Callea, Sonny Russo (tb); Herbie Steward, Frank Socolow, Al Cohn, Danny Bank (saxes).

Don Cherry and Artie Shaw at Decca recording session January 30, 1951.

Artie Shaw and Doris Dowling leaving London, November 1951. They were married in 1952, had a son, Jonathan, in 1953, and divorced in 1956.

Ad for the Conn Clarinet (1953).

The "Texas tour" band, spring 1953. This was the last road band Shaw led as a performer; there were no recordings. Personnel is unidentified except for drummer Tony Papa.

Artie Shaw and Evelyn Keyes in the home Shaw designed in Spain, late 1950s.

Artie Shaw fronting the Artie Shaw Orchestra, c. December 1983. Pictured (l to r) Dick Johnson (cl); Artie Shaw; Bob Patton (ts); Gary Johnson (d); Jay Branford (as); Rock Ciccerone (tb); Bob Bowlby (as).

102978	Picture Me Without You (vSA)	Vic.25392

NOTE: Short clarinet break on 102975; *Metronome* (September 1936, p. 41) noted: "Fine Artie Shaw clarinet work on Richard Himber's 'Me and the Moon.' " The other titles could not be reviewed.

Jack Shilkret and His Orchestra
New York, 31 July 1936

Artie Shaw(cl,as), Larry Stewart, Chick Bullock(v), others uncertain

19635	Dream Awhile (vLS)	ARC61009
19636	There Goes My Attraction (vLS)	ARC61003
19637	Shoe-Shine Boy (vCB)	—
19638	San Francisco (vCB)	ARC61009

NOTE: Shaw featured on clarinet on 19636 & 19637; no features on the others.

Ray Sinatra Hit Parade Orchestra
New York, c. early August 1936

Emil Weinstein, Fred Farrar, Russ Case(tp), Sam Lewis, Lloyd Turner, Will Bradley(tb), Arnold Brilhart, Toots Mondello, Artie Shaw, Henry Wade(reeds), Jo Baum, Tex Raymond, Pete Eisenberg, Dave Zayde, Fred Fenton, Walter Eddlstein, Joseph Dindault(vl), Harry Waller(vla), Lucien Smith(cello), Verlie Mills(harp), Ed Lassoff, Adrian Rollini-(vibes), Frank Signorelli(p), Dick McDonough(g), Ed Prager(tu), Alfred Kunze(b), Herb Quigley(d), Joey Nash(v)

> Am I in Love?
> On with the Dance (vJN)
> Down with Love (vJN)
> Mama I Want to Make Rhythm

NOTE: Shaw had clarinet solos on all titles except "Down with Love." These four performances allegedly were from Muzak transcriptions, but other titles recorded (if any) and exact details of the session are lacking. Personnel from a radio review of Ray Sinatra's orchestra at that time.

Dick McDonough and His Orchestra
New York, 5 August 1936

Artie Shaw(cl,as), Dick McDonough(g), Chick Bullock(v), others uncertain

19663	When the Moon Hangs High (vCB)	ARC61104

19664	Midnight Blue (vCB)	—, Jerry Disc EVA1700-2
19665	South Sea Island Magic (vCB)	ARC61101
19666	Afterglow (vCB)	—

NOTE: Shaw featured on clarinet on 19664; no features on the others.

Jack Shilkret and His Orchestra
New York, 29 August 1936

Sterling Bose(tp), Jack Jenney (tb), Artie Shaw, Sid Stoneburn(cl,as), Dick McDonough(g), Fred Huffsmith, Chick Bullock(v), others uncertain

19773	The World Is Mine (vFH)	ARC61115
19774	So Divine (vCB)	—
19775	Darling Not Without You (vCB)	ARC61109
19776	Fancy Meeting You (vCB)	ARC61107
19777	Out Where the Blue Begins (vCB)	—
19778	Here's Love in Your Eyes (vCB)	ARC61109

NOTE: Shaw confirmed clarinet solos on the last three titles. No features on others.

Dick McDonough and His Orchestra
New York, 17 September 1936

Artie Shaw(cl,as), Dick McDonough(g), Chick Bullock, Buddy Clark(v), others uncertain

19891	I'm One Step Ahead of My Shadow (vCB)	ARC61202
19892	Now or Never (vCB)	—
19893	Love What Are You Doing to My Heart? (vBC)	ARC61203
19894	You're Giving Me a Song and a Dance (vCB)	—

NOTE: Shaw had clarinet obbligatos on 19891; no features on the others.

Richard Himber and His Orchestra
New York, 13 October 1936

same or similar to 13 January 1936

02134	In the Chapel in the Moonlight (vSA)	Vic.25441

02135	Thru the Courtesy of Love (vSA)	Vic.25443
02136	Wintertime Dreams (vSA)	—
02137	You're Everything Sweet (vSA)	Vic.25441
02138	Where Have You Been All My Life? (vSA)	Vic.25457
02139	Twinkle Twinkle Little Star (vSA)	—

NOTE: Clarinet solo on 02136, short breaks on 02137; 02138 & 02139 not reviewed.

Dick McDonough and His Orchestra
New York, 3 November 1936

Artie Shaw(cl,as), Dick McDonough(g), Chick Bullock(v), others uncertain

| 20183 | With Thee I Swing (vCB) | ARC70107, Jerry Disc EVA1700-2 |
| 20184 | Tea on the Terrace (vCB) | ARC70111, — |

| 20185 | I'm in a Dancing Mood (vCB) | ARC70107, — |
| 20186 | There's Frost on the Moon (vCB) | ARC70111, — |

NOTE: Shaw featured on clarinet on 20184; no features on the others.

Mildred Bailey and Her Orchestra
New York, 9 November 1936

Ziggy Elman(tp), Artie Shaw(cl), Johnny Hodges(as), Ben Webster(ts), Teddy Wilson(p), Dave Barbour(g), John Kirby(b), Cozy Cole(d), Mildred Bailey(v)

20217	For Sentimental Reasons (vMB)	Vo.3367
20218	It's Love I'm After (vMB)	—
20219	'Long About Midnight (vMB)	Vo.3378, SoS122

NOTE: Short clarinet introduction on 20217; no features on the others. Shaw was absent from a fourth title from this session.

Alphabetical List of Tune Titles with Artie Shaw as Sideman: 1928–1936

The following list represents only the items shown in the discography section "Artie Shaw as Sideman" with date of recording and the band leader for the session indicated. For further details see the discography. As noted elsewhere, only titles known to include Shaw, featuring Shaw, or confirmed by Shaw are listed.

Afterglow (1936/08/05) w. Dick McDonough
Ain't Misbehavin' (1936/04/27) w. Frankie Trumbauer
Alabamy Bound (1931/08/?) w. Fred Rich
All I Do Is Dream of You (1934/06/07) w. Richard Himber
The Alpine Milkman (c. 1931–32) w. Blue Coal Minstrels
Am I in Love? (1936/08/?) w. Ray Sinatra
Annabelle Lee (c. 1931–32) w. Blue Coal Minstrels
As the Backs Go Tearing By (1931/10/?) w. Fred Rich
As Time Goes By (1931/09/10) w. Fred Rich
Auf Wiedersehen My Dear (1931/08/?) w. Fred Rich
Auf Wiedersehen My Dear (1932/02/04) w. Ben Selvin
Auld Lang Syne (1931/12/?) w. Fred Rich
Autumn in New York (1934/12/05) w. Richard Himber
Avalon (1934/10/05) w. Richard Himber
Ay-Ay-Ay (1931/08/?) w. Fred Rich

Baby Take a Bow (1934/06/07) w. Richard Himber
Bend Down Sister (1931/08/?) w. Fred Rich
Bend Down Sister (c. 1931–32) w. Blue Coal Minstrels
Between Showers (1934/10/15) w. Johnnie Davis
Billie's Blues (1936/07/10) w. Billie Holiday
Blue Coal Theme (c. 1931–32) w. Blue Coal Minstrels
Blue Moon (1934/11/20) w. Frankie Trumbauer
Blue Moon (1935/01/15) w. Connee Boswell
Blues in My Heart (c. 1931–32) w. Blue Coal Minstrels
Body and Soul (1935/11/25) w. Richard Himber
Broadway Rhythm (1935/06/19) w. Richard Himber
Broadway Rhythm (1936/03/?) w. Bill Challis
Bugle Call Rag (1931/08/?) w. Fred Rich
Butterfingers (1934/03/24) w. Adrian Rollini
By the Sycamore Tree (1931/08/?) w. Fred Rich
By the Taj Mahal (1934/08/01) w. Johnny Green

California Here I Come (1931/08/?) w. Fred Rich
Call Me Darling (1931/12/?) w. Fred Rich

Can This Be Love? (1932/spring) w. Ben Selvin
Carioca (1934/06/07) w. Richard Himber
Carolina's Calling Me (1932/02/04) w. Ben Selvin
Celebratin' (1936/04/06) w. Richard Himber
Charlie Cadet March (1931/08/?) w. Fred Rich
Cheek to Cheek (1935/10/08) w. The Boswell Sisters
Cheerful Little Earful (1932/ spring) w. Ben Selvin
Clarinet Marmalade (1936/02/24) w. Bill Challis
Cling to Me (1936/01/13) w. Richard Himber
Clouds (1935/01/15) w. Connee Boswell
Cocktails for Two (1934/06/07) w. Richard Himber
College Rhythm (1934/10/15) w. Johnnie Davis
Comin' Thru the Rye (1931/12/?) w. Fred Rich
Congratulate Me (1934/10/22) w. Johnnie Davis
Copenhagen (1931/08/?) w. Fred Rich
Crazy People (1932/05/12) w. Ben Selvin
Crazy People (1932/ film) w. R. W. Kahn
Crazy Rhythm (1932/ film) w. R. W. Kahn

Dancing on the Ceiling (1931/08/?) w. Fred Rich
Dancing with My Shadow (1934/12/05) w. Richard Himber
Dardanella (1936/02/24) w. Bill Challis
Darling Not Without You (1936/08/29) w. Richard Himber
Dawn (1934/12/05) w. Richard Himber
Dear Old Southland (1936/02/24) w. Bill Challis
Dear Old Southland (1936/06/23) w. Dick McDonough
Did I Remember? (1936/07/10) w. Billie Holiday
Diga Diga Doo (1936/03/?) w. Bill Challis
Dinah (1931/08/?) w. Fred Rich
Dinah (1932/film) w. R. W. Kahn
Dixie Jamboree (1931/08/?) w. Fred Rich
Do the New York (1931/08/?) w. Fred Rich
Don't Stop Me If You've Heard It (1934/10/22) w. Johnnie Davis
Down t' Uncle Bill's (1934/11/20) w. Frankie Trumbauer
Down with Love (1936/08/?) w. Ray Sinatra
Dream Awhile (1936/07/31) w. Jack Shilkret

Easy Like (1934/08/15) w. Wingy Manone
Ending with a Kiss (1934/03/19) w. Richard Himber
Evening in Caroline (1931/08/?) w. Fred Rich
Every Once in a While (1936/04/06) w. Richard Himber

Everything's Been Done Before (1935/02/11) w. Richard Himber

Falling in Love (1931/05/28) w. Paul Specht
Fancy Meeting You (1936/08/29) w. Jack Shilkret
Farewell My Lovely (1935/08/19) w. Richard Himber
Fine and Dandy (1931/08/?) w. Fred Rich
Fit as a Fiddle (1932/11/09) w. R. W. Kahn
Flamenco (1934/12/05) w. Richard Himber
Follow the Swallow (1931/08/?) w. Fred Rich
Footloose & Fancy Free (1935/05/04) w. Richard Himber
For Sentimental Reasons (1936/11/09) w. Mildred Bailey
Forever and Ever (1936/04/21) w. Richard Himber
The Fortune Teller (1934/08/01) w. Johnny Green
Freddie the Freshman (1931/08/?) w. Fred Rich
Frisco Squabble (1928/08/13) w. Joe Cantor
From the Top of Your Head (1935/08/19) w. Richard Himber
Fun to Be Fooled (1934/07/13) w. Richard Himber

Garbo Green (1936/01/28) w. Bob Howard
Get Thee Behind Me Satan (1936/01/16) w. Richard Himber
Get Thee Behind Me Satan (1936/02/24) w. Bill Challis
The Girl Friend (1928/08/13) w. Joe Cantor
Give a Broken Heart a Break (1935/05/04) w. Richard Himber
Goin' to Town (1931/08/?) w. Fred Rich
A Good Man Is Hard to Find (c. 1931–32) w. Blue Coal Minstrels
Good News (1934/06/07) w. Richard Himber
Goodnight Lovely Little Lady (1934/06/07) w. Richard Himber
Goodnight Moon (1931/08/?) w. Fred Rich
Goodnight My Love (1936/07/?) w. Carl Hoff
Goodnight Sweetheart (1931/08/?) w. Fred Rich
Goodnight Sweetheart (1931/11/09) w. Bing Crosby
Gosh Darn (1932/film) w. R. W. Kahn
Great Day (1936/02/24) w. Bill Challis
Gringola (1935/06/19) w. Richard Himber
Guilty (1931/08/?) w. Fred Rich
Guilty (c. 1931–32) w. Blue Coal Minstrels

Happy Feet (1932/spring) w. Ben Selvin
Have You Ever Been Lonely (1933/02/14) w. Adrian Rollini
Heartbroken and Lonely (1928/08/13) w. Joe Cantor
Here Am I (1935/11/25) w. Richard Himber
Here's Love in Your Eyes (1936/08/29) w. Jack Shilkret
Hiding in the Shadows of the Moon (1931/08/?) w. Fred Rich
Hiding in the Shadows of the Moon (1931/11/09) w. Carl Fenton
High and Low (1931/08/?) w. Fred Rich

Hiking Down the Highway (c. 1931–32) w. Blue Coal Minstrels
Home (1931/08/?) w. Fred Rich
Honest Really Truly (1931/08/?) w. Fred Rich
Hosanna (1931/08/?) w. Fred Rich
Hot Spell (1936/01/20) w. Manny Klein
How Can It Be a Beautiful Day (1934/03/24) w. Adrian Rollini
How Deep Is the Ocean (1936/04/21) w. Richard Himber
How Long Will It Last? (1931/08/?) w. Fred Rich
A Hundred to One It's You (1934/10/22) w. Johnnie Davis
Hunkadola (1935/11/25) w. Richard Himber
Hustlin' and Bustlin' for Baby (1933/02/14) w. Adrian Rollini

I Can't Believe It's True (1932/08/05) w. R. W. Kahn
I Can't Get Started (1936/04/13) w. Bunny Berigan
I Cried for You (1931/11/07) w. Bing Crosby
I Don't Know Why (1931/08/24) w. Red Nichols
I Don't Want to Make History (1936/04/21) w. Richard Himber
I Feel Like a Feather in the Breeze (1935/10/21) w. Richard Himber
I Found a Dream (1935/11/25) w. Richard Himber
I Found a Million Dollar Baby (1931/05/28) w. Paul Specht
I Idolize My Baby's Eyes (1931/08/24) w. Red Nichols
I Idolize My Baby's Eyes (1931/08/?) w. Fred Rich
I Know That You Know (1931/08/?) w. Fred Rich
I Love Louisa (1931/08/?) w. Fred Rich
I Never Saw a Better Night (1935/06/19) w. Richard Himber
I Surrender Dear (1934/09/26) w. Red Norvo
I Want to Count Sheep 'Til the Cows Come Home (1931/08/?) w. Fred Rich
I Wished on the Moon (1935/05/04) w. Richard Himber
I Woke Up Too Soon (1934/12/05) w. Richard Himber
I Wouldn't Change You for the World (1931/08/?) w. Fred Rich
I'd Love to Take Orders from You (1935/11/25) w. Richard Himber
I'd Rather Lead a Band (1936/01/13) w. Richard Himber
I'd Rather Listen to Your Eyes (1935/11/25) w. Richard Himber
I'll Make a Happy Landing (1931/08/?) w. Fred Rich
I'm Alone Without You (1934/08/15) w. Wingy Manone
I'm Going Down to Dance at Clancey's (1935/02/11) w. Richard Himber
I'm Gonna Sit Right Down and Write Myself a Letter (1936/01/06) w. The Boswell Sisters
I'm Grateful to You (1936/06/23) w. Dick McDonough
I'm in a Dancing Mood (1936/11/03) w. Dick McDonough
I'm in Love (1936/01/20) w. Manny Klein
I'm Just a Dancing Sweetheart (1931/08/?) w. Fred Rich
I'm Just a Dancing Sweetheart (1931 09/10) w. Fred Rich

I'm Just a Dancing Sweetheart (1931/10/?) w. Fred Rich
I'm One Step Ahead of My Shadow (1936/09/17) w. Dick McDonough
I'm Painting the Town Red (1935/10/21) w. Richard Himber
I'm Putting All My Eggs in One Basket (1936/02/12) w. The Boswell Sisters
I'm Sorry Dear (1931/08/?) w. Fred Rich
I'm Through with Love (1931/09/02) w. Bing Crosby
I'm with You (1931/08/24) w. Red Nichols
I'm with You (1931/08/?) w. Fred Rich
I've Got a Heavy Date (1936/04/06) w. Richard Himber
I've Got Five Dollars (1931/08/?) w. Fred Rich
Ida (c. 1931–32) w. Blue Coal Minstrels
If I Didn't Have You (1931/08/24) w. Red Nichols
If I Didn't Have You (1931/09/10) w. Fred Rich
If I Do It Again (1934/06/07) w. Richard Himber
If I Had a Million Dollars (1934/10/05) w. Richard Himber
If I Had to Go on Without You (1931/08/?) w. Fred Rich
If I Love Again (1934/06/07) w. Richard Himber
If I Should Lose You (1935/10/21) w. Richard Himber
If I Were King (c. 1931–32) w. Blue Coal Minstrels
If You Can't Sing, Whistle (c. 1931–32) w. Blue Coal Minstrels
In a Blue & Pensive Mood (1934/12/05) w. Richard Himber
In a Dream (1931/08/24) w. Red Nichols
In a Little Spanish Town (1936/03/?) w. Bill Challis
In the Chapel in the Moonlight (1936/10/13) w. Richard Himber
In the Slot (1934/08/15) w. Wingy Manone
In the Still of the Night (1936/02/24) w. Bill Challis
In the Twinkling of an Eye (1935/05/04) w. Richard Himber
Is I in Love? I Is (1932/05/12) w. Ben Selvin
It Don't Mean a Thing If It Ain't Got That Swing (1932/11/09) w. R. W. Kahn
It Happened in Monterey (1936/03/?) w. Bill Challis
It's Great to Be in Love (1931/08/?) w. Fred Rich
It's Love I'm After (1936/11/09) w. Mildred Bailey
It's Psychological (1934/03/19) w. Richard Himber
It's the Girl (1931/08/?) w. Fred Rich
It's the Girl (1931/09/?) w. Fred Rich

Jangle Fever (1934/06/07) w. Richard Himber
Japanese Sandman (1931/08/?) w. Fred Rich
Jericho (1931/08/?) w. Fred Rich
Juba (1936/01/20) w. Manny Klein
June in January (1934/10/05) w. Richard Himber
Just a Little Home for the Old Folks (1932/11/09) w. R. W. Kahn
Just Another Night Alone (1932/08/05) w. R. W. Kahn
Just Because She Made Those Googly Eyes (c. 1931–32) w. Blue Coal Minstrels
Just Friends (1931/08/?) w. Fred Rich

Just Hear That Slide Trombone (c. 1931–32) w. Blue Coal Minstrels
Just Once Too Often (1934/09/26) w. Chick Bullock
Just One More Chance (1931/08/?) w. Fred Rich
Just One More Chance (1931/09/02) w. Bing Crosby
Just One More Chance (1936/04/21) w. Richard Himber
Just One of Those Things (1935/10/21) w. Richard Himber

Kiss Me Goodnight (1931/09/10) w. Fred Rich
Kiss Me Goodnight (1935/06/19) w. Richard Himber

Let Yourself Go (1936/02/12) w. The Boswell Sisters
Let Yourself Go (1936/02/24) w. Bill Challis
Let's Face the Music and Dance (1936/02/24) w. Bill Challis
Let's Take a Walk Around the Block (1934/06/13) w. Richard Himber
Life Begins When You're in Love (1936/01/13) w. Richard Himber
Life Is a Song (1936/02/24) w. Bill Challis
Linda (1931/08/?) w. Fred Rich
A Little Bit Independent (1935/11/25) w. Richard Himber
A Little Bit Later On (1936/04/13) w. Bunny Berigan
A Little Robin Told Me So (1936/04/02) w. Jack Shilkret
Little Did I Dream (1934/03/24) w. Adrian Rollini
Little Dutch Mill (1934/06/07) w. Richard Himber
Little Girl (1931/09/?) w. Fred Rich
Little Mary Brown (c. 1931–32) w. Blue Coal Minstrels
Lo and Behold (1931/08/?) w. Fred Rich
Long About Midnight (1936/11/09) w. Mildred Bailey
Lost (1936/04/21) w. Richard Himber
Lost in a Fog (1934/09/26) w. Chick Bullock
Love Is Sweeping the Country (1935/11/25) w. Richard Himber
Love Makes the World Go Round (1935/08/19) w. Richard Himber
Love Me (1934/06/07) w. Richard Himber
Love Me Forever (1935/05/04) w. Richard Himber
Love Thy Neighbor (1934/03/19) w. Richard Himber
Love What Are You Doing to My Heart? (1936/10/17) w. Dick McDonough
Loveable (1931/08/?) w. Fred Rich
Lullaby of Broadway (1935/02/11) w. Richard Himber
Lullaby of the Leaves (1932/05/12) w. Ben Selvin
Lullaby of the Leaves (1932/film) w. R. W. Kahn

Mama I Want to Make Rhythm (1936/08/?) w. Ray Sinatra
Marching Home to You (c. 1931–32) w. Blue Coal Minstrels
The Marine's Hymn (1934/06/12) w. Richard Himber
Mary I'm in Love with You (1931/08/?) w. Fred Rich
May I? (1934/03/19) w. Richard Himber
May I? (1934/06/07) w. Richard Himber

May I Have the Next Romance with You? (1936/07/?) w. Carl Hoff

The Mayor of Alabam' (1936/04/27) w. Frankie Trumbauer

Me (1931/08/?) w. Fred Rich

Me and the Moon (1936/07/27) w. Richard Himber

A Melody from the Sky (1936/04/13) w. Bunny Berigan

A Melody from the Sky (1936/04/21) w. Richard Himber

Midnight Blue (1936/07/27) w. Richard Himber

Midnight Blue (1936/08/05) w. Dick McDonough

Mimi (1936/03/?) w. Bill Challis

Moan You Moaners (c. 1931–32) w. Blue Coal Minstrels

Monday in Manhattan (1935/06/19) w. Richard Himber

The Moon Was Yellow (1936/02/24) w. Bill Challis

Moonlight on the Colorado (1930/08/22) w. Irving Aaronson

More Than You Know (1936/03/?) w. Bill Challis

Much Too Much (1936/01/28) w. Bob Howard

The Music Goes Round and Round (1936/01/06) w. The Boswell Sisters

Must We Say Goodnight (1934/10/13) w. Richard Himber

My Bluebird's Back Again (1931/08/?) w. Fred Rich

My Foolish Heart (1935/08/19) w. Richard Himber

My Future Star (1934/09/26) w. Alice Faye

Never Had No Lovin' (1934/08/15) w. Wingy Manone

A New Moon over My Shoulder (1934/08/01) w. Johnny Green

New Orleans (1936/02/24) w. Bill Challis

New Sun in the Sky (1931/08/?) w. Fred Rich

The Night Is Blue (1934/10/04) w. Red Norvo

The Night Is Young (1936/07/?) w. Carl Hoff

Night on the Desert (1934/06/12) w. Richard Himber

99 out of 100 (1931/08/?) w. Fred Rich

No Greater Love (1936/04/21) w. Richard Himber

No Other One (1935/11/25) w. Richard Himber

No Regrets (1936/07/10) w. Billie Holiday

Nobody's Sweetheart (1931/08/?) w. Fred Rich

Nobody's Sweetheart (c. 1931–32) w. Blue Coal Minstrels

Now or Never (1936/10/17) w. Dick McDonough

Now That You've Gone (1931/11/09) w. Bing Crosby

Now the Show Is On (1936/07/?) w. Carl Hoff

Now's the Time to Fall in Love (1931/08/?) w. Fred Rich

Oh Say Can You Swing? (1936/07/?) w. Carl Hoff

Oh Susanna (c. 1931–32) w. Blue Coal Minstrels

Oh That Kiss (1931/08/?) w. Fred Rich

Old Fashioned Love (1934/09/26) w. Red Norvo

On a Sunday Afternoon (1935/06/19) w. Richard Himber

On the Beach at Bali-Bali (1936/06/04) w. Dick McDonough

On Treasure Island (1936/02/24) w. Bill Challis

On with the Dance (1936/08/?) w. Ray Sinatra

Once in a Lifetime (1934/06/07) w. Richard Himber

One Hamburger for Madame (1936/04/02) w. Jack Shilkret

One Man Band (1931/08/?) w. Fred Rich

One More Kiss (1931/08/?) w. Fred Rich

Out of a Clear Blue Sky (1931/08/?) w. Fred Rich

Out Where the Blue Begins (1936/08/29) w. Jack Shilkret

Paradise (1936/02/24) w. Bill Challis

Paris in the Spring (1936/02/24) w. Bill Challis

Picture Me Without You (1936/07/27) w. Richard Himber

Plantation Moods (1934/11/20) w. Frankie Trumbauer

Put On Your Old Gray Bonnet (1934/03/27) w. Ben Selvin

Rain on the Roof (1931/08/?) w. Fred Rich

Rain on the Roof (1932/02/04) w. Ben Selvin

Ramona (1936/03/?) w. Bill Challis

The Ranger's Song (March) (1931/08/?) w. Fred Rich

Reckless (1935/05/04) w. Richard Himber

Red Sails in the Sunset (1935/11/25) w. Richard Himber

Rhythm in My Nursery Rhymes (1936/03/?) w. Bill Challis

Rhythm Saved the World (1936/04/13) w. Bunny Berigan

The Riff Song (1931/08/?) w. Fred Rich

Ringside Table for Two (1936/O1/20) w. Manny Klein

River Stay 'Way from My Door (1931/08/24) w. Red Nichols

Riverboat Shuffle (1936/02/24) w. Bill Challis

Robins and Roses (1936/04/02) w. Jack Shilkret

Rockin' Chair (1936/02/24) w. Bill Challis

Roll on Mississippi (1931/08/?) w. Fred Rich

Roll on Mississippi (c. 1931–32) w. Blue Coal Minstrels

Rollin' Home (1934/06/12) w. Richard Himber

'S Wonderful (1936/04/27) w. Frankie Trumbauer

Sally (1934/06/07) w. Richard Himber

San (1931/08/?) w. Fred Rich

San Francisco (1936/07/31) w. Jack Shilkret

Save the Last Dance for Me (1931/08/?) w. Fred Rich

Say When (1934/10/23) w. Richard Himber

The Scene Changes (1936/06/04) w. Dick McDonough

Sheltered By the Stars (1932/08/05) w. R. W. Kahn

A Shine on Your Shoes (1932/11/09) w. R. W. Kahn

Shoe-Shine Boy (1936/07/31) w. Jack Shilkret

Sidewalks of Cuba (1936/03/?) w. Bill Challis

Sleepy Head (1934/06/07) w. Richard Himber

Slummin' on Park Avenue (1936/07/?) w. Carl Hoff

Smooth (1935/10/21) w. Richard Himber

Snuggled on Your Shoulder (1931/08/?) w. Fred Rich

So Are You (1931/08/?) w. Fred Rich

So Divine (1936/08/29) w. Jack Shilkret

So Help Me (1934/06/07) w. Richard Himber

So This Is Heaven (1936/01/13) w. Richard Himber

Some of These Days (1931/08/?) w. Fred Rich

Somebody Loves Me (1936/04/27) w. Frankie Trumbauer

Somebody Loves You (1931/08/?) w. Fred Rich

Somebody Stole My Gal (1931/08/?) w. Fred Rich
Something to Remember (1935/08/19) w. Richard Himber
Song of the Flame (1931/08/?) w. Fred Rich
South Sea Island Magic (1936/08/05) w. Dick McDonough
Southbound (1931/08/?) w. Fred Rich
Stars Fell on Alabama (1934/10/05) w. Richard Himber
Stars in My Eyes (1936/06/04) w. Dick McDonough
Straight from the Shoulder (1934/06/12) w. Richard Himber
Sugar (1931/08/?) w. Fred Rich
Summer Holiday (1936/06/23) w. Dick McDonough
Summertime (1936/04/21) w. Richard Himber
Summertime (1936/07/10) w. Billie Holiday
Sunny Skies (1931/08/?) w. Fred Rich
The Sun's in My Heart (1931/08/?) w. Fred Rich
Suzannah (1936/01/13) w. Richard Himber
Sweet and Hot (1932/film) w. R. W. Kahn
Sweet and Lovely (1931/08/?) w. Fred Rich
Sweet Jenny Lee (1931/08/?) w. Fred Rich
Sweetheart I'm on My Way (c. 1931–32) w. Blue Coal Minstrels

Take a Number from One to Ten (1934/10/15) w. Johnnie Davis
Take Me Back to My Boots and Saddle (1935/11/25) w. Richard Himber
Take My Heart (1936/06/04) w. Dick McDonough
Take My Heart (1936/07/20) w. Chick Bullock
Take This Ring (1935/08/19) w. Richard Himber
Tea for Two (1934/10/05) w. Richard Himber
Tea on the Terrace (1936/11/03) w. Dick McDonough
Tell Tales (1931/08/?) w. Fred Rich
Temptation (1936/03/?) w. Bill Challis
Tesario Mio (1935/11/25) w. Richard Himber
Thank You for a Lovely Evening (1934/06/07) w. Richard Himber
There Goes My Attraction (1936/07/31) w. Jack Shilkret
There's a Blue Note in My Love Song (1931/08/?) w. Fred Rich
There's a Small Hotel (1936/04/21) w. Richard Himber
There's Always a Happy Ending (1936/04/02) w. Jack Shilkret
There's Frost on the Moon (1936/11/03) w. Dick McDonough
These Foolish Things (1936/07/20) w. Chick Bullock
Things Might Have Been So Different (1935/02/11) w. Richard Himber
This Is the Missus (1931/08/?) w. Fred Rich
This Is the Missus (1931/11/09) w. Bing Crosby
This Year's Kisses (1936/07/?) w. Carl Hoff
A Thousand Goodnights (1934/03/19) w. Richard Himber
A Thousand Goodnights (1934/03/24) w. Adrian Rollini
Thrilled (1935/06/19) w. Richard Himber
Thru the Courtesy of Love (1936/10/13) w. Richard Himber

Thunder over Paradise (1935/10/21) w. Richard Himber
Tiger Rag (1931/08/?) w. Fred Rich
Time Will Tell (1935/05/04) w. Richard Himber
Tomboy (1934/10/04) w. Red Norvo
Too Late (1931/08/?) w. Fred Rich
Top Hat White Tie and Tails (1935/10/08) w. The Boswell Sisters
Tormented (1936/04/06) w. Richard Himber
Tormented (1936/04/21) w. Richard Himber
Touch of Your Lips (1936/04/21) w. Richard Himber
Troubled (1934/11/20) w. Frankie Trumbauer
True (1934/06/07) w. Richard Himber
Twilight Waltz (1935/10/21) w. Richard Himber
Twinkle Twinkle Little Star (1936/07/?) w. Carl Hoff
Twinkle Twinkle Little Star (1936/10/13) w. Richard Himber
Two Cigarettes in the Dark (1934/08/01) w. Johnny Green
Two Loves (1931/08/?) w. Fred Rich

Violets (1935/11/25) w. Richard Himber

WaDaDa (1928/08/13) w. Joe Cantor
Waitin' at the Gate for Katy (1934/03/24) w. Adrian Rollini
Waitin' at the Gate for Katy (1934/06/07) w. Richard Himber
Waiting for the Robert E. Lee (1931/08/?) w. Fred Rich
Was It Wrong? (1931/08/?) w. Fred Rich
Was That the Human Thing to Do? (1931/08/?) w. Fred Rich
Way Down Yonder in New Orleans (1932/ film) w. R. W. Kahn
Way Down Yonder in New Orleans (1936/06/23) w. Dick McDonough
Way Down Yonder in the Cornfield (c. 1931–32) w. Blue Coal Minstrels
Were You Foolin' (1934/10/22) w. Johnnie Davis
Were You Foolin' (1934/10/23) w. Richard Himber
What a Difference a Day Made (1934/10/23) w. Richard Himber
What a Wonderful World (1935/08/19) w. Richard Himber
What a Wonderful World (1935/11/25) w. Richard Himber
What Can You Say in a Love Song (1934/06/13) w. Richard Himber
What Is It? (1931/08/?) w. Fred Rich
What Makes You So Adorable? (1931/08/?) w. Fred Rich
When a Woman Loves a Man (1934/03/19) w. Richard Himber
When Love Comes Swinging Along (1934/10/23) w. Richard Himber
When My Dreamboat Comes Home (1936/07/?) w. Carl Hoff
When the Blue of the Night (Theme) (1931/11/09) w. Bing Crosby

When the Moon Hangs High (1936/08/05) w. Dick McDonough

When You Are in My Arms (1935/06/19) w. Richard Himber

When You Love (1936/04/06) w. Richard Himber

When You Love (1936/04/21) w. Richard Himber

Where Am I? (1935/11/25) w. Richard Himber

Where Have You Been All My Life (1936/10/13) w. Richard Himber

Whistle and Blow Your Blues Away (1932/05/12) w. Ben Selvin

Who's Afraid of Love? (1936/07/?) w. Carl Hoff

Whose Big Baby Are You? (1936/01/28) w. Bob Howard

Who's Your Little Whoosits? (1931/08/?) w. Fred Rich

Why Do I Dream Those Dreams (1934/06/07) w. Richard Himber

Why Have a Falling Out? (1935/02/11) w. Richard Himber

Why Have You Forgotten Waikiki? (1930/08/22) w. Irving Aaronson

Why Was I Born? (1935/11/25) w. Richard Himber

Wild Rose (1934/06/07) w. Richard Himber

Will I Ever Know (1936/04/21) w. Richard Himber

Will Love Find a Way (1935/11/25) w. Richard Himber

Winter Wonderland (1934/10/23) w. Richard Himber

Wintertime Dreams (1936/10/13) w. Richard Himber

With Every Breath I Take (1934/10/05) w. Richard Himber

With Love in My Heart (1931/08/?) w. Fred Rich

With My Eyes Open I'm Dreaming (1934/06/07) w. Richard Himber

With Plenty of Money and You (1936/07/?) w. Carl Hoff

With Thee I Swing (1936/11/03) w. Dick McDonough

Without a Word of Warning (1935/08/19) w. Richard Himber

The World Is Mine (1936/07/27) w. Richard Himber

The World Is Mine (1936/08/29) w. Jack Shilkret

Would You (1936/04/06) w. Richard Himber

Would You (1936/04/21) w. Richard Himber

Yes To You (1934/09/26) w. Alice Faye

You (1936/04/21) w. Richard Himber

You Call It Madness I Call It Love (1931/08/?) w. Fred Rich

You Call It Madness I Call It Love (1931/12/?) w. Fred Rich

You Didn't Know the Music (1931/08/?) w. Fred Rich

You Dropped Me Like a Red Hot Penny (1936/07/20) w. Chick Bullock

You Gotta Give Credit to Love (1934/10/15) w. Johnnie Davis

You Fit into the Picture (1935/01/15) w. Chick Bullock

You Forgot Your Gloves (1931/05/28) w. Paul Specht

You Hit the Spot (1935/10/21) w. Richard Himber

You Hit the Spot (1936/01/28) w. Bob Howard

You Must Believe Me (1933/02/14) w. Adrian Rollini

You Oughta Be in Pictures (1934/06/07) w. Richard Himber

You Started Me Dreaming (1936/04/21) w. Richard Himber

You Try Somebody Else (1931/08/?) w. Fred Rich

You Were My Salvation (c. 1931–32) w. Blue Coal Minstrels

You're a Builder Upper (1934/06/13) w. Richard Himber

You're Driving Me Crazy (1932/film) w. R. W. Kahn

You're Everything Sweet (1936/10/13) w. Richard Himber

You're Giving Me a Song and a Dance (1936/10/17) w. Dick McDonough

You're Laughing at Me (1936/07/?) w. Carl Hoff

You're Not the Kind (1936/07/20) w. Chick Bullock

You've Got Me in the Palm of Your Hand (1932/08/05) w. R. W. Kahn

You've Got Me Cryin' Again (1933/02/14) w. Adrian Rollini

Zing! Went the Strings of My Heart (1935/02/11) w. Richard Himber

Zonky (1931/08/?) w. Fred Rich

Artie Shaw Discography: 1936–1954

PART I: ART SHAW AND HIS ORCHESTRA, THE 1936–37 BAND

Art Shaw's Swing String Ensemble
Imperial Theatre, New York, 24 May 1936

Artie Shaw(cl), Harry Bluestone, Mannie Green(vl), Isadore Zir(vla), Rudy Simms(cel), Carl Kress(g), Artie Bernstein(b), Art Stein(d)

	Interlude in B-flat	Aircheck LP-1, BOMR71-7715

NOTE: Personnel from *Down Beat*, except Shaw identified the unnamed bassist (2). Location and date have been controversial.

Art Shaw and His Orchestra
New York, 11 June 1936

Willis Kelly(tp), Mark Bennett(tb), Artie Shaw(cl), Tony Zimmer(ts), Louis Klayman, Julie Schechter(vl), Sam Persoff(vla), James Oderich(cel), Fulton McGrath(p), Wes Vaughan(g,v), Hank Wayland(b), Sammy Weiss(d)

19434	Japanese Sandman	Br7688, Ajaz259, CK46156
19435	A Pretty Girl Is Like a Melody	—, —, —
19436	I Used to Be Above Love (vWV)	Br7698, —, —
19437	No Regrets	(rejected)

same
New York, 17 June 1936

19437	No Regrets (vWV)	Br7698, Ajaz259, CK46156

NOTE: "No Regrets" has been edited for some LP issues eliminating the vocal. This was a studio group, not a regular working group. Columbia CK46156 is a CD.

Art Shaw and His Orchestra
New York, 6 August 1936

Lee Castle, Dave Wade(tp), Mike Michaels(tb), Artie Shaw(cl), Tony Pastor(ts,v), Jerry Gray, Ben Plotkin(vl), Sam Persoff(vla), James Oderich(cel), Joe Lippman(p), Gene Stone(g), Ben Ginsberg(b), Sammy Weiss(d), Peg La Centra(v)

19667	South Sea Island Magic (vPL)	Br7721, Ajaz259, CK46156
19668	It Ain't Right (vPL)	—, —, —
19669	Sugar Foot Stomp	Br7735, —, —
19670	Thou Swell	—, —, —

NOTE: This band opened at the Silver Grill, Hotel Lexington, 21 August 1936, broadcasting on their first Wednesday evening and every Saturday and Sunday. The broadcasts were carried by CBS over WABC until the band closed on 6 October 1936, for a total of fifteen broadcasts.

same
New York, 17 September 1936

19895	You're Giving Me a Song and a Dance (vPL)	Br7741, Ajaz259, CK46156
19896	Darling Not Without You (vPL)	—, —, —
19897	One Two Button Your Shoe (vTP)	Br7750, —, —
19898	Let's Call a Heart a Heart (vPL)	—, —, —

NOTE: The band opened at the French Casino on 10 October 1936, and began broadcasting the next day on CBS. They continued to broadcast on Sundays and Thursdays until closing on 20 November 1936 for a total of eleven broadcasts. Several personnel changes occurred in this period.

Art Shaw and His Orchestra
New York, 30 October 1936

Lee Castle, Zeke Zarchy(tp), Mike Michaels(tb), Artie Shaw(cl), Tony Pastor(ts,v), Jerry Gray, Frank Siegfield(vl), Sam Rosenblum(vla), Bill Schumann(cel), Joe Lippman(p), Tony Gottuso(g), Ben Ginsberg(b), George Wettling(d), Peg La Centra(v)

20166	The Skeleton in the Closet	Br7771, Ajaz259, CK46156

20167	There's Something in the Air (vPL)	Br7778, —, —
20168	Take Another Guess (vTP)	—, Ajaz264, —
20169	There's Frost on the Moon (vPL)	Br7771, —, —

same
CBS/WABC Broadcast, French Casino, New York, 1 November 1936

	Take Another Guess (vTP)	air check
	There's Something in the Air (vPL)	—
	The Skeleton in the Closet	—
	There's Frost on the Moon (vPL)	—

Buddy Morrow(tb) for Michaels
New York, 30 November 1936

20342	Love and Learn (vPL)	Br7787, Ajaz264, CK53423
20343	Moon Face (vPL)	—, —, —
20344	The Same Old Line	Br7794, —, —
20345	You Can Tell She Comes from Dixie (vPL)	—, —, —

NOTE: The band was at the Paramount Theatre, New York City, 9–22 December 1936.

same
New York, 23 December 1936

20448	Sobbin' Blues	Br7806, Ajaz264, CK53423
20449	Copenhagen	Br7827, —, —
20450	Cream Puff	Br7806, —, —
20451	My Blue Heaven	Br7827, —, —

omit brass, piano, tenor sax; same session

| 20452 | Streamline Br | 7852, Ajaz264, CK53423 |
| 20453 | Sweet Lorraine | —, —, — |

NOTE: The band was at the Century Room, Adolphus Hotel, Dallas, Texas, from 6 January–2 February 1937, broadcasting regularly. Curtis Hurd(tp) was reported joining Shaw (replacing Zarchy) in *Metronome* (February 1937, p. 39).

Mike Bryan(g) for Gottuso
New York, 15 February 1937

20678	Love Is Good for Anything That Ails You	Br7841, Ajaz270, CK53423
20679	No More Tears (vPL)	Br7835, Ajaz264, —
20680	Moonlight and Shadows (vPL)	—, —, —
20681	Was It Rain? (vPL)	Br7841, Ajaz270, —

same; as Rhythm Makers
New York, 4 March 1937

06230	Love Is Good for Anything That Ails You	TT366, SW7001
	No More Tears (vPL)	—, —
	September in the Rain (vPL)	—, —
	The Mood That I'm In	—, —
06231	Trust in Me (vPL)	—, —
	A Message from the Man in the Moon	—, —
	Was It Rain? (vPL)	—, —
	Swing High Swing Low	—, —
06232	Sweet Is the Word for You (vPL)	TT370, —
	Moon Face (vPL)	—, —
	The Skeleton in the Closet	—, —
	Sobbin' Blues	—, —
06233	Cream Puff	TT377, —
	At Sundown	—, —
	Copenhagen	—, —
	My Blue Heaven	—, —
06234	When Your Lover Has Gone (vPL)	TT385, SW7002
	All Dressed Up and No Place to Go (vPL)	—, —
	How Come You Do Me Like You Do?	—, —
	The Blues	—, —

NOTE: The above date for this session was given by Ken Crawford in his discography on the Rhythm Makers provided by the International Association of Jazz Record Collectors, but all titles have unaccountably been issued on Swingdom dated 19 February 1937. On all Rhythm Makers sessions, Crawford's dating was used, as there were other problems with the dates provided by Swingdom.

The band was at the Meadowbrook Ballroom in New Jersey from 17 February through 9 March 1937, then disbanded.

PART II: ART SHAW AND HIS NEW MUSIC: THE 1937–38 BAND.

Art Shaw and His Music: as Rhythm Makers
New York, 28 April 1937

John Best, Tom DiCarlo, Malcolm Crain(tp), George Arus, Harry Rodgers(tb), Artie Shaw(cl), Les Robinson, Buddy Saffer(as), Tony Pastor(ts,v), Fred Petry(ts), Les Burness(p), Al Avola(g), Ben Ginsberg(b), Cliff Leeman(d), Dorothy Howe(v)

07884	Born to Swing	TT395, SW7002
	Milenburg Joys	—, —
	The Bus Blues	—, —
	Ubangi	—, —
07885	Twilight in Turkey	TT398, —
	Alibi Baby (vTP)	—, —
	Night over Shanghai	—, —
	Study in Brown	—, —
07886	I'll Never Tell You I Love You (vDH)	—, —
	All at Once (vDH)	—, —
	Without Your Love (vDH)	—, —
	The Love Bug Will Bite You (vTP)	—, —
07887	Johnny One Note	TT389, SW7003
	Never in a Million Years (vDH)	—, —
	Wake Up and Live	—, —
	I've Got Beginners Luck (vDH)	—, —
07888	Someday Sweetheart	TT402, —
	Symphony in Riffs	—, —
	In the Bottom	—, —
	Hold Your Hats	—, —
07889	Theme(Bus Blues) & Introduction	TT389, —
	Born to Swing	—, —
	Someday Sweetheart	—, —
	Night and Day	—, —
	Ubangi	—, —
	Theme(Bus Blues) & Close	—, —

NOTE: "The Bus Blues" was speeded up and retitled "Free for All" (18 October 1937). "Ubangi" became "The Chant" (4 August 1937, etc.). "In the Bottom" was the same composition as "Leapin' at the Lincoln" (Blue Room, 1 December 1938) and "Rockin' the State" (Old Gold show, 11 December 1938). The composition "Hold Your Hats" was *NOT* the same piece Shaw performed on broadcasts from the Blue Room in December 1938 titled "Hold Your Hat(s)." Add unidentified announcer on mx #07889, made as a simulated broadcast; these versions of tunes re-

corded earlier that day were different performances. Swingdom dated this session as 29 April.

Art Masters(as) for Saffer
New York, 13 May 1937

21134	All Alone	Br7899, Ajaz270, CK53423
21135	All God's Children Got Rhythm (vTP)	Br7895, —, —
21136	It Goes to Your Feet (vTP)	—, —, —
21137	Because I Love You	Br7899, —, —

Hank Freeman(as) for Masters
New York, 18 May 1937

21167	Night and Day	Br7914, Ajaz270
21168	I Surrender Dear	Br7907, —
21169	Blue Skies	—, —
21170	Someday Sweetheart	Br7914, —

NOTE: Beginning 21 May 1937, the band was at the Willows in Pittsburgh until 24 June, with regular Saturday night broadcasts through KDKA with an NBC coast-to-coast hookup. Following the Willows engagement, Peg La Centra returned as vocalist, replacing Dorothy Howe.

same; as Rhythm Makers
New York, 12 July 1937

011303	Whispers in the Dark	TT419, SW7003
	Don't Ever Change (vPL)	—, —
	If I Put My Heart into a Song	—, SW7004
	Love Is a Merry-Go-Round	—, —
011304	'Til the Clock Strikes Three	—, —
	The Moon Got in My Eyes (vPL)	—, —
	All You Want to Do Is Dance (vPL)	—, —
	It's the Natural Thing to Do (vPL)	—, —
011305	The Folks Who Live on the Hill (vPL)	TT426, —
	Can I Forget You? (vPL)	—, —
	The Things I Want (vPL)	—, —
	Posin'	—, —
011306	If You Ever Should Leave (vPL)	TT420, —

	The Loveliness of You	—, —
	Afraid to Dream (vPL)	—, —
	All Alone	—, —
011307	Because I Love You	TT433, —
	If I Had You	—, —
	Together	—, SW7005
	Just You Just Me	—, —

NOTE: Swingdom SW7005 is a four–LP set, which dated this session as 13 July.

same
New York, 22 July 1937

21423	Afraid to Dream (vPL)	Br7934, Ajaz270
21424	If You Ever Should Leave (vPL)	—, —
21425-1	Sweet Adeline (vTP)	Br7936, —
21425-2	Sweet Adeline (vTP)	Vo.4182
21426-1	How Dry I Am	Br7936, —
21426-2	How Dry I Am	Vo.4182

NOTE: These were the earliest alternate takes verified to have surfaced from the Brunswick/Vocalion series of recordings. A third take of 21425 with the vocal by Shaw is rumored to exist as a test pressing, but this is denied by Shaw.

Jules Rubin(ts) for Petry
New York, 4 August 1937

21458	Am I in Love? (vPL)	Br7942, Ajaz276
21459	Fee Fi Fo Fum	Br7952, —
21460	Please Pardon Us We're in Love (vPL)	Br7942, —
21461	The Chant	Br7952, —
21462-1	The Blues, A	Br7947, —, AFS1028
21462-2	The Blues, A	Vo.4401, —
21463	The Blues, B	Br7947, —, —

NOTE: "The Chant" was the same composition earlier titled "Ubangi," and "The Blues" has been retitled on LP issues as "The Blues March." AFS1028 is a CD.

Fred Petry(ts) for Rubin; Charlie Spivak(tp) for Best;
Bea Wain(v) for La Centra; add Leo Watson(v)
New York, 17 September 1937

21710	It's a Long Way to Tipperary	Br7965, Ajaz276, AFS1028
21711	I've a Strange New Rhythm in My Heart (vLW)	Br7971, —, —
21712	If It's the Last Thing I Do (vBW)	—, —, —

21713-1	Nightmare	Br7965, —, —
21713-2	Nightmare	Vo.4306
21714	Shoot the Likker to Me John Boy (vLW)	Br7976, —, —
21715	Free Wheeling (vLW)	—, —, —

Max Kaminsky, Chuck Peterson(tp) for Spivak &
Crain; Dolores O'Neill(v) for Wain as Rhythm Makers
New York, 17 October 1937

015507	A Strange Loneliness (vDO)	TT455, SW7005
	Have You Met Miss Jones? (vTP)	—, —
	I'd Rather Be Right	—, —
	Everything You Said Came True	—, —
015508	Rosalie (vTP)	—, —
	You Have Everything	—, —
	Shindig	—, —
	I've a Strange New Rhythm in My Heart	—, —
015509	Sweet Varsity Sue (vTP)	TT496, —
	I Want a New Romance	—, —
	Shoot the Likker to Me John Boy	—, —
	Free Wheeling	—, —
015510	S.O.S.	—, —
	How Dry I Am	—, —
	Black and Blue (vTP)	—, —
	Fee Fi Fo Fum	—, —
015511	I'm Yours	TT461, —
	Sweet Adeline (vTP)	—, —
	Old Black Joe	—, —
	It's a Long Way to Tipperary	—, —

same
New York, 18 October 1937

21895	Let 'er Go	Br7986, Ajaz276, AFS1028
21896	A Strange Loneliness (vDO)	—, —, —
21897	Monsoon	Br8019, Ajaz283, —
21898	I'm Yours	Br8010, —, —
21899	Just You Just Me	—, —, —
21900	Free for All	Br8019, —, —

Norman Ayres(tp) for DiCarlo; Nita Bradley(v) for
O'Neill; as Rhythm Makers
New York, 15 December 1937

017807	Goodnight Angel (vNB)	TT481, SW7005
	One Song (vNB)	—, —

	There's a New Moon over the Old Mill (vNB)	—, —
	Can't Teach My Old Heart New Tricks (vNB)	—, —
017808	You're Out of This World (vTP)	—, —
	You're a Sweetheart (vNB)	—, —
	Bob White (vTP)	—, —
	The Old Stamping Ground (vTP)	—, —
017809	Love for Sale	TT487, —
	Big Dipper	—, —
	The Lady Is a Tramp (vTP)	—, —
	Stalling for Time	—, —
017810	Monsoon	TT482, —
	Honeysuckle Rose	—, —
	I'll Be with You in Apple Blossom Time (vTP)	—, —
	Non-Stop Flight	—, —
017811	Nightmare	TT524, —
	My Bonnie Lies over the Ocean (vTP)	—, —
	Show Me the Way to Go Home	—, —
	Stealin' Apples	—, —

NOTE: Swingdom unaccountably dated the 17 October session as 16 October and the above as 18 October.

same
New York, 30 December 1937

22237-1	Whistle While You Work (vTP)	Br8050, Ajaz283
22237-2	Whistle While You Work (vTP)	SB207, AFS1028
22238	One Song (vNB)	Br8050, —, —
22239-1	Goodnight Angel (vNB)	Br8054, —, —
22239-2	Goodnight Angel (vNB)	—
22240	There's a New Moon Over the Old Mill (vNB)	Br8054, —, —
22241	Non-Stop Flight	Vo.S147, —, —
22242	I'll Be with You in Apple Blossom Time	Vo.4438, —, —

NOTE: An alternate take of 22238 allegedly exists but remains unconfirmed.

as Rhythm Makers
New York, 15 February 1938

Chuck Peterson, Max Kaminsky, Norman Ayres(tp), George Arus, Harry Rodgers(tb) Artie Shaw(cl), Les Robinson, Hank Freeman(ts), Tony Pastor, Fred Petry(ts), Les Burness(p), Al Avola(g), Sid Weiss(b), Cliff Leeman(d), Nita Bradley(v)

019825	The Toy Trumpet	TT501, SW7005
	Hillbilly from Tenth Avenue	—, —
	My Old Kentucky Home	—, —
	Any Old Time (vNB)	—, —
019826	Powerhouse	TT549, —
	Take My Word	—, —
	Azure	—, —
	Call of the Freaks	—, —
019827	The Old Apple Tree	TT500, —
	Lost in the Shuffle	—, —
	If Dreams Come True	—, —
	Moonlight on the Sunset Trail (vNB)	—, —
019828	More Than Ever	—, —
	I'll Never Let You Cry	—, —
	In the Shade of the New Apple Tree	—, —
	It's Wonderful (vNB)	—, —
019829	Blue Fantasy	TT567, —
	Love's Old Sweet Song (vNB)	—, —
	Indian Love Call	—, —
	Meade Lux Special	—, —

same session

Max Kaminsky(tp), George Arus(tb), Artie Shaw(cl), Tony Pastor(ts), Les Burness(celeste), Al Avola(g), Sid Weiss(b), Cliff Leeman(d)

019830	Sweet and Low	TT514, SW7005

NOTE: The above item was a New Orleans–style collective improvisation. The brass section and drums also recorded "7 Fanfares and 2 Drumrolls" issued on the same Thesaurus Transcription, but Shaw did not play.

The band opened at the Roseland Ballroom, Boston, on 22 March 1938, broadcasting two nights per week. They were listed as broadcasting at 6:30 p.m. every Tuesday and Saturday, and at midnight on Tuesdays. On other nights they were playing one-nighters on the circuit of Shribman ballrooms around New England. This situation lasted for the following three months. Air checks featuring Billie Holiday from this period have been rumored to exist, but have not surfaced at this writing.

PART III: ARTIE SHAW AND HIS ORCHESTRA, THE 1938–39 BAND

All of Artie Shaw's New York record sessions for Bluebird (and later Victor) were held in RCA's "Studio 2" on East 24th Street in New York City.

Art Shaw and His Orchestra
2:00–8:30 p.m. New York, 24 July 1938

Chuck Peterson, Claude Bowen, John Best(tp), Harry Rodgers, Ted Vesely, George Arus(tb), Artie Shaw(cl), Les Robinson, Hank Freeman(as), Tony Pastor(ts,v), Ronnie Perry(ts), Les Burness(p), Al Avola(g), Sid Weiss(b), Cliff Leeman(d), Billie Holiday(v)

024079-1	Begin the Beguine	BB7746, AXM2-5517
024080-1	Indian Love Call (vTP/band)	—, —
024081-2	Comin' On	BB7772, —
024082-2	Back Bay Shuffle	BB7759, —
024083-1	Any Old Time (vBH)	—, —
024084-2	I Can't Believe That You're in Love with Me	BB7772, —

NOTE: An alleged alternate take of the last title appeared in extremely low fidelity on an Artie Shaw Club special pressing from England (ASC-8), but it could not be confirmed that this performance may not be from another source. The RCA log sheet for this session showed two takes were recorded for each mx #, except 024080 (one take).

George Koenig(as) for Robinson *Magic Key of Radio*, **New York, 18 September 1938**

Begin the Beguine	ASC-4
What Is This Thing Called Love?	—

NOTE: The date for this broadcast also has been given as 16 September 1938.

Russell Brown(tb) for Vesely; Helen Forrest(v) for Holiday
7:00–11:45 p.m. New York, 27 September 1938

027229	Nightmare	BB7875, AXM2-5517
027230	Non-Stop Flight	—, —
027231	Yesterdays	BB10001, —
027232	What Is This Thing Called Love?	—, —
027233	You're a Sweet Little Headache (vHF)	BB7889, —
027234	I Have Eyes (vHF)	—, —

NOTE: RCA log sheets indicated only one take was made for each mx #, except 027233 (two takes), with no indication of which take was used; takes 1A & 2A were marked "Hold cast" while takes 1 & 2 are marked "Flowed." The band opened at the Blue Room, Hotel Lincoln, New York City, on 28 October 1938, broadcasting almost nightly.

All-Stars
***WNEW Jam Session*, New York, 9 November 1938**

Yank Lawson(tp), Tommy Dorsey(tb), Artie Shaw(cl), Chu Berry(ts), Jess Stacy(p), Alan Reuss(g), John Kirby(b), O'Neil Spencer(d)

Limehouse Blues	Merritt LP-21

NOTE: Recording faded on the Merritt release following Berry's solo, as Tommy Dorsey's solo began; but Lawson, Shaw and Stacy's solos preceded Berry's. This show was held on Wednesdays, but the Merritt LP unaccountably dated this performance as 11 November 1938 (a Friday).

Art Shaw and His Orchestra
1:30–6:08 p.m. New York, 17 November 1938

Chuck Peterson, Claude Bowen, John Best(tp), George Arus, Harry Rodgers, Russell Brown(tb), Artie Shaw(cl), Les Robinson, Hank Freeman(as), Tony Pastor(ts,v), Ronnie Perry(ts), Les Burness(p), Al Avola(g), Sid Weiss(b), Cliff Leeman(d), Helen Forrest(v)

028973	Between a Kiss and a Sigh (vHF)	BB10055, AXM2-5517
028974	Thanks for Everything (vHF)	—, —
028975	Deep in a Dream (vHF)	B10046, —
028976	Day after Day (vHF)	—, —
028977	Softly as in a Morning Sunrise	BB10054, —
028978	Copenhagen	—, —

NOTE: The RCA log sheets indicated only one take of each mx # was made.

add Dick Todd(v) for Old Gold shows
Rehearsal, Old Gold show, 18 November 1938

The Yam	JG1001, LL15757
Two Sleepy People (vDT)	(unissued)
Begin the Beguine	—
Softly as in a Morning Sunrise	JHCD1009

NOTE: The weekly Old Gold show *Melody and Madness* radio series featuring Artie Shaw and his orchestra with Robert Benchley as host, began broadcasting on Sunday, 20 November 1938 at 10 p.m. Rehearsals for at least the first several shows also have been preserved.

same
Old Gold show, 20 November 1938

The Yam	JHCD1009
Two Sleepy People (vDT)	(unissued)

| Softly as in a Morning Sunrise | — |
| Non-Stop Flight | JG1001 |

Bernie Privin(tp) for Bowen
Rehearsal, Old Gold show, 25 November 1938

Begin the Beguine	unissued)
When I Go A-Dreamin' (vDT)	—
Who Blew Out the Flame (vHF)	—
Shoot the Rhythm to Me John Boy	JG1001

same
7:00–7:30 p.m. Blue Room, 25 November 1938

Theme(Nightmare) & Introduction	FF28-128
Sobbin' Blues	—, Vic.LPT6000
I Can't Believe That You're in Love with Me	—, SoS125
They Say (vHF)	—, ASC-8
It Had to Be You	—, HBCD502
My Reverie (vHF)	—, Vic.LPT6000
Sweet Adeline (vTP)	—, SoS126, HSR176, HSR401, HBCD502
Who Blew Out the Flame (vHF)	—, SoS117, ASC-9
Copenhagen	—, SoS125
Theme(Nightmare) & Closing	—

same
Old Gold show, 27 November 1938

Begin the Beguine	(unissued)
When I Go A-Dreamin' (vDT)	—
Who Blew Out the Flame (vHF)	JG1001, JHCD1009
Back Bay Shuffle	—

same
Vitaphone Movie Short *Artie Shaw and His Orchestra*, 28/29 November 1938

Theme(Nightmare)	MGM (laserdisc) ML 103 928, J3004, ASC-11
Begin the Beguine	—, —, —
Let's Stop the Clock (vHF)	—, —, —

| Non-Stop Flight | —, —, — |
| Prosschai (vTP) | —, —, — |

NOTE: The band reportedly filmed on the 28th, and recorded sound on the 29th.

same
12:00–12:30 a.m. Blue Room, 29 November 1938

Theme(Nightmare)	HSR139
April in My Heart	—
Night over Shanghai (vHF)	—, HBCD502
Small Fry (vTP)	—, HSR401
What Is This Thing Called Love?	—, —
Comin' On (incomplete)	(unissued)
Theme(Nightmare)	HSR139

Les Jenkins(tb) for Brown; George Wettling(d) for Leeman
11:00–11:30 p.m. Blue Room, 1 December 1938

Theme(Nightmare)	HSR139
Non-Stop Flight	Vic.LPT6000
Just a Kid Named Joe (vTP)	(unissued)
When I Go A-Dreamin' (vHF)	HSR139
Leapin' at the Lincoln (= In the Bottom)	—, HBCD502
Theme(Nightmare)	—
April in My Heart	(unissued)
Lambeth Walk	HSR139, —, HSR401
They Say (vHF)	—
Shine On Harvest Moon	—, —, —

NOTE: According to Ken Seavor's "Artie Shaw—The Sustaining Broadcasts 1938 to 1939" in *In Tune* [undated], the version of "Just a Kid Named Joe" on HSR139 was from 20 December 1938, but issued in place of the above version.

same
Rehearsal, Old Gold show, 2 December 1938

Yesterdays
What Is This Thing
   Called Love?
Have You Forgotten?
   (vDT)
Copenhagen

same
7:00–7:30 p.m. Blue Room, 2 December 1938

| Theme(Nightmare) | HSR139 |
| Out of Nowhere | —, HBCD502 |

Simple and Sweet (vHF)	—, HSR401
Blue Interlude	—, HBCD502
I'll Be with You in Apple Blossom Time (vTP)	—
Theme(Nightmare)	HSR140
Deep in a Dream (vHF)	—
Softly as in a Morning Sunrise	—, HSR401
I Won't Tell a Soul (vHF)	—
Back Bay Shuffle	(unissued)
Theme(Nightmare)	HSR140

same
Old Gold show, 4 December 1938

Yesterdays	JG1001, JHCD1009
What Is This Thing Called Love?	—
Have You Forgotten? (vDT)	(unissued)
Copenhagen	JG1001

NOTE: Issued titles sometimes dated as from the 2 December 1938 rehearsal.

same
12:00–12:30 a.m. Blue Room, 6 December 1938

Theme(Nightmare)	HSR140
If I Had You	—, HBCD502
Thanks for Everything (vHF)	—, HSR401
I Used to Be Color Blind (vTP)	—, HBCD502
Together	—, HSR401
Star Dust	—, —
Who Blew Out the Flame (vHF)	—
The Old Stamping Ground (vTP)	Vic.LPT6000
Copenhagen	(unissued)
Theme(Nightmare)	HSR140

same
Old Gold show, 11 December 1938

It Had to Be You	JG1001
Simple and Sweet	—, JHCD1009, LL15757
I'm Madly in Love with You (vDT)	—, —, —
Rockin' the State (= In the Bottom)	—, —, —

NOTE: All titles on Jazz Guild 1001 also on Phontastic PCD 7609.

same
12:00–12:30 a.m. Blue Room, 13 December 1938

Theme(Nightmare)	(unissued)
Begin the Beguine	Vic.LPT6000
Monday Morning (vHF)	HSR176
The Old Stamping Ground (vTP)	(unissued)
I Can't Believe That You're in Love with Me	HSR176, 401, HBCD502
Any Old Time (vHF)	(unissued)
It Had to Be You	—
Summer Souvenirs (vHF)	—
Shine On Harvest Moon	—
Theme(Closing)	—

same
12:00–12:30 a.m. Blue Room, 14 December 1938

Theme(Nightmare)	(unissued)
I Cover the Waterfront	—
Jeepers Creepers (vTP)	—
They Say (vHF)	—
Ya Got Me	HBCD502
April in My Heart	(unissued)
The Yam	HBCD502
I Won't Tell a Soul (vHF)	(unissued)
Back Bay Shuffle	—
Theme(Nightmare)	Vic.LPT6000

same
"Special short-wave broadcast to Lima, Peru": Blue Room, 14 December 1938

Theme(Nightmare)	Natasha Imports NI4013
Begin the Beguine	—
Deep in a Dream (vHF)	—
Back Bay Shuffle	—
Theme(Closing)	—

same
11:00–11:30 p.m. Blue Room, 15 December 1938

Theme(Nightmare)	(unissued)
Out of Nowhere	—
Prosschai (vTP)	—
I Haven't Changed a Thing (vHF)	HBCD502
Non-Stop Flight	(unissued)
In the Mood	Vic.LPT6000
I Have Eyes (vHF)	(unissued)
The Chant	Vic.LPT6000

Georgie Auld(ts) for Perry; Bob Kitsis(p) for Burness
7:00–7:30 p.m. Blue Room, 16 December 1938

Free Wheeling	ASC-2, J1041, GE15006
Softly as in a Morning Sunrise	—, —
Jungle Drums	—, —

NOTE: All titles also on Big Band Gems BBG094.

same
Rehearsal, Old Gold show, 16 December 1938

My Reverie (vDT)	(unissued)
Just You Just Me	JHCD1009

NOTE: This material allegedly was from Old Gold show rehearsals from about this time (probably the above date). As Georgie Auld can be heard soloing and the drummer sounds like George Wettling, these performances must originate from around this time (see next entry).

same
Old Gold show, 18 December 1938

Ya Got Me	JG1001, JHCD1009, LL15757
My Reverie	(unissued)
In the Mood	JG1001, —

NOTE: The above unissued title may contain a Dick Todd vocal (see preceding entry).

same
1:30–5:30 p.m. New York, 19 December 1938

030731	A Room with a View (vHF)	BB10075, AXM2-5517
030732	Say It with a Kiss (vHF)	BB10079, —
030733	They Say (vHF)	BB10075, —
030734	It Took a Million Years (vHF)	BB10079, —
030735	Jungle Drums	BB10091, —
030736	It Had to Be You	—, —

NOTE: The RCA log sheet shows only one take made for each mx #, except 030731 (two takes, with no indication of which take was used); all takes note "Flowed."

same
12:00–12:30 a.m. Blue Room, 20 December 1938

Theme(Nightmare)	HSR140
Yesterdays	(unissued)
Prosschai (vTP)	—

Between a Kiss and a Sigh (vHF)	HSR140, HBCD502
Just You Just Me	—, HSR401
Just a Kid Named Joe (vTP)	HSR139, —
Let's Stop the Clock (vHF)	HSR140
In the Mood	—, —
Diga Diga Doo	—

same
11:00–11:30 p.m. Blue Room, 22 December 1938

Theme(Nightmare)	(unissued)
Begin the Beguine	—
Jeepers Creepers (vTP)	—
Two Sleepy People (vHF)	HSR176, HBCD502
It Had to Be You	(unissued)
Theme(Nightmare)	—
Theme(Nightmare)	—
Jungle Drums	—
You're a Sweet Little Headache (vHF)	—
I Surrender Dear	—
Copenhagen	—
Theme(Closing)	—

same
7:00–7:30 p.m. Blue Room, 23 December 1938

Theme(Nightmare)	Reader's Digest 056C
Star Dust	Vic.LPT6000, —
Ya Got Me	(unissued)
Thanks for Everything (vHF)	—
Together	Vic.LPT6000

Artie Shaw with Paul Whiteman and His Orchestra
Carnegie Hall, 25 December 1938

Artie Shaw(cl), Bob Cusumano, Charlie Teagarden, Harry Goldfield(tp), Jack Teagarden, Jose Gutierrez, Hal Matthews(tb), Al Gallodoro, Frank Gallodoro, Jack Bell, Art Drelinger, Murray Cohan, Vincent Capone, George Ford, Sal Franzella, Walter Hegner, Harold Feldman(reeds), Al Duffy, Jules Schacter, Maurice Ancher, Kurt Dieterle, Emmanuel Green, Maximillian Pilzer, Harry Struble(violins), Harry Waller, Herb Borodkin(violas), Abraham Borodkin(cello), Frank Signorelli(p), Allan Reuss(g), Norman McPherson(tu), Art Shapiro(b), George Wettling(d)

The Blues	Aircheck LP-l, BOMR71-7715

Artie Shaw and His Orchestra
Old Gold show, 25 December 1938

Chuck Peterson, Bernie Privin, John Best(tp), Harry Rodgers, Les Jenkins, George Arus(tb), Artie Shaw(cl), Les Robinson, Hank Freeman(as), Georgie Auld(ts), Tony Pastor(ts,v), Bob Kitsis(p), Al Avola(g), Sid Weiss(b), Buddy Rich(d), Dick Todd, Helen Forrest(v)

Shine On Harvest Moon	JG1001, JHCD1009
Deep in a Dream (vDT)	(unissued)
Jeepers Creepers (vTP)	JG1003, —
Hold Your Hat	—, LL15757

NOTE: The above and following composition "Hold Your Hat" is *NOT* the same composition as "Hold Your Hats" (29 April 1937), although it has been listed as "Hold Your Hats" on some issues. Part of this arrangement was used in "Table d' Hote" for the film short, *Class in Swing* (c. January 1939).

same
Blue Room, 27 December 1938

Theme(Nightmare)	(unissued)
Out of Nowhere	—
Prosschai (vTP)	—
Between a Kiss and a Sigh (vHF)	—
Non-Stop Flight	—
Deep in a Dream (vHF)	—
Serenade to a Savage	—
Any Old Time (vHF)	—
Hold Your Hat	HBCD502
Theme(Nightmare)	HSR139

same
11:00–11:30 p.m. Blue Room, 29 December 1938

Theme(Nightmare)	(unissued)
I Cover the Waterfront	HSR176, 401, HBCD502
Jeepers Creepers (vTP)	Vic.LPT6000
They Say (vHF)	(unissued)
Softly as in a Morning Sunrise	—
Theme(Nightmare)	—
Theme(Nightmare)	—
Simple and Sweet (vHF)	—
Diga Diga Doo	—
When I Go A–Dreamin' (vHF)	—
Shine On Harvest Moon	—
Theme(Nightmare)	—

NOTE: The second half of this broadcast has circulated with the erroneous date of 1 November 1939, but the announcer clearly states it was from the Blue Room.

same
7:00–7:30 p.m. Blue Room, 30 December 1938

Theme(Nightmare)	FF28-128
Begin the Beguine	—
You're a Sweet Little Headache (vHF)	—, SoS126
The Old Stamping Ground (vTP)	—
What Is This Thing Called Love?	—, —
Jungle Drums	—
It Had to Be You	—, —
Thanks for Everything (vHF)	—, —
Copenhagen	—
Theme(Nightmare)	—

same
Old Gold show, 1 January 1939

I've Been Saving Myself for You	JG1003
They Say (vDT)	(unissued)
Indian Love Call (vTP/ band)	JG1003
Time Out	—, LL15757

NOTE: Shaw reportedly took a week's vacation in Cuba "right after the New Year."

same
Old Gold show, 8 January 1939

Serenade to a Savage	JG1003
My Reverie (vDT)	(unissued)
Softly as in a Morning Sunrise	JG1003
Diga Diga Doo	—, LL15757

same
Paramount Movie Short *Class in Swing*, New York, c. early January 1939

Theme (Nightmare)	ASC-9, J3004
Table d' Hote	—, —
I Have Eyes (vHF)	—, —
Shoot the Likker to Me John Boy	—, —

NOTE: Sound track includes announcer "explaining" the band's performances.

same
7:00–7:30 p.m. Blue Room, 13 January 1939

Serenade to a Savage	ASC-2, Aircheck-11
Any Old Time (vHF)	—

same
Old Gold show, 15 January 1939

Begin the Beguine	JG1003
A Room With a View (vDT)	JHCD1009
My Heart Belongs to Daddy	JG1003
Prosschai (vTP)	—

same
1:00–5:00 p.m. New York, 17 January 1939

031491	Lover Come Back to Me	BB10126, AXM2-5517
031492	My Heart Stood Still	BB10125, —
031493	Rosalie (vTP)	BB10126, —
031494	Supper Time (vHF)	BB10127, —
031495	Vilia	BB10128, —

NOTE: RCA log sheet shows only one take made for each mx #, except 031493 (two takes, with no indication of which take was used); take 1A states "Hold cast" while takes 1 & 2 state "Flowed" (no take 2A was listed).

same
12:00–12:30 a.m. Blue Room, 18 January 1939

Theme(Nightmare)	JHCD1031, SoS126, FTR1501
Rose Room	—, —, ASC-5
Rosalie (vTP)	—, —, ASC-8
Any Old Time (vHF)	—, —, —
My Heart Stood Still	—, —, HSR401
Jungle Drums	—, —, —
This Can't Be Love (vHF)	—, SoS117, —, HBCD502, HSR176, ASC-9
Lover Come Back to Me	—, SoS126, —, —
Copenhagen	—, —, ASC-7
Theme(Nightmare)	—, —, —

NOTE: This broadcast was issued complete on ASC-12 and Joyce J1041.

same
Old Gold show, 22 January 1939

Rose Room	Jazz Hour JHCD1050
My Reverie (vDT)	—
Softly as in a Morning Sunrise	—
Oh Lady Be Good	—

NOTE: JHCD1050 allegedly contains the complete show including Robert Benchley presenting Shaw with the *Down Beat* trophy for "Band of the Year" for winning the polls. This dialogue also appeared on JHCD1009, also introducing "Softly as in a Morning Sunrise" but the performance on that CD was not from this show. It has been reported that JHCD1050 uses performances from other shows to "recreate" this one as well, but this could not be checked.

same
2:00–5:30 p.m. New York, 23 January 1939

031823	Man I Love	128, AXM2-5517
031824	The Donkey Serenade	BB10125, —
031825	Bill (vHF)	BB10124, —
031826	Zigeuner	BB10127, —
031827	Carioca	BB10124, —

NOTE: RCA log sheets indicate only one take made of each mx # except 031826 (two takes, with take 1 marked "Flowed" and take 2 marked "Hold Flowed").

same
Old Gold show, 29 January 1939

Rose Room	JG1003
This Can't Be Love (vDT)	(unissued)
My Own (vHF)	JG1003
At Sundown	—, LL15757

NOTE: The band was reported playing a dance at Syracuse University on 30 January 1939, cited as its "first location away from the Lincoln" in the announcement.

same
1:30–4:45 p.m. New York, 31 January 1939

031864	Alone Together	BB10148, AXM2-5533
031865	Rose Room	—, —
031866	I Want My Share of Love (vHF)	BB10134, —
031867	It's All Yours (vHF)	BB10141, —
031868	This Is It (vHF)	—, —
031869	Delightful Delirium (vTP)	BB10134, —

NOTE: RCA log sheets indicate only one take was made for each mx #. All take 1s were marked "Flowed" and all take 1As marked "Hold Cast."

The band opened at the Strand Theatre in New York City on 3 February 1939.

same
Vitaphone Movie Short *Symphony of Swing*, c. early February 1939

Alone Together	MGM (laserdisc) ML 103 928, ASC-11, J3004

Jeepers Creepers (vTP)   —, —, —
Deep Purple (vHF)   —, —, —
Oh Lady Be Good   —, —, —

NOTE: This film reportedly was done while the band was at the Strand. Some of the visuals are unusual for a band short.

Shaw, trumpeter Bernie Privin, the rhythm section, and possibly others out of the band reportedly recorded an acetate with Lee Wiley at Nola Studios while the band was at the Strand, but no further details have surfaced.

same
Old Gold show, 5 February 1939

Good for Nothin' But   (unissued)
  Love (vDT)
I Have Eyes (vHF)   JG1005
Carioca   —, ASC-2, Aircheck-11,
                             GE15006
Zigeuner   —

same
Old Gold show, 12 February 1939

My Heart Stood Still   JG1005
I'm Coming Virginia   —, ASC-2, Aircheck-11,
                             GE15006
This Is It (vHF)   (unissued)
Alone Together   —

NOTE: Titles from the 5th & 12th on ASC-2 etc. originally were issued misdated as 13 January 1939. The opening chorus of "I'm Coming Virginia" was edited to begin at Shaw's solo on all issues except Jazz Guild 1005, which is complete. "My Heart Stood Still" on Jazz Guild 1005 is distorted by skips and edits.

same
Old Gold show, 19 February 1939

Diga Diga Doo   JG1005
Deep Purple (vHF)   —
You Must Have Been a   JHCD1009
  Beautiful Baby (vDT)
Shoot the Rhythm to Me   JG1005
  John Boy

same
Old Gold show, 26 February 1939

This Can't Be Love   (unissued)
  (vDT)

I Cried for You (vHF)   JG1005, JHCD1009
Back Bay Shuffle   —, —
Together   —

same
Old Gold show, 5 March 1939

Rosalie (vTP)   JG1005
Jungle Drums   —
I Want My Share of Love   —, LL15757
  (vHF)
Non-Stop Flight   JG1007

same
Old Gold show, 12 March 1939

My Heart Belongs to   JG1007
  Daddy
The Chant   —
Double Mellow   —, LL15757

NOTE: Evidently the band went directly from their Old Gold show broadcast to the RCA studios for the following record session.

same
11:30 pm–4:00 a.m. New York, 12 March 1939

032961	Any Old Time (vHF)	Vic.20-1575, AXM2-5533
032962	I'm in Love with the Honorable Mr. So & So (vHF)	BB10188, —
032963	Prosschai (vTP)	—, —
032964	Deep Purple (vHF)	BB10178, —
032965	I'm Coming Virginia	BB10320, —
032966	Pastel Blue	BB10178, —

NOTE: RCA log sheets indicate one take made of each mx #, except 032961 & 032962 (two takes each) with both take 2s marked "Held in N.Y." and "Flowed." 032966 was listed as "Blue Dilemma" with a handwritten note of the title change.

same
1:30–6:00 p.m. New York, 17 March 1939

032999	You Grow Sweeter as the Years Go By (vHF)	BB10195, AXM2-5533
035300	You're So Indifferent (vHF)	BB10215, —
035301	Snug as a Bug in a Rug (vTP)	—, —
035302	If You Ever Change Your Mind (vHF)	BB10195, —

035303	One Night Stand	BB10202, —
035304	One Foot in the Groove	—, —

NOTE: RCA log sheets show only one take of each mx #, with all take 1s marked "Flowed" and all take 1As marked "Hold cast."

same
Old Gold show, 19 March 1939

Better Than the Average Girl (vTP)	JG1007

NOTE: This is the only performance reported from this show.

same
Old Gold show, 26 March 1939

Gangbusters	JG1007, LL15757
Pastel Blue	—, —
It's All Yours	—
Prosschai (vTP)	—

same
Old Gold show, 2 April 1939

One Foot in the Groove	JG1007, JHCD1050
Nightmare	—, —
I'm in Love with the Honorable Mr. So & So (vHF)	—, —
I'm Coming Virginia	—, —

NOTE: Jazz Hour JHCD1050 includes the complete show.

After a cross-country tour the band opened at the Palomar Ballroom in Los Angeles on 19 April 1939. Shaw collapsed on stage during the show and was out of the band for five weeks. Jerry Gray directed the band for the Old Gold show broadcasts, and Tony Pastor fronted the band at the Palomar. Shaw's solo spots were taken primarily by Auld on tenor sax, but some spots were given to other instruments.

omit Shaw
Old Gold show, 23 April 1939

Rosalie (vTP)	JG1009
Serenade to a Savage	—
You're So Indifferent (vHF)	—, LL15757
Copenhagen	—

same
Old Gold show, 7 May 1939

At Sundown	JG1009
Supper Time (vHF)	—
Snug as a Bug in a Rug (vTP)	—
Diga Diga Doo	—, ASC-2, BBG094

same
Old Gold show, 14 May 1939

I'm Coming Virginia	JG1009
Prosschai (vTP)	—
One Foot in the Groove	ASC-2, BBG094

same
Palomar Ballroom, 16 May 1939

Blue Skies	ASC-2, BBG094
Copenhagen	—, —

same
Palomar Ballroom, 19 May 1939

I Ain't Comin'	ASC-2, BBG094
One Night Stand	—, —

add Shaw
Old Gold show, 23 May 1939

Begin the Beguine	JG1009
Shoot the Rhythm To Me John Boy	—
Carioca	—

same
Palomar Ballroom, 28 May 1939

I Ain't Comin'	ASC-12, Aircheck-11, GE15006, LL15757
The Chant	—, ASC-3, —, —, —

same
Old Gold show, 30 May 1939

It Had to Be You	JG1009
Traffic Jam	—

same
2:00–5:30 p.m. Hollywood, 5 June 1939

036237	Octoroon	BB10319, AXM2-5533

036238	I Poured My Heart Into a Song (vHF)	BB10307, —
036239	When Winter Comes (vTP)	—, —
036240	All I Remember Is You (vHF)	BB10319, —
036241	Out of Nowhere	BB10320, —

NOTE: Session held in RCA's Hollywood Recording Studio. The log sheets are very confusing for the 1939 Hollywood sessions. The mx #s indicate (for example) that 2 takes were made for 036237, but only show take 6 FOLLOWED by take 5; 036238 shows only take 4 followed by take 3; one take each for 036239 and 036240 but labelled take 7 and take 1 respectively; and 036241 shows take 3 followed by take 1. John Harding has explained that he believes the "biscuits" used as masters had independent numbers having no relationship to the actual recording activity.

same
Old Gold show, 6 June 1939

Blue Skies	(unissued)
Octoroon	—
Don't Worry 'Bout Me (vHF)	—

same
Palomar Ballroom, 10 June 1939

Shoot the Rhythm to Me John Boy	ASC-2, Aircheck-11, GE15006
One Night Stand	—, ASC-6, ASC-12
Begin the Beguine (part/ into Theme)	—

same
1:00–6:30 p.m. Hollywood, 12 June 1939

036264	I Can't Afford to Dream (vTP)	BB10324, AXM2-5533
036265	Comes Love (vHF)	—, —
036266	Go Fly a Kite (vTP)	BB10347, —
036267	A Man and His Dream (vHF)	—, —
036268	Traffic Jam	BB10385, —
036269	Serenade to a Savage	AXM2-5580

NOTE: (see "NOTE" for 5 June session); it appears that two takes each were made of 036264, 036265, & 036268, and one take each of the others. The RCA log sheet indicated that 036269 was remade on the 22nd (see below).

same
Old Gold show, 13 June 1939

Zigeuner	(unissued)
Comes Love (vHF)	—
When Winter Comes (vTP)	—
One Night Stand	—

same
Old Gold show, 20 June 1939

Together	(issued)
Show Your Linen Miss Richardson (vTP)	—
Non-Stop Flight	—

same
1:30–4:30 p.m. Hollywood, 22 June 1939

036269	Serenade to a Savage	BB10385, AXM2-5533
036291	Easy to Say (vHF)	BB10345, —
036292	I'll Remember (vHF)	—, —
036293	Moonray (vHF)	BB10334, —
036294	Melancholy Mood (vHF)	—, —

NOTE: (see 5 June); one take of mx #s 036291 & 036293; two takes of the others.

same
Old Gold show, 27 June 1939

I Never Knew Heaven Could Speak (vHF)	(unissued)
Copenhagen	JHCD1009

NOTE: Shaw could not play on the above date due to a tonsillectomy, according to the announcer, who presented him with the *Radio Guide* award for "Best Swing Band" on this show. This dialogue is also on JHCD1009.

same
Old Gold show, 4 July 1939

unknown titles	(unissued)

NOTE: *Down Beat* reported that Robert Benchley would be taking a thirteen-week holiday from the Old Gold shows, leaving Shaw and his band more room, starting on 4 July. However, transcriptions and data on this show and subsequent Old Gold shows have not surfaced as consistently as earlier shows in this series.

same

MGM Film *Dancing Co-ed*: Hollywood, 12–31 July 1939

Theme(Nightmare)	(film sound track)
Non-Stop Flight	—
Stars & Stripes Forever	—
(untitled instrumental)	—
Traffic Jam	—
I'm Coming Virginia	—
Double Mellow	—
Jungle Drums	—
Gangbusters	—
Back Bay Shuffle	
One Foot in the Groove	

same

3 July 1939

I'm Yours	Rhino CD R2 72721
Donkey Serenade	—

same

4 July 1939

At Sundown	—

NOTE: All titles on movie sound track incomplete and serve as background to dialogue and action but "Traffic Jam" is complete on a promotional clip. Shaw not heard in the sound track on "I'm Coming Virginia" or "Double Mellow." The untitled instrumental (no melody played) is by Shaw and rhythm section only. Latter five titles not used in available copies of the film; last three titles issued on Rhino with dates shown. It was erroneously reported in several sources that this film was made by Warner Bros. After filming and a cross-country tour the band opened at the Summer Terrace of the Ritz-Carlton Hotel in Boston on 18 August 1939.

same

Summer Terrace, 19 August 1939

Theme(Nightmare)	HSR148, HBCD502
Rose Room	—, HSR401
Go Fly a Kite (vTP)	—, —
Comes Love (vHF)	(unissued)
Donkey Serenade	—
Moonray (vHF)	—
One Foot in the Groove	—
Don't Worry 'Bout Me (vHF)	HSR148, —

Carioca	—, Vic.LPT6000
Theme(Nightmare)	—

NOTE: According to Ken Seavor in his "Artie Shaw—The Sustaining Broadcasts 1938 to 1939" (*In Tune*, [undated], p. 337), the recording of the above version of "Moonray" was interrupted in changing the transcription discs during the initial recording, and Hindsight substituted the version from 19 October in programming HSR148 and HBCD502. Similarly, "Comes Love" from 20 October was used in the above sequence for these issues.

same

Old Gold show, 22 August 1939

Theme(Nightmare)	J1010, Aircheck-11, ASC-11
Donkey Serenade	—, —, —
The Lamp Is Low (vHF)	—, —, LL15757
Octoroon	—, —, —

Harry Geller(tp) for Best 12:00–4:00 p.m. New York, 27 August 1939

042605	Put That Down in Writing (vTP)	BB10406, AXM2-5556
042606	Day In Day Out (vHF)	—, —
042607	Two Blind Loves (vHF)	BB10412, —
042608	The Last Two Weeks in July (vHF)	—, —
042609	Oh Lady Be Good	BB10430, —
042610	I Surrender Dear	—, —

NOTE: RCA log sheets show only one take was made of each mx #, with all take 1s marked "Fld." and all take 1As marked "Hold Cast."

same

Summer Terrace, 31 August 1939

Copenhagen	(unissued)
Theme(Nightmare)	—

NOTE: Available copies of this broadcast excerpt have a clipped beginning on "Copenhagen."

same

Old Gold show, 19 September 1939

Lover Come Back to Me	ASC-9
Man from Mars	Aircheck-11

add the King Sisters: Alyce, Louise, Donna, Yvonne(v), with Shaw & rhythm section only; Kitsis played celeste; same show.

Volga Boat Song (vKS)   J1041, ASG5

NOTE: This "Volga Boat Song" performance also has erroneously been attributed to the Andrews Sisters from a *Saturday Night Swing Club* show, and was falsely issued as a Gramercy 5 item on ASG5.

same
Old Gold show, 26 September 1939

Them There Eyes (vTP)   Aircheck-11, ASC-6

same
11:00–1:00 p.m. New York, 28 September 1939

042755	Many Dreams Ago (vHF)	BB10446, AXM2-5556
042756	A Table in a Corner (vHF)	BB10468, —
042757	If What You Say Is True (vTP)	BB10446, —
042758	Without a Dream to My Name (vHF)	BB10468, —

NOTE: RCA log sheets indicate one take each made of 042755 & 042758, and two takes for each of the others, but noted "compressor loss cut position" for both take 2 items. There also was a note stating "Flowed waxes are 'wide Range' " [*sic*].

Shaw's final appearance on the Old Gold show was 3 October 1939. Band opened at the Cafe Rouge of the Hotel Pennsylvania in New York City on 19 October 1939.

same
Cafe Rouge, 19 October 1939

Theme(Nightmare)	HSR148
Out of Nowhere	(unissued)
Put That Down in Writing (vTP)	HSR148, HBCD502
Many Dreams Ago (vHF)	—
What Is This Thing Called Love?	(unissued)
Day In Day Out (vHF)	HSR148, —
One Foot in the Groove	—, —
Moonray (vHF)	—, —
St. Louis Blues	—, —
Theme(Nightmare)	—

NOTE: According to Ken Seavor's listing, "Out of Nowhere" from 28 October was used in place of the above version on HSR148.

same
Cafe Rouge, 20 October 1939

Theme(Nightmare)	HSR149
You're Mine You	(unissued)
You're a Lucky Guy (vTP)	HSR149, HBCD502
Comes Love (vHF)	HSR148, —
I'm Coming Virginia	HSR149, —
Moonray (vHF)	(unissued)
Everything Is Jumpin'	Vic.LPT6000
A Table in a Corner (vHF)	HSR149
Copenhagen	(unissued)
Theme(Nightmare)	—

NOTE: According to Ken Seavor's listing, the performance of "You're Mine You" used on HSR149 in the above sequence was from the 4 November 1939 broadcast.

same
Cafe Rouge, 21 October 1939

Theme(Nightmare)	HSR149
Yesterdays	—, HBCD502
I'm Sorry for Myself (vTP)	—, Vic.LPT6000
Melancholy Lullaby (vHF)	(unissued)
Traffic Jam	HSR149, HBCD502
Two Blind Loves (vHF)	(unissued)
My Heart Stood Still	HSR149, —
Moonray (vHF)	(unissued)
Man from Mars	—
Theme(Nightmare)	—

NOTE: According to Ken Seavor's listing, the performances of "Melancholy Lullaby," "Man From Mars," and the closing "Theme" used for HSR149 in the above sequences were from 28 October 1939.

same
Cafe Rouge, 25 October 1939

Theme(Nightmare)	(unissued)
I'm Yours	—
Oh You Crazy Moon (vTP)	HSR176, HBCD502
Many Dreams Ago (vHF)	(unissued)
At Sundown	Vic.LPT6000
A Table in the Corner (vHF)	(unissued)
Maria My Own	Vic.LPT6000
Moonray (vHF)	(unissued)
Everything is Jumpin'	—
Theme(Nightmare)	—

same

1:30–3:45 p.m. New York, 26 October 1939

043316	Love Is Here (vHF)	BB10482, AXM2-5556
043317	All in Fun (vHF)	BB10492, —
043318	All the Things You Are (vHF)	—, —
043319	You're a Lucky Guy (vTP)	BB10482, —

NOTE: RCA log sheets show only one take each except for mx # 043319 (two takes, with take 2 marked "Hold in N.Y." and "Flowed").

same

Cafe Rouge, 26 October 1939

Theme(Nightmare)	(unissued)
You're Mine You	—
I've Got My Eyes on You (vHF)	Vic.LPT6000
Got the Mis'ry (vTP)	HBCD502
Sweet Sue	Vic.LPT6000
Moonray (vHF)	(unissued)
One Foot in the Groove	—
Day In Day Out (vHF)	—
Back Bay Shuffle	HBCD502
Theme(Nightmare)	(unissued)

same

Cafe Rouge, 28 October 1939

Theme(Nightmare)	(unissued)
Out of Nowhere	HSR148
I Can't Give You Anything But Love (vTP)	HSR176, 401, HBCD502
The Last Two Weeks in July (vHF)	HSR149
The Donkey Serenade	(unissued)
Moonray (vHF)	Vic.LPT6000
Man from Mars	—, HSR149, —
Melancholy Lullaby (vHF)	—, —
St. Louis Blues	—
Theme(Nightmare)	—, —

same

Cafe Rouge, 1 November 1939

(unknown titles)

NOTE: This broadcast is reported to exist (information from John Harding). However, known dubs circulating with this date are of a Blue Room broadcast apparently from 29 December 1938.

Dave Barbour(g) for Avola

Cafe Rouge, 3 November 1939

Theme(Nightmare)	JHCD1031
I'm Yours	—, HSR176, 401, HBCD502
El Rancho Grande (vTP)	—, Vic.LPT6000
What's New? (vHF)	—, HSR176, 401, —
Man from Mars	—
Any Old Time (vHF)	—
It Had to Be You	—
Melancholy Lullaby (vHF)	—
St. Louis Blues	—
Theme(Nightmare)	—

same

Cafe Rouge, 4 November 1939

Theme(Nightmare)	(unissued)
You're Mine You	HBCD502, HSR149
If What You Say Is True	—
Over the Rainbow (vHF)	—, HSR176
Sweet Sue	—, —
Last Night (vHF)	—
Maria My Own	—
Any Old Time (vHF)	—
Back Bay Shuffle	Jazz Hour JHCD1031
Theme(Nightmare)	(unissued)

same

1:30–4:00 p.m. New York, 9 November 1939

043367-1	Shadows	BB10502, AXM2-5580
043367-2	Shadows	CAL908, AXM2-5556
043368-1	I Didn't Know What Time It Was (vHF)	BB10502, —
043369-?	Do I Love You (vHF)	BB10509, —
043370-1	When Love Beckoned (vHF)	—, —

NOTE: The versions of "Shadows" listed disagrees with the liner notes to the RCA albums *The Complete Artie Shaw*, but agrees with the music on the records; the log sheet shows takes 1A & 2A marked "Hold cast" and takes 1 & 2 marked "Flowed." The log sheet also shows a take 2 for mx #043369; take 1A is marked "Hold cast" while takes 1 & 2 were marked "Flowed," with no indication of which take was used for processing (there was no take 2A listed).

same

Cafe Rouge, 10 November 1939

Theme(Nightmare)	SoS126
You're Mine You	—, ASC-11

Oh You Crazy Moon (vTP)	—, ASC-3
Many Dreams Ago (vHF)	(unissued)
Serenade to a Savage	SoS126, ASC-11
Day In Day Out (vHF)	—
One Foot in the Groove	—
Moonray (vHF)	(unissued)
Copenhagen	—
Theme(Nightmare)	—

same
Cafe Rouge, 11 November 1939

Theme(Nightmare)	(unissued)
I'm Yours	—
Diga Diga Doo	Vic.LPT6000
Lilacs in the Rain (vHF)	HSR149, HBCD502
My Blue Heaven	Vic.LPT6000
Moonray (vHF)	(unissued)
Everything Is Jumpin'	HSR176, —
I Didn't Know What Time It Was (vHF)	—
El Rancho Grande (vTP)	(unissued)
Theme(Nightmare)	—

NOTE: Several titles were issued on Victor LPT6000 and by Hindsight Records dated 28 November 1939, but Shaw walked out on the band at about 11 p.m. on the night of 14/15 November 1939. Presumably the original air check disc was mislabeled. Ken Seavor has suggested the correct date for those items was 28 October 1939, but other suggestions have included 1, 2, or 8 November 1939.

PART IV: ARTIE SHAW AND HIS ORCHESTRAS WITH STRINGS 1940–42

Artie Shaw and His Orchestra
8:00 p.m.–1:15 a.m. Hollywood, 3–4 March 1940

Manny Klein, George Thow, Charlie Margulis(tp), Randall Miller, Bill Rank, Babe Bowman(tb), Artie Shaw(cl), Blake Reynolds, Bud Carleton(as), Jack Stacy, Dick Clark(ts), Joe Krechter(bcl), Martin Ruderman(fl), Phil Nemoli(oboe), John Cave(Fh), Mark Levant, Harry Bluestone, Peter Eisenberg, Robert Barene, Sid Brokaw, Dave Cracov, Jerry Joyce, Alex Law(vl), David Sterkin, Jack Ray, Stanley Spiegelman(vla), Irving Lipschultz, Julius Tannebaum(cel), Stanley Wrightsman(p), Bobby Sherwood(g), Jud DeNaut(b), Carl Maus(d), Pauline Byrne(v)

042546-1	Frenesi	Vic.26542, AXM2-5556
042547-1	Adios Marquita Linda	—, —
042548-1	Gloomy Sunday (vPB)	Vic.26563, —
042549-1	My Fantasy (vPB)	Vic.26614, —

| 042550-1 | A Deserted Farm | — |
| 042551-1 | Don't Fall Asleep (vPB) | Vic.26563, — |

NOTE: All arrangements by William Grant Still with Artie Shaw, except Still scored "A Deserted Farm," which contains no improvisation, and was not issued initially due to inability to obtain permission from MacDowell's estate. RCA log sheets show two takes made for each mx # and the take 2 mx's held. No alternates have surfaced at this writing. Personnel from Musicians' Union Local 47 files.

Art Shaw and His Orchestra
10:00 p.m.–2:15 a.m. Hollywood, 13–14 May 1940

Harry Geller, Manny Klein, George Thow(tp), Artie Shaw(cl), Ben Kanter, Lyall Bowen(as), Jack Stacy, Harold Lawson(ts), Joe Krechter(bcl), John Cave(Fh), Sid Brokaw, Harry Bluestone, Bill Brower, Bob Morrow, Jerry Joyce, Mischa Russell(vl), David Sterkin, Sam Freed(vla), Cy Bernard(cel), Skitch Henderson(p), Bobby Sherwood(g), Jud DeNaut(b), Spencer Prinz(d), Martha Tilton, Jack Pearce(v)

049687-1	Dreaming Out Loud (vMT)	Vic.26642, AXM2-5556
049688-1	Now We Know (vMT)	—, —
049689-1	Mister Meadowlark (vJP)	Vic.26614, —
049690-1	April in Paris	Vic.26654, —
049691-1	King for a Day	—, —

NOTE: RCA log sheets show two takes made for each mx # and the take 2 mx's held. The March and May sessions were with studio musicians, not regular orchestras. No alternates have surfaced at this writing. Personnel from union files.

Shaw formed a new orchestra in June 1940 that starred on the *Burns and Allen Show* broadcasting weekly starting 1 July 1940, and appeared in the Paramount feature film *Second Chorus*, produced by Borros Morros, starring Fred Astaire, Paulette Goddard, and Burgess Meredeth. Shaw has stated the personnel for his new orchestra essentially was in place by the first *Burns and Allen Show* (2).

Art Shaw and His Orchestra
***Burns and Allen Show*, 1 July 1940**

probably: Billy Butterfield, Jack Cathcart, George Wendt(tp), Bruce Squires, Elmer Smithers, Vernon Brown(tb), Artie Shaw(cl), Les Robinson, Neely Plumb(as), Bus Bassey, Jerry Jerome(ts), Mischa Russell, Sid Brokaw, Bill Brower, Bob Morrow, Alex Beller, 1 unk.(vl), Harry Rumpler, Sam Freed(vla), 1 unk.(cel), Johnny Guarnieri(p), Al Hendrickson(g), Jud DeNaut(b), Nick Fatool(d)

| Frenesi | Hep CD19 |

same
Burns and Allen Show, **8 July 1940**

Alice Blue Gown	Hep CD19

same
Burns and Allen Show, **15 July 1940**

(unknown title)	unissued

same
Burns and Allen Show, **22 July 1940**

(unknown title)	unissued

omit strings
Paramount Movie *Second Chorus*, **26/27/29 July 1940**

NOTE: Local Union 47 files show recording sessions for this film on 26, 27, and 29 July, with Bobby Hackett(tp) added; Hackett and Butterfield played trumpets on the sound track for Astaire and Meredith in scenes showing them playing, but Shaw did not play in those sequences.

add strings
Burns and Allen Show, **29 July 1940**

Temptation	Hep CD19

same
Burns and Allen Show, **5 August 1940**

Sweet Sue	Hep CD19

similar
Paramount Movie *Second Chorus*, **10 August 1940**

NOTE: Additional French horns and woodwinds appeared at this recording session, which probably was for Fred Astaire's final dance sequence with a larger orchestra, which did not include Shaw.

same
Burns and Allen Show, **12 August 1940**

Frenesi	Hep CD19

add Louis Feiler, Mischa Levienne, Sol Kindler, Julian Brodetsky(vl); Sam Noble, Ovady Julber(vla) for Freed; Karl Rossner, Bob Sevely(cel); Charles Hutchinson(g) for Hendrickson
8:00–11:05 p.m. Paramount Movie *Second Chorus*, **16 August 1940**

Concerto for Clarinet [4:40]	AFRS BML, Hep CD19
Concerto for Clarinet [3:25]	HSLP-404, ASC-7, J3004
(unknown title—excerpt)	—

NOTE: Since the 1980s the entire film has been available on several home video issues, but some video issues omit the 3:25 "Concerto" used in the soundtrack.

same
Burns and Allen Show, **19 August 1940**

King for a Day	Hep CD19

omit Smithers, strings; add Fred Astaire(v)
9:00 p.m.–1:00 a.m. Paramount Movie *Second Chorus*, **25–26 August, 1940**

Opening Theme	HSLP-404, ASC-7
Everything is Jumpin'	—, J3004
Love of My Life (vFA)	—
Double Mellow	—

NOTE: From available data, this seems the most likely of sessions listed by the union for the above recordings to have occurred; union files do not indicate what actually was recorded at recording sessions for *Second Chorus*. There were additional numbers in this film not including Shaw.

add strings
Burns and Allen Show, **26 August 1940**

Out of Nowhere	Hep CD19

same
Burns and Allen Show, **2 September 1940**

Jungle Drums	Hep CD19

Artie Shaw and His Gramercy 5
8:00–12:00 p.m. Hollywood, 3 September 1940

Billy Butterfield(tp), Artie Shaw(cl), Johnny Guarnieri(harpsichord), Al Hendrickson(g), Jud DeNaut(b), Nick Fatool(d)

055061-1	Special Delivery Stomp	Vic.26762, AXM2-5556, CD7637-2-RB
055062-1	Summit Ridge Drive	Vic.26763, —, —
055063-1	Keepin' Myself for You	Vic.26762, —, —
055064-1	Cross Your Heart	Vic.26763, AXM2-5572, —

NOTE: RCA log sheets show only one take of each mx # was made.

Art Shaw and His Orchestra
9:00 p.m.–12:45 a.m. Hollywood, 7–8 September 1940

George Wendt, Jack Cathcart, Billy Butterfield(tp), Jack Jenney, Vernon Brown(tb), Artie Shaw(cl), Les Robinson, Neely Plumb(as), Jerry Jerome, Bus Bassey(ts), Truman Boardman, Ted Klages, Bill Brower, Bob Morrow, Alex Beller, Eugene Lamas(vl), Al Harshman, Keith Collins(vla), Fred Goerner(cel), Johnny Guarnieri(p), Al Hendrickson(g), Jud DeNaut(b), Nick Fatool(d), Anita Boyer(v)

055067-1	If It's You (vAB)	Vic.26760, AXM2-5572
055068-1	Old Old Castle in Scotland (vAB)	—, —
055069-1	Temptation	Vic.27230, —
055070-1	Chantez Les Bas	Vic.27354, —

NOTE: Last title co-arranged by Shaw and William Grant Still. RCA log sheets show only one take of each mx #, except 055067 (two takes, holding take 2).

same
***Burns and Allen Show*, 9 September 1940**

| Begin the Beguine | Hep CD55 |

The orchestra opened at the Palace Hotel, San Francisco, on 12 September 1940.

same
***Burns and Allen Show*, 16 September 1940**

| Rose Room | Hep CD55 |

same
***Burns and Allen Show*, 23 September 1940**

| My Romance | Hep CD55 |

same
***Burns and Allen Show*, 30 September 1940**

| My Heart Stood Still | Hep CD55 |

same
***Burns and Allen Show*, 7 October 1940**

| Through the Years | Hep CD55 |

same
9:30 p.m.–12:45 a.m. Hollywood, 7–8 October 1940

055095-1	Love of My Life (vAB)	Vic.26790, AXM2-5572
055096-1	A Handful of Stars (vAB)	—, —
055097-1	Star Dust	Vic.27230, —
055098-1	Marinella	Vic.27362, —
055099-1	Danza Lucumi	Vic.27354, —

NOTE: Last two titles coarranged by Shaw and William Grant Still. RCA log sheets indicated only one take was made of each mx #.

same
***Burns and Allen Show*, 14 October 1940**

| Star Dust | Hep CD55 |

same
***Burns and Allen Show*, 21 October 1940**

| Temptation | Hep CD55 |

same
Palace Hotel, 26 October 1940

Looking for Yesterday (vAB)	Aircheck-11, ASC-6, Hep-19, CD19
Everything Is Jumpin'	—, —, —, —
Along the Santa Fe Trail (vAB)	—, —, —, —

NOTE: Some sources state a version of "Star Dust" also was on this broadcast.

same
***Burns and Allen Show*, 28 October 1940**

| Love of My Life (vAB) | Hep CD55 |

same
***Burns and Allen Show*, 4 November 1940**

| Blues (from Lenox Avenue Suite) | Hep CD55 |

same
***Burns and Allen Show*, 11 November 1940**

    Prelude in C Major   Hep CD55

same
***Burns and Allen Show*, 18 November 1940**

    Sugar   Hep CD55

same
***Burns and Allen Show*, 25 November 1940**

    What Is There to Say?   Hep CD55

same
***Burns and Allen Show*, 2 December 1940**

    Diga Diga Doo ASC-5,   Hep CD55

same
1:00–4:00 p.m. Hollywood, 3 December 1940

055184	This Is Romance	Vic.27343, AXM2-5572
055185-1	What Is There to Say?	Vic.27432, —
055185-2	What Is There to Say?	AXM2-5580
055186	Pyramid	Vic.27343, —
055187	You Forgot About Me (vAB)	Vic.27236, —
055188	Whispers in the Night (vAB)	—, —

NOTE: The original RCA log sheet shows only one take of each mx #; however, an added sheet headed "re-recording" (*NOT* "re-made") and dated 5 December 1940 listed each mx # as take 2 (with identical timings). These probably were studio transfers from the original masters: 055185-2 probably was from a test pressing.

same
2:00–5:15 p.m. Hollywood, 4 December 1940

055191	Blues (from Lenox Avenue Suite), Part 1	Vic.27411, AXM2-5572
055192	Blues (from Lenox Avenue Suite), Part 2	—, —
055193-1	Who's Excited?	Vic.27385, —
055193-2	Who's Excited?	AXM2-5580
055194-1	Prelude in C Major	Vic.27432, —
055194-2	Prelude in C Major	AXM2-5580

NOTE: "Blues" (from William Grant Still's "Lenox Avenue Suite") coarranged by Shaw and Still. The original

RCA log sheet shows only one take of each mx # but a "corrected log sheet" (otherwise identical) is also in the file that cited only take 3 for mx #s 055191 & 055192, and only take 2 for 055193 & 055194.

Art Shaw and His Orchestra
2:00–6:00 p.m. Hollywood, 5 December 1940

Billy Butterfield(tp), Artie Shaw(cl), Johnny Guarnieri(harpsichord), Al Hendrickson(g), Jud DeNaut(b), Nick Fatool(d)

055195-1	Dr. Livingstone, I Presume?	Vic.27289, AXM2-5572
055196-1	When the Quail Come Back to San Quentin	—, —
055197-1	My Blue Heaven	Vic.27432, —
055198-1	Smoke Gets In Your Eyes	Vic.27335, —

NOTE: All titles also on RCA CD 7637-2-RB. RCA log sheets show only one take of each mx # was made.

Art Shaw and His Orchestra
***Burns and Allen Show*, 9 December 1940**

George Wendt, Jack Cathcart, Billy Butterfield(tp), Jack Jenney, Vernon Brown(tb), Artie Shaw(cl), Les Robinson, Neely Plumb(as), Jerry Jerome, Bus Bassey(ts), Truman Boardman, Ted Klages, Bill Brower, Bob Morrow, Alex Beller, Eugene Lamas(vl), Al Harshman, Keith Collins(vla), Fred Goerner(cel), Johnny Guarnieri(p), Al Hendrickson(g), Jud DeNaut(b), Nick Fatool(d), Anita Boyer(v)

    Yesterdays   Hep CD55

Orchestra opened at the Hollywood Palladium on 12 December 1940, and broadcast regularly until closing on 22 January 1941.

same
***Burns and Allen Show*, 16 December 1940**

    Dancing in the Dark   Hep CD55

add Ray Conniff(tb)
1:30–5:00 p.m. Hollywood, 17 December 1940

055224-1	The Calypso (vAB)	Vic.27315, AXM2-5572
055225-1	Beau Night in Hotchkiss Corners (vAB)	—, —

055226-1	Concerto for Clarinet, Part 1	Vic.36385, —
055227-1	Concerto for Clarinet, Part 2	—, —

NOTE: RCA log sheets show only one take of each mx # was made.

same
Burns and Allen Show, **23 December 1940**

(unknown title)	unissued

same
Burns and Allen Show, **30 December 1940**

(unknown title)	unissued

same
Burns and Allen Show, **6 January 1941**

There'll Be Some Changes Made	ASC-3, Hep CD55

same
Burns and Allen Show, **13 January 1941**

Nobody Knows the Trouble I've Seen	ASC-8, Hep CD55

same
Burns and Allen Show, **20 January 1941**

Jungle Drums	ASC-9, Hep CD55

same
[Gramercy 5 as above = (G5)] Hollywood Palladium, 21 January 1941

Alice Blue Gown	(unissued)
Do You Know Why? (vAB)	Hep-l9
Cross Your Heart (G5)	(unissued)

same
Hollywood Palladium, 22 January 1941

Frenesi	Hep-19, CD19
Whispers in the Night (vAB)	—, —

Jungle Drums (as Canto Karabali)	—, —
There I Go (vAB)	—, —
Prelude in C Major	—, —
Dr. Livingstone, I Presume? (G5)	—, —
Nobody Knows the Trouble I've Seen	—, —

NOTE: This was the orchestra's final night at the Palladium. Following the next day's Victor record date, Shaw left the West Coast for New York City (relocating with the *Burns and Allen Show* in time for their next broadcast), but some personnel chose to remain behind and were replaced by New York musicians.

Clyde Hurley(tp) for Cathcart
1:30–5:00 p.m. Hollywood, 23 January 1941

055256-1	Dancing in the Dark	Vic.27335, AXM2-5572
055257-1	I Cover the Waterfront	Vic.27362, —
055258-1	Moonglow	Vic.27405, —
055259-1	Alone Together	Vic.27385, —

NOTE: RCA log sheets show only one take for each mx # was made.

Art Shaw and His Orchestra
Burns and Allen Show, **27 January 1941**

Billy Butterfield, Lee Castle, Bernie Privin(tp), Jack Jenney, Vernon Brown, Ray Conniff(tb), Artie Shaw(cl), Les Robinson, Toots Mondello(as), Jerry Jerome, Bus Bassey(ts), Kurt Dieterle, Truman Boardman, Leo Pevsner, Leo Kahn, Dave Kahn, Dave Herman(vl), Bernard Ocko, Keith Collins(vla), Fred Goerner(cel), Johnny Guarnieri(p), Sam Herman(g), Ed McKinney(b), Nick Fatool(d)

Rockin' Chair	Hep CD55

NOTE: The above New York personnel is as cited on Hep CD55.

same
Burns and Allen Show, **3 February 1941**

Georgia on My Mind	Hep CD55

same
Burns and Allen Show, **10 February 1941**

There'll Be Some Changes Made	unissued

same
Burns and Allen Show, **17 February 1941**

    Deep River   Hep CD55

same
Burns and Allen Show, **24 February 1941**

    Sometimes I Feel Like a   Hep CD55
    Motherless Child

same
Burns and Allen Show, **3 March 1941**

    Little Gate's Special   ASC-4, Hep CD55

same
Burns and Allen Show, **10 March 1941**

    Swing Low Sweet   Hep CD55
    Chariot

same
Burns and Allen Show, **17 March 1941**

    (unknown title)   unissued

NOTE: The unissued material from the *Burns and Allen Show* broadcasts cited throughout reportedly exist.

same
12:00–3:30 a.m. New York, 20 March 1941

062767-1	If I Had You	Vic.27536, AXM2-5572
062768-1	Georgia on My Mind	Vic.27499, AXM2-5576
062769-1	Why Shouldn't I?	—, —
062770-1	It Had to Be You	Vic.27536, —

NOTE: RCA log sheets show only one take of each mx #, except 062769 (two takes, with take 2 held).

same
Burns and Allen Show, **24 March 1941**

    To a Broadway Rose   Hep CD55

Artie Shaw and His Gramercy 5
unknown location, c. September 1940–March 1941

Billy Butterfield(tp), Artie Shaw(cl), Johnny Guarnieri(harpsichord), Al Hendrickson(g), Jud DeNaut(b), Nick Fatool(d)

    No Name Blues   ASG5

NOTE: Various sources and dates have been circulated concerning this broadcast. It has not been possible to be certain of its exact source. There were many undocumented broadcasts from the orchestra's two locations and from the *Burns and Allen Show* during the above indicated period of the band's existence.

After completing the *Burns and Allen Show* on 24 March 1941, Shaw disbanded.

Artie Shaw and His Orchestra
1:30–6:00 p.m. New York, 26 June 1941

Henry "Red" Allen(tp), J. C. Higginbotham(tb), Artie Shaw(cl), Benny Carter(as), Leo Krusczak, Kurt Dieterle, Max Silverman, Sergei Kotlarsky, Louis Edlin, Lee Kahn, Harry Urbant, Dave Norman(vl), Bernard Ocko, Sol Deutsch(vla), Lucien Schmidt, Abe Borodin(cel), Sonny White(p), Jimmy Shirley(g), Laura Newell(harp), Billy Taylor, Fred Zimmerman(b), Shep Shepherd(d), Lena Horne(v)

066146-1	Confessin'	CAL584, AXM2-5576
066147-1	Love Me a Little Little (vLH)	Vic.27509, —
066148-1	Beyond the Blue Horizon	—
066149-1	Don't Take Your Love from Me (vLH)	—, —

NOTE: This was a studio session with arrangements by Shaw. RCA log sheets show only one take of each mx # was made.

Shaw began rehearsing a new orchestra with strings during August 1941.

Artie Shaw and His Orchestra
6:30 p.m.–12:30 a.m. New York, 2–3 September 1941

Oran "Hot Lips" Page(tp,v), Steve Lipkins, Max Kaminsky, Lee Castle(tp), Jack Jenney, Ray Conniff, Morey Samuels(tb), Artie Shaw(cl), Les Robinson, Charlie DiMaggio(as), Georgie Auld, Mickey Folus(ts), Artie Baker(bari), Leo Persner, Bernard Tinterow, Raoul Poliakine, Leonard Posner, Max Berman, Irving Raymond, Bill Ehrenkranz, Alex Beller, Truman Boardman(vl), Morris Kohn, Sam Rosenblum, Leonard Atkins(vla), George Taliarkin, Fred Goerner, Ed Sodero(cel), Johnny Guarnieri(p), Mike Bryan(g), Ed McKinney(b), Dave Tough(d), Bonnie Lake(v)

067735-1	This Time the Dream's on Me (vBL)	(unissued)
067735-2	This Time the Dream's on Me (vBL)	Vic.27609, AXM2-5576
067736-1	Blues in the Night (vLP)	(unissued)
067736-2	Blues in the Night (vLP)	Vic.27609, —
067737-1	Nocturne	Vic.27703, —

67738-1	Rockin' Chair	Vic.27664, —
067739-1	Through the Years	Vic.27703, —
067740-1	If I Love Again	Vic.27664, —

NOTE: All titles arranged by Shaw or co-arranged by Shaw with Lennie Hayton except 067736, arranged by Bill Challis, and 067737, arranged by Jerry Sears. RCA log sheets show only one take of each mx #, except 067735 & 067736 (two takes each) with the note that Shaw preferred "take 2" of 067736. The unissued takes have been reviewed and show significant variations in Shaw's solos. The issued takes generally were slightly more forcefully delivered, as if the earlier take was a warm-up performance.

Art Shaw and His Orchestra
3:30–7:00 p.m. New York, 3 September 1941

Lee Castle(tp), Ray Conniff(tb), Artie Shaw(cl), Les Robinson(as), Georgie Auld(ts), Leo Persner, Bernard Tinterow, Raoul Poliakine, Leonard Posner, Max Berman, Irving Raymond, Bill Ehrenkranz, Alex Beller, Truman Boardman(vl), Morris Kohn, Sam Rosenblum, Leonard Atkins(vla), George Taliarkin, Fred Goerner, Ed Sodero(cel), Johnny Guarnieri(p), Mike Bryan(g), Ed McKinney(b), Dave Tough(d)

066148-2	Beyond the Blue Horizon	Vic.27641, AXM2-5576
067747-1	Is It Taboo?	—, —
067747-2	Is It Taboo?	(unissued)
067748-1	I Ask the Stars	Vic.27719, —

NOTE: Arrangements by Artie Shaw. RCA log sheets show two takes of each mx # were made with the second takes held; 066148 was a remake from the 26 June session. 067747 was listed on the log sheet as "Swing By Any Other Name"; the unissued take listed has been reviewed and is an excellent performance with variations in solos (particularly Shaw's) evident. It is not known if the other unissued takes still exist.

Art Shaw and His Orchestra
Steel Pier, Atlantic City, 6 September 1941

Oran "Hot Lips" Page(tp,v), Steve Lipkins, Max Kaminsky, Lee Castle(tp), Jack Jenney, Ray Conniff, Morey Samuels(tb), Artie Shaw(cl), Les Robinson, Charlie DiMaggio(as), Georgie Auld, Mickey Folus(ts), Artie Baker(bari), Leo Persner, Bernard Tinterow, Raoul Poliakine, Leonard Posner, Max Berman, Irving Raymond, Bill Ehrenkranz, Alex Beller, Truman Boardman(vl), Morris Kohn, Sam Rosenblum, Leonard Atkins(vla), George Taliarkin, Fred Goerner, Ed Sodero(cel), Johnny Guarnieri(p), Mike Bryan(g), Ed McKinney(b), Dave Tough(d), Bonnie Lake(v)

Theme(Nightmare)	(unissued)
Frenesi	Hep-19
Dancing in the Dark	(unissued)
Time Was (vBL)	Hep-19
There'll Be Some Changes Made	—, CD19, FTR1513
Blues in the Night (vLP)	ASC-3, —
Little Gate's Special	ASC-4, —, IAJRC17

NOTE: The issued performance of "Little Gate's Special" is edited from several sources for ASC-4 and from more than one source for IAJRC17; it has not been possible to sort them out completely or to determine if a complete broadcast exists for this date.

Paula Kelly(v) for Lake
1:00–4:50 p.m. Chicago, 30 October 1941

070342-1	Take Your Shoes Off Baby (vLP)	Vic.27719, AXM2-5576
070342-1	Make Love to Me (vPK)	(unissued)
070343-2	Make Love to Me (vPK)	Vic.27705, —
070344-1	Solid Sam	—, —
070344-2	Solid Sam	(unissued)
070345-1	Just Kiddin' Around	Vic.27806, —
070345-2	Just Kiddin' Around	(unissued)

NOTE: Arrangements by Bill Challis, Lennie Hayton, Fred Norman, and Ray Conniff, respectively. RCA log sheet shows location marked as "Studio 'A'—Chicago" and two takes made for each mx #, except 070342 (one take). All takes were marked "Flowed" and "Process," but there was no indication which takes were used for issue. The above distribution of take numbers was provided by John Harding. The unissued takes have been reviewed and are excellent performances with notable variations in most solos but particularly in Shaw's solos.

same
6:00–10:00 p.m. New York, 12 November 1941

068194-1	To a Broadway Rose	Vic.27838, AXM2-5576
068194-2	To a Broadway Rose	(unissued)
068195-1	St. James Infirmary, Part 1 (vLP)	—
068195-2	St. James Infirmary, Part 1 (vLP)	Vic.27895, —
068195-1	St. James Infirmary, Part 2	RCA ND82432
068196-2	St. James Infirmary, Part 2	Vic.27895, —
068197-1	Deuces Wild	(unissued)
068197-2	Deuces Wild	Vic.27838, —

NOTE: 068194 arranged by Conniff, 068197 arranged by Marjorie Gibson; both originally were listed on the log sheet as "Will Send In Name" with the above titles penciled in. The arrangement of the two-sided ten-inch 78-rpm version of "St. James Infirmary" reportedly was a head arrangement and therefore attributable to Shaw (see Appendix 3: "Artie Shaw as Composer/Arranger"). RCA log sheets show two takes of each mx # were made, apparently with takes being issued as indicated (data from John Harding). The unissued takes have been reviewed and, again, all are excellent performances with solo variations evident, particularly Shaw's.

same
Loew's State Theatre, New York, 8 December 1941

It Had to Be You	air check
Blues in the Night (vLP)	—
Suite #8	—
Theme(Nightmare)	—

same
3:30–7:45 p.m. New York, 23 December 1941

068803-1	Evensong	Vic.28-0405, AXM2-5576
068803-2	Evensong	(unissued)
068804-1	Suite #8	Vic.28-0405, —
068805-1	Someone's Rocking My Dreamboat (vPK)	Vic.27746, —
068806-1	I Don't Want to Walk Without You (vPK)	—, —

NOTE: 068803-1 & 068804 made up a twelve-inch 78-rpm record, and were composed and arranged by Paul Jordan. The vocals were arranged by Lennie Hayton. The RCA log sheet indicated 068803 originally was titled "Dusk" and that a take 2 of only 2:15 duration also was recorded (take 1 is timed at 4:07). Nevertheless, a full-length alternate has been reviewed and is excellent. The other titles apparently were recorded in one take each.

Fredda Gibson(v) for Kelly
6:00–9:00 p.m. New York, 20 January 1942

071701-1	Somebody Nobody Loves (vFG)	Vic.27798, AXM2-5576
071702-?	Not Mine (vFG)	Vic.27779, —
071703-1	Absent Minded Moon (vFG)	—, —
071704-1	Hindustan	Vic.27798, —

NOTE: Vocals probably all arranged by Lennie Hayton; 071704 by Paul Jordan. The RCA log sheet indicated only one take was made of each mx #, except 071702 (two takes, with no clear indication of which was used; the alternate may be lost).

same
6:00–9:30 p.m. New York, 21 January 1942

071709-1	Carnival	Vic.27860, AXM2-5579
071709-2	Carnival	AXM2-5580
071710-1	Needlenose	Vic.27860, —
071711-1	Two in One Blues	Vic.20-1526, —
071712-1	Sometimes I Feel Like a Motherless Child (vLP)	Vic.27806, —

NOTE: 071709 & 071711 composed and arranged by Paul Jordan; 071710 composed and arranged by Ray Conniff; 071712 arranged by Lennie Hayton. The RCA log sheet indicated the original title for 071710 was "Juke Box Joe" and that all mx #s were made in only one take, except 071709 (two takes) with take 2 marked "hold." Shaw disbanded following this record date.

Following his marriage to Elizabeth Kern in early March, Shaw went on the road for a few weeks with a big band organized for him by Lee Castle, which remains undocumented. Shaw then enlisted in the Navy in late April 1942.

PART V: ARTIE SHAW, 1943–44

Artie Shaw and Navy Band 501
Honolulu, Hawaii, 30 January 1943

Frank Beach, John Best, Conrad Gozzo, Max Kaminsky(tp), Tasso Harris, Dick LeFave, Tak Takvorian(tb), Artie Shaw(cl), Mack Pierce, Ralph LaPollo(as), Sam Donahue, Joe Aglora(ts), Charlie Wade(bari), Harold Wax(p,acc), Rocky Coluccio(p), Al Horesh(g), Barney Spieler(b), Dave Tough(d)

Theme(Nightmare)	air check
Begin the Beguine	—

NOTE: This dub, from an "America Salutes the President" broadcast for President Roosevelt's birthday, has been the only known recording of this band.

Art Shaw and His Orchestra
AFRS *Command Performance #124*, 10 June 1944

Artie Shaw(cl), with studio orchestra including big band with strings

Long Ago and Far Away	air check

NOTE: Nothing more could be discovered concerning details of this orchestra.

Artie Shaw with Count Basie
AFRS *Jubilee #198*, Hollywood, 25 September 1944

Artie Shaw(cl), Harry Edison, Al Killian, Ed Lewis(tp), Ted Donnelly, Eli Robinson, Louis Taylor, Dickie Wells(tb), Earl

Warren, Jimmy Powell(as), Jimmy Keith, Buddy Tate(ts), Rudy Rutherford(bari), Count Basie(p), Freddie Green(g), Rodney Richardson(b), Buddy Rich(d)

| Oh Lady Be Good | Hindsight HCD224 |
| Oh Lady Be Good | SoS125, Kaydee-2 |

same session(s)

Artie Shaw(cl), Count Basie(p), Freddie Green(g), Rod Richardson(b), Buddy Rich(d)

| Bird Calls | Hindsight HCD224 |
| Bird Calls | SoS125, Kaydee-2 |

NOTE: Session also erroneously dated 10 October 1944. "Bird Calls" also issued as "Blues Jam Session" (SoS125) and "Artie's Blues" (Kaydee-2); Shaw did not play on other titles on this broadcast (that clarinetist is Rudy Rutherford). "One O'Clock Jump" from another AFRS broadcast by the Basie band in October, on the LP *Artie Shaw: The Jazz Years* (SoS125), features Rudy Rutherford on clarinet. Above "alternate takes" on the Count Basie Hindsight CD HCD224 are without audience noises, apparently from rehearsals earlier that afternoon.

All-Stars
AFRS *Command Performance*, Hollywood,
30 September 1944

Ziggy Elman(tp), Tommy Dorsey(tb), Artie Shaw(cl), Illinois Jacquet(ts), Lionel Hampton(vibes), Count Basie(p), Les Paul(g), Ed McKinney(b), Buddy Rich(d).

| Honeysuckle Rose | SoS125 |

NOTE: Several photos of this group appeared in music publications in the fall of 1944, erroneously captioned to the effect that this was Shaw's first public performance since returning from the Navy.

Shaw organized his new big band, consisting of four trumpets, four trombones, five reeds, and four rhythm (no string section), on the West Coast in the early fall of 1944.

PART VI: ARTIE SHAW AND HIS ORCHESTRA: THE 1944–45 BAND

Artie Shaw and His Orchestra
10:30 p.m.–3:00 a.m. Hollywood, 23–24 November 1944

Roy Eldridge, Ray Linn, George Schwartz, Jimmy Pupa(tp), Harry Rodgers, Ray Conniff, Pat McNaughton, Charles Coolidge(tb), Artie Shaw(cl), Les Clarke, Tommy Mace(as),

Herbie Steward, Jon Walton(ts), Charles Gentry(bari), Dodo Marmarosa(p), Barney Kessel(g), Morris Rayman(b), Lou Fromm(d), Imogene Lynn(v)

1052-1	Ac-Cent-Tchu-Ate the Positive (vIL)	Vic.20-1612, AXM2-5579
1053-1	Lady Day	Vic.20-1620, —
1054-1	Let's Take the Long Way Home (vIL)	—, —
1055-1	Jumpin' on the Merry-Go-Round	Vic.20-1612, —

NOTE: Arrangements by Ray Conniff except 1053 by Jimmy Mundy. RCA log sheets indicate only one take was made of each mx #.

Paul Cohen, Tony Faso(tp) for Linn & Pupa
1:30–9:00 p.m. New York, 9 January 1945

0028-6	I'll Never Be the Same	Vic.20-1638, AXM2-5579
0029-11	Can't Help Lovin' That Man (vIL)	Vic.20-1931, —
0030-2	'S Wonderful	Vic.20-1638, —
0031-10	Bedford Drive	Vic.20-1696, —

NOTE: 0028 and 0030 arranged by Ray Conniff, 0029 by Bobby Sherwood, 0031 by Buster Harding. RCA log sheets indicate the above number of takes for each item with the last take marked "MASTER" and all others marked "NP" in all cases. It is likely "NP" means "not processed" and thus probably destroyed.

Artie Shaw and His Gramercy 5
10:00 p.m.–1:00 a.m. New York, 9–10 January 1945

Roy Eldridge(tp), Artie Shaw(cl), Dodo Marmarosa(p), Barney Kessel(g), Morris Rayman(b), Lou Fromm(d)

| 0032-4 | The Grabtown Grapple | Vic.20-1647, AXM2-5579 |
| 0033-4 | The Sad Sack | —, — |

NOTE: All titles also on RCA CD 7637-2-RB. The RCA log sheet indicates four takes of 0032 and five takes of 0033 were recorded, with the above indicated takes cited as "MASTER" and the others as "NP" (see above). The log sheet also showed the original title of 0033 was "What Happened to Ace?"

omit Eldridge
Bing Crosby *Kraft Music Hall* Show, Hollywood,
15 March 1945

I Was Doing All Right	Music Hall ll9, ASG5
I Was Doing All Right	—
You Took Advantage of Me	—, —

You Took Advantage of   —
  Me

NOTE: Music Hall 119 is from rehearsals; the other takes from the broadcast.

Art Shaw and His Orchestra
8:00–11:00 p.m. Hollywood, 5 April 1945

Roy Eldridge, Paul Cohen, Bernie Glow, George Schwartz(tp), Harry Rodgers, Gus Dixon, Ollie Wilson, Bob Swift(tb), Artie Shaw(cl), Rudy Tanza, Lou Prisby(as), Herbie Steward, Jon Walton(ts), Chuck Gentry(bari), Dodo Marmarosa(p), Barney Kessel(g), Morris Rayman(b), Lou Fromm(d)

1045-1	September Song	Vic.20-1668, AXM2-5579
1046-2	Little Jazz	—, —

NOTE: 1045 arranged by Conniff; 1046 composed and arranged by Buster Harding. The RCA log sheet states the recordings were made on 33⅓-rpm acetates and transferred for 78-rpm pressings. It appears four "false starts" (designated "NG") were made on 1045 before "take 1" was designated "MASTER." 1046 shows two "NG" entries, a "take 1" marked "hold," another "NG," and a "take 2" marked "MASTER."

same
Fitch Bandwagon Broadcast, 8 April 1945

Begin the Beguine	(unissued)
My Heart Stood Still	—
Little Jazz	ASC-9
Limehouse Blues	ASC-5, GE15006

NOTE: The unissued broadcast titles were the prewar arrangements.

Ralph Rosenlund(ts) for Steward
2:00–11:50 p.m. Hollywood, 17 April 1945

1047-1	But Not for Me	Vic.20-1745, AXM2-5579
1048-1	Tea for Two	Vic.PM42403, —
1091-1	Summertime	Vic.28-0406, AXM2-5580
1091-2	Summertime	Vic.LPM1648, AXM2-5579

NOTE: 1047 arranged by Dick Jones, 1048 by Jimmy Mundy. "Summertime" was an extended arrangement by Eddie Sauter originally issued on a twelve-inch 78-rpm record, with an alternate take appearing on LPM1648 in the 1950s as shown, contrary to the programming on the indicated *The Complete Artie Shaw* reissues. RCA log sheets, however, only cite one take of each master being made. It is

probable that the alternate originally was from a test pressing made from the acetate but not given a "take" number (see "NOTE" for the 5 April 1945 session).

Stan Fishelson(tp) for Cohen
8:00–12:00 p.m. Hollywood, 5 June 1945

1054	Kasbah	rejected?
1055	Lament	—

NOTE: Some sources cited one or both the above takes as the issued versions. The RCA log sheet indicated two takes made of each mx #; 1054 was listed as "Untitled as yet" and 1055 was listed as "Nostalgia." There was no indication of either take being processed or held.

same
8:00–11:30 p.m. Hollywood, 7 June 1945

1056-1	Easy to Love	Vic.20-1934, AXM2-5579
1057-1	Time on My Hands	Vic.20-1930, —
1058-1	Tabu	Vic.20-1696, —

NOTE: 1056 arranged by Dick Jones, 1057 by Dave Rose, 1058 by Artie Shaw. The RCA log sheet indicated second takes of the first two titles were made but marked "NP."

same
2:00–5:30 p.m. Hollywood, 8 June 1945

1059-1	A Foggy Day	Vic.20-1933, AXM2-5579
1060-1	These Foolish Things	Vic.20-1930, —
1061-1	Lucky Number	AXM2-5580

NOTE: 1059 arranged by George Siravo, remainder by Ray Conniff. The RCA log sheet indicated second takes of the first two titles were made but marked "NP."

add Dorothy Allen(v)
2:00–5:00 p.m. Hollywood, 9 June 1945

1061-2	Lucky Number	(unissued)
1062-1	You Go to My Head (vDA)	AXM2-5579

NOTE: 1062 arranged by Harry Rodgers. The RCA log sheet indicated one take of each mx # made, with 1061-2 marked "NP (HOLD)" and a note on the earlier recording.

same
2:00–5:00 p.m. Hollywood, 12 June 1945

1067-1	The Man I Love	AXM2-5579
1068-1	I Could Write a Book	—, Vic.20-1933

NOTE: 1067 arranged by Eddie Sauter, 1068 by George Siravo. The RCA log sheet indicated only one take of each mx # was recorded.

same
3:00–6:00 p.m. Hollywood, 13 June 1945

| 1061-3 | Lucky Number | (unissued) |
| 1069-1 | Thrill of a Lifetime | Vic.20-1937, AXM2-5579 |

NOTE: 1069 arranged by Harry Rodgers. The RCA log showed only these takes made.

same
12:30–3:00 pm Hollywood, 14 June 1945

1054-3	Kasbah	Vic.20-1932, AXM2-5579
1055-3	Lament	—, —
1061-4	Lucky Number	Vic.20-1937, —

NOTE: Arrangements by Ray Conniff. RCA log sheet showed only the indicated takes.

same
2:00–5:00 pm Hollywood, 3 July 1945

| 1070-1 | Love Walked In | Vic.20-1745, AXM2-5579 |
| 1071-1 | Soon | Vic.20-1742, AXM2-5580 |

NOTE: Arrangements by George Siravo. RCA log sheets show take 2s of both numbers as "NP."

same
(Roy Eldridge also sings) 2:00–5:30 p.m. Hollywood, 6 July 1945

1072-1	Keepin' Myself for You	Vic.20-1936, AXM2-5580
1073-1	No One But You	Vic.LPV-582
1074-1	Natch (vRE)	—, —

NOTE: 1072 arranged by George Siravo, 1073 composed and arranged by Siravo, 1074 arranged by Buster Harding (according to best information available). The RCA log sheet showed one take of each except a take 2 marked "NP" for 1072.

add Hal Stevens(v)
2:00–5:00 p.m. Hollywood, 11 July 1945

| 1075-1 | That's for Me (vHS) | Vic.20-1716, AXM2-5580 |
| 1076-1 | They Can't Take That Away from Me | — |

NOTE: Arranger for 1075 is unknown. 1076 has been attributed to both Siravo and Conniff but most sources credit

Conniff. RCA log sheets show take 2s marked "NP" for both titles.

same
2:00–5:30 p.m. Hollywood, 14 July 1945

1076-2	They Can't Take That Away from Me	Vic.20-1743, AXM2-5580
1079-1	Our Love Is Here to Stay	—, —
1080-1	I Was Doing All Right	Vic.20-1742, —

NOTE: Arrangements for last two items by George Siravo. 1076-2 is marked "remake" and 1080 shows a take 2 marked "NP."

same
2:00–5:00 p.m. Hollywood, 17 July 1945

| 1081-1 | Someone to Watch over Me | Vic.20-1744, AXM2-5580 |
| 1082-1 | Things Are Looking Up | —, — |

NOTE: 1081 arranged by Eddie Sauter or George Russell; 1082 by George Siravo. The log sheet shows only the indicated takes made.

same
3:00–6:00 p.m. Hollywood, 19 July 1945

| 1101-1 | The Maid with the Flaccid Air | Vic.28-0406, AXM2-5580 |

NOTE: Arranged by Eddie Sauter. This performance also was issued on a twelve-inch 78-rpm. The RCA log sheet indicated one take of 1101 was all that was recorded that day.

same
9:00 p.m.–12:30 a.m. Hollywood, 20–21 July 1945

| 1073-2 | No One But You | Vic.20-1935, AXM2-5580 |

NOTE: Arranged by George Siravo. RCA log sheet indicates this was a remake and all previous versions should be marked "NG."

same
8:45–11:45 p.m. Hollywood, 21 July 1945

| 1089-1 | They Didn't Believe Me | Vic.20-1931, AXM2-5580 |

NOTE: Arranged by Eddie Sauter. The RCA log sheet showed only one take made.

same
2:00–5:00 p.m. Hollywood, 24 July 1945

| 1090-1 | Dancing on the Ceiling | Vic.LPT1020, AXM2-5580 |
| 1091-1 | I Can't Get Started with You | Vic.20-1934, — |

NOTE: Arrangers uncertain; 1091 probably George Siravo. The RCA log sheet showed only one take of each mx # was made.

same
3:00–6:00 p.m. Hollywood, 26 July 1945

| 1096-1 | Just Floatin' Along | Vic.20-1935, AXM2-5580 |

NOTE: Arranged by George Siravo. RCA log sheet showed only the one take made.

same
2:00–5:00 p.m. Hollywood, 28 July 1945

| 1097-1 | Don't Blame Me | AXM2-5580 |
| 1098-1 | Yolanda (vHS) | —, Vic.20-1716 |

NOTE: 1097 arranged by George Siravo; arranger for 1098 unknown. RCA log sheet showed only one take of each mx # was made.

same
1:00–4:00 p.m. Hollywood, 30 July 1945

| 1047-2 | But Not for Me | (unissued) |
| 1099-1 | I Can't Escape from You | Vic.20-1936, AXM2-5580 |

NOTE: Arranged by George Siravo. RCA log sheet shows only the above takes made, with no indication that 1047-2 was used. A test pressing of 1047-2 was auctioned off by Warren Hicks in 1993 but it has not been possible to review a dub.

Art Shaw and His Orchestra
1:00–7:10 p.m. Hollywood, 31 July 1945

Roy Eldridge(tp), Artie Shaw(cl), Dodo Marmarosa(p), Barney Kessel(g), Morris Rayman(b), Lou Fromm(d)

| 1102-1 | Scuttlebutt | Vic.20-1929, AXM2-5580 |

NOTE: RCA log sheet shows only the one take of this mx # recorded that day.

same
2:00–5:00 p.m. Hollywood, 2 August 1945

1103-1	The Gentle Grifter	Vic.20-1929, AXM2-5580
1104-1	Mysterioso	Vic.20-1800, —
1104-2	Mysterioso	Vic.LPV-582, —
1105-1	Hop Skip and Jump	Vic.20-1800, —

NOTE: All titles also on RCA CD 7637-2-RB. RCA log sheets only show one take of each mx # being made, but an alternate take of 1104 has appeared as shown (see "NOTE" for 17 April 1945 for a likely explanation).

Art Shaw and His Orchestra
Los Angeles, c. August–September 1945

Herb Steward(ts) for Roselund

5408	Let's Walk	(test pressing)
5408	Let's Walk	Mus.357, MVS503, MVSCD50
5416	Love of My Life	Mus.378, —, MVSCD51
5417	Ghost of a Chance (vHS)	Mus.357, —, —
5418	How Deep Is the Ocean (vHS)	Mus.409, —, —
5419	The Glider	Mus.378, —, MVSCD50
5420	The Hornet	Mus.409, —, MVSCD51

NOTE: 5408 arranged by George Siravo and Artie Shaw, 5416 by Artie Shaw, 5419 & 5420 by Buster Harding; others uncertain. The date usually has been given as 14 or 16 November (see text). Dubs of #5408s test pressing circulate.

same
Naval Hospital, San Diego, 12 September 1945

Theme(Nightmare)	Spotlight Bands 894, J1003
Tabu	—, —
Little Jazz	—, —
Summit Ridge Drive (G5)	—, ASG5
Lucky Number	—, —
Begin the Beguine (incomplete)	—, —

same
Fort Ord, California, 19 September 1945

Theme(Nightmare)	Spotlight Bands 897, J1003
My Heart Stood Still	—, —
On the Atcheson Topeka and Santa Fe (vIL)	—, ASC-3

Scuttlebutt (G5)	—, ASG5
Gotta Be This or That (vIL)	—, ASC-4
Just Floatin' Along (incomplete)	—, —

**Ray Linn(tp) for Eldridge
(no trumpet with Gramercy 5) San Luis Obispo,
California, 26 September 1945**

Theme(Nightmare)	Spotlight Bands 900, J1003
Blue Skies	—, —
On the Sunny Side of the Street	—, —
Hop Skip and Jump (G5)	—, ASG5
Jumpin' on the Merry-Go-Round	—, —
Hop Skip and Jump (incomplete) (G5)	—, —

**same
Santa Ana Army Air Force Base, 3 October 1945**

Theme(Nightmare)	Spotlight Bands 903, J1010
Bedford Drive	—, ASC-6
Along the Navajo Trail (vIL)	—, ASC-9
The Sad Sack (G5)	—, ASG5
'S Wonderful	—

**same
Huff General Hospital, Santa Barbara, 10 October 1945**

Theme(Nightmare)	Spotlight Bands 906, J1010
Hindustan	—, ASC-9
Love Walked In	—, —
Can't You Read Between the Lines (vIL)	—, —
The Glider	—, ASC-7

**same
Fitch Bandwagon Broadast, 7 November 1945**

'S Wonderful	(unissued)
Night and Day	GE15078
Let's Walk	—, ASC-8
No One But You	(unissued)

NOTE: Arrangers as previously noted or unknown for titles on above broadcasts.

The 1944–45 band was reported disbanded as of 18 November 1945. Shaw did not have another regular working unit until 1949.

PART VII: ARTIE SHAW ON MUSICRAFT, 1946

During 1946, Shaw did not have a regular touring band. He convened studio orchestras for recording sessions for Musicraft during the spring, summer, and fall. All arrangements in this section by Artie Shaw (2). The Musicrafts have long been in the public domain and thus appeared on numerous budget labels such as Allegro, Royale, Viking, Rondo-lette, Tops, Everest's Archive of Folk & Jazz Music label, etc. In 1997, Luiz Carlos do Nascimento Silva discovered full personnel data for these sessions in the files of AFM Local 47, Hollywood. All sessions took place at Radio Recorders in Los Angeles.

**Art Shaw and His Orchestra
2:00–6:30 p.m. Los Angeles, 30 April 1946**

Artie Shaw(cl), Manny Klein, Ray Linn, Zeke Zarchy, Clyde Hurley(tp), Elmer Smithers, Ollie Wilson, Hoyt Bohannon(tb), Les Robinson, Heinie Beau, Deacon Dunn, Don Raffell, Chuck Gentry(reeds), David Frisina, Nicholas Pisani, Samuel Cytron, Peter Ellis, George Kast, Mark Levant, Walt Edelstein, Mischa Russell, William Bloom(vl), David Sterkin, Sam Freed, Stan Spiegelman(vla), Fred Goerner, Charles Gates, Nicholas Ochi-Albi(cel), Tommy Todd(p), Al Hendrickson(g), Phil Stevens(b), Nick Fatool(d), Mel Torme, the Mel-Tones (Ginny O'Connor, Betty Beveridge, Bernie Parks, Les Baxter)(v)

| 5473 | I Got the Sun in the Morning (vMT&M-T) | Mus.365, MVS503, Lion70058 |
| 5474 | Along with Me (vMT) | —, — |

NOTE: Both titles on CD on MVSCD50.

**Art Shaw and His Orchestra
1:00–4:30 p.m. Los Angeles, 6 June 1946**

Artie Shaw(cl), Fred Fox, Jack Kirksmith, James Decker, Harry Parshal(Fh), Gordon Pope(oboe), Harold Lewis(fl), Jules Seder, Charles Graver(bassoon), Skeets Herfurt, Joe Krechter, Harold Lawson, Herman Berardinelli, Chuck Gentry(reeds), Marshall Sosson, James Cathcart, Morris King, Mark Levant, Joseph Chassman, Vincenzo Pometti, George Barres, Marvin Limonick, James Getzoff, Howard Halbert, Oscar Wasserberger, Eugene Lamas(vl), David Sterkin, Stan Spiegelman, Harry Rumpler, Alvin Dinkin(vla), Julius Tannenbaum, Fred Goerner, Edgar Lustgarten, Kurt

Reher(cel), Gail Laughton(harp), Mark McIntyre(p), Dave Barbour(g), Nat Gangursky, Manny Stein, Art Shapiro(b), Lou Singer(d), Teddy Walters(v)

5544	You Do Something to Me (vTW)	Mus.391, MVS503, Lion70058
5547	In the Still of the Night	Mus.390, —, —

NOTE: Both titles on CD on MVSCD51. Contrary to previously published data, only these pieces were recorded on this date: although matrix numbers for the entire series of Cole Porter tunes were assigned in advance, they were not recorded in order of matrix number. It is possible that rejected takes of the other pieces with this instrumentation were attempted, however.

Art Shaw and His Orchestra
7:30–11:00 p.m. Los Angeles, 13 June 1946

Artie Shaw(cl), Manny Klein, Ray Linn, Zeke Zarchy, Clyde Hurley(tp), Si Zentner, Elmer Smithers, Joe Howard(tb), Skeets Herfurt, Joe Krechter, Harold Lawson, Don Raffell, Chuck Gentry(reeds), Marshall Sosson, Mischa Russell, George Kast, Harry Bluestone, Harold Halbert, Eugene Lamas, Dan Lube, Jan Russell, Sam Freed(vl), Paul Robyn, Stan Spiegelman, David Sterkin(vla), Cy Bernard, Fred Goerner, Edgar Lustgarten(cel), Milt Raskin(p), Dave Barbour(g), Art Shapiro(b), Nick Fatool(d), Kitty Kallen(v)

5545	Begin the Beguine	Mus.391, MVS503, AFJ248
5546	My Heart Belongs to Daddy (vKK)	Mus.392, —, Lion70058

NOTE: Both titles on CD on MVSCD51.

Nicholas Pisani, Olcott Vail(vl) for Russell and Freed (Freed plays viola, replacing Sterkin); Mel Tormé, Mel-Tones(v) for Kallen
7:30–11:30 p.m. Los Angeles, 19 June 1946

5543-1	Night and Day	Mus.389, AFJ248
5543-2	Night and Day	Lion70058, MVS503, MVSCD51
5548-1	What Is This Thing Called Love? (vMT&M-T)	Mus.390, AFJ248
5548-2	What Is This Thing Called Love? (vMT&M-T)	Lion70058, MVS507, MVSCD50

NOTE: These are the only 1946 Musicraft alternates to have surfaced to date. The issues for the "take 2" performances are the only ones known; all other LP issues reviewed have the originally issued "take 1" versions.

Art Shaw and His Orchestra
7:30 p.m.–12:30 a.m. Los Angeles, 25–26 June 1946

Artie Shaw(cl), Vincent DeRosa, James Stagliano, Jack Kirksmith, Richard Perissi(Fh), Gordon Pope(oboe), Harold Lewis(fl), Jules Seder, Charles Graver(bassoon), Skeets Herfurt, Jack Mayhew, Harold Lawson, Herman Berardinelli, Chuck Gentry(reeds), Harry Bluestone, Marshall Sosson, Mischa Russell, Nicholas Pisani, Howard Halbert, Eugene Lamas, Olcott Vail, David Frisina, Peter Ellis, Samuel Cytron, Morris King, George Kast(vl), David Sterkin, Sam Freed, Maurice Perlmutter, Paul Robyn(vla), Fred Goerner, Edgar Lustgarten, Cy Bernard, Nicholas Ochi-Albi(cel), Kathryn Thompson(harp), Mark McIntyre(p), Dave Barbour(g), Art Shapiro, Manny Stein, Nat Gangursky(b), Lou Singer(d), Mel Tormé(v)

5541	I've Got You Under My Skin	Mus.392, MVS507, Lion70058
5542	Get Out of Town (vMT)	Mus.389, —, —

NOTE: Both titles on CD on MVSCD50.

Art Shaw: *The Pied Piper of Hamelin*
CBS *Columbia Workshop*, 21 July 1946

Artie Shaw(cl), 2(tp), 1(tb), 2(Fh), 1(tu), 2(fl), 2(cl), 2(oboe), 2(bassoon), 1(harp), 12(vl), 3(vla), 3(cel), l(p), 1(g), 2(b), 1(d), Harry von Zell(narr), Ed Max(Pied Piper), Arthur Q. Bryan(Mayor of Hamelin)

The Pied Piper of Hamelin	air check

NOTE: A low-fidelity dub of this broadcast circulates among collectors. Personnel probably similar, if not identical, to the following session.

Art Shaw: *The Pied Piper of Hamelin*
CBS *Columbia Workshop*, 28 July 1946

Artie Shaw(cl), Mannie Klein, Don Anderson(tp), Ed Kusby(tb), John Cave, Huntington Burdick(Fh), Henry Stern(tu), Archie Wade, Richard Linden(fl), Vincent Donatelli, George Smith(cl), Gordon Pope, George Moore(oboe), Jules Seder, Charles Graver(bassoon), Harry Bluestone, Marshall Sosson, Joseph Livoti, James Cathcart, George Kast, Fred Olson, Edgar Bergman, Sam Middleman, Dan Lube, Marvin Limonick, Victor Arno, Joseph Quadri(vl), Paul Robyn, Louis Kievman, William Baffa(vla), Cy Bernard, Kurt Reher, Jack Sewell(cel), Gail Laughton(harp), Mark McIntyre(p), Barney Kessel(g), Simon Green, Art Shapiro(b), John Jacobs(d), Harry von Zell(narr), Ed Max(Pied Piper), Arthur Q. Bryan(Mayor of Hamelin)

5625	The Pied Piper of Hamelin, Part 1	Mus.5004
5630	The Pied Piper of Hamelin, Part 2	Mus.5005
5631	The Pied Piper of Hamelin, Part 3	Mus.5006
5632	The Pied Piper of Hamelin, Part 4	—
5633	The Pied Piper of Hamelin, Part 5	Mus.5005
5634	The Pied Piper of Hamelin, Part 6	Mus.5004

NOTE: Shaw composed, arranged, and conducted this work. It was recorded in two sessions that day: 9:30 a.m.–12:30 p.m. for parts 1–3, and 7:00–10:00 p.m. for parts 4–6.

Art Shaw and His Orchestra
8:15 p.m.–12:45 a.m. Los Angeles, 16–17 August 1946

Artie Shaw(cl), Manny Klein, Ray Linn, Zeke Zarchy, Clyde Hurley(tp), Elmer Smithers, Ollie Wilson, Ed Kusby(tb), Les Robinson, Harry Klee, Babe Russin, Don Raffell, Chuck Gentry(reeds), David Frisina, Nicholas Pisani, Samuel Cytron, Sam Freed, George Kast, Harold Halbert, Marshall Sosson, Mischa Russell, Harry Bluestone(vl), David Sterkin, Stan Spiegelman, Paul Robyn(vla), Fred Goerner, Arthur Kafton, Nicholas Ochi-Albi(cel), Dodo Marmarosa(p), Al Hendrickson(g), Phil Stevens(b), Lou Singer(d), Mel Tormé, Mel-Tones(v)

| 5629 | For You For Me Forevermore (vMT) | Mus.412, MVS507, MVSCD50 |
| 5635 | Changing My Tune (vMT&M-T) | —, —, — |

Art Shaw and His Orchestra
8:30–12:00 p.m. Los Angeles, 10 September 1946

Manny Klein, Ray Linn, Zeke Zarchy, Clyde Hurley(tp), Si Zentner, Ed Kusby, Joe Howard(tb), Skeets Herfurt, Harry Klee, Babe Russin, Don Raffell, Morton Friedman(reeds), Marshall Sosson, Mischa Russell, George Kast, Harry Bluestone, Nicholas Pisani, Harold Halbert, Eugene Lamas, Olcott Vail, Peter Ellis, Samuel Cytron(vl), David Sterkin, Stan Spiegelman, Paul Robyn(vla), Cy Bernard, Arthur Kafton, Fred Goerner(cel), Milt Raskin(p), Alan Reuss(g), Art Shapiro(b), Nick Fatool(d), Mel Tormé(v)

| 5636 | Love for Sale | Mus.391, MVS507, Lion70058 |
| 5647 | They Can't Convince Me (vMT) | Mus.441, —, MVS503 |

NOTE: Both titles on CD on MVSCD50. These are the pieces for which Shaw had to overdub his solos later, due to

problems with his teeth. In a 1948 discography of Artie Shaw's recordings by Orrin Keepnews, a typographical error listed mx #5647 ("They Can't Convince Me") as mx #5467. This was obviously a typo, as all other information was correct and all copies of the disc, Musicraft 441, bore mx #5647. However, later discographers perpetuated this accident to the point of attributing the recording date of "They Can't Convince Me" to an April 1946 session due to the apparent proximity of master numbers. Shaw's Musicraft recordings eventually were issued in matrix number order on Musicraft LPs MVS503 and (less in order) MVS507; this title appeared in both sequence locations (as it has in some discographies, showing identical issues). This indicates neither the discographers nor the reissuing company had access to the original files, as all examined issues of this title were the identical performance.

add Artie Shaw(cl), Carl Loeffler(tb), Mel-Tones(v); Walt Edelstein(vl) for Cytron
8:30–12:00 p.m. Los Angeles, 19 September 1946

| 5648 | Guilty (vMT&M-T) | Mus.428, MVS507, MVSCD51 |
| 5649 | Anniversary Song | —, —, — |

Art Shaw and His Orchestra
7:00–10:30 p.m. Los Angeles, 17 October 1946

Artie Shaw(cl), Ray Linn, Zeke Zarchy, Frank Beach, Mannie Klein(tp), Bill Schaefer, Ed Kusby, Joe Howard, Elmer Smithers(tb), Skeets Herfurt, Harry Klee, Babe Russin, Harold Lawson, Bob Lawson(reeds), Sam Freed, Lewis Elias, Mischa Russell, Nicholas Pisani, Olcott Vail, George Kast, Alex Law, Edgar Bergman, Samuel Cytron, Walt Edelstein(vl), David Sterkin, Maurice Perlmutter, Harry Weiss (vla), Cy Bernard, Fred Goerner, Jack Sewell(cel), Dodo Marmarosa(p), Alan Reuss(g), Phil Stevens(b), Nick Fatool(d), Mel Tormé, Mel-Tones, Ralph Blane(v)

5650	And So to Bed (vMT&M-T)	Mus.441, MVS507, MVSCD50
5651	Connecticut (vRB)	Mus.445, —, —
5701	Don't You Believe It Dear (vMT&M-T)	—, —, —

Art Shaw and His Orchestra
12:30–4:15 p.m. Los Angeles, 9 November 1946

Artie Shaw(cl), Ray Linn, Zeke Zarchy, Frank Beach, Mannie Klein(tp), Bill Schaefer, Ed Kusby, Joe Howard, Si Zentner(tb), Skeets Herfurt, Harry Klee, Babe Russin, Harold Lawson, Bob Lawson (reeds), Sam Freed, Felix Slatkin,

Morris King, Harry Bluestone, Mischa Russell, Marshall Sosson, Nicholas Pisani, Olcott Vail, George Kast, Peter Ellis, Howard Halbert, Samuel Cytron(vl), David Sterkin, Maurice Perlmutter, Stanley Spiegelman(vla), Cy Bernard, Fred Goerner, Jack Sewell(cel), Dodo Marmarosa(p), Dave Barbour(g), Art Shapiro(b), Nick Fatool(d), Mel Tormé, Lillian Lane(v)

5702	It's the Same Old Dream (vMT)	Mus.492, MVS507, MVSCD51
5703	I Believe (vMT)	—, —, —
5704	When You're Around (vLL)	Mus.512, —, —

NOTE: On the LP *Artie Shaw Plays Cole Porter and Irving Berlin* issued by MGM as Lion 70058, there was a spurious track on which Shaw was not involved: "There's No Business Like Show Business" by Mel Tormé with Sonny Burke's studio orchestra (mx #5803), recorded in 1947.

Artie Shaw retired from performing music completely during 1947 and 1948, devoting himself to writing (books, not music) at his home in Connecticut, and developing as a classical soloist.

PART VIII: ARTIE SHAW AS CLASSICAL SOLOIST, 1949

Artie Shaw: *Modern Music for Clarinet*
New York, 11 March 1949

Artie Shaw(cl), with Studio Orchestra, Walter Hendl(cond)

41059	Valse (Poulenc)	Co. 17600, ML4260
41060	Habanera (Ravel)	Co. 17597, —
41061	Guadalajira (Gould)	—, —
41062	Corcovado (Milhaud)	Co. 17598, —
41063	A Short Story (Kabalevsky)	—, —
41064	Petite Piece (Debussy)	Co. 17599, —
41065	Prelude (Shostakovich)	Co. 17600, —
41066	Andaluza (Granados)	Co. 17599, —

NOTE: Orchestrations by Hershey Kay except 41060 by Arthur Hoeree.

Adventures in Jazz
CBS TV, New York, 18 March 1949

Artie Shaw(cl), Virginia Passecantandro(p)

| | Habanera (Ravel) | (unissued) |
| | Rendezvous (Shulman) | — |

WOR Radio Broadcasts
New York, c. March 1949

Artie Shaw(cl), unk.(vl), unk.(p)

| | Clarinet Trio in E-flat (K.498) (Mozart) | (unissued) |

Artie Shaw(cl), WOR String Quartet.

| | Clarinet Quintet in A Major (K.581) (Mozart) | BOMR71-7715 |
| | Hebrew Sketches (Krein) | — |

NOTE: The BOMR set liner notes dated these performances as 1947 (see text).

National Youth Symphony with Artie Shaw
New York, 18 April 1949

Artie Shaw(cl), National Youth Symphony, Leon Barzin(-cond)

| | Concerto for Clarinet (Berezowsky) | BOMR71-7715 |

NOTE: The BOMR set liner notes dated this performance as from 1948, but the above date is certain.

Art Shaw and His Orchestra
New York, 31 May 1949

Artie Shaw(cl), Julius Baker, H. Moskovitz(fl), R. Gomberg, H. Davidson(oboes), P. Lorr, A. Kubey(bassoons), B. Erle, S. Gralnik, M. Lomask, D. Sackson, S. Shulman, L. Fishzohn, M. Raimondi, B. Sonofsky, S. Goldshield(violins), W. Trampler, P. Goldberg(violas), H. Grosser, C. Adam(cellos), Janet Putram(harp), Gene di Novi(p), Arnold Fishkin(b), Irv Kluger(d)

40813-1	The Man I Love	(unissued)
40813-2	The Man I Love	Co. 38775, ML4260, Ajaz291
40814-1	I Concentrate on You	—, —, —

NOTE: 40813 arranged by Shaw and Hershey Kay; 40814 by Shaw and Alan Shulman. The "take 1" of 40813 apparently was only available from a test pressing.

Art Shaw and His New Music String Quartet
(same session)

Artie Shaw(cl), Janet Putram(harp), New Music String Quartet

| 40815 | Mood in Question | Co. 55048, ML4260, Ajaz291 |

omit Putram

40816   Rendezvous (for Clarinet   —, —, —
              and Strings)

NOTE: Both titles composed and arranged by Alan Shulman.

Artie Shaw with Symphony Orchestra
Temple Shalom, Chicago, 9 November 1949

Artie Shaw(cl), Symphony Orchestra, Alfredo Antonini (cond)

              Fantasie on 3 American   private recording
              Songs

NOTE: A low-fidelity dub of this performance circulates among collectors.

Artie Shaw–Norman Dello Joio
film clip, c. 1949–50

Artie Shaw(cl), Norman Dello Joio(p)

              Concerto for Clarinet   Berman film
              (Dello Joio):
              Andante(excerpt)

Artie Shaw–Connecticut Symphony
Westport, Connecticut, c. 1949–50

Artie Shaw(cl), Connecticut Symphony, unk.(cond)

              Concerto for Clarinet   private recording
              (Dello Joio)

NOTE: Shaw has an acetate dub of this performance (2).

PART IX: ARTIE SHAW AND HIS ORCHESTRA, 1949–50

Arranger credits for some of the following are unknown or controversial. Those pieces also recorded for Decca give arranger credit there. Other previously recorded titles were the former arrangements (re-orchestrated, where necessary, to omit the string sections), except for "I Concentrate on You." New originals were arranged by their composers. Shaw released a MusicMasters CD in 1990 titled *Artie Shaw '1949'* (CIJD60234M, reissued on MusicMasters CD 65026 as *Last Recordings Vol. II*), with certain tunes retitled as shown below.

Art Shaw and His Orchestra
New York, c. late December 1949

Don Fagerquist, Don Paladino, Dale Pierce, Victor Ford(tp), Sonny Russo, Porky Cohen, Freddie Zito, Bart Varselona(tb), Artie Shaw(cl), Herb Steward, Frank Socolow(as), Al Cohn, Zoot Sims(ts), Danny Bank(bari), Gil Barrios(p), Jimmy Raney(g), Dick Niveson(b), Irv Kluger(d), Pat Lockwood(v)

D9	MM2463 Star Dust	TT1556, SOL508, CIJD60234M
	Tea for Two	—, —, —
	They Can't Take That Away from Me	—, —, —
	Things Are Looking Up	—, —, —
	Softly as in a Morning Sunrise	—, —, —
D9 MM2464	He's Funny That Way (vPL)	—, TT1557, —
	I Only Have Eyes for You (vPL)	—, —, —
	Let's Fall in Love (vPL)	—, —, —
	So in Love (vPL)	—, —, —
	You Do Something to Me (vPL)	—, —, —
D9 MM2465	I Get a Kick Out of You	TT1573, —, —
	Begin the Beguine	—, —, TT1559
	I Concentrate on You	—, —, —
	'S Wonderful	—, —, —
	Orinoco	—, —, —
D9 MM2466	Carnival	TT1577, SOL509, —
	Comes Love	—, —, —
	I Cover the Waterfront	—, —, —
	Krazy Kat	—, —, —
	Love Walked In	—, —, —
D9 MM2467	Moonglow	TT1558, —, —
	So Easy	—, —, —
	Innuendo (as "Minnesota" on SoS118)	—, —, —
	Gue-le-le (as "Mucho de Nada" on CIJD)	—, —, —
D9 MM2468	Theme(Nightmare) & Narration by Shaw	TT1559, SOL508
D9 MM2469	Cool Daddy	TT1596, SOL509
	Easy to Love	—, SOL510
	Minnesota (as "Aesop's Foibles" on CIJD)	—, —, —
	Smooth and Easy	—, —, —

NOTE: Arranger credit for the vocal items has been attributed to Gene Roland. All titles on MusicMasters

CIJD60234M also on MusicMasters CD 65026-2. Shaw did not play on "He's Funny That Way" or "So in Love."

add Jose Manguel, Ubal Nieto, Chino Pozo, Bobby Rodriguez(Latin percussion)
New York, 30 December 1949

75639	Orinoco	De.24889, Ajaz291
75640	Mucho de Nada	—

NOTE: Arrangements by John Bartee (who also did the above "Gue-le-le").

omit Latin percussionists
New York, 3 January 1950

75641	Love Is the Sweetest Thing	De.DL74462, Ajaz291
75642	I Get a Kick Out of You	De.2469, —

NOTE: 75641 arranged by Johnny Thompson; 75642 by Johnny Mandel. (Information from Artie Shaw).

Trudy Richards(v) for Lockwood
New York, c. early January 1950

E0 MM600	Don't Take Your Love from Me (vTR)	TT1584, SOL510
	Exactly Like You (vTR)	—, —
	How Deep Is the Ocean (vTR)	—, —
	Together (vTR)	—, —
	Too Marvelous (vTR)	—, —
E0 MM601	The Very Thought of You	TT1589, —
	Love Is the Sweetest Thing	—, —
	Bedford Drive	—, —
	Love of My Life	—, —
EO MM602	Fred's Delight	TT1599, —, CIJD60234M
	Love for Sale	—, —
	Similau	—, —, —
	Time on My Hands	—, —
(?)	Mucho de Nada (as "Afro-Cubana" on CIJD)	—

NOTE: Arranger credit for the vocal items has been attributed to Gene Roland. All titles on MusicMasters CIJD60234M also on MusicMasters CD 65026-2. "Mucho de Nada" evidently was from a test pressing, according to discographer Ken Crawford. Shaw did not play on "Don't Take Your Love from Me."

Artie Shaw and His Gramercy 5
New York, c. early January 1950

Don Fagerquist(tp), Artie Shaw(cl), Gil Barrios(p), Jimmy Raney(g), Dick Niveson(b), Irv Kluger(d)

E0 MM603	Summit Ridge Drive	TT1564/65, SOL509
	The Grabtown Grapple	—, —
	Smoke Gets in Your Eyes	—, —
	The Pied Piper Theme	—, —
	Cross Your Heart	—, —

add Mary Ann McCall(v)
New York, 6 January 1950

75677	There Must Be Something Better Than Love (vMM)	De.24870, Ajaz291
75678	Nothin' from Nothin' (vMM)	—, —

Art Shaw and His Orchestra
New York, 6 January 1950

Don Fagerquist, Don Paladino, Dale Pierce, Victor Ford(tp), Sonny Russo, Porky Cohen, Freddie Zito, Bart Varselona(tb), Artie Shaw(cl), Herb Steward, Frank Socolow(as), Al Cohn, Zoot Sims(ts), Danny Bank(bari), Gil Barrios(p), Jimmy Raney(g), Dick Niveson(b), Irv Kluger(d)

75679	Love Walked In	De.24869, Ajaz291
75680	So Easy	De.DL74462, —

NOTE: 75679 was the 1945 George Siravo arrangement; 75680 composed and arranged by Tadd Dameron.

Shaw disbanded following the above recording session. He re-formed with a band organized for him by Lee Castle for an appearance at Bop City in March 1950.

Art Shaw and His Orchestra
New York, 4 April 1950

Steve Lipkins, Lee Castle, Louis Mucci(tp), Eddie Bert, Porky Cohen, Sonny Russo(tb), Artie Shaw(cl), Bill Shine, Al Block(as), Don Lanphere, Eddie Wasserman(ts), Gil Barrios(p), Jimmy Raney(g), Teddy Kotick(b), Dave Williams(d)

76079	He's Gone Away	De.27009, Ajaz291
76080	Foggy Foggy Dew	—, Ajaz298

| 76081 | The Continental | De.27056, — |
| 76082 | I'll Remember April | —, — |

NOTE: above four items arranged by Artie Shaw.

Artie Shaw and His Gramercy 5
New York, 7–8 April 1950

Lee Castle(tp), Artie Shaw(cl), Don Lanphere(ts), Gil Barrios(p), Jimmy Raney(g), Teddy Kotick(b), Dave Williams(d)

| 76099 | Crumbum | De.27196, Ajaz298 |
| 76100 | The Shekomeko Shuffle | —, — |

Shaw toured with the above big band and Gramercy 5 until June 1950, but later recordings for Decca used studio groups, not his regular working units.

PART X: ARTIE SHAW ON DECCA 1950–53

Arranging credits for all Deccas in this section belong to Artie Shaw. He has stated that he sketched all arrangements at his farm and delegated the scoring. Sessions co-led with Sy Oliver and Gordon Jenkins were co-arranged with them (2).

Dick Haymes with Artie Shaw, His Strings and Woodwinds
New York, 27 April 1950

Artie Shaw(cl), Tom Parshley(fl), Sam Amato(oboe,Eh), James Chambers(Fh), Jack Margolies, Mac Ceppos, Harry Melnikoff, Bernard Ocko, Marshall Moss, Sam Rand, Zolly Smirnov (vl), Julius Shaier, Izzy Zer(vla), Maurice Brown, Harvey Shapiro(cel), Al Lerner(p), Teddy Kotick(b), Irv Kluger(d), Dick Haymes(v)

| 76196 | Count Every Star (vDH) | De.27042, Ajaz298 |
| 76197 | If You Were Only Mine (vDH) | —, — |

Artie Shaw with Gordon Jenkins Orchestra & Chorus
New York, 29 May 1950

Tony Faso, Charlie Margulis, Louis Mucci(tp), Bob Alexander, Kai Winding(tb), Artie Shaw(cl), Hymie Shertzer, Milt Yaner(as), Jack Greenberg, Sam Gargason(ts), Stan Webb (bari), Gordon Jenkins, Al Lerner(p), Trigger Alpert(b), John Blowers(d), unidentified string section, Choral Group(v)

| 76426 | I'm Forever Blowing Bubbles (vCG) | De.27186, Ajaz298 |
| 76427 | You're Mine You (vCG) | —, — |

Artie Shaw and His Orchestra
New York, 31 May 1950

Lee Castle, Carl Poole, Yank Lawson(tp), Will Bradley, Charlie Castaldo(tb), Artie Shaw(cl), Hymie Shertzer, Milt Yaner(as), Al Klink, Art Rollini(ts), Billy Kyle(p), Everett Barksdale(g), Joe Benjamin(b), Jimmy Crawford(d), Don Cherry, Gwen Davies, Trio: Ray Charles, Artie Malvin, Eugene Lowenthal(v)

| 76434 | I Love the Guy (vGD& T) | De.27085, Ajaz298 |
| 76435 | Just Say I Love Her (vDC) | —, — |

Art Shaw and His Orchestra
New York, 19 July 1950

Yank Lawson, Bernie Privin, Carl Poole(tp), Will Bradley, Jack Satterfield(tb), Artie Shaw(cl,v), Hymie Shertzer, Milt Yaner(as), Art Drelinger(ts), Stan Webb(ts,bari), Bob Kitsis(p), Everett Barksdale(g), Bob Haggart(b), Bunny Shawker(d), Don Cherry, Jane Ford, Chelsea 3(v)

76669	Don't Worry 'Bout Me (vDC)	De.27213, Ajaz298
76670	Blue Again (vJF)	(unissued)
76671	It's a Long Way to Tipperary (vCT)	De.27434, —
76672	Show Me the Way to Go Home (vCT,AS)	—, —

Artie Shaw, His Strings and Woodwinds
New York, 12 September 1950

Julie Shacter, Harry Glickman, Zolly Smirnov, Jack Margolies, Rebecca Lynch, Harry Melnikoff(vl), Julius Shaier, Leon Frengut(vla), Maurice Brown, Harvey Shapiro(cel), Artie Shaw(cl), Art Ralston(fl,cl), Eddie Brown(fl,cl,Eh), Will Blanchard(Fh), Billy Taylor(p), John Collins(g), Joe Benjamin(b), Charlie Smith(d), Trio(v)

| 76843 | Autumn Leaves | (unissued) |
| 76844 | White Christmas (vT) | — |

Art Shaw and His Orchestra
New York, 14 September 1950

Tony Faso, Chris Griffin, Bert Wallace(tp), Will Bradley, Jack Satterfield(tb), Artie Shaw(cl), Hymie Shertzer, Milt Yaner(as), Art Drelinger(ts), Stan Webb(ts,bari), Billy Taylor(p), John Collins(g), Joe Benjamin(b), Charlie Smith(d), Chickering 4: Ray Charles, Artie Malvin, Eugene Lowenthal, Sid Bennett(v)

76845	Jingle Bells (vCF)	De.27243, Ajaz426
76846	Where or When	De.DL74462, —
76847	Blue Again	(unissued)

Artie Shaw and His Strings and Woodwinds
New York, 5 October 1950

Julie Shacter, Harry Glickman, Kurt Dieterle, Jack Margolies, Arnold Eidus, Rebecca Lynch(vl), Julius Shaier, Leon Frengut(vla), Rudy Sims, Harvey Shapiro(cel), Irving Horowitz, John Fulton(woodwinds), John Barrows(Fh), Artie Shaw(cl), Sanford Gold(p), Frank Worrell(g), Bob Haggart(b), Bunny Shawker(d), Gwen Davies(v)

76953	White Christmas (vGD)	De.27243, Ajaz426
76954	Autumn Leaves	De.27270, —
76955	Serenade in Blue	—, —

Don Cherry, Artie Shaw, Sy Oliver Orchestra & Chorus
New York, 25 January 1951

Charlie Shavers(tp), Artie Shaw(cl), Hymie Shertzer, Artie Baker(as), Art Drelinger(ts), Bill Holcomb(bari), Billy Kyle(p), George Barnes(g), Sandy Block(b), Jimmy Crawford(d), Don Cherry, Chorus(v)

80461	Beautiful Madness (vDC&C)	De.27475
80462	Chapel of the Roses (vDC&C)	—
80463	I've Got to Pass Your House (vDC&C)	De.28768
80464	The Thrill Is Gone (vDC&C)	(unissued)

NOTE: Personnel from Decca log sheet. Artie Shaw has stated that he may not have played clarinet on this session (2). Records could not be reviewed.

Don Cherry–June Hutton–Artie Shaw:
New York, 30 January 1951

Artie Shaw(cl), Stan Freeman(p), Don Perry(g, Bob Haggart(b, Bunny Shawker(d), June Hutton, Don Cherry & Chorus(v)

80473	Bring Back the Thrill (vDC&C)	De.27484
80474	I Apologize (vDC&C)	—
80475	My Kind of Love (vJH)	De.27580, Ajaz426
80476	Dancing on the Ceiling (vJH)	—, —

NOTE: The Don Cherry features from this session could not be found for review.

Trudy Richards–Artie Shaw–Sy Oliver
New York, 23 April 1952

Harold Johnson, Jimmy Nottingham, Bernie Privin(tp), Mort Bullman, Bobby Byrne, Henderson Chambers(tb), Hymie Shertzer, Milt Yaner(as), Art Drelinger, Al Klink(ts), Bill Holcomb(bari), Billy Taylor(p), George Barnes(g), Sandy Block(b), John Blowers(d), Trudy Richards(v), Artie Shaw(cond)

82732	I Waited a Little Too Long (vTR)	De.28190, Ajaz426
82733	I May Hate Myself in the Morning (vTR)	—, —
82734	Travelin' All Alone	MCA2-4081

NOTE: Artie Shaw conducted but did not play on this session.

Connee Boswell–Artie Shaw
New York, 1 August 1952

Artie Shaw(cl), Bob Kitsis(p), George Barnes(g), Trigger Alpert(b), Buddy Schutz(d), Connee Boswell(v)

| 83203 | Where There's Smoke There's Fire (vCB) | De.28377, Ajaz426 |
| 83204 | My Little Nest of Heavenly Blue (vCB) | —, — |

Artie Shaw and His Orchestra
New York, 2 July 1953

Billy Butterfield, Andy Ferretti, Dale McMickle, Bart Wallace(tp), Bob Alexander, Will Bradley, Jack Satterfield, Kai Winding(tb), John Barrows, Jim Buffington(Fh), Artie Shaw(cl), Hymie Shertzer, Milt Yaner(as), Al Klink, Romeo Penque(ts), Manny Thaler(bari), Sylvan Shulman, Jack Zayde, Tosha Samaroff, Manny Green, Sam Rand, Max Hollander, Harry Melnikoff, Harry Urbant, Felix Orlewitz, Bernie Robbins, Stan Kraft(vl), Harold Colletta, Julie Brand, Harold Furmansky, Sid Bracker(vla), Lucien Schmidt, Allen Shulman(cel), Bernie Leighton(p), Barry Galbraith(g), Trigger Alpert(b), Don Lamond(d)

84799	These Foolish Things	De.DL5524, Ajaz426
84800	In the Still of the Night	—, —
84801	That Old Black Magic	—, Ajaz431
84802	I'll Be Seeing You	—, —

Art Shaw and His Orchestra
New York, 6 July 1953

Billy Butterfield, Chris Griffin, Dale McMickle(tp), Bob Alexander, Lou McGarity(tb), Jim Buffington(Fh), Artie

Shaw(cl), Hymie Shertzer, Milt Yaner(as), Romeo Penque, Al Klink(ts), Sylvan Shulman, Zolly Smirnov, Raoul Poliakin, Harry Melnikoff, Mac Ceppos, Harry Glickman, Julie Brand, Paul Melnikoff, Felix Orlewitz(vl), Izzy Zer, Sol Deutsch, Sid Brecker(vla), Maurice Brown, Maurice Balkin(cel), Bernie Leighton(p), Art Ryerson(g), Trigger Alpert(b), Don Lamond(d)

84817	It Could Happen to You	De.DL5524, Ajaz431
84818	They Can't Take That Away From Me	—, —
84819	All the Things You Are	—, —
84820	September Song	—, —

NOTE: Recitation of the lyrics for these pieces was overdubbed by Doris Dowling and Robert Pastrone on all eight items from July 1953 for their original 10-inch LP issue, *Speak to Me of Love* (Decca DL5524). Later reissues did not contain the overdubbed recitations. On 12-inch LP reissues on Decca and Ace of Hearts, the album usually has been filled out with the four titles from November 1955 on which Shaw conducted but did not play (see "Discographical Addenda & Ephemera" section).

During September 1953, Shaw formed a new Gramercy 5.

PART XI: ARTIE SHAW AND HIS GRAMERCY 5, 1953–54

Artie Shaw and His Gramercy 5
New York, c. early December 1953

Artie Shaw(cl), Joe Roland(vibes), Hank Jones(p), Tal Farlow(g), Tommy Potter(b), Irv Kluger(d)

5003	Besame Mucho	Bell 706, Ajaz431
5004	That Old Feeling	—, —
5005	Tenderly	Bell 700, —
5006	Stop and Go Mambo	—, —
C1664	Sunny Side Up	Clef 89117
C1647	Imagination	—

same
New York, c. late February–early March 1954

The Sad Sack	MGC-159, MGV-2014, Ajaz431, BOMR71-7715, MM65071-2
I've Got a Crush on You	—, —, —, —, MM65101-2
Sequence in B-flat (= The Chaser)	—, —, —, Ajaz440, —
Sequence in B-flat (= The Chaser)	—, —, —, —, MM65071-2
Tenderly	MGC-160, —, —, —, —

When the Quail Come Back to San Quentin	—, —, —, —, —
Sunny Side Up	—, —, Ajaz446, —, MM65119-2
Autumn Leaves (tk.5)	—, —, —, MM65101-2, —
Autumn Leaves (tk.6)	—, —, —, —, —
Pied Piper Theme	MGC-645, SoS125, Ajaz440, —, —
Pied Piper Theme	MM65071-2
Dancing in the Dark	—, —, —, —, MM65101-2
That Old Feeling	—, —, —, —
Someone to Watch over Me	—, —, —, —, MM65071-2
Stop and Go Mambo	—, —, Ajaz446, —, MM65101-2
Besame Mucho	—, —, —, —, MM65071-2
Love of My Life	—, —, —, —, —
Grabtown Grapple	MGV-2015, —, —, —, MM65101-2
I Can't Get Started	—, —, —, —, —
I Can't Get Started	—, —, —, —, MM65071-2
Lugubrious	—, —, —, —, —
Lugubrious	—, —, —, —, —
Lyric —	—, —, —, —, —
Imagination	—, —, —, —, —
Imagination	—, —, —, —, —
Crumbum (as Mysterioso)	—, —, —, —, —
Begin the Beguine	—, —, —, —, MM65101-2
Don't Take Your Love from Me	—, —, —, —, —
Cross Your Heart	—, —, —, —, —
Back Bay Shuffle	—, —, —, —, —
How High the Moon	—, —, —, —, —
Star Dust	—, —, —, —, —
Summit Ridge Drive	—, —, —, —, —
Scuttlebutt	—, —, —, —, —
Frenesi	—, —, —, —, —

NOTE: The matrix numbers for the December 1953 items were artifacts of the issuing record companies. Shaw has consistently stated in discussing these sessions that he recorded the sextet himself after hours while the band was appearing at The Embers, in New York City, and leased the tapes for issue. However, he could not be explicit about exact dating of the recording sessions. The Bell titles have erroneously been dated as early as September 1953 in some discographies. However, as noted in the text, when the group formed that month, the drummer was Denzil Best, who remained with the group until replaced by Irv Kluger in October. Also, as noted in the text, Shaw recalled annoyance at having to hold the timing of "three records" (six sides) to the three-minute time limit for 78-rpm releases, for issue by Bell, and associated this episode with the approach of Christmas. This difficulty also would have been in effect for the two titles for the Clef 78-rpm record. As Shaw recalled "three records" being made under these circumstances, and the *Globe & Mail* article discussed in the text indicated that the Bell records (*AND* longer versions of the same numbers) were recorded in December, it appears the dating for at least these six items should be early December 1953. Shaw was certain *ALL* other titles by the sextet were recorded during the band's second engagement at The Embers, in late February–early March 1954. The MusicMasters MM65071-2 and MM65101-2 items are CD issues.

Artie Shaw and His Gramercy 5
Hollywood, c. June 1954

Artie Shaw(cl), Hank Jones(p), Joe Puma(g), Tommy Potter(b), Irv Kluger(d)

Rough Ridin'	Clef MGC-630, Ajaz451, RWJ1001
Rough Ridin'	—, —, MM65071-2
My Funny Valentine	—, —, —
Dancing on the Ceiling	—, —, —
Dancing on the Ceiling	—, —, —
Too Marvelous	—, —, —
Yesterdays	—, —, —
S'posin'	—, —, —
Bewitched, Bothered & Bewildered	—, —, —
September Song	—, —, MM65101-2

NOTE: Shaw has stated that there remains considerable material from these sessions that has never been issued. This quintet disbanded in early July 1954, and following a brief tour of Australia in late July with a pick-up group, Shaw ceased performing on clarinet. He was certain nothing had been recorded by the groups in Australia.

Artie Shaw has conducted many other ensembles since 1954, but has not otherwise performed himself (see "Discographical Addenda & Ephemera" following the index).

Appendix 1

Alphabetical List of Tune Titles with Composer Credits and Recording Dates

The following list alphabetically arranges all titles of pieces recorded by Artie Shaw under his own name, with composers and lyricists (where known) following in parentheses, and dates of recording shown below. The sources of this information were primarily the records themselves, where such information was given (occasionally erroneously; where errors were found, corrections were made); Kinkle's *Encyclopedia of Popular Music and Jazz 1900–1950* (New Rochelle, N.Y.: Arlington House, 1974); and, where titles were still elusive, various other sources, including *Lissauer's Encyclopedia of Popular Music in America 1888 to the Present* (New York: Paragon House, 1991). Where the piece was based on traditional material, "(traditional)" is the notation for composer credit. In the few cases where nothing could be discovered, I have left a question mark "(?)" in that entry.

It is of interest to note the frequency of appearance by various popular song composers. Much has been made of Shaw's decision to base his band library on the best tunes by the best popular composers of the day. There are seven composers represented by ten or more tunes each, as follows:

Cole Porter	19
George Gershwin	16
Richard Rodgers	15
Irving Berlin	13
Harry Warren	12
Jerome Kern	11
Jimmy McHugh	10

Together they account for 96 titles of the more than 530 recorded by Shaw throughout his career, or less than 20 percent of the total number of songs he recorded during his career as a bandleader. As noted, Shaw himself composed or co-composed over 75 titles. Another sixteen composers are represented by five or more titles apiece:

Harold Arlen	9
Ray Conniff	9
Jimmy Van Heusen	9
Saul Chaplin	8
Harry Revel	8
Arthur Schwartz	8
Art Johnston	7
Richard Whiting	7
Hoagy Carmichael	6
Sam Coslow	6
Sammy Fain	6
Buster Harding	6
Larry Clinton	5
Vernon Duke	5
Ben Oakland	5
Vincent Youmans	5

Shaw has been cited as cocomposer on several titles with other notable composers, including Ray Conniff ("Prelude in C Major"), Buster Harding (at least two of the Gramercy 5 titles, and some sources cite "Bedford Drive" as well), and Ben Oakland ("If It's You"). (See also the section "Artie Shaw as Composer/Arranger.") For obvious reasons lyricists are not included in the above tables.

(untitled instrumental excerpt in *Dancing Co-ed*) (?)
  (1939/07/12–31)
(untitled instrumental excerpt in *Second Chorus*) (Artie Shaw)
  (1940/08/16)
Absent Minded Moon (Jimmy Van Heusen—Johnny Burke)
  (1942/01/20)
Ac-Cent-Tchu-Ate the Positive (Harold Arlen—Johnny Mercer)
  (1944/11/23)
Adios Marquita Linda (Marcos Jiminez)
  (1940/03/03)

Afraid to Dream (Harry Revel—Mack Gordon)
(1937/07/12)
(1937/07/22)
Alibi Baby (Vee Lawnhurst—Tot Seymour—Ed Heyman)
(1937/04/28)
Alice Blue Gown (Harry Tierney—Joseph McCarthy)
(1940/07/08)
(1941/01/21)
All Alone (Irving Berlin)
(1937/05/13)
(1937/07/12)
All at Once (Richard Rodgers—Lorenz Hart)
(1937/04/28)
All Dressed Up and No Place to Go (?)
(1937/03/04)
All God's Children Got Rhythm (Bronislaw Kaper—Walter Jurmann—Gus Kahn)
(1937/05/13)
All I Remember Is You (Jimmy Van Heusen—Eddie DeLange)
(1939/06/05)
All in Fun (Jerome Kern—Oscar Hammerstein)
(1939/10/26)
All the Things You Are (Jerome Kern—Oscar Hammerstein)
(1939/10/26)
(1953/07/06)
All You Want to Do Is Dance (Art Johnston—Johnny Burke)
(1937/07/12)
Alone Together (Art Schwartz—Howard Dietz)
(1939/01/31)
(1939/02/?)
(1941/01/23)
Along the Navajo Trail (Eddie DeLange)
(1945/10/03)
Along the Santa Fe Trail (Will Grosz—Al Dubin—E. Coolidge)
(1940/10/26)
Along with Me (Harold Rome)
(1946/04/30)
Am I in Love? (Harry Warren—Al Dubin)
(1937/08/04)
And So to Bed (Harry Revel—Mack Gordon)
(1946/10/18)
Andaluza (Enrico Granados)
(1949/03/11)
Anniversary Song (Al Jolson—Saul Chaplin)
(1946/09/19)
Any Old Time (Artie Shaw)
(1938/02/15)
(1938/07/24)
(1938/12/13)

(1939/01/13)
(1939/01/18)
(1939/03/12)
(1939/11/03)
April in My Heart (Hoagy Carmichael—Helen Minardi)
(1938/11/29)
(1938/12/01)
April in Paris (Vernon Duke—E. Y. Harburg)
(1940/05/13)
Artie's Blues (= Bird Calls, Blues Jam Session) (Artie Shaw—Count Basie)
(1944/09/25)
At Sundown (Walter Donaldson)
(1937/03/04)
(1939/01/29)
(1939/07/14)
(1939/10/25)
Autumn Leaves (Joe Kosma—Johnny Mercer—Jacques Prevert)
(1950/09/12)
(1950/10/05)
(1954/03/?)
Azure (Duke Ellington)
(1938/02/15)

Back Bay Shuffle (Artie Shaw—Teddy McRae)
(1938/07/24)
(1938/11/27)
(1938/12/02)
(1938/12/14)
(1939/02/26)
(1939/07/12–31)
(1939/10/26)
(1954/03/?)
Beau Night in Hotchkiss Corners (Herb Magidson—Ben Oakland)
(1940/12/17)
Beautiful Madness (?)
(1951/01/25)
Because I Love You (Irving Berlin)
(1937/05/13)
(1937/07/12)
Bedford Drive (Buster Harding)
(1945/01/09)
(1945/10/03)
(1950/01/?)
Begin the Beguine (Cole Porter)
(1938/07/24)
(1938/09/16)
(1938/11/18)
(1938/11/25)
(1938/11/27)
(1938/11/28)

(1938/12/13)
(1938/12/14)
(1938/12/30)
(1939/01/15)
(1939/05/23)
(1939/06/10)
(1940/09/09)
(1943/01/30)
(1945/04/08)
(1945/09/12)
(1946/06/13)
(1949/12/?)
(1954/03/?)
Besame Mucho (Consuelo Velasquez—Sunny Skylar)
(1953/12/?)
(1954/03/?)
Better Than the Average Girl (Maxwell)
(1939/03/19)
Between a Kiss and a Sigh (Art Johnston—Johnny Burke)
(1938/11/17)
(1938/12/20)
Bewitched, Bothered & Bewildered (Richard
    Rodgers—Lorenz Hart)
(1954/06/?)
Beyond the Blue Horizon (Leo Robin—Richard Whiting)
(1941/06/26)
(1941/O9/03)
Big Dipper (Larry Clinton)
(1937/12/15)
Bill (Jerome Kern—Oscar Hammerstein)
(1939/01/23)
Bird Calls (= Artie's Blues, Blues Jam Session) (Artie
    Shaw—Count Basie)
(1944/09/25)
Black and Blue (Fats Waller—Andy Razaf)
(1937/lO/17)
Blue Again (Jimmy McHugh—Dorothy Fields)
(1950/07/l9)
(1950/09/14)
Blue Fantasy (Frankie Carle)
(1938/02/15)
Blue Interlude (Benny Carter)
(1938/12/02)
Blue Skies (Irving Berlin)
(1937/05/18)
(1939/06/06)
(1945/09/26)
The Blues (Artie Shaw)
(1937/03/04)
The Blues (Artie Shaw)
(1938/12/25)
Blues (from Lenox Avenue Suite), Pts.1/2 (William Grant
    Still)

(1940/11/04)
(1940/12/04)
The Blues A/B (= The Blues March (Artie Shaw)
(1937/08/04)
Blues in the Night (Harold Arlen—Johnny Mercer)
(1941/09/02)
(1941/09/06)
(1941/12/08)
Blues Jam Session (= Artie's Blues, Bird Calls) (Artie
    Shaw—Count Basie)
(1944/09/25)
Bob White (Bernie Hanighen—Johnny Mercer)
(1937/12/15)
Born to Swing (Artie Shaw)
(1937/04/28)
Bring Back the Thrill (Pete Rugolo—Ruth Poll)
(1951/01/30)
The Bus Blues (= Free for All) (Artie Shaw)
(1937/04/28)
(1937/10/18)
But Not for Me (George Gershwin—Ira Gershwin)
(1945/04/17)

Call of the Freaks (Luis Russell)
(1938/02/15)
The Calypso (Herb Magidson—Ben Oakland)
(1940/12/17)
Can I Forget You? (Jerome Kern—Oscar Hammerstein)
(1937/07/12)
Can't Help Lovin' That Man (Jerome Kern—Oscar
    Hammerstein)
(1945/01/09)
Can't Teach My Old Heart New Tricks (Richard
    Whiting—Johnny Mercer)
(1937/12/15)
Can't You Read Between the Lines (Jule Styne—Sammy
    Kahn)
(1945/10/10)
Canto Karabali (see Jungle Drums) (Ernesto Lecuona—C.
    O'Flynn—C. Lombardo)
Carioca (Vincent Youmans—Edward Eliscu—Gus Kahn)
(1939/01/13)
(1939/01/23)
(1939/02/05)
(1939/05/23)
(1939/08/19)
Carnival (Paul Jordan)
(1942/01/21)
(1949/12/?)
Changing My Tune (George Gershwin—Ira Gershwin)
(1946/08/16)
The Chant (= Ubangi) (Artie Shaw)
1937/04/28
1937/08/04

1938/02/15)
1939/03/12)
1939/05/28)
Chantez Les Bas (W. C. Handy)
(1940/09/07)
Chapel of the Roses (Abel Baer)
(1951/01/25)
The Chaser (= Sequence in B flat) (Artie Shaw)
1954/03/?)
Clarinet Quintet in A Major (K.581) (W. A. Mozart)
(1949/03/?)
Clarinet Trio in E–flat (K.498) (W. A. Mozart)
(1949/03/?)
Comes Love (Sam Stept—Charles Tobias—Lew Brown)
(1939/06/12)
(1939/06/13)
(1939/08/19)
(1939/10/20)
(1949/12/?)
Comin' On (Artie Shaw)
(1938/07/24)
(1938/11/29)
Concerto for Clarinet (Nikolai Berezowski)
(1949/04/18)
Concerto for Clarinet (Norman Dello Joio)
(c.1949–50)
Concerto for Clarinet (Artie Shaw)
(1940/08/16)
(1940/12/17)
Confessin' (Al Neiberg—Dan Dougherty—Ellis Reynolds)
(1941/06/26)
Connecticut (Hugh Martin—Ralph Blane)
(1946/10/16)
The Continental (Con Conrad—Herb Magidson)
(1950/03?)
Cool Daddy (Artie Shaw)
(1949/12/?)
Copenhagen (Walter Melrose—Charlie Davis)
(1936/12/23)
(1937/03/04)
(1938/11/17)
(1938/11/25)
(1938/12/04)
(1938/12/06)
(1938/12/30)
(1939/01/18)
(1939/06/27)
(1939/08/31)
(1939/10/20)
(1939/11/10)
Corcovado (Darius Milhaud)
(1949/03/11)

Count Every Star (Bruno Coquatrix—Sammy Gallop)
(1950/04/27)
Cream Puff (Artie Shaw—Franklin Marks)
(1936/12/23)
(1937/03/04)
Cross Your Heart (Buddy DeSylva—Lou Gensler)
(1940/09/03)
(1941/01/21)
(1950/01/?)
(1954/03/?)
Crumbum (Artie Shaw)
(1950/04/08)
(1954/03/?)

Dancing in the Dark (Art Schwartz—Howard Dietz)
(1940/12/16)
(1941/01/23)
(1941/09/06)
(1954/03/?)
Dancing on the Ceiling (Richard Rodgers—Lorenz Hart)
(1945/07/24)
(1951/01/30)
(1954/06/?)
Danza Lucumi (Ernesto Lecuona)
(1940/10/07)
Darling Not Without You (Abner Silver—Al Sherman—Ed Heyman)
(1936/09/17)
Day After Day (Richard Himber—Bud Green)
(1938/11/17)
Day In Day Out (Rube Bloom—Johnny Mercer)
(1939/08/27)
(1939/10/19)
(1939/11/10)
Deep in a Dream (Jimmy Van Heusen—Eddie DeLange)
(1938/11/17)
(1938/12/02)
(1938/12/14)
(1938/12/25)
Deep Purple (Peter DeRose)
(1939/02/19)
(1939/03/12)
(1939/02/?)
Deep River (Henry Thacker Burleigh)
(1941/02/17)
Delightful Delirium (Bickley Reichner—Clay Boland)
(1939/01/31)
A Deserted Farm (Edward MacDowell)
(1940/03/03)
Deuces Wild (Margie Gibson)
(1941/11/12)
Diga Diga Doo (Jimmy McHugh—Dorothy Fields)
(1938/12/20)

(1938/12/29)
(1939/01/08)
(1939/02/19)
(1939/11/11)
(1940/12/02)
Do I Love You? (Cole Porter)
(1939/11/09)
Do You Know Why? (Jimmy Van Heusen—Johnny Burke)
(1941/01/21)
Don't Blame Me (Jimmy McHugh—Dorothy Fields)
(1945/07/28)
Don't Ever Change (Lou Handman—Walt Hirsch)
(1937/07/12)
Don't Fall Asleep (Artie Shaw—Art Quenzer)
(1940/03/03)
Don't Take Your Love from Me (Henry Nemo)
(1941/06/26)
(1950/01/?)
(1954/03/?)
Don't Worry 'Bout Me (Rube Bloom—Ted Koehler)
(1939/06/06)
(1939/08/19)
(1950/07/19)
Don't You Believe It Dear (Artie Shaw—Johnny Lehman)
(1946/10/18)
Donkey Serenade (Rudolf Friml)
(1939/01/23)
(1939/07/13)
(1939/08/19)
(1939/08/22)
Double Mellow (Artie Shaw—Teddy McRae)
(1939/03/12)
(1939/07/12–31)
(1940/08/25)
Dr. Livingstone, I Presume? (Artie Shaw)
(1940/12/05)
(1941/01/22)
Dreaming Out Loud (Sam Coslow)
(1940/05/13)

Easy to Love (Cole Porter)
(1945/06/07)
(1949/12/?)
Easy to Say (Artie Shaw—Art Quenzer)
(1939/06/22)
El Rancho Grande (Silvano Ramos—Bartley Costello)
(1939/11/03)
Evensong (Paul Jordan)
(1941/12/23)
Everything Is Jumpin' (Artie Shaw)
(1939/10/20)
(1939/10/25)
(1939/11/11)

(1940/08/25)
(1940/10/26)
Everything You Said Came True (Dane Franklyn—Cliff Friend)
(1937/10/17)
Exactly Like You (Jimmy McHugh—Dorothy Fields)
(1950/01/?)

Fee Fi Fo Fum (Artie Shaw—Al Avola)
(1937/08/04)
(1937/10/17)
A Foggy Day (George Gershwin—Ira Gershwin)
(1945/06/08)
Foggy Foggy Dew (traditional)
(1950/04/04)
The Folks Who Live on the Hill (Jerome Kern—Oscar Hammerstein)
(1937/07/12)
For You For Me Forevermore (George Gershwin—Ira Gershwin)
(1946/08/16)
Fred's Delight (Tadd Dameron)
(1950/01/?)
Free for All (= The Bus Blues) (Artie Shaw)
(1937/04/28)
(1937/10/18)
Free Wheeling (Artie Shaw)
(1937/09/17)
(1937/10/17)
(1938/12/16)
Frenesi (Alberto Dominguez)
(1940/03/03)
(1940/07/01)
(1940/08/12)
(1941/01/22)
(1941/09/06)
(1954/03/?)

Gangbusters (Artie Shaw—Teddy McRae)
(1939/03/26)
(1939/07/12–31)
The Gentle Grifter (Artie Shaw)
(1945/08/01)
Georgia on My Mind (Hoagy Carmichael—Stuart Gorrell)
(1941/02/03)
(1941/03/20)
Get Out of Town (Cole Porter)
(1946/06/25)
Ghost of a Chance (Victor Young—Bing Crosby—Ned Washington)
(1946/08-09)
The Gilder (Count Basie—Buster Harding)
(1945/08–09)
(1945/10/10)

Gloomy Sunday (Lazlo Janor—Rezso Seress)
   (1940/03/03)
Go Fly a Kite (James Monaco—Johnny Burke)
   (1939/06/12)
   (1939/08/19)
Good for Nothin' But Love (Jimmy Van Heusen—Eddie
      DeLange)
   (1939/02/05)
Goodnight Angel (Herb Magidson—Allie Wrubel)
   (1937/12/15)
   (1937/12/30)
Got the Mis'ry (Willie Smith)
   (1939/10/26)
Gotta Be This or That (Sunny Skylar)
   (1945/09/19)
The Grabtown Grapple (Artie Shaw—Buster Harding)
   (1945/01/09)
   (1950/01/?)
   (1954/03/?)
Guadalajira (Morton Gould)
   (1949/03/11)
Gue-le-le (John Bartee)
   (1949/12/?)
Guilty (Richard Whiting—Gus Kahn—Harry Akst)
   (1946/09/19)

Habanera (Maurice Ravel)
   (1949/03/11)
   (1949/03/17)
A Handful of Stars (Jack Lawrence—Ted Shapiro)
   (1940/10/07)
Have You Forgotten? (?)
   (1938/12/04)
Have You Met Miss Jones? (Richard Rodgers—Lorenz
      Hart)
   (1937/10/17)
He's Funny That Way (Richard Whiting—Neil Moret)
   (1949/12/?)
He's Gone Away (traditional)
   (1950/04/04)
Hebrew Sketches (Alexander Krein)
   (1949/03/?)
Hillbilly from Tenth Avenue (M. K. Jerome—Jack Scholl)
   (1938/02/15)
Hindustan (Lew Wallace—Harold Weeks)
   (1942/01/20)
   (1945/10/10)
Hold Your Hat (Artie Shaw)
   (1938/12/25)
   (1938/12/27)
Hold Your Hats (Artie Shaw)
   (1937/04/28)

Honeysuckle Rose (Fats Waller—Andy Razaf)
   (1937/12/15)
   (1944/09/30)
Hop Skip and Jump (Artie Shaw)
   (1945/08/01)
   (1945/09/26)
The Hornet (Buster Harding)
   (1945/08-09)
How Come You Do Me Like You Do? (Gene Austin—Roy
      Bergere)
   (1937/03/04)
How Deep Is the Ocean (Irving Berlin)
   (1945/08-09)
   (1950/01/?)
How Dry I Am (traditional)
   (1937/07/22)
   (1937/10/17)
How High the Moon (Morris Lewis—Diane Hamilton)
   (1954/03/?)

I Ain't Comin' (Artie Shaw)
   (1939/05/28)
I Apologize (Al Hoffman—Al Goodhart—Ed Nelson)
   (1951/01/30)
I Ask the Stars (Artie Shaw)
   (1941/09/03)
I Believe (Jule Styne—Sammy Cahn)
   (1946/11/08)
I Can't Afford to Dream (Sam Stept—Charles Tobias—Lew
      Brown)
   (1939/06/12)
I Can't Believe That You're in Love with Me (Jimmy
      McHugh)
   (1938/07/24)
   (1938/11/25)
   (1938/12/13)
I Can't Escape from You (Richard Whiting—Leo Robin)
   (1945/07/30)
I Can't Get Started (Vernon Duke—Ira Gershwin)
   (1945/07/24)
   (1954/03/?)
I Can't Give You Anything But Love (Jimmy
      McHugh—Dorothy Fields)
   (1939/10/28)
I Concentrate on You (Cole Porter)
   (1949/05/31)
   (1949/01/?)
I Could Write a Book (Richard Rodgers—Lorenz Hart)
   (1945/06/12)
I Cover the Waterfront (Johnny Green—Ed Heyman)
   (1938/12/29)
   (1941/01/23)
   (1949/12/?)

I Cried for You (Gus Arnheim—Abe Lyman—Art Freed)
(1939/02/26)

I Didn't Know What Time It Was (Richard
Rodgers—Lorenz Hart)
(1939/11/O9)
(1939/11/11)

I Don't Want to Walk Without You (Jule Styne—Frank
Loesser)
(1941/12/23)

I Get a Kick Out of You (Cole Porter)
(1949/12/?)
(1950/01/03)

I Got the Sun in the Morning (Irving Berlin)
(1946/04/30)

I Have Eyes (Ralph Rainger—Leo Robin)
(1938/09/27)
(1939/02/05)
(1939/01/?)

I Haven't Changed a Thing (Henry Nemo)
(1938/12/15)

I Love the Guy (Cy Cohen)
(1950/05/31)

I May Hate Myself in the Morning (George Weiss)
(1952/04/23)

I Never Knew Heaven Could Speak (Harry Revel—Mack
Gordon)
(1939/06/27)

I Only Have Eyes for You (Harry Warren—Al Dubin)
(1949/12/?)

I Poured My Heart into a Song (Irving Berlin)
(1939/06/05)

I Surrender Dear (Harry Barris—Gordon Clifford)
(1937/05/18)
(1939/08/27)

I Used to Be Above Love (Vernon Duke—Ira Gershwin)
(1936/06/11)

I Used to Be Color Blind (Irving Berlin)
(1938/12/06)

I Waited a Little Too Long (Sidney Miller—Donald
O'Connor)
(1952/04/23)

I Want a New Romance (Burton Lane—Sam Coslow)
(1937/10/17)

I Want My Share of Love (Saul Chaplin—Sammy Cahn)
(1939/01/31)
(1939/03/05)

I Was Doing All Right (George Gershwin—Ira Gershwin)
(1945/03/15)
(1945/07/14)

I Won't Tell a Soul (Ross Parker—Hughie Charles)
(1938/12/02)

I'd Rather Be Right (Richard Rodgers—Lorenz Hart)
(1937/10/17)

I'll Be Seeing You (Sammy Fain—Irving Kahal)
(1953/07/02)

I'll Be with You in Apple Blossom Time (Albert von
Tilzer—Neville Fleeson)
(1937/12/15)
(1937/12/30)
(1938/12/02)

I'll Never Be the Same (Gus Kahn—M. Malneck—F.
Signorelli)
(1945/01/09)

I'll Never Let You Cry (Lew Pollack—Sidney Mitchell)
(1938/02/15)

I'll Never Tell You I Love You (Will Hudson—Irving Mills)
(1937/04/28)

I'll Remember April (Don Raye—Gene DePaul—Pat
Johnston)
(1950/04/04)

I'll Remember (Burton Lane—Art Freed)
(1939/06/22)

I'm Coming Virginia (Will Cook—Don Heywood)
(1939/01/13)
(1939/02/12)
(1939/03/12)
(1939/04/02)
(1939/07/12–31)
(1939/10/20)

I'm Forever Blowing Bubbles (Jean Kenbrovin—John
Kellette)
(1950/05/29)

I'm in Love with the Honorable Mr. So-and-So (Sam
Coslow)
(1939/03/12)
(1939/04/02)

I'm Madly in Love with You (J. F. Coots—Benny Davis)
(1938/12/11)

I'm Sorry for Myself (Irving Berlin)
(1939/10/21)

I'm Yours (Johnny Green—E. Y. Harburg)
(1937/10/17)
(1937/10/18)
(1939/07/13)
(1939/10/25)
(1939/11/03)

I've a Strange New Rhythm in My Heart (Cole Porter)
(1937/09/17)
(1937/10/17)

I've Been Saving Myself for You (Saul Chaplin—Sammy
Cahn)
(1939/01/01)

I've Got a Crush on You (George Gershwin—Ira Gershwin)
(1954/03/?)

I've Got Beginner's Luck (George Gershwin—Ira
Gershwin)
(1937/04/28)

I've Got My Eye on You (Cole Porter)
(1939/10/26)
I've Got to Pass Your House (Lew Brown)
(1951/01/25)
I've Got You Under My Skin (Cole Porter)
(1946/06/25)
If Dreams Come True (Edgar Sampson—Benny
      Goodman—Irving Mills)
(1938/02/15)
If I Had You (Ted Shapiro—Jimmy Campbell—Reg
      Connely)
(1937/07/12)
(1938/12/06)
(1941/03/20)
If I Love Again (J. P. Murray—Ben Oakland)
(1941/09/02)
If I Put My Heart into a Song (Sam Coslow)
(1937/07/12)
If It's the Last Thing I Do (Saul Chaplin—Sammy Cahn)
(1937/09/17)
If It's You (Artie Shaw—Milt Drake—Ben Oakland)
(1940/09/07)
If What You Say Is True (Henry Nemo)
(1939/09/28)
(1939/11/04)
If You Ever Change Your Mind (G. Watts—B. Green—M.
      Sigler)
(1939/03/17)
If You Ever Should Leave (Saul Chaplin—Sammy Cahn)
(1937/07/12)
(1937/07/22)
If You Were Only Mine (isham Jones—Charles Newman)
(1950/04/27)
Imagination (Jimmy Van Heusen—Johnny Burke)
(1953/12/?)
(1954/03/?)
In the Bottom (= Leapin' at the Lincoln, Rockin' the State)
      (Artie Shaw)
(1937/04/28)
(1938/12/01)
(1938/12/11)
In the Mood (Joe Garland—Andy Razaf)
(1938/12/15)
(1938/12/18)
(1938/12/20)
In the Shade of the New Apple Tree (Harold Arlen—E. Y.
      Harburg)
(1938/02/15)
In the Still of the Night (Cole Porter)
(1946/06/12)
(1953/07/02)
Indian Love Call (Rudolf Friml—Otto Harbach—Oscar
      Hammerstein)

(1938/02/15)
(1938/07/24)
(1939/01/01)
Innuendo (Johnny Mandel)
(1949/12/?)
Interlude in B-flat (Artie Shaw)
(1936/05/24)
Is It Taboo? (Edgar Leslie—Albert Debru)
(1941/09/03)
It Ain't Right (Joseph Meyer—Bob Rothberg)
(1936/08/06)
It Could Happen to You (Jimmy Van Heusen—Johnny
      Burke)
(1953/07/06)
It Goes to Your Feet (Sammy Fain—Lew Brown)
(1937/05/13)
It Had to Be You (isham Jones—Gus Kahn)
(1938/11/25)
(1938/12/11)
(1938/12/13)
(1938/12/19)
(1938/12/30)
(1939/05/30)
(1939/11/03)
(1941/03/20)
(1941/12/08)
It Took a Million Years (Larry Clinton—William Wolfe)
(1938/12/19)
It's a Long Way to Tipperary (Jack Judge—Harry Williams)
(1937/09/17)
(1937/10/17)
(1950/07/19)
It's All Yours (Art Schwartz—Dorothy Fields)
(1939/01/31)
(1939/03/26)
It's the Natural Thing to Do (Art Johnston—Johnny Burke)
(1937/07/12)
It's the Same Old Dream (Jule Styne—Sammy Cahn)
(1946/11/08)
It's Wonderful (Stuff Smith—Mitchell Parish)
(1938/02/15)

Japanese Sandman (Richard Whiting—Ray Egan)
(1936/06/11)
Jeepers Creepers (Harry Warren—Johnny Mercer)
(1938/12/25)
(1938/12/29)
(1939/02/?)
Jingle Bells (John Pierpoint)
(1950/09/14)
Johnny One Note (Richard Rodgers—Lorenz Hart)
(1937/04/28)

Jumpin' on the Merry-Go-Round (Ray Conniff)
(1944/11/23)
(1945/09/26)
Jungle Drums (= Canto Karabali) (Ernesto Lecuona—C.
O'Flynn—C. Lombardo)
(1938/12/16)
(1938/12/19)
(1938/12/30)
(1939/01/18)
(1939/03/05)
(1939/07/12–31)
(1940/09/02)
(1941/01/20)
(1941/01/22)
Just a Kid Named Joe (Jerry Livingston—Mack David)
(1938/12/01)
(1938/12/20)
Just Floatin' Along (Artie Shaw—George Siravo)
(1945/07/26)
(1945/09/19)
Just Kiddin' Around (Ray Conniff)
(1941/10/30)
Just Say I Love Her (Jimmy Dale)
(1950/05/31)
Just You Just Me (Jesse Greer—Norman Klages)
(1937/07/12)
(1937/10/18)
(1938/12/20)
(1938/12/?)

Kasbah (Ray Conniff)
(1945/06/14)
Keepin' Myself for You (Vincent Youmans—Sidney Clare)
(1940/09/03)
(1945/07/06)
King for a Day (Sam Lewis—Joe Young—Ted Fiorito)
(1940/05/13)
(1940/08/19)
Krazy Kat (Johnny Mandel)
(1949/12/?)

Lady Day (Jimmy Mundy)
(1944/11/23)
The Lady Is a Tramp (Richard Rodgers—Lorenz Hart)
(1937/12/15)
Lambeth Walk (Noel Gay)
(1938/12/01)
Lament (Ray Conniff)
(1945/06/14)
The Lamp Is Low (Buddy DeSylva—Bert
Shafter—Mitchell Parish)
(1939/08/22)

Last Night (Nick & Charles Kenny—Austin Groom-
Johnson)
(1939/11/04)
The Last Two Weeks in July (Sam Lewis—Abel Baer)
(1939/08/27)
(1939/10/28)
Leapin' at the Lincoln (= In the Bottom, Rockin' the State)
(Artie Shaw)
(1938/12/01)
Let 'er Go (Larry Clinton)
(1937/10/18)
Let's Call a Heart a Heart (Art Johnston—Johnny Burke)
(1936/09/17)
Let's Fall in Love (Harold Arlen—Ted Koehler)
(1949/12/?)
Let's Stop the Clock (Peter DeRose—Haven Gillespie)
(1938/11/28)
(1938/12/20)
Let's Take the Long Way Home (Harold Arlen—Johnny
Mercer)
(1944/11/23)
Let's Walk (Artie Shaw—George Siravo)
(1945/08-09)
(1945/11/07)
Lilacs in the Rain (Peter DeRose—Mitchell Parish)
(1939/10/28)
Limehouse Blues (Phil Braham—Doug Furber)
(1938/11/09)
(1945/04/08)
Little Gate Special (Ray Conniff)
(1940/12/02)
(1941/03/03)
(1941/09/06)
Little Jazz (Buster Harding)
(1945/04/05)
(1945/04/08)
(1945/09/12)
Long Ago and Far Away (Jerome Kern—Ira Gershwin)
(1944/06/10)
Looking for Yesterday (Jimmy Van Heusen—Eddie
DeLange)
(1940/10/26)
Lost in the Shuffle (?)
(1938/02/15)
Love and Learn (Art Schwartz—Ed Heyman)
(1936/11/30)
The Love Bug Will Bite You (Pinky Tomlin)
(1937/04/28)
Love for Sale (Cole Porter)
(1937/12/15)
(1946/09/10)
(1950/01/?)

Love Is a Merry-Go-Round (Rube Bloom—Johnny Mercer)
    (1937/07/12)
Love Is Good for Anything That Ails You (Lou
    Handman—Walt Hirsch)
    (1937/02/15)
    (1937/03/04)
Love Is Here (Artie Shaw—Art Quenzer)
    (1939/10/26)
Love Is the Sweetest Thing (Ray Noble)
    (1950/01/03)
    (1950/01/?)
Love Me a Little Little (Herb Holmes—Howard
    Smith—Ellen Orr)
    (1941/06/26)
Love of My Life (Artie Shaw—Johnny Mercer)
    (1940/08/25)
    (1940/10/07)
    (1940/10/28)
    (1945/08-09)
    (1950/01/?)
    (1954/03/?)
Love Walked In (George Gershwin—Ira Gershwin)
    (1945/07/03)
    (1945/10/10)
    (1949/12/?)
    (1950/01/06)
The Loveliness of You (Harry Revel—Mack Gordon)
    (1937/07/12)
Love's Old Sweet Song (A. C. Bingham—J. L. Molloy)
    (1938/02/15)
Lover Come Back to Me (Sigmund Romberg—Oscar
    Hammerstein)
    (1939/01/17)
    (1939/01/18)
    (1939/09/19)
Lucky Number (Ray Conniff)
    (1945/06/08)
    (1945/06/14)
    (1945/09/12)
Lugubrious (Artie Shaw)
    (1954/03/?)
Lyric (Artie Shaw)
    (1954/03/?)

The Maid with the Flaccid Air (Eddie Sauter)
    (1945/07/19)
Make Love to Me (Kim Gannon—Paul Mann—Stephen
    Weiss)
    (1941/10/30)
A Man and His Dream (James Monaco—Johnny Burke)
    (1939/06/12)
Man from Mars (Artie Shaw)
    (1939/09/19)

    (1939/10/21)
    (1939/10/28)
    (1939/11/03)
The Man I Love (George Gershwin—Ira Gershwin)
    (1939/01/23)
    (1945/06/12)
    (1949/05/31)
Many Dreams Ago (Fred Ahlert—Al Stilman)
    (1939/09/28)
    (1939/10/19)
    (1939/10/25)
    (1939/11/10)
Maria My Own (Ernesto Lecuona—Wolfe Gilbert)
    (1939/10/25)
    (1939/11/04)
Marinella (Artie Shaw—J. Serrano—Romero)
    (1940/10/07)
Meade Lux Special (Artie Shaw)
    (1938/02/15)
Melancholy Lullaby (Benny Carter—Ed Heyman)
    (1939/10/21)
    (1939/10/28)
    (1939/11/03)
Melancholy Mood (Walter Schumann—Victor Knight)
    (1939/06/22)
A Message from the Man in the Moon (Bronislaw Caper)
    (1937/03/04)
Milenburg Joys (Paul Mares—Leon Roppolo—Jelly Roll
    Morton)
    (1937/04/28)
Minnesota (Johnny Mandel)
    (1949/12/?)
Mister Meadowlark (Walter Donaldson—Johnny Mercer)
    (1940/05/13)
Monday Morning (Lindsay Buckingham)
    (1938/12/13)
Monsoon (Artie Shaw)
    (1937/10/18)
    (1937/12/15)
Mood in Question (Alan Shulman)
    (1949/05/31)
The Mood That I'm In (Abner Silver—Al Sherman)
    (1937/03/04)
Moon Face (Art Schwartz—Ed Heyman)
    (1936/11/30)
    (1937/03/04)
The Moon Got in My Eyes (Art Johnston—Johnny Burke)
    (1937/07/12)
Moonglow (Will Hudson—Eddie DeLange—Irving Mills)
    (1941/01/23)
    (1949/12/?)
Moonlight and Shadows (Fred Hollander—Leo Robin)
    (1937/02/15)

Moonlight on the Sunset Trail (?)
  (1938/02/15)
Moonray (Artie Shaw—Art Quenzer)
  (1939/06/22)
  (1939/08/19)
  (1939/10/19)
  (1939/10/20)
  (1939/10/21)
  (1939/10/25)
  (1939/11/10)
  (1939/11/11)
More Than Ever (isham Jones—Bud Green)
  (1938/02/15)
Mucho de Nada (Manuel Rojas—John Bartee)
  (1949/12/?)
  (1949/12/30)
My Blue Heaven (George Whiting—Walter Donaldson)
  (1936/12/23)
  (1937/03/04)
  (1939/11/11)
  (1940/12/05)
My Bonnie Lies over the Ocean (traditional)
  (1937/12/15)
My Fantasy (Paul Whiteman—Jack Meskill—Joan
  Edwards)
  (1940/03/03)
My Funny Valentine (Richard Rodgers—Lorenz Hart)
  (1954/06/?)
My Heart Belongs to Daddy (Cole Porter)
  (1939/01/15)
  (1939/03/12)
  (1946/06/13)
My Heart Stood Still (Richard Rodgers—Lorenz Hart)
  (1939/01/17)
  (1939/01/18)
  (1939/02/12)
  (1939/10/21)
  (1940/09/30)
  (1945/04/08)
  (1945/09/19)
My Kind of Love (Louis Altier—Joe Trent)
  (1951/01/30)
My Little Nest of Heavenly Blue (Franz Lehar—S. Spaeth)
  (1952/08/01)
My Old Kentucky Home (Stephen Foster)
  (1938/02/15)
My Own (Jimmy McHugh—Harold Adamson)
  (1939/01/29)
My Reverie (Claude Debussy—Larry Clinton)
  (1938/11/25)
  (1938/12/?)
  (1938/12/18)
  (1939/01/08)

My Romance (Richard Rodgers—Lorenz Hart)
  (1940/09/23)
Mysterioso (Artie Shaw)
  (1945/08/01)

Natch (Artie Shaw—Nat Leslie)
  (1945/07/06)
Needlenose (Ray Conniff—Ed McKinney)
  (1942/01/21)
Never in a Million Years (Harry Revel—Mack Gordon)
  (1937/04/28)
Night and Day (Cole Porter)
  (1937/04/28)
  (1937/05/18)
  (1945/11/07)
  (1946/06/19)
Night Over Shanghai (Harry Warren—Johnny Mercer)
  (1937/04/28)
  (1938/11/29)
Nightmare (Artie Shaw)
  (1937/09/17)
  (1937/12/15)
  (1938/09/27)
  (1939/04/02)
  (1949/12/?)
No More Tears (Burton Lane—Art Freed)
  (1937/02/15)
  (1937/03/04)
No Name Blues (Artie Shaw)
  (1940-41)
No One But You (Artie Shaw—George Siravo—Nat Leslie)
  (1945/07/06)
  (1945/07/20)
  (1945/11/07)
No Regrets (Harry Tobias—Roy Ingraham)
  (1936/06/17)
Nobody Knows the Trouble I've Seen (traditional)
  (1941/01/13)
  (1941/01/22)
Nocturne (Thomas Griselle)
  (1941/09/02)
Non-Stop Flight (Artie Shaw)
  (1937/12/15)
  (1937/12/30)
  (1938/09/27)
  (1938/11/20)
  (1938/11/28)
  (1938/12/01)
  (1939/03/05)
  (1939/06/20)
  (1939/07/12–31))
Not Mine (Victor Schertzinger—Johnny Mercer)
  (1942/01/20)

Nothin' from Nothin' (Morton Gould—Dorothy Fields)
  (1950/01/06)
Now We Know (Willard Robison—Ray Mayer)
  (1940/05/13)

Octoroon (Harry Warren)
  (1939/06/05)
  (1939/06/06)
  (1939/08/22)
Oh Lady Be Good (George Gershwin—Ira Gershwin)
  (1939/02/?)
  (1939/08/27)
  (1944/09/25)
Oh You Crazy Moon (Jimmy Van Heusen—Eddie Delange)
  (1939/10/25)
  (1939/11/10)
The Old Apple Tree (M. K. Jerome)
  (1938/02/15)
Old Black Joe (Stephen Foster)
  (1937/10/17)
Old Old Castle in Scotland (Herb Magidson—Ben Oakland)
  (1940/09/07)
The Old Stomping Ground (Willie Smith—La
    Freniere—Bishop)
  (1937/12/15)
  (1938/12/06)
  (1938/12/13)
  (1938/12/30)
On the Atcheson Topeka and Santa Fe (Harry Warren)
  (1945/09/19)
On the Sunny Side of the Street (Jimmy McHugh—Dorothy
    Fields)
  (1945/09/26)
One Foot in the Groove (Artie Shaw—Wen D'Aurey)
  (1939/03/17)
  (1939/04/02)
  (1939/07/12–31)
  (1939/08/19)
  (1939/10/19)
  (1939/11/10)
One Night Stand (Artie Shaw)
  (1939/03/17)
  (1939/06/10)
  (1939/06/13)
One Song (Frank Churchill—Larry Morey)
  (1937/12/15)
  (1937/12/30)
One Two Button Your Shoe (Art Johnston—Johnny Burke)
  (1936/09/17)
Opening Theme (Artie Shaw)
  (1940/08/25)
Orinoco (Manuel Rojas—John Bartee—Roger Segure)
  (1949/12/?)
  (1949/12/30)

Our Love Is Here to Stay (George Gershwin—Ira Gershwin)
  (1945/07/14)
Out of Nowhere (Johnny Green—Ed Heyman)
  (1938/12/02)
  (1939/06/05)
  (1939/10/19)
  (1939/10/28)
  (1940/08/26)
Over the Rainbow (Harold Arlen—E.Y. Harburg)
  (1939/11/04)

Pastel Blue (Artie Shaw—Charlie Shavers))
  (1939/03/12)
  (1939/03/26)
Petite Piece (Claude Debussy)
  (1949/03/11)
The Pied Piper of Hamelin (Artie Shaw)
  (1946/07/21)
  (1946/07/28)
The Pied Piper Theme (Artie Shaw)
  (1950/01/?)
  (1954/03/?)
Please Pardon Us We're in Love (Harry Revel—Mack
    Gordon)
  (1937/08/04)
Posin' (Saul Chaplin—Sammy Cahn)
  (1937/07/12)
Powerhouse (Raymond Scott)
  (1938/02/15)
Prelude (Dimitri Shostakovich)
  (1949/03/11)
Prelude in C Major (Artie Shaw—Ray Conniff)
  (1940/11/11)
  (1940/12/04)
  (1941/01/22)
A Pretty Girl Is Like a Melody (Irving Berlin)
  (1936/06/11)
Prosschai (Saul Chaplin—Sammy Cahn)
  (1938/11/28)
  (1938/12/20)
  (1939/01/15)
  (1939/03/12)
  (1939/03/26)
Put That Down in Writing (Harry Warren—Al Dubin)
  (1939/08/27)
  (1939/10/19)
Pyramid (Duke Ellington—Juan Tizol—Irving Mills)
  (1940/12/03)

Rendezvous (for Clarinet and Strings) (Alan Shulman)
  (1949/03/18)
  (1949/05/31)

Rockin' Chair (Hoagy Carmichael)
    (1941/01/27)
    (1941/09/02)
Rockin' the State (= In the Bottom, Leapin' at the Lincoln)
    (Artie Shaw)
    (1938/12/11)
A Room with a View (Al Stillman—Einar Swain)
    (1938/12/18)
    (1939/01/15)
Rosalie (Cole Porter)
    (1937/10/17)
    (1939/01/17)
    (1939/01/18)
    (1939/03/05)
Rose Room (Art Hickman—Harry Williams)
    (1939/01/18)
    (1939/01/29)
    (1939/01/31)
    (1939/08/19)
    (1940/09/16)
Rough Ridin' (Hank Jones—Ella Fitzgerald)
    (1954/06/?)

'S Wonderful (George Gershwin—Ira Gershwin)
    (1945/01/09)
    (1945/10/03)
    (1945/11/07)
    (1949/12/?)
S.O.S. (Artie Shaw)
    (1937/10/17)
S'posin' (Paul Denniker—Andy Razaf)
    (1954/06/?)
The Sad Sack (Artie Shaw—Buster Harding)
    (1945/01/09)
    (1945/10/03)
    (1954/03/7)
The Same Old Line (Tot Seymour—Vee Lawnhurst)
    (1936/11/30)
Say It with a Kiss (Harry Warren—Johnny Mercer)
    (1938/12/19)
Scuttlebutt (Artie Shaw)
    (1945/07/31)
    (1945/09/19)
    (1954/03/?)
September in the Rain (Harry Warren—Al Dubin)
    (1937/03/04)
September Song (Kurt Weill—Maxwell Anderson)
    (1945/04/05)
    (1953/07/06)
    (1954/06/?)
Sequence in B-flat (= The Chaser) (Artie Shaw)
    (1954/03/?)
Serenade in Blue (Harry Warren—Mack Gordon)
    (1950/10/05)

Serenade to a Savage (Joe Garland)
    (1939/01/08)
    (1939/01/13)
    (1939/06/22)
    (1939/11/10)
    (1939/06/12)
Shadows (Frankie Carle—Chet Thompson—Jules Loman)
    (1939/11/09)
The Shekomeko Shuffle (Artie Shaw)
    (1950/04/08)
Shindig (Artie Shaw)
    (1937/10/17)
Shine On Harvest Moon (Nora Bayes—Jack Norworth)
    (1938/12/01)
    (1938/12/13)
    (1938/12/25)
    (1938/12/29)
Shoot the Likker [Rhythm] to Me John Boy (Artie Shaw)
    (1937/08/17)
    (1937/10/17)
    (1938/11/25)
    (1939/01/?)
    (1939/02/19)
    (1939/05/23)
    (1939/06/10)
A Short Story (Dimitri Kabalevsky)
    (1949/03/11)
Show Me the Way to Go Home (Reg Connelly—Jimmy
    Campbell)(as "Irving King")
    (1937/12/15)
    (1950/07/19)
Show Your Linen Miss Richardson (Bernie
    Hanighen—Johnny Mercer)
    (1939/06/20)
Similau (Eddie Sauter)
    (1950/01/?)
Simple and Sweet (Sammy Fain—Irving Kahal)
    (1938/12/02)
    (1938/12/11)
    (1938/12/29)
The Skeleton in the Closet (Art Johnston—Johnny Burke)
    (1936/10/30)
    (1936/11/01)
    (1937/03/04)
Small Fry (Hoagy Carmichael—Frank Loesser)
    (1938/11/29)
Smoke Gets in Your Eyes (Otto Harbach—Jerome Kern)
    (1940/12/05)
    (1950/01/?)
Smooth and Easy (Eddie Sauter)
    (1949/12/?)
Snug as a Bug in a Rug (Marty Malneck—Frank Loesser)
    (1939/03/17)

So Easy (Tadd Dameron)
(1949/12/?)
(1950/01/06)
So in Love (Cole Porter)
(1949/12/?)
Sobbin' Blues (Art Kassel—Dick Burton)
(1936/12/23)
(1937/03/04)
(1938/11/25)
Softly as in a Morning Sunrise (Sigmund Romberg)
(1938/11/17)
(1938/11/18)
(1938/11/20)
(1938/12/02)
(1938/12/16)
(1938/12/29)
(1939/01/08)
(1939/01/22)
(1949/12/?)
Solid Sam (Fred Norman)
(1941/10/30)
Somebody Nobody Loves (Sy Miller)
(1942/01/20)
Someday Sweetheart (John Spikes—Ben Spikes)
(1937/04/28)
(1937/05/18)
Someone to Watch over Me (George Gershwin—Ira
    Gershwin)
(1945/07/17)
(1954/03/?)
Someone's Rocking My Dreamboat (Leon & Otis
    Rene—Emerson Scott)
(1941/12/23)
Sometimes I Feel Like a Motherless Child (traditional)
(1941/02/24)
(1942/01/21)
Soon (George Gershwin—Ira Gershwin)
(1945/07/03)
South Sea Island Magic (Andy Iona Long—Lysle Tomerlin)
(1936/08/06)
Special Delivery Stomp (Artie Shaw)
(1940/09/03)
St. James Infirmary Pts. 1 & 2 (Joe Primrose)
(1941/11/12)
St. Louis Blues (W. C. Handy)
(1939/10/19)
(1939/10/28)
(1939/11/03)
Stalling for Time (Artie Shaw)
(1937/12/15)
Star Dust (Hoagy Carmichael—Mitchell Parish)
(1938/12/06)
(1938/12/23)

(1940/10/07)
(1940/10/13)
(1949/12/?)
(1954/03/?)
Stars & Stripes Forever (J. P. Sousa)
(1939/07/21–31)
Stealin' Apples (Fletcher Henderson)
(1937/12/15)
Stop and Go Mambo (Artie Shaw)
(1953/12/?)
(1954/03/?)
A Strange Loneliness (Sammy Mysels—Bob Burke)
(1937/10/17)
(1937/10/18)
Streamline (Artie Shaw)
(1936/12/23)
Study in Brown (Larry Clinton)
(1937/04/28)
Sugar (Maceo Pinkard—Sidney D. Mitchell)
(1940/11/18)
Sugar Foot Stomp (King Oliver—Louis Armstrong)
(1936/O8/06)
Suite #8 (Paul Jordan)
(1941/12/08)
(1941/12/23)
Summer Souvenirs (J. Fred Coots—Charles Newman)
(1938/12/13)
Summertime (George Gershwin—Ira Gershwin)
(1945/04/17)
Summit Ridge Drive (Artie Shaw)
(1940/09/03)
(1945/09/12)
(1950/01/?)
(1954/03/?)
Sunny Side Up (Artie Shaw)
(1953/12/?)
(1954/03/?)
Supper Time (Irving Berlin)
(1939/01/17)
Sweet Adeline (Harry Armstrong—Richard H. Gerard)
(1937/07/22)
(1937/10/17)
(1938/11/25)
Sweet and Low (Joseph Barnaby)
(1938/02/15)
Sweet Is the Word for You (Ralph Rainger—Leo Robin)
(1937/03/04)
Sweet Lorraine (Cliff Burwell—Mitchell Parish)
(1936/12/23)
Sweet Sue (Victor Young—Will Harris)
(1939/10/26)
(1939/11/04)
(1940/08/05)

Sweet Varsity Sue (Charles Tobias—Al Lewis)
  (1937/10/17)
Swing High Swing Low (Burton Lane—Art Freed)
  (1937/03/04)
Swing Low Sweet Chariot (traditional)
  (1941/03/10)
Symphony in Riffs (Benny Carter)
  (1937/04/28)

Table d'Hote (Artie Shaw)
  (1939/01/?)
A Table in a Corner (Sam Coslow—Dana Suesse)
  (1939/09/28)
  (1939/10/20)
  (1939/10/25)
Tabu (Margarita Lecuona)
  (1945/06/07)
  (1945/09/12)
Take Another Guess (Murray Mencher—Charles
    Newman—Al Sherman)
  (1936/10/30)
  (1936/11/01)
Take My Word (Benny Carter)
  (1938/02/15)
Take Your Shoes off Baby (Gene Austin)
  (1941/10/30)
Tea for Two (Vincent Youmans—Irving Caesar)
  (1945/04/17)
  (1949/12/?)
Temptation (Art Freed—Herb Brown)
  (1940/07/29)
  (1940/O9/07)
  (1940/10/21)
Tenderly (Walter Gross—Jack Lawrence)
  (1953/09/?)
  (1954/03/?)
Thanks for Everything (Harry Revel—Mack Gordon)
  (1938/11/17)
  (1938/12/06)
  (1938/12/23)
  (1938/12/30)
That Old Black Magic (Harold Arlen—Johnny Mercer)
  (1953/07/02)
That Old Feeling (Sammy Fain—Lew Brown)
  (1953/09/?)
  (1954/03/?)
That's for Me (Richard Rodgers—Oscar Hammerstein)
  (1945/07/11)
Them There Eyes (Maceo Pinkard—William Tracy—Doris
    Tauber)
  (1939/09/19)
There I Go (Irving Weiser—Hy Zaret)
  (1941/01/22)

There Must Be Something Better Than Love (Morton
    Gould—Dorothy Fields)
  (1950/01/06)
There'll Be Some Changes Made (Bill Higgins—W.
    Overstreet)
  (1941/01/06)
  (1941/09/06)
There's a New Moon over the Old Mill (Allie
    Wrubel—Herb Magidson)
  (1937/12/15)
  (1937/12/30)
There's Frost on the Moon (Fred Ahlert—Joe Young)
  (1936/10/30)
  (1936/11/01)
There's Something in the Air (Jimmy McHugh—Harold
    Adamson)
  (1936/10/30)
  (1936/11/01)
These Foolish Things (Jack Strachey—Holt
    Marvell—Harry Link)
  (1945/06/08)
  (1953/07/02)
They Can't Convince Me (Allan Roberts—Doris Fisher)
  (1946/09/10)
They Can't Take That Away from Me (George
    Gershwin—Ira Gershwin)
  (1945/07/11)
  (1945/07/14)
  (1949/12/?)
  (1953/07/06)
They Didn't Believe Me (Jerome Kern—Michael E.
    Rourke)
  (1945/07/21)
They Say (Paul Mann—Stephan Weiss)
  (1938/11/25)
  (1938/12/01)
  (1938/12/19)
  (1938/12/29)
  (1939/01/01)
Things Are Looking Up (George Gershwin—Ira Gershwin)
  (1945/07/17)
  (1949/12/?)
The Things I Want (Jerome Kern—Oscar Hammerstein)
  (1937/07/12)
This Can't Be Love (Richard Rodgers—Lorenz Hart)
  (1939/01/18)
  (1939/01/29)
  (1939/02/26)
This Is It (Art Schwartz—Dorothy Fields)
  (1939/01/31)
This Is Romance (Vernon Duke—Ed Heyman)
  (1940/12/03)

This Time the Dream's on Me (Harold Arlen—Johnny
    Mercer)
    (1941/09/02)
Thou Swell (Richard Rodgers—Lorenz Hart)
    (1936/08/06)
The Thrill Is Gone (Ray Henderson—Lew Brown)
    (1951/01/25)
Thrill of a Lifetime (Sam Coslow—Fred Hollander—C.
    Lombardo)
    (1945/06/13)
Through the Years (Vincent Youmans)
    (1940/10/07)
    (1941/09/02)
Till the Clock Strikes Three (Billy Hill)
    (1937/07/12)
Time on My Hands (Vincent Youmans)
    (1945/06/07)
    (1950/01/?)
Time Out (Eddie Durham)
    (1939/01/01)
Time Was (Miguel Prado—S. K. Russell)
    (1941/09/06)
To a Broadway Rose (Ray Conniff)
    (1941/03/24)
    (1941/11/12)
Together (Ray Henderson—Buddy DeSylva—Lew Brown)
    (1937/07/12)
    (1938/12/06)
    (1938/12/23)
    (1939/02/26)
    (1939/06/20)
    (1950/01/?)
Too Marvelous for Words (Richard Whiting—Johnny
    Mercer)
    (1950/01/?)
    (1954/06/?)
The Toy Trumpet (Raymond Scott)
    (1938/02/15)
Traffic Jam (Artie Shaw—Teddy McRae)
    (1939/05/30)
    (1939/06/12)
    (1939/07/12–31)
    (1939/10/21)
Travelin' All Alone (J. C. Johnson)
    (1952/04/23)
Trust in Me (Milt Ager—Jean Schwartz—Ned Wever)
    (1937/03/04)
Twilight in Turkey (Raymond Scott)
    (1937/04/28)
Two Blind Loves (Harold Arlen—E. Y. Harburg)
    (1939/08/27)
    (1939/10/21)

Two in One Blues (Paul Jordan)
    (1942/01/21)
Two Sleepy People (Hoagy Carmichael—Frank Loesser)
    (1938/11/18)
    (1938/11/20)
    (1938/12/22)

Ubangi (see The Chant) (Artie Shaw)

Valse (Frances Poulenc)
    (1949/03/11)
The Very Thought of You (Ray Noble)
    1950/01/?)
Vilia (Franz Lehar—Harry Johnson)
    (1939/01/17)
Volga Boat Song (traditional)
    (1939/09/19)

Wake Up and Live (Harry Revel—Mack Gordon)
    (1937/04/28)
Was It Rain? (Lou Handman—Walter Hirsch)
    (1937/02/15)
    (1937/03/04)
What Is There to Say? (Vernon Duke—E. Y. Harburg)
    (1940/11/25)
    (1940/12/03)
What Is This Thing Called Love? (Cole Porter)
    (1938/O9/16)
    (1938/O9/27)
    (1938/11/29)
    (1938/12/04)
    (1938/12/30)
    (1939/10/19)
    (1946/06/19)
What's New? (Bob Haggart—Johnny Burke)
    (1939/11/03)
When I Go A-Dreamin' (Clay Boland—Bickley Reichner)
    (1938/11/25)
    (1938/11/27)
    (1938/12/01)
    (1938/12/29)
When Love Beckoned (Cole Porter)
    (1939/11/09)
When the Quail Come Back to San Ouentin (Artie Shaw)
    (1940/12/05)
    (1954/03/?)
When Winter Comes (Irving Berlin)
    (1939/06/05)
    (1939/06/13)
When You're Around (Artie Shaw—Johnny Lehman)
    (1946/11/08)
When Your Lover Has Gone (Einar Swan)
    (1937/03/04)

Where or When (Richard Rodgers—Lorenz Hart)
(1950/09/14)
Where There's Smoke There's Fire (J. Levinson—Marty Symes)
(1952/08/01)
Whispers in the Dark (Fred Hollander—Leo Robin)
(1937/07/12)
Whispers in the Night (Artie Shaw—Jack Owens)
(1940/12/03)
(1941/01/22)
Whistle While You Work (Frank Churchill—Larry Morey)
(1937/12/30)
White Christmas (Irving Berlin)
(1950/09/12)
(1950/10/05)
Who Blew Out the Flame (Sammy Fain—Mitchell Parish)
(1938/11/25)
(1938/11/27)
(1938/12/06)
Who's Excited? (Artie Shaw)
(1940/12/04)
Why Shouldn't I? (Cole Porter)
(1941/03/20)
Without a Dream to My Name (Artie Shaw—Art Quenzer)
(1939/09/28)
Without Your Love (Fred Stryker—Johnny Lange)
(1937/04/28)

The Yam (Irving Berlin)
(1938/11/18)
(1938/11/20)
(1938/12/14)
Yesterdays (Jerome Kern—Otto Harbach)
(1938/09/27)
(1938/12/04)
(1938/12/20)
(1939/10/21)
(1940/12/09)
(1954/06/?)
Yolanda (Harry Warren—Art Freed)
(1945/07/28)
You Can Tell She Comes from Dixie (Milt Ager—Marty Symes)
(1936/11/30)
You Do Something to Me (Cole Porter)
(1946/06/12)
(1949/12/?)

You Forgot About Me (Dick Robertson—Jim Hanley—Sam Mysels)
(1940/12/03)
You Go to My Head (J. Fred Coots—Haven Gillespie)
(1945/06/09)
You Got Me (Clay Boland—Bickley Reichner)
(1938/12/14)
(1938/12/18)
(1938/12/23)
You Grow Sweeter as the Years Go By (Johnny Mercer)
(1939/03/17)
You Have Everything (Art Schwartz—Howard Dietz)
(1937/10/17)
You Must Have Been a Beautiful Baby (Harry Warren—Johnny Mercer)
(1939/02/19)
You Took Advantage of Me (Richard Rodgers—Lorenz Hart)
(1945/03/15)
You're a Lucky Guy (Saul Chaplin—Sammy Cahn)
(1939/10/20)
(1939/10/26)
You're a Sweet Little Headache (Ralph Rainger—Leo Robin)
(1938/09/27)
(1938/12/30)
You're a Sweetheart (Jimmy McHugh—Harold Adamson)
(1937/12/15)
You're Giving Me a Song and a Dance (Milt Ager—Marty Symes)
(1936/09/17)
You're Mine You (Johnny Green—Ed Heyman)
(1939/10/20)
(1939/11/04)
(1939/11/10)
(1950/05/29)
You're Out of This World (Jule Styne—Kim Gannon)
(1937/12/15)
You're So Indifferent (Sammy Fain—Mitchell Parish)
(1939/03/17)

Zigeuner (Noel Coward)
(1939/01/23)
(1939/02/05)
(1939/06/13)

Appendix 2

Discographical Addenda and Ephemera

Many fans of the 1938–39 Shaw band have been intrigued by the recordings made by Georgie Auld and the remnants of the former Shaw band for Varsity in early 1940, before their final breakup. Their legacy appears to be:

Georgie Auld and His Orchestra
New York, c. January 1940

Chuck Peterson, Bernie Privin, Johnny Best(tp), George Arus, Les Jenkins, Harry Rodgers(tb), Les Robinson, Hank Freeman(as), Georgie Auld, Ronnie Perry(ts), Bob Kitsis(p), Al Avola(g), George Horvath(b), Ralph Hawkins(d), Kay Foster(v)

1241	Angel (vKF)	Varsity 8152
1242	I Want My Mama (vKF)	—
1243	This Is Romance	Varsity 8159
1244	Juke Box Jump	—
1245	Man from Mars	Varsity 8163
1246	Lover Come Back to Me	—

same
New York, c. February 1940

1379	Shake Down the Stars (vKF)	Varsity 8199
1380	With the Wind and the Rain in Your Hair (vKF)	Varsity 8212
1381	Sweet Sue	—
1382	Imagination	Varsity 8199

This band naturally preserved much of the feel it had while Shaw still was fronting the group. In a sense, it was a parallel situation to the May 1939 period, at the Palomar while Shaw was out sick. Nevertheless, Shaw was gone and they were Georgie Auld's recording sessions, although the band's style and even some of its arrangements were retained.

It is interesting to note that Fred Astaire recorded three titles from the film *Second Chorus* for Columbia on 22 Sep-

tember 1940, shortly after the film was completed. The band on that date was made up of studio musicians and the tunes from the movie were "Love of My Life," "Poor Mr. Chisholm," and "Dig It." Versions of the latter two titles from the film sound track have been issued on Artie Shaw albums, although Shaw neither composed nor performed on those titles.

Air checks by the Sam Donahue Navy band, which retained some of the personnel from the Rangers and toured Europe after a rest following their return from the Pacific, also have evoked interest. However, Donahue reportedly used an entirely new library of arrangements, so there was far less connection with Shaw's Rangers than the above Georgie Auld titles had with Shaw's music.

Recordings attributed to Artie Shaw, but not by Shaw, have occasionally appeared. Bandleader Jerry Wald modeled his band and clarinet playing so closely on Shaw's that two titles by his groups have appeared on Artie Shaw Club albums as if they were by Shaw: "Tuxedo Junction" and "Blue Prelude," both evidently recorded in the mid-1940s. Another clarinetist-bandleader modeled on Shaw was Tommy Reynolds, although apparently his records have not been mistaken for Shaw's so far. There also was the Mel Tormé with Sonny Burke's Orchestra record of "There's No Business Like Show Business" for Musicraft which appeared on the Shaw LP *Artie Shaw Plays Cole Porter and Irving Berlin* in the 1950s, as mentioned in the text.

Besides the "real" Artie Shaw records that did not feature Shaw (as noted in the text or discography), there was another Decca session held in November 1955, over a year after Shaw's final break with playing the clarinet, evidently to fulfill contract obligations. Shaw conducted a studio big band with strings through the following four titles:

Art Shaw and His Orchestra
New York, 21 November 1955

Jimmy Nottingham, Jimmie Maxwell, R. D. McMickle(tp), Will Bradley, Lou McGarity, Kai Winding(tb), James Buffington, Octavia DeRosa(Frh), Toots Mondello(as), Milt Yaner(as,fl), Romeo Penque(ts,oboe), Boomie Richmond(ts, bcl), Phil Bodner(bari,bcl), Sylvan Shulman, Arnold Eidus, Mac Ceppos, Raoul Poliakine, Tom Frost, Sol Deutsch, Harry Melnikoff, Sam Rand, Julie Held, Izzy Zir, Howard Kay(vl), Maurice Brown, Sid Edwards(cel), Bernie Leighton(p), Art Ryerson(g), Eddie Safranski(b), Don Lamond(d), Artie Shaw(cond)

88922	Long Ago and Far Away	DL 8309
88923	I Remember You	—
88924	More Than You Know	—
88925	My Funny Valentine	—

On these performances there was nothing of jazz interest, despite restrained solos by Art Ryerson on 88922, Will Bradley on 88923, Toots Mondello and Jimmie Maxwell on 88924, and Boomie Richmond on tenor and Milt Yaner on flute on 88925. These pieces were similar to the backgrounds for the July 1953 Deccas and have usually been issued with them on LP by Decca, Ace of Hearts, and other labels.

Along with other albums in the nostalgia field re-creating the original arrangements of various big band hits, many of Shaw's performances have been imitated by Glen Gray, Billy May (on the Time–Life *Swing Era* sets), Dave Pell, and Francis Bay, among others.

One exceptional re–creation album was a 1968 session for Capitol Records conducted by Shaw himself, with Walt Levinsky playing the clarinet parts. Occasionally, performances from this album have been reissued in collections without identifying them as re–creations, to Shaw's chagrin. Since Shaw was conducting these items they are of slightly greater interest than the usual imitations:

Art Shaw and His Orchestra
New York, c. 1968

collective personnel: Artie Shaw(cond), Bernie Privin, Mel Davies(tp), Buddy Morrow(tb), Walt Levinsky(cl), Toots Mondello(as), Al Klink, Bill Slapin(ts), Bernie Leighton(p), Don Lamond(d), others unknown

Traffic Jam	Cap.ST2992
Begin the Beguine	—
Lover Come Back to Me	—
What Is This Thing Called Love?	—
It Had to Be You	—
Softly as in a Morning Sunrise	—
Octoroon	—
Nightmare	—
Back Bay Shuffle	—
Jungle Drums	—
Copenhagen	—
Zigeuner	—

As noted in the text, since the early 1980s Shaw has again conducted a big band, playing old and new arrangements, with Dick Johnson on clarinet. This band toured with Shaw conducting and providing commentary, appeared with him in the film *Artie Shaw: Time is All You've Got*, and recorded at least two LPs worth of material which Shaw said remains unissued as he was not satisfied with the results. It continues to tour as the twentieth century draws to a close.

Also as noted in the text, Shaw can be heard playing an excerpt from Edward A. MacDowell's "A Deserted Farm" on piano for part of the sound track of *Artie Shaw: Time is All You've Got*. This was performed for Brigitte Berman and her crew at the time the film interviews were taking place at Shaw's home near Los Angeles in 1983.

In 1998, Shaw produced a test pressing of a CD containing his extended compositions "The Pied Piper of Hamelin" and "The Emperor and the Nightingale," which he had scripted and scored in 1941 as described in the text. The former is projected as a reissue of his 1946 recording for Musicraft, but for the latter, which Shaw had never recorded or even heard performed until creating this CD, he provided the voice for certain characters and electronic effects for certain sequences.

Appendix 3

Artie Shaw as Composer/Arranger

Artie Shaw with his various bands recorded over seventy-five pieces attributed to Shaw as composer or cocomposer (usually with a lyricist collaborator when another name is cited). This represents nearly 15 percent of his total released recorded output of about 530 or so individual compositions (depending on how one counts). It is interesting to note that of his eight million-selling titles for Victor during the period of his greatest popularity, four were his own compositions, and all were his arrangements:

> Begin the Beguine
> Back Bay Shuffle   (Shaw composition)
> Nightmare   "
> Traffic Jam   "
> Summit Ridge Drive   "
> Frenesi
> Star Dust
> Dancing in the Dark

"Nightmare" is of special interest not only because it was Shaw's theme song (other bandleaders had theme songs that they composed and arranged that were major hits, e.g., Glenn Miller's "Moonlight Serenade"), but also because of its structure. The entire composition was built on a four-note ostinato pattern, moving chromatically up and down an interval of a second in quarter notes. The effect of this pattern is ominous and hypnotic (incidentally used as theme music for the James Bond film *Goldfinger*). Shaw then wrote a wailing phrase descending in a bluesy pattern to introduce his solo, which made up the bulk of the full-length versions recorded. The drone-like ostinato provided a foundation reminiscent of textures utilized for establishing the tonic in non-Western musical traditions, particularly in India or the Mid-East, over which improvisation on the given scale or mode occurs. On the five recorded full-length versions of "Nightmare" that have become available, all from the 1937–39 band, Shaw's solos had a similar basic feel, but varied considerably in their decorative patterns and passing tones. All had a definite Cantorial aura, especially the rarest version (apparently only available in its original 78-rpm

issue on Vocalion 4306). It was an alternate take of the commonly reissued version originally issued in 78-rpm on Brunswick. On this take, Shaw's choices of notes and phrasing were particularly evocative.

Given the unusually broad exposure of this number to the public, it is impossible to ignore Shaw's likely influence on the eventual evolvement of the "modal" approach in jazz (often attributed to beginning with Miles Davis twenty years later, despite George Russell's experiments with modes for over a decade prior to that time). Since this piece was Shaw's theme song throughout his career as a bandleader, it was performed to open and close all broadcasts. This indicates it was heard, on radio at least, over ten times per week during his stay at the Blue Room alone, for example. Since it also was a million-selling hit record and Shaw's was the most popular band in North America during 1938–39 (and widely heard before and after), it would be surprising if the effect of his theme song failed to imprint musicians' musical consciousness. Clearly it would not be necessary for musicians to study Eastern modes to find an example of this approach in order to be influenced in this direction. And certainly it would be rare to find any musician developing during the generation that grew up to develop "modal" approaches to jazz composition and improvisation who could have been unaware of Artie Shaw's theme song. True modal jazz is a rare exception, since most so-called modal pieces feature some modulations, and most jazz improvisors regularly use passing tones in soloing. Consequently, as the term is generally used when applied to jazz, there is no doubt that "Nightmare" represents the most prominent pioneering example of the genre.

Titles attributed to Shaw as composer or co-composer generally fall into two broad categories: pieces based on the blues form, and pieces based on popular song forms (the AABA structure), occasionally with chord changes based on existing "standards." Many items in both categories were obviously "head arrangements" for which it might be said the entire band were co-composers. Shaw has stated that the band often would make up tunes on the stand, assembling riffs or patterns from other arrangements interspersed with solos into a unique form, which by any reasonable definition can be asserted to be a distinctive composition even if never repeated or written down. Count Basie stated in his autobiography that this was common practice in his band and among the big bands of the era in general, and that the leader would assume composer credit for the piece if it got on a record, as a matter of course, regardless of the sources of the patterns used. Obvious instances of this practice in Shaw's band would include pieces such as "Double Mellow," based on the riff patterns the band used in its arrangement of "Oh Lady Be Good," and "Gangbusters," which used a riff pattern from Shaw's version of Fletcher Henderson's "Stealin' Apples" (which differed from the patterns used in Henderson's own version of his composition).

An example of an "original" built on a standard piece was "The Chant" (which has often been referred to as "Artie's answer to Benny Goodman's 'Sing Sing Sing' " because of its clarinet-drums interplay passages). Originally titled "Ubangi" on its initial recording for Thesaurus, "The Chant" was almost a paraphrase of "St. James Infirmary," and it becomes an exercise in the psychology of perception to make the hairline division between a "version" of an established pattern and a distinct if similar "original" composition. (It also is worth noting that the piece was recorded prior to Goodman's famous recording of "Sing Sing Sing," but who would dare to suggest "Sing Sing Sing" was Goodman's answer to "The Chant"?)

It also has been pointed out that "The Chant" was closely related to the traditional Jewish melody "Mazel Tov," which again brings up the influence of Shaw's Jewish heritage on his music. The most prominent example of direct influence was the frahlich cadenza concluding "Dr. Livingstone, I Presume?" by the 1940–41 Gramercy 5. Interestingly, this cadenza was heard earlier, in Shaw's conclusion to the clarinet-drum section of "The Chant" on the air check from the Palomar in June 1939. Interestingly, he concluded his original Thesaurus version of "The Chant" with a cadenza that also appeared again later, as a major climactic passage in his "Concerto for Clarinet" recorded on the 12-inch Victor record in 1940, but this cadenza bore little relationship to any ethnic overtones.

Parts of Shaw's "Concerto for Clarinet" (basically a blues set off by cadenzas) also can be heard in the blues performance Shaw played with Paul Whiteman at the Carnegie Hall concert on Christmas 1938. This latter item, which featured Shaw improvising over Whiteman's orchestra performing Irving Szathmary's orchestration of an arrangement dictated by Shaw, offered a good example for discussion of various roles in creating an arrangement and for defining terms. For this composition, Shaw "dictated" an arrangement of the blues to Szathmary, who then orchestrated the piece, writing out the parts for the various instruments in the ensemble.

The "blues" is a traditional form, and has been used as a foundation underlying many compositions. Often the basic structure of the piece may also be freshly invented by a composer. Nevertheless, frequently, established patterns are used, among which the twelve-bar blues is prominent along with the "AABA" structural form of many popular songs of the era, and so forth.

It is difficult to analogize these concepts into other media, but these terms could perhaps be clarified by thinking of visual art situations. By analogy, artists planning a painting select a subject (landscape, still life, figure study, etc.) and "compose" their ideas. In sketching them out and deciding what colors and forms are to appear, they perform the role of the "arranger," and in applying the paint, the role of "orchestrator." Of course, it is well known that, historically, in some schools of art, this task may be "delegated" along with specific guidelines, as in paint-by-number sets (which are even more specific in this sense than children's coloring books). Similarly, the architect designs the building ("composing" and/or "arranging") while the engineer takes care of the details of structure and internal building materials (analogous to being the "orchestrator").

In this sense Shaw affirmed that he was the "arranger" for the entire repertoire of his bands for the 1936–37 "String Swing" ensemble, the 1937–39 big band, the 1940–41 orchestra, the 1946 Musicraft material, and all material he recorded for Decca from April 1950 on. In discussing these roles, Shaw stated in 1991, "Few people understand the difference between an arranger and an orchestrator, and the terms are often misused" (2).

Thus, for example, Sonny Burke usually was credited as arranger on the 1946 Musicraft sessions (along with Dick Jones on some of the tunes on the Cole Porter album), but actually he was orchestrating Shaw's arrangements, which had been sketched out pretty specifically. Similarly, Shaw maintained that Jerry Gray, Harry Rodgers, Joe Lippman, Al Avola, etc., in his earlier bands, or Lennie Hayton with the 1940–41 orchestra, actually were orchestrators for the material for which they often are cited as arranger in the liner notes to recordings and other written accounts of their roles in Shaw's music. Shaw also noted that for the 1941–42 Orchestra, and the 1944–45 and 1949–50 big bands, he hired arrangers whose work interested him and would perform their work without altering the arranger's intentions. Of course these bands also performed many of Shaw's own arrangements as well. It is also worth recalling that all Gramercy 5 pieces were "head arrangements."

Shaw also dismissed the role of "co-composers" (except for lyricists) in credits for compositions under his name. In fact "John Carleton" (cited as co-composer with Shaw in six of the Gramercy 5 compositions) was a pen name invented by Shaw's lawyer, Andrew Weinberger, for legal purposes. The authentic co-composer credits refer to lyricists, on compositions in the category of "lyrical ballads" which represent one dimension of Shaw's composing.

In this body of work, Arthur Quenzer is credited on five items:

Easy to Say	(1939)
Love Is Here	"
Moonray	"
Without a Dream to My Name	"
Don't Fall Asleep	(1940)

Quenzer was a popular songwriter and lyricist active in the late 1930s and had been in Irving Aaronson's sax section alongside Shaw in 1930. In 1938 he also received screen credits for music for the film *Swiss Miss*.

Shaw also used lyricists Jack Owens ("Whispers in the Night"), Johnny Mercer ("Love of My Life"), and Johnny Lehman on two items for Musicraft in 1946 ("Don't You Believe It Dear" and "When You're Around"), and credit was also given to Ben Oakland and Milt Drake for "If It's You" in 1940. The latter tune was used in the Marx Brothers' film *The Big Store*, where it was sung by Tony Martin. In discussing composer credits in this instance, Shaw was not aware of the identity of "Milt Drake," stating, "How did he get on there? These things are a mystery!" (2)

The remaining items with vocals composed by Shaw included two "novelty" numbers, "Shoot the Likker to Me John Boy" and "Natch," and the classic romantic ballad "Any Old Time." These are credited to Shaw alone. "Pastel Blue" (credited to Shaw and Charlie Shavers) had lyrics added by Dick Todd and was retitled "Why Begin Again?" but Shaw never recorded it as a vocal.

Despite Shaw's interest in the small group with strings ensembles, he did not compose very extensively for these groups. For the clarinet with string quartet and pianoless rhythm section, Shaw only recorded "Interlude in B-flat" and "Streamline." His "Cream Puff" added the horns and piano to this 1936 ensemble. "I Ask the Stars" was done for the 1941 session, which added another saxophone and more strings to this approach. Nevertheless, Shaw lavished much attention to arranging for these and his larger ensembles with strings.

Although Shaw began arranging for the Joe Cantor band in about 1927, and stated that all the arrangements performed by Cantor's band at their one recording session were his (including "Wabash Blues," Shaw's very first arrangement), no confirmed recordings of Shaw arrangements prior to his 1936 group could be located or are known to have surfaced. Shaw stressed that *ALL* the arrangements recorded under his name, up to the 1941–42 band, were his. He stated unequivocally, "I had my hand on every note. I either wrote the whole thing out myself, or sketched it out and revised what came back from the orchestrators" (2).

Learning to write for strings was a challenge. Shaw was surprised to learn of Glenn Miller's recordings with a string quartet and small jazz group that had been made a year prior to Shaw's first recorded efforts along these lines. When discussing any influences on his work at that time, Shaw stated:

> I asked Glenn Miller about writing for tenor clef, because we were working in the studios together and I knew he was studying arranging with [Joseph] Schillinger. Then I studied Schillinger's method, to learn how to write for string quartets. I didn't know Glenn [Miller] recorded with a string quartet and a jazz group with similar instrumentation to mine until just this minute, so I certainly didn't get the idea from his work. Actually I was sketching things like that on the farm [in 1933]. (2)

Miller's experiment with this instrumentation was recorded at his first recording session under his own name, two years before his next recordings with his first conventional big band. Except for the extra trombone, this also was the instrumentation Shaw used for most of his 1936–37 band's arrangements.

Glenn Miller and His Orchestra
New York, 25 April 1935

Charlie Spivak, Bunny Berigan(tp), Jack Jenney, Glenn Miller(tb), Johnny Mintz(cl), Eddie Miller(ts), Harry Bluestone, Vladimir Solinsky(vl), Harry Waller(vla), Bill Schumann(cel), Claude Thornhill(p), Larry Hall(g), Delmar Kaplan(b), Ray Baduc(d), Smith Ballew(v)

17379	A Blues Serenade (vSB)	Col.3051
17380	Moonlight on the Ganges (vSB)	—
17381	In a Little Spanish Town	Col.3058

The fourth title made at this session, "Solo Hop," omitted Jenney and the strings. Gunther Schuller, in *The Swing Era* (pp. 663–64) discussed these works and Miller's having studied with Joseph Schillinger. Schuller called these records "eclectic in the extreme" and "a veritable kaleidoscope of all known styles and effects in jazz and popular music" with even classical touches ("the direct lift from Tchaikovsky's 'Romeo and Juliet' in 'A Blues Serenade' "). Nevertheless, the effect was less interesting than Shaw's achievements the following year. Oddly, Schuller praised Miller's arrangements but wrote disparagingly of Shaw's work, despite Shaw's greater originality and scope.

It is clear Shaw has not received the recognition due for his experiments anticipating the developments of the so-called Third Stream movement of the 1950s.

Shaw's intentions in using strings were examined in the relevant chapters in context, but it also is important to recall the influence he exerted on other bands in doing so. Most leading swing bands at least experimented with using string sections shortly afterward, including Tommy Dorsey, Harry James, and Benny Goodman.

Of course, most of Shaw's compositions were for the big band format, with a few premiered by the big bands with string sections, but many appeared only in Gramercy 5 renditions (the variously titled blues quintet number with Basie in 1944 was not properly a Gramercy 5 situation):

> Crumbum
> Dr. Livingstone, I Presume?
> Hop Skip and Jump
> Lugubrious
> Lyric
> Mysterioso
> No Name Blues
> Scuttlebutt
> Sequence in B-flat
> Special Delivery Stomp
> Stop and Go Mambo
> Summit Ridge Drive
> Sunny Side Up
> The Gentle Grifter
> The Grabtown Grapple
> The Pied Piper Theme
> The Sad Sack
> The Shekomeko Shuffle
> When the Quail Come Back to San Quentin

Other Shaw compositions recorded by Gramercy 5 units were premiered earlier in big band versions, e.g., "Back Bay Shuffle" and "Love of My Life" from the 1954 sessions. Of course "The Pied Piper Theme" was taken from Shaw's extended work "The Pied Piper of Hamelin," and "Special Delivery Stomp" was derived from his earlier big band number "Man from Mars."

Few popular bandleaders of the era could claim such a large percentage of original compositions in their repertoire, let alone among million-sellers. Few, if any, were as extensively involved in arranging as Shaw was, especially in his peak years, when all arrangements were carefully sketched out by him before being turned over to his orchestrators. When contemplating this prodigious output it is even more remarkable to recall that Shaw also was his own primary soloist. Few major bandleader soloists were also their own arranger to any significant extent.

Comments by band members on Shaw's arranging were quoted in the liner notes to RCA AXM2-5533. Pianist Bob Kitsis said,

> Artie made a very specific point of keeping the stuff in our library simple and light. He allowed the soloists the freedom to do as they preferred, but let them know he favored directness and lack of complication. His own playing, however, was highly sophisticated.

Shaw solos, placed against the uncluttered ensembles, still are something to hear.

Bert Korall noted, "The charts were written in reasonable registers for the players and, therefore, generally were easy and pleasant to perform." He then quoted Bernie Privin:

> Though we played hard and aggressively during the course of an evening, we never were whipped or destroyed by what was down there on paper, as happened with other bands.
> With Benny Goodman, for example, the arrangements could beat hell out of you—simple as many of them sounded—especially if you were in the brass section.

In the liner notes to RCA AXM2-5556, Les Robinson noted, "The [sax] section things were like solos, only arranged for saxophones."

Along with Shaw's own comments as quoted in the text, a portrait of Shaw as an arranger emerges that indicates unusual skill in handling parts. Not only did he achieve the clear transparency in the arrangements, but he achieved this by writing "naturally" for the instruments involved. Buddy Rich was quoted in the liner notes to RCA AXM2-5533,

> There was only one minor problem when it came to playing the music. Because it was natural, it took a great deal of concentration to keep it that way. Otherwise it was straight ahead!

His arranging philosophy, method and results seem evident from the above comments taken in total, but only careful listening reveals the subtlety and sophistication written into the arrangements. Coupling the arrangements with Shaw's skill in bringing out the best in his soloists and sections accounted for the uncanny sense of appropriateness most performances of his arrangements by most of his bands offered. It must be stressed that only working bands with long experience performing given arrangements can be expected to bring out all the subtle nuances Shaw wanted. Therefore, studio groups led by Shaw, and especially imitations by others, could never achieve the same aura or "feel" in the music, even when reading the same notes. Obviously, the unity Shaw could achieve through arranging the pieces he was performing and training the working bands to phrase exactly as he wished would result in the ultimate expressions of his intentions. This would be even more true if he had also composed the tunes in question.

The following list of Shaw compositions represents all known titles composed by Shaw that he recorded, with dates of recording. Where titles changed, the later titles indicate the original title, which lists the dates (except for "Ubangi"/"The Chant," which is so much better known under its later title).

Artie Shaw Compositions	Dates of Recording
Any Old Time	(1938/02/15)
	(1938/07/24)
	(1938/12/13)
	(1939/01/13)
	(1939/01/18)
	(1939/03/12)
	(1939/11/03)
Artie's Blues (see Bird Calls)	
Back Bay Shuffle	(1938/07/24)
	(1938/11/27)
	(1938/12/02)
	(1938/12/14)
	(1939/02/26)
	(1939/07/12–31)
	(1939/10/26)
	(1954/03/?)
Bird Calls (aka Blues Jam Session, etc.)	(1944/09/25)
Born to Swing	(1937/04/28)
Comin' On	(1938/07/24)
	(1938/11/29)
Concerto for Clarinet	(1940/08/16)
	(1940/12/17)
Cool Daddy	(1949/12/?)
Cream Puff	(1936/12/23)
	(1937/03/04)
Crumbum	(1950/04/08)
	(1954/03/?)
Don't Fall Asleep	(1940/03/03)
Don't You Believe It Dear	(1946/10/18)
Double Mellow	(1939/03/12)
	(1939/07/12–31)
	(1940/08/25)
Dr. Livingstone, I Presume?	(1940/12/05)
	(1941/01/22)
Easy to Say	(1939/06/22)
Everything Is Jumpin'	(1939/10/20)
	(1939/10/25)
	(1939/11/11)
	(1940/08/05)
	(1940/10/26)
Fee Fi Fo Fum	(1937/08/04)
	(1937/10/17)
Free for All (see The Bus Blues)	
Free Wheeling	(1937/09/17)
	(1937/10/17)
	(1938/12/16)
	(1939/03/26)
Gangbusters	(1939/03/26)
	(1939/07/12–31)
Hold Your Hat	(1938/12/25)
	(1938/12/27)
Hold Your Hats	(1937/04/28)

Hop Skip and Jump	(1945/08/01)
	(1945/09/26)
I Ain't Comin'	(1939/05/28)
I Ask the Stars	(1941/09/03)
If It's You	(1940/09/07)
In the Bottom	(1937/04/28)
	(1938/12/01)
	(1938/12/11)
Interlude in B-flat	(1936/05/23)
Just Floatin' Along	(1945/07/26)
	(1945/09/19)
Leapin' at the Lincoln (see In the Bottom)	
Let's Walk	(1945/11/07)
	(1945/11/14)
Love Is Here	(1939/10/26)
Love of My Life	(1940/08/25)
	(1940/10/07)
	(1940/10/28)
	(1945/11/14)
	(1950/01/?)
	(1954/03/?)
Lugubrious	(1954/03/?)
Lyric	(1954/03/?)
Man from Mars	(1939/09/19)
	(1939/10/21)
	(1939/10/28)
	(1939/11/03)
Marinella	(1940/10/07)
Meade Lux Special	(1938/02/15)
Monsoon	(1937/10/18)
	(1937/12/15)
Moonray	(1939/06/22)
	(1939/08/19)
	(1939/10/19)
	(1939/10/20)
	(1939/10/21)
	(1939/10/25)
	(1939/11/10)
	(1939/11/11)
Mysterioso	(1945/08/01)
Natch	(1945/07/06)
Nightmare	(1937/09/17)
	(1937/12/15)
	(1938/09/27)
	(1939/04/02)
	(1949/12/?)
No Name Blues	(c.1940–41)
No One But You	(1945/07/06)
	(1945/07/20)
	(1945/11/07)
NonStop Flight	(1937/12/15)
	(1937/12/30)
	(1938/09/27)

	(1938/11/20)		(1945/09/12)
	(1938/11/28)		(1950/01/?)
	(1938/12/01)		(1954/03/?)
	(1939/03/05)	Sunny Side Up	(1953/12/?)
	(1939/06/20)		(1954/03/?)
	(1939/07/12–31)	Table d'Hote	(1939/01/?)
One Foot in the Groove	(1939/03/17)	The Blues	(1937/02/19)
	(1939/04/02)	The Blues	(1938/12/25)
	(1939/07/12–31)	The Blues, A/B (= The Blues March)	(1937/08/04)
	(1939/08/19)	The Bus Blues	(1937/04/28)
	(1939/10/19)		(1937/10/18)
	(1939/11/10)	The Chant (= Ubangi)	(1937/04/28)
One Night Stand	(1939/03/17)		(1937/08/04)
	(1939/06/10)		(1938/12/15)
	(1939/06/13)		(1939/03/12)
Opening Theme	(1940/08/25)		(1939/05/28)
Pastel Blue	(1939/03/12)	The Chaser (see Sequence in B-flat)	
	(1939/03/26)	The Gentle Grifter	(1945/08/01)
Prelude in C Major	(1940/12/04)	The Grabtown Grapple	(1945/01/09)
	(1941/01/22)		(1950/01/?)
Rockin' the State (see In the Bottom)			(1954/03/?)
S.O.S.	(1937/10/17)	The Pied Piper of Hamelin	(1946/07/21)
Scuttlebutt	(1945/07/31)		(1946/07/28)
	(1945/09/19)	The Pied Piper Theme	(1950/01/?)
	(1954/03/?)		(1954/03/?)
Sequence in B-flat	(1954/03/?)	The Sad Sack	(1945/01/09)
Shindig	(1937/10/17)		(1945/10/03)
Shoot the Likker to Me John Boy	(1937/08/17)		(1954/03/?)
	(1937/10/17)	The Shekomeko Shuffle	(1950/04/08)
	(1938/11/25)	Traffic Jam	(1939/05/30)
	(1939/01/?)		(1939/06/12)
	(1939/02/19)		(1939/07/12–31)
	(1939/05/23)		(1939/10/21)
	(1939/06/10)	Ubangi (see The Chant)	
Special Delivery Stomp	(1940/09/03)	When the Quail Come Back to San Quentin	(1940/12/05)
Stalling for Time	(1937/12/15)		(1954/03/?)
Stop and Go Mambo	(1953/12/?)	When You're Around	(1946/11/08)
	(1954/03/?)	Whispers in the Night	(1940/12/03)
Streamline	(1936/12/23)		(1941/01/22)
Summit Ridge Drive	(1940/09/03)	Who's Excited?	(1940/12/04)
		Without a Dream to My Name	(1939/09/28)

Appendix 4

Artie Shaw and Vocalist

Examining Artie Shaw's recordings from the aspect of vocal renditions is of special relevance because of his often stated negative attitude toward lyrics and vocal treatments of tunes. In the interesting interview/article by John McDonough in *Down Beat* (22 January 1970, pp. 12, 13, 38) titled "Artie Shaw: Nonstop Flight from 1938," Shaw stated:

> I'm not interested in lyrics . . . used vocalists only because it was commercially necessary, and whenever possible, it was a put-on, like Tony Pastor doing "Indian Love Call" or "Rosalie." Today it's just about the same as then, a big, bloody bore.

Shaw also often complained that he had been pressured into making records he didn't feel were suitable, and it takes little reading between the lines to conclude that he was referring to some of the banal popular songs being pushed by the song pluggers in the music industry. While his musical relationship with Billie Holiday clearly was an exception to these generalizations concerning singers, ironically, this was one of the least documented episodes of Shaw's career as a leader. It also is apparent that his rapport with Helen Forrest, who succeeded Billie Holiday as the band's primary vocalist during Shaw's peak years of 1938–39, was of more than usual musical vitality (see text for details). She also recorded over half-again more surviving performances while with Shaw than any other singer in his career as a leader (with 115 performances listed during 1938–39, compared to Tony Pastor's 68 over his total tenure with Shaw's bands throughout 1936–39). While these figures for recorded pieces are an artifact of what has become available, as opposed to what was performed, this recorded legacy is, after all, what survives to be examined. Unless unknown air checks become available it will not be possible to evaluate, for example, how Patty Morgan sounded with the Shaw band in the summer of 1938.

It is necessary to distinguish between the number of performances and the number of titles under discussion. For example, Helen Forrest has eight performances of one title alone (Shaw's original ballad, "Moonray") as cited in the discography, five of them unissued and all but the Bluebird record from broadcasts. She actually recorded 41 titles for

Bluebird. In addition, there were also 23 different titles preserved only from broadcast performances, for a total of 64 unique titles among her 115 performances.

There were also 11 titles for Bluebird that year sung by Tony Pastor (out of his total of 40 unique titles among his 68 performances). This gave a total of 52 vocal titles among the Bluebird records (Helen Forrest remade Billie Holiday's one item). Thus, there were only 32 instrumental titles for Bluebird out of the total of 84 titles recorded by the 1938–39 band. One can play with numbers and percentages this way with great amusement and gain insight into Shaw's legacy and the sense of proportion derived, but the quantities are not as relevant as the quality of the music concerned. As noted in the text, the vocal performances generally are the least interesting examples of the band-in-question's work, and in view of Shaw's perspective, would represent the items in his legacy of lesser interest in evaluating what Shaw wanted to do. Nevertheless, during his career as a bandleader, Shaw used a total of forty different singers who recorded with him, plus (depending on how one counts) five vocal groups. These vocalists are listed below in order of number of known recordings, and then alphabetically. Those who worked publicly for Shaw over any extended period were listed with just inclusive dates. The remainder show the affiliation that produced the collaboration. The majority were hired for special record dates, or just for radio shows (Dick Todd and the King Sisters) or (in the case of Fred Astaire) a movie.

Vocalist	Number of Performances	Dates
Helen Forrest	15	1938–39
Tony Pastor	68	1936–39
Peg La Centra	36	1936–37
Dick Todd	14	(Old Gold Show 1939)
Anita Boyer	14	1940–41
Nita Bradley	13	1937–38
Mel Tormé	13	(Musicraft 1946)
Don Cherry	8	(Decca 1950–51)

Oran "Hot Lips" Page	8	1941–42
Imogene Lynn	7	1944–45
Trudy Richards	7	(Thesaurus and Decca 1950/1952)
Dorothy Howe	5	(Thesaurus 1937)
Pat Lockwood	5	1949
Paula Kelly	4	1941
Hal Stevens	4	(Victor and Musicraft 1945)
Pauline Byrne	3	(Victor 1940)
Fredda Gibson (Georgia Gibbs)	3	(Victor 1942)
Bonnie Lake	3	1941
Leo Watson	3	(Brunswick 1937)
Connee Boswell	2	(Decca 1952)
Gwen Davies	2	(Decca 1950)
Dick Haymes	2	(Decca 1950)
Lena Horne	2	(Victor 1941)
June Hutton	2	(Decca 1951)
Mary Ann McCall	2	(Decca 1950)
Dolores O'Neill	2	1937
Martha Tilton	2	(Victor 1940)
Wes Vaughan	2	(Brunswick 1936)
Dorothy Allen	1	(Victor 1945)
Fred Astaire	1	(Movie *Second Chorus* 1940)
Ralph Blane	1	(Musicraft 1946)
Roy Eldridge	1	1945
Jane Ford	1	(Decca 1950)
Billie Holiday	1	1938
Kitty Kallen	1	(Musicraft 1946)
Lillian Lane	1	(Musicraft 1946)
Jack Pearce	1	(Victor 1940)
Bea Wain	1	(Brunswick 1937)
Teddy Walters	1	(Musicraft 1946)

It should be noted that this tally does not include the anonymous scat-singer/whistler heard on both takes of Tony Pastor's vocal feature "Whistle While You Work" (30 December 1937). It has been suggested that it was Shaw, but he denied it, stating, "I'm not sure who that was; maybe Maxie [Kaminsky]" (2).

The vocal groups on Shaw's recordings, in chronological order, included:

Vocal Group	Number of Performances	Date
The King Sisters	1	(Old Gold Show 1939)
The Mel-Tones (with Mel Tormé)	1	(Musicraft 1946)
Gordon Jenkins Choir	2	(Decca 1950)

Trio/Chelsea 3/ Chickering 4	4	(Decca 1950; same basic men)
Chorus (with Don Cherry)	6	(Decca 1951)

In most cases the result was clearly commercial popular music. The "put-ons" Shaw referred to in the cases of Tony Pastor's "novelty" numbers also clearly extended to the items by Leo Watson, Roy Eldridge, and Hot Lips Page for the most part, but these all represented high-spirited fun. Shaw often sounded like he was enjoying himself thoroughly, judging by the way he played on most of these pieces. On "Show Me the Way to Go Home" (19 July 1950) Shaw himself sang briefly. Often the fun was overt satire, as in "Indian Love Call," with its take-off on Tommy Dorsey's big hit "Marie" (the band's answering vocal fills commenting on the singer's lyrics like a mock Greek chorus's asides). On a few numbers, however, even Pastor functioned in the role of "boy crooner," as opposed to his more stimulating "hep" renditions showing influences from Louis Armstrong and Fats Waller.

With a few of the female singers who were well represented, many items of transcendent artistic merit served to balance the items that were obvious commercial concessions. Naturally this was most evident in the work of Helen Forrest and Peg La Centra, who were as ahead of the rest in quality as in quantity. Intuitively, however, one assumes that the air checks known to exist featuring Billie Holiday would provide a new perspective, should they ever become available.

Shaw composed thirteen songs that have been recorded by his bands in vocal versions. A few have appeared more often as instrumentals, namely "Shoot the Likker to Me John Boy" (Leo Watson's vocal on the original version is the only vocal rendition) and "Love of My Life" (which Shaw recorded in several contexts over the years). Others were recorded many times, while eight titles appeared only in their studio recording version. "Shoot the Likker to Me John Boy" and "Natch" were novelty pieces, but the remaining eleven were romantic ballads. In chronological order of initial recording, the thirteen titles were:

Shoot the Likker to Me John Boy	(1937)	(1 vocal version, 6 instrumental)
Any Old Time	(1938)	(7 versions, 3 different singers)
Easy to Say	(1939)	
Love Is Here	"	
Moonray	"	(8 versions)
Without a Dream to My Name	"	
Don't Fall Asleep	(1940)	
If It's You	"	

Love of My Life   *"*   (6 versions, 3 vocals)
Whispers in the Night   *"*   (2 versions)
Natch   (1945)
Don't You Believe It   (1946)
    Dear
When You're Around   *"*

As noted elsewhere, Shaw collaborated with lyricists on most of these titles. Other singers have recorded some of his tunes, including Fred Astaire doing "Love of My Life" with a studio orchestra, Tony Martin singing "If It's You" in the Marx Brothers' movie *The Big Store,* and the situation of Dick Todd with "Pastel Blue" as discussed in the text. "Moonray" was a popular hit for Shaw in 1939, and versions also were recorded by Teddy Wilson and Jack Jenney in that era; it was recorded in a vocal version by Chris Connor in the 1950s, and in 1962 by Roland Kirk as an instrumental.

The following lists of tune titles (arranged alphabetically with source and date of recording) are provided for each of the vocalists who are represented among the known recordings by Artie Shaw's various bands. Lists for the three singers most heavily represented are followed by an alphabetical list of the remaining vocalists and their repertoire. All vocalists recording at least five titles with bands under Artie Shaw's name appear in the photo section.

Helen Forrest Vocals with Artie Shaw

All I Remember Is You (Bb.1939/Jun.5)
All In Fun (Bb.1939/Oct.26)
All the Things You Are (Bb.1939/Oct.26)
Any Old Time (b'cast.1938/Dec.13)
    "   (b'cast.1939/Jan.13)
    "   (b'cast.1939/Jan.18)
    "   (Bb.1939/Mar.12)
    "   (b'cast.1939/Nov.3)
Between a Kiss and a Sigh (Bb.1938/Nov.17)
    "   (b'cast.1938/Dec.20)
Bill (Bb.1939/Jan.23)
Comes Love (Bb.1939/Jun.12)
    "   (O.G.S.1939/Jun.13)
    "   (b'cast.1939/Aug.19)
    "   (b'cast.1939/Oct.20)
Day After Day (Bb.1938/Nov.17)
Day In Day Out (Bb.1939/Aug.27)
    "   (b'cast.1939/Oct.19
    "   (b'cast.1939/Nov.10)
Deep in a Dream (Bb.1938/Nov.17)
    "   (b'cast.1938/Dec.2)
    "   (b'cast.1938/Dec.14)
Deep Purple (film.1939/Feb.?)

    "   (O.G.S.1939/Feb.19)
    "   (Bb.1939/Mar.12)
Do I Love You? (Bb.1939/Nov.9)
Don't Worry 'Bout Me (O.G.S.1939/Jun.6)
    "   (b'cast.1939/Aug.19)
Easy to Say (Bb.1939/Jun.22)
I Cried for You (O.G.S.1939/Feb.26)
I Didn't Know What Time It Was (Bb.1939/Nov.9)
    "   (b'cast.1939/Nov.11)
I Have Eyes (Bb.1938/Sept.27)
    "   (film.1939/Jan.?)
    "   (O.G.S.1939/Feb.5)
I Haven't Changed a Thing (b'cast.1938/Dec.15)
I Never Knew Heaven Could Speak (O.G.S.1939/Jun.27)
I Poured My Heart Into a Song (Bb.1939/Jun.5)
I Want My Share of Love (Bb.1939/Jan.31)
    "   (O.G.S.1939/Mar.5)
I Won't Tell a Soul (b'cast.1938/Dec.2)
I'll Remember (Bb.1939/Jun.22)
I'm In Love with the Honorable Mr. So-and-So (Bb.1939/Mar.12)
    "   (O.G.S.1939/Apr.2)
If You Ever Change Your Mind (Bb.1939/Mar.17)
It Took a Million Years (Bb.1938/Dec.19)
It's All Yours (Bb.1939/Jan.31)
I've Got My Eyes on You (b'cast.1939/Oct.26)
The Lamp Is Low (O.G.S.1939/Aug.22)
The Last Two Weeks in July (Bb.1939/Aug.27)
    "   (b'cast.1939/Oct.28)
Last Night (b'cast.1939/Nov.4)
Let's Stop the Clock (film.1938/Nov.28–29)
    "   (b'cast.1938.Dec.20)
Lilacs in the Rain (b'cast.1939/Oct.28)
Love Is Here (Bb.1939/Oct.26)
A Man and His Dream (Bb.1939/Jun.12)
Many Dreams Ago (Bb.1939/Sept.28)
    "   (b'cast.1939/Oct.19)
    "   (b'cast.1939/Oct.25)
    "   (b'cast.1939/Nov.10)
Melancholy Lullaby (b'cast.1939/Oct.21)
    "   (b'cast.1939/Oct.28)
    "   (b'cast.1939/Nov.3)
Melancholy Mood (Bb.1939/Jun.22)
Monday Morning (b'cast.1938/Dec.13)
Moonray (Bb.1939/Jun.22)
    "   (b'cast.1939/Aug.19)
    "   (b'cast.1939/Oct.19)
    "   (b'cast.1939/Oct.20)
    "   (b'cast.1939/Oct.21)
    "   (b'cast.1939/Oct.25)
    "   (b'cast.1939/Nov.10)
    "   (b'cast.1939/Nov.11)
My Own (O.G.S.1939/Jan.29)

My Reverie (b'cast.1938/Nov.25)
Night over Shanghai (b'cast.1939/Nov.4)
A Room with a View (Bb.1938/Dec.19)
    "   (b'cast.1939/Oct.25)
    "   (b'cast.1939/Oct.25)
Say It with a Kiss (Bb.1938/Dec.19)
Simple and Sweet (b'cast.1938/Dec.2
    "   (b'cast.1938/Dec.29)
Summer Souvenirs (b'cast.1938/Dec.13)
Supper Time (Bb.1939/Jan.17)
    "   (O.G.S.1939/May 7)
Thanks for Everything (Bb.1938/Nov.17)
    "   (b'cast.1938/Dec.23))
    "   (b'cast.1938/Dec.30)
They Say (b'cast.1938/Nov.25)
    "   (b'cast.1938/Dec.1)
    "   (Bb.1938/Dec.19)
    "   (b'cast.1938/Dec.29)
This Can't Be Love (b'cast.1939/Jan.18)
This Is It (Bb.1939/Jan.31)
Two Blind Loves (bb.1939/Aug.27)
    "   (b'cast.1938/Dec.22
Two Sleepy People (b'cast.1938/Dec.22)
What's New? (b'cast.1939/Nov.3)
When I Go A-Dreamin' (b'cast.1938/Dec.1)
    "   (b'cast.1938/Dec.29)
When Love Beckoned (Bb.1939/Nov.9)
Who Blew Out the Flame (O.G.S.1938/Nov.25)
    "   (b'cast.1938/Nov.25)
    "   (O.G.S.1938/Nov.27)
    "   (b'cast.1938/Dec.6)
Without a Dream to My Name (Bb.1939/Sept.28)
You Grow Sweeter as the Years Go By (Bb.1939/Mar.17)
You're a Sweet Little Headache (Bb.1938/Sept.27)
    "   (b'cast.1938/Dec.30)
You're So Indifferent (Bb.1939.Mar.17)
    "   (O.G.S.1939/Apr.23)

For convenience, just her Bluebird records are also listed below.

Helen Forrest Vocals with Artie Shaw: For Bluebird

All I Remember Is You (Bb.1939/Jun.5)
All In Fun (Bb.1939/Oct.26)
All the Things You Are (Bb.1939/Oct.26)
Any Old Time (Bb.1939/Mar.12)
Between a Kiss and a Sigh (Bb.1938/Nov.17)
Bill (Bb.1939/Jan.23)
Comes Love (Bb.1939/Jun.12)
Day After Day (Bb.1938/Nov.17)
Day In Day Out (Bb.1939/Aug.27)

Deep in a Dream (Bb.1938/Nov.17)
Deep Purple (Bb.1939/Mar.12)
Do I Love You? (Bb.1939/Nov.9)
Easy to Say (Bb.1939/Jun.22)
I Didn't Know What Time It Was (Bb.1939/Nov.9)
I Have Eyes (Bb.1938/Sept.27)
I Poured My Heart into a Song (Bb.1939/Jun.5)
I Want My Share of Love (Bb.1939/Jan.31)
I'll Remember (Bb.1939/Jun.22)
I'm In Love with the Honorable Mr. So-and-So (Bb.1939/
    Mar.12)
If You Ever Change Your Mind (Bb.1939/Mar.17)
It Took a Million Years (Bb.1938/Dec.19)
It's All Yours (Bb.1939/Jan.31)
The Last Two Weeks in July (Bb.1939/Aug.27)
Love Is Here (Bb.1939/Oct.26)
A Man and His Dream (Bb.1939/Jun.12)
Many Dreams Ago (Bb.1939/Sept.28)
Melancholy Mood (Bb.1939/Jun.22)
Moonray (Bb.1939/Jun.22)
A Room with a View (Bb.1938/Dec.19)
Say It with a Kiss (Bb.1938/Dec.19)
Supper Time (Bb.1939/Jan.17)
A Table in a Corner (Bb.1939/Sept.28)
Thanks for Everything (Bb.1938/Nov.17)
They Say (Bb.1938/Dec.19)
Two Blind Loves (Bb.1939/Aug.27)
When Love Beckoned (Bb.1939/Nov.9)
Without a Dream to My Name (Bb.1939/Sept.28)
You Grow Sweeter as the Years Go By (Bb.1939/Mar.17)
You're a Sweet Little Headache (Bb.1938/Sept.27)
You're So Indifferent (Bb.1939/Mar.17)

Tony Pastor Vocals with Artie Shaw

Alibi Baby (Thes.1937/Apr.29)
All God's Children Got Rhythm (Br.1937/May 13)
Better Than the Average Girl (O.G.S.1939/Mar.19)
Black and Blue (Thes.1937/Oct.17)
Bob White (Thes.1937/Dec.15)
Delightful Delirium (Bb.1939/Jan.31)
El Rancho Grande (b'cast.1939/Nov.3)
Go Fly a Kite (Bb.1939/June.12)
    "   (b'cast.1939/Aug.19)
Got the Mis'ry (b'cast.1939/Oct.26)
Have You Met Miss Jones? (Thes.1937/Oct.17)
I Can't Afford to Dream (Bb.1939/Jun.12)
I Can't Give You Anything But Love (b'cast.1939/Oct.28)
I Used to Be Color Blind (b'cast.1938/Dec.6)
I'll Be With You in Apple Blossom Time (Thes.1937/
    Dec.15)
    "   (b'cast.1938/Dec.2)

I'm Sorry for Myself (b'cast.1939/Oct.21)
If What You Say Is True (Bb.1939/Sept.28)
Indian Love CAll (Bb.1938/Jul.24)
    ″   (O.G.S.1939/Jan.1)
It Goes to Your Feet (Br.1937/May 13)
Jeepers Creepers (O.G.S.1938/Dec.25)
    ″   (b'cast.1938/Dec.29)
    ″   (film.1939/Feb.?)
Just a Kid Named Joe (b'cast.1938/Dec.1)
    ″   (b'cast.1938/Dec.20)
The Lady Is a Tramp (Thes.1937/Dec.15)
The Love Bug Will Bite You (Thes.1937/Apr.29)
My Bonnie Lies over the Ocean (Thes.1937/Dec.15)
Oh You Crazy Moon (b'cast.1939/Oct.25)
    ″   (b'cast.1939/Nov.10)
The Old Stamping Ground (Thes.1937/Dec.15)
    ″   (b'cast.1938/Dec.6)
    ″   (b'cast.1938/Dec.13)
    ″   (b'cast.1938/Dec.30)
One Two Button Your Shoe (Br.1936/Sept.17)
Prosschai (film.1938/Nov.28/29)
    ″   (b'cast.1938/Dec.20)
    ″   (O.G.S.1939/Jan.15)
    ″   (Bb.1939/Mar.12)
    ″   (O.G.S.1939/Mar.12)
    ″   (O.G.S.1939/May 14)
Put That Down in Writing (Bb.1939/Aug.27)
    ″   (b'cast.1939/Oct.19)
Rosalie (Thes.1937/Oct.17)
    ″   (Bb.1939/Jan.17)
    ″   (b'cast.1939/Jan.18)
    ″   (O.G.S.1939/Mar.5)
    ″   (O.G.S.1939/Apr.23)
Show Your Linen Miss Richardson (b'cast.1939/Jun.20)
Small Fry (b'cast.1938/Nov.29)
Snug as a Bug in a Rug (Bb.1939/Mar.17)
    ″   (O.G.S.1939/May 7)
Sweet Adeline (Br.1937/Jul.22) (two takes)
    ″   (Thes.1937/Oct.17)
    ″   (b'cast.1938/Nov.25)
Sweet Varsity Sue (Thes.1937/Oct.17)
Take Another Guess (Br.1936/Oct.30)
    ″   (b'cast.1936/Nov.1)
Them There Eyes (b'cast.1939/Sept.19)
When Winter Comes (Bb.1939/Jun.5)
    ″   (b'cast.1939/Jun.13)
Whistle While You Work (Br.1937/Dec.30) (two takes)
You're a Lucky Guy (b'cast.1939/Oct.20)
You're Out of This World (Thes.1937/Dec.15)

Peg La Centra Vocals with Artie Shaw

Afraid to Dream (Thes.1937/Jul.13)
    ″   (Br.1937/Jul.22)

All Dressed Up and No Place to Go (Thes.1937/Feb.19)
All You Want to Do Is Dance (Thes.1937/Jul.13)
Am I in Love? (Br.1937/Aug.4)
Can I Forget You? (Thes.1937/Jul.13)
Darling Not Without You (Br.1936/Sept.17)
Don't Ever Change (Thes.1937/Jul.13)
    ″   (Br.1937/Jul.22)
The Folks Who Live on the Hill (Thes.1937/Jul.13)
It Ain't Right (Br.1936/Aug.6)
It's the Natural Thing to Do (Thes. 1937/Jul.13)
Let's Call a Heart a Heart (Br.1936/Sept.17)
Love and Learn (Br.1936/Nov.30)
Moon Face (Br.1936/Nov.30)
    ″   (Thes.1937/Feb.19)
The Moon Got in My Eyes (Thes.1937/Jul.13)
Moonlight and Shadows (Br.1937/Feb.15
No More Tears (Br.1937/Feb.15)
    ″   (Thes.1937/Feb.19)
Please Pardon Us We're in Love (Br.1937/Aug.4)
September in the Rain (Thes.1937/Feb.19)
South Sea Island Magic (Br.1936/Aug.6)
Sweet Is the Word for You (Thes.1937/Feb.19)
There's Frost on the Moon (Br.1936/Oct.30)
    ″   (b'cast.1936/Nov.1)
There's Something in the Air (Br.1936/Oct.30)
    ″   (b'cast.1936/Nov.1)
The Things I Want (Thes.1937/Jul.13)
Trust in Me (Thes.1937/Feb.19)
Was It Rain? (Br.1937/Feb.15)
    ″   (Thes.1937/Feb.19)
When Your Lover Has Gone (Thes.1937/Feb.19)
You Can Tell She Comes from Dixie (Br.1936/Nov.30)
You're Giving Me a Song and a Dance (Br.1936/Sept.17)

Singers on Twelve or Fewer Titles with Artie Shaw

Allen, Dorothy	You Go to My Head (Vic.1945/Jun.9)
Astaire, Fred	Love of My Life (film.1940/Aug.?)
Blane, Ralph	Connecticut (Mus.1946/Oct.18)
Boswell, Connee	My Little Nest of Heavenly Blue (Decca.1952/Aug.1)
	Where There's Smoke There's Fire (Decca.1952/Aug.1)
Boyer, Anita	Along the Santa Fe Trail (b'cast,1940/Oct.26)
	Beau Night in Hotchkiss Corners (Vic.1940/Dec.17)
	The Calypso (Vic.1940/Dec.17)
	Do You Know Why? (b'cast,1941/Jan.21)

A Handful of Stars (Vic.1940/
Oct.7)

If It's You (V1c.1940/Sept.7)

Looking for Yesterday
(b'cast,1940/Oct.26)

Love of My Life (Vic.1940/
Oct.7)

    " (*Burns & Allen Show*,
1940/Oct.28)

Old Old Castle in Scotland
(Vic.1940/Sept.7)

There I Go (b'cast,1941/Jan.22)

Whispers in the Night
(Vic.1940/Dec.3)

    " (b'cast,1941/Jan.22)

You Forgot About Me (Vic.1940/
Dec.3)

Bradley, Nita   Any Old Time (Thes.1938/
Feb.15)

Can't Teach My Old Heart New
Tricks (Thes.1937/Dec.15)

Goodnight Angel (Thes.1937/
Dec.15)

    " (Br.1937/Dec.30)
(two takes)

It's Wonderful (Thes.1938/
Feb.15)

Love's Old Sweet Song
(Thes.1938/Feb.15)

Moonlight on the Sunset Trail
(Thes.1938/Feb.15)

One Song (Thes.1937/Dec.15)
    " (Br.1937/Dec.30)

There's a New Moon over the
Old Mill (Thes.1937/Dec.15)
    " (Br.1937/Dec.30)

You're a Sweetheart (Thes.1937/
Dec.15)

Byrne, Pauline   Don't Fall Asleep (Vic.1940/
Mar.3)

Gloomy Sunday (Vic.1940/
Mar.3)

My Fantasy (Vic.1940/Mar.3)

Chelsea 3   It's a Long Way to Tipperary
(Decca.1950/Jul.19)

Show Me the Way to Go Home
(Decca.1950/Jul.19)

Cherry, Don   Don't Worry 'Bout Me
(Decca.1950/Jul.19)

Just Say I Love Her
(Decca.1050/May 31)

    " (& Chorus)   Beautiful Madness (Decca.1951/
Jan.25)

"   Bring Back the Thrill
(Decca.1951/Jan.30)

"   Chapel of the Roses
(Decca.1951/Jan.25)

"   I Apologize (Decca.1951/Jan.30)

"   I've Got to Pass Your House
(Decca.1951/Jan.25)

"   The Thrill Is Gone (Decca.1951/
Jan.25)

Chickering 4   Jingle Bells (Decca.1950/
Sept.14)

Davies, Gwen   White Christmas (Decca.1950/
Oct.5)

    " (& Trio)   I Love the Guy (Decca.1950/
May 31)

Eldridge, Roy   Natch (Vic.1945/Jul.6)

Ford, Jane   Blue Again (Decca.1950/Jul.19)

Gibson, Fredda   Absent Minded Moon
(Vic.1942/Jan.20)

Not Mine (Vic.1942/Jan.20)

Somebody Nobody Loves
(Vic.1942/Jan.20)

Gordon Jenkins Choir   I'm Forever Blowing Bubbles
(Decca.1950/May 29)

You're Mine You (Decca.1950/
May 29)

Haymes, Dick   Count Every Star (Decca.1950/
Apr.27)

If You Were Only Mine
(Decca.1950/Apr.27)

Holiday, Billie   Any Old Time (Bb.1938/Jul.24)

Horne, Lena   Don't Take Your Love from Me
(Vic.1941/Jun.26)

Love Me a Little Little
(Vic.1941/Jun.26)

Howe, Dorothy   All at Once (Thes.1937/Apr.29)

I'll Never Tell You I Love You
(Thes.1937/Apr.29)

I've Got Beginners Luck
(Thes.1937/Apr.29)

Never in a Million Years
(Thes.1937/Apr.29)

Without Your Love (Thes.1937/
Apr.29)

Hutton, June   Dancing on the Ceiling
(Decca.1951/Jan.30)

My Kind of Love (Decca.1951/
Jan.30)

Kallen, Kitty   My Heart Belongs to Daddy
(Mus.1946/Jun.13)

Kelly, Paula   I Don't Want to Walk Without
You (Vic.1941/Dec.23)

	Make Love to Me (Vic.1941/ Oct.30) (two takes)	Richards, Trudy	Don't Take Your Love from Me (Thes.1950/Jan.?)
	Someone's Rocking My Dreamboat (Vic.1941/Dec.23)		Exactly Like You (Thes.1950/ Jan.?)
King Sisters	Volga Boat Song (O.G.S.1939/ Sept.19)		How Deep Is the Ocean (Thes.1950/Jan.?)
Lake, Bonnie	This Time the Dream's on Me (Vic.1941/Sept.2) (two takes)		I May Hate Myself in the Morning (Decca.1952/Apr.23)
	Time Was (b'cast,1941/Sept.6)		I Waited a Little Too Long (Decca.1952/Apr.23)
Lane, Lillian	He's Funny That Way (Thes.1949/Dec.?)		Together (Thes.1950/Jan.?)
	I Only Have Eyes for You (Thes.1949/Dec.?)		Too Marvelous (Thes.1950/ Jan.?)
	Let's Fall in Love (Thes.1949/ Dec.?)	Stevens, Hal	Ghost of a Chance (Mus.1945/ Nov.14)
	So in Love (Thes.1949/Dec.?)		How Deep Is the Ocean (Mus.1945/Nov.14)
	You Do Something to Me (Thes.1949/Dec.?)		That's for Me (Vic.1945/Jul.11)
Lynn, Imogene	Ac-Cent-Tchu-Ate the Positive (Vic.1944/Nov.23)		Yolanda (Vic.1945/Jul.28)
	Along the Navajo Trail (b'cast.1945/Oct.3)	Tilton, Martha	Dreaming Out Loud (Vic.1940/ May 13)
	Can't You Read Between the Lines (b'cast.1945/Oct.10)		Now We Know (Vic.1940/May 13)
	Can't Help Lovin' That Man (Vic.1945/Jan.9)	Todd, Dick	A Room with a View (O.G.S.1939/Jan.15)
	Gotta Be This or That (b'cast.1945/Sept.19)		Deep in a Dream (O.G.S.1938/ Dec.25)
	Let's Take the Long Way Home (Vic.1944/Nov.23)		Good for Nothin' But Love (O.G.S.1939/Feb.5)
	On the Atcheson Topeka & Santa Fe (b'cast.1945/Sept.19)		Have You Forgotten? (O.G.S.1938/Dec.4)
McCall, Mary Ann	Nothin' from Nothin' (Decca.1950/Jan.6)		I'm Madly in Love with You (O.G.S.1938/Dec.11)
	There Must Be Something Better Than Love (Decca.1950/ Jan.6)		My Reverie (O.G.S.1939/Jan.8) They Say (O.G.S.1939/Jan.1) This Can't Be Love
O'Neill, Dolores	A Strange Loneliness (Thes.1937/Oct.17)		(O.G.S.1939/Jan.29) 〃 (O.G.S.1939/Feb.26)
	〃 (Br.1937/Oct.18)		Two Sleepy People (O.G.S.1938/ Nov.18)
Page, "Hot Lips"	Blues in the Night (Vic.1941/ Sept.2) (two takes)		〃 (O.G.S.1938/Nov.20)
	〃 (b'cast,1941/Sept.6)		When I Go A-Dreamin' (O.G.S.1938/Nov.25)
	〃 (b'cast,1941/Dec.8)		〃 (O.G.S.1938Nov.27)
	Sometimes I Feel Like a Motherless Child (Vic.1942/ Jan.21)		You Must Have Been a Beautiful Baby (O.G.S.1939/Feb.19)
	St. James Infirmary, Pt.1 (Vic.1941/Nov.12) (2 takes)	Tormé, Mel	Along with Me (Mus.1946/ Apr.30)
	Take Your Shoes off Baby (Vic.1941/Oct.30)		For You For Me Forevermore (Mus 1946/Aug.16)
Pearce, Jack	Mister Meadowlark (Vic.1940/ May 13)		Get Out of Town (Mus.1946/ Jun.25)
			I Believe (Mus.1946/Nov.8)

It's the Same Old Dream
(Mus.1946/Nov.8)

They Can't Convince Me
(Mus.1946/Sept.10)

" (& Mel-Tones)   And So to Bed (Mus.1946/
Oct.18)

"   Changing My Tune (Mus.1946/
Aug.16)

"   Don't You Believe It Dear
(Mus.1946/Oct.18)

"   Guilty (Mus.1946/Sept.19)

"   I Got the Sun in the Morning
(Mus.1946/Apr.30)

"   What Is This Thing Called
Love? (Mus.1946/Jun.19)
(two takes)

Vaughan, Wes   I Used to Be Above Love
(Br.1936/Jun.11)

                  No Regrets (Br.1936/Jun.17)

Wain, Bea   If It's the Last Thing I Do
(Br.1937/Sept.17)

Walters, Teddy   You Do Something to Me
(Mus.1946/Jun.12)

Watson, Leo   Free Wheeling (Br.1937/
Sept.17)

                  I've a Strange New Rhythm in
My Heart (Br.1937/Sept.17)

                  Shoot the Likker to Me John Boy
(Br.1937/Sept.17)

Appendix 5

Annotated Selective Bibliography

Given Artie Shaw's celebrity status, it is not surprising that the number of references to him in print is monumental. Most references repeat familiar information and misinformation. Thus, there is little point in cataloging such items. This would include most liner notes to the various issues of his records, superficial articles both during and since his rise to fame (which have appeared in newspapers and magazines of all levels of quality and availability) and the standard accounts in musical and other encyclopedias, books on jazz or popular music, and so forth. During the active years of his career, newspapers in the various cities where he would appear usually offered advertisements, articles, and photos, as well as reviews of his appearances. The major music magazines of the era, *Metronome* and *Down Beat*, along with the major entertainment industry magazine, *Billboard*, were the most fertile primary sources in providing reviews of records and shows, the band's itinerary, articles and interviews, advertisements, and (in *Metronome* and *Down Beat*) photos. Perusing the entire run of these titles during the years in question, in chronological order, is highly recommended as an exercise in gaining perspective on the era and on Shaw and his bands. Libraries with good archival collections occasionally have these titles at least on microfilm. More obscure magazines of the era, such as *Swing* or *Upbeat*, are far rarer and more difficult to examine.

Shaw can be seen in a variety of advertisements, aside from those for his Bluebird and Victor records and his appeal to the jukebox trade as a "nickel-nabbing magnet" as the *Billboard* ads put it. He appeared in several Selmer ads, both alone and with his reed section. He also appeared in an ad for Martin instruments along with members of his brass section in 1940–41, and in a Gretch drums ad along with Nick Fatool in the same period. Not surprisingly, he also appeared in several ads for reeds. In 1939, he was endorsing Conrad reeds. During 1940–41 he was shown smiling out of an ad for "Enduro" plastic reeds, manufactured by his old friend from the CBS studio years, Arnold Brilhart.

Brilhart also designed and manufactured woodwind mouthpieces, and in 1941 produced an Artie Shaw clarinet mouthpiece. The ads quoted Shaw:

This new mouthpiece, co-designed by Arnold Brilhart and myself, fills a long-felt need for a really fine clarinet mouthpiece to meet the demands of the modern clarinetist.

Shaw also contributed to the *Brilhart Bulletin*, available free from Brilhart dealers in those days. *Brilhart Bulletin #4* featured Shaw explaining high-note technique, tone control, improvising, and "How to practice." A later ad for the Artie Shaw Mouthpiece announced,

By popular request, the title of *Brilhart Bulletin #10* is "How to develop your style" by Artie Shaw.

Another collaboration between Shaw and Brilhart was a clarinet method book, titled *Artie Shaw Clarinet Method: A School of Modern Clarinet Technic* (New York: Robbins Music Corp., 1941). This instruction book also contained transcriptions of several Shaw solos from his Bluebird and Victor records, along with exercises and advice. Some of the solo transcriptions were published in *Down Beat* around that period as well.

Some of Shaw's arrangements were also published. As early as 1939, Harms Inc., a music publisher in New York, was advertising the "Artie Shaw Dance Series," as noted in the text. In 1941, Robbins Music Corporation published a collection of Shaw solos with piano accompaniment titled *Artie Shaw Rhythm Hits For Clarinet*. This collection contained the following:

If I Had You	I'm Coming Virginia
I Never Knew	Back Bay Shuffle
I Cried for You	At Sundown
My Blue Heaven	Whispering
Just You, Just Me	Rose Room

It is interesting to note that Shaw never commercially recorded some of these titles with any of his bands; not even broadcast versions have appeared.

Many of Shaw's compositions also appeared as sheet music, but often they were not published, and in any case publication data would be difficult to establish. The Library of Congress Catalogs for pre-1956 imprints are very sketchy and only list Shaw's autobiography, the above clarinet method, and the published version of *Concerto for Clarinet* (New York: Mills Music, 1941).

Another intriguing advertisement showed Shaw playing into, and smiling over, a Presto portable home recording system. In those pre-tape days, acetate discs were used. The Presto machine was capable of recording a fifteen-minute program on two sides of a 12-inch disc, at either 78-rpm or 33⅓-rpm. The ad read in part:

ARTIE SHAW CHECKS UP ON ARTIE SHAW with a Presto recorder . . . Artie Shaw makes Presto recordings during rehearsals, then lets his men hear themselves as they play new numbers and arrangements. Presto recordings help him explain faults . . . save time training new men . . . speed up rehearsals.

As noted in the text, Shaw was in the practice of doing something like this as early as 1936. Although he confirmed these activities, he had no idea what may have become of such recordings.

The ultimate source of information on Shaw's point of view and early life is Shaw's autobiographical *The Trouble with Cinderella*. It was first published by Farrar, Straus & Young in 1952. It next appeared slightly edited in England, published by Jarrolds (London) in 1955. This edition contained twelve photographs. The Farrar, Straus & Young version was reissued in paperback by Collier Books in 1963. In 1979, Da Capo Press reprinted it again, with a new introduction by Shaw, all the photos from the Jarrolds edition, and two new photos; in 1992 this version was reprinted by Fithian Press of Santa Barbara, with some changes among photos. Although more specific dates would have been helpful, and more details concerning his music and musical life after his early years would have been welcome, it stands as the definitive self-portrait alongside the music itself. The book has been praised as a major contribution not only to the literature of jazz and popular culture, but also to the literature of introspection. As a document describing the confrontation between the artist and his public in that era, and of the twentieth century materialistic North American culture generally, it is equally insightful.

Shaw's other writings on music are harder to track down. His fiction (aside from the *Education of Albie Snow* trilogy in process) has little to do with music. Many of his articles on music have appeared only in obscure magazines at that time. One of the most important is also one of the most accessible: "Music Is a Business" in the 2 December 1939 issue of *The Saturday Evening Post*. One of his earliest articles on music was "Artie Shaw Expresses His Opinions on Swing and Its Various Forms," which appeared in *The Bandstand*, vol. 1, no. 2 (February 1939), page 1. This was

a magazine published by Tommy Dorsey devoted to swing. The next month, an article by Shaw titled "I Am Not a Monster" appeared in *Upbeat* (March 1939), as noted in the text. Probably the last article he wrote for publication during his career as a leader was the "Dixie, Swing, Bop or What?" item in *See* magazine, also described in the text. It actually appeared the month following his final tour of Australia. If his many interviews are counted, including items done after he left music, the total number of references on Shaw expressing himself in print on music would run into the hundreds.

Shaw's autobiography and the above article from *The Saturday Evening Post* have been the most frequently quoted sources of Shaw's own comments on music and his career. Some of the most complete and accurate articles not among the references cited are:

1) Albertson, Chris. "Artie Shaw" in *The Swing Era 1937-1938* (New York: Time-Life Records, 1971, pp. 30–39).
NOTE: This series was a multivolume set accompanying records which recreated hit tunes from the Swing Era. The orchestras were led primarily by Billy May (some by Glen Gray). Abe Most took Shaw's role on clarinet for the recreations. The books accompanying the records contain informative articles and photographs.
2) Duckham, Henry. "A Masterclass with Artie Shaw" in *The Clarinet*, vol. 12, no. 3 (spring 1985): pp. 10–16.
NOTE: This was an informative interview/article with several good photos.
3) Ruhlmann, William. "The Trouble with Artie Shaw" in *Goldmine*, vol. 18, no. 11 (29 May 1992): pp. 20+
NOTE: This was the most complete account, with fewest errors, that was available to date. It includes discussions of which Shaw records were placing on the pop charts during his active years.

The best articles and reviews found have been quoted and cited in the text, where relevant, as far as possible. Since the 1980s and Shaw's reemergence into the public eye with his fronting a band again and the release of the two-hour Academy Award-winning documentary film *Artie Shaw: Time Is All You've Got*, articles and interviews have appeared occasionally in various jazz-oriented music magazines such as *Coda* or *Jazz Journal*, or even in the classical-oriented *The Instrumentalist*; general news magazines such as *People* magazine; and so forth. Aside from the aforementioned items in *Goldmine* and *The Clarinet*, these have been generally superficial rehashes. In the latter 1990s more substantial articles also have appeared in the *IAJRC Journal* containing previously unpublished discographical details and discussions of newly discovered recordings. Another article in *The Clarinet*, by Tsuneya Hirai, "Homage to Artie Shaw" (vol. 14, no. 4 [Summer 1987]: pp. 30–33, dealt specifically with

Shaw's clarinet technique during 1953–54, and included transcriptions of solos.

Liner notes to recordings also have generally been superficial rehashes. Those cited in the text were obvious exceptions. The notes to the Hindsight Records series of 1938–39 broadcast air checks were also excellent in quoting Shaw's comments on the performances released. The liner notes by Bert Korall for the seven-volume set on RCA titled *The Complete Artie Shaw*, as broken down in the discography, were most heavily quoted. These volumes were:

The Complete Artie Shaw Volume I / 1938–1939	AXM2-5517
The Complete Artie Shaw Volume II / 1939	AXM2-5533
The Complete Artie Shaw Volume III / 1939–1940	AXM2-5556
The Complete Artie Shaw Volume IV / 1940–1941	AXM2-5572
The Complete Artie Shaw Volume V / 1941–42	AXM2-5576
The Complete Artie Shaw Volume VI / 1942–1945	AXM2-5579
The Complete Artie Shaw Volume VII / 1939–1945— Retrospective	AXM2-5580

As these were LP record releases, they have gone out of print with the advent of compact discs, but may of course be reissued in that format.

Biographies and autobiographies by various performers and celebrities who had contact or interaction with Shaw abound. The most useful are among the footnoted references. Many, such as Charlie Barnet's autobiography, *Those Swinging Years* (Baton Rouge: Louisiana State University Press, 1984) contain an anecdote or two of marginal interest. In this case there was brief mention of their record date together with Red Norvo in 1934; the story of Barnet's elopement with Shirley Lloyd summarized in the text; and brief mention of Barnet and Shaw working across the street from each other in Las Vegas in 1954. While it may be interesting to contemplate their proximity twenty years apart at the dawn and twilight of Shaw's most important years as a performer, and the story of the elopement is fun, there was not much of substance to draw from. Others not listed or referred to contain erroneous information Shaw refuted, or merely superficial rehashes. As noted, this also applies to most books on the Swing Era, jazz encyclopedias, and so forth. The discussions in Gunther Schuller's *The Swing Era* (New York: Oxford University Press, 1989), as noted in the text, are a case in point.

In the 1970s, Edmund L. Blandford, who started the Artie Shaw Club in England, published two similar accounts of Shaw's musical life himself: *Swinging Shaw* (Hastings, England: Castle Books, 1973) and *Artie Shaw: The Man & The Music* (Hastings, England: The Author, 1975). Both books mostly were extensive but uncritically selected quotes, otherwise often very inaccurate, and generally unobtainable. The Artie Shaw Club also issued over a dozen "collector's label" (bootleg) LPs and published *The Artie Shaw Club Journal*. This publication primarily contained enthusiastic fan-style reviews, correspondence, and occasional information. It ran through about two dozen issues, first under Blandford, then under David Cooper, before expiring in 1974.

Prior to the 1970s, no attempt to publish a complete Artie Shaw discography materialized. The best one could do was to combine entries in Brian Rust's *Jazz Records A–Z, 1932 to 1942* (Hatch End, England: The Author, 1965) with Jorgen Grunnet Jepsen's *Jazz Records 1942–1962, Vol. 7: S–Te* (Holte, Denmark: Karl Emil Knudson, 1964). These were combined with some added data by Walter Bruyninckx in *60 Years of Recorded Jazz* (Belgium: The Author, various datings). None of these can be considered very accurate beyond the general contours, and do not include sideman sessions within entries on leaders' work. Searching for Shaw's name among others' records in these and other discographies yielded many spurious sessions, as well as revealing many omissions.

The first attempt at a discography including records, transcriptions and broadcasts by Shaw's bands was Alastair Robertson's *Artie Shaw '36–'55* (Edinburgh, Scotland: The Author, 1971). Blandford's books had similar efforts, with his *Swinging Shaw* listing sideman sessions for which Shaw's name was suggested by Rust, without corrections or additions. In 1974, Bill Korst and Charles Garrod published *Artie Shaw and His Orchestra* (Spotswood, N.J.: Joyce Music Publications, 1974). This effort to chronologically list everything Shaw recorded as a leader, under his own name, although containing many errors and spurious items, has remained the best effort to date.

In 1998, *Non-Stop Flight: A Life of Artie Shaw* by John White (New York: Paul & Company Publishers Consortium, Inc., 1998) was announced as forthcoming in its publisher's catalog, but it has not been possible to preview a copy.

References

Sources that are referred to frequently in the text are listed here. They are referred to in the text by the reference number shown below. Other references are cited in full in the text; they are further mentioned in appendix 5, the annotated selective bibliography. Magazine and newspaper references are fully cited at the point where relevant quotes were used.

(1) Shaw, Artie. *The Trouble with Cinderella*. New York: Da Capo Press, 1979.

(2) Shaw, Artie. Personal communications with author, 1973, 1989–1998.

(3) Feather, Leonard. " 'Happy at Last!' Says Shaw" in *Down Beat*, 29 June 1951, pp. 1 ff.

(4) Connor, D. Russell. *B.G.—On the Record*. New Rochelle, N.Y.: Arlington House, 1969.

(5) Kaminsky, Max. *My Life in Jazz*. New York: Harper & Row, 1963.

(6) Simon, George T. *Simon Says*. New York: Galahad Books, 1971.

(7) Frank, Gerold. *Judy*. New York: Harper & Row, 1975.

(8) Shaw, Artie. "Music Is a Business" in *The Saturday Evening Post*, 2 December 1939, pp. 14, 15, 66 ff.

(9) McDonough, John. "Artie Shaw: Non-Stop Flight from 1938" in *Down Beat*, 22 January 1970, pp. 12, 13, 38.

(10) Simon, George T. *The Big Bands*. New York: Macmillan, 1967.

(11) Palmer, Robert. "Middle-Aged Man Without a Horn" in *The New Yorker*, 19 May 1962, pp. 47 ff.

(12) Forrest, Helen. *I Had the Craziest Dream*. New York: Coward, McCann & Geoghegan, 1982.

(13) Morella, Joe, and Edward Z. Epstein. *Lana: The Public and Private Lives of Miss Turner*. New York: Dell, 1971.

(14) Turner, Lana. *Lana: The Lady, The Legend, The Truth*. New York: Dutton, 1982.

(15) Tormé, Mel. *Traps—the Drum Wonder: The Life of Buddy Rich*. New York: Oxford University Press, 1991.

(16) Ulanov, Barry. "Shaw in '44" in *Metronome*, September 1944, p. 18.

(17) Flamini, Roland. *Ava*. New York: Coward, McCann & Geoghegan, 1983.

Name Directory

All names mentioned in the text or discography are listed alphabetically, with a tag indicating their relevance in Shaw's musical career, except for the names of later writers on Shaw (subsequent to his career as a performer, who were mentioned in the preface or annotated bibliography). Writers mentioned in the text who wrote about Shaw during his career as a performer are identified by the significance of their contribution at that time. Others noted as "writer" were friends of Shaw in that era. Similar identification tags are cited for those actors, etc., mentioned in the text. If the individual was a musician or singer for whom Shaw worked or recorded as a sideman, they are suitably indicated as having "led session," with applicable dates cited. Those also known to be along on such sessions are cited as "with (whoever led the session)" and the date. If the musician recorded under Shaw's leadership, only the dates the musician was active in Shaw's bands are cited, inclusively by year for multiple sessions in working bands, or by specific date for unique sessions as part of a studio group. Composers of pieces Shaw performed are listed here only if mentioned in the text (as they are in any case cited in the "Composers' Credits" appendix, along with their tune titles) and are simply cited as "composer" or "popular songwriter" in most cases.

It is hoped the entries are otherwise self-explanatory. Generally, more information can be found in the text, except for names found only in the discography. Spelling variations in names, or name changes, may not have always been caught, and thus some individuals may be listed twice, under two or more different spellings or names as given in various sources, if it could not be confirmed they were the same person. (For example, Ike SEAR, Irving and Isadore ZIR in the 1930s, and Izzy ZER in the 1950s, all string players). Spelling has been checked where possible in the sources listed below, but are otherwise given as found. For more information on musicians and singers, the *New Grove Dictionary of Jazz* (ed. Barry Kernfeld; London: Macmillan, 1988), Roger Kinkle's *Encyclopedia of Popular Music and Jazz 1900–1950* (New Rochelle, N.Y.: Arlington House, 1974), Chilton's *Who's Who of Jazz: Storyville to Swing Street* (New York: Chilton Book Co., 1972) and Leonard Feather's various editions of the *Encyclopedia of Jazz* are particularly recommended, but more obscure figures would not be listed. For composers and songwriters, the *New*

Grove Dictionary of American Music would include most of the major figures.

AARONSON, Irving. Prominent bandleader 1920s–1930s; Shaw in band most of 1930; led session1930/August 22.

ABBOTT, Larry(as,cl). With Carl Hoff 1936.

ABBOTT, Stan. Pseudonym for Stuart Allen(v) on Richard Himber transcriptions.

ADAM, C.(cello). 1949/May 31.

ADLER, Rudy(reeds). Probably took the bass clarinet solos with Fred Rich 1931 and Ben Selvin 1932/May 12; with Bill Challis 1936.

AGLORA, Joe(ts). In The Rangers 1942–43.

ALEXANDER, Bob(tb). 1950/May 29; 1953/July.

ALEXANDER, Willard. Booking agent.

ALLEN, Dorothy(v). 1945/June 9.

ALLEN, Gracie. Comedienne/actress of the *Burns and Allen Show*.

ALLEN, Henry "Red"(tp). 1941/June 26.

ALLEN, Marge. Shaw's second wife, with him at Bucks County farm 1933–34.

ALLEN, Stuart(v). With Richard Himber 1935–36.

ALLEY, Ben(v). With Fred Rich 1931/October.

ALPERT, Trigger(b). 1950/May 29; 1952/August 1; 1953/July.

AMATO, Sam(oboe,Eh). 1950/April 27.

AMOROSO, Sam(harp). With Richard Himber 1935.

ANCHER, Maurice(vl). With Paul Whiteman, Christmas 1938.

ANDERSON, Don(tp). 1946/July 28.

ANDREWS SISTERS, THE (Patty, Maxine, LaVerne). Prominent vocal group from 1930s.

ANTONIONI, Alfredo(cond). With Shaw at Temple Shalom concert 1949.

ARLEN, Harold. Popular songwriter.

ARMSTRONG, Jack(vl,v). With Irving Aaronson 1930/August 22.

ARMSTRONG, Louis(tp,v). Major innovator/stylist in jazz during 1920s.

ARNAUD, Leo(tb,cello). With Roger Wolfe Kahn 1932/August 5.

ARNHEIM, Gus. Prominent bandleader, emerged in 1920s.

ARNO, Victor(vl). 1946/July 28.

ARQUETTE, Les(ts,v). With Joe Cantor 1928/August 13.

ARSHAWSKY, Abraham Isaac. Artie Shaw's Hebrew name.

ARSHAWSKY, Harry. Artie Shaw's father.

ARUS, George(tb). Trombone soloist with Shaw 1937–39.

ASH, Paul. Popular bandleader.

ASTAIRE, Fred(v). Dancer/movie star; in *Second Chorus* (1940).

ATKINS, Leonard(vla). With Shaw 1941–42.

AULD, Georgie(ts). Prominent soloist with Shaw's 1938–39 and 1941–42 bands.

AVOLA, Al(g). With Shaw 1937–39; assisted with arrangements.

AYRES, Lew. Movie star.

AYRES, Norman(tp). With Shaw 1937–38.

BAFFA, William(vla). 1946/July 28.

BAILEY, Buster(cl). Important clarinet stylist emerging in 1920s.

BAILEY, Mildred(v). Led session 1936/November 9.

BAKER, Artie(as,bar). With Shaw 1941–42; 1951/January 25.

BAKER, Benny(tp). With Don Voorhees 1934.

BAKER, Chet(tp,v). Emerged in 1950s; a star as "cool jazz" symbol.

BAKER, Dan. Organist on Paramount Theatre bill, 1936.

BAKER, Julius(fl). 1949/May 31.

BALKIN, Maurice(cello). 1953/July 6.

BALLEW, Smith(v). Prolifically recorded bandleader/singer of 1930s.

BANK, Danny(bar). With Shaw 1949–50.

Bar Harbor Society Orchestra. A Ben Selvin recording unit.

BARBOUR, Dave(g). With Mildred Bailey 1936/November 9; with Shaw 1939/November; 1946.

BARENE, Robert(vl). 1940/March 3.

BARGY, Roy(p). With Frank Trumbauer 1934/November 20; 1936/April 27.

BARKSDALE, Everett(g). 1950/May 31 & July 19.

BARLOW, Howard. Led radio orchestra including Shaw in 1930s.

BARNES, George(g). 1951/January 25; 1952/April 23 & August 1.

BARNET, Charlie(ts). With Red Norvo 1934/September 26 & October 4; prominent swing era bandleader.

BARRES, George(vl). 1946/June 6.

BARRIOS, Gil(p). With Shaw 1949–50.

BARRON, Blue. Popular "sweet" bandleader.

BARROWS, John(Fh). 1950/October 5; 1953/July 2.

BARRYMORE, John. Movie star.

BARTEE, John. Composer/arranger of three Latin-style numbers Shaw used in 1949–50.

BARZIN, Leon(cond). 1949/April 18.

BASIE, Count(p). Led session 1944/September 25; in All-Stars 1944/September 30.

BASSEY, Bus(ts). With Shaw 1940–41.

BAUM, Jo(vl). With Ray Sinatra 1936.

BAXTER, Les(v). With the Mel-Tones, 1946.

Bea and the Bachelors(v). Popular vocal group including Bea Wain and Al Rinker; with Bill Challis 1936.

BEACH, Frank(tp). In The Rangers 1942–43; with Shaw's 1946 studio bands.

BEAU, Heinie(reeds). 1946/April 30; played Shaw's role in Ace Hudkins's 1948 Shaw-styled band.

BECHET, Sidney(cl,ss). Major stylist; emerged 1920s.

BECKER, R. Whitney. *Down Beat* writer of the era.

BEECHER, Gene(bjo,g). With Shaw in early New Haven bands.

BEIDERBECKE, Bix(tp,p). Major stylist emerged in 1920s and Shaw's friend.

BELL, Jack(reeds). With Paul Whiteman, Christmas 1938.

BELLER, Alex(vl). With Shaw 1940–42.

Bellevue Ramblers. Band including Shaw in New Haven, mid-1920s.

BENCHLEY, Robert. Humorist; with Shaw on Old Gold show 1938–39.

BENJAMIN, Joe(b). 1950/May 31; 1950/September.

BENNETT, Mark(tb). 1936/June.

BENNETT, Sid(v). With Chickering 4 vocal group, 1950/September 14.

BENNY, Jack. Famed comedian.

BERARDINELLI, Herman(reeds). With Shaw's 1946 studio bands.

BEREZOWSKY, Nikolai. Composed clarinet concerto Shaw recorded 1949/April 18.

BERGMAN, Dewey(p,arranger). With Carl Hoff 1936.

BERGMAN, Edgar(vl). With Shaw's 1946 studio bands.

BERGNER, Walt(p). With Joe Cantor 1928/August 13.

BERIGAN, Bunny(tp,v). Major jazz soloist and bandleader in 1930s. With CBS House Band 1931–32; Adrian Rollini 1934/March 24; Frank Trumbauer 1934/November 20; Richard Himber 1934–36; Bob Howard 1936/January 28; led session 1936/April 13; with Dick McDonough 1936/June 4 & 23; Billie Holiday 1936/July 10.

BERLIN, Irving. Major popular song composer.

BERLINER, Emile. Early inventor/manufacturer of phonographs.

BERMAN, Billy(tp). With Shaw in the Bellevue Ramblers.

BERMAN, Brigitte. Produced documentary films on Beiderbecke and Shaw.

BERMAN, Max(vl). With Shaw 1941–42.

BERMAN, Sonny(tp). Star with Woody Herman's First Herd.

BERNARD, Cy(cello). 1940/May 13; 1946.

BERNIE, Al. Comedian on same bill as Shaw in theatres 1936–37.

BERNIE, Ben. Popular bandleader.

BERNSTEIN, Artie(b). Prominent bassist in the era & Shaw's roommate in 1931. With Red Nichols 1931/August 24; Frank Trumbauer 1934/November 20; The Boswell Sisters 1936/January 6; Manny Klein 1936/January 20; Bill Challis 1936; Shaw 1936/May 24.

BERRY, Chu(ts). On WNEW jam 1938/November 9.

BERT, Eddie(tb). 1950/April 4.

BEST, Denzil(d). In 1953 Gramercy 5 to mid-October; no recordings.

BEST, Johnny(tp). With Shaw 1937–39; in The The Rangers 1942–43.

Betty and the Troubadors(v). Pseudonym for vocal group "Bea and the Bachelors" on Bill Challis' transcriptions, 1936.

BEULER, George(v). With Johnny Green 1934/August 1.

BEVERIDGE, Betty(v). With the Mel-Tones 1946.

BIAGINI, Hank. Bandleader from whom Shaw recruited several sidemen in 1937.

BIGARD, Barney. Important clarinet stylist from 1920s.

BINYON, Larry(reeds). With Roger Wolfe Kahn 1932; Frank Trumbauer 1934/November 20; Bill Challis 1936.

BLANCHARD, Will(Fh). 1950/September 12.

BLANE, Ralph(v). Songwriter/singer, 1946/October 17.

BLANTON, Jimmy(b). Major innovator/stylist; with Duke Ellington 1939–42.

BLOCK, Al(as). 1950/April 4.

BLOCK, Martin. WNEW announcer & disc jockey.

BLOCK, Sandy(b). 1951/January 25; 1952/April 23.

BLOOM, William(vl). 1946/April 30.

BLOWERS, John(d). 1950/May 25; 1952/April 23.

Blue Coal Minstrels. Band on radio show of same name featuring Shaw, 1931–32.

BLUESTONE, Harry(vl). With Red Nichols 1931/August 24; Bill Challis 1936; with Shaw 1936/May 24; 1940/March 3 & May 13; 1946.

BOARDMAN, Truman(vl). With Shaw 1940–42.

BODNER, Phil(reeds). 1955/November 21.

BOHANNON, Hoyt(tb). 1946/April 30.

BOLDEN, Buddy(tp). Legendary New Orleans jazz innovator at turn of century.

BOOKER, Beryl(p). Led trio opposite Shaw at The Embers in 1954.

BOOP, Betty. Cartoon character popular in the era.

BORDONI, Irene(v). Star of Cole Porter musical revue *Paris* in late 1920s–early 1930s.

BORNE, Hal. Songwriter; worked on movie *Second Chorus*.

BORODIN, Abe(cello). 1941/June 26.

BORODIN, Alexander. Russian composer.

BORODKIN, Abraham(cello). With Richard Himber 1936; Bill Challis 1936; Paul Whiteman, Christmas 1938.

BORODKIN, Herb(vla). With Paul Whiteman, Christmas 1938.

BOSE, Sterling(tp). With Jack Shilkret 1936/August 29.

BOSWELL SISTERS, THE (Connee, Helvetia, Martha)(v).

Led sessions 1935/October 28; 1936/January 6 and February 12.

BOSWELL, Connee(v). Led session 1935/January 15; with Shaw 1952/August 1.

BOTKIN, Perry(g). With Roger Wolfe Kahn 1932; Johnny Green 1934/August 1.

BOWEN, Claude(tp). With Shaw 1938.

BOWEN, Lyle(reeds). With Don Voorhees 1934; Richard Himber 1936; Shaw 1940/May 13.

BOWER, Bob(vl). With Shaw 1940–41.

BOWMAN, Babe(tb). 1940/March 3.

BOYER, Anita(v). With Shaw 1940–41.

BOYER, Charles. Movie star.

BRADFORD, Larry. Pseudonym on World Transcriptions for Richard Himber.

BRADLEY, Nita(v). With Shaw 1937–38.

BRADLEY, Will(tb). With Red Nichols 1931/August 24; The Boswell Sisters 1935/October 8 and 1936/February 12; Bill Challis 1936; Ray Sinatra 1936; with Shaw 1950; 1953/July 2; 1955/November 21.

BRAND, Julie(vl,vla). 1953/July.

BRECKER, Sid(vla). 1953/July.

BRIERS, Larry(p,cond). Led Blue Coal Minstrels including Shaw 1931–32.

BRILHART, Arnold(reeds). With Don Voorhees 1934; Richard Himber 1934; Ray Sinatra 1936. Later manufactured quality reeds and mouthpieces which Shaw endorsed; Coauthored clarinet book with Shaw.

BRODETSKY, Julian(vl). 1940/August 16.

BRODSKY, Irving(p). With Fred Rich 1931.

BROKAW, Sid(vl). With Shaw 1940.

BROWER, Bill(vl). With Shaw 1940–41.

BROWN, Eddie(reeds). 1950/September 12.

BROWN, Maurice(cello). 1950/April 27 & September 12; 1953/July 6; 1955/November 21.

BROWN, Ray(b). With Ella Fitzgerald's group opposite Shaw at Bop City 1949.

BROWN, Russell(tb). With Shaw 1938.

BROWN, Vernon(tb). With Shaw 1940–41.

BRUBECK, Dave(p). Prominent modernist since 1940s.

BRYAN, Arthur Q. Played "Mayor" in Shaw's "Pied Piper of Hamelin" in 1946.

BRYAN, Don(tp). With Carl Hoff 1936.

BRYAN, Mike(g). With Shaw 1941–42.

Bucktown Five. Group led by Muggsy Spanier in 1924.

BUFFINGTON, Jim(Fh). 1953/July; 1955/November 21.

BULLMAN, Mort(tb). 1952/April 23.

BULLOCK, Chick(v). Led sessions 1934/September 26, 1935/January 15, 1936/July 20; with Jack Shilkret 1936/April 2, July 31 & August 29; Bunny Berigan 1936/April 13; Dick McDonough 1936/June 4, August 5, September 17 & November 3.

BUMPUS, Dudley. Sammy Cahn's pseudonym as Shaw's "doctor" in 1939.

BURDICK, Huntington(Fh). 1946/July 28.

BURKE, Sonny. Orchestrated Shaw's Musicraft arrangements.

BURNESS, Les(p,celeste). With Shaw 1937–38.

BURNS, George. Comedian/actor; Shaw on the *Burns and Allen Show* 1940–41.

BURNS, Ralph. Pianist/arranger prominent in the 1940s.

BUSHKIN, Joe(p). With Bunny Berigan 1936/April 13; Billie Holiday 1936/July 10.

BUTTERFIELD, Billy(tp). Soloist with Shaw's 1940–41 orchestra and Gramercy 5.

BUTTERFIELD, Charles(tb). With Fred Rich 1931; Don Voorhees 1934.

BUYNAK, Vic(ts). With Joe Cantor 1928/August 13.

BYRNE, Bobby(tb). 1952/April 23.

BYRNE, Pauline(v). 1940/March 3.

BYRNS, Hans. Conductor of Berlin Opera Orchestra with whom Shaw studied, 1941.

CAHN, Sammy. Songwriter; friend of Shaw's in 1939–40.

California Ramblers. Famed New York recording group of 1920s.

CALLEA, Ange(tb,arr). With Shaw 1949–50.

CALLOWAY, Cab. Prominent bandleader/singer.

CAMARATA, Toots. Prominent popular bandleader.

CAMPBELL, Chuck(tb). With Bill Challis 1936.

CAMPBELL, Colin. Friend of Eddie Condon's.

CANTOR, Charlie(d). With Joe Cantor 1928/August 13; got Shaw into Cantor's band.

CANTOR, Joe(vl). Led band including Shaw in Cleveland in 1927–28; led session 1928/August 13.

CAPONE, Vincent(reeds). With Paul Whiteman, Christmas 1938.

CAPOZIE, Ernie(g). With Richard Himber 1934–36.

Captivators, The. Pseudonym for Red Nichols group, 1931.

CARLETON, Bud(as). 1940/March 3.

CARLETON, John. Pseudonym for Shaw for "co-composer" business reasons.

CARLSON, Russ(p). With Roger Wolfe Kahn 1932.

CARMICHAEL, Hoagy. Prominent songwriter.

CARNS, Jane. Shaw's first wife; marriage annulled.

CARSON, Johnny. TV talk show host.

CARTER, Benny(as). 1941/June 26.

CARUSO, Enrico. Famed turn-of-century operatic tenor.

CARVER, Wayman. Flute soloist with Chick Webb's band in 1930s.

CASE, Russ(tp). With The Boswell Sisters 1935/October 8, 1936/January 6 & February 12; Ray Sinatra 1936.

CASTALDO, Charlie(tb). 1950/May 31.

CASTALDO, Lee. see CASTLE, Lee.

CASTLE, Irene. Half of famed dance team of 1910s.

CASTLE, Lee(tp). With Shaw 1936–37; 1941–42; 1950.

CASTLE, Vernon. Half of famed dance team of 1910s.

CATHCART, Jack(tp). With Shaw 1940–41.

CATHCART, James(vl). With Shaw's 1946 studio bands.

Cavaliers, The. Ben Selvin recording unit.

CAVALLARO, Johnny. Prominent New Haven bandleader with whom Shaw played in mid-1920s.

CAVE, Jack(Fh). 1940/March 3 & May 13; 1946/July 28.

CEPPOS, Mac(vl). 1950/April 27; 1953/July 6; 1955/November 21.

Cerney Twins. Dance act on same bill as Shaw on theater tours 1941–42.

CHALLIS, Bill. Prominent arranger of the era. Led band including Shaw 1936.

CHAMBERS, Henderson(tb). 1952/April 23.

CHAMBERS, Jack(Fh). 1950/April 27.

CHAPLIN, Charlie. Famed actor/comedian/movie star emerged in 1910s.

CHAPLIN, Saul. Songwriter.

CHAPMAN, Ann. Socialite Shaw rescued in the Acapulco surf in 1940.

CHARLES, Ray(v). In Shaw's vocal groups 1950/May 23 & September 14.

CHARLES, Teddy(vibes). In Shaw's road band late spring 1950 (no recordings).

CHASE, Frank(reeds). With Don Voorhees 1934; Bill Challis 1936.

CHASSMAN, Joseph(vl). 1946/June 6.

Chelsea 3. One of Shaw's vocal groups for Decca 1950; also used as name of small groups out of earlier Shaw orchestras, but did not record under that name.

CHERRY, Don(v). 1950/May 31 & July 19; 1951/January 25 & 30.

CHERWIN, Dick(b). With The Boswell Sisters 1935/October 8; 1936/February 12.

CHESTER, Bob. Popular bandleader in Swing Era.

Chickering 4. One of Shaw's vocal groups for Decca, 1950.

CHRISTIAN, Charlie(g). Major innovator/stylist; with Benny Goodman in 1939–42.

CIBELLI, Sal(vl,v). With Irving Aaronson 1930/August 22.

Cities Service Quartet(v). With Don Voorhees 1934.

CLARK, Buddy(v). With Dick McDonough 1936/June 23 & September 17.

CLARK, Dick(ts). 1940/March 3.

CLARKE, Kenny(d). Major drum innovator in 1940s; with Ella Fitzgerald group at Bop City opposite Shaw, 1949.

CLARKE, Les(as). With Shaw 1944–45.

CLINTON, Larry. Bandleader/composer popular in Swing Era.

COFFEE, John. Shaw's partner in wood-chopping business, Bucks County, 1933–34.

COHAN, Murray(reeds). With Paul Whiteman, Christmas 1938.

COHEN, Paul(tp). With Shaw 1945.

COHEN, Porky(tb). With Shaw 1949–50.

COHEN, Teddy(vibes)—SEE Teddy CHARLES.

COHN, Al(ts). With Shaw 1949–50.

COLE, Ben. Shaw's road manager 1938–41.

COLE, Cozy(d). With Bunny Berigan 1936/April 13; Billie Holiday 1936/July 10; Mildred Bailey 1936/November 9.

COLEMAN, Emile. Bandleader.

COLLETTA, Harold(vla). 1953/July 2.

COLLINS, John(g). 1950/September.

COLLINS, Keith(vla). With Shaw 1940–41.

COLONNA, Jerry(tb). With Fred Rich 1931; Richard Himber 1935; Australian tour, 1954/July. Also noted as a comedian.

Colstons, The. Dance team on same bill with Shaw in December 1941.

COLUCCI, Tony(g). With Manny Klein 1936/January 20.

COLUCCIO, Rocky(p). In The Rangers 1942–43.

COLUMBO, Russ. Popular bandleader in Swing Era.

CONDON, Eddie(g). Prominent stylist emerged in 1920s; with Shaw 1936 at Paramount Theatre (no recordings with Shaw).

CONDON, Pat. Eddie Condon's brother.

CONLEY, Bob. Pseudonym for Bill Challis 1936.

CONNIFF, Ray(tb,arr). With Shaw 1941–42 & 1944–45.

CONRAD, Lew(vl). With Fred Rich 1931.

CONSIDINE, J. F. *Metronome*'s Boston correspondent 1938.

CONSUMANO, Bob(tp). With Paul Whiteman, Christmas 1938.

COOGAN, Jackie. Movie actor.

COOLIDGE, Charles(tb). With Shaw 1944–45.

COOPER, Jackie. Movie star of the era and friend of Judy Garland.

COOPER, Jane. Dancer on Paramount bill 1936.

CORDARO, John(cl,as). With Frank Trumbauer 1936/April 27.

CORNEOL, Jess(reeds). With Richard Himber 1935–36; Manny Klein 1936/January 28; Carl Hoff 1936.

CORNWALL, Frank(vl). With Squibb Dentifrice radio show 1936.

COSLOW, Sam. Popular song composer.

CRACOV, Dave(vl). 1940/March 3 & May 13.

CRAIN, Malcolm(tp). With Shaw 1937.

CRAMER, Irving(reeds). With Carl Hoff 1936.

CRAWFORD, Forrest(ts). With Bunny Berigan 1936/April 13.

CRAWFORD, Jimmy(d). 1950/May 31; 1951/January 25.

CROSBY, Bing(v). Major star emerged in 1920s. Shaw on Crosby's radio shows in 1931–32 & 1945.

CROSBY, Bob(v). Popular bandleader.

CROSEN, Jimmy(reeds). With Don Voorhees 1934.

CROSS, Glen(v). With Carl Hoff 1936.

CYTRON, Samuel(vl). With Shaw's 1946 studio bands.

CZERNY, Carl. Wrote widely used piano method books.

D'ISERE, Guy. Shaw's literary mentor at CBS in early 1930s.

DAILEY, Frank. Owner of Meadowbrook Ballroom, New Jersey; booked Shaw, 1937.

DAMERON, Tadd. Major pianist/arranger from 1940s.

DAVIDSON, H.(oboe). 1949/May 31.

DAVIES, Gwen(v). 1950/May 31 & October 5.

DAVIES, Mel(tp). With Shaw's studio re-creation band, 1968.

DAVIS, Bette. Major movie actress.

DAVIS, Johnnie "Scat"(tp,v). Worked with Shaw in Cleveland in late 1920s; with Red Nichols 1931/August 24; led sessions 1934/October 15 & 22.

DAVIS, Miles(tp). Major bop pioneer, prototype of "cool" trumpet style.

DEBUSSY, Claude. Classical composer.

DECKER, James(Fh). 1946/June 6.

DeFAUT, Volly(cl). Early solo stylist from 1924 on.

DeFRANCO, Buddy(cl). Important stylist in bop period.

DELLO JOIO, Norman(p,comp). Composed clarinet concerto on commission from Shaw; film c.1949–50.

DeNAUT, Jud(b). With Shaw 1940–41.

DeROSA, Octavia(Fh). 1955/November 21.

DeROSA, Vincent(Fh). 1946/June 25.

DERWIN, Hal(v)(= Hal STEVENS). With Shaw 1945.

DESMOND, Paul(as). "Cool" jazz stylist.

DEUTSCH, Sol(vl,vla). With Bill Challis 1936; Carl Hoff 1936; Shaw 1941/June 26; 1953/July 6; 1955/November 21.

DEXTER, Dave. *Down Beat* writer of the era.

DIAMOND, David. American composer with whom Shaw studied in 1941.

DiCARLO, Tom(tp). With Shaw 1937.

Dick, Don, & Dinah. Acrobatic team on bill with Shaw at Strand Theatre 1939.

DICK, Ruth(v). With Carl Hoff 1936.

DIETERLE, Kurt(vl). With Bill Challis 1936; Paul Whiteman, Christmas 1938; Shaw 1941/June 2 & 1950/October 5.

DiMAGGIO, Charles(as). With Shaw 1941–42.

DINDAULT, Joseph(vl). With Ray Sinatra 1936.

DINKIN, Alvin(vla). 1946/June 6.

DISKEN, Bernie. Original leader of New Haven band, the Bellvue Ramblers.

DISNEY, Walt. Cartoonist.

DIXON, Gus(tb). With Shaw 1945.

DIXON, Joe(reeds). Prominent clarinet soloist of the era.

DODDS, Johnny. Major jazz clarinetist from 1920s.

DODDS, Warren "Baby"(d). Great jazz drummer.

DONAHUE, Sam(ts). In The Rangers 1942–43.

DONATELLI, Vincent(cl). 1946/July 28.

DONNELLY, Ted(tb). With Basie 1944/September 5.

Dorsey Brothers Orchestra. Famous band in early 1930s.

DORSEY, Jimmy(cl,as). Major stylist from 1920s on; with CBS House Band 1931–32; led important swing band.

DORSEY, Tommy(tb). Major Swing Era bandleader. With CBS House Band 1931–32; Adrian Rollini 1933/February 14; Richard Himber 1934; WNEW Jam Session 1938/November 9; All-Stars 1944/September 30.

DOUCETTE, Bob. *Down Beat* columnist in late 1930s.

DOUGLAS, Kirk. Movie star.

DOUGLAS, Paul. NBC announcer of the era.

DOWLING, Doris(recitation). 1953/July. Movie actress and Shaw's seventh wife.

DRAKE, Milt. Cocomposer credit for song "If It's You" with Shaw and Ben Oakland.

DRELINGER, Art(reeds). With Paul Whiteman, Christmas 1938; with Shaw 1950/July 19 & September 14; 1951/January 25; 1952/April 23.

DRESLIN, Dorothy(v). With Dick McDonough 1936/June 4.

DUCHIN, Eddie(p). Popular bandleader.

DUFFY, Al(vl). With Paul Whiteman, Christmas 1938.

DUKE, Vernon. Popular songwriter.

Dukes of Dixieland. Popular dixieland band during 1950s.

DUNN, Deacon(reeds). 1946/April 30.

DuPONT, Ann(cl). Bandleader billed as "The Female Artie Shaw" in 1939–40.

DuPONT, Bob. Juggler on same bill with Shaw, December 1941.

DURANTE, Jimmy(p). Led early ragtime/jazz band. Later actor/comedian/singer.

ECKSTINE, Billy(tb,v). Led innovative big band in early 1940s.

EDELSTEIN, Walter(vl). With Ray Sinatra 1936; with Shaw's 1946 studio bands.

EDISON, Harry(perc). With Don Voorhees 1934.

EDISON, Harry(tp). With Basie 1944/September 25.

EDLIN, Louis(vl). 1941/June 26.

EDWARDS, Sid(cello). 1955/November 21.

EFFROS, Bob(tp). With Fred Rich 1931.

EHRENKRANTZ, Bill(vl). With Shaw 1941–42.

EIDUS, Arnold(vl). 1950/October 5; 1955/November 21.

EISENBERG, Peter(vl). With Carl Hoff 1936; Ray Sinatra 1936; Shaw 1940/March 3.

EISENHOWER, Dwight D. President of the United States 1952–60.

ELDRIDGE, Roy(tp,v). Major jazz stylist. In Shaw's 1944–45 band & Gramercy 5.

ELIAS, Lewis(vl). 1946/October 17.

ELLINGTON, Duke(p). Major innovative composer/bandleader from 1920s on. Pianist in trio with Shaw and Chick Webb at UHCA session 14 March 1937.

ELLINGTON, Eddie(v). With Carl Hoff 1936.

ELLIS, Peter(vl). With Shaw's 1946 studio bands.

ELLISHER, Frank. Musical instrument dealer in Pittsburgh; helped band in 1937.

ELMAN, Ziggy(tp). With Mildred Bailey 1936/November 9; All-Stars 1944/September 30.

EMGE, Charles. *Down Beat* writer in 1940.

ENGLE, Victor(d). With Red Nichols 1931/August 24.

EPS, Fred, van. American composer.

ERLE, B.(vl). 1949/May 31.

ERWIN, Pee Wee(tp). With Johnny Green 1934/August 1.

ETTING, Ruth(v). Shaw in Johnny Green's band on her radio show in 1934.

EUROPE, James Reese. Led black ragtime orchestra accompanying the Castles dance team in 1910s.

Evans & Mayer. Dance team on bill at Strand with Shaw, 1939.

EVANS, Alfie(reeds). With Don Voorhees 1934, Bill Challis 1936.

EVANS, Gil. Innovative arranger with Claude Thornhill and later Miles Davis.

EVANS, Pop(tp). With Don Voorhees 1934.

FAGERQUIST, Don(tp). In Shaw's 1949–50 band and Gramercy 5.

FAIN, Sammy. Popular song composer.

FARLEY, Max(reeds). With Roger Wolfe Kahn 1932.

FARLOW, Tal(g). Major jazz guitarist; in Shaw's 1953–54 Gramercy 5.

FARMER, Frances. Movie actress.

FARRAR, Fred(tp). With Don Voorhees 1934, Ray Sinatra 1936.

FASO, Tony(tp). 1945/January 9; 1950/May 29 & September 14.

FATOOL, Nick(d). With Shaw 1940–41; 1946.

FAYE, Alice(v). Popular singer/movie star; led session 1934/September 6.

FAZOLA, Irving(cl). Influential New Orleans clarinet star with Bob Crosby.

FEATHER, Leonard. Prominent jazz writer since 1930s.

FEILER, Louis(vl). 1940/August 16.

FELDKAMP, Elmer(reeds,v). With Fred Rich 1931; Roger Wolfe Kahn 1932.

FELDMAN, Harold(reeds). With Paul Whiteman, Christmas 1938.

FELDMAN, Stan(d). In Shaw's road band spring 1950 (no recordings).

FENTON, Carl(cond). Conducted orchestra for Bing Crosby Cremo radio show 1931.

FENTON, Fred(vl). With Ray Sinatra 1936.

FERDINANDUS, Johnny(p). With Shaw in the Bellevue Ramblers.

FERRETTI, Andy(tp). 1953/July 2.

FINELLI, Tony(g). With Bunny Berigan 1936/April 13.

FINZI, Gerald. American composer.

FISCHER, Clifford. Follies d'Amour Showgirls promoter, French Casino, 1936.

FISHELSON, Stan(tp). With Shaw 1945.

FISHKIN, Arnold(b). 1949/May 31.

FISHZOHN, L.(vl). 1949/May 31.

FITZGERALD, Ella(v). On Bop City bill with Shaw 1949.

FOLUS, Mickey(ts). With Shaw 1941–42.

FORD, George(reeds). With Paul Whiteman, Christmas 1938.

FORD, Jane(v). 1950/July 19 (unissued).

FORD, Victor(tp). With Shaw 1949–50.

FORREST, Helen(v). With Shaw 1938–39.

FORRESTAL, James. Undersecretary of the U.S. Navy during WW II.

FOSTER, Kay(v). With Georgie Auld's "ex-Shaw" band in 1939–40.

FOUNTAIN, Pete(cl). Irving Fazola disciple, very popular from late 1950s on.

Four Clubmen, The. Vocal group on Old Gold show 1939 (no known recordings).

Four Jacks and a Jill. Vocal group from which Shaw recruited Terry Swope, 1950.

FOWLER, Gene. Writer.

FOX, Fred(Fh). 1946/June 6.

FRADKIN, Fred(vl). With Richard Himber 1934–35.

FRANKEL, Jerry. *Billboard*'s "Air Briefs" columnist in the era.

FRANZELLA, Sal(reeds). With Paul Whiteman, Christmas 1938.

FRAZIER, George. *Down Beat* writer of the era.

Fred's Friendly Five. Band led by Fred Rich for Jarman Shoes radio show = Shaw's first gig for CBS 1931.

FREED, Sam(vla). With Shaw 1940; 1946.

FREEMAN, Bud(ts). With Wingy Manone 1934/August 15.

FREEMAN, Hank(as,bar,bcl). With Shaw 1937–39.

FREEMAN, Stan(p). 1951/January 30.

FRENGUT, Leon(vla). 1950/September 12 & October 5.

FRIEDMAN, Morton(reeds). 1946/September 19.

FRISINA, David(vl). With Shaw's 1946 studio bands.

FROMM, Lou(d). With Shaw 1944–45.

FROST, Tom(vl). 1955/November 21.

FUDD, Elmer. Cartoon character, voice by Arthur Q. Bryan.

FULTON, John(reeds). 1950/October 5.

FURMANSKY, Harold(vla). 1953/July 2.

GALBRAITH, Barry(g). 1953/July 2.

GALLODORO, Al(reeds). With Paul Whiteman, Christmas 1938.

GALLODORO, Frank(reeds). With Paul Whiteman, Christmas 1938.

GANGURSKY, Nat(b). With Shaw's June 1946 studio bands.

GARDNER, Ava. Movie star and Shaw's fifth wife.

GARFIELD, John. Movie actor.

GARGASON, Stan(ts). 1950/May 29.

GARLAND, Judy. Movie star; close friend of Shaw's.

GATES, Charles(cello). 1946/April 30.

GEARSDORF, Rae(v). On Squibb Dentifrice radio show, 1936.

GELLER, Harry(tp). With Shaw 1939; 1940/May 13.

GENNER, Russ(tb). With The Boswell Sisters 1936/January 6.

GENTRY, Chuck(bar). With Shaw 1944–46.

GEORGE, Izzy(tp). With Joe Cantor 1928/August 13.

Georgians, The. Paul Specht's small-group recording unit.

GERSHWIN, George. Prominent pianist/composer/songwriter; Shaw in pit band of Gershwin's *Pardon My English* 1932–33.

GETZOFF, James(vl). 1946/June 6.

GIARDINA, Felix(tb). With Carl Hoff 1936.

GIARDINA, Phil(tb). With Roger Wolfe Kahn 1932; Johnny Green 1934/August 1.

GIBBS, Georgia(v). = Fredda GIBSON.

GIBSON, Fredda(v). 1942/January 20.

GIBSON, Marjorie. Arranger/composer.

GILLESPIE, Dizzy(tp). Major bebop innovator/stylist.

GINSBERG, Ben(b). With Shaw 1936–37.

GIUFFRE, Jimmy. Prominent reedman/composer/arranger 1940s on.

GLEASON, Ralph J. Jazz writer/critic of the era.

GLICKMAN, Harry(vl). 1950/September 12 & October 5; 1953/July 6.

GLOVER, Elwood. Announcer at Canadian National Exposition, Toronto 1939.

GLOW, Bernie(tp). With Shaw 1945.

GODDARD, Paulette. Movie star; female lead in *Second Chorus*.

GOERNER, Fred(cello). With Shaw 1940–42; 1946.

GOLD, Sanford(p). 1950/October 5.

GOLDBERG, P.(vla). 1949/May 31.

GOLDFIELD, Harry(tp). With Paul Whiteman, Christmas 1938.

GOLDKETTE, Jean. Prominent jazz-oriented bandleader of 1920s.

GOLDSHIELD, S.(vl). 1949/May 31.

GOLDSTEIN, Betty. Early girlfriend of Shaw's.

GOMBERG, R.(oboe). 1949/May 31.

GOODMAN, Al. Led radio orchestra including Shaw in mid-1930s.

GOODMAN, Benny(cl,as). Famed as "King of Swing"; in CBS House Band 1931; with Richard Himber, 1934/March 19; Adrian Rollini 1934/March 24.

GOODMAN, Freddie. Benny Goodman's brother; Shaw's 1944–45 road manager.

GOODWIN, Alice. Pseudonym for female vocalist on Richard Himber transcriptions.

GOOL, Danny. Arranged for Carl Hoff 1936.

GORDON, Lee. Promoter organized 1954 Australian tour.

GUSSLEIN, Jack(vl). With Bill Challis 1936.

GOTTUSO, Tony(g). With Shaw 1936–37.

GOZZO, Conrad(tp). In The Rangers 1942–43.

GRABLE, Betty. Movie star. Shaw's girlfriend 1939.

GRALNIK, S.(vl). 1949/May 31.

Gramercy 5. Name of Shaw's small-group recording units 1940–54.

GRANT, Cary. Movie star; played Cole Porter in 1946 movie.

GRANZ, Norman. concert promoter and Verve/Clef record company director.

GRAU, Gil. Arranger.

GRAVER, Charles(bsn). With Shaw's 1946 studio bands.

GRAY, Glen. Prominent bandleader.

GRAY, Jack(vla). 1940/March 3 & May 13.

GRAY, Jerry(vl). With Shaw 1936–37; scored most arrangements 1936–39.

GRAY, Milt. Shaw's road manager 1950.

GREEN, Emanuel(vl). With Paul Whiteman, Christmas 1938.

GREEN, Freddie(g). With Count Basie 1944/September 25.

GREEN, George(perc). With Fred Rich 1931.

GREEN, Johnny(p). Songwriter/bandleader; led radio orchestra including Shaw for Ruth Etting's radio show, 1934; led session 1934/August 1.

GREEN, Manny(vl). With Shaw at Imperial Theatre 1936/May 24; 1953/July 2.

GREEN, Simon(b). 1946/July 28.

GREENBERG, Jack(ts). 1950/May 29.

GREER, Sonny(d). With Wingy Manone 1934/August 15.

GRIFFIN, Chris(tp). 1950/September 14.

GROSS, Walter(p). With Fred Rich 1931.

GROSSER, H.(cello). 1949/May 31.

GRUPP, Dave(d). With Don Voorhees 1934; Carl Hoff 1936.

GUARNIERI, Johnny(p,hpsch). With Shaw 1940–42.

GUMM, Frances. = Judy GARLAND.

GUSSAK, Bill(d). With Red Norvo 1934/September 26 & October 4.

GUTIERREZ, Jose(tb). With Paul Whiteman, Christmas 1938.

HACKETT, Bobby(tp). Played trumpet off-screen for Burgess Meredith's trumpet-playing sequences in *Second Chorus*.

HAGGART, Bob(b). 1950/July 19 & October 5; 1951/January 30.

HALBERT, Howard(vl). With Shaw's 1946 studio bands.

HALL, Lionel(b). With Frank Trumbauer 1934/November 20.

HALL, Sleepy. Pseudonym for Red Nichols' recording unit 1931.

HAMMOND, John. Produced Manone and Norvo sessions 1934.

HAMPTON, Lionel(vibes). With All-Stars 1944/September 30.

HANDY, W. C. Composer.

HANIGHEN, Bernie. Songwriter. Worked on *Second Chorus*.

HARDING, Buster. Arranger/composer.

HARLOW, Jean. Movie star.

Harmonians, The. Ben Selvin recording unit.

HARPER, Chet. Pseudonym for Carl Hoff on World Transcriptions.

HARRIS, Tasso(tb). In The Rangers 1942–43.

HARRISON, Guy Frasser(cond). With Rochester Symphony, featured Shaw 1949.

HARSHMAN, Al(vla). With Shaw 1940–41.

HART, Lorenz. Lyricist.

HAWKINS, Coleman(ts). Major innovator/stylist/influence; emerged in 1920s.

HAWKINS, Ralph(d). Replaced Buddy Rich with Shaw, 1939 (no recordings); stayed with band led by Georgie Auld after Shaw left.

HAYES, Mutt(ts). With Frank Trumbauer 1936/April 27.

HAYMER, Herbie(reeds). 1946/November 9.

HAYMES, Dick(v). 1950/April 27.

HAYNES, Polly. Claude Thornhill's widow and old friend of Shaw's.

HAYTON, Lennie. Orchestrator/arranger (especially for Shaw's 1940–42 orchestras).

HEGNER, Walter(reeds). With Paul Whiteman, Christmas 1938.

HEISTAND, John. Announcer on the *Burns and Allen Show* 1940–41.

HELBOCK, Joe. Proprietor of Onyx Club; promoter of Imperial Theatre concert.

HELD, Julie(vl). With Roger Wolfe Kahn, 1932; with Shaw 1955/November 21.

HENDERSON, Fletcher(p,comp,arranger). Pioneer bandleader/arranger emerged 1920s.

HENDERSON, Skitch(p). 1940/May 13.

HENDL, Walter(cond). 1949/March 11.

HENDRICKSON, Al(g). With Shaw 1940–41; 1946.

HENTOFF, Nat. Prominent jazz writer since 1950s.

HERFURT, Skeets(as). With Shaw's 1946 studio bands.

HERMAN, Dave(vl). With Shaw 1941.

HERMAN, Sam(g). With Shaw 1941.

HERMAN, Woody(cl,as,v). Prominent bandleader from 1930s.

HEUSEN, Jimmy, Van. Songwriter.

HIGGINBOTHAM, J. C.(tb). 1941/June 26.

HILL, Henry. Shaw's first teacher from Wrozina's music store in New Haven.

HILLERSON, S. *Metronome*'s Pittsburgh correspondent in 1937.

HIMBER, Richard. Prominent bandleader in 1930s; featured Shaw 1934–36.

HINES, Earl(p). Major stylist and bandleader emerged in 1920s.

HIRT, Al(tp). Popular New Orleans Dixieland Revival star.

HITZ, Ralph. Hotel chain owner.

HODGES, Johnny(as). With Mildred Bailey 1936/November 9.

HOEREE, Arthur. Orchestrator for some of Shaw's early 1949 repertoire.

HOFF, Carl. Led radio orchestra including Shaw 1936.

HOLCOMB, Bill(bar). 1951/January 25; 1952/April 23.

HOLIDAY, Billie(v). Led session 1936/July 10; with Shaw 1938.

HOLLANDER, Max(vl). 1953/July 2.

HOPE, Bob. Popular comedian.

HOPKINS, Claude. Bandleader.

HORESH, Al(g). In The Rangers 1942–43.

HORN, Art(reeds). With Carl Hoff 1936.

HORNE, Lena(v). 1941/June 26.

HOROWITZ, Irving(reeds). 1950/October 5.

HORVATH, George(b). With Georgie Auld 1940.

HOWARD, Bob(v). Led session 1936/January 28.

HOWARD, Joe(tb). With Shaw's 1946 studio bands.

HOWE, Dorothy(v). 1937/April 29.

HUDKINS, Dave(d). = Ace Hudkins, Dave YUDKIN. With Shaw 1936; Shaw's road manager off and on; led Artie Shaw "ghost" orchestra 1948–49.

HUFFSMITH, Fred(v). With Jack Shilkret 1936/August 29.

HUGHES, Howard. Famous eccentric millionaire.

HULL, Warren. Radio announcer for Old Gold show 1939.

HURD, Curtis(tp). Replaced Zeke Zarchy in Shaw's band at Century Ballroom, 1937.

HURLEY, Clyde(tp). 1941/January 23; 1946.

HUTCHINRIDER, Clarence. Worked with Shaw in Cleveland in 1920s.

HUTCHINSON, Charles(g). 1940/August 16.

HUTTON, Betty(v). Singer/dancer popular in 1930s–1940s.

HUTTON, Ina Ray. Female bandleader and sister of June Hutton.

HUTTON, June(v). 1951/January 30.

HYDE, Alex(cond). Led band at Olympia in New Haven including Shaw in 1926.

HYLTONE, David. *Down Beat* writer in 1939.

JACOBS, John(d). 1946/July 28.

JACOBS, Merle(d). Led jazz band including Shaw in Cleveland, 1928.

JACQUET, Illinois(ts). With All-Stars 1944/September 30.

Jazz Wizards. Early recording group with Albert Nicholas(cl).

JENKINS, Gordon(p,arr.). 1950/May 29.

JENKINS, Les(tb). With Shaw 1938–39.

JENNEY, Jack(tb). With Red Norvo 1934/September 26 & October 4; Manny Klein 1936/January 20; Bill Challis 1936; Jack Shilkret 1936/August 29; Shaw 1940–41.

JEROME, Jerry(ts). With Shaw 1940–41.

JOHNSON, Bobby(g). With Red Norvo 1934/September 26 & October 4.

JOHNSON, Bunk(tp). Old-time New Orleans stylist; catalyst for Dixieland Revival movement of 1940s–1950s.

JOHNSON, Dick(cl). Played Shaw's spots in 1980s–1990s Artie Shaw band.

JOHNSON, Harold(tp). 1952/April 23.

JOHNSON, James P.(p). Founded innovative Harlem Stride style of piano playing.

JOHNSON, Stanley(d,v). With Irving Aaronson 1930/August 22.

JOHNSTON, Art. Songwriter.

JONES, Bill. Pseudonym for male vocalist on Richard Himber transcriptions.

JONES, Casey. "Air Briefs" announcer on Jarman Shoes radio shows, 1931–32.

JONES, Dick. Orchestrator/arranger.

JONES, Hank(p). With Shaw's 1953–54 Gramercy 5s.

JONES, Jo(d). Innovative drummer with Count Basie in the 1930s.

JORDAN, Paul. Composer/arranger.

JOYCE, Jerry(vl). 1940/March 3 & May 13.

JULBER, Ovady(vla). 1940/August 16.

KAFTON, Arthur(cello). With Shaw's 1946 studio bands.

Kahn-a-Sirs, The(v). Vocal group with Roger Wolfe Kahn 1932.

KAHN, Dave(vl). With Shaw 1941.

KAHN, Leo(vl). With Shaw 1941.

KAHN, Otto. Millionaire father of Roger Wolfe Kahn.

KAHN, Roger Wolfe. Led dance band including Shaw 1932.

KALLEN, Kitty(v). 1946/June 11.

KAMINSKY, Max(tp). With Shaw 1937–38; 1941–42; The Rangers 1942–43.

KANTER, Ben(reeds). With Bill Challis 1936; Shaw 1940/May 13.

KARDINER, Abram. Shaw's analyst in New York.

KARLE, Milton. *Down Beat*'s Pittsburgh correspondent 1939.

KAST, George(vl). With Shaw's 1946 studio bands.

KAY, Eunice. *Down Beat*'s Cleveland correspondent 1939.

KAY, Hershey. Orchestrator for much of Shaw's early 1949 repertoire.

KAY, Howard(vl). 1955/November 21.

KAYE, Sammy. Led popular "sweet" band.

KEENE, Bob(cl). Imitated Shaw on some re-creation recordings.

KEITH, Jimmy(ts). With Basie 1944/September 25.

KELLNER, Murray(vl). With Richard Himber 1934–35; Carl Hoff 1936.

KELLY, Gene. Dancer/movie star.

KELLY, Paula(v). 1941/October 30 & December 23.

KELLY, Willis(tp). With Joe Cantor 1928/August 13; with Shaw 1936/June.

KENTON, Stan(p). Led modern big band 1940s on.

Kentuckians, The. Band Shaw toured with in 1926.

Kentucky Serenaders, The. Ben Selvin recording unit.

KEPPARD, Freddie(tp). New Orleans pioneer.

KERN, Elizabeth. Jerome Kern's daughter and Shaw's fourth wife.

KERN, Jerome. Popular songwriter.

KESSEL, Barney(g). With Shaw 1944–46.

KEYES, Evelyn. Movie star and Shaw's eighth wife.

KIEVMAN, Louis(vla). 1946/July 28.

KILLIAN, Al(tp). With Basie 1944/September 25.

KIMMEL, Jack(b). With Richard Himber 1934–35.

KINDLER, Sol(vl). 1940/August 16.

KING, Morris(vl). With Shaw's 1946 studio bands.

KING SISTERS, THE (Alyce, Donna, Louise, Yvonne)(v). Popular vocal group; on Old Gold show with Shaw 1939.

KING, Stan(d). With The Boswell Sisters 1935/October 8, 1936/January 6 & February 20; Bob Howard 1936/January 28; Frank Trumbauer 1936/April 27.

King's Men, The(v). Vocal group with Lennie Hayton's orchestra, 1936.

KIRBY, John(b). With Wingy Manone 1934/August 15; Mildred Bailey 1936/Nov.9; WNEW Jam 1938/November 9.

KIRK, Warren(as). With Shaw 1937 (no recordings).

KIRKSMITH, Jack(Fh). With Shaw's June 1946 studio bands.

KITSIS, Bob(p,celeste). With Shaw 1938–39; 1950/July 19; 1952/August 1.

KLAGES, Ted(vl). With Shaw 1940–41.

KLAYMAN, Lou(vl). 1936/June.

KLEE, Harry(reeds). With Shaw's 1946 studio bands.

KLEIN, Dave. Contracted studio orchestras for Shaw in 1946 (brother of Manny Klein).

KLEIN, Manny(tp). With CBS House Band 1931–32; Adrian Rollini 1933/February 14; led session 1936/January 20; Bill Challis 1936; Shaw 1940/March 3 & May 13; 1946.

KLINK, Al(ts). 1950/May 31; 1952/April 23; 1953/July; 1968.

KLUGER, Irv(d). With Shaw 1949–50 & 1953–54 Gramercy 5.

Knickerbockers, The. Ben Selvin recording unit.

KOENIG, George(as). With Shaw 1938.

KOERNER, Gil(reeds). With Don Voorhees 1934.

KOHN, Morris(vla). With Shaw 1941–42.

KONITZ, Lee(as). Major exponent of "cool" jazz style from 1940s.

KOSTELANETZ, Andre. Led radio orchestra including Shaw in 1930s.

KOTICK, Teddy(b). 1950/April.

KOTLARSKY, Sergei(vl). 1941/June 26.

KRAFT, Stan(vl). 1953/July 2.

KRAMER, Henry, Jr. *Down Beat*'s Baltimore correspondent 1938.

KRAMER, Maria. Manager of Hotel Lincoln.

KRECHTER, Joe(reeds). 1940/March 3 & May 13; 1946.

KRESS, Carl(g). With Ben Selvin 1932/May 12; The Boswell Sisters 1935/October 8; Frank Trumbauer 1936/April 27; Shaw 1936/May 24.

KRUPA, Gene(d). With Ben Selvin 1932.

KRUSCZAK, Leo(vl). 1941/June 26.

KUBEY, A.(bassoon). 1949/May 31.

KUNZE, Alfred(b). With Ray Sinatra 1936.

KUSBY, Ed(tb). With Shaw's 1946 studio bands.

KYLE, Billy(p). 1950/May 31; 1951/January 25.

KYSER, Kay. Led entertainment band.

LA CENTRA, Peg(v). With Johnny Green 1934/August 1; with Shaw 1936–37.

LACEY, Jack(tb). With Richard Himber 1936; Bill Challis 1936; Manny Klein 1936/January 20.

LADEN, Les. Leader of Yale Collegians band including Shaw in mid-1920s.

LAINE, Jack.

LAKE, Bonnie(v). 1941/September.

LAMAS, Eugene(vl). With Shaw 1940–41; 1946.

LAMOND, Don(d). 1953/July; 1955/November 21; 1968.

LANE, Bobby. Acrobatic team (with Edna Ward) on same bill as Shaw in 1941.

LANE, Kenny(v). With Bill Challis 1936.

LANE, Lillian(v). 1946/November 9.

LANG, Eddie(g). With Fred Rich 1931; Adrian Rollini 1933/February 14.

LANPHERE, Don(ts). With Shaw's spring 1950 band and Gramercy 5.

LANTHIER, Ronnie. Shaw's bus driver 1937.

LAPIN, Al(d). With Carl Hoff 1936.

LaPOLLO, Ralph(as). In The Rangers 1942–43.

LaPORTA, John(cl). Prominent in Third Stream settings 1940s—1950s.

LASSOFF, Ed(vibes). With Ray Sinatra 1936.

LAUGHTON, Gail(harp). With Shaw's 1946 studio bands.

LAW, Alex(vl). 1940/March 3; 1946/October 17.

LAWSON, Bob(reeds). With Shaw's 1946 studio bands.

LAWSON, Harold(reeds). 1940/May 13; 1946.

LAWSON, Yank(tp). WNEW Jam 1938/November 9; 1950/May 31 & July 19.

LEACH, Lem(vibes). On Squibb Dentifrice radio show 1936.

LEEMAN, Cliff(d). With Shaw 1937–38.

LeFAVE, Dick(tb). In The Rangers 1942–43.

LEHMAN, Johnny. Lyricist.

LEIGHTON, Bernie(p). 1953/July; 1955/November 21; 1968.

LEONARD, Terry(v). With Shaw's March 1942 band (no recordings).

LERNER, Al(p). 1950/April 27; 1950/May 29.

LEVANT, Mark(vl). 1940/March 3; 1946.

LEVIENNE, Mischa(vl). 1940/August 16.

LEVINE, Aaron(g). With Carl Hoff 1936.

LEVINE, Henry(tp). With Johnny Green 1934/August 1.

LEVINE, Nat(d). With Richard Himber 1934–36.

LEVINSKY, Walt(cl). Imitated Shaw on 1968 recreations for Capitol.

LEVY, Dave(p). With Richard Himber 1935.

LEWIS, Ed(tp). With Count Basie 1944/September 25.

LEWIS, George(cl). New Orleans stylist.

LEWIS, Harold(fl). 1946/June.

LEWIS, Lennie. Shaw's road manager 1949–50.

LEWIS, Meade Lux(p). Boogie Woogie stylist.

LEWIS, Sam(tb). With Don Voorhees 1934; Carl Hoff 1936; Ray Sinatra 1936.

LEWIS, Sinclair. Writer friend of Shaw's.

LEWIS, Ted(cl,v). Early popular entertainer/bandleader.

LEY, Ward(b). With Roger Wolfe Kahn 1932.

LIGHT, Ed(bari). On Squibb Dentifrice radio show 1936.

LIMONICK, Marvin(vl). With Shaw's 1946 studio bands.

LINDEN, Richard(fl). 1946/July 28.

LINN, Ray(tp). With Shaw 1944–46.

LINDWORM, Joe(tp). With Don Voorhees 1934.

LIPKINS, Steve(tp). With Shaw 1941–42; 1950/April 4.

LIPPMAN, Joe(p,celeste). With Shaw 1936–37.

LIPSCHULTZ, Irving(cello). 1940/March 3.

LIVOTI, Joseph(vl). 1946/July 28.

LLOYD, Shirley. Vocalist with Ozzie Nelson in 1936.

LOCKWOOD, Pat(v). With Shaw 1949.

LOEFFLER, Carl(tb). 1946/September 19.

LOMASK, M.(vl). 1949/May 31.

LOMAX, Alan. Eminent folklorist.

LOMBARDO, Guy. Led popular "sweet" band; emerged in 1920s.

LONDON, Jack. Writer.

LOPEZ, Vincent. Led band including Shaw in 1932.

LORR, P.(bassoon). 1949/May 31.

LOWENTHAL, Eugene(v). With Shaw vocal groups 1950/May 31 & September 14.

LOWTHER, Betty(v). Pseudonym for Peg La Centra on Rhythm Makers transcriptions.

LUBE, Dan(vl). With Shaw's 1946 studio bands.

LUSTGARTEN, Edgar(cello). With Shaw's June 1946 studio bands.

LYNCH, Rebecca(vl). 1950/September 12 & October 5.

LYNN, Imogene(v). With Shaw 1944–45.

LYON, Russ(as,v). With Red Nichols 1931/August 24.

LYTELL, Jimmy(ts). Prominent early 1920s clarinet soloist; with Johnny Green 1934/August 1.

MacDOUGAL, Dick. *Down Beat*'s Toronto correspondent in 1938.

MacDOWALL, Edward A. American composer.

MACE, Tommy(as). With Shaw 1944–45.

MacGREGOR, Chummy(p). With Irving Aaronson 1930/August 22.

MACHITO (= Frank Grillo). Led Afro-Cuban big band, 1940s on.

MAGNANTE, Charles(acc). With Adrian Rollini 1933/February 14.

MALTBY, Richard. Arranger.

MALVIN, Artie(v). With Shaw vocal groups for Decca 1950/May 31 & Sept.14.

MANDEL, Johnny. Arranged several items for Shaw's 1949–50 band.

MANGUEL, Jose(perc). 1949/December 30.

MANN, June. Half of comedy team (with Ross Wise) on same bill as Shaw, 1945.

MANONE, Wingy(tp,v). Led session 1934/August 15.

MANTZ, Paul. Pilot who rented chartered flights in Hollywood in 1940.

MARGOLIES, Jack(vl). 1950/April 27, September 12 & October 5.

MARGULIS, Charlie(tp). With Richard Himber 1934–35; Bill Challis 1936; Manny Klein 1936/January 20; Shaw 1940/March 3; 1950/May 29.

MARMAROSA, Dodo(p). With Shaw 1944–46 & 1949.

MARSALA, Joe(cl). Prominent figure in 1930s & 1940s.

MARTIN, David Stone. Artist; did album covers for Shaw's Clef LPs.

MASON, Melissa. Double-jointed dancer featured in the Roger Wolfe Kahn film *The Yacht Party*, 1932.

MASTERS, Art(as). 1937/May 13.

MATTHEWS, Dave. Arranger.

MATTHEWS, Hal(tb). With Paul Whiteman, Christmas 1938.

MAUS, Carl(d). 1940/March 3.

MAX, Ed(narration). Voice of Pied Piper 1946/July.

MAXWELL, Jimmie(tp). 1955/November 21.

MAY, Billy. Led band re-creating Shaw's hits for Time-Life Records.

MAYHEW, Jack(reeds). 1946/June 25.

McCALL, Mary Ann(v). 1950/January 6.

McCARTHY, Joe. U.S. senator sponsored House Un-American Activities Committee.

McCARTY, Walter. *Down Beat* writer in 1939.

McCONVILLE, Leo(tp). With Don Voorhees 1934.

McCOY, Clyde(tp). Popular bandleader.

McDEVITT, B. Shaw's press agent on West Coast 1939.

McDONOUGH, Dick(g). With Adrian Rollini 1934/March 24; Bill Challis 1936; The Boswell Sisters 1936/January 6 & February 12; Billie Holiday 1936/July 10; Jack Shilkret 1936/August 29; Ray Sinatra 1936; Squibb Dentifrice Show, spring 1936; led sessions 1936/June 4 & 23; August 5; September 17; November 3.

McGARITY, Lou(tb). 1953/July 6; 1955/November 21.

McGRATH, Fulton(p). With Adrian Rollini 1933/February 14 & 1934/March 4.

McHUGH, Jimmy. Popular songwriter.

McINTYRE, Arthur "Traps"(d). The Lion's drummer at Pod's and Jerry's 1930–31.

McINTYRE, Mark(p). With Shaw's 1946 studio bands.

McINTYRE, Maurice(reeds). AACM musician emerged in 1960s.

McKINNEY, Ed(b). With Shaw 1941–42; with All-Stars 1944/September 30.

McMICKLE, Dale(tp). 1953/July; 1955/November 21.

McNAUGTON, Pat(tb). With Shaw 1944–45.

McPHERSON, Norman(tu). With Paul Whiteman, Christmas 1938.

McRAE, Teddy. Jazz composer/arranger.

McSHANN, Jay(p,v). Kansas City bandleader.

Mel-Tones, The. Mel Torme's vocal group; recorded with Shaw 1946.

MELNIKOFF, Harry(vl). 1950/April 27 & September 12; 1953/July; 1955/November 21.

MELNIKOFF, Paul(vla). 1953/July.

MERCER, Johnny. Lyricist; lyrics for "Love of My Life" with Shaw.

MEREDITH, Burgess. Movie actor in *Second Chorus*.

MERTZ, Paul(p). With Irving Aaronson 1930/August 22; Red Nichols 1931/August 24.

MESSING, Marcus(b). On Squibb Dentifrice radio show 1936.

MICHAELS, Mike(tb). With Shaw 1936.

MIDDLEMAN, Sam(vl). 1946/July 28.

MILLER, Artie(b). With Adrian Rollini 1933/February 14 & 1934/March 24.

MILLER, Eddie(ts). Prominent sax star of the era.

MILLER, Glenn(tb). Famed popular bandleader. With Frank Trumbauer 1934/November 20.

MILLER, Randall(tb). 1940/March 3.

MILLER, William. *Down Beat*'s Australian correspondent 1943.

MILLS, Dick(tp). In Shaw's road band and Gramercy 5, spring 1950 (no recordings).

MILLS, Verlie(harp). With Richard Himber 1934–35; Carl Hoff 1936; Ray Sinatra 1936.

MOK, Michael. Columnist for *The New York Post* in 1930s.

MOLE, Miff(tb). Major figure in 1920s; in CBS House Band 1931–32; with Don Voorhees 1934.

MONDELLO, Toots(as). With Irving Aaronson 1930;

Manny Klein 1936/January 20; Ray Sinatra 1936; with Shaw 1941; 1955/November 21; 1968.

MONK, Thelonious(p). Major innovator emerged in 1940s.

MONROE, Clark. Proprietor of Monroe's Uptown House in Harlem.

MOORE, Brew(ts). In Kai Winding's group opposite Shaw at Bop City 1949.

MOORE, Don(tp). With Red Nichols 1931/August 24.

MOORE, George(oboe). 1946/July 28.

MOREHOUSE, Chauncey(d). With Roger Wolfe Kahn 1932; Bill Challis 1936; Manny Klein 1936/January 20.

MORGAN, Patty(v). With Shaw 1938 (no recordings).

MORGAN, Russ(tb). With Paul Specht 1931/May 28; led ARC House Band in 1934–36.

MORRIS, Johnny(d). In Vincent Lopez's band with Shaw 1932.

MORRIS, William. Head of booking agency of same name.

MORROS, Borros. Hollywood producer; credit for *Second Chorus*.

MORROW, Bob(vl). With Shaw 1940–41.

MORROW, Buddy(tb) = Moe ZUDEKOFF. With Shaw 1936–7; 1968.

MORTON, Jelly Roll(p). Major jazz pioneer. With Wingy Manone 1934/August 15.

MOSKOVITZ, H.(fl). 1949/May 31.

MOSS, Joe. Popular bandleader.

MOSS, Marshall(vl). 1950/April 7.

MOST, Abe(cl). Imitated Shaw on re-creation recordings.

MOST, Sam(cl,fl). Modernist in 1950s.

MOTEN, Benny. Led early Kansas City style big band.

MOZART, W. A. Classical Composer.

MUCCI, Louis(tp). 1950/April 4 & May 29.

MULCAHEY, Tex(tb). With Shaw 1938 (no recordings).

MULLIGAN, Gerry(bar). With Kai Winding opposite Shaw at Bop City 1949.

MUNDY, Jimmy. Arranger/composer.

MUNRO, John. *Down Beat* writer, profiled Shaw's band 1938.

MURPHY, Larry(v). With Fred Rich 1931.

MURPHY, Turk. Led dixieland revival band from 1940s.

MURRAY, Lyn(v). Director of vocal group The Four Clubmen, on Old Gold show 1939.

NAPOLI, Ralph(g,bjo,v). With Irving Aaronson 1930/August 22.

NASH, Joey(v). With Adrian Rollini 1933/February 14 & 1934/March 4; Richard Himber 1934–35; Ray Sinatra 1936.

National Youth Symphony. Accompanied Shaw at Carnegie Hall 1949/April 18.

NATOLI, Nat(tp). With Frank Trumbauer 1934/November 20.

NELSON, Ozzie. Popular bandleader.

NEMOLI, Phil(oboe). 1940/March 3.

New Music String Quartet. 1949/May 31.

New Orleans Rhythm Kings. Important early jazz band.

NEWELL, Laura(harp). With Bill Challis 1936; Shaw 1941/June 26.

Newport Society Orchestra. Ben Selvin recording unit.

NICHOLAS, Albert(cl). Prominent figure; emerged in 1920s.

NICHOLS, Loring "Red"(tp). Led session 1931/August 24.

NIESEN, Gertrude(v). With Roger Wolfe Kahn 1932.

NIETO, Ubal(perc). 1949/December 30.

NIMITZ, Chester. WW II admiral and Naval tactician.

NIVESON, Dick(b). With Shaw 1949–50.

NOBLE, Ray. Bandleader/composer.

NOBLE, Sam(vla). 1940/August 16.

NOONE, Jimmy(cl). Major influence on jazz clarinetists from 1920s on.

NORMAN, Dave(vl). 1941/June 6.

NORMAN, Fred. Arranger.

NORVO, Red(xylophone). Led sessions 1934/September 26 & October 4.

NOTTINGAM, Jimmy(tp). 1952/April 23; 1955/November 21.

NOVI, Gene, di(p). 1949/May 31.

OAKLAND, Ben. Songwriter.

O'BRIEN, Floyd(tb). Chicago-style trombonist active in 1920s.

O'BRIEN, Jack(p). With Shaw 1937 (no recordings).

O'CONNOR, Ginny(v). In Mel-Tones 1946.

O'HARA, John. Prominent writer.

O'NEILL, Dolores(Dodie)(v). 1937/October; in 1950 band.

OAKLAND, Ben. Popular songwriter.

OBERSTEIN, Eli. RCA record producer/executive.

OCHI-ALBI, Nicholas(cello). With Shaw's 1946 studio bands.

OCKO, Bernard(vl,vla). With Shaw 1941; 1950/April 27.

ODERICH, James(cello). With Shaw 1936.

Oivero Trio. Acrobatic act at the Palomar on same bill as Shaw, 1939.

OLIVER, King(tp). Important early New Orleans recording artist/bandleader.

OLIVER, Sy(arr). Coarranged with Shaw for Decca 1951/Jan. 25 & 1952/April 23.

OLSON, Fred(vl). 1946/July 28.

Original Dixieland Jazz Band. Made first jazz records and popularized the idiom.

ORLEWITZ, Felix(vl). 1953/July 6.

ORY, Kid(tb). Early New Orleans stylist.

OSBORNE, Will. Popular bandleader.

OWENS, Jack. Lyricist.

PAGE, Oran "Hot Lips"(tp,v). With Shaw 1941–42.

PAGE, Walter(b). Important figure, with Count Basie in the 1930s.

PALADINO, Don(tp). With Shaw 1949–50.

PAPA, Tony(d). Organized band for Shaw's spring 1953 Texas tour.

PAPILE, Phil(acc). On Squibb Dentifrice radio show 1936.

PARENTI, Tony(cl). With CBS in early 1930s; Don Voorhees 1934.

PARGER, Frank(cello). With Carl Hoff 1936.

PARKER, Charlie(as). Major bebop innovator in 1940s.

PARKER, Dorothy. Writer.

PARKS, Bernice(v). With Johnny Green 1934/August 1.

PARKS, Bernie(v). With Mel-Tones 1946.

PARSHAL, Harry(Fh). 1946/June 6.

PARSHLEY, Tom(fl,bcl). 1950/April 27.

PASSECANTANDRO, Virginia(p). Shaw's classical accompanist 1949; TV 1949/03/18.

PASTOR, Tony(ts,v). With Irving Aaronson 1930/August 22; Shaw's bands 1936–39.

PASTRONE, Robert(recitation). 1953/July.

PATENT, Harry(b). With Richard Himber 1936.

PAUL, Les(g). With All-Stars 1944/September 30.

PEARCE, Jack(v). 1940/May 13.

PEARLMAN, Ted(d). With Shaw in the Bellvue Ramblers.

PENQUE, Romeo(ts). 1953/July; 1955/November 21.

PERISSI, Richard(Fh). 1946/June 25.

PERLEMAN, S. J. Writer.

PERLMUTTER, Maurice(vla). With Shaw's 1946 studio bands.

PERRY, Don(g). 1951/January 30.

PERRY, Ronnie(ts). With Shaw 1938.

PERSOFF, Sam(vl,vla). With Richard Himber 1935; Shaw 1936.

PESTRITTO, Tony = Tony PASTOR.

Peter Pan Novelty Orchestra. Shaw's first band in New Haven.

PETERSON, Chuck(tp). With Shaw 1937–39.

PETERSON, Pete(b). With Bob Howard 1936/January 28; Billie Holiday 1936/July 10.

PETERSON, Tweet(tp). With Shaw 1937 (no recordings).

PETRILLO, Joseph Cesare. Perennial president of Musicians' Union in that era.

PETRY, Fred(ts). With Shaw 1937–38.

PETTIFORD, Oscar(b). Influential bop stylist.

PEVSNER, Leo(vl). With Shaw 1941–42.

PFAFF, Fred(tu). With Don Voorhees 1934.

PHILBURN, Al(tb). With Adrian Rollini 1934/March 24.

PICOU, Alphonse(cl). New Orleans pioneer.

PIERCE, Dale(tp). With Shaw 1949–50.

PIERCE, Jack(tu). With Don Voorhees 1934.

PIERCE, Mack(as). In The Rangers 1942–43.

PILZER, Max(vl). With Bill Challis 1936; Carl Hoff 1936; Paul Whiteman, Christmas 1938.

PINARO, Frank(vl). With Carl Hoff 1936.

PISANI, Nicholas(vl). With Shaw's 1946 studio bands.

PITT, Merle. Bandleader.

PLATT, Ralph. Leader of The Kentuckians.

PLOTKIN, Ben(vl). With Shaw 1936.

PLUMB, Neely(as). With Shaw 1940–41.

PLUNKETT, Jimmy. Owner/manager/bartender of musicians' hangout, Plunkett's.

POLIAKINE, Raoul(vl). With Shaw 1941–42; 1953/July 6; 1955/November 21.

POLLACK, Ben(d). Led band including Benny Goodman in late 1920s.

POLLARD, Snub(tp). With Red Nichols 1931/August 24.

POMETTI, Vincenzo(vl). 1946/June 6.

POOLE, Carl(tp). 1950/May 31 & July 19.

POPE, Gordon(oboe). With Shaw's 1946 studio bands.

PORTER, Cole. Major songwriter.

PORTER, Del(reeds,v). With Roger Wolfe Kahn 1932.

POSNER, Leonard(vl). With Shaw 1941–42.

POTTER, Tommy(b). With Shaw's 1953–54 Gramercy 5.

POWELL, Jimmy(as). With Count Basie 1944/September 25.

POZO, Chino(perc). 1949/December 30.

PRAGER, Ed(tu). With Ray Sinatra 1936.

PRAGER, Gerald(b). With Carl Hoff 1936.

PRAGER, Irving(vl). With Carl Hoff 1936.

PRAGER, Sam(p). With Fred Rich 1931; Carl Hoff 1936.

PRINZ, Spencer(d). 1940/May 13.

PRISBY, Louis(as). With Shaw 1945.

PRIVIN, Bernie(tp). With Shaw 1938–39; 1941; 1950/July 19; 1952/April 23; 1968.

PROKOFIEV, Sergei. Classical composer.

PROPHET, Clarence(p). Led trio on 52nd Street during swing era.

PUGH, Marshall. British reporter.

PUMA, Joe(g). In 1954 Gramercy 5.

PUMIGLIO, Pete(reeds). With Richard Himber 1935

PUPA, Jimmy(tp). 1944/November 23.

PUTRAM, Janet(harp). 1949/May 31.

QUADRI, Joseph(vl). 1946/July 28.

QUENZER, Arthur(reeds). With Irving Aaronson 1930/August 22; later was lyricist-collaborator with Shaw.

QUIGLEY, Herb(d). With Ray Sinatra 1936.

QUINTO, Marty(g). With Don Voorhees 1934.

RADERMAN, Lou(vl). With Richard Himber 1934–36; Bill Challis 1936.

RAE, Johnny(v). Popular "sob-singer" stylist in early 1950s.

RAEBURN, Boyd. Led advanced big band in 1940s.

RAFFELL, Don(reeds). With Shaw's 1946 studio bands.

RAGUSO, Tony(s). With Shaw 1949–1950.

RAIMONDI, M.(vl). 1949/May 31.

RALSTON, Art(fl,cl). 1950/September 12.

RALSTON, Bill(v). Pseudonym for Tony Pastor on Rhythm Makers transcriptions.

RAND, Sam(vl). 1950/April 27; 1953/July; 1955/November 21.

RANEY, Jimmy(g). With Shaw 1949–50.

Rangers, The. Shaw's 1942–43 Navy band.

RANK, Bill(tb). 1940/March 3.

RASKIN, Milt(p). With Shaw's 1946 studio bands.

RATTINER, Angie(tp). With Roger Wolfe Kahn 1932; Bill Challis 1936.

RAUB, Mel(tu). With Carl Hoff 1936.

RAVEL, Maurice. Classical composer.

RAY, Jack(vl). 1940/March 3.

RAYES, Bobby. Juggler on same bill with Shaw, Chicago 1941.

RAYMAN, Morris(b). With Shaw 1944–45.

RAYMOND, Irving(vl). With Shaw 1941–42.

RAYMOND, Tex(vl). With Ray Sinatra 1936.

REARDON, Caspar(harp). On Squibb Dentifrice radio show 1936.

REHER, Kurt(cello). With Shaw's 1946 studio bands.

Reilley's, The. Dance act at the Strand on same bill as Shaw, fall 1939.

REINHARDT, Django. Belgian Gypsy guitarist.

REISMAN, Leo. Popular society bandleader in era; Shaw in band early 1930s.

REUSS, Alan(g). WNEW Jam 1938/Novewmber 9; Paul Whiteman, Christmas 1938; with Shaw's 1946 studio bands.

REVEL, Harry. Popular songwriter.

REYES, Benn. Promoter organized 1954 Australian tour.

REYNOLDS, Blake(as). 1940/March 3.

REYNOLDS, Tommy(cl). Led Artie Shaw-styled big band from 1939 on.

Rhinelander 4. One of Shaw's small groups (no recordings).

Rhythm Boys, The(v). Paul Whiteman vocal group including Bing Crosby, Al Rinker, and Harry Barris in late 1920s into 1930.

Rhythm Girls, The(v). With Lennie Hayton's Hit Parade Orchestra 1936.

Rhythm Makers. Pseudonym for transcription recordings for several bands including Shaw's in 1937.

RIBAUD, Joe. Vincent Lopez's contractor in 1932.

RICCI, Paul(reeds). With Richard Himber 1936; Manny Klein 1936/January 20.

RICE, Sunny. Tapdancer on same bill as Shaw at Strand in 1945.

RICH, Buddy(d). With Shaw band 1938-39; With Count Basie 1944/September 25; All-Stars 1944/September 30; on Australian tour 1954.

RICH, Fred. CBS House Orchestra bandleader in early 1930s; Shaw in orchestra from September 1931—June 1932.

RICHARDS, Trudy(v). 1950/January; 1952/April 23.

RICHARDSON, Rodney(b). With Count Basie 1944/September 25.

RICHMOND, Boomie(reeds). 1955/November 21.

RICHMOND, June(v). With Jimmy Dorsey in late 1930s.

RINKER, Al(v). With Bill Challis 1936.

ROBBINS, Bernie(vl). 1953/July 2.

ROBERTS, Whitney. M. C. at the Palomar 1939.

ROBERTSON, Dick(v). With Frank Trumbauer 1934/November 20.

ROBINSON, Eli(tb). With Count Basie 1944/September 25.

ROBINSON, Les(as). Lead alto with Shaw 1937–39 and 1940–42; 1946.

ROBSON, Flora. Movie actress; rented Shaw's house in Hollywood 1939–40.

ROBYN, Paul(vla). With Shaw's 1946 studio bands.

ROCHESTER, Charlie. Manager of Hotel Lexington 1936.

ROCKWELL, Tommy. Booking agent; managed Shaw off and on.

RODGERS, Harry(tb). With Shaw 1937–39 & 1944–45; also arranger.

RODGERS, Richard. Popular songwriter.

RODRIGUEZ, Bobby(perc). 1949/December 30.

ROGERS, Ginger. Movie actress; Fred Astaire's dance partner in many films.

ROGERS, Will. Comedian; had radio show for which Shaw played in early 1930s.

ROLAND, Gene. Arranger for some of Shaw's 1949–50 band's charts.

ROLAND, Joe(vibes). With Shaw's 1953–54 Gramercy 5.

ROLLINI, Adrian(vibes,bs). Led sessions 1933/February 14; 1934/March 24; with Richard Himber 1934–36; with Ray Sinatra 1936.

ROLLINI, Art(ts). With Adrian Rollini 1933/February 14 & 1934/March 24; Shaw 1950/May 31.

ROMBERG, Sigmund. Popular songwriter; led radio orchestra including Shaw 1935.

ROMM, May. Shaw's analyst in Los Angeles.

ROONEY, Mickey. Movie actor.

ROOSEVELT, Franklin D. U.S. president during Swing Era.

ROPPOLO, Leon(cl). Innovative stylist with New Orleans Rhythm Kings.

ROSE, Dave. Arranger.

ROSELLI, Jimmy(tp). With Richard Himber 1935.

ROSENBLATT, Joseph(vla). With Carl Hoff 1936.

ROSENBLUM, Sam(vl,vla) = Sam ROSS. With Shaw 1936–37 & 1941–42.

ROSENLUND, Ralph(ts). With Shaw 1945.

ROSS, David. CBS announcer in 1930s; Jarman Shoes radio show etc.

ROSS, Diana. Movie actress/singer; played Billie Holiday in movie.

ROSS, Joe(vla). With Roger Wolfe Kahn 1932.

ROSS, Lee. Signed Shaw for 1954 Australian tour.

ROSS, Sam(vl,vla) = Sam ROSENBLUM.

ROSSNER, Karl(cello). 1940/August 16.

ROWLAND, Helen(v). With Fred Rich 1931/December.

RUBIN, Jules(ts). 1938/August 4.

RUDERMAN, Martin(fl). 1940/March 3.

RUMPLER, Harry(vla). With Shaw 1940; 1946/June 6.

RUSSELL, Bill. American Records producer, catalyst for Dixieland Revival.

RUSSELL, Curley(b). With Kai Winding's group opposite Shaw at Bop City 1949.

RUSSELL, George(p). Prominent jazz composer/arranger from 1940s on.

RUSSELL, Guy(v). With Richard Himber 1934/June 12.

RUSSELL, Jan(vl). 1946/June 11.

RUSSELL, Luis. Composer/bandleader.

RUSSELL, Mischa(vl). With Shaw 1940; 1946.

RUSSELL, Pee Wee(cl). Prominent stylist emerged in 1920s.

RUSSIN, Babe(ts). With Red Nichols 1931/August 24; Bob Howard 1936/January 28; with Shaw's 1946 studio bands.

RUSSO, Andy(tb). With Roger Wolfe Kahn 1932.

RUSSO, Sonny(tb). With Shaw 1949–50.

RUTHERFORD, Rudy(reeds). With Count Basie 1944/September 25.

RYERSON, Art(g). 1953/July 6; 1955/November 21.

SACCO, Tony(g,v). With Red Nichols 1931/August 24.

SACKSON, D.(vl). 1949/May 31.

SAFFER, Buddy(as). 1937/April 29.

SAFRANSKI, Eddie(b). 1955/November 21.

SAMAROFF, Tosha(vl). 1953/July 2.

SAMSON, Edgar. Jazz composer/arranger.

SAMUELS, Morey(tb). With Shaw 1941–42.

SAROYAN, William. Writer.

SATTERFIELD, Jack(tb). 1950/July 19 & September 14; 1953/July 2.

SAUTER, Eddie. Jazz composer/arranger.

SAX, Adolph. Invented saxophone c.1840.

SAXE, Phil(reeds). With Irving Aaronson 1930/August 22.

SCHACTER, Jules(vl). 1936/June; with Carl Hoff 1936; Paul Whiteman, Christmas 1938; Shaw 1950/September 12 & October 5.

SCHAEFER, Bill(tb). With Shaw's 1946 studio bands.

SCHERTZER, Hymie(as). Lead alto with Shaw's Decca studio bands 1950–53.

SCHILLINGER, Joseph. Music theoretician; developed arranging method in 1930s.

SCHMIDT, Lucien(cello). 1941/June 26; 1953/July 2.

SCHNEIDER, Isadore. Poet whose farm in Bucks County, Pa. Shaw purchased in 1933.

SCHOEN, Vic. Popular bandleader.

SCHOEPP, Franz. Clarinet teacher in Chicago in 1920s.

SCHULLER, Gunther. Composer/conductor/jazz writer; coined term "Third Stream."

SCHUMANN, Bill(cello). With Shaw 1936.

SCHUTZ, Buddy(d). 1952/August 1.

SCHWARTZ, Arthur. Popular songwriter.

SCHWARTZ, George(tp). With Shaw 1944–45.

SCOBEY, Bob. Led Dixieland Revival band from 1940s.

SCOTT, Raymond. Popular songwriter.

SCOTT, Tony(cl). Important stylist emerged in 1940s.

SEAR, Ike(vla). With Bill Challis 1936.

Searles & Lene. Dance team on same bill as Shaw at Palomar 1939.

SEARS, Jerry. Arranger.

SEDER, Jules(bsn). With Shaw's 1946 studio bands.

SELINSKY, Vladimir(vl). With Bill Challis 1936.

SELVIN, Ben. Popular bandleader & Columbia recording contractor; led many record sessions and radio shows including Shaw, e.g., 1932/February 4; 1932/May 12; Blue Coal Minstrels & Devoe Painters radio shows 1931–32.

SEVELY, Bob(cello). 1940/August 16.

SEWELL, Jack(cello). With Shaw's 1946 studio bands.

SHAIER, Julius(vla). 1950/April 27, September 12 & October 5.

SHANK, Chuck(g). With Joe Cantor 1928/August 13.

SHAPIRO, Art(b). With Paul Whiteman, Christmas 1938; with Shaw's 1946 studio bands.

SHAPIRO, Harvey(cello). 1950/April 27, September 12 & October 5.

SHAPIRO, Sam(vl). With Manny Klein 1936/January 20.

SHARON, Ralph(p). British pianist led trio opposite Shaw at The Embers 1953.

SHAVERS, Charlie(tp). 1951/January 25.

SHAW, Jonathan. Shaw's son by Doris Dowling.

SHAW, Steven. Shaw's son by Elizabeth Kern.

SHAWKER, Bunny(d). 1950/July 19 & October 5; 1951/January 30.

SHEARING, George(p). Led popular jazz combos.

SHEPHERD, Beresford "Shep"(d). 1941/June 26.

SHERMAN, Tommy(cond). With Little Orchestra Society 1949–50.

SHERWOOD, Bobby(g,arr). 1940/March 3 & May 13.

SHIELDS, Larry(cl). With Original Dixieland Jazz Band.

SHILKRET, Jack. Led sessions 1936/April 2, July 31 & August 29.

SHILKRET, Nat. Led radio band including Shaw in 1930s.

SHINE, Bill(as). 1950/April 4.

SHIRLEY, Jimmy(g). 1941/June 26.

SHORE, Jack(as). With Frank Trumbauer 1934/November 20.

SHRIBMAN, Si & Charlie. Brothers operating chain of New England ballrooms.

SHULMAN, Alan(cello,comp,arr.). 1949/May 31.

SHULMAN, Sylvan(vl). With Carl Hoff 1936; Shaw 1949/May 31; 1953/July; 1955/November 21.

SIEGFIELD, Frank(vl). With Bill Challis 1936; with Shaw 1936-37.

SIGNORELLI, Frank(p). With Manny Klein 1936/January 20; Bob Howard 1936/January 28; Bill Challis 1936; Ray Sinatra 1936; Paul Whiteman, Christmas 1938.

SILVERMAN, Max(vl). 1941/June 26.

SILVERS, Phil. Comedian; friend of Shaw in early 1940s.

SIMEON, Omer(cl). Important New Orleans stylist.

SIMMONS, Bob(v). With Carl Hoff 1936.

SIMON, George T. Prominent jazz writer since 1930s; editor of *Metronome*.

SIMS, Rudy(cello). 1936/May 24; 1950/October 5.

SIMS, Zoot(ts). With Shaw 1949–50.

SINATRA, Ray. Led Hit Parade orchestra featuring Shaw 1936.

SINGER, Lou(d). With Shaw's 1946 studio bands.

SINGLETON, Zutty(d). Major stylist emerged in 1920s; with Shaw briefly 1936.

SIRAVO, George. Jazz composer/arranger; many arrangements for Shaw in 1944–45.

Six Brown Brothers, The. Ragtime saxophone ensemble, pre–WW I.

Six Hits and a Miss. Vocal group on Bob Hope radio show including Pauline Byrne.

SKYLES, Marlin(p,v). With Roger Wolfe Kahn, 1932 (led vocal group The Kahn-a-Sirs).

SLAPIN, Billy(ts). With Shaw's studio re-creation band, 1968.

SLATKIN, Felix(vl). 1946/November 9.

SMALL, Paul(v). With Fred Rich 1931/December; Ben Selvin 1932/February 4.

SMEDBURG, Johnny(v). With Bill Challis 1936.

SMELSER, Cornell(acc). With CBS house bands 1931–32.

SMIRNOV, Zolly(vl). 1950/April 27 & September 12; 1953/July.

SMITH, Bill(cl). Modernist; later known as William O. Smith, composer.

SMITH, Charlie(d). 1950/September.

SMITH, Ernie. Jazz film collector.

SMITH, Georgia(cl). 1946/July 28.

SMITH, Kate(v). Popular singer 1930s–1950s; possibly with Blue Coal Minstrels 1931–32.

SMITH, Lucien(cello). With Ray Sinatra 1936.

SMITH, Mamie(v). First blues recordings 1920.

SMITH, Stuff(vl). Important stylist of the era.

SMITH, Tick. Buffalo promoter who sued Shaw in 1939.

SMITH, Willie "The Lion"(p). Important stylist emerged in 1920s & Shaw's friend and mentor around Harlem 1930–31.

SMITHERS, Elmer(tb). With Shaw band for movie *Second Chorus* (1940); 1946.

SMOOTHIES, THE(v). Vocal group on the *Burns and Allen Show* 1940–41.

SOCOLOW, Frank(as). With Shaw 1949–50.

SOCON, Paul. *Billboard* writer in 1945.

SODERO, Ed(cello). With Shaw 1941–42.

SONOFSKY, B.(vl). 1949/May 31.

SOSSON, Marshall(vl). With Shaw's 1946 studio bands.

SOUTH, Eddie(vl). Prominent stylist emerged in 1920s.

SPANIER, Muggsy(tp). Major figure; emerged in early 1920s.

SPEAR, Sammy(tp). With Bill Challis 1936.

SPECHT, Paul(vl). Led session 1931/May 28.

SPENCER, O'Neil(d). WNEW Jam 1938/November 9.

SPIEGELMAN, Stanley(vla). 1940/March 3; 1946.

SPIELER, Barney(b). In The Rangers 1942-43.

SPIVAK, Charlie(tp). With Paul Specht 1931/May 28; with Shaw 1937/September 17.

SQUIRES, Bruce(tb). With Shaw band in movie *Second Chorus*.

SROKA, Joseph. *Metronome* writer.

STACY, Jack(as). 1940/March 3 & May 13.

STACY, Jess(p). WNEW Jam 1938/November 9.

STAGLIANO, James(Fh). 1946/June 25.

STANDARD, Eddie(reeds). With Don Voorhees 1934.

STANLEY, Red(tb,v). With Irving Aaronson 1930/August 22.

STEARNS, Marshall. Jazz writer; founded Institute of Jazz Studies.

STEEDEN, Peter van. Led radio band including Shaw in 1930s.

STEELE, Blue. Bandleader; Shaw in band briefly in 1926.

STEIN, Art(d). 1936/May 24.

STEIN, Manny(b). With Shaw's June 1946 studio bands.

STEINBERG, Ed(p). With Richard Himber 1934–35.

STENROSS, Charlie(tb). With Joe Cantor 1928/August 13.

STEPHENS, Phil(b). With Shaw's 1946 studio bands.

STERKIN, David(vla). 1940/March 3 & May 13; 1946.

STERN, Art(d). With Shaw 1936.

STERN, Hank(vla). With Bill Challis 1936.

STERN, Henry(tu). 1946/July 28.

STERNS, Hank(b). With Fred Rich 1931.

STEVENS, Hal(v)(= Hal DERWIN). 1945/July; 1945/November 14.

STEVENS MALE TRIO. Vocal group for Richard Himber transcriptions 1934/June 7.

STEWARD, Herbie(ts). With Shaw 1944-45.

STEWART, Larry(v). With Jack Shilkret 1936/July 31.

STILL, William Grant. Prominent black composer/arranger; coarranged several items with Shaw 1940–42.

Stomp Six. Group led by Muggsy Spanier 1925.

STONE, Gene(g). With Shaw 1936.

STONEBURN, Sid(reeds). With Jack Shilkret 1936/August 29.

STRAUSS, Sarah. Artie Shaw's mother's maiden name.

STRAVINSKY, Igor. Prominent major twentieth century composer.

Streamliners, The. Strings-and-rhythm small group from Shaw's 1936–37 band (announced as such in public, but not on records by this instrumentation).

STRICKLAND, Cliff(ts). With Shaw 1938 (no recordings).

STRUBLE, Harry(vl). With Paul Whiteman, Christmas 1938.

STUHLMAKER, Mort(b). With Bunny Berigan 1936/April 13.

STURKIN, David(vla). 1940/March 3 & May 13.

SULLIVAN, Joe(p). With Roger Wolfe Kahn 1932–33.

SWEATMAN, Wilbur(cl). Early ragtime/jazz bandleader.

SWIFT, Bob(tb). With Shaw 1945.

Swing 8. Small group out of Shaw's 1941–42 orchestra (no recordings).

SWOPE, Terry(v). With Shaw at The Iceland, 1950 (no recordings).

SYKES, Marlin(p,v). With Roger Wolfe Kahn 1932.

SZATHMARY, Irving. Paul Whiteman arranger; orchestrated Shaw's "Blues" 1938.

TAKVORIAN, Tak(tb). In The Rangers 1942–43.

TALIARKIN, George(cello). With Shaw 1941–42.

TANNENBAUM, Julius(cello). 1940/March 3; 1946/June 6.

TANSMAN, Alexandre. Classical composer.

TANZA, Rudy(as). With Shaw 1945.

TARTO, Joe(b). With Don Voorhees 1934.

TATE, Buddy(ts). With Count Basie 1944/September 25.

TAYLOR, Billy(b). 1941/June 26.

TAYLOR, Billy(p). 1950/September; 1952/April 23.

TAYLOR, Dub. Comedian on bill at Palomar June 1939.

TAYLOR, Jimmy(tp,v). With Irving Aaronson 1930/August 22.

TAYLOR, Louis(tb). With Count Basie 1944/September 25.

TEAGARDEN, Charlie(tp). With Roger Wolfe Kahn 1932; Frank Trumbauer 1936/April 27; Paul Whiteman, Christmas 1938.

TEAGARDEN, Jack(tb). With Frank Trumbauer 1936/April 27; Paul Whiteman, Christmas 1938.

TESCHEMACHER, Frank(cl,as). Influential Chicagoan in late 1920s–early 1930s.

THALER, Manny(bar). 1953/July 2.

THOMPSON, Johnny. Arranger.

THOMPSON, Kathryn(harp). 1946/June 25.

THOMPSON, Lucky(ts). Prolific figure emerged in 1940s.

THOMPSON, Tommy. Shaw's band boy in 1950.

THORNHILL, Claude(p). Led duo with Shaw for private recording 1936/April 24; Shaw's close friend from Cleveland on; toured with Shaw's Navy band; prominent bandleader in 1940s.

THOW, George(tp). 1940/March 3 & May 13.

TILTON, Martha(v). 1940/May 13.

TINTEROW, Bernard(vl). With Shaw 1941–42.

TIO, Lorenzo et al. Prominent family of New Orleans clarinet masters.

TODD, Dick(v). On Old Gold shows with Shaw 1938–39.

TODD, Tommy(p). 1946/April 30.

TORME, Mel(v). On Shaw's 1946 Musicraft dates and remained friendly into 1990s.

TORRENCE, John & Edna. Dance team on same bill with Shaw in Dallas 1937.

TOUGH, Dave(d). With Shaw 1941-42 orchestra; in The Rangers 1942-43.

TOWNE, Jack(reeds). With Fred Rich 1931.

Towne & Knott. Dance team at Century Room in Dallas, 1937.

Trafalgar 7. One of Shaw's small groups (no recordings).

TRAMPLER, W.(vla). 1949/May 31.

TRAVERS, Vincent. Bandleader sharing bill with Shaw at French Casino 1936.

TRISTANO, Lennie(p). Major stylist emerged in 1940s.

TRONE, Bill(melophone). With Don Voorhees 1934.

TROTTA, Charlie(tp,v). Worked with Shaw in New Haven in 1920s; with Irving Aaronson 1930/August 22.

TRUMBAUER, Frankie(C-mel). Led sessions 1934/November 20; 1936/April 27.

TURNER, Lana. Movie star; in *Dancing Co-Ed* (1939); Shaw's third wife.

TURNER, Lloyd(tb). With Fred Rich 1931; Richard Himber 1936; Carl Hoff 1936; Ray Sinatra 1936.

ULANOV, Barry. Jazz writer of the era.

URBANT, Harry(vl). With Roger Wolfe Kahn 1932; Bill Challis 1936; with Shaw 1941/June 26; 1953/July.

VAIL, Olcott(vl). With Shaw's 1946 studio bands.

VALENTINO, Rudolph. Movie star/dancer; backed by Yale Collegians (including Shaw) during New England tour in mid–1920s.

VALLEE, Rudy(as,v). Played in Yale Collegians along with Shaw in 1920s.

Vanderbilt 6. One of Shaw's small groups (no recordings).

VARSELONA, Bart(tb). With Shaw 1949–50.

VAUGHAN, Sarah(v). Major song stylist emerged in 1940s.

VAUGHAN, Wes(g,v). 1936/June.

VELDE, Harold. Chairman of House Un-American Activities Committee, 1953.

VENTRANO, Mike. Shaw's road manager briefly in 1941.

VENUTI, Joe(vl). Major figure; with CBS House Band 1931–32; Adrian Rollini 1933/February 14.

VESELY, Ted(tb). With Shaw 1938.

VETTEL, Fred(v). With Blue Coal Minstrels 1931–32.

VICTOR, Frank(g). With Wingy Manone 1934/August 15.

VOORHEES, Don. Led radio orchestra including Shaw on Ed Wynn's radio show, 1934.

WADE, Archie(fl). 1946/July 28.

WADE, Charlie(bar). In The Rangers 1942–43.

WADE, Dave(tp). With Shaw 1936.

WADE, Ed(tp). With The Boswell Sisters 1935/October 8; Frank Trumbauer 1936/April 27.

WADE, Henry(reeds). With Don Voorhees 1934; Richard Himber 1934–35; Ray Sinatra 1936.

WAIN, Bea(v). With Manny Klein 1936/January 20; Bill Challis 1936; Shaw (as Beatrice Wayne) 1937/September 17.

WALD, Jerry(cl). Led Shaw-styled dance band from 1940s.

WALKER, Max(b). With Irving Aaronson 1930/August 22.

WALLACE, Bert(tp). 1950/September 14; 1953/July 2.

WALLACE, Spike. President of Los Angeles Musicians' Union 1940–41.

WALLER, Harry(vla). With Bill Challis 1936; Ray Sinatra 1936; Paul Whiteman, Christmas 1938.

WALLER, Thomas "Fats"(p,v,comp). Major stylist emerged in 1920s.

WALLINGTON, George(p). With Kai Winding opposite Shaw at Bop City 1949.

WALTERS, Teddy(v). 1946/June 6.

WALTON, John(ts). With Shaw 1944–45.

WARNER, Audree(v). With Shaw 1938 (no recordings).

WARREN, Earl(as). With Count Basie 1944/September 25.

WARREN, Ernie(as). With Paul Specht in 1920s.

WARREN, Harry. Popular songwriter.

WASSERBERGER, Oscar(vl). 1946/June 6.

WASSERMAN, Eddie(ts). 1950/April 4.

WATKINS, Ralph. Owner of Bop City and The Embers.

WATSON, Leo(v). 1937/September 17.

WAX, Harold(acc). In The Rangers 1942–43.

WAYLAND, Hank(b). With Frank Trumbauer 1934/November 20; Shaw 1936/June.

WAYNE, Beatrice(v) = Bea Wain.

WAYNE, Chuck(g). Rehearsed with 1953 Gramercy 5.

WEBB, Chick(d). Major stylist and bandleader of 1930s; in UHCA trio session with Shaw and Duke Ellington, March 14, 1937 (not recorded).

WEBB, Stan(ts,bar). 1950/May 29, July 19 & September 14.

WEBSTER, Ben(ts). With Mildred Bailey 1936/November 9.

WEEMS, Ted. Popular bandleader.

WEIL, Herb(d). With Adrian Rollini 1934/March 24.

WEINBERGER, Andrew. Shaw's lawyer from 1930s on.

WEINSTEIN, Ruby(tp). With Roger Wolfe Kahn 1932; Richard Himber 1935–36; Manny Klein 1936/January 20; Bill Challis 1936; Carl Hoff 1936; Ray Sinatra 1936.

WEINSTOCK, Manny(tp). With Carl Hoff 1936.

WEISS, Harry(vla). 1946/October 17.

WEISS, Sammy(d). With Shaw 1936.

WEISS, Sid(b). With Shaw 1938–39.

WELK, Lawrence. Popular bandleader emerged 1920s.

WELLS, Dickie(tb). With Wingy Manone 1934/August 15; Count Basie 1944/Sept.25.

WENDT, George(tp). With Shaw 1940–41.

WETTLING, George(d). With Shaw 1936–37; December 1938; Paul Whiteman, Christmas 1938.

WEXLEY, John. Writer; friend of Shaw's in Bucks County.

WHITE, Sonny(p). 1941/June 26.

WHITEMAN, Paul. Prominent bandleader from 1920; featured Shaw, Christmas 1938 and on radio shows.

WHITING, Richard. Popular songwriter.

WHITMAN, Ernie "Bubbles." Announcer for AFRS shows 1944/September.

WIEDOEFT, Rudy(as). Popular early virtuoso entertainer.

WILEY, Lee(v). Important jazz song stylist emerged in 1930s.

WILLIAMS, Clarence(p,comp). Leader on several classic jazz records.

WILLIAMS, Dave(d). 1950/April.

WILLIAMS, Jack(d). With Frank Trumbauer 1934/November 20.

WILLIAMS, Lloyd(tp). With Don Voorhees 1934.

WILLIAMS, Mary Lou(p,comp,arr). Important figure emerged 1930s.

WILSON, Earl. Columnist for *The New York Times* in the era.

WILSON, Ollie(tb). With Shaw 1945–46.

WILSON, Teddy(p). With Wingy Manone 1934/August 15; Red Norvo 1934/ September 26 & October 4; Mildred Bailey 1936/November 9.

WINDING, Kai(tb). Led combo opposite Shaw at Bop City 1949; with Shaw 1950/May 29; 1953/July 2; 1955/November 21.

WINSOR, Kathleen. Best-selling novelist and Shaw's sixth wife.

WITHERSPOON. Shaw's pseudonym at political meetings in the 1940s.

WITTSTEIN, Eddie. New Haven bandleader of the 1920s.

WOLFSON, Herman(ts). With Ben Selvin 1932/May 12; Richard Himber 1934–35.

WOODS, George. Pedestrian killed by Shaw's car in NYC, October 1930, causing Shaw to become stranded in New York.

WOODWORTH, Julian(b,tu). With Joe Cantor 1928/August 13.

WOR String Quartet. 1949/March.

WORRELL, Frank(g). 1950/October 5.

WRIGHTSMAN, Stan(p). 1940/March 3.

WYLIE, Austin. Prominent Cleveland bandleader in 1920s; Shaw in band 1928–30; Shaw's road manager 1941–42.

WYNN, Ed. Popular radio entertainer; Shaw in Don Voorhees band on show in 1934.

WYSE, Ross & June Mann. Comedy team on bill with Shaw at Strand 1945.

Yale Collegians. Band including Shaw backing Rudolph Valentino's show.

YANER, Milt(reeds). On Shaw's Decca studio recordings 1950, 1951, 1953, 1955.

YOUMANS, Vincent. Songwriter.

YOUNG, Lester(cl,ts). Major innovator emerged in 1930s; friend of Shaw.

YOUNG, Victor. Led radio band including Shaw in 1930s.

YUDKIN, Dave(d) = Dave "Ace" Hudkins.

ZARCHY, Zeke(tp). With Shaw 1936–37; 1946.

ZAYDE, Dave(vl). With Ray Sinatra 1936.

ZAYDE, Jack(vl). With Richard Himber 1934–36; Carl Hoff 1936; Shaw 1953/July 2.

ZELL, Harry, von(narr). 1946/July on Shaw's *Pied Piper of Hamelin* album and radio special.

ZENTNER, Si(tb). With Shaw's 1946 studio bands.

ZER, Izzy(vla). 1950/April 27; 1953/July 6.

ZIMMER, Tony(ts). 1936/June.

ZIMMERMAN, Fred(b). 1941/June 26.

ZIR, Irving(vla). With Richard Himber 1935–36.

ZIR, Isadore(vl). 1936/May 24; 1955/November 21.

ZITO, Freddy(tb). With Shaw 1949–50.

ZUDEKOFF, Moe(tb)(= Buddy MORROW). With Shaw 1936–37.

ZULLO, Frank(tp). With Roger Wolfe Kahn 1932.

Index

Note: "pi" references are to photo insert pages.

Aaronson, Irving, 6, 21
abortion, 87
Adler, Rudy, 28–29
Adolphus Hotel (Dallas), 47–48
advertisements and advertising: for Conn instruments, 129; income from, 43; of Shaw appearances, pi5, pi11; Shaw endorsements, 245, 246, pi7, pi11, pi30
African percussion, 3
AFRS Command Performance session, pi23
agranulocytosis, 72
Aircheck Records, 28
air checks, 8
Ajazz record label, 48, 135, 136
albums, 68
alcohol, 27; musicians' use of, 32, 100, 137. *See also* drugs
Allen, Henry "Red," 94, pi18
Allen, Marge, 34, 36, 56, pi4
American Federation of Musicians, 38, 126. *See also* Musicians' Union
American Records label, 12
anti-Semitism, 17
Armed Forces Radio Service, 105, 108
Armstrong, Louis, 4, 5, 22, 67; Decca recording, 123; Imperial Theatre concert, 44; mentors, 12
Arnheim, Gus, 21
Arquette, Les, 20, pi2
arrangements: head, 89, 123, 136, 231–32; redone, 90
arrangers, 232; band leaders as, 14; Shaw use of, 105, 107, 119; staff, 13
Arshawsky, Arthur. *See* Shaw, Artie
Arshawsky, Harry, 17, 25
Arshawsky, Sarah Strauss, 17, 87, 103, 110, pi26
Artie Shaw—A Legacy, 13–14
Artie Shaw Archives, University of Arizona, 127
"Artie Shaw Clarinet Method," pi19
Artie Shaw: Time Is All You've Got, 1, 140
Arus, George "Swami," 71; photos, ii(p), pi8, pi9, pi14; with Shaw bands, 51, 53, 56, 57, 76

ASCAP (American Society of Composers, Authors and Publishers), 90
Astaire, Fred, 3, 237, 239; *Second Chorus*, 88, 89, pi15
Attiner, Angie, pi2
audience, 64; band members' reaction to, 69–70, 77; reaction to classical concerts, 117; service members, 100; Shaw view of, 79–80, 109. *See also* fans
Auld, George "Killer," 71, 72, 77; on audiences, 80; as band leader, 11, 82; photos, pi9, pi10, pi14; recordings, 229; with Shaw groups, 66, 67, 76, 95, 96, 97
Avola, Al "Mouthpiece," 71; on "Begin the Beguine," 63; as composer, 53; photos, ii(p), pi8, pi9, pi14; with Shaw bands, 51, 81
Ayres, Lou, 22

Bailey, Buster, 6
Bailey, Mildred, 41, 44, 60
Baker, Benny, pi3
Baker, Chet, 133
ballads, 11, 36
ballrooms, 8, 58
band bus, 51
band/orchestra leader's role, 40
bands: development of, 55, 56; names, 31; repertoire, 11. *See also specific group names*
Bank, Danny, pi28
Barbour, Dave, 81
Barlow, Howard, 37
Barnet, Charlie, 46, 136
Barrios, Gil, 120, 121, 123, 124, pi28
Barris, Harry, 22
Barron, Blue, pi19
Bartee, John, 120, 121
Basie, Count, 11, 105, pi23
Bassey, Bus, 88, pi17
Baxter, Les, pi25
Beacon Theater (New York), 23
Beau, Heinie, 113
bebop, 10–11, 12, 133; clarinet in, 13
Bechet, Sidney, 5, 12, 26, 113
Beecher, George, 18

"Begin the Beguine," 8, 62, 63, 65, 112
Beiderbecke, Bix, 4, 5, 13; death, 27, 32; with Dorsey band, 26, 27
Bell record label, 131, 134, 136
Beller, Alex, pi17
Bellevue Ramblers, 18
Benchley, Robert, 66, 75
benefit performances, 43, 66
Benjamin, Joe, 124
Berezowsky, Nicolai, 117–18
Berigan, Bunny, 27, 28, 30, 43; band, 51; with CBS house band, 35; with Holiday, 41; recordings, 39, 41, 51
Berman, Billy, 18
Berman, Brigitte, 1, 139–40
Berman, Sonny, 18
Bernie, Al, 47
Bernie, Ben, 21
Bernstein, Artie, 26, 27, 38
Berry, Chu, 66, 67
Best, Denzil, 131, 133
Best, Johnny "Colonel," 71; leaving Shaw bands, 53, 54, 76; photos, ii(p), pi8, pi9; with Shaw bands, 57, 59, 76; as soloist, 72
The Best of Intentions, 26, 140
Beveridge, Betty, pi25
Biagini, Hank, 51
Big Band Era, 7, 12
big band format, 234
big bands: jazz, 4; popularity of, 12; strings in, 10; swing, 49
Bigard, Barney, 5, 12
Billboard magazine, 21
Billy Taylor Quartet, 124
Binyon, Larry, pi2
Black Swan record company, 4
Blane, Ralph, 112
Blanton, Jimmy, 11
Blossom Room (Roosevelt Hotel), 22
Blue Coal Minstrels program, 30–31
Blue Note Cafe (Chicago), 120
Blue Room (Hotel Lincoln, New York), 65
Bluebird record label, 65, 68
blues form, 231, 232
Bluestone, Harry, 26, 27, 111, pi4

BMI (Broadcast Music, Inc.), 90
Boardman, Truman, pi17
Bob Crosby's Bobcats, 11, 12
Bobcats, 11, 12
Bolden, Buddy, 2
booking agencies, 9, 89, 93. *See also specific agencies*
bookings: joint, 51; problems with, 58, 134
Bop City (New York), 116
Boston Commons concert, 76
Boswell, Connee, 37, 126
The Boswell Sisters, 37, 38, 126
Botkin, Perry, pi2
Bowen, Claude, 61, 66, ii(p)
Bowen, Lyle, 27, 28, pi3
Bower, Bob, pi17
Bowlby, Bob, pi32
Boyer, Anita, 90, 91, 92, pi17
Bradley, Nita, 55, 63; with Shaw big band, 56, 59, 60
Bradley, Will, 26, 27
Branford, Jay, pi32
The Breakers (Hawaii), 99
Brilhart, Arnold, 147, 245, pi3
broadcasting: from live engagements, 45, 46, 52, 58, 59, 62, 66; as part of nightclub engagements, 6; Radio Tokyo, 101; recording for, 8, 28, 29 (*see also* recordings); Shaw problems with repertoire, 90, 92, 107. *See also* radio; radio shows
Brown, Ray, 117
Brown, Russell, ii(p), 64, 66, pi8
Brown, Vernon, 88, pi15, pi17
Brubeck, Dave, 13, 133
Bryan, Arthur Q., 112
Bryan, Martin F., 28
Bryan, Mike, 47
Bucks County (Pennsylvania) farm, 32, 34, 140
Bucktown Five, 4
Bullock, Chick, 36, 37, 39, 41
Burke, Sonny, 111, 232
Burness, Les, 51, 53, 56, 57, 59, pi8
Burns, Les, ii(p)
Burns, Ralph, 119
Burns and Allen radio show, 87, 88, 89, 90, 92
Bushkin, Joe, 41, 44
Butterfield, Billy, 88, 89, 91; photos, pi15, pi16, pi17
Butterfield, Charles, Jr., pi3
Butterfield, Charles, Sr., pi3
Byrne, Pauline, 87
Byrns, Hans, 93, 94, 112

cadenzas, 232
Cahn, Sammy, 80

California Ramblers, 5, 6, 20
Callea, Angie, 119, pi28
Calloway, Cab, 21
Canadian National Exposition tour, 76–78
Cantor, Charlie "Chuck," 20, pi2
Cantor, Joe, 20, 233, pi2
Capitol Records, 139
Capitol Theatre (Washington, D.C.), 52
career, context of, 2, 14
Carleton, John, 232
Carns, Jane, 32
Carter, Benny, 7, 11, 26, 94, pi18
Carver, Wayman, 11
Casa Loma Orchestra, 7, 21, 43
Castaldo, Charlie, 51
Castle, Lee, 48, 98; band organization by, 122, 123; with Shaw groups, 92, 122
Castle, Vernon and Irene, 3
Catagonia Club, 25
Cathcart, Jack, pi15, pi17
Catlett, Sid, 121
Cavallaro, Johnny, 18, 19
CBS house band, 6, 26, 27–31, 35
CDs, 48
celebrities, 1, 2, 6, 8
celebrity: effect of, 137; Shaw as, 14, 67, 76, 86; of Shaw big band, 69–71
Century Room (Adolphus Hotel), 47–48
Challis, Bill, 5, 38
"The Chant," 76, 232, 234
Chapman, Ann, 82, 86
Chase, Frank, 44, pi3
Chase Hotel (St. Louis), 65
Chelsea 3 vocal group, 123, 124
Cherry, Don, 123, 124, 125, pi29
The Chicagoans, 5, 22, 46
Chick Webb's Little Chicks, 11
Chickering 4 vocal group, 123, 125
children's music, 12, 93, 112
Christian, Charlie, 11
Ciccerone, Rock, pi32
Circle Records, 38
Cities Service Quartet, pi3
Clambake 7, 11, 44
Clarence Prophet Trio, 94
clarinets, 5–6, 12–13; Buffet, 129, 135; makers, 129; Selmer, 129, 135; types, 67
Clarke, Kenny, 11, 117
Cleveland, 20–21
Club Alabam, 4
co-composers, 232
Coffee, John, 34
Cohen, Phil, 49
Cohen, Porky, pi28
Cohen, Teddy, 124
Cohn, Al, 119, 121, pi28

Cold War era, 13
Cole, Ben, 61, 77
Cole, Cozy, 41
Coleman, Emile, 41
Collins, John, 124
Collins, Keith, pi17
Colonna, Jerry, 46, 137
Coluccio, Ricky, 100
Columbia Broadcasting System. *See* CBS house band
Columbia Records, 115, 116, 118; Shaw contract with, 120
Columbia University, 32, 36
combat fatigue, 102, 103
Command Performances broadcasts, 105
commercial music: need for, 79; Shaw Decca recordings, 123; Shaw dislike for, 8, 14, 30, 31, 37; vocalists on, 57
commercial studio records, 8
communism, 113, 127
composers, 211; band as co-composers, 231–32
composition, 1, 231–32. *See also* improvisation
"Concerto for Clarinet" (Shaw), 88, 91, 232
concerts, "battle of bands" type, 59, 64
Condon, Eddie, 26, 39, 44; with Shaw band, 46–47
Conn instrument company, 129
Conniff, Ray, 90, pi17, pi21, pi24; with Shaw groups, 94, 106
contract breaches, 77–78, 124
cool jazz, 12, 13, 131
Cooper, Jackie, 85
Cornwall, Frank, 41
covers, 46
Crain, Malcolm, 51
Crawford, Forrest, 39
Cremo Cigars, 29
Creole Jazz Band, 4
Crosby, Bing, 22, 29
Crosby, Bob, 12, 44
Crosen, Jimmy, pi3
cross-cultural music, 13

Dailey, Frank, 48
dairy farming, 125
Dameron, Tadd, 119, 121
dance bands/orchestras, 4–5, 6; demise of, 133
dance music: commercial, 30; hotel ballroom style, 27; Shaw and, 62, 65, 119; tempos, 45
dances, 8, 23
Davies, Gwen, 123, 125
Davis, Bette, 105
Davis, Johnny "Scat," 21, 36

Davis, Miles, 13, 231
Decca Records, 12, 120–22; contract artists, 123; Shaw contract obligations, 126, 139
DeFaut, Volly, 4
DeFranco, Buddy, 13
Dello Joio, Norman, 116, 122
DeNaut, Jud, 88, 89, 91, pi16, pi17
Desmond, Paul, 13
Diamond, David, 93, 103
DiCarlo, Tom, 51, 53, 57
discography, 143
D'Isere, Guy, 30, 32
Disken, Bernie, 18
Dixieland bands, 2
Dixieland Revival, 12, 13
Dodds, Johnny, 4, 6
Dodds, Warren "Baby," 4, 7
Dominguez, Alberto, 90
Don Voorhees Orchestra, 35, pi3
Donahue, Sam, 99, 229, pi22
Dorsey, Jimmy, 20, 26, 28; attributions, 36; bands, 12, 58; California Ramblers and, 5; influences on, 6; jams, 38; recordings, 30; as session player, 147; studio work, 30
Dorsey, Tommy, 20, 26, 28, 43, pi23; band formation, 48; California Ramblers and, 5; Clambake 7, 11, 44; cooperative booking and, 9; in CBS house band, 29; string use, 98, 234; studio work, 30; as trombonist, 66
Dorsey Brothers' Orchestra, 28
Dorseyland Jazz Band, 12
doubling: by instrumentalists, 3, 52, 145, pi8; need for, 19
Douglas, Paul, 43
Dowling, Doris, 1, 126, 127, 128, 139, pi29
Drake, Milt, 233
dressmaking, 17, 24
drugs, 27, 66, 77; Shaw use, 87
Duchin, Eddie, 35, 55
Dukes of Dixieland, 12
DuPont, Ann, 83
Durante, Jimmy, 3
Dwight Street School, 17
dynamics, 19–20

Eastern music, 231
Easton, Walt, pi2
Eckstine, Billy, 11
Eddie Wittstein's Society Band, 19
Edison, Harry, pi3
The Education of Albie Snow, 26, 27, 32, 140
Eldridge, Roy, 106, 107, 108–9, pi24, pi25
Ellington, Duke, 3, 6, 49, pi6; orchestra, 21; style, 7

Ellisher, Frank, 52
Elman, Ziggy, 71, 88, pi23
The Embers (New York), 131–32
ensembles within big bands, 10–11. *See also* Shaw small groups
entertainment, 8; acts in addition to bands, 74, 78, 97, 106; Shaw view of, 22, 45
Etting, Ruth, 35
Europe, James Reese, 3
Evans, "Pop," pi3
Evans, Gil, 13
Evanss, Alfie, pi3
exhaustion, 21

Fagerquist, Don, 120, 121, pi28
fan clubs, 70
fans, 69, 76, 80. *See also* audience
Far East Orchestra, 20, pi2
Farley, Max, pi2
Farlow, Tal, 131, 132, 133, 135, 136
Farmer, Frances, 8
Farrar, Fuzzy, pi3
Fatool, Nick, 88, 89, pi16, pi17
Faye, Alice, 36
Fazola, Irving, 12
Feldman, Stan, 124
Fenton, Carl, 29
Ferdinandus, Johnny, 18
film shorts, 7, 33, 75, pi7–9; Paramount, 68; Vitaphone, 66
firewood business, 34
Fitzgerald, Ella, 59, 60, 117, 123, 137
Ford, Jane, 124
Ford, Vic, pi28
Forrest, Helen, 71, 237, 238; autobiography, 66, 77; band members and, 70; on Hollywood work, 75; photos, pi9, pi10, pi14; Shaw big band vocals, 65, 69, 74, 76, 78, 81
Forrestal, James, 10, 98
Fountain, Pete, 12
The Four Clubmen, 75
Fred's Friendly Five, 15, 27
Freeman, Hank "Spanky," 52, 71, 145; on "Begin the Beguine," 63; photos, ii(p), pi8–10, pi14; on Shaw style, 63
French Casino, 46
"Frenesi," 87, 88, 90, 95, 120
Fromm, Lou, pi25

GAC. *See* General Amusement Corporation
Gardner, Ava, 1, 109, 110, 113, pi26
Garfield, John, 8
Garland, Judy, 45, 72, 81; relationship with Shaw, 73, 74–75, 85, 86
Geller, Harry, 76, 82
General Amusement Corporation (GAC), 56, 124

Gennett Records, 4, 20
Gentry, Chuck, pi24
Germany, Nazi, 9
Gershwin, George, 34
Giardina, Phil, pi2
Gibbs, Georgia, 98
Gibson, Fredda, 98
Gillespie, Dizzy, 11, 13, 120
Ginsberg, Ben, 47, 51, 55
Giuffre, Jimmy, 13
Glen Gray's Casa Loma Orchestra, 7, 21, 43
Goddard, Paulette, 88, 89, pi15
Goerner, Fred, pi17
Golden Gate Theatre (San Francisco), 75
Golden Pheasant Chinese Restaurant, 21
Goodman, Al, 34
Goodman, Benny, pi13, pi19; arrangers, 10; classical studies, 6; cooperative booking and, 9; dance band tours, 8; illness, 87–88; recordings with Selvin, 31; rivalry with Shaw, 9, 58, 68, 69, 87; Shaw work with, 35; "Sing Sing Sing," 232; string use, 234; studio work, 30, 147
Goodman, Freddy, 103
Gordon, Lee, 137
Gordon Jenkins Choir, 123
Gottuso, Tony, 47
Gozzo, Conrad, 100
Grable, Betty, 75, 76, 80, 85, 86
Gramercy 5: 1940–1941 version, pi16; 1945 version, 106, pi25; 1949 version, 120; 1950 sextet, 122, 124–25; 1953–1954 version, 13, 131–37; broadcast, 91; debut, 89; recordings, 92, 107, 108; repertoire, 121, 234; vocal backing, 125, 126
Granada Cafe (Chicago), 22
Granz, Norman, 43, 133, 134, 135, 136
Gray, Glen, 44; orchestra, 7, 21, 43
Gray, Jerry, 10, 63, pi5; as copyist, 44; as orchestrator, 51, 70
Gray, Milt, 123
Great Depression, 25
Green, Freddie, 11
Green, Johnny, 35
Grupp, Dave, pi3
Guarneri, Johnny, 11, 88, 89, 91; photos, pi16, pi17

Hackett, Bobby, 88, 89
Hammond, John, 43
Hampton, Lionel, 11, pi23
Hampton Beach Casino (New Hampshire), 61
Handy, W. C., 90
Hank Biagini orchestra, 51
Harding, John, 144
Harlem, 25

Harlem Stride piano, 26
harpsichord, 89, 131
Harshman, Al, pi17
Hawkins, Coleman, 4, 11, 123
Hawkins, Ralph, 81
Haymes, Dick, 123, 125
Haynes, PollyThornhill, 35
Hayton, Lennie, 27, 38, 90
head arrangements, 89, 132, 136, 231–32
Helbock, Joe, 39, 43
Held, Julie, pi2
Henderson, Fletcher, 4, 6, 7, 10
Hendl, Walter, 116
Hendrickson, Al, 91, pi16, pi17
Herfurt, Skeets, 112
Herman, Woody, 12, 120
Higginbotham, J. C., 94, pi18
Hill, Henry, 18
Himber, Richard, 35, 37–38, 39, 41
Hindenburg, 52
Hines, Earl, 5, 11, 12
Hirt, Al, 12
Hitz, Ralph, 47
Hodges, Johnny, 41
Hoeree, Arthur, 116
Hoff, Carl, 40
Holiday, Billie, 64, 237, 238; Brunswick
    contract, 63; Decca recording, 123; leav-
    ing band, 66; photo, pi6; Shaw backing,
    41; Shaw hiring of, 8; Shaw meeting, 6,
    26; with Shaw big band, 57, 58–59, 60–
    63, 65
Horne, Lena, 94
Hotel Lexington, 41, 44–45
Hotel Lincoln, pi19
House Un-American Activities Committee,
    13, 127
Howard, Bob, 39
Howe, Dorothy, 52, 53
Hudkins, Dave "Ace," 18, 45, 54, 96, 113
Hurd, Curtis, 48
Hutchinrider, Clarence, 21
Hutton, Betty, 66
Hutton, June, 125, 126
Hyde, Alex, 19, 20

imitations, 229–30
Imperial Theatre concert, 39, 40, 43–44
improvisation: defined, 1; early jazz, 3; by
    entire band, 231–32; length, 60; on-air,
    90; in repeated numbers, 128; in solos,
    91; style, 22–23. See also composition
innovators, 11
insomnia, 21
instruments: financing, 52; weather and,
    101–2
"Interlude in B-flat," 43

intonation, 52; vocalists, 44, 87
intuition, 7
Irving Aaronson's Commanders, 6, 21
isolation, 25, 80

Jacobs, Merle, 20–21
Jacquet, Illinois, pi23
Jaimel, Victor, 127
jam sessions, 8, 22, 27, 38; Master Studios,
    49; on-air, 66; at Onyx Club, 43; Roxwell
    Apartments, 26
James, Harry, 234, pi19
jazz: chamber ensembles, 8; classical influ-
    ences, 4–5; concerts, 43; cool, 12, 13,
    131; in Europe, 8–9; evolution of, 7, 14;
    genesis, 2; modal approach, 231; modern,
    11, 13; originality in, 26; popular material
    as, 49; popularity of, 12, 13; progressive,
    133; Shaw on, 109; studying, 5, 7
Jazz Age, 4
Jazz at the Philharmonic series, 43
jazz bands, 2–3
jazz/classical fusion, 12
jazz history, 2–14
Jenkins, Les "Tex," 66, 71, 76, pi9, pi14
Jenney, Jack, 21, 38, 96, pi17; with Shaw
    groups, 88, 90–91, 94, 97
Jerome, Jerry, 88, pi15, pi17
Jewish music, 232
Joe Cantor's Far East Orchestra, 20, pi2
Johnny Cavallaro's Orchestra, 18, 19
Johnson, Bunk, 12
Johnson, Dick, 140, pi32
Johnson, Gary, pi32
Johnson, James P., 26
Jones, Casey, 28
Jones, Dick, 111
Jones, Hank, 117, 131, 133, 136
Jones, Jo, 11, 105
Jordan, Paul, 98

Kahn, Roger Wolfe, 32–33, pi2
The Kahn-a-sirs, 33
Kallen, Kitty, 111, 112
Kaminsky, Max, 32, 63, 96, pi21; with Navy
    band, 99, 101, 102–3; with Shaw big
    band, 54, 55, 56, 57, 59, 61, 62
Kansas City style, 11
Kardiner, Abram, 10
Kay, Hershey, 116, 117, 118
Keene, Bob, 113
Kelly, Paula, 96, 97
Kelly, Willis, 20, 44, pi2
Kenton, Stan, 11
The Kentuckians, 19
Keppard, Freddie, 3
Kern, Elizabeth (Betty), 98, 99, 101, 103,
    105

Kern, Jerome, 98, 99
Kessel, Barney, 106, pi25
Keyes, Evelyn, 1, 139, 140, pi31
Kid Ory's Sunshine Orchestra, 4
King Oliver's Creole Jazz Band, 4
King Sisters, pi13
Kirby, John, 66
Kirk, Warren, 51
Kitsis, Bob, 66, 71, 126, 234; photos, pi9,
    pi14
Klages, Ted, pi17
Klein, Dave, 111
Klein, Manny, 28, 30, 38, 39, 43
Kluger, Irv, 121, 131, 136, pi28
Koenig, Gene, 64
Koerner, Gil, pi3
Konitz, Lee, 13
Korall, Bert, 63, 88, 234, 247
Kostelanetz, Andre, 37
Kotick, Teddy, 123, 124
Kramer, Maria, pi19
Krein, Alexander, 115, 116
Kress, Carl, 44
Krupa, Gene, 31
Kyser, Kay, 88

La Centra, Peg, 36, 40, 238, pi5; on Rhythm
    Makers recording, 48; with Shaw bands,
    44–48, 53
Lacey, Jack, 38
Laden, Les, 19
Laine, Jack, 2
Lake, Bonnie, 94, 95, 96
Lane, Lillian, 112
Lanphere, Don, 122, 123, 124
Lanthier, Ronnie, 51
LaPorta, John, 13, 119
Lawson, Yank, 66, 67
lawsuits: auto accident, 23–24; contract
    breaches, 78, 80, 124; re walkout, 86
Leach, Les, 41
Lee, Sonny, 46
Leeman, Cliff, 55, ii(p), pi8; illness, 66, 67;
    with Shaw groups, 51, 54, 59
Lehman, Johnny, 233
Leonard, Terry, 98
Les Laden's Yale Collegians, 19
Levinsky, Walt, 139
Lewis, George, 12
Lewis, Lennie, 123
Lewis, Meade Lux, 44
Lewis, Sammy, pi3
Ley, Ward, pi2
libraries/music books, 44, 51, 52
Light, Eddie, 41
Lindworm, Joe, pi3
liner notes, 11, 247

Linn, Ray, 108, 109
Lion records, 112
Lippman, Joe, 44, 51
Little Chicks, 11
Lloyd, Shirley, 46
Lockwood, Pat, 120, 121, pi27, pi28
Lomax, Alan, 7
Lombardo, Guy, 21
loneliness, 25, 80
Lopez, Vincent, 32
Louis Armstrong's Hot Five, 22
Lumas, Eugene, pi17
Lunceford, Jimmy, 66
Lynn, Imogene, 105, 106
lyricists, 231, 233, 239
lyrics, Shaw attitude toward, 237. *See also*
    vocalists

MacDowell, Edward A., 87
MacGregor, Chummy, 22
magazines, pi7
Magic Key of Radio, 64
Make Believe Ballroom radio show, 66
Mandel, Johnny, 119, 121
Manone, Wingy, 36, 43
Margulis, Charlie, 38
Marmorosa, Dodo, 106, 120, pi25, pi26
Marsalis, Branford, 116
Martin, Tony, 239
Mason, Melissa, 33
Masters, Art, 52
Matthews, Dave, 119
Max, Ed, 112
MCA. *See* Music Corporation of America
McCall, Mary Ann, 120, 121
McCarthy, Joe, 13, 127
McConville, Leo, pi3
McDonough, Dick, 40, 41, 44, 49
McIntyre, Arthur "Traps," 26
McIntyre, Kalaparusha Maurice, 18
McKinney, Ed, pi23
McNamee, Graham, pi3
McShann, Jay, 11
Meadowbrook Ballroom, 48
megaphone, 132–33
Melody and Madness (Old Gold) radio
    show, 22, 66, 75, 79
The Mel-Tones, 111–12, pi25
Mercer, Johnny, 233
Meredith, Burgess, 88
Messing, Marcus, 41
Michaels, Mike, 46
Miller, Eddie, 27
Miller, Glenn, 9, 10, 49, 233
Mills, Dick, 124
minstrel shows, 2
modal approach, 231

Mole, Miff, 30, pi3
Mondello, Toots, 23
Monk, Thelonious, 11
Moore, Brew, 117
Morehouse, Chauncey, pi2
Morgan, Patty, 62, 63, 237, ii(p)
Morgan, Russ, 27, 37
Morrow, Bob, pi17
Morrow, Buddy, 46
Morton, Jelly Roll, 36
Moss, Joe, 26
Most, Sam, 13
Moten, Bennie, 11
movies, 8. *See also* film shorts
Mulcahy, Tex, 59
Mulligan, Gerry, 13, 117
Murphy, Larry, 28
Murphy, Turk, 12
music: American, 94; artistic conflicts re,
    79; quality of, 30, 31, 34; Shaw view of,
    64, 87, 109; types of, 10
music business: Shaw dislike of, 14, 32, 79,
    109–10; Shaw stress from, 89
Music Corporation of America (MCA), 56
music publishing, 70
music reading, 47
musical notation, 7
musicians: Americans in Europe, 8–9;
    black, 94, 96; booking agencies' treat-
    ment of, 9; in film, 89; pay, 37, 38; pro-
    fessional requirements, 19; recruitment
    of, 87, 99; Shaw demands on, 67, 77; stu-
    dio, 30, 40, 35, 111, 122; substitutes, 35;
    work available in 1920s and 1930s, 6
Musicians' Union, 10; foreign recording
    blockage, 126; residency requirements,
    24, 25; Shaw problems with, 88
Musicraft records, 111

narration, 128
Nash, Joey, 34, 35, 36, 37, 41
National Swing Club concert, 74
Navy band, 10, 98–103, pi22
New Haven (Connecticut), 17
New Haven High School, 17
New Music String Quartet, 118
New Orleans, 4
New Orleans ensemble style, 3
New Orleans Rhythm Kings (NORK), 4, 5
Nicholas, Albert, 5, 12
Nichols, Red, 5, 7, 20, 27
nicknames, pi10, pi14
Niesen, Gertrude, 8, 33
"Nightmare," 46, 52, 53, 95, 231
Niveson, Dick, pi28
Noble, Ray, 121
Noone, Jimmy, 5–6

NORK. *See* New Orleans Rhythm Kings
Norvo, Red, 36, 44, 60
nostalgia, 12, 13, 131
novelty numbers, 11, 238

Oakland, Ben, 233
Oberstein, Eli, 86, 108, 109
O'Brien, Floyd, 22
O'Brien, Jack, 51
O'Connor, Ginny, pi25
ODJB. *See* Original Dixieland Jazz Band
Old Gold radio show, 22, 66, 75, 79
Oliver, King, 4, 12
Olympia Theatre (New Haven), 19, 20
O'Neill, Dodie, 122, 123, 124
O'Neill, Dolores, 54, 55
Onyx Club (New York), 39, 43, 46
orchestras, 21, 37. *See also* bands; *specific
    group names*
orchestrators, 10, 90, 232
Original Dixieland Jazz Band (ODJB), 3
overdubbing, 113, 128
Owens, Jack, 233

Page, Oran "Hot Lips," pi21; with Shaw
    groups, 94, 95, 96–97, 98
Page, Walter, 11
Palace Hotel (San Francisco), 89, 90–91
Palace Theatre (Cleveland), 78
Palladino, Don, 121, pi28
Palladium Ballroom (Hollywood), 87, 91,
    92, pi17
Palomar Ballroom (Los Angeles), 71, 74, 75
Papa, Tony, 126, pi31
Papile, Phil, 41
Paramount Theatre (New York), 46–47, 49
Parenti, Tony, 28, 30, 147, pi3
Parker, Charlie, 11, 92
Parks, Bernie, pi25
Passecantandro, Virginia, 116
Pastor, Tony "Emcee," 21, 23, 71, 237, 238;
    as band leader, 72, 82, 83; with 1936
    Shaw band, 44, 45, 47; photos, ii(p), pi5,
    pi7–9, pi14; relationship with band mem-
    bers, 83; with Shaw big band, 51, 53, 56,
    57; Shaw big band vocals, 52, 54, 55, 63,
    65, 74, 76, 81
Pastrone, Robert, 128
Patton, Bob, pi32
Paul, Les, pi23
Pearce, Jack, 87
Pearlman, Ted, 18
percussion, African, 3. *See also* rhythm sec-
    tion
Perry, Ronnie, 59, ii(p), pi8
Pestritto, Tony. *See* Pastor, Tony
Peter Pan Novelty Orchestra, 18

Peterson, Chuck, 63, 70–71, 76; photos, ii(p), pi8, pi9, pi14
Peterson, Tweet, 51, 59
Petry, Fred, 51, 56, 57, 59
Pettiford, Oscar, 11
Pfaff, Fred, pi3
photography studio, 17
Picou, Alphonse, 5
The Pied Piper of Hamelin, 12, 112
Pierce, Dale, pi28
Pierce, Jack, pi3
Platt, Ralph, 19
The Plaza at Hunt's Inn (New Jersey), 53
Plotkin, Ben, 45
Plumb, Neely, pi15, pi17
Plunkett's (New York), 26
Poli's Palace Theatre, 18
popular music, 2; commercial, 237, 238; conflict with artistry, 58–59; jazz in, 111; pressure to perform, 94, 109; song forms, 231; vocalists, 12, 13, 57. *See also* commercial music
Potter, Tommy, 131, 133, 136
poverty, 25
Prager, Sammy, 27, 28
press, Shaw relations with, 91
Privin, Bernie "Crazyman," 71, 72, 234; photos, pi8, pi9, pi14; with Shaw big band, 66, 67, 76; on Shaw's leaving, 82, 83
pseudonyms, 38, 48
Puma, Joe, 135, 136

Quenzer, Arthur, 87, 233
Quinto, Marty, pi3

racial incidents, 64, 66, 96, 108
radio, 6, 58
radio shows, 28; personnel variation in, 35; Shaw on 14–15, 64–65. *See also specific show names*
Rae, Johnny, 126
Raeburn, Boyd, 11, 13
ragtime, 2, 3
Raguso, Tony, pi28
Raney, Jimmy, 121, pi28
The Rangers. *See* Navy band
Rayman, Morris, pi25
Raymor Ballroom (Boston), 51
RCA-Victor record company, 108, 109; contract disputes, 112; Shaw big band, 62
Reade's Casino (New Jersey), 59
Reardon, Caspar, 41, 44
record companies and early jazz, 4
record players, 2
record sales, 6; Gramercy 5 hits, 89; Shaw hits, 8, 10, 14, 90, 92
recording bans, 10, 12

recording format, 143; limitations, 108, 134
recording sessions, 48
recording technology, 2, 5, 29, 48; devices, 246; quality of, 66
recordings: availability of, 2, 48; for broadcast, 8, 28, 29 (*see also* broadcasting; radio shows); constraints on, 60; contract disputes re, 112; control of, 111; during Depression, 34; as documentation, 66; early jazz/swing, 36; issuance of, 2, 147; live, 66, 92; multiple, 237; in 1930s, 6; releases, 36; re-recordings, 120–21; Shaw (*see* Shaw recordings); types of, 8. *See also record company names*
Red Norvo's Swing Septet, 36
Red Norvo's Swingtette, 44
Reed's Casino, 51
rehearsals, 37
Reinhardt, Django, 8
Reisman, Leo, 26, 32
releases, 53, 109
repetition, 128
Reyes, Benn, 137
Reynolds, Tommy, 83, 229
The Rhythm Boys, 22
Rhythm Makers, 48, 52; Shaw band as, 54
rhythm section: Basie's, 11; Latin, 120; ODJB, 3; Shaw 1936 band, 46–47
Ricci, Paul, 39
Rich, Buddy, 69–70, 71, 121, 234; in Australia, 137; with Basie band, 105; leaving band, 81, 82; photos, pi9, pi14, pi23; with Shaw big band, 66, 67, 76
Rich, Fred, 15, 27; CBS house band, 26, 27–28; recordings, 29–30, 31
Richards, Trudy, 120, 121, 126, pi27
Richmond, June, 58
Ritz-Carlton Hotel (Boston), 76
Roaring '20s, 4
Robinson, Les "Dapper Dan," 64, 71, 234; photos, ii(p), pi7–10, pi14, pi15, pi17; on Shaw arrangements, 63; with Shaw bands, 51, 52, 88
Rochester, Charlie, 45
Rochester Civic Orchestra (New York), 115
rock and roll, 13
Rockwell, Tommy, 45
Rockwell-O'Keefe Agency, 44
Rodgers, Harry "Muscles," 51, 71; photos, ii(p), pi8, pi9, pi14
Rodriquo, Nano, 64
Rogers, Ginger, 3
Roland, Gene, 119, 121
Roland, Joe, 131, 132, 133, 135, 136
Rollini, Adrian, 5, 34, 35, 44
Rollini, Art, 5

Romberg, Sigmund, 37
Romm, May, 10
Roppolo, Leon, 4, 5
Roseland State Ballroom (Boston), 51, 57, 61
Rosenblum, Sam, 45
Ross, David, 27, 28, 37
Ross, Joe, pi2
royalties, 90
Russell, Bill, 12
Russell, Curley, 117
Russell, George, 231
Russin, Babe, 35, 39, 112
Russo, Andy, pi2
Russo, Sonny, 121, pi28

Sacco, Tony, 27
Saffer, Buddy, 52
Sam Donahue Navy band, 229
Samson, Edgar, 10
satire, 63, 238
Saturday Night Swing Club, 49, 53, 56, 61
Sauter, Eddie, 41, 107, 108, 119, 121
Savitt, Jan, 74
Savoy Ballroom (Chicago), 65
Saxophone Sextet, 44
saxophones, 2, 18, 19
Schuller, Gunther, 10
Scobey, Bob, 12
scoring, 20. *See also* orchestrators
Scott, Tony, 13
Second Chorus, 87, 88, 89, pi15
Second Herd, 12
Selvin, Ben, 27, 30, 31, 35
session players and playing, 147
Shank, Chuck, pi2
Sharon, Ralph, 131
Shaw, Artie: acting, 22, 139; alcohol use, 77, 87, 137; artistic/commercial conflicts, 14; artistic evolution, 15, 107, 113; artistic goals, 14; artwork, 140; auto accidents, 23–24, 124; as band leader (*see* Shaw as band leader/conductor); birth, 17; Bucks County farm, 32, 34, 140; childhood poverty, 14; children, 101, 103, 128, pi23, pi28; as clarinetist, 8, 14, 19, 79, 131; classical pursuits, 12, 23, 39–40, 113, 115–18; Columbia University courses, 32, 36; dental problems, 113; disparagement of, 9–10; drug use, 77, 87; early professional jobs, 18, 19–24; economic opportunities, 8; education, 32, 33, 35, 36; England trip, 125–26; essay contest, 21; fame (*see* celebrity); family bankruptcy, 17; family support by, 18; father's death, 25; film distribution business, 139; film score possibilities, 85, 86;

as flutist, 147; gallbladder illness, 120, 121–22; gun shop, 139; Harlem connections, 26; harmonic sophistication, 11; hearing problems, 102; hobbies, 139; in Hollywood, 22, 92; illnesses, 9, 72, 73–74, 75, 101, 103; income, 14, 20, 43, 124–25, 126, 131; intellect, 110; intellectual mentors, 30; jazz and, 1, 5, 13, 21, 32; job stress, 20, 21; knee injury, 82, 85; lecturing, 139; lifestyle, 93; marriage to Allen (Marge), 34, 36, 56; marriage to Carns (Jane), 32; marriage to Dowling (Doris), 126, 127, 128, 139, pi28; marriage to Gardner (Ava), 110, 113; marriage to Kern (Elizabeth), 98, 99, 101, 103, 105; marriage to Keyes (Evelyn), 139, 140; marriage to Turner (Lana) , 85–86, 87, 91–92, pi12; marriage to Winsor (Kathleen), 113; marriages, 1, 14; Mexico trip, 81–82; misinformation re, 245, 247; mother, 17, 87, 103, 110, pi26; movie work, 87; as multi-instrumentalist, 5; music for income, 124, 125, 126, 131; music study, 17, 18; name, 65; Navy service, 10, 12, 98, 99; near-death experiences, 17, 72; in New York (1930), 24, 25, 26; Onyx Club membership, 43; personality, 127; piano lessons, 17; political interests, 13, 127; psychoanalysis, 103, 105; reading, 17; relationship with Judy Garland, 73, 74–75, 85, 86; retirement desire, 31, 34, 73, 80; retirements, 12, 14, 34, 37, 81, 113, 123; returns to music, 9, 12, 13; rivalry with Goodman, 9, 58, 68, 69, 87; role models, 5; romance with Betty Grable, 80, 85, 86; romances, 1, 21, 22; roommates, 26, 27; as saxophonist, 8, 14, 18, 19, 147; school experiences, 17–18, 19, 36; Shekomeko farm, 125, 126, 139, 140; as sideman (*see* Shaw as sideman); sight-reading, 19; singing, 22, 124; Spain, residence in, 139, 140; style range, 14; tax problems, 13, 131, 139; tonsillectomy, 75; ukelele playing, 17; vacation, 79; vaudeville viewing, 18; wartime illnesses, 101, 103; wristwatch collection, 80; writing (*see* Shaw as writer)

Shaw as band leader/conductor, 79, 229–30; band members' view of, 109; financing band, 41; formation of first group, 39–40; groups (*see listing for "Shaw band . . . "*); guest conducting, 87–88; interviews, 79; large orchestra plans, 86; limiting activity as, 107; recruiting players, 99; relationship with band members, 68, 77, 80, 82–83; stage personality, 78, 81, 97, 106, 132; touring, 41; treatment of members, 71–72; vocalists with, 237; walkout, 81

Shaw as composer/arranger, xiii, 14, 231–36; children's music, 12, 93, 112; classical pieces, 116; for Decca recordings, 123, 128; for film, 88; initial efforts, 20; instrumental combinations, 39–40; "Interlude in B-flat," 39–40; for Joe Cantor band, 233; modernization, 133; for own groups, 39–40, 44, 51, 108; part handling, 234; performances of own music, 10; for pop vocalists, 12; publications, 245–46; for radio, 21; rearrangements, 120–21; satisfaction with work, 56; for small ensembles, 95, 233; for strings, 86–87, 233–34; studies, 93, 94, 103, 112; for Wylie, 21

Shaw as sideman, 25–41; Australian gigs, 137; backing Holiday, 41; college gigs, 26; commercial recordings, 38–41; on Crosby radio show, 29; discography, 165–70; after forming own band, 44; freelancing, 8, 34, 35, 37; for income, 41, 49; instruments played, 34; jam sessions, 22, 27; jazz recordings, 36; music tastes, 14; radio shows, 41; solos, 14 (*see also* Shaw as soloist); style, 13; with Ben Selvin bands, 31; with Berigan swing group, 44; with CBS house band, 27–31, 35; with Challis orchestra, 38; with Cornwall band, 41; with Green orchestra, 35–36; with Hayton orchestra, 38; with Himber orchestra, 35, 36, 37–38, 39, 41; with Hoff band, 40; with Kahn band, 33–34; with Manone jazz band, 36; with McDonough band, 40, 41; with Nichols band, 27; with Norvo's Swing Septet, 36; with Selvin's orchestra, 35; with Shilkret, 41; with Specht orchestra, 27; with Vincent Lopez orchestra, 32; with Voorhees orchestra, 35

Shaw as soloist, 10, 14–15, 234; baritone sax, 33; classical, 113, 115–118, 120, 122; control of nuance, 15; development as, 15, 121, 136–37; flute, 33; guest appearances, 66–67; originality, 15; radio recordings, 28, 29, 31; on saxophone, 28; sideman recordings, 38–39; technique, 65; variation in, 90, 95; with Basie band, 105; with Norvo's Swing Septet, 36; with own band, 44; with Trumbauer, 36

Shaw as writer, 8, 14, 34; autobiography (*see The Trouble with Cinderella*); *The Education of Albie Snow*, 26, 27, 32, 140; on music, 246; novels, 32; short stories, 26, 140

Shaw, Elizabeth Kern, pi23

Shaw, Jonathan, 128, pi28

Shaw, Stephen, 101, 103, pi23

Shaw band (1936), 44–49

Shaw band (1937–1938), 8, 51–62; air checks, 59; evolution of, 63; financing, 51, 54, 55; morale, 55; popularity of, 53, 57, 61; recording dates, 52, 53–54, 55, 62; reviews, 52–53, 53–54, 57, 60–62; road managers, 51, 54, 61; transcription recordings, 51–52, 53, 54, 55, 56

Shaw band (1938–1939), 63–83, ii(p); air checks, 65; broadcasting, 66, 74; evolution of, 66; fans, 69, 76, 80; film work, 75; imitators, 83; income, 68; personnel changes, 67; pop repertoire, 79; popularity of, 63, 65, 68–70; problems in, 68; RCA recordings, 65, 68, 69, 76; recording dates, 63; reviews, 65, 74, 76, 78, 80–81; without Shaw as leader, 82–83

Shaw band (1940), 87–88

Shaw band (1940–1941), 90–92, pi17

Shaw band (1941), 98

Shaw band (1941–1942), 94–98, pi20

Shaw band (1944–1945), 12, 103, 105–10, pi24; personnel changes, 107; reviews, 106–7

Shaw band (1949–50), 12, 119–22, pi28

Shaw band (1950), 122

Shaw band (1950 road group), 123

Shaw band (1953 Texas tour), 126–28, pi31

Shaw early appearances, 18, 19–20; with Austin Wylie, 21–22; with Irving Aaronson's Commanders, 21, 22–24; with Joe Cantor's Far East Orchestra, 20; with Merle Jacobs, 20–21

Shaw orchestra (1983), pi32

Shaw orchestras, 9, 90–92, 94–98

Shaw recordings, 27; attributions, 30–31; as sideman, 37; big band for Brunswick, 52, 53, 54, 55; for Brunswick Records, 44, 46, 47, 48; classical, 115–16; Cole Porter album, 111–12; commercial record dates, 38–39; control of, 108, 109; Decca, 122, 123, 124, 125, 128, 131; Gramercy 5, 89; jazz/string combination, 94; material, 57; 1937–1938 big band, 52, 53–54, 55, 57; 1937 transcriptions, 51–52; 1940–1941 orchestra, 90, 91, 92; 1940–1950 big band, 120–21; 1941 orchestra, 95, 96, 97–98; 1944–1945 band, 105–6, 107, 109; quality of, 60, 66; RCA, 63, 86; reissues, 140; re-recordings (1968), 139; Shaw opinion of, 56, 57; small groups, 95; with Aaronson, 23; with Gramercy 5 (1953–1954), 134–35, 136; with Joe Cantor, 20; with Kahn band, 34; with large orchestra, 86; with Specht, 27; with studio group, 111

Shaw small groups, 59, 89, 95, 107. *See also* Gramercy 5; Swing 8

Shekomeko farm, 125, 126, 139, 140
Shepherd, Beresford "Shep," 94, pi18
Shields, Larry, 5
Shilkret, Jack, 37, 39, 41
Shilkret, Nat, 37
Shirley, Jimmy, 94, pi18
Shoepp, Franz, 6
Shribman, Charlie, 58
Shribman, Si, 58, 59
Shulman, Alan, 118
sidemen: identification of, 37; recording listings of, 147; with Thornhill, 13
sight-reading, 37
Signorelli, Frank, 38, 39
Silver Grill (Hotel Lexington), 40, 45, pi5
Silvers, Phil, 74, 85, 87
Simeon, Omer, 5
Sims, Zoot, 121
Sinatra, Ray, 40–41
Singleton, Zutty, 64
The Six Brown Brothers, 2, 3
Small, Paul, 28
Smith, Charlie, 117, 124
Smith, Kate, 31, 33
Smith, Mamie, 4
Smith, Stuff, 43
Smith, William O. "Bill," 13
Smith, Willie "The Lion," 6, 25, 26, 44, 140
Socolow, Frank, pi28
soloists: domination by, 7; filling in, 72; identifying, 28–29
solos, 147, 234; in early jazz, 3; style, 4, 12
Spanier, Muggsy, 4, 22
Specht, Paul, 18, 27
Spencer, O'Neil, 66
Spirituals to Swing concerts, 43
Spivak, Charlie, 18, 27, 53–54
sponsors, 29, 30, 58–59, pi3. *See also* radio shows
Squires, Bruce, pi15
Stacy, Jess, 23, 66, 67
Standard, Eddie, pi3
standards, 231
"Star Dust," 90
Steele, Blue, 19
Stenross, Charles, pi2
Stern, Art, pi4
Stevens, Hal, 108
Steward, Herbie, pi28
Still, William Grant, 86, 87, 90
Stomp Six, 4
Stoneburn, Sid, 41
Strand Theatre (New York), 78, pi24
Strickland, Cliff, 59
strings, 10; in "Interlude in B-flat," 44; for jazz work, 94; reviews of, 96; Shaw use of, 44, 86, 88, 92, 105; writing for, 233–34

style: arranging, 11; documenting, 7; evolution of, 7, 10; improvisation, 22–23; individuality in, 7; Kansas City, 11; Latin, 120; New Orleans, 3; personal, 5; popular, 10; Shaw, 60, 131; Shaw big band, 76; of solos, 4, 12; swing, 7, 36
success: problems with, 68; Shaw reaction to, 67–68; Shaw view of, 79–80, 83
Sullivan, Joe, 22, 33
Sunshine Orchestra, 4
Sunshine record company, 4
Sweatman, Wilbur, 3
swing, 7, 36, 39, 49
Swing 8, 96, 98
Swing Era, 7, 8, 10
Swope, Terry, 124, 126
Sykes, Marlin, pi2
Szathmary, Irving, 67, 232

takes, 48, 143–44; alternate, 15, 53, 95, 135
Tarto, Joe, pi3
Taylor, Billy, 124, pi18
Teagarden, Charlie, 33, 44, pi2
Teagarden, Jack, 5, 12, 39, 44
television, 13
Teschemacher, Frank, 6, 23
test pressings, 2
Texaco radio sponsorship, pi3
theme song, 52, 231. *See also* "Nightmare"
Thesaurus Transcription Service, 41, 48; Shaw bands, 51, 53, 120
Third Stream movement, 10, 13, 97–98, 233; in classical music, 118, 120
Thompson, Lucky, 9
Thornhill, Claude, 13, 21, 35, 39, 46, 99
Tilton, Martha, 87
Tio, Lorenzo, Jr., 6
Tio family, 5
titles, multiple recordings of, 237
Todd, Dick, 69, 75, 68, 237, 239
Tommy Dorsey's Clambake 7, 11, 44
tone, 19, 115
tone color, 49, 86
Tormé, Mel, 80, pi25; recordings with Shaw, 111–12, 123
Torrence, John and Edna, 47
Tough, Dave, 95, 99, 100–101, 102–3, 121
touring, 32; colleges (1936), 46; delays, 77; Gramercy 5 (1953–1954), 133, 134; income from, 86, 94; Navy band, 99–102; road life, 55, 61, 69–70; Shaw big band (1949), 120
Towne, Jack, 28–29
Towne and Knott (dance team), 47
transcriptions, 8, 28, 29, 51–52; NBC disks, 48; for performance checks, 46; surviving, 35. *See also* recordings

Tristano, Lennie, 13
Trone, Bill, pi3
Trotta, Charlie, 21, 23
The Trouble with Cinderella, 1, 12, 125, 126, 129, 139
Trumbauer, Frank, 5, 10, 13, 18, 39, 44
Turner, Lana, 1, 75; marriage to Shaw, 85–86, 87, 91–92, pi12
Turner, Lloyd, 29

"Ubangi." *See* "The Chant"
uniforms, 47
United Hot Clubs of America, 49, pi6
United States, 4, 10
Urbant, Harry, pi2

Vallee, Rudy, 19
Van Steeden, Peter, 37
vaudeville, 2, 18
Vaughan, Sarah, 119
Vaughan, Wes, 44
Ventrano, Mike, 96
Venuti, Joe, 28
Verve/Clef Records, 133, 134, 136
Vesely, Ted, 59, 64
vibraphone, 131
vibrato, 115–16
Victor record label, 3, 65
Vocalion records, 53, 65
vocalists, 237–44; with big bands, 58, 66; contracts, 124; period, 39, 41; pop music, 12, 13, 57; sexual politics of, 72; Shaw view of, 111, 121, 133, 237; Shaw use of, 57
Voorhees, Don, 35, pi3

Wade, Henry, pi3
Wain, Bea (Beatrice Wayne), 38, 53, 54
Wald, Jerry, 229
Waller, Thomas "Fats," 26
Wallington, George, 117
Walters, Teddy, 112, 123
Warner, Audree, 63
Warren, Ernie, 18
Watkins, Ralph, 116
Watson, Leo, 53, 238
Wax, Harold, 100
Wayne, Chuck, 131
Webb, Chick, 6, 26, 49, 121, pi6; groups, 11, 59–60
Webster, Ben, 41
Weems, Ted, 21, 22
Weinberger, Andrew, 58, 126, 232
Weinstein, Ruby, pi2
Weiss, Sid, 55, 59, 71, 140; photos, ii(p), pi8, pi9, pi14
Wendt, George, pi15, pi17

Wettling, George, 46, 51; in Shaw big band, 51, 66, 67
Wexley, John, 34, 35
White, Sammy, pi18
White, Sonny, 94
Whiteman, Paul, 4–5, 44, 232; orchestra, 21, 22, 44; Shaw guesting with, 59, 62, 67; symphonic jazz by, 95; trophy presentation by, 74
Wiedoeft, Rudy, 2, 3, 6, 18
Willard Alexander Agency, 124
William Morris Agency, 89, 98
Williams, John (Jack), 36

Williams, Lloyd, pi3
Williams, Mary Lou, 119
The Willows (Pennsylvania), 52
Wilson, Teddy, 36
Winding, Kai, 117
Winsor, Kathleen, 1, 113, pi26
Wittstein, Eddie, 19
The Wolverines, 4
women, 27, 70
Woody Herman's Second Herd, 12, 120
workaholism, 21
World Transcriptions, 38, 39, 40
World War II, 10, 76, 97

Wylie, Austin, 6, 21, 96
Wynn, Ed, 35, 38, pi3

Young, Lester, 11, 13, 18, 105
Young, Victor, 37
Your Hit Parade radio show, 40
Yudkin, Dave. *See* Hudkins, Dave "Ace"

Zarchy, Zeke, 46, 48
Zell, Harry Von, 112
Zimmer, Tony, 44
Zito, Fred, 121, pi28
Zudekoff, Moe, 46

About the Author

Vladimir Simosko was born in Pittsburgh, Pennsylvania, in 1954. He is Music Librarian at the University of Manitoba and former Curator of the Institute of Jazz Studies at Rutgers University, has taught jazz history courses, and is also a musician. He has published more than 130 articles and reviews in various magazines including *Coda* and *The Journal of Jazz Studies* since 1973. His first book, *Eric Dolphy: A Musical Biography and Discography* (The Smithsonian Institution Press, 1974) has been published in several languages and editions. Simosko is also the author of *Serge Chaloff: A Musical Biography and Discography,* also in the Studies in Jazz Series published by Scarecrow Press.